Deep Things out of Darkness

The Book of Job

Essays and a New English Translation

David Wolfers

Pharos

WILLIAM B. EERDMANS PUBLISHING COMPANY
GRAND RAPIDS, MICHIGAN

© 1995 Kok Pharos Publishing House – Kampen – the Netherlands
P.O. Box 5016, 8260 GA Kampen, the Netherlands
Kok ISBN 90 390 0104 9
NUGI 632

Published jointly 1995
in the Netherlands by Kok Pharos
and in the United States of America by
Wm. B. Eerdmans Publishing Co.
255 Jefferson Ave. S.E., Grand Rapids, Michigan 49503

Printed in the United States of America

00 99 98 97 96 95   7 6 5 4 3 2 1

CIP-GEGEVENS KONINKLIJKE BIBLIOTHEEK, DEN HAAG

Wolfers, David

Deep things out of darkness : the book of Job : essays and a new English translation /
by David Wolfers. – Kampen : Kok Pharos. – Ill.
Met lit. opg., reg.
ISBN 90-390-0104-9
NUGI 632
Trefw.: Job (bijbelboek)

Library of Congress Cataloging-in-Publication Data

Wolfers, David, 1927–
Deep things out of darkness: the book of Job, essays and a
new English translation / David Wolfers.
p.   cm.
Includes bibliographical references and index.
ISBN 0-8028-4082-5 (pbk.: alk. paper)
1. Bible. O.T. Job — Criticism, interpretation, etc.
I. Bible. O.T. Job. English. Wolfers. 1995. II. Title.
BS1415.2.W65   1995
223'.106 — dc20   95-4625
                                          CIP

Note: Over the past ten years earlier versions of substantial parts of this book
have appeared in the *Jewish Bible Quarterly* (Dor leDor) and *Vetus Testamentum*.

To the memory of my parents,
Abraham and Mary Wolfers,
who taught me to love the Hebrew Bible,
and of my brother Philip (1926-1955),
who demonstrated that the righteous
do indeed perish

"Scripture does not state its doctrine as doctrine, but by telling a story, and without exceeding the limits set by the nature of a story. It uses the methods of story-telling to a degree, however, that world literature has not yet learned to use; and its cross-references and interconnections, while noticeable, are so unobtrusive that a perfect attention is needed to grasp its intent — an attentiveness so perfect that it has not yet been fully achieved. Hence it remains for us latecomers to point out the significance of what has hitherto been overlooked, neglected, insufficiently valued."

MARTIN BUBER

Table of Contents

Acknowledgments

It is a pleasure to acknowledge the critical assistance of Rabbis Ronald Lubofsky of Melbourne, Australia, and Uzi Weingarten of Jerusalem, who read and discussed large portions of this work and contributed many helpful suggestions.

Preface

Best known and least well understood of books, the Book of Job is a favourite of philosophers and poets, but not of priests. For while its intellectual messages attest to truths that have not changed in the nearly thirty centuries since its composition, its religious messages are profoundly shocking to modern believers. They have been nurtured on a sentimental parody of a loving God who watches the fall of every sparrow, not that honest appraisal of the Lord, Who "formed light and created darkness; made peace and created evil" (Isa. 45:7) to which the Hebrew prophets attained more than 2500 years ago.

I was about twelve years old when I first heard of the Book of Job. My English teacher, Mr. Anderson of Sydney High School, introducing his class to the novel, suggested that the first example of that genre was this Biblical work. This unusual judgement was to influence the later part of my life unpredictably and overwhelmingly. Immediately on returning home from school, I sat down with the Bible, and read the Book of Job.

On first reading, I found the work (in the King James translation) to be full of irreconcilable obscurities and self-contradictions which, at the time, I attributed to my own incapacity as a young reader. I was sure that everyone else understood it perfectly well. As the years passed I returned to Job again and again, but neither age, nor experience, nor increased comprehension skills did anything to clarify the obscurities or resolve the contradictions. Finally, in middle life, still as baffled and intrigued by Job as I was a child, I determined to devote whatever time was necessary – and it turned to be the rest of my life – to penetrating the mysteries of this deepest of books.

One of the first facts that I discovered was that in innumerable of the cruxes of comprehension, the Hebrew text did not say precisely (or indeed in many cases even approximately) what any of the numerous translations of Job into modern languages assumed it to mean. Each translation gives the impression of having been produced in a mind at least half made-up in advance as to what the book was about, and when the text contradicted the thesis, all too often it was the text which was jettisoned.

The faithful translator, however, is not over-concerned with the suspicion that the text says something incongruous, or even blasphemous. The translator's duty is unequivocal. He has to translate the words that are there, not those he thinks ought to be, or wishes were. Only when we cease trying to reconcile the Book of Job with theories of wisdom literature, guesses as to the location of Uz, conjectures of date and setting, and accept the text at its face value, can we begin to fathom its true meaning.

On the religious level, we can hardly avoid seeing it as a didactic work, aimed at demonstrating or maintaining, or at least arguing that a God-fearing approach to life is consistent with all the events and accidents which appear to contradict it. But the character of the God we must fear, and where He is to be found, are surprises in store for the reader of this book.

Inasmuch as "religion" in the ancient world encompassed the whole, or almost the whole, of men's attempts to make sense of the Universe, to create an intellectual model of it, how it came into being and how it operated, all for the salutary purpose of manipulating it to their own advantage, this book must be acknowledged as occupying a solitary peak.

At its most accessible level of understanding, it carries monotheism, which is surely before atheism, the ultimate evolutionary simplification of theistic belief, to its closest possible encounter with reality. In resolving, which it does, the problem, inescapable for well-intentioned man, of the apparent incompatibility between a fundamentally injust Universe, capable of inflicting untold pain on the innocent, and a fundamentally benevolent Creator-Governor, it offered a new lease of life to God on honourable terms. It offered an alternative to the existential nightmare of Ecclesiastes. The spokesmen for God in the established religions were never able to accept those terms which included, as a bare minimum, a ruthless clarity of vision, an uncompromising acceptance of terrible truths about the Universe.

But there is an entirely different dimension to the Book of Job, and it is to making this dimension accessible that the present work has principally been devoted.

The relationship between the Israelite nation and its Lord God was governed from the time of the Sinaitic revelation, by the terms of three Convenants, in the Books of Exodus, Leviticus and, in a revised form, Deuteronomy. Quotations from each of these solemn agreements are to be found in the text of the Dialogue, while that of Deuteronomy is the disguised but unmistakable model for the descriptions of the prosperity and downfall of Job in the Prologue.

The most obvious novelty of my interpretation, based on textual evidence rather than preceding it, is that Job is primarily an allegorical figure representing the people of Judah and their King Hezekiah in the time of the Assyrian conquests. This is not the hardly-conscious device of merging the individual with community which we find in many of the Psalms[1], where the spontaneous outpouring of pain at the trials of the people finds expression in the laments of a poet speaking for them in the first person, but a supremely conscious employment of a literary device, in a work whose every aspect is sculptured with professional craft.

This national-historical underpinning of an allegorical Job is emphatically not an optional alternative for readers. It is the essential carrier of its most profound messages. Almost nothing of the final portion of the book, its resolution, makes any sense at all if we do not read the whole of it as an allegory. Indeed it is the veiled story of national disaster, the rupture of Convenants between the tribal desert God and His chosen people, and the trial of faith of Israel in exile which is the true theme of the book, while the superficial layer, treating of personal disaster, betrayal and temptation, is merely an exceptionally effective and compelling disguise and vehicle.

The purpose of the author in writing the Book of Job was, I believe, to re-draw the nature of the relationship between the people of Israel and their God by demonstrating that the Covenants were no longer in operation, that they had been unilaterally abrogated by the Lord, or in the alternative, so transgressed by the people, that they had become inoperative. We can easily see, on reading the story with this thought as a considered possibility, that Job representing the Israelite nation, believed the betrayal to have been the Lord's, while the Lord was equally convinced that His people had deserted Him and His ways.

The bases of these Covenants had been something new in national and religious history. While the surrounding nations structured their relationships with their tutelary gods on the premise of deities whose actions had all the caprice deduced from the behaviour of their own venal lords, kings and emperors[2], reserving laws and rules of social behaviour for the lower realm, Israel attempted an exercise in transcendence. In what we would now term a quantum leap of sophistication, the architects of the Jewish religion re-ordered the rules of conduct required to gain favour in the upper sphere so that they coincided with the conduct rationally calculated to promote a particular value system - orderly society, safe conduct among men and women in their dealings with each other, security for the State, peace between the generations, secure tenure and orderly transfer of property, harmony of home life, husbandry of resources for the future. The demands of the Lord became codified not on the basis of the arbitrary and contemptibly selfish spirits of gods fabricated from the raw materials of human cupidity, but on the best interests of the earthly society, The divine realm became sponsor of a Code of Laws for the benefit of the public – Ten Commandments and 603 more.

The force of these agreements, the Covenants, while hinting at individual behaviour and individual disfavour, was essentially a collectivist contract. You, as a people, obey my laws and I, as your God, will ensure your prosperity, survival and harmony. Disobey, and immeasurable disaster will follow. The Covenants, so understood, had a very good chance of proving self-fulfilling, for they did indeed spell out conduct required to give internal and external strength to a society, to preserve it from the principal dangers of internal conflict and disintegration which in time must inevitably turn the strongest into victims.

But it was inevitable that among the common people, this simply splendid, rational, serviceable system of justice should degenerate to the personal level, that the idea would spread that a good and just man would earn a good life, and a wicked one, disaster. Indeed, as an underlying superstition, this belief is enormously widespread amongst believing Jews and Christians to this day.

Perhaps on a psychological level this proposition too has validity, but in the simple terms on which it was understood, that virtue conferred prosperity and immunity from the pitfalls of life – it is demonstrably false in every time and place. Despite this falsehood, the proposition was widely accepted in Israel that the Lord Who would reward and punish right and wrong of the nation must do the same for each individual within it, posing a theological conundrum over which debate has never ceased. This proposition seems to have become the evolved dogma of the Israelite view of its Covenants and its God, and also its Wisdom at the time of the writing of the Book of Job. It is certainly the "Wisdom" propounded repreatedly by Job's friends.

The author sought to upset these Covenantal interpretations of the truths about the Universe essentially because events – the Assyrian conquests – and the mundane facts of personal lives had demonstrated their invalidity. Therefore the very survival of the Hebrew God, and by unavoidable corollary, the Israelite nation, was in jeopardy. A new and even more realistic foundation for the faith had become an urgent necessity.

Surely rightly, the author judged that the tribal-god relationship of Israel and the Lord, no different in essence from those of other more prosperous and successful nations, nations celebrating in triumph over the downfall of Israel, could not survive the appalling and undeserved reverses of the "Age of Empires". The people in exile and at home would surely transfer their allegiance to one who seemed a more powerful or faithful god. Indeed this was the fate of the ten tribes of Israel in exile. Signs of this fear recur throughout the Book of Job. He therefore wrote this book to point the way to a different form of relationship between man and god, one no longer dependent on reward and punishment, reciprocal rights and duties, bur relying on an internalised god, a devotion to righteousness of necessity in the teeth of the "living God who denied me (Job) justice, the Almighty Who embittered my soul". In doing so, he also freed the Lord to move from His exclusive partnership with His chosen people towards that universality which has left Him in the Western world as the One Sole God, with no rival in the heavens or on the earth.

Briefly, this is the Book of Job: an heretical interpretation of the downfall of the Israelite polity as the unilateral rupture by the Lord of the Covenants between God and His people, rather than as their fulfillment. It hints at a purpose and timing for this rupture analogous to the severance of the umbilical cord between mother and offspring, and points the way into a future where the monotheistic concept of Judaism might evolve in the direction of universality. It seems to harbour as an ultimate purpose the liberation of the human sense of justice and right behaviour from all dependence on supernatural reward or sanction. Thus the Book of Job contains religious innovations as momentous as the Ten Commandments, innovations so far in advance of their time that neither Judaism nor Christianity has yet been willing fully to absorb them.

It has taken me more than half a century to arrive at these conclusions, but in the last twenty years, in which I have been exploring this magical text and making discoveries like an archaeologist uncovering artefacts, burrowing ever deeper into darkness to find ever deeper truths, I have lived in his company whom I believe the wisest man who ever put quill to papyrus, and loved every hour of my days.

Melbourne, June 1994.

Notes Preface

1. II. Wheeler Robinson, *Inspiration and Revelation in the Old Testament*, Oxford, *1964*, pp. 70 and 264.

2. See, for example the Sumerian "Prayer to every God" (Pritch. p. 391f) which contains such complaints as:

"The sin which I have committed, indeed I do not know. The forbidden thing which I have eaten indeed I do not know. The prohibited place on which I have set foot, indeed I do not know. The lord in the anger of his heart looked at me; the god in the rage of his heart confronted me..." etc.

PART 1

INTRODUCTION

Introduction

Biblical scholarship has always been a closed field, immune from external criticism and appraisal except on such narrow grounds as the literary quality of its product. Only from within has it been possible to debate the methods and results of textual analysis. This reservation of the field to an intimate elite has led to errors systematically becoming entrenched, perpetuated, and passed on from teacher to student. In it, it has become all too easy to brush aside the occasional protest against procedures whose best justification has been the high reputations of those who practiced them.

All the problems and inadequacies of Biblical scholarship are intensified and concentrated when the yet narrower specialty of Book of Job studies is concerned. For this is not only the Biblical work most sophisticated in both literary technique and intellectual content, it is also textually by far the most difficult to decipher.

M. Dahood, the great authority on Ugaritic – North-West Semitic – asserted extravagantly that 30% of the verses in the Book of Job remain untranslated[1] (without a faithful translation). If he was right, or anywhere near being right, this provides some explanation of the startling fact that since I started work on the Book of Job twenty years ago, new translations have appeared under the banner of the Jewish Publication Society, by Habel, by Hartley, by Mitchell, a half-translation by Clines has seen the light and a partial one by Van Selms; goodness knows how many more are taking shape in university libraries and theological departments; besides these there have appeared commentaries by McKenna, Janzen, Guyon, Eaton, Vawter, Garland, Simundsen, Epp, Penn-Lewis and Gibson, and doubtless others I have not seen.

Indeed, in the modern age of Biblical studies, there have been many dozens of translations of the Book of Job, particularly into English and German, and the majority have been accompanied by commentaries and explanations seeking to justify the selections which have been made. In this word "selections" is a major clue as to what has being going on. All the recent translators of Job (perhaps not Mitchell) have been enormously erudite scholars, steeped in the literature of Job as deeply as, if not more deeply than, in the Book of Job itself. What they seem to have done has been to examine all the many versions to which their predecessors have given birth, comparing them either critically or indulgently with the Hebrew text, and making selections from them. There are many scores of verses in Job where

radically different versions have circulated in past literature, so that there
is scope for innumerable possible combinations, none of them original.

But if Dahood was right, this process will never get any closer
to tapping the true meaning of the work, for if a verse has never been
correctly translated, what boots it which of the wrong versions one
selects? Conceding a little exaggeration, I believe Dahood was right,
and it is not by erudition, or the multiplication of selections from such
scholarship, that any progress will be made. Indeed, heresy though it
be, I feel constrained to suggest that the more one is immersed in the
mistakes of the past, the harder it becomes to solve the problems of
the text with the fresh insights that are needed.

How we may suspect that Dahood was about right is that
whichever version of the Book of Job we pick up, or however we mix
and match parts of versions together, we will always end up with a
mass of contradictions, illogicalities, inelegancies, which we must then
try to explain away as well as we can. What is more, we are bound to
find in our collection of dismembered and re-assembled fragments of
past versions, innumerable obvious examples of rude assaults on the
Hebrew text of natures which owe nothing at all to the sort of rigour
which ought to govern all scholarships and scientific enquiry.

For this reason, it seemed to me pointless to include any
review of the literature in this book. Where I have been happy with
another's translations, I have uses or paraphrased it, frequently without
acknowledgement. The skeleton I have used for my translation is the
old JPS one, which itself was the AV made conformable to Jewish
understanding, and where I have accepted the common view of a verse
or passage, I have written what is close to a mildly modernised version
of that. Only where there has been controversy, and I have felt I had
something to contribute, have I entered the lists.

The Book of Job is poetic throughout, and almost entirely
formally poetic. The spirit of the present age of Biblical scholarship
seems to be quite strongly anti-poetic. To read the great Hebrew
trumpet-blast of Genesis 1:1 in the New JPS translations is to realise
to what an extent the very style of these direct and compact poets has
become an embarrassment. "When God began to create heaven and
earth – the earth being unformed and void, with darkness over the
surface of the deep and a wind from God sweeping over the water –
God said "Let there be light". One may argue that such a version
recreates the meaning of the Hebrew, but it would be very difficult to
sustain the argument that it does anything to the spirit but murder it!

Introduction

No poet, I have nevertheless attempted to maintai
poetic diction and spirit in the translation, and, where specific devices,
as rhyme, assonance, alliteration, have been employed by the author,
I have done my best to reproduce them.

The world of Biblical scholarship has been swept in the past
century and a half by successive <u>theories</u> relating to the composition
of its books, the rules governing the grammer and syntax of its prose
and poetry, its laws of prosody, analyses of its <u>genres</u> and their
purposes, so that we have reached a state where we can classify the
scholarly works we read by the theory which has influenced them.
There is no theory in my translation, other than that translation
depends on the faithful rendition of words and sentences to recreate as
closely as possible, first the meaning and then the emotional and
intellectual ambience of what the translator believed to be the
intention at the time of writing.

This book is not a text-book of the Book of Job, nor is it in
any way a review of the literature, nor does it contain one. For those
who do want one, I suggest they consult the first volume of Clines,
and await the second.

Comments on the translation are largely restricted to where I
have felt them to be necessary, and the greater part goes without. But
there are points which, even after the translation has been given and
justified, need explanation. For example, the first author, the Deutero-
nomist, or Moses, or God, depending on your point of view, to speak
of *sore lesions from the sole of the foot to the crown of the head*, and to
mean something entirely different from the literal sense, had to explain
it a little later in the text. So did the second, Isaiah, to ensure that he
was not misinterpreted. But the author of Job was the third, and he
perhaps felt that by now the expression had taken on a metaphorical
mask of its own, and needed no laborious anti-paraphrase to correct
the literalist's impression. The modern translator has to mend this
omission with direct comment.

To generalise, where meaning in the Hebrew depends not
simply on the words, but also on their associations, the translator has
an obvious obligation to tell the reader so. This can happen very
frequently in a book which consists largely of a debate between a
group of well-educated gentlemen who, like all scholars, delighted in
displaying their scholarship by quotation and reference.

I
The Art of Mistranslation

The trouble with the Book of Job is quite simply stated. It has been misunderstood and mistranslated with unerring consistency for as far back as our knowledge stretches. Let me give the example of one very simple verse as a sample justification of that statement. Job 40:26 is a question asked of Job by God about *Leviathan*.

התשים אגמן באפו   ובחוח תקב לחיו

The words used in it are straightforward. An אגמן is the kind of reed which grows at the foot of trees - apart from grass, the lowest (in height) form of vegetable matter. Rightly or wrongly, it is often considered to mean *bulrush* (AV of Isaiah 58:5). The word recurs as probably vegetable matter producing smoke when burnt in the next chapter of Job. חוח is a brier or a bramble and also occurs elsewhere in Job - 31:40, where it is the sterile substitute for wheat invoked in a curse. The verse itself appears to be a parody of Isaiah 37:29 addressed by God to Sennacherib as though a horse:

ושמתי חחי באפך ומתגי בשפתיך

And I shall put My hook in your nose, and My bridle in your lips.

It is fairly clear then that the Job verse asks

> *Will you put a reed in his nose*
> *And pierce his jaw with a bramble?*

and it is not the task of the translator to explain why. That task belongs to the interpreter. When they are both the same, the translator must do his job first, and only then may he get to work on it as interpreter. The primary requisite is an accurate translation.

Here are the versions of 40:26 of LXX, Vg and QT:
LXX: *Will you fasten a ring in his nostril and bore his lip with a clasp?*
Vg: *Can you put a ring in his nose and pierce his jaw with a bracelet?*
QT: *Will you place a muzzle on his nose, and will you pierce his jaw with your engraving tool?*

This requires diagnosing.

What is going on that in three ancient translations, two words have achieved five different senses between them, none of which corresponds to the correct (as far as we now know) meaning of either word?[2] I suggest there is one explanation only, and that explanation spreads its wings to explain half the errors in translation of the Book of Job from that time to this. The persons responsible for these versions were not translating what the writer wrote, but what they thought he ought to have written or meant to have written. They could not believe their eyes when they read of passing a reed through the nose of a leviathan and piercing his jaw with a bramble. What nonsense! So bless them! they corrected his mistakes for him! Scholars have been correcting the mistakes of one of the world's greatest poets ever since.

It will be instructive to see how our five new versions (Clines has not reached Chapter 40 yet) have coped with the problem of this verse. NJPSV mates LXX's *ring* with the splendidly non-commital *barb*. Both Habel and Hartley copy *barb* and face it with *rope* (H.) and *cord* (Hartley). Mitchell demotes this into *string* and cracks Leviathan's jaw with a *pin*. Van Selms scores top marks not only amongst these five, but in all the history of the Book of Job with *bulrush* and *thorn*. If only he had not added an explanation[3]!

The *cord, rope, string* rendition of אגמן derives from the assumption that what means a reed can also mean a rope plaited of reeds. Both Pope and Gordis ingeniously draw attention to the ancient Greek *schoinos* which means both a reed (the aromatic rush) and a rush-rope. It is a pity for this argument that the LXX did not employ this word in their translation. The proponents of this version refer either to methods of carrying or of capturing fish as known or thought to be known from ancient inscriptions and pictures.

Of course the general fault of everybody here is an inability to tolerate fun. The Lord is having fun at the expense of Job. Look for a moment at 40:29:

> *Will you make sport with him like a bird?*
> *And will you cage him for your maidens?*

This too is asked about *Leviathan*. Even if one accepted the most pathetic of all Biblical misconceptions and regarded *Leviathan*, the mighty chaos-sea-monster and enemy-agent of God and Creation, as a prosaic crocodile, one could hardly fail to recognize the deliberate and ludicrous unreality of this image. The preposterous picture of Job attempting to capture a vast, fire-breathing monster by passing a reed through his incandescent nose and a bramble through his cast-iron jaw is exactly the image which the Lord intends to project. As will be seen from Chapter 5, p. 174, the origin of the vegetables is v. 40:22.

There is a two-stage process involved in achieving mistranslations of this kind. First it is necessary to misunderstand the author's intentions, to misconceive the passage to be translated; then it is necessary to rewrite the passage to conform to this misconception. The example of the reed and bramble is a crude one, where the technique of mistranslation consists simply of giving the wrong meaning to one or more key words. Translators are usually more resourceful in disguising what they have done. There is an art of mistranslation which has to be learned, and at the risk of being thought flippant, I will add that it is taught in the Bible study departments of Universities!

To speak of mistranslation at all is, I know, provocative and, in this age of scholarly urbanity, unmannerly. Nor am I unaware that there is no such thing as an exact translation, particularly of a poetic passage, only a better or a worse compromise. Still, what has gone on with reeds and brambles above merits no other word. It is not a matter of approaching more or less closely to the intentions of the author, or interpreting his mood or poetic nuance. It is really a failure to translate at all, a betrayal of the task. In this, we are dealing with poles of true and false mediations of the text, with errors, not of judgement, but of fact.

There are surely errors in translations of most if not all Biblical books, but equally surely they are nowhere so frequent as in this Book of Job, and for this there are good reasons. One is the often remarked unique difficulty both of the Hebrew of the book and of its gnomic prosodic form. This may account for what I shall call innocent errors. But many translational errors in the Book of Job (including the *reed and bramble*) are not of this kind. An innocent error is one that occurs for no other reason than a mistake, a misjudgement, a lacuna in knowledge, personal or general, reliance on unreliable tradition, or a lack or wandering of attention.

The second type of error is culpable error. This depends on some precondition in the mind of the translator which induces him to reject, consciously or unconsciously, the appropriate set of plausible translations, and to search for a way around them to a different meaning altogether. Such errors have both motive and method, while innocent errors lack motive. The motive in the errors discussed above was to achieve a verisimilitude which the author had gone to considerable lengths to avoid.

It is quite common for translators under the influence of theories of Biblical composition, from Wellhausen to Lowth to the committee of NJPSV, to contrive ways of inducing a text to support, or at least to conform to, such theories, and this can lead to unacceptable versions of any text. Religious certainty can interfere with translation, as in the famous crux of the "virgin" of Isaiah 7:14. So can political hatred, as when the word Zion is excised from the Bible by one Christian sect, and the gender of the Deity changed by another! In the Book of Job there is an additional and special motive in the necessity, felt by virtually all scholars, to find the text supporting a restricted interpretation of the story-line from which all geographical, historical, national and religious specificity is excluded. How intensely this necessity is felt to operate may be judged from the fact that the majority deny its individuality even to the River Jordan when it makes an appearance in the Book of Job (v. p. 176ff). Wherever the text makes some specific reference within one of these parameters, it will be found that culpable errors abound.

I now propose to discuss briefly the sundry methods of error which I have encountered in my study of the Book of Job. This may serve to explain the hostility towards scholarship as such which the astute reader will have detected already in this introduction. Nothing is less acceptable to a scientifically inclined mind than interference with data.

1. Impugning the Whole Text

There have been strange theories mooted about the origin of the Book of Job. Tur-Sinai insisted that its present text is a botched translation from an Aramaic original, granting himself the licence to *correct* the text to bring it into conformity with this imaginary ideal. For a scholastic horror story, readers should skim Introduction IV, pages XL to L of Tur-Sinai's Introduction. Guillaume[4] held that the original language was Arabic.

The wonderful thing about translations is that they are always clearer than the originals. The translator is obliged to choose between pairs of ambiguities, to find some lucid way of expressing the deepest obscurities, to make decisions and to incorporate them in a version. The extreme opacity of the Hebrew Book of Job, the very argument which has led these writers to assume an original in another tongue, is the most powerful reason for rejecting their contentions. Besides this, there is the pervasive presence of word-play - punning - in the Hebrew text. Except fortuitously, word-play cannot be translated. For these two reasons, as well as the absence of any convincing reason to favour such hypotheses, we have to reject these theories and assert that the Book of Job was written in literary Hebrew, and carry that conclusion to its full logical conclusion.

2. The Comparative Method

This last remark engenders far-reaching implications. Translators and commentators of the Book of Job, from as long ago as Rashi and Ibn Ezra down to the present day, have developed the habit of dealing with certain difficulties in the text by assuming a foreign meaning for particular words, *even though those words be perfectly acceptable Biblical Hebrew*. In the course of this book, we shall be encountering *all* those examples of this device which have become established wisdom about the text, and every one of them will be rejected decisively. It is, for example, no more acceptable to translate the Hebrew פחד as "thigh" (40:17), to give us the anatomically inconceivable *The sinews of his thighs are intertwined* in place of the metaphorically sound, *His sinews of fear are intertangled!*, than it is to translate the German *kind* as "well-disposed". The search of cognate languages for the meaning of Hebrew words is justified only where the Hebrew words are otherwise entirely unknown, and even in these cases conclusions drawn from such discoveries should be entertained with the utmost wariness. פחד in Hebrew would not have meant "thigh" even had Job 40:17 been the only example of the word, a *hapax legomenon*.

It is more than 120 years since the great Anglican divine, Dr. Pusey, expressed his outrage at this approach[5], but if anything, it has become more accepted, even to the point of being seen as an indispensable resource, in the intervening time. Dr. Pusey wrote,

> *But the comparison of the cognate dialects opened for a time an*
> *unlimited licence of innovation. Every principle of interpretation,*
> *every rule of language was violated. The Bible was interpreted with*
> *a wild recklessness to which no other book has ever been subjected.*
> *A subordinate meaning of some half-understood Arabic word was*
> *always at hand to remove whatever one misliked.*

Not a decade later an even greater Anglican clergyman, Pusey's protege
Charles Dodgson[6], published *Alice Through The Looking-Glass* where
Humpty Dumpty declared,

     "When I use a word, it means just what I choose it to mean -
neither more nor less."

     "The question is," said Alice, "whether you can make words
mean so many different things."

     "The question is," said *Humpty Dumpty*, "which is to be master
- that's all."

     Exactly the same practice is as widespread today. Gordis writes
in the introduction to his monumental translation/commentary of Job

> *No significant work in Biblical research is possible today without the*
> *use of the comparative method, the full utilization of extra-Biblical*
> *sources from the ancient Near East, Semitic, Hamitic, and even*
> *further afield.*

G divided this method into two components,

> *horizontal, reaching out in space from the biblical heartland to the*
> *surrounding peoples, cultures and religions of the Middle East, and*
> *vertical, reaching out in time to later periods in the historical*
> *experience of the Jewish people.*

He adds a very necesssary caveat:

> Indeed comparative material is so much in vogue that it is often permitted to take precedence ... even over intrinsic Biblical evidence at hand when it points in another direction. Often the text is emended to conform to the extra-Hebrew parallel, even when the Hebrew usage supports the Masoretic text.

Nonetheless, Gordis adheres as avidly as any other scholar to the error against which he warns.

Although G is undoubtedly exaggerating, there is no gainsaying the enormous value of viewing Biblical texts in the contexts of their contemporary geographical, social and historical settings. It is when the Hebrew *language* is deprived of its individuality and integrity that serious trouble ensues. What was going on in the countries around Israel can be employed to cast the brightest of lights on the understanding and interpretation of Biblical passages, but not on their translation. It cannot be allowed to infest the language with foreign words.

3. Quotations and Similar Figures

The indefatigable Gordis recognized eleven different forms of "quotation" in the Bible, and claimed that seven of these are to be found in Job[7]. The use which he, and many others, have made of the "recognition" of quotations is as follows: A statement is made by one of the speakers which, in the opinion of the scholar, is inappropriate or incomprehensible. He therefore declares that this statement is a *virtual quotation*, either recording what another speaker has said (although there be no record of this), or recording a view the speaker himself once held but has now abandoned, or a view which he imputes to someone else. That this is a very dangerous weapon indeed is readily apparent. With it, it is possible actually to *reverse* the intention of any passage at will. Its lavish employment by Gordis is perhaps the major flaw in his commentary. We shall encounter, and refute, a considerable number of "Gordian quotations" in the course of this study, but here I give one example, one of the most seriously damaging. Chapter 24:18-24 are difficult verses. Gordis converts all of them into a direct speech "quotation" by prefixing to them the phrase *You say to me* (of which there is no trace or hint in the Hebrew) - *You say to me, "They* penalty for wickedness in this life, when in fact they are his own words decrying God's indifference to the sufferings of the poor!

It is unfortunate that it cannot be said categorically that the only true quotations in the Book of Job are ones which are introduced in such a way as to make it clear that a quotation is to follow. There *are* wholly unintroduced quotations, but we only know this because we can identify the passage quoted. Some are immediately recognizable and universally acknowledged. 22:18 *The counsel of the wicked, far be it from me!* is the same as 21:16. 42:3 *Who obscures counsel without knowledge?* is obviously a variant of 38:2. 7:17 *What is man that you magnify him?* must be a close relation of Psalm 8:5. When it comes, however, to 2:7 as Deut 28:35, 1:14-19 as Deut 28:31,32, 17:6 as Deut 15:6, neither the facts nor their significance is commonly mentioned (v. Chap. 1). Indeed, where it does not suit the purposes of the commentators to mention them, or when they do not see the purpose of the quotation, no notice is taken even of direct quotations *within* the book itself - 41:4 (לא אחריש בדיו) as a quotation of 11:3 (בדיך מתים יחרישו) for example.

Thus not only are non-quotations regularly identified as quotations, but quotations are regularly treated as nonquotations. The tolerance of this practice is another result of the immunity enjoyed by the field of Biblical study from outside appraisal.

A further problem lies in the identification of those aggregations of words, to be found in all languages, called collocations, where the same phrase is used again and again in divers contexts, but where the element of true quotation does not really exist. The passage 19:15-19, seemingly dependent on sundry sources, is probably an elaborate example of this. Yet another problem is in determining whether a certain passage might not be a quotation from Psalm 151 a classic example of the question what song the sirens sang. This is not as fanciful as it sounds for many scholars "identify" 17:5 and 11:12, and even the peerless 1:21 as well-known sayings of the author's time, of which no other trace has survived. The almost central problem of the so-called "folk-tale of Job" is a problem in this category. See below in the section "How Many Authors?".

Again, we face problems in determining, after identifying a quotation from elsewhere in the Bible or ME literature, who is quoting whom. Is Job 3:3 a quotation of Jeremiah 20:14,15, or *vice versa*? Such questions cannot be answered without definitive datings of both books. Without them, it is fatally easy to invent sophistic arguments to support any hypothesis.

Granted that a *recognizable* quotation does not require any introduction, and this of course is true in any language, what introduction is required to establish an unrecognizable passage as a quotation? Or pehaps we should clean up our nomenclature a little and speak here not of a quotation but an *attribution*. "You said," "He said," even "I said" are straightforward. Most commentators recognize 22:19b *An innocent man would deride them* as an introduction to the words the innocent will speak, and they are surely right for what follows is scornful and contemptuous. But what of 12:4 *I am a mockery to His friends*? Is not what follows this *He who calls upon God and He answers him is a just and innocent jest* just as much the mockery forecast in that line? Strangely this solution is not accepted (v.i.). Is 24:12c *But God imputes nothing amiss* not a proper introduction to what God does impute? I strongly suggest it is. כי by itself undoubtedly serves in 27:3 to mark the intensification of Job's statement with "I avow" or "I swear". Should it not also be regarded as the introduction to a direct speech attribution in 31:18, allowing the verse to make sense without assuming a preposterous "he grew up to me" for גדלני?

Yet another puzzle. Does ועתה (*and now* or perhaps *and then*) after an attribution of direct or indirect speech (35:15; 37:21) indicate that a further and subsequent attributed statement is to follow?

It is clearly necessary to systematise our approach to the vexed question of "quotation" and "attribution" which is endemic in a book whose principal content is a prolonged debate. The most liberal view imaginable must cavil at many of the examples treated as attributions by Gordis and other modern scholars. Even if we accept that the least resemblance in what is said to what was said elsewhere is justification for treating one as a quotation of the other, and that the least hint of a comment by someone else (or at some other time) in the flow of a speech is justification for reading what is said into another mouth or time, attributing it away from the one who is saying it, we shall still look in vain for support for many now fully accepted attributions in the Book of Job. The unrestricted assumption that the scholar may choose into whose mouth he will place any words spoken by anyone in the debate at the heart of Job means that he has usurped the right to make the book say what he wants it to say, thinks it ought to have said, rather than what it does indeed record. The commentator and translator must always be searching for rules which will constrain freedom, not liberate imagination.

4. *Distortions of Grammar*

The changing from one language to another or one speaker to another only scratch the surface of the resources available to one determined to find the text conformable to his preconceptions. For instance, the sense of a passage may be effectively reversed by placing it in the jussive mood. This is a Biblical Hebrew variation of the imperfect (but only the imperfect) tense which changes a sentence from a statement into a wish - "Let it be" in place of "it is, was, or will be". The heart of that same passage which Gordis turned into a quotation, 24:18-20, was read as jussive as long ago as in LXX, and as recently as NJPSV the whole section 18-24 is still so treated (*May they be flotsam on the face of the water*) though in the section of seven verses there are three examples of verbs in the wrong form for the jussive as well as one verb in the perfect tense. There are even noun clauses, which it might be thought could not by any stretch of the imagination be made desiderative. Similar defects afflict other passages where this same illegitimate device is employed, e.g. 21:19,20, which has the distinction of being mistreated both as a false attribution in 19a, and as a false jussive in 19b and 20!

   A lax attitude to grammar may lead to the distortion or inversion of the meaning of a passage in other ways, imagining hermaphrodite sentences with feminine subjects and masculine verbs (they do sometimes occur). Particularly taking a singular verb and tacking it onto a plural subject or the opposite, can turn a statement by or about one party into one by or about another. The passage, 24:17-21, which has been surfacing repeatedly in this indictment, presents so singular a congeries of examples of this device that the only choice left to an uncommitted student is to determine whether it was the author or all the translators who were deranged! The "they" who *perish swiftly* in Gordis, and who are destined to be *flotsam* in NJPSV are represented by the non-negotiably singular word הוא in the Hebrew!

   There is a body of opinion, reflected *par excellence* in the NEB translation of the Bible, which actually believes that Hebrew verse is not constrained by grammatical rules at all or at least by none known.

Noel Freedman[8] wrote

> *Don't take anything for granted, least of all the idea that prose rules govern Hebrew poetry, with a few exceptions. It is the other way round: poetry has its own rules, and occasionally the results coincide with prose usage, but not always or often, and there is always the possibility of a different arrangement or analysis, and we must reckon with the possibility of multiple meanings and different levels of discourse.*

This is either a counsel of despair or the determination to treat the text as a palimpsest upon which the commentator is free to inscribe essentially his own composition. To read 15:28:

וישכון ערים נכחדות   בתים לא־ישבו למו   אשר התעתדו לגלים

The city where he lives will lie in ruins, his house will be deserted; it will soon become a heap of rubble. (NEB)

is truly to play author. There are indubitably deviations from prose syntax and grammar in Hebrew poetry, particularly in the extremely contracted sentence formations used in the Book of Job. The absence of the *nota accusativa* and the sparing use of the definite article, the way in which suffixes are allowed to spread their influence to parallel nouns and verbs which lack them are all very obvious. The far greater laxity in the use of the tenses is disconcerting to a diligent translator. But none of this adds up to justification for disregard of the normal rules of grammar. Indeed, it is difficult to imagine how in any language such a situation might arise that grammatical rules for prose and poetry could be radically different, and this least of all in Hebrew, a language where the difference between the two modes of writing is so indistinct, so graduated.

5. *Denaturing the Idiom*

Allied to the misprision of Masoretic grammar is the technique of dismissing the idiomatic sense of a phrase in favour of its long discarded literal meaning, as when כפי (30:18) is translated "as the mouth of", אל־פיהו (40:23) as "to his mouth"; מי־יתן? (14:4) as "who will give?" (JPS), "who will extract?" (H), "who can distinguish?" (G), "who will produce?" (NJPSV), "who can make [into]?" (C). In this last example it is apparent that the translators are drawing courage from each others' follies, and concentrating their skills on novel ways of reproducing the errors of the past rather than on how to correct them. We might expect a badly programmed computer to misrepresent stock phrases in these ways. The worst aspect of this practice is the selectivity with which it is applied. מי־יתן is given by all translators as an idiom in almost all locations. לעשות עם is always taken as thoroughly idiomatic in 10:12, but never in 40:15. This favouritism is impossible to justify.

    It is true that the possibility of making startling use of the literal sense of an idiomatic phrase is open to the inventive writer. I would even suggest that there are at least two such examples in the Book of Job - 1:5 and 21:33. But the exposure of such examples requires close argument, and at the very least a clear demonstration that the idiomatic sense is not applicable in the context.

6. *Reattribution per se*

Quite crudely we find commentators simply reattributing speeches or parts of speeches to speakers other than those whom the text announces. There is, for example, close to unanimous consensus (this writer of course dissenting) that major portions of Chapters 24, 26 and 27 (yes, sometimes including 24:18-24) are incorrectly attributed to Job in the MT, although strangely, no two scholars seem to be in full agreement as to which portions of which speeches should be reallocated to which of the comforters. With engaging disingenuousness, D&G[9] put it thus:

> *The probability is great, not that to the third cycle Sophar contributed nothing and Bildad less than half a dozen distichs, but that the speeches of the third cycle have through some accident reached us in a very imperfect form, part of them having been lost, the remainder dislocated. This* single hypothesis *(my italics) of mutilation of the text accounts at once for the whole of the peculiarities of the existing close of the third cycle...*

Again we encounter a method of exegesis which can be used to cut any Gordian knot and relieve us of the necessity of struggling with the significance of a recalcitrant part of the work. The formulation of such single hypotheses as allow the translator to work his will unconstrained upon the text should always be resisted. Later in this book (Chap. 9), I shall demonstrate how the elements of this so-called "third cycle" belong together where they have been put, and how the apparent contradictions which the text suggests may properly be resolved without recourse to surgery. Indeed this whole theory of a disordered "third cycle" has arisen because of prior translational malpractices sedulously copied from generation to generation.

7. Prising Stones from a Mosaic

If we go back in time a few decades and turn to the work of Christian exegetes, we find all textual problems summarily dissolved by the expedient of expunging from the text any portion which caused difficulty. Each Biblical book was treated as a mosaic of different authors, peppered with interpolations and glosses, and the game played was to restore a mythical original, or more than one, which was perfectly self-consistent and sensible, although sometimes reduced in size to but a small fraction of the transmitted work. With regard to the Book of Job, this process reached its absurd climax, or nadir, in the analysis of Baumgartel[10] (1933), who allowed just 168 verses to survive from Chapters 4 to 31 (out of almost 700) and denied all authenticity to any other part of the book! When it comes to consideration of Elihu (Chaps 32-37), present-day commentators of all denominations have no hesitation in applying this Wellhausian approach, and wishing them out of the way. Chapter 28 scarcely fares better.

While it is true that, like rolling snowballs, simple and popular compositions, especially those like ballads, which are sung to repetitive tunes, tend to gather additional material as the years pass, this does not happen to such elaborate literary works as the Book of Job. The most that has been established in this regard is the occasional addition of a few explanatory lines at the end of such compositions. This we know happened in the LXX Book of Job, though it is noteworthy that the addition has long ago been shed. It is also possible that the last six over-specific verses (42:12-17) of the present MT version, which are absent from the QT and, significantly, also from the commentary of Berechiah, are not a part of the original work. The possibility that Chapters 28 and 32-37 are interpolations is, I believe, negligible.

8. *Corruption per se*

The text of the Bible is, in parts, as many as 3000 years old, and has been transmitted for a large part of that time by manual copyists. The precautions against error or corruption creeping into the text have been formidable, but it is in the nature of reality that imperfections have been introduced. The original text was without vowels, and for many centuries the vocalization was transmitted by word of mouth - essentially by song. The dangers in this are too obvious to state. That there are errors in the text we know for certain because of the existence of variant texts in different ancient manuscripts of the Bible.

The problem of detecting and correcting such errors is not susceptible of any unique and perfect solution. A conservative attitude will seek to accept as much of the text as possible and to assume corruption only as a last resort, and this surely is the right way. My finding has been that errors in the Masoretic Text are extremely rare in the Book of Job, perhaps no more than two dozen, and those all of a most minor nature. There are in Hebrew letters which resemble each other, ד and ר; ה and ח, but I know of no instance in Job where it is reasonable to suspect that confusion has occurred between either of these pairs. The sort of error which is to be found is a metaplasm - שלמותי for שמלתי, a dropped letter, את for אתה, or a confusion between *sureq* and *holem*.

On the other hand the *assumption* of corruption of the text is very common amongst Job scholars, although there is great variation, with those claiming to be relying on the MT tending to be far more conservative than others. Tur-Sinai made use of the assumption of corruption to an extent which is agreed to be excessive by almost everyone. But the practice of even the most conservative commentators and translators succeeds in generating as many maimed and mangled words as wounded soldiers on a battlefield.

It should, I think, be an unbreakable rule that, in the absence of extrinsic evidence of corruption (variant readings in old manuscripts or deduced from LXX, Vg, Peshitta, etc.) the assumption of corruption is barred if the word under suspicion exists at all in Hebrew. The fact that one or more commentators cannot understand what is written should not suffice to justify changing the text. I offer here only one example to illustrate the lightness with which this very serious course is habitually undertaken.

Eliphaz declares in 5:7 that *Man is born to Trouble*, a simple poetic statement whose literal meaning is that Trouble is the parent of man. Many commentators consider that this statement does not quite fit into its context, and that what the poet really meant to say was that *Man begets trouble*. From this it is no distance at all for them to make the decision that this after all must have been what he did say. They therefore take the Puʻal verb יוּלָד of the MT and revocalize it to the hapax deficient Hiphʻil form יוֹלִד, achieving their ends, and destroying altogether the carefully crafted architecture of Eliphaz's extended discourse on the subject of the parentage of man and Trouble and affliction. At the same time the parallelism of the verse which has in stich b the sons of one god, *Reshef*, and in stich a the sons of another, *Amal*, is destroyed.

That any scholar should imagine that his trade gives him the freedom to change a perfectly good יולד into something else, and that a form unattested in the Bible, is testimony to a terribly wrong attitude which has somehow flourished in the profession uncorrected for decades or centuries. I cannot see that we can go on permitting changes of this kind to be made in the text of these revered books. Some form of self-discipline must one day prevail. No fewer than fifteen distinguished Biblical scholars[11] have insisted on this mischievous change of vocalization, for which there is no reason whatever but their own imperfect understanding of the text and appreciation of its ramifications and subtleties.

This one example could be multiplied a hundred-fold. The fact is that many scholars, although they might not wish to admit it, actually prefer making an emendation to accepting the MT, other things being equal. The scope for ingenuity is, of course, limitless.

9. *The Massacre of the Particles*

Another form of violence to the text, one which has been systematised in the NJPSV throughout the Bible can be described as the demolition of road signs. A vital ingredient in language is the small directional words, conjunctions and prepositions, which govern the relationships between substantive words, verbs and nouns. There is nothing to complain of in NJPSV's *statement* of its practice in this regard[12]; it is impeccable.

> A further obvious difference between this translation and most of the older ones is in the rendering of the Hebrew particle waw, which is usually translated "and." Biblical Hebrew demanded frequent use of the waw, but in that style it had the force not only of "and" but also of "however," "but," "yet," "when," and any number of other such words and particles, or none at all that can be translated into English. Always to render it as "and" is to misrepresent the Hebrew rather than be faithful to it. Consequently the committee translated the particle as the sense required, or left it untranslated.

They left it untranslated 450 times in the 1043-verse Book of Job alone, displaying rather than the judicious care foreshadowed by the above, a lust for indiscriminate destruction which is ludicrous and astonishing. What is more it is not only waws which have succumbed to the long knives of JPS, but numerous other prepositions and conjunctions of none of which can it be said that they have the force of no word at all which can be translated into English. Having rid themselves of these authentic roadsigns, the translators then had to face the necessity of replacing them with new ones of their own, for no language can function effectively without a sufficiency of particles. They did not flinch from this.

In Jeremiah 25 there is a passage in which a large number of

place-names from the region is assembled in a comprehensive imprecation. A study of this list shows that it contains enough information to
locate reasonably accurately on the map a considerable number of
places whose position is otherwise unknown. Amongst them is the
Land of Uz, the setting of the Book of Job[13] (see Chap. 2). However,
in order to follow the information contained in this list, it is necessary
to pay the closest attention to the presences and absences of <u>waws</u>.
There are in all thirty <u>waws</u> in the entire passage, but woe to him who
relies on NJPSV to decipher it, for only thirteen of them have
survived, and upon what principle these and no others, who can tell?

There is no substitute for unfailing respect for the text,
enduring to the least <u>jot</u>, <u>tittle</u>, <u>waw</u> and <u>dagesh</u>.

10. Questionable Questions

Another way of achieving the pernicious objective of reversing the
meaning of a statement is to treat it as a rhetorical question demanding
a negative answer. A signal example of this is 40:24a, בעיניו יקחנו, almost
always rendered, with the aid of denaturing the idiom בעיניו, to suggest
Job's inability to capture *Behemoth* (*Shall any take him by the eyes?*)
when it actually refers to *Behemoth*'s confidence in his ability to
capture Nahar (*In his opinion he can take him.*) There are also examples
of indicatives treated as imperatives and *vice versa* with similar effect.

11. Misorientation

The concepts of "quotation" and "attribution" are not clear-cut. At
some point we decline into "reference". Particularly in the Book of
Job, because it is unique amongst Biblical books as a debate or
discussion, "references" by one speaker to remarks made by another
must be frequent, and to identify them is an important part of the art,
both of translation and of interpretation. Of translation as well as
interpretation because if a word is a reference to the same word
elsewhere, it *must* be translated by the same word the second time.
This does not necessarily apply in other circumstances (see e.g. תחת in
34:24 and 34:26 where it has quite different meanings).

Consider the following sample list. Is גדיש in 21:32, usually
taken to mean a tomb or tombstone, a reference to the same word in

5:26? Is כי־חמה, utterly mysterious in 36:18, a reference to the same phrase in 19:29? What of מתקו־לו רגבי־נחל in 21:33 and מתקו רמה in 24:20? Once attention has been drawn to it, is there any doubt that 41:19 *He treats iron as straw and brass as rotten wood* is a true reference to 40:18, *His bones are ingots of brass, His skeleton cast-iron?* No-one has dared to notice it! For once it is recognized, and with it the opposition between *Behemoth* and *Leviathan*, the whole structure of the common understanding of the Book of Job falls in its ramifications like a row of dominoes. שמץ דבר in 26:14 can be nothing but a reference to דבר...שמץ in 4:12, flooding Chapter 26 with wholly unfamiliar light. Going farther afield, is it possible that there is no element of reference in the fact that the phrase שחק־בו occurs twice only in the whole Bible, in Job 40:29 and Psalm 104:26, both times in reference to an entity called *Leviathan*. Can they really be different *Leviathans?*

H, who devoted unparalleled attention to teasing out the interplay of words between different chapters and different speakers in Job, noted only one of the above internal references, that between 24:20 and 21:33.

It is essential that a proper consistency be maintained both in identifying genuine references, and in eschewing false ones. While we must rigorously avoid assuming quotations gratuitously, we must not overlook the innumerable to-and-fro references whereby the speakers, including the Lord, taunt, deprecate and answer one another and expand and develop their own arguments through thesis and antithesis.

Even the question of identifying internal and external references is not the final relevant attenuation of the problem of orienting passages towards one another in this book. We must consider also the way in which words are used, and whether we have a right to expect consistency in this. Is it reasonable, for example, to allow that the author might have used the word שחקים to mean *the skies* in 37:21 but mean *clouds* in the sense of individual aggregations of vapour in 38:37? Could he have intended התערר to mean *become hostile to* in 17:8 and *to triumph* in 31:29? Can the word קדרים have entirely different meanings in Chapters 5 and 6? Does the Po`lal חוללת mean *Were you brought forth?* in 15:7, while יחוללו, also Pol`al, means *they writhe* in 26:5?

12. Bare-faced Mistranslation

Here we return to where we began, finding words like reed and bramble exchanged for metallic hardware. Because the next example is in itself of surpassing triviality, yet the subject of the lengthiest and most fascinating commentary in the whole of Delitzsch's two-volume masterpiece[14], I propose to add one final sample of this inexcusable technique. 34:36 is אָבִי יִבָּחֵן אִיּוֹב עַד־נֶצַח בְּאַנְשֵׁי־אָוֶן, which only produces difficulties if the translator decides to make them. G comments as follows, אבי *manifestly not "my Father" (Ra, Ibn E.), a term never applied to God in the book*; P. *Certainly the word does not mean "my father" (so Vulg.) here and probably not in I Sam xxiv 12 (sic) and II Kings v 13*; D&G *My father (V pater mi) is out of the question*; H `*my father' is meaningless at this point and should probably be deleted as a dittograph for* `*Job'.* (!)

Manifestly; certainly; out of the question; meaningless".

Strong words, these!

The real trouble here lies in the resolute determination of all commentators to read the verse as an expression of desire *Let Job be tried...!* It does not seem to have occurred to anyone how utterly perverse such a sentiment would have been at this point in the story. If the Satan had uttered it in Chapter 1 it would have been comprehensible, but here when Job in the understanding of these commentators is destitute, bereaved of all his children, smitten with foul disease, deserted by all, scorned by all, sitting on his ash-heap scratching his sores, one must ask in bewilderment, what further trial does Elihu recommend? And what sort of character can a man have to say this to or about Job?
    I have searched in vain for a straightforward translation of the first line (leaving aside the controversial אבי). But surely, in modern idiom, what this line says is:

Job is being tested to destruction

and the next gives Elihu's view of the reasons for this.
    As for אבי, despite the magnificent study of Delitzsch, and the ingenuity exercised by modern authors in finding new ways of expressing their conformity to a fashion, the word has only one real

meaning in Hebrew, and all the variations on the dialects of the
Hauran area which fill the pages of the commentaries cannot alter this.
אבי is *my father*. As in English, this also means *Sire!*, a form of address
offered to one who far outranks the speaker. This is how the word
should be translated in II Kings 5:13, when the servants of Naaman
sought delicately to persuade him to follow Elisha's prescription. This
address is not directed to God as those who reject *my Father* assume,
but Eliphaz, and has a modicum of sarcasm in the obsequy. Elihu
promised not to *bestow titles* on any man, but, having something of a
Uriah Heep nature, he cannot altogether avoid it. The passage is
discussed on p. ?

13. Translating off-centre

Every word of independent meaning in every language has what we
have come to call a semantic range, an umbra and penumbra of
meaning surrounding the primary dictionary definition of the word.
It is a function of context to direct us where in this complex to locate
the precise sense attaching to any particular word in a passage. Most
of the time we shall find our answer in the bull's-eye, the lexical or
dictionary definition. Often it will be close to this but not exactly it;
occasionally we shall find the appropriate meaning well off centre.

     Mistranslation reaches its zenith of artistry in devising
meanings for well-understood words which, while close enough to
arouse no suspicion of mistranslation, yet combine to convey an
impression quite different from that which would be obtained from
unimaginative and uninspired adherence to dictionary meanings of the
words. Consider the two-verses 15:4,5. Almost every version of this
admonition contains renditions of the seven key words and phrases
חפר, יראה, תגרה, שיחה, לפני-אל, יאלף and ערומים, none of which can be
proved to be actually wrong, but none of which corresponds closely
to the normal meaning of the word or phrase. The result is a total
misrepresentation of the passage. Always the adoption of a novel
meaning, or the choice of a rare and deviant one, requires especial
justification, and where a concentration of such exceptions is required
to sustain a particular interpretation, that interpretation should be
abandoned. See p. 479ff.

14. Faith in and with the Text

Ultimately these questions of the identification of references, of threading the way through syntactic jungles, of deciphering words in languages long dead and gone, come down to a question of how much one respects the craftsmanship, integrity and alertness of the author of the book, and the scribes who laboured to transmit his writing intact to an only-imagined future. Did both he and they make a whole lot of careless mistakes in putting the book together and transmitting it, or is this in fact one of the most refined and delicately chiselled poems that the world has ever been bequeathed, lovingly *embalmed and treasured up on purpose to a life beyond life*? I do not find it necessary to believe that the work, or the Bible as a whole, was divinely inspired to conclude that this second is the correct alternative.

There is another way of resolving what appear to be selfcontradictions and inconsistencies and hopeless obscurities, one which does not involve transparently illegitimate forms of textual mutilation practiced on the words and sentences anaesthetised during the transfer between languages. That is to attempt, by patience and reflection, to ascertain what the author of the book was really up to, letting it tell its story without interrupting it to coerce into any predetermined channel.

This methodology requires that one put up with the consequences of acceptance of the accuracy and reliability of the work. It requires more from the interpreter and less from the translator. It is for the former to resolve inconsistencies, contradictions and paradoxes faithfully transcribed by the latter. In every enterprise of translation/interpretation, interpretation must wait upon translation. The text must always rule.

In the translation of the Book of Job which is the centrepiece and purpose of this book, I present a translation which is truly based on the Masoretic text. It takes as fundamental assumptions that the Book of Job was written in literary Hebrew, that it employs standard Hebrew grammar and syntax within the constraints of its gnomic form, that it says what it wishes to say economically, that it contains nothing redundant or unnecessary to its purpose, nor any detritus accumulated from external sources, that it lets the reader know by one means or another when it is being interrogative, imperative or imploring, and when it is invoking material from sources other than the immediate speaker. Also I have assumed that the number of errors which has accumulated in the transmission of the text is small, and their nature invariably simply explicable in mechanical terms. I have not, however, accepted any restraints on interpretation other than plausibility and sense. Least of all have I accepted any derived from speculations about the literary category of the work.

II
Some Aspects of the Provenance of the Book of Job

Of what *genre* is the Book of Job? When was it composed? Who was the author or authors? Was there more than one author? What was the purpose in writing it?

1. Genre

Anyone who reads some part of the recent literature relating to the Book of Job will gather that it has been almost fully accepted that it belongs to that corpus of ancient international literature known as "Wisdom Literature". Taking books at random from this section of the library I read:

Job has commonly and *appropriately* been classed with Pr., Qoh., Sir., and Wisdom as belonging to the "Wisdom" or reflective literature of the Jews in which human life is considered broadly without the overruling national interest that characterizes most other Hebrew literature. D&G

The Book of Job represents the supreme achievement of Hebrew Wisdom. In form and approach, as well as in background and content, its affinities with both conventional and unconventional Wisdom teaching are striking. When the full scope of biblical wisdom is kept in mind, it is clear that by virtue of its literary form Job belongs in this category. G

The Book of Job, of course, falls into the category of Wisdom Literature. The speeches of the friends are orthodox or conventional wisdom, while Job's discourses may be termed "anti-wisdom wisdom". P

These examples of ancient eastern literature belong to what is usually called Wisdom literature, and to the same category we also assign the Book of Job, although...it is an emphatic protest against the prevailing wisdom of the time in Israel and the Near East. T-S

We have in our Old Testament three wisdom books, Proverbs, Job, and Ecclesiastes. Bewer[15]

There have, however, been occasional dissenting voices and caveats against this confident categorisation. Crenshaw[16] writes with commendable balance, if without decision, on the subject:

> *What if the Book of Job does not belong to wisdom literature? After all, Chapter 31 has the form of Egyptian ritual texts. As a matter of fact, a case can be made against Job as wisdom writing (Claus Westerman, Der Aufbau des Buches Hiob [Stuttgart: Calwer, 1977], original publication 1956). None can deny strong affinity between Job and complaints within the book of Psalms and related laments in Mesopotamian texts. The book can certainly be viewed as an example of an answered lament, a model for the appropriate manner of responding to suffering. It also has the form of a disputation, specifically, a mythological prologue, a debate, and a divine resolution. In addition the book freely incorporates material from prophetic literature, especially Isaiah 40-55, and traditions concerning the divine self manifestation. The ending of the poetic dialogue, specifically God's approach to humans, belongs to prophetic and narrative texts but is ill at home in wisdom contexts.*

Let us for a moment take up Crenshaw's "what if..." Why is it important to what category this book, or any book belongs? The clue in this case lies in the sentence of D&G in the first illustration above. It has long been concluded that Wisdom Literature is *without the overruling national interest that characterises most other Hebrew literature.* Once the decision has been made by a commentator that the Book of Job belongs in this category, he becomes resistant, if not impervious, to any evidence that national concerns are involved in, let alone central to, the work. No matter that this reasoning is perfectly circular, it nonetheless in practice imposes an estoppal on particular lines of thought.

Ancient contemporary critics did not make rigid distinctions between different categories of literature. This is a relatively modern imposition. No-one set out to write a piece of Wisdom Literature; he just set out to write. Whenever such categorizations are *post facto*, they are invalid for imposing restrictions on content or form. Our knowledge of the restrictions and characteristics of any type of literature, other than those subject to contemporary definition, like the Pindaric Ode or the Sonnet, is arbitrary, reflecting nothing but our own decisions as to which works to place into which categories. The statement *Job is Wisdom Literature* cannot be allowed to influence our views as to the content of the Book of Job. It can, however, influence our view as to what may properly be contained within the category of Wisdom. The content of a book is to be determined from the book itself, alone and isolated from every other consideration. If Job has national concerns, this means either that it is wrong to regard it as Wisdom Literature, or that the restriction placed on Wisdom Literature as devoid of national interest must be revised. But no conclusion can flow backward from category to content.

Personally, I do not believe that there are good grounds for assigning the Book of Job to this category, even though there is an undeniably philosophic theme running from beginning to end of the book. There is too much beside. The hallmarks of the *genre* are not so much missing from the work as stamped in reverse. Wisdom Literature is enquiry, but above all calm and dispassionate enquiry, armchair enquiry. Passion rages through the Book of Job like a fire blown by a hurricane. Between *Perish the day in which I was born* and *When the stars of the morning rang out in unison*, every colour in the emotional rainbow has been dashed on the pages, every stop in the emotional organ has been pulled out. What have despair, and longing, and terror, and pride, defiance, and anger, and contempt, and humiliation, grief, and faith, and pity, and stubborness, and exaltation, and menace, and outrage, and *hubris* to do with Wisdom? Surely one cannot claim for Wisdom Literature, as an object-lesson, the uninhibited parade of all that negates it.

Wisdom deals with God-at-a-distance; no intimacy, no involvement. He is the remote Ruler Who has laid down the laws for men to follow. Wisdom teaches men how to keep out of His skirts; how to get through life without attracting His attention: *Be not rash with thy mouth, and let not thy heart be hasty to utter a word before God; for God is in heaven and thou upon earth; therefore let thy words be few* (Ecc. 5:1). This is the authentic voice of Wisdom. Can one say other than that in all literature there is no example of the disregard of this advice more extreme than that of Job? Job is man in desperate pursuit of communication with God. He is the prophet in reverse, relentlessly pursuing God with the call to duty and justice.

Wisdom enquires how men should deal with men, with women, and with God. In the widest sense it seeks to understand the Universe, but not through the immediacy of revelation, as Job does, but through quiet reflection, the study of tradition, and meticulous

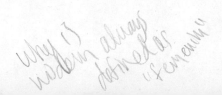

observation. The Book of Job tells how God should deal with man. It weighs Him and finds Him wanting, exploring theology to the depths.

The range of concerns in the Book of Job so far exceeds the concerns of "other" wisdom literature as to testify to a whole new intellectual universe. For in addition to the "wisdom" themes of innocent suffering, man's place in the Universe, the doctrine of reward and punishment, and the need for men to walk on egg-shells in the sight of God, this book deals with predestination, free-will and original sin; sin in thought, word and deed; the absolutism of right and wrong; the afterlife and resurrection; penitence and mediation; dreams and their meaning; vicarious and surrogate sacrifice; Dualism; the Divine role in history; modes of communication between God and man; the meaning of election; the Divine need for man's service and the Divine obligations to man and beast; even the several obligations of each to the very soil itself. The Book of Job is an arrow shot to the heart of the forbidden question, the character and composition of the Creator.

In form too, while clearly the Book of Job has borrowed (and transformed) devices from works which lie firmly within the Wisdom tradition - in particular, disputation, it has borrowed from every other Hebrew literary tradition as well. While there are a number of genuine proverbs in the book, it is a small number, and the use to which they are put is much the same as we should expect in any argumentative work; at no time are they *ex cathedra* pronouncements as is the proverb of the Wisdom school. There are, as Crenshaw remarks, laments and Psalmic episodes recurring throughout the book. The two phrases, *He who calls upon God and He answers him* (12:4, referring to Job), and *an intercessor, the one in a thousand, to declare His uprightness to man* (33:23, referring to Elihu [see p.295ff]) together virtually define the prophets, whilst all the addresses between men and God and God and men in the book are, as Crenshaw declares, prophetic literature, or they are fiction, but never Wisdom. Innumerable writers have commented on the large share of the book devoted to jurisprudence, to the conduct of a legal tussle between Job and God. This too is quite foreign to Wisdom. That there is a major, indeed a primary, theme of historicity in the Book of Job is a principal thesis of this work, and this decisively excludes it from the category, Wisdom, as presently understood.

In truth the Book of Job is *sui generis*, an unique work, whose amplitude bursts free of every attempt at confinement within a defined literary sphere. It is the realisation of the combination of forms,

we can not put into a category

wisdom, prophecy, psalm, drama, contest, lament, theodicy, history, and allegory, fused in the crucible of genius to be one of a kind for all time.

2. The Date

Centuries have been credited with the composition of this book ranging from the third millenium to the second century before the Common era, but modern opinion is strongly weighted in favour of an early post-exilic date. The (to my mind) absolutely decisive reference to the Book of Job in the writings of Ezekiel is not merely brushed aside, but made somehow to serve as additional evidence for this late date. So-called Aramaisms also are invoked to testify to a post-exilic composition, but as Habel, quoting Snaith and others, points out *the identification of a word or root as an Aramaism which necessarily belongs to the postexilic period is a precarious exercise. The absence of any prior reference to a particular word or root in earlier Biblical texts is no proof that such a word did not exist, as the recent findings from Ugarit have demonstrated.*[17]

There are very many apparent quotations from and references to other Biblical books in the Book of Job, but each of these, before it can be pressed into the service of "dating" it, must first itself be dated, and then be shown, by what means I hardly know, to have or not to have priority over the Job text. Unfortunately, where it is clear that Job is quoting a prior source, as for example the dependence of Job 7:17 on Psalm 8:5, we have no idea at all of the date of the source. The same applies to the certain dependence of a considerable number of verses in both Prologue and Dialogue on the 28th chapter of Deuteronomy. We really do not know when Deuteronomy was written, nor if it was all written in one period. Some writers find a heavy dependence of Job on Jeremiah, but I see little evidence of this. One certain resemblance, Job 3 and Jeremiah 20, is equivocal, with a possibility that both passages depend on a common extraneous formula - the exclamation *Perish the day I was born!* was surely first uttered by a Neanderthal caveman. Resemblances between Job and the first Isaiah, particularly their shared use of mytho-allegorical terminology (*Behemoth, Leviathan, Nahar, Rahab*) have in general passed unacknowledged. There has long been an unresolved dispute over priority between Job and Deutero-Isaiah.

The verse 17:6, if understood without recourse to inventing Hebrew verbs (תוף) and distorting Hebrew idiom (לפנים), gives us a date earlier than which the Book cannot have been composed, for it contains the phrase *Tophet of yore* - i.e. of former times (so NJPSV). The high place at Tophet in the Gehinnom valley (? the site of what has long been known as *Job's Spring*) was twice abolished, once by Hezekiah in 715 (II Kings 18:4) and the second time by Josiah in 622 (II Kings 23:10). A date earlier than the last decade of the 8th Century therefore seems impossible. However, the majority of scholars would probably reject this evidence because it provides a geographical focus inside Judah for a book which they are convinced deals with events outside its borders, and because it is anachronistic to the patriarchal period which they believe it reconstructs.

The Ezekiel references to Job (14:14,20) are nearly unanimously accepted as testifying to the prior existence of a folk-tale of Job rather than an acquaintance by the prophet with the Book of Job itself. This folk-tale theory is discussed below and found extremely improbable. Ezekiel speaks of Job as the third of a group of ultra-righteous men, Noah, Danel and Job. Not only is this taken as evidence of the antiquity of Job (as a folk-hero), but also of his non-Israelite status, Danel being identified with the virtuous pagan king in the Ugaritic *Tale of Aqhat*[18]. This identification is intrinsically unlikely, for acknowledgement of the supreme virtue of a pagan would have run counter to Ezekiel's life purpose. Noah, of course, though no Israelite, was also no pagan. More likely is it that the Danel of Ezekiel is a precursor of the Daniel of the eponymic book, perhaps from a story first told in relation to the earlier Assyrian exile. Noah, Daniel and Job, as described in the Bible, share the distinction of being the most righteous men of their respective generations, and it is surely this distinction which prompted their choice as exemplars by the prophet. At no point in the *Tale of Aqhat* is Danel credited with this exceptional rank in virtue. Inasmuch as the characteristics of Job in the surviving Book of Job make him a fit companion for Noah in Ezekiel's illustration, and as Ezekiel's comment seems to reflect Job 22:30[19], it is proper to regard the citation as very powerful evidence that the present Book of Job was known to Ezekiel, establishing a date later than which it could not have been written. This is early in the 6th Century.

Analysis of the text of the Book of Job contained in this work shows an allegorical level in which the book is concerned throughout with events taking place during the 8th Century BCE, culminating in the siege of Jerusalem in 701 (or 700). While a discussion of these events and their significance might, of course, have taken place at any time after that date - such debates are still taking place in *yeshivoth* throughout the world - there is a high probability that such a literary treatment would have been undertaken shortly after the events. Indeed, because the catastrophe of the Assyrian conquests of Israel and Judah was ultimately dwarfed by the Babylonian conquest culminating in the sack of Jerusalem in 587, it is unlikely that such a discussion would have been regarded as topical in the Babylonian or the post-exilic period. The final conquest of Assyria by Babylon (and Medea) occurred in 608. These considerations lead me to date the composition of the Book of Job to the 7th Century, and most probably quite or very early in that century.

The dependence of the Book of Job on Deuteronomy is crucial, not only to the comprehension of the book, but to its dating. It is scarcely going too far to describe the Book of Job as an elaborate *midrash* on Deut 28, on the whole idea of a covenant enforced by threats and promises from on high. This theme is dealt with at length in Chapter 2 of this book and I shall not anticipate. It is, however, almost beyond comprehension that innumerable commentaries on Job have been written, and almost all without even passing reference to the many close resemblances, amounting again and again to direct quotation, between the Book of Job and Chap. 28 of Deuteronomy. Most recently Hartley affects to list all parallels of phrase and metaphor between the Book of Job and other Biblical books (pp.11,12), but does not even mention Deuteronomy.

There is a strong body of opinion that the Book of Deuteronomy was composed during the reign of King Josiah (640-609), and was the book of the law "discovered" in the Temple in 621[20]. If this were correct it would impose an additional restriction on the possible date of the Book of Job as being later than 621. But this view has never been universally accepted. Driver[21], for example, maintains *it is probable that its composition is not later than the reign of Manasseh*. Manasseh's dates are 687-642. The evidence of Isaiah 1:5,6 in which the situation in Jerusalem during the siege of 701 is expressed in the present tense in terms which appear, like Job 2:7, to be a direct quotation of Deut 28:35, would seem to push the date back by a further quarter of a century.

From the evidence presented in this introduction and in several of the essays which follow, any date between 701 and the Babylonian exile is possible for the composition of the Book of Job, but any later date is improbable. Such a later date would require a reinterpretation of the historical occasion for the composition, equating the second round of Job's misfortunes with the destruction of Jerusalem and the Temple, and the exile to Babylon. This is very nearly incompatible with Job 2:6 *But his life you shall spare*, and contradicts the many clues (v. Chap. 5) to the symbolic association between Leviathan and Sennacherib. Crucially, it leaves Ezekiel's reference to Job without any acceptable explanation.

3. The Author

If one thing is certain, it is that we shall be very lucky indeed ever to find conclusive evidence of the name of the author of this peerless work. All that can be done with this problem is to speculate, so what follows is mere speculation and should be treated as such.

The author of the Book of Job was first of all a man of exceptional education and erudition; secondly he was as great a poet as ever lived, which means that this could not have been his only essay into literature; thirdly, if I am correct in the above discussion of dates, his lifetime included the early part of the 7th Century; fourthly, he was certainly an Israelite or a Judean. The suggestion has been made that he was widely travelled, particularly in Egypt (P, p.xli) but there is little or no compulsion to accept this. Not all knowledge is the result of experience. He must have had a considerable acquaintance with legal procedure, a good knowledge of zoology and astronomy, and a compendious literacy.

There is one known person who possessed all these attributes, the poet-prophet Isaiah (c.765-?, but certainly later than 701). As we penetrate the Book of Job, we shall find again and again that there are words, phrases and whole passages which cannot be understood without reference to the Book of Isaiah. This is particularly the case with the two final chapters of the poem, 40 and 41, which are replete with symbols whose significance is directly derived from the work of the prophet. Indeed, the reader who examines Chap. 5 of this book attentively can hardly escape the conviction that Chapters 40 and 41 of Job are approximately contemporaneous with the first Isaiah, and that their author either was he, or someone closely associated with him.

There are various ways in which this theory might be examined, some of them highly technical, involving computer analysis of the texts of the two works. As this is speculation only, and not an important prop of this work, I propose only to examine a part of a single episode in Isaiah, Chaps. 38 and 39, which I suggest, has a special relationship with the Book of Job.

In these chapters, Isaiah records the "illness" which Hezekiah suffered "in those days". Those days were the time of the Assyrian siege of Jerusalem and occupation of the rest of Judah. *In those days*, writes Isaiah, *was Hezekiah sick unto death*. Immediately this should raise the question "was Hezekiah actually ill, or was Isaiah translating the political situation into an allegorical form?" The narrative continues with Isaiah reporting (using the third person for himself) that he came to Hezekiah and warned him to prepare for death. Hezekiah reacted to this by turning his face to the wall and praying to the Lord *Remember now (זכר־נא), O Lord, I beseech Thee, how I have walked before Thee in truth and with a whole heart, and have done that which is good in Thy sight.* Then word comes to Isaiah commanding him to say to Hezekiah *I have heard thy prayer, I have seen thy tears; behold I will add unto thy days fifteen years. And I will deliver thee and this city out of the hand of the king of Assyria; and I will defend this city.* The Lord then provides a sign to Hezekiah (the returning of the shadow on the sun-dial) that He will indeed do these things.

The next section consists of *the writing of Hezekiah, King of Judah, when he had been sick and was recovered from his sickness.* This is an eleven-verse hymn of thanksgiving which is remarkable in many ways, including both its sentiments and its vocabulary, for its resemblances to sundry passages in the Book of Job. The chapter concludes *And Isaiah said, `Let them take a cake of figs, and lay it for a plaster upon the boil (שחין), and he shall recover.'* Almost the same story is told in II Kings 20:1-11, but with omissions and additions.

The suggestion I make regarding Isaiah 38 is, first that it was wholly composed by the prophet, including the two passages attributed to Hezekiah, and second that it constitutes a very first sketch of the idea which ultimately flowered into the finished Book of Job. The juxtaposition of the promise *(Behold I will heal thee; on the third day thou shalt go up into the House of the Lord.) And I will add unto thy days fifteen years* with *And I will deliver this city out of the hand of the king of Assyria* most powerfully suggests the allegorical nature of the illness. In exactly the same way, I shall suggest later (Chaps 1 & 3), is Job's illness an allegory of the destruction of the cities of Judah and the siege of Jerusalem (cf. also Isa 1:5,6; Deut 28:35). The fact that the name of Hezekiah's "illness" is the same as that of Job is also suggestive. Further "coincidences" between Job and Hezekiah are noted in Chap. 1.

The especial evocations of the Book of Job in Hezekiah's thanksgiving are the following:

ISAIAH

JOB

בשערי שאול :10c
To the gates of Sheol

בדי שאול 17:16
To the babble (or bars) of Sheol

פקדתי יתר שנות :10d
I am deprived of the residue of my years

הלא־נסע יתרם בם? 4:21
Surely their life-line is uprooted in them?

אמרתי לא־אראה יה :11
יה בארץ חיים לא־אביט אדם
עוד עם־יושבי חדל
I said: I shall not see the Lord, Even the Lord in the land of the living; I shall behold man no more with the inhabitants of the world.

זכר כי רוח היי 7:7f
לא־תשוב עיני לראות טוב
לא־תשורני עין ראי
Remember, for my life is but a breath, my sight will not return to seeing good. The eye that sees me will see me no more.

ואחר עורי נקפו־זאת 19:26
And (that) in my flesh I should see God!

דורי נסע ונגלה מני 12a
My habitation is plucked up carried away from me.

יגל יבול ביתו 20:28
Let the wealth of his house and be carried away.

קפדתי כארג חיי 12c
I have rolled up like a weaver my life

ימי קלו מני־ארג 7:6
My days are swifter than a weaver's shuttle.

מיום עד־לילה תשלימני 12d,13c

מבקר לערב יכתו 4:20

From day even to night wilt Thou make an end of me.

Between morning and eve they are swatted.

שויתי עד־בקר כארי 13a,b
כן ישבר ישבר כל־עצמ ותי
The more I make myself as a lion until morning, the more it breaketh all my bones!

אמ־אמרי אשכחה שיחי... 9:27f
יגרתי כל־עצבתי
If I say, "I will forget my complaint, I will discard my frown and be of good cheer," I dread all my tribulations.

דלו עיני למרום 14c
Mine eyes fail from looking up.

ותכח מכעש עיני 17:7
My sight is dimmed with frustration.

יהוה עשקה־לי ערבני 14d
O Lord, I am oppressed, Give a pledge (for) me!

שימה נא ערבני עמך 17:3
Display (some sign)! Give a pledge (for) me with You!

מה־אדבר ואמר־לי והוא עשה 15a,b

What shall I say? He hath both spoken unto me, and Himself hath done it.

והוא באחד ומי ישיבנו? 23:13
ונפשו אותה ויעש
But He is One, and who can annul Him? And His spirit wills, and it is done.

אדדה כל־שנותי על־מר נפשי 15c
I shall go softly all my days for the bitterness of my soul

אדברה במר נפשי 10:1
I will speak in the bitterness of my soul.

ואתה חשקת נפשי 17b,c
משחת בלי

Thou hast in love to my soul delivered it from the pit of corruption.

ויחננו ויאמר 33:24
פדעהו מרדת שחת
מצאתי כפר
Then He will be gracious to him saying, "Save him from going down to the pit: I have found a ransom.

כי־השלכת אחרי גוך 17d
כל־חטאי

לא תשמר על־חטאתי 14:16b,17
חתם בצרור פשעי
ותטפל על־עוני

Thou hast cast all my sins	Not watch for my every flaw.
behind Thy back.	My transgression would be sealed
	in a bag and You would white-
	wash over my iniquity.

None of these resemblances is so close as to be fairly describable as a quotation, but the cumulative effect of the thirteen similarities in a very small number of consecutive verses is very persuasive.

Chapter 39 records a further consequence of Hezekiah's illness. The son of the king of Babylon sent congratulations and a gift to Hezekiah on his recovery, and Hezekiah

> *was glad of them, and showed them his treasure house, the silver, and the gold, and the spices, and the precious oil, and all the house of his armour, and all that was found in his treasures; there was nothing in his house, nor in all his dominion, that Hezekiah showed them not. Isa 39:2.*

This indiscretion of Hezekiah's elicited a strong reaction from Isaiah:

> *Hear the word of the Lord of hosts: Behold, the days come, that all that is in thy house, and that which thy fathers have laid up in store until this day, shall be carried to Babylon; nothing shall be left, saith the Lord. And of the sons that shall issue from thee, whom thou shalt beget, shall they take away; and they shall be officers in the palace of the king of Babylon. Isa 39:5-7.*

It is not difficult to imagine that, if indeed Isaiah were the author of the Book of Job, the seed of the opening scene between God and the Satan, in which the Lord does for the Satan precisely what Hezekiah did for the messengers from Babylon, lies in this incident.

> *And the Lord said unto the Satan, "Hast thou considered My servant Job, that there is none like him in the earth, a whole-hearted and an upright man, one that fears God and shuns evil?*

This too is a king gratuitously displaying his treasure to an emissary of a foreign power, and the destructive consequences were no less.

4. How Many Authors?

The Folk-tale Theory

Among the many unsubstantiated and insubstantial theories about the Book of Job, one of the most firmly entrenched is that the present book is based on an ancient folk-tale, the remnants of which are preserved in Prologue and Epilogue. To a certain type of mind this theory will appear as unlikely as the tales of *Atlantis* and *Lemuria*, but to those with a penchant for believing most firmly in what is least based on solid evidence - like the latest lay-inspired cancer cure, or the planet Vulcan, or the imminence of the Mahdi or the Messiah, it will seem totally convincing. The strongest expression of conviction I have encountered is that of Rick Moore[22], *The obvious and drastic difference between the idyllic, stylized character of the narrative and the passionate, existential creativity of the poetry places a virtually unbearable burden of proof on anyone who would resist seeing evidence of two literary hands - indeed, of two literary worlds.* To which one must reply, "two literary worlds surely, but not necessarily two literary hands."

The decision to read the introductory two chapters as allegorical raises immediately in the most acute form this problem of the relationship between prose Prologue-Epilogue and the poetic heart of the book. The questions which need to be resolved seem at first sight to be doubled by this decision, for if even when taken at a literal level the two sections of the book already display not only an extreme formal contrast in their modes of composition, but an inescapable if not precisely definable, sense of reciprocal contradiction, then with the complexity of an allegorical interpretation of the Prologue, there is raised the additional spectre of a possible contradiction between Job as a symbol in one part reacting with Job as a real man in the other.

It is in the contradictions between the two sections that the main justification for the folk-tale theory, which is in fact largely taken for granted by modern scholars (H is a welcome exception) lies. The only supporting evidence offered has been the reference to Job in Ezekiel (which is only supporting if it be assumed and accepted that the poem of Job was written after the time of Ezekiel) and the discovery of alleged precursors of Job in Akkadian and Sumerian literature[23]. To an extent these two pieces of evidence contradict one another, for if Ezekiel is referring to a folk-tale, it is one in which the name of the main protagonist is JOB, and as there is no Job in any so-called precursor, they can hardly be relevant. In fact these so-called precursors resemble the Book of Job only in that they relate the advent of misfortune to persons who had done nothing to merit it - a common enough theme - but they share little or nothing else with the Book of Job. Indeed it is likely that the so-called "Babylonian Job" *(Ludlul Bel Nemeqi)* is no more than a mnemonic poem for students of the healing art! In any case, the existence of true precursors, even if it were established, would provide no real evidence for or support of the theory of a prior folktale. The external evidence must therefore be considered so weak as to be of no significance.

We are left therefore to consider what is intrinsic to the text, and rather than speak of "unbearable burdens of proof", we might perhaps go so far as to say that there is a *prima facie* case which can be made out to suggest multiple authorship, in which the Prologue-Epilogue is some sort of survival of an older and more popular version of the tale. But even the contradictions between the sections may be no anomaly at all. The expressions at the ends of each of the two Prologue chapters, *In all this Job neither sinned nor ascribed anything amiss to God* and *In all this Job did not sin with his lips* properly understood and considered together, convey with unrivalled economy that to the end of the Prologue Job had not spoken one word of what was seething in his heart towards God. They therefore in fact carry the promise of that all-embracing contradiction between Prologue and Dialogue which troubles so many readers.

There are, I suggest, three possible theories to entertain:

1. The Prologue-Epilogue is a literal transcription of an old folk-tale, to which the poet has grafted the Dialogue.

2. The Prologue-Epilogue is based on an old folk-tale, but has been substantially re-written and brought up to date by the author of the poem.

3. The Book is an integrated whole, and the Prologue-Epilogue is as much a part of the original conception of the author of the poem as is the poem itself.

The first of these theories is essentially untenable. In the first place linguistic evidence (for what it is worth) is said to rule out an early date for the writing of this part of the work; indeed, linguistic experts consider that, if anything, it post-dates the poem[24]. In the second place, serious anachronism is involved in treating the Satan, as he appears in the Prologue to Job, as an archaic figure. Leaving aside the Book of Job, *The Satan as the standing appellation of a particular angel first appears around 520 BCE in Zechariah 3* (Encyclopaedia Judaica, 14, 902). E.J. assumes Job post-dates this, but far more likely, particularly in view of the limitless inventive capacity of the author of Job, is that this use of the Satan was initiated by him, and Zechariah depends upon it. The welding of the *adversary* of man with the *spirit* of the heavenly host from I Kings 22 to produce an *adversary of God*, which is how the Satan of Job functions, is precisely the sort of imaginative poetic leap that abounds in Job. In any case, the *invention* of the Satan in a folk-tale is unthinkable. Perforce, folk-tales make use of the material already available to the culture of their time and place. In addition to these objections, the resemblances between the Prologue of Job and Deuteronomy 28 are unaccountable under this theory, for there is no realistic possibility that the blessings and curses which Deuteronomy attributes to Moses actually depend on Job or his hypothetical folk-tale.

Examined logically, the second theory scarcely provides any advantage over the third in the resolution of the contradictions between the divisions of the work which constitute the case in favour of the folk-tale theory. If the author assumed the freedom to rewrite a folk-tale as drastically as the introduction of the Satan, the hint of the division between Job's lips and his heart, and the quotations from and allusions to Deuteronomy suggest, it was surely open to him to re-write it in such a way as to remove the contradictions between it and the poem he intended to fit to it. It is extremely difficult to imagine what sort of folk-tale of Job could have existed without the Satan and those particulars of Job's prosperity and his losses which are culled from Deut. 28. We can, in fact, refer almost the whole of the Prologue of Job to material antecedent to the Babylonian exile, but later than any reasonable date for a pre-existent folk-tale.

So we may say that on either the second or the third theories it is apparent that the contrasts between the two sections of the work are *deliberate*, and if this is so, we are deprived of all reason to consider an hypothesis of multiple authorship, and left with only the third possibility. We should then concentrate on trying to find the reason that the author introduced or allowed the mismatch between the sections of his work, rather than engaging in what Alter terms *excavative research* into the text[25]. Nor should we forget that there are numerous other stories in the Bible where a self-contradictory duality is apparent, and recognize that in some of these cases as well it may be that a stylistic convention foreign to modern ideas of story-telling is at work, rather than a crude amalgamation of sections from different sources. Indeed, looking at the "writing" section of the Bible with an unprejudiced eye, we have to concede or claim that no writing anywhere is further from crudity in construction or expression. We draw simplistic conclusions at our peril.

An absolutely decisive objection to the first theory must surely lie in the text of the Prologue itself. Few short pieces of literature exhibit such careful crafting, such balancing of elements, such symmetry of characters and situations. These are [the] opposite to the characteristics of folk-tales, stories which grow by accretion, shapeless, planless and rambling. This objection ought by rights to be accorded equal validity against the second theory, for so alien to the art of folk stories is the art of the Prologue, that it is impossible to visualise how a folk story could have been transmuted into the Prologue and yet have retained any of its features. We may be sure that if there was a precursor to the Book of Job, it was no example of folk-art. It was as contrived and skillful a composition as the present Prologue.

There are, in addition to these intrinsic reasons for rejecting the theory of a folk-tale, two very powerful extrinsic reasons, albeit negative. One is the total "disappearance" of the original work. Neither in the library of Ashurbanipal comprising 600,000 tablets, nor in the huge collection at Ugarit, is there a trace of it. The other, more convincing still, is the complete silence of the whole of the vast corpus of antique Middle Eastern literature so far unearthed on the subject of Job or of a character with his experiences. As soon as it was told, the story of Job must have been recognized as archetypical, as sounding chords dominant in all human experience. Even today, it seems hardly possible for authors to write seriously about the human condition without referring to or quoting from Job. In the years following its appearance in its present form (which I suggest, v.s., was between 690 and 700 BCE) it was quoted from, used by, or referred to by Jeremiah, Ezekiel, Deutero-Isaiah, Zechariah, Ecclesiastes and James, among the small company of Biblical writers. The beginning of this dependence on the story of Job to illustrate the pain of life, which has continued in spate through the two and a half thousand years to our own time, establishes, I suggest, an independent *terminus a quo* for the "publication" of the story itself.

One may infer a whole dynosaur from a single toe-bone, but there is not even a finger-nail upon which to build the ancient folk-tale of Job.

In the light of these considerations, it is worth considering that an allegorical interpretation of the Prologue may provide not an added complication of the problem of the relationship between the two parts, but its explanation. In the smooth modulation at the end of Chapter 2, which takes us from the hectic narrative pace of the Prologue to the time suspension of the Dialogue, and from the conspicuous unreality of schematic herds, households, assemblies of children and angels, and wholesale destruction by fire and tempest, war and disease, to the group of four flesh-and-blood men sitting appalled upon the ground in bewildered silence, it is surely possible also to discern a modulation from allegory to reality, or from one form and level of allegory to another quite different. For myself, when I read this transition, I always remember the introduction to the great Laurence Olivier film of Henry V, when the schematic tapestry-like picture of the fleet merges gradually into the real thing.

If it is recognized that the reality which succeeds the formality of the Prologue is related to the reality which lies behind the Prologue, the actual events which it allegorises, and not just to the allegorical disguise which they are wearing, then it will also be recognized that contradictions between the two sections of the book are inevitable, although of course it remains to be demonstrated that the contradictions which exist are those to be expected on this assumption. I trust that in the course of this book, it will become apparent that they are.

There is, however, an important artistic constraint which maintains a degree of obscurity over this issue. That is that allegory must never be explicitly unmasked. A properly designed allegory must always proceed simultaneously on both levels of understanding. Ambiguity is its essence. Terms which are capable of interpretation in a dual sense may be expected to abound. So we shall find the people of Judah referred to as Job's children (Ch. III inf.), and also as God's; their foes referred to as "the wicked" (Ch. IV inf.), and their trials never precisely specified so as to conform unequivocally to either one or the other of the two levels of interpretation. Even at the very end of the poem, when the Lord addresses Himself exclusively to the plight of Judah, He does so in His own allegorical terms, masking the protagonists of the historical conflict as titanic beasts (Ch. V).

Thus, although it is contended here that the strange "events" of the Prologue, properly read, expand into a vast panorama of history, with marching armies, columns of captives, flaming cities, dethroned kings, extinguished and triumphant empires, and that the discussions between Job and his friends, the homilies of Elihu and the final Self-justification of the Lord are all directed to these historical upheavals, it is not to be expected that this will ever be made absolutely and unambiguously clear, or at least not until the final moment of the work. Throughout the book the problem raised by the literal wording of the Prologue is also under discussion.

That problem, often referred to as the problem of innocent suffering, is really nothing of the kind. There is no exploration in the book of reasons for unmerited suffering. The problems addressed by the Book of Job non-allegorically are those of the survival of faith in adversity and the questionable existence of unmerited suffering. While the question arises as to whether there is such a thing as unmerited suffering, there is no debate about the hypothetical causes of it. Job is sure his suffering is unmerited and attributes it to God, as indeed he attributes everything to God; his three friends are sure it is a sign of sin and therefore deserved, and Elihu raises the possibility that it is admonitory and also therefore deserved. While it may well be argued that God's first speech, Chapters 38 and 39, does address the cause of suffering unconnected with sin, revealing the ineradicable injustice of the Universe, this is an answer to a question that was never asked, and cannot colour the understanding of the preceding thirty-seven chapters which do not address it.

Throughout the Dialogue, and the speeches of Elihu and the Lord which follow, attention is being paid both to the discussion of these non-allegorical problems, the straightforward literal meaning of the Prologue, and at the same time to the allegorised historical events which lie in the background. At times the author succeeds in a perfect ambiguity, but at other times one interpretation or the other is the more relevant to a particular passage, or even applies to it exclusively.

The alternation between allegorical and nonallegorical is best evidenced in the Lord's speeches at the conclusion of the work, for the first of these (Chaps 38 & 39) speaks to the essentially personal problem of the intrinsic injustice of life, while the second is incomprehensible unless it is understood as a resolution of the historic crux at the end of the 8th Century.

Elihu

The second area where there is strong support for the idea of multiple authorship is in the speeches of Elihu, Chaps. 32 to 37. The majority of scholars favour the theory that these are a late interpolation. Some of this support derives from the supposedly inferior literary quality of these speeches, but this is subjective opinion by Biblical scholars who are not especially well qualified to make such judgements. Other evidence derives from an alleged greater frequency of "Aramaisms" in Elihu's chapters than in the rest of the work. Even accepting as Aramaisms all those words which have been so descibed from time to time, a statistical analysis shows no significant difference in frequency between Elihu and the rest of the book. A further line of reasoning asserts that there is nothing in the speeches of Elihu but what the three comforters have already said to Job. This argument is factually false.

The main reason for discarding the Elihu speeches from the hypothetical original composition is the awkwardness with which they interrupt the pace and flow of the book, and the failure of the earlier parts to prepare for Elihu and of the later parts to dispose of him. There are however good reasons for accepting that these speeches are aboriginal, despite the validity of this last objection. The way in which Elihu's arguments are integrated into the rest of the book by means of numerous quotations and allusions to previous remarks by the speakers is impressive. The introduction of Elihu into the discussion is in fact elaborate and adequate, even though no explicit explanation for his presence is given. The integration of Elihu's speeches with what succeeds them, provided it is not overlooked, is also ample, for at the conclusion of his part of the book, Elihu describes the approach of the storm from which God delivers his reply (37:2-4). Without Elihu we should doubtless be complaining of the abruptness of God's appearance on the scene and asking "What whirlwind?" in relation to 38:1 *Then the Lord answered Job out of the whirlwind.* The deficiencies in integration of the speeches could easily have been remedied by an interpolator had he existed. The vital and indispensable legal function which Elihu appears to perform is discussed in Chapter X.

Bearing in mind that a responsible attitude to an ancient text requires us to accept the integrity of the text as it has been transmitted to us unless there are overwhelming reasons to question it, I incline strongly towards the acceptance of the Elihu speeches as part of the original composition.

Other Suggested Interpolations
Suggestions have been made at various times that Chap. 28, the so-called "independent" poem on Wisdom, and Chaps. 40 and 41, the Lord's second speech, are later additions to the work. Fortunately there are few adherents of the second of these suggestions, for as will become clear from Chapter V, the amputation of these chapters would be the equivalent of beheading the Book of Job, leaving it without resolution of any of its major concerns. The place of Chap. 28 (see Chap. 3:VIII) is by no means so secure, but the presence in it of the striking and mysterious phrase, בני־שחץ, which is found only elsewhere in Job 41:26, and the quotation of Job 1:1 which concludes it, argue strongly for common authorship.

There is, however, real and sound reason for considering 42:12-17, the last seven verses of the MT Job, to be a late addition. These verses do not appear in the oldest surviving version of the book - the QT - and they have a quality of over-explicitness, spelling out the numbers of his restored livestock and children, giving the names of his new daughters, and specifying the doubling of his life span to 140 additional years. Certainly the most likely place for an addition to a book to be located is at the end, and we find a clear parallel in the additions of LXX which extend v.17 by an additional sentence and append pseudo-biographical notes on the four main characters. Berechiah either came to the same conclusion, or worked with a manuscript which did not contain these verses. A similar speculation exists regarding the final two verses of Ecclesiastes, but without any corroborative evidence of the kind provided in this case by QT and Berechiah.

5. *The Purpose of the Book of Job*
The idea that there should be an underlying or hidden purpose in the composition of a Biblical work does not arise for all, or indeed for many of the books of the Bible. It certainly does arise in the cases of the Books of Jonah and Ruth, of Deuteronomy, and for some readers,

the Song of Songs. It is readily apparent that Genesis, Exodus, Numbers, Joshua, Judges, the two Samuels and the two Kings are proto-histories and interpretations of history, as also are the later books of Nehemiah, Ezra and the two Chronicles. Leviticus is a book of laws and regulations. Deuteronomy is revised or as moderns would say, re-written, history which always has an ulterior aim. It is reasonable to speculate to what use the Psalms were put, and whether Ecclesiastes and Proverbs were texts for academies of a class of Israelite youth, but the books present no great mystery. There is no problem about thirteen of the fifteen eponymic prophetic books which seem genuinely to record the utterances and writings of a political and moral opposition established as a sort of fourth estate in the land. Of the other two, Jonah is a work of fiction with a moral message, and Joel an allegorical prophetic poem rather than a record of prophetic struggle and/or instruction. Esther is a sort of fairy-tale, and Daniel a conflation of the same with a burgeoning mysticism, and Lamentations is what its name purports it to be. But what and why is Job?

Job shares with the Books of Ruth, Jonah and Esther the quality of being a unitary literary composition. It was written originally by a single author as a self-contained work. This holds even for those who believe it contains accretions contributed by later interpolators or incorporates foundations from the remote past.

Unlike the other three works, which are prose, Job is a poem framed within a partly prose Prologue and Epilogue. As with the three other books, there is little or no possibility that the events which it records actually occurred. The work is therefore either pure fiction, or an allegory, ideational, politico-historical, or of some other nature. The books of Ruth and Esther are fictional although in each of them there is a purpose ulterior to entertainment, Ruth dealing with problems of intolerance of proselytes, and Esther perhaps designed to combat national pessimism and defeatism. These two books are early examples of the tradition in which Dickens's novels of social reform were written. Jonah is very clearly an allegory almost surely ideational (if politico-historical the reference events have been lost) in which both characters and events symbolise systems of thought which the author sought to parody and hold up to examination. It is of a class with *Penguin Island* and *Gulliver's Travels*.

The common view of the Book of Job would place it in a quite different class from any of these, as similar to the *Socratic Dialogues*, or *Galileo's Dialogues*, although Job's dialogues do not proceed in the

same orderly way as these philosophic and scientific ones. Galileo and
Socrates operated in a tradition which sought to uncover truths about
the Universe by dialectic, and there is no doubt that the application of
this description in its broadest sense would bring the Book of Job into
the same category. But the truths sought in the Book of Job are
theological truths rather than scientific ones, and the method of
arriving at them is by revelation sweeping away all the earlier
conclusions of dialectic. *Who*, asks the Great Panjandrum, *is this that
is obfuscating counsel in words without knowledge?* We should however
recognize that the distinction between science and theology, as well as
the scientific method, is a late development of human thought, with
science having branched out of theology in the time of ancient Greece.
Much of the theology of the Book of Job is in fact concerned with
matters which we should call scientific; Chapters 38 and 39 are
compendia of scientific conundrums.

      Not only is the Book of Job a theological work - the only one
in the Hebrew Bible. It is unquestionably a theodicy, an essay in the
justification of the ways of God to man. The God who appears at the
end of the work is on the defensive, however well He follows the
dictum that the best defence is a good offence. In order to determine
the purpose in writing of this book, we have to ask which of the ways
of God does it seek to justify? If we accept the book on a strictly
literal level, the answer must be that it seeks to justify the arbitrary
dispensation of injustice by God for His private ends, and we have to
conclude that as theodicy it fails. Job succeeds in establishing against
the three comforters that he has indeed been subjected to gross
injustice, and the Lord's first reply, while raising the whole question
of whether individual justice is possible in so complex an engine as the
Universe, gives no justification at all for deliberate injustice. The
Lord's second reply does not seem to touch the issue at all. Indeed,
despite numerous ingenious attempts down the centuries to establish
its relevance, taken literally this speech remains close to gibberish. It
can only reveal its meaning and relevance to the rest of the book if
understood on an allegorical level.

      So for this reason, as well as many others which will be discussed
in the course of this work, we can hardly be satisfied with the simple
answer to the question of which of the ways of God the book seeks to
justify. Many writers have complained bitterly of the futility of this
literal reading of the Book of Job, displaying a God of staggering
immorality and irresponsibility. The dean of these is surely Carl Jung[26].

The alternative solution is that the Book of Job is a politi-co-historical allegory in the tradition of Dryden's *Absalom and Achitophel*, and that it seeks to justify God's assumed role in certain historical reversals which are symbolised by the catastrophes of Job. This idea has the initial merit that it brings the Book of Job at once into the ambit of the normative concerns of the Hebrew Bible, as part of the continuing demonstration of God active as the shaper of history with far-ranging moral and credal aims. That such matters were subject of debate in ancient Israel can hardly be doubted. The survival of so cynical a saying as *The fathers have eaten sour gapes and the children's teeth are set on edge*[27] testifies to lively popular concern and dissatisfaction with the ready prophetic explanation of all such reversals as manifestations of Divine displeasure, i.e. that all the suffering of Israel was retributive, the point of view of Eliphaz and his associates towards Job's sufferings.

I shall be presenting throughout this book evidence that the true occasion for the writing of the Book of Job was as a contribution to just such a debate over the significance of the destruction of the kingdoms of Israel and Judah by successive Assyrian monarchs, with a particular emphasis on the spectacular injustice of the "punishment" of Judah at just that time when there reigned a virtuous king who *did that which was right in the eyes of the Lord, according to all that David, his father, had done* (II Chron 29:2; II Kings 18:3), who, *in every work that he began in the service of the house of God, and in the law, and in the commandments, to seek his God, he did it with all his heart* (II Chron 31: 21), who *trusted in the Lord, the God of Israel; so that after him was none like him among all the kings of Judah, nor among them that were before him* (II Kings 18:5).

The destruction of Judah in the time of Hezekiah at the hand of Sennacherib seemed at the time as wanton an act of arbitrary injustice by God as the events described in the first two chapters of the Book of Job still seem. To justify it, no ordinary prophetic response would have sufficed, and indeed, none is recorded. Instead, we have the Book of Job.

The Book of Job goes beyond the merely sterile debate to hint at God's purpose in withdrawing His captaincy from the armies of Israel and Judah. At the very end of the work, in 42:10, we find the future vocation of the nation spelled out:

And the Lord turned the captivity of Job when he prayed for his friends, and the Lord gave Job twice as much as was previously his.

Thus the future blessing of Job/Judah, like the past blessing of Israel is conditional, now on what one might call the fulfillment of a mission to the gentiles. The ultimate and deepest concern of the Book of Job is with the conversion of the God of Abraham into the universal God of all mankind, a conversion which could occur only after the severance of the partisan tie which bound him to His own treasured people.

6. The Historical Background

The events reflected in the Book of Job, whose occurence led to the analyses of the conduct, character and purposes of God which culminated in the writing of this work, were the whole history of the Israelite nation between the time of King David and King Hezekiah, that is from approximately 1000 BCE to precisely 700 BCE.

To save the reader unfamiliar with this history the trouble of reading it elsewhere, this bare-bones outline tells what is needed to understand the argument of the Book of Job.

King David came to the throne of the United Kingdom of Israel in 1010 BCE. He was a successful military leader and in a forty-year reign stretched the boundaries of the country widely in all directions. He established what was to prove a short-lived Israelite Empire. Cf. Job 12:23,

> He increased the nations and then destroyed them, Spread the nations abroad and then abandoned them.

and 24:24,

> When they rise up a little, He is gone; And they are brought low like all men. They retract And are lopped off, like a head of corn.

He was succeeded by Solomon, who also reigned for about forty years, an interregnum of peace and construction, marked, however, by growing internal disaffection because of high taxation.

> *And Judah and Israel dwelt safely, every man under his vine and under his fig-tree, from Dan even to Beer-Sheba, all the days of Solomon* (I Kings 5:5).

The only echo of Solomon's reign found in the Book of Job is in the initial description of Job's prosperity and wealth which seems to have some element of parody of the description of Solomon's wealth and wisdom in I Kings 5. Of especial concern is I Kings 5:10:

> *And Solomon's wisdom excelled the wisdom of all the Children of the East (כל־בני־קדם), and all the wisdom of Egypt,*

which must be juxtaposed to Job 1:3,

> *So that this man was greater* (i.e. wealthier) *than any of the Children of the East* (מכל־בני־קדם).

Upon the death of Solomon, the country split into two, a northern kingdom of Israel under Jeroboam, and a southern kingdom of Judah under Rehoboam. The northern kingdom encompassed the notorious ten tribes, two and a half in transJordan and seven and a half in cis-Jordan. Job 1:2

> *And there were born to him seven sons and three daughters.*

From the beginning, Jeroboam committed what were considered religious crimes, insisting on setting up his own places of worship with calves of gold, and nominating his own feast days ("which he had devised of his own heart"). See Job 1:4:

> *And his sons used to go and hold a feast in the house of each one upon his day.*

In the following two hundred years the two kingdoms remained separate, sometimes allying themselves against a common foe, sometimes fighting each other. They enjoyed a brief resurgence of military power from about 780 to 750. The religious iniquities, and social injustices, practiced by the northern kingdom were, if the histories which have come down to us are reliable, more outstanding and consistent than those of the southern kingdom. However the majority of our sources are southern.

In accordance with Jewish historiography, interpretation of the plan behind history, the failure of the people and their rulers to be faithful to God and to His laws was to result in their conquest by foreign foes and their extirpation from the Land (sundry sources, but especially Deut. 28). It was in these terms that the prophets and, as far as can be ascertained, the people as well, understood the successful attacks by the Assyrians against the northern kingdom throughout the second half of the 8th century. At first under Tiglath-Pileser III, they conquered three provinces of the northern kingdom. Cf. Job 1:17

> *The Chaldeans formed into three troops and fell upon the camels*

and then under Sargon, conquered the capital, Samaria, and deported the inhabitants to become the lost tribes, bringing the independence of the kingdom to a permanent end. Job 1:19

> *And behold there came a great gale from beyond the desert, and smote the four corners of the house, and it fell upon the young people, and they are dead.*

This was in 721 BCE.

In 716 Hezekiah became king of Judah. Of him it is written that

> *He did that which was right in the eyes of the Lord, according to all that David, his father, had done.* (II Kings 18:3, II Chron 29:2)

Contemporary with him, and active well before his accession to the throne was the greatest of all the prophets, Isaiah.

The relations between Judah and Assyria at this time are difficult to unravel, and seem to have constituted an uneasy co-existence, with Judah taking risks by participating in defensive alliances with Egypt, Edom, Philistia and Moab, against the advice of Isaiah. It was at this time that the famous Shiloah tunnel was constructed to internalise the water supply of Jerusalem. In 704, Sennacherib succeeded Sargon to the throne of Assyria, and he at once displayed an unwelcome interest in the Land of Israel. In 701 (700 according to the insistence of Cambridge Ancient History) he invaded the Land, besieged Lachish and devoted it, captured forty-six walled cities and deported over two hundred thousand Judeans and much booty back to Assyria (Sennacherib's own account). He then, according to Biblical sources in which two different campaigns appear to be amalgamated (Isaiah, II Kings and II Chronicles), sent his troops on to besiege Jerusalem where, after a considerable siege, the Assyrian army was decimated by a plague (145,000 fatalities - *when they arose in the morning, behold, they were all dead men* II Kings 19:35). Hezekiah and Judah could well claim

I escaped by the skin of my teeth (Job 19:20b)

The coincidence in time of this devastating defeat of Judah with the occupation of its throne by a king of unparalleled virtue appeared to invalidate the basic premise of the Jewish understanding of history. It is the contention of this book that the Book of Job is a record of the fierce debate which raged over the dilemma posed by this, with Job representing the Jewish people and Hezekiah, and his apparently unmerited suffering being the symbol of what happened to the people both of Israel and of Judah in the 8th Century.

7. The Social Setting

Inasmuch as they pretend to belong to periods in the distant past, several Biblical books could be described as historical romances. The impression created by the Book of Job is that it, too partakes of this convention, with a setting contemporary with the patriarchs. We find the following evidence for this[28]:

1. Job's wealth is measured in livestock and servants.
2. His religious worship is the domestic sacrifice of burnt offerings, and the names of God used by the speakers are archaic.
3. The only unit of currency mentioned is the ancient קשיטה.
4. Job describes his home repeatedly as "my tent".
5. His life-span exceeds 150 and perhaps 200 years.

If, however, we examine in detail all the hints which are given in the book, we find a situation which does not conform to any single genuine social milieu.

1. Job's wealth in fact comprises oxen, asses, sheep, camels, land and servants. Land, which the oxen were ploughing (1:14), and which was farmed by tenants (31:39), implies a long settled abode, while sheep and camels argue a nomadic existence.

2. While Job apparently lived in a tent, when a wind from the desert struck his children's house, its downfall killed all ten of them. This is intended to be a permanent stone dwelling, not a tent.

3. The way of life of the patriarchs was nomadic-rural, and their contact with city-dwellers casual and occasional. Job, however, played a leading role in the life of a city (29:7-17, 21-25). Even as early as Chapter 2 we have evidence in 2:8 that he was a town-dweller, for the ash-heap is an urban rubbish-dump and has no rural or desert equivalent.

4. The "law" of the patriarchs is the social custom of the desert, and their religious practice purely domestic. Job's law is fully organized, with judges and counsel for prosecution and defence, witnesses and arbiters and established penalties. In part this law is what we should understand as civil/criminal (31:11, relating to adultery) and in part religious (31:28, relating to false worship). In Chap. 12 there is reference to priests and many other members of the hierarchy of national society.

5. The apparent longevity of Job in reality testifies to a typical life-span of seventy years, for it is in the context of the doubling of all that Job had before that he is granted an additional 140 years of life (42:10,16), almost certainly, as Andersen[29] pointed out, in recognition of the double indemnity awarded in Jewish law to the victim of theft (Ex 22:3).

6. The קשיטה[30] is mentioned elsewhere in the Bible only in reference to the purchase by Jacob of a plot of land in Shechem (Gen 33:19, Josh 24:32). Certainly the use of the word is part of the attempt to impart an antique flavour to the story. It is revealing that no commentator sees it as evidence of an Israelite location for the story. Shechem is in the very heart of the Land of Israel and currency is usually local. I would suggest that the true significance of the use of the term is its relation to the purchase of land, and the analogies which should be drawn with Job 42:11

and each one gave him a קשיטה and each one a golden ring

are Ezra 1:6

> And all they that were round about strengthened their hands with vessels of silver, with gold, with goods, and with beasts

with Exodus 12:35

> And the children of Israel ... asked of the Egyptians jewels of silver, and jewels of gold, and raiment

and with the modern *Jewish National Fund*, all of which illustrate the funding of the return from exile as specified in Job 42:10, the immediately preceding verse.

⌈Taking all this together, we find no single social setting which accounts for all the features of Job's existence as detailed in the book. We are indeed confronting an imaginary man from an imaginary time which, while it has superficial resemblance to the patriarchal period, infringes its own authenticity in several important ways.⌉

8. The Names of God

The names by which God is referred to in the Book of Job have been the subject of much comment by numerous writers, and many of them have attempted to draw far-reaching conclusions from them.

The facts are as follows: In the Prologue, God is referred to on earth by the name אלהים, and in heaven by the name יהוה. In the Dialogue between Job and his three friends the names אל and אלוה occur with equal frequency and are the most common names. שדי is the next most frequent, אלהים is rare, יהוה occurs once only, as does אדני. In Elihu's speeches אל occurs with three times the frequency of אלוה which is found exactly as often as שדי. אלהים is found twice. Strangely, in the final speeches of the Lord (Chaps. 38-41), the Lord Himself employs אלהים, אל (three times), אלוה (twice) and שדי. In the final scene, the Epilogue, only יהוה is used. In addition to the above, Job uses three rare names for God as well as אדני in Chapter 28 - קדוש, גאלי, שפטי. The name עשה, Maker, is used by Eliphaz, Elihu twice, and by the Lord. It may have some lost significance that Bildad uses only אל and, in parallel with that, שדי.

The "narrator" employs only the word יהוה, except when he refers to Job as God-fearing, when he uses אלהים.

Any conclusion that, because the name יהוה is absent from the Dialogue (except for its one use in Chapter 12), there is an essentially non-Israelite background to this section of the book is adequately refuted by the frequent appearance of the name שדי. This is as exclusively an Israelite name for God as the tetragrammaton. The same applies to אלהים. The conclusion which is to an extent justified by the absence of יהוה is that the author, who knew God by that name, wished to preserve the illusion that the events he was describing were pre-Mosaic (v. Ex 6:2,3):

> And God spake to Moses ... "I am the Lord (יהוה); and I appeared unto Abraham, unto Isaac and unto Jacob as God Almighty (אל שדי), but by My name יהוה I made Me not known to them."

But to this conclusion 12:9 is an embarrassment. Nor should we accept the explanation that the author nodded. This was not a nodding author.

The use of the names אלהים, אלוה, אל, by "The Lord" Himself confers on them complete legitimacy as equivalents for the one God, and the pagan associations of the singular forms elsewhere in the Bible (and in the case of אל in other Middle Eastern literature) should be entirely discounted. It is wrong to do as Habel has done, and render אל as *El*, אלוה as *Eloah*, שדי as *Shaddai*. This is transliteration rather than translation. It is probable that the ringing of the changes between these four forms has little more significance than a poetic requirement for both variety and frequent synonymous parallel. Nor can any special significance be read into the differing frequencies with which the different forms are used by the five principal speakers, all of whom with the exception of Bildad (v.s.) make use of all four of the common terms.

There is, however, a very definite significance attached to the use of the name יהוה, in every context where it appears. It is used exclusively as the *personal name* of God in contradistinction to the references to God as a concept or a force. Wherever God appears or speaks in person, He is יהוה. Wherever His power, His actions, His opinions, His demands, His needs, His doctrines, are in question, some other name is employed. יהוה is God Himself; the other names are God conceived as an operating Being. It is this distinction which leads to the solitary use of the word יהוה in the Dialogue, where the knowledge of the actions of God, not by men, but by beast, fish, fowl and the inanimate earth is described. These do not conceptualise, and consequently their knowledge of God is direct and *personal*. For this reason the personal name is used.

Job fears God not as one fears a man or a lion, but as one respects the *concept* of virtue and obedience. Therefore he does not fear יהוה, but אלהים. So says the narrator (1:1). So also says the Lord Himself (1:8; 2:3). The use of the alternative names of God by the Lord Himself is unique to Job. The Lord speaks of "God" in the third person in exactly the same way as the human speakers do. The ostrich has no fear for her young because אלוה has denied her wisdom. The raven's young cry to אל for food. Job is asked if he has an arm like אל's. *Behemoth* is the first in the ways of אל. Most extraordinary of all, the Lord describes Job as one who has contended with שדי and argued with אלוה. Nor is it that the Lord entirely avoids referring to Himself as "I" and "Me". Both of these words, as well as "My" are found throughout the Lord's speeches and in both Prologue and Dialogue. We are thus certainly encountering in the Book of Job a convention in the use of the Divine names which is unique to that Book, with a very meticulous restriction placed on the use of "The Lord" as an indication of His "presence" and personality as distinct from His function, status or power.

The commonly voiced opinion, that the differences in the names of God used in the Prologue-Epilogue and by the narrator from those employed by the several speakers in the Dialogue indicates separate authorship or origin, does not seem to conform with the facts. Even after explaining away the word יהוה in 12:9, it leaves unexplained the variety of terms used in Chapters 38-41, particularly the personal pronouns which match the usage of the Prologue-Epilogue.

9. About this Book

The principal object of this book is to present a new translation of the Book of Job, together with an interpretation derived from that translation. The translation itself differs from all others in that it is based strictly upon the Masoretic text of the book and Biblical practice in the use of the Hebrew language. On the few occasions where a clear meaning could not be derived, one of two superscripts has been inserted - * indicating that an assumption of corruption of the text has been conceded, and #, indicating that no confident translation could be reached, but that I wished to leave no blanks in the version.

Unless otherwise specified, all English quotations from the Bible other than those from the Book of Job are from the first JPS translation.

Besides this introduction, and the translation itself, the book contains a number of essays, of which the majority deals with a single important facet of the Book of Job or its interpretation. Because of the nature of the Book of Job, it frequently occurs that evidence relating to what is a single point of interpretation is to be found scattered through as many as a dozen different chapters. Unless these several linked but separated references are brought together and considered side by side, the force of any interpretative scheme is hopelessly dissipated. It is thus the nature of the Book of Job itself which has dictated the way in which this translation has been presented. The conventional chapter by chapter textual analysis with notes and commentary cannot cope with the mutliple thematic problems involved. Hence, while textual analysis is given here, it is in the main disseminated throughout the series of thematic essays, rather than attached page by page to the translation.

Even more briefly: I suppose that this work actually embodies a novel approach to the translation of a Biblical text. But even after saying all the above, I find this a statement hard to believe. It seems to me that all I have done is to apply a common-sense approach to a difficult piece of writing on the not-improbable assumptions that it was all written in one language, has been transmitted from antiquity in a remarkably faithful form, and that it is the work of a man of genius in both senses of that word - a man of inspired creativity, and one with an infinite capacity for taking pains.

Notes Part 1

1. Fr. M. Dahood *Northwest Semitic Texts & Textual Criticism of the Hebrew Bible*, 174, p.19

2. The words are unsatisfactorily treated by LXX and Vg at other points in the Bible. In Isaiah 58:5 both seek consistency by translating אגמן 'ring' in a context where this is impossible - *bend down your neck like a ring*, while where the word is clearly metaphorical in the phrase כפה ואגמן LXX provides *great and small* in Isa 9:13, but *beginning or end* in Isa 19:15; Vg *incurvantem et refrenantem* in both places. This seems to mean *bent and restrained*, and its relevance to *head and tail* is difficult to establish. Mgr. R. Knox (*The Old Testament Newly Translated from the Latin Vulgate*, Burns Oates & Washbourne Ltd. London, 1949) has this comment: "*Pliant reed and stubborn bough*; literally *him, who bends down and him who holds back*. The Hebrew text has *both the palm-branch and the reed*, which is commonly understood as meaning *both high and low*, but seems to be interpreted by the Latin translator as meaning *both the stubborn* (senator) *and the pliant* (prophet), so as to correspond with the 'head' and the 'tail,' as explained in verse 15" - [*What is the head, but the Senator who holds his head so high? What is the tail, but the prophet that gives lying assurances?*]. This very fascinating piece would seem to confirm that אגמן is some form of reed, notable in Vg because it is pliant, and in later translations because it is low.

3. p.152. *When a fish is caught people run a long bulrush or thorn through the gills, to be able to carry it home with ease. Will you perhaps do that with a crocodile?* This is, of course, sheer fantasy, and besides, the crocodile has no gills.

4. A. Guillaume, *Studies in the Book of Job*, E.J. Brill, Leiden, *1968*. Guillaume postulated that the Book of Job related to the destruction of the community at Tema by the Babylonian king, Nabonidus, who settled there c.549 BCE.

5. E.B. Pusey (*1828-1882*), quoted in the Preface to H.H. Bernard's *Book of Job*, Adams & Co. London, *1864*.

6. Pusey nominated Dodgson for his life-long occupation as "scholar" at Christ Church, Oxford in 1852 (TB Strong [Dean of Christ Church, writing in 1898] in *Aspects of Alice*, Ed. Robert Phillips, Penguin, *1974*, 69). There can be little doubt that Humpty Dumpty's attitude to language reflects Pusey's strong views on the abuse of cognates by Biblical scholars.

7. BGM, Chap. XIII, p. 169-189.

8. Personal communication.

9. p. xxxix.

10. F. Baumgartel, *Der Hiobdialog* (BZAW 4/9. Stuttgart Kohlhammer, *1933*.)

11. Beer, Budde, Buttenweiser, Clines, Duhm, Dhorme, Gordis, Hartley, Hesse, Holscher, Mitchell, Moffatt, Rowley, Terrien, Weiser; also the *Jerusalem Bible*, the *New American Bible* and the *Good News Bible* (the bulk of this list from C)

12. Jewish Publication Society, *Tanakh*, JPS, Philadelphia, *1985*, xviii.

13. The only authority I have found to have detected this is A. Elzas (*The Book of Job*, Trubner & Co., London, *1872*, p. 5). His discovery has been ignored or forgotten, but certainly never refuted. He wrote *The Land of Uz appears to have been between Egypt and Philistia, Jer 25:20, where the order of the places seems to have been accurately observed in reviewing the different nations from Egypt to Babylon.* The location of Uz

and Jeremiah's verbal "map" of the Middle East are discussed in Chapter II below.

14. pp. 261-265.

15. J.A. Bewer, *Literature of the Old Testament*, Columbia U. Press, NY, *1922*, 308-9.

16. J.L. Crenshaw, *Old Testament Wisdom*, SCM Press, *1982*, p.16.

17. p.40.

18. Pritchard, p. 149-155.

19. Ezekiel 14:14,20: *Though these three men, Noah, Dan'el and Job were in it* (a land that sinneth against Me grievously), *they should deliver but their own souls by their righteousness, saith the Lord God...they shall deliver neither sons nor daughters; they only shall be delivered, but the land shall be desolate.*

Job 22:30: *He will deliver him that is not innocent, And he will be delivered through the purity of your hands.*

20. See e.g. O.Eissfeldt, *The Old Testament, An Introduction*, Harper & Row, NY, *1965* trans. pp. 171ff.

21. S.R. Driver, *Introduction to the Literature of the Old Testament*, T&T Clark, Edinburgh, *1913*, p. 87.

22. R.D. Moore, *The Integrity of Job*, Catholic Bible Quarterly, 45, *1983*, p.18.

23. Andersen discusses and rightly dismisses as precursors the Ugaritic story of Keret; *Ludlul Bel Nemeqi*, the so-called "Babylonian Job"; the Sumerian poem titled by Pritchard *Man and His God; The Babylonian Theodicy;* the Egyptian *Protests of the Eloquent Peasant, Dispute over Suicide* and *Admonitions of Ipu-wer;* the Akkadian *Pessimistic Dialogue between Master and Servant*, and several other even less likely candidates. English translations of all these are available in Pritchard.

24. See e.g. J.C. Greenfield, *The Language of the Book of Job* in *The Book of Job*, JPS, Philadelphia, *1980*, p.xiv.

25. R. Alter, *The Art of Biblical Narrative*, Basic Books Inc. NY, *1981*, p.13.

26. C.G. Jung, *Answer to Job*, (Trans. R.F.C. Hull) Routledge & Kegan Paul, London, *1954* (orig. German *1952*).

27. Jer 31:29 and Ezek 18:2.

28. D&G p.lxvi.

29. p. 293.

30. The reference to the payment of a hundred קשׂיטה by Jacob seems anachronistic if the קשׂיטה is taken as a minted coin. The *Interpreter's Dictionary of the Bible* (Vol 4 p.832) has this to say:

> The qesita (*קְשִׂיטָה*) is an enigma. The LXX translates by amnos ("male lamb") in Gen 33:19 and by amnas ("female lamb")in Josh 24:32; Job 42:11. The weight may have been in metal in the form of a lamb. Another suggestion is that amnas is an expanded form of mna ("mina"). Jacob paid Hamor of Shechem a hundred qesitahs for a parcel of land. In Job's final state all his relatives and friends came to him, each bringing a qesitah and a gold earring. The Arabic qesita has been estimated at 1,429 grams or 3.15 pounds. Still another suggestion is that it was a quantity of silver equal to the price of a lamb.

PART 2

COMMENTARY

I
The Identity of Job

If there is one aspect of the Book of Job upon which all scholars seem in agreement, it is that the hero of the book is not an Israelite. This conviction is based on two main lines of argument and supported by two less impressive pieces of evidence. The main pillars holding up the view are that the action takes place in the Land of Uz, and that Job is identified in Chapter 1 as a member of a group called *Bene Kedem*, the Children of the East. The supporting evidence derives from the names of the protagonists, specifically Job's three friends, which are all of "foreign" origin, and the absence of all reference to Israelite worship, law, ritual, etc. and of all reference to place names within the Land of Israel in the text.

In accordance with the strategy of this book, which is to take absolutely nothing for granted, I propose to examine in some detail these four pieces of evidence.

1. The Land of Uz

The Land of Uz is mentioned three times in the Hebrew Bible, but nowhere else in Middle Eastern literature[1]. It is ארץ עוץ in Job 1:1 and in Lam 4:21, but ארץ העוץ in Jer 25:20. The assumption has been made almost universally that the name of the land is eponymic, and the choice of its derivation is made between Uz, the grandson of Shem through his son Aram, and Uz, the grandson of Seir through his son Dishan, the brother of Hor[2]. The first supports the Arabic tradition of a location in the Hauran mountains; the second a location within Edom, or even synonymity with Edom.

The form ארץ העוץ is, however, grammatically incompatible with an eponymic origin for the phrase, infringing the barrier against double determination in Hebrew[3]. This obliges us to choose between three hypotheses – 1. That the Jeremiah citation is corrupt. 2. That there are two different Lands of Uz, one of eponymic origin and one not. 3. That the designation of the Land is descriptive rather than eponymic.

There is no way to account both for the introduction and the survival of such a corruption as the addition of a ה to an eponymically-named

Land. It sticks out like a sore thumb as though one spoke of *The the Land of Israel*.

The second hypothesis is preposterous, that there should be two lands of the same name in the same area, and both of unknown location. Particularly is this so in the light of the evidence of Jer 20:14-18 and Job 3:3 that whichever of the two authors came later knew of the writings of the other, and the general feeling that Lamentations was either written by Jeremiah, or (to appropriate an old joke) by someone else of the same name.

The third is therefore by far the most likely explanation of what is thus only an apparent anomaly. Maimonides[4] did not hesitate to treat the word עוץ as a common noun, pointing out that it is the imperative of "to take advice or counsel": *The name Uz therefore expresses an exhortation to consider well this lesson, grasp its ideas and comprehend them, in order to see which is the right view*. Such a reading, however, implies that the name of the land in which the Book of Job was to be set was the invention of its author, and this implication is very nearly incompatible with the appearance of the same name indicating a real geographic location in other Biblical books and contexts, and certainly so if these are taken as being of earlier vintage than The Book of Job. The same objection must be raised against the rather more sophisticated suggestion of Weiss[5], that the Land of Uz is an imaginary and symbolic land of Wisdom – the land where the tenets of the Wisdom school prevail – and that the Book of Job is devoted to its demolition.

Any identification of the Land of Uz must account not only for its being the setting of Job's ordeal, but also for the citations of the Land in the precise places and ways in which it is spoken of in Jeremiah and Lamentations. The Jeremiah passage in fact imposes an incontrovertable definition on the Land of Uz. It is the name of a real, not an imaginary territory, for it occurs in the midst of a list of the names of lands and cities, twenty-five in all, all of which are known contemporary geographical localities.

> *Then took I the cup at the Lord's hand, and made all the nations to drink, unto whom the Lord had sent me: Jerusalem, and the cities of Judah, and the kings thereof, and the princes thereof, to make them an appalment, an astonishment, a hissing and a curse, as it is this day. Pharaoh king of Egypt, and his servants, and his princes, and all his people; and all the mingled people; and all the kings of the Land of Uz, and all the kings of the Land of the Philistines, and Ashkelon, and Gaza, and Ekron, and the remnant of Ashdod; Edom, and Moab, and the children of Ammon; and all the kings of Tyre, and all the kings of Zidon, and the kings of the isle which is beyond the sea; Dedan and Tema and Buz, and all that have the corners of their hair polled; and all the kings of Arabia, and all the kings of the mingled peoples that dwell in the wilderness; and all the kings of Zimri, and all the kings of Elam, and all the kings of the Medes; and all the kings of the north, far and near, one with another; and all the kingdoms of the world, which are upon the face of the earth; and the king of Sheshach (Babylon in àtbash'code[6]) shall drink after them.*
>
> Jer. 25:17-26.

Careful attention to the punctuation of this passage (see Introduction, pp. 40f) reveals that it is a fully organized geographical list. Jerusalem and Babylon, Jeremiah's prime targets, frame the list, and within there are three sub-lists meticulously demarcated. The three sub-lists trace three sweeps through the Middle East, each from South to North, and each sweep further East than its predecessor – see fig. 1. This feature has previously been noted by A. Elzas (*The Book of Job*, Trubner & Co., London, 1872, p. 5).

Uz is in the first of the sub-lists, and falls between "the mingled people" and Philistia. Edom is the first nation in the second sweep, followed by Moab, Ammon, Tyre, Sidon and Cyprus, while the northern Arabian tribes of Dedan, Tema and Buz commence the third sweep. The irresistible logic of this passage rules out both Edom and Arabia as possible sites for the Land of Uz, and places it to the west of both. "The mingled people","distinguished from "the mingled people that dwell in the wilderness (of Arabia)" can only be the inhabitants of the Sinai, and the location of Uz is thereby pinpointed to somewhere in the Negev of Judah, between the Sinai and the territory of the Philistines.

The reference to the Land of Uz in Lamentations 4:21 is:

> *Rejoice and be glad, O daughter of Edom*
> *That dwellest in the Land of Uz:*
> *The cup shall pass over unto thee also;*
> *Thou shalt be drunken and make thyself naked, etc.*

and this has frequently been construed as settling the matter in favour of an Edomite location for Uz. Examining the reason for this furious attack on the Edomites, we find from Obadiah that, like the Italian "jackals", to use Churchill's word, ripping their piece from the carcass of France in 1940, the Edomites had spilled over from their homeland into the Negev of Judah and the *cities of the South* when Nebuchadnezzar's campaign left them relatively defenceless.

> *Thus saith the Lord God concerning Edom: ...*
> *Thou shouldst not have entered into the gate of My people*
> *n the day of their calamity;*
> *Yea, thou shouldst not have gazed on their affliction*
> *In the day of their calamity,*
> *Nor have laid hands on their substance*
> *In the day of their calamity...*
>
> *As thou hast done it shall be done unto thee;*
> *Thy dealings shall return on thine own head.*
> *For as ye have drunk upon My holy mountain*
> *So shall all the nations drink continually,*
> *Yea they shall drink and swallow down,*
> *And shall be as though they had not been...*
>
> *And they of the South shall possess the mount of Esau,*
> *And they of the Lowland the Philistines;*
> *And they shall possess the field of Ephraim,*
> *And the field of Samaria;*
> *And Benjamin shall possess Gilead.*
> *And the captivity of this host of the children of Israel*
> *That are among the Canaanites, even unto Zarephath,*

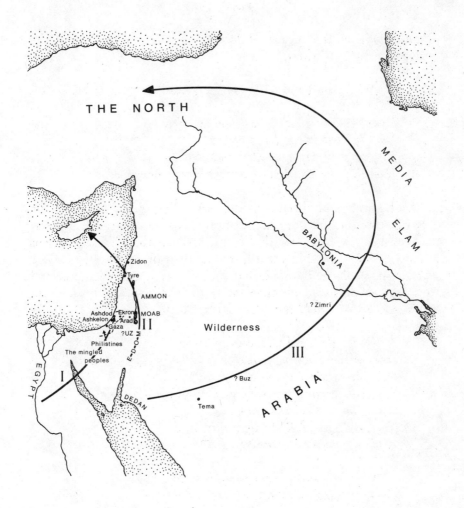

Map 1. *The Loci of Jeremiah's Imprecation*

> *And the captivity of Jerusalem, that is in Sepharad,*
> *Shall possess the cities of the South.*
> *And saviours shall come up on mount Zion*
> *To judge the mount of Esau;*
> *And the kingdom shall be the Lord's.*

So Obadiah. The Mount of Esau is Mount Seir, Edom.

There is archaological confirmation of the Edomite assault on the Negev of Judah and its occupation of the cities of the South in the Arad ostraca, particularly:

> *... from Arad 50 and from Kina[h one hundr]ed; and you shall send them to Ramah of the Nege[b un]der Malkiyahu son of Qerabúr, and he will entrust them to Elisha son of Jeremiah in Ramah of the Negeb, lest anything happen to the city. And the word of the king is strictly incumbent upon you. Behold, I have sent to admonish you: [Get] the men to Elisha, lest Edom should come thither!*

This is interpreted in the World History of the Jewish People[7] as follows:

> *Here again Arad appears as a major fortress in the Negeb, whose commanders transmit the king's orders for reinforcements in order to ward off the Edomites who were threatening Ramah of the Negeb. Arad itself probably also fell victim to this attack, apparently launched in the third year of Zedekiah, in the tenth month, if we can rely upon the dates on two ostraca. In other words, in Tebeth 595 BCE, the Edomite attack ended the hegemony of Judah over the Negeb, or, in the words of Jeremiah:* The cities of the Negeb are shut up, with none to open them *(Jer. 13:19).*

With this background, we can certainly say that the probable dynamic of the passage in Lamentations is similar to the saying "Make hay

while the sun shines!" The only hint which the poet gives of the sins
of the Edomites is that line *That dwellest in the Land of Uz*. Rather
than a mere pointless gloss, as it would be were Edom and Uz
interchangeable names, the phrase explains both what the daughter of
Edom has to rejoice over in the present, and for what she is to suffer
in the future – the conquest and occupation of the Land of Uz – the
Negev of Judah. Let us retranslate the passage, recalling the primary
sense of the verb ישׁב:

> *Rejoice and be glad, O daughter of Edom,*
> *Squatting in the Land of Uz!*

Both the extra-Jobian references thus appear to support the view that
Uz is an area in the South (the Negev) of Judah, with a considerable
probability that the cities of Arad and Ramah, known to have fallen
to the Edomites in the time of Nebuchadnezzar, were included in the
territory. The witness of Uz against the Jewishness of Job stands
discredited.

2. The Children of the East

בני קדם is a vague term for any or all of the tribes and kingdoms in the
desert areas to the east of the River Jordan and the Aravah[8]. By
definition it excludes the Children of Israel as the *locus* of reference.
Job 1:3 states that, because of his vast possessions, Job was גדל מכל
בני־קדם, which means *greater than any of the Children of the East*. In
English, this phrase is actually incompatible with Job's membership of
the group, as one might say of an English, but not of a Swedish
woman, that she was fairer than any Swede.

Solomon was certainly an Israelite, but in a description of
which Job 1:3 is perhaps an imitation or even a deliberate contrast, his
wisdom is described as *exceeding the wisdom of any of the Children of
the East, and any of the wisdom of Egypt* (I Kings 5:10). It has become
customary to weaken these phrases by substituting "all" for "any" as
the rendition of the Hebrew כל, allowing more ambiguity about the
inclusion or exclusion of Job (and Solomon) from the group compared.
BDB, however, is quite emphatic that *in a comparative or hypothetical
sentence כל is = any, and with a negative, = none*[9].

In Hebrew it is not possible to assert, as in English, that the phrase rules out the possibility of Job's membership of the בני קדם, for Hebrew usage was not so strict as English. *The serpent was more subtle than any of the beasts of the field* (Gen 3:1) really means *more subtle than any other of the beasts of the field.* There seems, however, little more reason to class Job with the children of the East than Solomon. As the expression is used as a standard of comparison both for wealth and wisdom, it is also possible that קדם in these contexts has a temporal rather than a spatial sense, meaning *the former days*, as e.g. in Job 29:2.

Although C concedes that *that Job's wealth surpassed that of all the "sons of the East" does not necessarily imply that he is one of them*, this is the assumption made by almost all commentators without further discussion. D&G say indeed only that it is *implied* that Job is one of them, but many like G translate in such a way as to close the issue *this man was the greatest among all the people of the East.*

The reference to בני קדם is however no more conclusive evidence of the non-Israelite status of Job than his dwelling in the Land of Uz.

3. *The Names of the Protagonists*

It is not disputed that Job's three friends, Eliphaz, Bildad and Zophar were neither Israelites nor Judeans, but as they each journeyed some considerable distance from his home to *to share his grief and to comfort him* (2:11), their ethnic identities are not to be expected to be the same as Job's. There is no hint in the book that the four shared a tribal affiliation, and indeed, if we found that one of the friends was an Israelite, it would add to our doubts that Job was. The usual view is that all three were Edomites. As Edom bordered the Negev of Judah, this does not impede the idea that Job himself was a Judean maintaining good neighbourly relations with the inhabitants of the land over the border (Cf. Elimelech and the Moabites, Ruth 1:1-4).

The identities and circumstances of the comforters are revealed in Chapter 18 of the Book of Job and discussed in Chapter VI below. There we shall find that they were apparently members of a group of non-Israelites of whom some at least had resided for centuries in the northern Negev of Judah. The designation of the comforters as Temanite, Shuhite and Naamathite cannot themselves be devoid of significance. Teman was an Edomite town on the border of the Judean

Negev. Shuah is unknown, and Naamah (Jos 15:41) was a Judean town
on the border of Philistia, to the Northwest of the Negev. Those
commentators (not Ley[10]) who discuss this last location (e.g. D&G
p.xxviiif) tend to dismiss it out of hand simply because it was a Judean
town. It is, I think, of considerable interest that if we draw a line on
the map joining the probable locations of Teman and Naamah, it
passes precisely through Arad (v.s.), with its half-way point somewhat
to the south-east of that town.

Of far greater significance than the non-Israelite names and
identities of the three friends who journeyed to see Job, is the
unmistakably Jewish name of Elihu. Elihu is represented as one of the
audience to the debate, i.e. one who is accidentally present, presumably
therefore a native or resident of the Land of Uz, not like the others,
a distant visitor. His nationality and Job's may fairly be assumed to be
the same. The only way this evidence[11] can be gainsaid is by rejecting
Elihu and his six speeches as all spurious, and this is what the majority
of scholars has done[12]. Even then, Elihu testifies that someone much
closer to the problem than we (Elihu's speeches are present intact in
both QT and LXX) identified Uz as a land peopled by Jews.

The origin of the name Job, איוב, remains unknown, although
a number of similar names has come to light from documents of the
second millenium B.C.E.[13] The earliest known attempt to elucidate it
is that of the note appended to the LXX translation, identifying the
name as a diminutive of Jobab, and the man as an Edomite king.
Another very old suggestion of Talmudic origin is that it is a metaplasm of איוב, "enemy"[14]. Derivation from an Arabic root meaning
"penitent" has also been proposed[15]. There is nothing other than the
Septuagint to connect the name with Edom. The possibility that it is
an anagram of ארץ יהודה ובנימן, "The Land of Judah and Benjamin" is
not altogether preposterous. Albright[16] considers the possibility of a
contraction of איה אב, "Where is the Father?", drawing parallels from
several Semitic sources.

We have to conclude that there is nothing in Job's name to
favour or hinder any particular theory as to the identity the author
wished to confer upon his subject.

The wide variety of names of God used in the Book of Job is
discussed in the Introduction. Conclusions have been drawn in favour
of a non-Jewish Job by some authors on the basis of the absence of the
tetragrammaton from the body of the work. In fact, however, the
tetragrammaton is present in the poem, and its Qere equivalent אדני

also. It is drawing conclusions not from the evidence but in its teeth to proceed to secondary deductions from the assumption that these examples are late interpolations, amendments, or unconscious slips. The presence of the name שׁדי in profusion in the speeches of all the participants is in itself sufficient evidence of the Jewish Israelite background to the discussions, for this word is used exclusively for the God of Abraham, Isaac and Israel, and is found nowhere else but in the Bible.

4. Israelite Themes and Places

The only explicit references to devotional practices in the Book of Job are to homespun sacrifices. The argument goes that "if the book were concerned with a Jewish hero and the testing of the Jewish people, we should expect references to (law), the Temple, the priesthood, sacrifices, the Sabbath, the festivals, *kashrut*, the Messianic ideal of God in history, the election of Israel etc."[17]

In a legalistic way we might answer that there are two cogent replies to this – 1. That if, as G and many others insist, the Book of Job is to be judged as Wisdom Literature, the expectation of such parochial Jewish themes is unjustified, even though the allegorical meaning of the work were of a specifically Jewish nature. Without doubt, whether the work is an historical allegory or not, it was the author's intention to emphasise the universalistic aspects of his story, and detailed references to these matters would have spoiled his aim. 2. That there are in fact clear references to almost all the matters which Gordis raises.

LAW: In 31:26-28 the worship of sun and moon is described as "an offence for the judges", that is a specific offence against a published law carrying a stated penalty. Such a law is unthinkable in the ancient world in any but a Jewish context. The only other offence so designated in the Book of Job is adultery which, like the worship of the heavenly bodies, carried the death penalty in the Deuteronomic Code (Deut 17:2-5; 22:22)[18].

PRIESTHOOD & TEMPLE: In 12:19. in a passage which appears to describe the steady undermining of a national integrity by God Himself (v.i.), Job says that *He conducted the priests (כהנים) away barefoot*, while G himself is responsible for the innovation of reading the next line *and (drives) temple votaries into confusion*, giving references to both priesthood and Temple. It is reasonable to connect the first line with the information implicit in II Kings 17:27,28 that specifically the priests of Samaria were carried into captivity by the Assyrians.

SACRIFICE: It is true that the only generally recognized explicit references to sacrifice in the Book of Job are those in the Prologue and Epilogue which take place outside any institutionalised setting. However, even here there is a specifically Israelite flavour to the sacrifices in the reference to preliminary *sanctification* of Job's sons. This concept of preparation for making sacrifice is absent both from those portions of the Bible which deal with the patriarchal period and from all pagan literature. It appears, see II Chron 30, to have belonged to the practices of the priesthood. Purification after contact with articles of pagan worship is recorded in Gen 35:2.

KASHRUT (Dietary laws): It is not reasonable to expect a book of this nature to refer in any deliberate or specific way to dietary law, a subject of low priority in the discussion of moral problems. However as it happens there are two incidental references to the Israelite dietary laws in the Book of Job.

In 18:3 Bildad asks Job (in the plural as though spokesman of the Jews – see Chapter 6) *Why are we accounted beasts, Unclean in your eyes? Kashrut*, of course, deals with the question of what "beasts" are "clean" and what "unclean". Amongst those which are unclean are all which have been torn טרף. Indeed, this word *tref* is used universally by Jews as the opposite of *kosher*. Bildad's next line is *You, who tears* (טרף) *himself in his anger* (a reference in this multifaceted interchange to 16:9 *His anger has torn me*). We must read the full import of Bildad's complaint as: "How can you, who are self-admittedly unclean by virtue of being torn (though you blame it on God rather than yourself) keep on treating us as unclean animals?" The entire success of this debating ploy of Bildad depends upon the reader understanding that underlying it are the Biblical laws of *kashrut*[19].

Animals are *kosher*, permitted, clean, if they fulfill two other conditions besides not being torn or otherwise diseased or defective. They must chew the cud and have cloven hoofs. This concept of *kashrut* has remained unnoticed in the strange phrase used at the outset of the description of Behemoth, who *eats grass like the cattle*. This means that he chews the cud (and is therefore not a hippopotamus), and it has other important implications as well, discussed at length in Chap V.

The Messianic Idea of God in History

It is, as the attentive reader of these essays will have gathered, my contention that the entire Book of Job is in one sense a thesis on the Messianic idea of God in history. But besides this, there are a number of specific references to the apocalyptic appearance of God – the first verse of Chap. 24 (see Chap. IX), the phrase שׁוֹד כִּי יָבוֹא of Eliphaz in 5:21 (a reference to Isa 13:6 – *Howl ye! for the day of the Lord is at hand; as destruction from the Almighty shall it come —* כְּשֹׁד מִשַּׁדַּי יָבוֹא.), and the mysterious אַחֲרוֹן עַל־עָפָר יָקוּם of 19:25 (See Chap. 3.VIII.5).

The Election of Israel

Again *en passant* there are two emphatic references to the election of Israel, but both have remained undetected largely, I suppose, because the mind remains closed to possibilities it has excluded *ab initio*. If Job is not an Israelite, then there cannot be any references to election. The first is 17:5 (cf. also 31:2), in which is invoked Deut 32:9, *For the portion of the Lord is His people* (see Chap. XI), and the second, presenting the same authentic and depressing view of election as Amos 3:2, is 21:19 (also Chap. XI).

Sabbath & Festivals

If we exclude the Prologue reference to feasting each on his day which it is suggested above was the equivalent of Jeroboam's changing the date of the festival to one in a month after his own heart, I find no reference to either Sabbath or festivals in the Book of Job.

The Bible

No two scholars will agree on how many quotations, near quotations and straightforward allusions there are in the Book of Job to prior Biblical texts, but none will contest that there are very many. It is in these signs of the dependence of the Book of Job on Israelite traditions, values and preoccupations that we find the most solid evidence that it is a Jewish book and that its characters, for ever drawing their inspiration and their illustrations from Jewish literature, operated in a Jewish milieu. It is difficult to see how this can be swept aside because certain aspects of Judaism are selectively neglected. No-one would suggest that the Book of Job arose from the priestly tradition of Israel. The author surely belonged to the prophetic party, and had no interest in promoting the non-ethical aspects of the creed.

The Geography
There are two Judean place-names which testify from the Book of Job
to its setting. Each has given rise to an elaborate theory to discount its
presence[20]. These are *Jordan* in 40:23 and *Tophet*, 17:6. They are
discussed, together with the attempts to explain them away, in Chaps.
V and XI respectively.

Two other references, both from the speeches of Elihu, 37:17
בהשקט ארץ מדרום, *In the still calm of the South land*, and the word ראים
(34:26), meaning in its context *seers*, i.e. *prophets* (see Chap. IV), add
their testimony to the solution of the geographical enigma.

Although there are also references to non-Israelite localities in
the book – Tema and Sheba, Ophir, these never leave any doubt that
they are not the site of the action of the book.

5. Job's Afflictions, a General Comment

There remain three obstructions to a clear view of Job, deriving from
the events described in the Prologue – the death of his ten children,
the loss of his possessions, and the affliction of a visible disease. Are
these to be considered literal or allegorical? In the Prologue they are
equivocal events. Devoid of all verisimiltude they have to be taken as
symbolic, but of what? Of the personal downfall of a man, or the
collective downfall of a nation? Do they become real in the Dialogue,
or do they fade away? Are they death, loss and disease as a man
understands and experiences them or are they what a nation understands by those terms? What Moses understood by them when he
addressed the nascent people of Israel? There is no doubt that the Job
of the Dialogue is suffering and afflicted; the question is from what is
he suffering and how is he afflicted?

It is necessary to examine with care all references in the poetic
section of the book to Job's illness, to his bereavement and his
children, and to his possessions in livestock and land. This requires
examining testimony from a number of different sources within the
book, and is so fundamental to its understanding, that I have felt
obliged to devote an entire chapter, Chap. III, to an analysis of every
conceivable reference within the Dialogue and the speeches of Elihu to
Job's illness and to his children. The conclusion of this analysis is the
startling one that there is no genuine reference to physical illness (as
distinct from mental anguish) of any kind in these portions of the

book. The status of Job's children is more ambiguous, for there is evidence pointing in two opposite directions, indicating both the survival and the extinction of Job's progeny.

6. *Job in the Poem*

We may make the confident identification of the Job of the Prologue as an allegorical figure representing the Jewish people, but a transformation occurs at the end of Chapter 2, and the Job whom his friends visit sitting on the ash-heap and scratching his sores is undoubtedly a flesh and blood human, operating in a dimension of reality quite different from the stylized fantasy of the prose. In this dimension, time is arrested, while it raced hectically through the centuries in the Prologue, character is complex and human where it was previously flat and functional, and all the props have acquired depth where previously they were schematic and symbolic. The technique of the author is very similar to the ultramodern cinematographic device of presenting a stylized painted scene on the screen and then merging it with a flesh and blood copy which "comes to life".

The story of Job is very nearly complete, whole and perfect by the end of the Prologue. When Job asks rhetorically, if somewhat sycophantically, *Shall we accept the good from associating with the God, and the evil not accept?*, it seems that nothing remains for the tale but for God to collect on His wager with the Satan (How? except by lording it over him?) and reward Job for his unshakeable faith.

Instead, in one of those infinitely economical flashes of genius which only the Bible can exhibit, the author tells us in a single word that we have not yet heard the first true word of the story! *In all this*, he writes, *Job did not sin with his lips* (בשפתיו). Brilliantly evoking *it may be that my sons have cursed God in their hearts,* it draws our attention to the fact that all we have seen and learned of Job so far has been his public *persona* – the posture he has adopted towards God. Now we are to be conducted into his heart, to see what aspect he will show when God's face is turned away. The Job we are about to meet functions primarily as an individual within the community of Judah, and his reactions and emotions are those of one man caught up in events that tore his nation to pieces. Let us explore the clues which tell us what manner of man this was.

7. Job's Rank

In the Prologue, the extreme dramatic effect of Job's fall is achieved by initially placing him at the pinnacle of the human hierarchy, *greater than any of the Bene Kedem*, richest, most virtuous and most blessed of men, and allowing him to fall to destitution, to lose his health and his family. The contrast is maximal and so designed. In the Poem, our direct knowledge of the poles between which Job fell derives principally from Chapters 29 and 30, in the first of which he laments his previous high state, and in the second deplores his present plight. "Fell" is the *leitwort* of Chap. 1.

Chapter 29 shows Job as a person commanding enormous respect. The scene which dominates the chapter is Job at the city-gate, the court of justice, where his word always prevails, where young men fade away from his presence and the elders rise to their feet. Here Job dispenses justice with charity and discretion, takes pride in it, and faces the future with confidence born of it. The intimate of God, he serves as a model for other men. The chapter concludes with this summary:

> *I made their decisions and sat as chief,*
> *And I lived as the king of an host,*
> *As he that comforts the mourners.*

Job, then, was legislative, executive, and spiritual leader of his community.

In Chapter 30, Job is treated with contempt by the lowest of society. *They disdain my course. They cast up against me their own paths to perdition.* Even his *justice*, which in Chap. 29 he symbolised as his *garments*, is perverted to give him neither comfort nor warmth (v.18). God's intimacy is gone, to be replaced by implacable hostility – *You have changed Yourself into a Being cruel to me; With all Your strength, You detest me.* There is an earlier passage in Chapter 19, *He has stripped me of my honour and lifted the crown from my head*; all his family and friends have turned against him and abandoned him. The ambience of these two chapters suggests that Job is being portrayed as a regional, perhaps provincial, leader, possibly one of those "kings" of the Land of Uz in Jeremiah's list (v.s.).

This impression is reinforced by the passage, 5:3-8, in Eliphaz's first speech, in which he appears to deliver to Job a lesson in wise statecraft (see Chap. 3.VIII.1) as from one ruler to another. Another broad hint of Job's eminence is to be found in Elihu's opening remarks (32:22) in which he states that he will not give titles to those he is addressing, leaving us to wonder to what titles their ranks lay claim.

When we come to the final speech of the Lord, however, it is very apparent that there is nothing provincial about the Job being challenged. He is the representative of the entire people of Judah. Whether this is to be interpreted as the simple equivalence, Job = Hezekiah, or as a shift in the focus of the allegory back towards the original symbolism of the Prologue, with Job shedding his personal form in favour of a collective *persona* as the nation itself, is a difficult choice to make.

8. Job's Fear

Another way of approaching the problem of Job's identity is through his state of mind during the discussions. A prominent feature of this is fear. Job's professed fear antedates his catastrophes. In 3:25 he tells his friends פחד פחדתי ויאתיני ואשר יגרתי יבא לי – *I feared a horror and it came to me, and that which I dreaded is upon me*. Is this perhaps related to Job's Prologue fear that his sons may have cursed God in their hearts? Or is it simply the insecurity which so often accompanies great happiness and prosperity? Was his fear for himself, his children, or for his nation?

In 4:5 Eliphaz accuses Job *It touches you and you take fright* and, I would suggest in amplification in the immediately following verse 4:6 הלא יראתך כסלתך?, *Is not your fear your folly?* (There is no precedent nor I think justification for reading יראתך as *your fear of God* either here or in 15:4, and the only other example of the word כסלה (Psalm 85:9) has the meaning *folly*, not *confidence*). So LXX[Job is thus seen clearly to be in a continuing state of fear.] He expects worse disaster to follow, and this cannot be his personal death, for this he has repeatedly declared he would welcome. Later in his speech (5:18-23) Eliphaz advises Job to apply to God for help and promises that if he does so he need no longer fear famine, war, slander, devastation (שוד), or the beasts of the field.

Job retorts (6:4) that the terrors of God are arrayed against him, and a little later accuses his friends themselves of harbouring a fear caught by infection from Job's own fear, the fear of being asked to contribute something to his relief, i.e. to *rescue me from the hands of the foe or ransom me from the tyrant's grip* (6:21-23). This important passage with its firm indication of the historical and political meaning of the events being discussed has always (except by Guillaume) been understood as a purely hypothetical list of demands which Job has not made, bearing no relation to his actual position.

In Chapter 7 Job describes how God is terrifying him with nightmares (vv.4,5 and 14) so that he would prefer to die rather than continue his burdensome existence. In 9:28 he asserts that he cannot put on a cheerful appearance because יגרתי כל־אצבתי *I dread all my tribulations.* Again it is something still to come which haunts Job awake and asleep. In 9:34 Job asks God to stop terrifying him. Zophar in 11:19 assures Job that if he stretches out his hands to God then he will be secure and able to lie down *with none to make you afraid. Many will entreat your favour, But the eyes of the wicked will fail ...And their hope will be the breathing out of life.*

Almost the last of the references to Job's persuasive fear is Eliphaz's again misunderstood reference to יראה in 15:4, enjoining Job *Therefore must you have done with fear and moderate your complaint in the presence of God* (See Chapter 12 below). Here too LXX will not accept *fear* as standing for *fear of God.* Fear reappears in the highly ambiguous 22:4, either meaning *Is it because He is Job-fearing that He rebukes you?* or *Is it because of your fear that He rebukes you?*

It is, however, not until Chapter 23 that we begin to be told what it is that a man who has already lost family, health and wealth, and who cares nothing for life, still has to fear. The passage (23:13-17) runs:

> But He is One; and who can annul Him? And His spirit wills, and He does it. Thus will He execute my decree, And He has myriads of the like to deal with. Therefore am I nervous in His presence. When I think it over I am terrified of Him, Yes, God dissolves my courage And the Almighty intimidates me Because I was not cut off before the darkness Nor did He cover my face from the gloom.

The reference here to a sentence still to be executed is the clearest of indications that Job believes there is still something for him to lose more important to him than life. The last verse suggests with great conviction that this final blow is one that might have been allowed to fall after Job had been removed from the scene – allowed to die. That is to say that it is not a personal disaster at all, but one to fall on those whom Job loves, or feels responsible for – his people.

There are Biblical precedents for the sentiment expressed in this last verse – the message of Huldah the prophetess to Josiah:

> *As touching the words which you have heard, because you were fearful and did humble yourself before the Lord when you heard what I spoke against this place, and the inhabitants thereof, that they shall become an astonishment and a curse, and rent your clothes and wept before Me, I also have heard you, saith the Lord. Therefore, behold, I will gather you to your fathers, and you shall be gathered to your grave in peace, neither shall your eyes see all the evil which I shall bring upon this place* (II Kings 22:18-20) (my trans.)

and Isa 57:1,2,

> *The righteous perisheth, And no man layeth it to heart, And godly men are taken away, None considering That the righteous is taken away from the evil that is to come. He entereth into peace, They rest in their beds, Each one that walketh in uprightness.*

If these parallels mean anything, and it is difficult to find any purpose for 23:17 which leaves them out of account, then what Job fears is God's *coup de grace* against the people and nation of Judah. He fears *the Day of the Lord* as described in Isaiah 2:12ff and 13:6-22 in which His full vengeance will be unleashed upon all mankind, including and especially on Judah. Job 24:1, immediately following 23:17, makes specific reference: *Those who know Him did not see His days*, while the remainder of Chapter 24 portrays the situation in the country in such a way as to demonstrate that *The Day of the Lord* has already dawned over it.

Job's fear is that of a national leader and representative. The distinction between Job as a person and Job as a nation is attenuated in these passages. There is a hint of the same sense of inseparability as is expressed in Jefferson's *I tremble for my country when I reflect that*

God is just. Inasmuch as these are the sentiments of an individual, they are those of the one individual who bears the weight of the nation on his shoulders, ruler or prophet.

9. Job's Dual Persona

There are other outbursts where Job speaks as though he were the nation rather than an individual. *He set me to be a ruler of nations* (17:6) surely does not mean as Berechiah suggests, that he will be a moral example to all around him. *Why have You averted Your face and reckoned me as an enemy?* (13:24) and *Does it do You some good to persecute, that You reject the work of Your hands But you shed radiance on the counsel of the wicked?* (10:3) are national rather than personal complaints. Like the speaker of many of the laments in Psalms, Job is an ambiguous figure, bearing a dual *persona*, part man, part people, the John Bull or the Uncle Sam of the Jewish state.

In Chapters 40 and 41, the individuality of Job begins a final dissolution back into the collective Job of the Prologue, so that by the beginning of the Epilogue there is no real trace left of the individual, and the full force of the initial allegory again prevails.

10. The Specification of Job's Complaint in the Poem

We have already seen that in many of the complaints and expressions of fear which Job utters, there is a mystifying lack of specificity, leaving the reader in a perpetual state of uncertainty as to whether or not he really knows what has happened to this victim of God's caprice. None of the specifics of the Prologue reappears in the Dialogue in any but the most ambiguous way. Job certainly complains of having become *declasse*. He has a feeling of being besieged (16:12-14; 19:12) and of being subject to excessive hostile scrutiny by God (7:12-21; 10:2-22; 13:24-27) alongside the complaint of having been abandoned by Him (23:3-9; 29:2-5). None of this is at all helpful in the actual identification of Job's wrongs. There is, however, one passage in which Job spells out in detail just what God has done to "him". This is 12:17-25, but in order to understand it, we have first to understand Chapter 12 itself[21].

Chapter 12

The opening complaint (see Chap XI. below) is that Job is becoming a laughing-stock. People who once offered their loyalty to God now consider that to be in His confidence is a sure path to destruction. This, says Job, is the wrong way of looking at it. Everything that has happened has been by His direction. He then sets out to "prove" this proposition in a semi-syllogistic way, introducing his "proof" with the challenge *Does not the ear test words as the palate tastes its food?* (12:11). The words to be tested follow. They are two contrasting proverbs, the first of which, *Wisdom is with the aged And length of days has understanding* is a deduction from Bildad's 8:8-10:

> *For ask, I suggest, the generations past,*
> *And ascertain what their fathers discovered –*
> *For creatures of yesterday are we, and know nothing;*
> *For our days on earth are but a shadow –*
> *Surely they can teach you, and speak to you,*
> *And utter these words from their hearts:*

and the second, *With Him is wisdom and might. He has counsel and understanding* is a variant of Prov 8:14. The first attributes control of events to the old and wise; the second to God. The apposition of these contrasting proverbs is followed by four sharp sentences, each a paraphrase of a statement by one of the comforters, in which they acknowledged the irreversibility of God's actions. These four statements constitute the "evidence" from which judgement between the two proverbs is to be made. In v.16 the judgement is delivered and its corollary announced *With Him are strength and sagacity; His, misleader and misled!* At this point Job feels that he has proved conclusively that everything that happens on earth does so by the will and act of the Lord – a defintive statement of the omnipresence of God in history and a metaphysical rejection of free will.

From v.17 to the end of the chapter, v.25, Job proceeds to specify the events for which he holds God responsible, the זֹאת – this – of which he asked in v.9 *Which does not know of all these that the hand of the Lord wrought this?* and which reappears as the זֹאת of 17:8 and 19:26 (see Chap. 3.VIII.5). This description runs as follows[22].

> *He it was Who led the councillors away barefoot*
> *And made fools of the judges;*
> *Who slackened the bond of kings*
> *And bound their loins with a slave-band.*
> *Who led priests away barefoot*
> *And subverted those established of old;*
> *Who robbed the faithful of speech*
> *And diverted the judgement of the elders,*
> *Pouring contempt upon princes*
> *And undermining the morale of the legions;*
> *It was He uncovered deep things out of darkness;*
> *He brought out into light the shadow of Death!*
> *He increased the nations and destroyed them;*
> *Spread the nations abroad, and abandoned them,*
> *Disheartening the chiefs of the People of the Land*
> *When He left them to wander a trackless waste.*
> *They groped in the dark, for there was no light,*
> *And He made them to stagger, like drunkards.*

and then, to remove any doubt that this is a recital of real events, rather than, as is usually understood, potential powers of God, the tell-tale 13:1 *Behold, my eyes have seen it all; My ears have heard and understood it.*

The above passage encapsulates the history of the rise, the decline and the fall of a nation, almost certainly Israel, as the expression *People of the Land* shows. It has no relevance to a patriarchal sheikh living his family life, but that it is intended as Job's definitive description of his own tragedy is hard to doubt once the dynamics of Chapter 12 have been successfully penetrated. Tied in with this description as a part of Job's personal experience is that strange challenge (v.s.) of 6:23 *(Did I say)* `Rescue me from the hands of the foe' or `Ransom me from the tyrant's grip'? I believe it is straining credulity too far to treat all this as entirely irrelevant, mere inflated rhetoric. But the phrasing of both the recital of Chap.12 and the questions of Chap.6 raise the problem of a further ambiguity in Job's condition. Has he been captured and taken into exile? Have his "sons"? i.e. his people?

11. Captivity

As the Book of Job is about to end, the Lord sets about restoring to the hero all that has been taken from him. Strangely, however, while his possessions are restored double, and his family is reconstituted, no mention is made of his health, the curing of his putative skin ailment. In place of this expected sentence we find the following:

ויהוה שב את־שבית איוב

The meaning of this (42:10) is:

And the Lord turned the captivity of Job.

Of all the innumerable indications of a national and historical allegorical meaning to the Book of Job, this is the most explicit and impossible to deny, but it is nevertheless universally denied. The customary solution is to translate the phrase:

And the Lord restored the fortunes of Job

but in thirty Biblical contexts the phrase with slight variations recurs always with the meaning of return from captivity. Not that there is not weighty authority behind the deviant view of the meaning in Job, and even the view that שבות or שבית are no more than replications of the verb שוב[23].

Spiegel[24] seems to voice almost a consensus when he writes that the phrase,

"although undoubtedly (!) including the miracle of his cure as well, has a wider range of meaning. *Restitutio in integrum* (not the Vg reading, DW) does not exhaust it, nor does it sound as a term borrowed from the legal sphere or prophethic eschatology. It seems older than both, and to reach back to the world of myth and fable, where time is reversible, and death not beyond remedy as in stubborn reality.

> In that dreamland a loss can be retrieved, life recalled from the
> beyond, and the joys of a former day restored by the grace and
> goodness of a god who can make *bygones come back*."

This beautiful idyll is unsupported by any vestige of evidence, and has
no connection at all with the literary collocation, שׁב את־שׁבית. The only
time this phrase is used without direct reference to the physical
captivity of a people is Ezek 16:53, when the prophet threatens the
return of the *captivity* of Sodom and *her daughters*. But this is a wildly
metaphorical and hyperbolic passage in which the idea of the return
of captives from the Netherworld is entirely in place as a poetic image.
By coincidence, it is this verse too which demonstrates the identity of
the roots of שׁבית and שׁביה (captive) by using the phrase שׁבית שׁביתיך
בתוכהנה – *the captivity of your captives in their midst*.

Another passage from Ezekiel, 29:13-15, clearly and finally distinguishes the *return from captivity* from the *restoration of fortunes*, or any such
status quo ante as is implied by reading the phrase "turn the turning
of".

> *At the end of forty years will I gather the Egyptians from the peoples*
> *where they are scattered; and I will turn the captivity of Egypt, and*
> *will cause them to return to the land of Pathros, into the land of*
> *their origin; and they shall be there a lowly kingdom. It shall be the*
> *lowliest of kingdoms, neither shall it any more lift itself up above*
> *the nations; and I will diminish them, that they shall no more rule*
> *over the nations.*

The fact that this explicit phrase occurs elsewhere so often, and only
in connection with a people or a country, never an individual, is the
most convincing evidence that Job in the Prologue-Epilogue at least is
not an individual. The sentence, occurring at the very end of the book,
is the equivalent of the dropping of the domino at the end of the
masquerade.

        The main indirect evidence for a significant role for exile in the
Book of Job is the conclusion of Bildad's first speech, Chapter 8. The

bulk of this speech is devoted to a parable, based upon Psalm 1, of two plants, one resembling the wicked, one the righteous. A crucial *leitwort* of this speech is House. The wicked's trust is *a spider's house; when he relies on his house it will not stand; when he holds fast to it, it will not endure.* The righteous, however, בית אבנים יחזה, literally, *beholds a house of stones.* There is one simple way to decipher this puzzling expression, which is to view the א of אבנים as ʾprosthetic'. A[25] in a different context has drawn attention to a number of other examples of אבן/אבני as a bi-form of בן/בני, and quotes Blommerde as having advanced others. In this case the meaning would be *He beholds the House of his descendants*, an amplification of the earlier expression related to the plant metaphor רטב הוא לפני־שמש – *He is for ever green* (Not *green under the sun*). Alternatively *A house of stone*, meaning a permanent House, may also be taken as a symbol of an enduring posterity. The word "house" in the Book of Job almost always means family, clan, tribe or nation, not the simple physical structure. 1:19 is of course an apparent exception.

Proceeding from this, Bildad states *If one destroy him from out of his place, and repudiate him, "I know you not!", Behold, this is the joy of his way* – ומעפר אחר יצמחו – *That from alien soil they will sprout anew.* אחר in this sentence cannot, as often postulated, be the subject of the plural יצמחו. This is either the (א)בנים, *children*, or, with the metaphor unmixed, the *roots and shoots* of the plant which are referred to immediately before the House of stones (Note עפר אחר as *fresh soil* in Lev 14:42. B concurs).

There does not seem to be any possible interpretation of this little homily of Bildad's but an assurance that if the righteous is transplanted from his home into a foreign environment, he and his descendants will prosper in it, nor does there seem to be any occasion for such a consolation unless this transplantation has in fact occurred, and is a part at least of Job's occasion for grief.

Nonetheless, there are many passages in the book which seem incompatible with the idea that Job, as an individual, is in exile. Particularly Chapter 24 which records the situation in Job's home territory, seems to place him still in that environment. When we recall that Sennacherib recorded[26] the capture of 200,150 Judeans (together, perhaps significantly [v. 1:14-17], with camels, asses, and big and small cattle), we see that there is no incompatibility in the assumption that the exile of the better part of the nation was a substantial part of Job's lament.

We shall not, I suggest, come closer to the identification of Job the man than we have done to this point. A leading Judean, either a local or national ruler, complaining bitterly amidst the ruin of his nation and the exile and degradation of the population, and obsessed with the fear of its final extinction seems the best that the deliberately hazy clues that the author has left will allow. The patriarchal sheikh, however, is surely no more than an allegorical mask.

Notes Chapter I

1. There is a star named Uz in Akkadian astronomical records (Pritchard p.333).

2. Gen 10:23 and Gen 36:28 respectively.

3. Gesenius #125, 1a; #127, a(a).

4. M. Maimonides, *Guide for the Perplexed*, (c.1194 C.E.) Dover Publications Inc. NY, *1956*, p.296.

5. M. Weiss, *The Story of Job's Beginning*, Magnes Press, Jerusalem, *1983*, pp. 23-24.

6. An ancient Hebrew code in which the twenty-two letters of the alphabet are arranged in order in two facing columns, of eleven letters each, the first descending and the second ascending, and each letter is interchanged with that facing it, so that א = ת, ב = שׁ etc.

7. *The World History of the Jewish People*, Vol 4 – I, Ed. A. Malamat, Massada Press, Jerusalem, *1979*, pp. 302-3.

8. BDB, p.869.

9. BDB, p.482e.

10. J. Ley, *Das Buch Hiob, Verlag der buchhandlung des Waisenhauses, 1903*, p.27 (quoted by D&G).

11. The name is Hebrew, *He is my God* (according to some, *Jahve is my God*). There are four other Israelites of the same name in the Hebrew Bible.

12. For those *pro* and *con* the authenticity of Elihu's interpolation into the debate, see G (BGM) p.106 and notes, p.332f.

13. Tel-el-Amarna Letter No. 256, where Job is prince of Ashtaroth, capital of Bashan, which fell to Tiglath-Pileser III in 732. See also the Mari document and the Al alakh Tablets.

14. *Baba Bathra*, 16a.

15. By H.G.A. Ewald.

16. W.F. Albright, JAOS, 74, *1954*, pp. 225-6, 232.

17. R. Gordis, personal communication.

18. S.R. Driver (*Introduction to the Old Testament*, T & T Clark, Edinburgh, *1891*, p.432) sees more: "Though references to distinctive observances of Israel's religion (as in Wisdom literature generally) are rare, an acquaintance with law seems here and there to betray itself: e.g. 22:6, 24:9 (pledges, Ex 22:26f, Dt 24:17) 22:27 (vows), 24:2 (landmarks; Dt 19:14 *al*) 31:9-11, 26-28 (judicial procedure against those guilty of adultery or worship of the sun and moon; cf. Dt 22:22, 4:19, 17:3-7)".

19. As explained with care in Josiah Derby *The Strange History of Kasher* (JBQ [Dor LeDor] XXI, 3, *1993* 164-9) the concept of what was fit and unfit for eating in the Bible was contained in the concept of what was *clean* and *unclean* – טהר and טמא.

20. The illusion is fostered that the word *Jordan*, which appears over one hundred times in the Bible as the name of a specific river, but never in a non-specific sense, may be used for any river. T-S is one of the boldest proponents of this view

> ירדן. does not mean specifically the Jordan, but a river or stream generally; a river or stream (ירדן) runs downhill (ירד) into the valley, whence Arabic *warada* `to go (down) to the water, to the watering-place' (*wird*).

Hartley, unjustly claiming support from Rowley, Kissaine, T-S, and Dhorme writes

> "Since the term *Jordan* may be used symbolically for any river with a strong
> current, here it represents the Nile at flood stage."

P sits on the fence, but, with G, refers to the absence of the definite article as though
it were of significance. As a general rule, definite articles are omitted in the Book of
Job. Until someone is able to cite another text in which the word does not stand for
the River of Israel, all these special pleadings must be dismissed as wishful thinking.
Tophet is habitually treated by most modern commentators as an anomalous derivative
of an imaginary Hebrew verb, תוּף, "to spit". C's note summarises the history:

Lit. "a spitting in the face," i.e. one in whose face people spit. It is more than
doubtful, that תפת is derived from the place Tophet as a symbol of shame
(Blommerde); NJPS suggests "I have become like Tophet [that swallowed
children; Jer 7:31] of old (לפנים)," but the connection with Job is not very
evident. KJV "tabret" ("aforetime I was as a tabret") took the word as
equivalent to תף "drum" (following Rashi). Blommerde took עמים as "my
relatives" and לפנים as "for my ancestors", which is more ingenious than
convincing. Others read תפת "a portent" (Perles, Budde, Terrien, claiming
support from Vg exemplum; cf. Deut 28:46; Ps 71:7); but the parallel in 30:9-10
confirms the present text (Dhorme).

All this would be well if there were such a verb as תוּף, but there isn't. All that there
is is a place called Tophet where children were passed through the fire to Moloch
which, until its abolition, was notorious in Judah. The normal meaning of לפנים is
"formerly".

21. See D. Wolfers, *Greek Logic in the Book of Job*, Dor Ledor, XV, 3, *1987*, pp.
166-172.

22. See Gesenius #116f,

By an exhaustive examination of the statistics, Sellin (*Ueber die verbal-nominale
Doppelnatur der hebraischen Participien und Infintive etc.* Lpz. *1889*, p.40ff)
shows that the participle when construed as a verb expresses a single and
comparatively transitory act, or relates to particular cases, historical facts, and
the like, while the participle construed as a noun indicates repeated, enduring,
or commonly occurring acts, occupations and thoughts.

In this passage, the construction of participles is verbal (the vocalization of מגלה in
v.22 removes the ambiguity).

23. H.G.A. Ewald, *Jahrb. Bibl. Wiss.* v. p.216f.

24. S. Spiegel, *Noah, Danel and Job*, Louis Ginzberg Jubilee Volume, American Academy for Jewish Research, NY, *1945*.

25. p.122, n.3.

26. *Annals of Sennacherib*, Pritchard, p.288.

II
Job and the Deuteronomic Covenant

The 28th Chapter of Deuteronomy, addressed through Moses to the people of Israel, is the specification of the rewards and punishments annexed to the Covenant between God and His people. It comprises two lists of promises, each introduced conditionally, the first with the condition

> *If thou shalt hearken diligently unto the voice of the Lord thy God, to observe to do all His commandments which I command thee this day...*,

the second with this,

> *If thou wilt not hearken unto the voice of the Lord thy God, to observe to do all His commandments and His statutes which I command thee this day...*

At first sight, this solemn recital of the operative clauses of a Divine-human contract has nothing whatever to do with the Book of Job, composed as though set many centuries before Moses, but on closer inspection there seem to be connections on two levels. The first of these might be dismissed as coincidental. It is that the dispute between God and the Satan in the Prologue to Job addresses a problem which is native to just this aspect of the Covenant. That is, that if a certain course of action is attended contractually by material benefits, then there is no easy way of ascertaining the spontaneous inclination of the party profiting. The Satan correctly points out that *Job does not serve God for nought*, and infers from this that if reward is witheld and punishment substituted, Job's attitude to God will follow in the wake of this reversal and change from obedient service to rebellion and hatred. The plot of the Book of Job is, on one level of understanding, the study of what happens in the heart of Job when the Satan is permitted to put this theory to the test.

Without any closer connection, it would be open to any commentator, and reasonable as well, to extrapolate from this individual experience of Job's to the more general experience of God's people, whose spontaneous orientation towards Him and His commandments and statutes, God might at some time in history, have sought to ascertain.

There is, however, a second, and far more intimate, level of relevance between Job and Deuteronomy 28. For the Book of Job, and most particularly the prose narrative Prologue, contains multiple references to and quotations of the blessings and curses of the Deuteronomic Covenant. The key passages in which these two books approach one another are so important for understanding what the Book of Job is really about, that we must examine them in full and with great care. That they are rarely if ever noted in commentaries must not be allowed to influence our assessment of their importance. With one exception, these Deuteronomy references are all to Chap. 28. Other references, especially to Deut 32, will be considered elsewhere as the need arises.

The parallel passages are these:

DEUTERONOMY	BOOK OF JOB
The Lord will make thee <u>over-abundant for good</u>, in <u>the fruit of thy body</u>, and in the <u>fruit of thy cattle</u>, and in the <u>fruit of thy land</u>, in the land which the Lord swore unto thy fathers to give thee. (28:11)	*His possessions <u>burst bounds in the land</u>. (1:10) There were born to him <u>seven sons and three daughters</u>. His possessions were <u>7000 sheep, and 3000 camels</u> and <u>500 yoke of oxen and 500 she-asses</u>. (1:2,3)*
The Lord will...<u>bless all the work of thy hand</u>. (28:12)	*<u>The work of his hands You have blessed</u>. (1:10)*
And thou shalt <u>grope at noonday</u> as the blind gropeth in darkness. (28:29)	*<u>They groped in the dark</u>, for there was no light. (12:25)*
	<u>In the daytime they encountered darkness, and they groped in the noontide as in the night</u>. (5:14)

Thine ox shall be slain before thine eyes, and thou shalt not eat thereof; thine ass shall be violently taken away from before thy face, and shall not be restored to thee; thy sheep shall be given unto thine enemies, and thou shalt have none to save thee. Thy sons and thy daughters shall be given unto another people, and thine eyes shall look, and fail with longing for them all the day, and there shall be nought in the power of thy hand. (28:31,32)

The oxen they were ploughing and the asses they were feeding beside them, and Sheba fell and seized them. The fire of God fell from the skies and burned up the sheep and the servants and consumed them... Your sons and your daughters were eating and drinking wine in the house of their first-born brother, when behold, there came a great gale from beyond the desert and struck the four corners of the house, and it fell upon the young people, and they died. (1:14-19)

The eyes of His children long in vain. (17:5)

The Lord will smite thee in the knees and in the legs, with a sore boil, whereof thou canst not be healed, from the sole of thy foot unto the crown of thy head. (28:35)

And the Satan left the precincts of the presence of the Lord and smote Job with a sore boil from the sole of his foot to the crown of his head. (2:7)

Thou shalt rule over many nations. (15:6)

He set me to be a ruler of nations. (17:6)

The Lord...will set thee on high above all the nations of the earth. (28:1)

Having hidden their hearts from understanding, You therefore will not exalt them. (17:4)

Thou shalt carry much seed into the field and shalt gather little in; for the locust shall consume it.

Naked, they tramp unclad, And hungry, they hump the grain. Between the bullocks they trundle the olive-press;

Thou shalt plant vineyards and *dress them, but thou shalt neither drink of the wine nor gather the grapes;* *for the worm shall eat them.* *Thou shalt have olive-trees* *throughout thy borders,* *but thou shalt not anoint thyself with the oil;* *for thine olives will drop off.* *(28:38-40)*	*they tread the winepress and* *thirst.* *(24:10,11)*
	He will rob – as a vine *his own* *grapes. He will shed* *– as an oli-ve-tree* *his own blossom.* *(15:33)*

Therefore *thou shalt serve thine enemy* *whom the Lord shall send against thee,* *in hunger, and in thirst, and in nakedness, and in want of all things;* *and he shall put a yoke of iron upon thy neck until he have destroyed thee. (28:48)*

In the morning thou shalt say: *"Would it were even!" and* *at even thou shalt say "Would it were morning!" for the fear of thy heart which thou shalt fear,* *and for the sight of thine eyes which thou shalt see. (28:67)*	*If I lie down, then I say, "When* *shall I arise?" But the night is endless, and* *I am surfeited with nightmares until dawn.* *(7:4)*
	(LXX & Vg have in addition *When I rise, I say `when will it be even?'* after *"arise?").*

Some of these similarities are closer than others, but taken together and considering that they are all but one from a single chapter of Deuteronomy, their cumulative effect should be overwhelming. This is particularly the case with the two recitals of Job's catastrophes, the loss of his livestock and his children in the same sequence as in Deuteronomy, and the *smiting* (דְּ) *with* שְׁחִין רָע, *sore boils,* מכף רגלו עד קדקדו from the sole of his foot to the crown of his head. Indeed, in this last case we are faced with unquestionable word for word quotation and have an obligation to account for it. *From the sole of the foot to the crown of the head* is certainly a collocation, but the faithful reproduction of the two other elements in the expression (יד and שחין רע) rules out mere happenstance as the cause of the coincidence of terms.

The affliction with boils threatened in Deuteronomy is not intended to be regarded as literal skin disease, nor, although it is

addressed to "thee" in the singular, is there any doubt that it is
intended as a collective threat to the community, as are all the curses
of this chapter. The same singular "thou" is employed for instance in
v.25 *Thou shalt go out one way against them* (thine enemies), *and shalt
flee seven ways before them.* The use of the singular is a device to imply
that whatever afflicts the community will afflict each of its members
singly as well. We are in the happy position of knowing precisely how
a more or less contemporary Judean, Isaiah, understood this threat to
the skin, for he also "quotes" from this verse in Deuteronomy in the
first chapter of his prophecies:

> *On what part will ye yet be stricken,*
> *Seeing ye stray away more and more?*
> *The whole head is sick*
> *And the whole heart faint;*
> <u>*From the sole of the foot even unto the head*</u>
> *There is no soundness in it;*
> *But <u>wounds and bruises and festering sores:</u>*
> *They have not been pressed, neither bound up,*
> *Neither mollified with oil.*

and then:

> *Your country is desolate;*
> *Your cities are burned with fire;*
> *Your land, strangers devour it in your presence,*
> *And it is desolate, as overthrown by the foe*,*
> *And the daughter of Zion (Jerusalem) is left*
> *As a booth in a vineyard,*
> *As a lodge in a garden of cucumbers,*
> *As a besieged city.*

* JPS translation of this line is inaccurate. This is my translation.

In this passage there is no question but that the image of visible disease
(wounds, bruises, sores) is used as a metaphor for invasion, destruction,
uprooting of population – the disintegration of the nation under
foreign assault. The picture conforms exactly to the state of Judah at
the time of the siege of Jerusalem by Sennacherib in 701. That Isaiah
should have chosen deliberately to invoke the Deuteronomic curse

with this image shows how the curse was understood in the time when it was current. What Isaiah is roaring at the people is: Everything that was predicted for you (in Deuteronomy) is already upon you! What are you waiting for? Turn your path around at once before the whole edifice comes tumbling down!

Although it has been the almost unvarying strategy of commentators on the Book of Job, it is not a valid strategy of biblical exegesis to ignore these indications entirely in interpreting the first and second chapters of the book. The Deuteronomic curse was a harbinger of national disaster, and so it was understood by those living at the time. The Job affliction by the Satan is exactly the same as the Deuteronomic curse, and is therefore open to interpretation also as national disaster. It is reasonable and just analysis to equate the "Thee" of Deuteronomy with Job, and to see Job therefore as the individual and collective Israelite and his sufferings as the ruin of his nation(s). The possibility of a mere coincidence of phraseology between Job 2:7 and Deut 28:35 is reduced to zero because of the additional coincidences of oxen, asses, sheep and sons and daughters, and the blessing of the work of Job's hands.

Once the suggestion is admitted that there is some connection between Job and Deuteronomy 28, it becomes necessary to re-examine the whole of the Book of Job in its light, for whatever is concealed beneath the literal words describing Job's trials is concealed beneath the whole book, the whole and all its parts.

This line of reasoning leads inevitably to the conclusion that Job's trials must be interpreted as the fulfillment of the curses in the Covenant between God and Israel. For this to be the case Job must be a figure representative of the people of Israel, and the events of the Prologue an allegorical presentation of national events affecting the people, specifically the destruction, or near destruction, of the nation on one of the several historic occasions on which it occurred. This suggestion, it must be emphasised, is not novel. It seems first to have been proposed by the Kabbalist, Solomon Molch (1500-1532), but the Midrash which restates Job 3:26 in these terms: *I had no ease from Babylon, no peace from Medea, no rest from Greece, and agony – from Edom*[1] implies that the idea has been around for much longer. It received its most extensive airing (if we except such theories as Guillaume's[2] which see an entirely different national setting for the work) in Napier's *Song of the Vineyard*[3]. But Napier brings almost no textual evidence to support what was little more than an intuitively apprehended theory. Napier further was handicapped by working exclusively with the RV, and thus disqualified from correcting the translational errors with which that, as all foreign language versions, abounds.

Looked at as a probable political allegory, the Prologue to Job immediately comes alive with allusions and possibilities. Job's ten children become the Ten Tribes of Israel (seven sons in cis-Jordan, three daughters in trans-Jordan) obliterated by that *great gale from beyond the desert* (what a telling expression!), Assyria, their final demise taking place in *the House of their first-born brother*, Samaria in the territory of Ephraim[4]. Job and his wife then represent the surviving kingdom of Judah with the tribe of Benjamin. The unpatriarchal independence, of the "children," appointing their own feasts and dwelling apart in their own homes, would signify the separation of the kingdoms and the recurrent sinfulness of Israel, just as the appointment of a feast day *in the month which he had devised of his own heart* by Jeroboam was used to symbolise this separation, and regarded by the redactor as a great sin (I Kings 12:32,33).

Job's ritual of *sending to and sanctifying* his children might reflect Hezekiah's celebration of the passover feast when he *sent* to the remnants of the ten tribes to celebrate in Jerusalem, and arranged for his priests to make sacrifices for them as they were not *sanctified* for the ritual. Either or both of II Chron 29:20-24 and II Chron 30:1-20 may be relevant to Job's ritual. There still remain some discrepancies, for while the *fire of God* can readily be equated with the great earthquake of 749 BCE, and Chaldeans may be taken as referring to Assyrians (Isa 23:13), it is difficult to find any equivalent for the Sabeans in Israelite history. The *three bands* of Chaldeans represent three-pronged assault of Tiglath-Peleser which detached the Sharon, the Galil and the Gilead from Israel (Isa 8:23).

Job's designation by God on every occasion that He speaks of him as *My servant, Job* is likewise explained on this hypothesis for the people of Israel is very often so designated.

We might also speculate as to the significance of the use of the word ברך to mean its opposite, *curse*, (1:5, etc.) and ask whether this does not reflect the way in which, apparently causelessly, the Lord converted His own blessing into a curse. By no means is it clear at this stage whether, if indeed the Prologue deals with the invocation of the Covenant curses, the Covenant was broken by Israel, or by God. The admission by the Lord that He was moved לבלע חנם, *to destroy him without cause* (2:3), favours the latter reading.

There is another area where apparently a systematic dependence of the Book of Job on Deuteronomy, and specifically the Deuteronomic treatment of the Covenant, can be demonstrated. This is the Song of Moses, Chapter 32. Besides the reference found in Chapter 17 (p.280), there are sundry other direct and indirect quotations in Job from this Poem. Some are discussed in Chapter 3.VIII.1, p.468ff.

In considering why the connections between Job and Deuteronomy have systematically been ignored in the study of Job, we must realise that deductions made long ago about the location of The Land of Uz and Job's membership of the *Bene Kedem* have made the dependence virtually unthinkable. If, as is universally assumed, Job was not Jewish (not intended to be Jewish by the author), then *a priori* there could be no message concealed in his story about the Deuteronomic Covenant. The best thing that could be done with these strange resemblances was to ignore them.

Notes Chapter II

1. Exodus Rabbah, Chap. 26 (900-1000 C.E.)
2. See Introduction, Note 4, p.79.
3. B.D.Napier, *Song of the Vineyard*, Harper, NY, *1962*
4. Cf. Gen 48:17 where the blessing of the first-born is ostentatiously conferred on Ephraim rather than Menasseh by Jacob.

III

The Nature of Job's Illness and the Fate of his Children

A. The Illness

The search for accurate diagnoses for illnesses recorded in the literature of antiquity is not one of the most rewarding forms of activity. Nevertheless, ideas on the subject will continue to occur to people, usually medical men, and they will continue to be aired. The illness of Job, of which the most popular diagnosis has been *elephantiasis* (which does not occur in the dry Middle East) is in a special category, for there is every reason to believe that Job as a man was a creature of his author's imagination. Further, as all the other events in the prose Prologue where the illness is first introduced are best explained as typological, if not metaphorical, and without attempt at verisimilitude, there is every cause to believe the same of Job's illness. That is, that if typological, it corresponds to no specific disease, but merely represents disease as such, while if metaphorical it does not even correspond to disease at all as it is ordinarily understood.

    I have asserted in the previous chapter that the expression *And the Satan...smote Job with sore boils from the sole of his feet to the crown of his head* is no more to be understood literally than the similar expressions in Deuteronomy and Isaiah, where it is apparent that the meaning is that God will bring (or in Isaiah, has brought) devastation upon the Israelite nation. While this assertion could survive the discovery in the subsequent Dialogue of further references to this type of illness, it is far more comfortable without them. There is no doubt that in all translations and commentaries there are sundry passages which have always been understood as providing these references. I propose therefore to examine all these passages in detail.

    So far as I have been able to ascertain, JPS has missed no possibly relevant passages and I shall therefore examine all that appear in that version. They are 6:6-7; 7:4-5; 13:28; 16:8; 17:7; 19:17; 19:20; 30:16-18; 30:30; 33:19-21. By no means all of these allude to the skin as a site of illness, but all in one way or another, allude to the "fact" that Job is suffering from some form of physical disorder. Some indicate entirely non-specific symptoms, similar to those described in many passages in Psalms and elsewhere, indicating mental anguish, or even the disintegration of national life, and these do not support the literal interpretation of 2:7.

1. The Sickness of my Flesh?

6:6-7 is fascinating. It is a four-line passage which concludes in JPS with the simile *They,* (whatever "they" are) *are like the sickness of my flesh,* giving support without specificity to the idea that Job's flesh is diseased. We may dispose very simply of this translation. The Hebrew of this last line reads המה כדוי לחמי, and לחמי is not *my flesh* but *my bread.* Under no circumstances can לחם mean "flesh". It is true that in Arabic it may have the sense "meat" as P points out, but no-one speaks of his own flesh as meat, particularly not in a context relating to his own appetite, and what he can and cannot, will or will not eat, as is the case here.

Certainly the simplest way out of the conundrum is to regard the odd expression as somehow meaning *they are as though my food had turned putrid* or something like this, but in fact the only literate meaning I can extract from the phrase as it stands is *They are like the sickness of Lahmi,* with Lahmi a man's name. There is a person of this name in the Bible, closely associated with the physical deformity of *polydactily.* In the description of the slaying of the family of Goliath[1] in I Chron 20, Lahmi is mentioned as a brother of Goliath immediately before another member of the family whose name is not given and who had six digits on each hand and foot. The phrase may therefore be understood as "an unnatural monstrosity" which fits the context well enough.

The full context of the figure is one of the most opaque in the book, and will be discussed in Chapter 3.VIII.2, p. 470ff. What is important here is that this phrase does not relate to any sort of illness of Job's.

2. Worms, Dust, and Festering Sores?

7:5 has been habitually understood as referring in explicit terms to Job's skin eruptions. In the Hebrew it reads:

לבוש בשרי רמה וגוש עפר   עורי רגע וימאס

while the English in JPS runs typically:

> *My flesh is clothed with worms and clods of dust*
> *My skin closeth up and breaketh out afresh.*

There has been no recent repentance of this version, for NJPSV reads *My flesh is covered with maggots and clods of earth; My skin is broken and festering*; H *My flesh is clad in worms and dust; My skin dries hard and suppurates*, while C goes quite overboard with *My flesh is covered with pus and scabs; My skin grows firm and then oozes.*

The first line seems to have been translated faithfully (except by C) in all of these versions, but as T-S alone[2] has pointed out, the picture which it portrays is not one of disease, but of death. *Worms and dust* are symbols of the grave, not of festering skin. It is true that there is a variety of tropical ulcer in which worms habitually breed, but it is not found within a thousand miles of the Middle East, and the *clod(s) of dust* are foreign to every form of skin ailment.

The translations of the second line, however, bear virtually no resemblance to the Hebrew text in any of these versions. רגע does not mean *hardens* or *is broken* or *closes,* nor does ימאס mean *breaks out, festers, suppurates* or *oozes.* All these wildly imaginative distortions derive from the search of cognate languages for alternatives to the true and known meanings of the Hebrew words. רגע has been translated as though it were Ethiopic, and ימאס as though Aramaic (and even then in a highly speculative manner). The falsity of the translation is in fact evident to anyone reading it without reference to the Hebrew, for the prepositioning of the repair of the skin before its rupture is unnatural.

There is no need whatever to understand the words in any way other than their normal Hebrew senses. The line means *My skin lies still and is discarded,* but we might better render עור as *shell* or *body.* As the first line indicates, Job describes a vision of himself lying in the grave. This vision is fully prepared by the preceding verse, in which the meaning of the hapax word נדדים has been incorrectly understood. This verse 7:4 is:

> *When I lie down I say, "When shall I arise?"*
> *But the night is endless,*
> *And I am surfeited with נדדים until dawn -*

If we understand נדדים to be nightmares, then v.5 neatly specifies the content of the nightmares. However it is customary to take *tossings to and fro* as the meaning. The root of the word נדד means, according to

BDB, *retreat, flee, depart, stray, wander, flutter* which are hard to connect with tossing to and fro, but accord well with nightmares in which the soul, as it were, departs from the body to wander in strange realms, and which themselves flee at the approach of dawn. The authenticity of "bad dreams" is attested by the specific association in Job 20:8 *Like a dream he will fly away and none find him, And he will be put to flight like a vision of the night*, where *put to flight* is the Hophal of נדד. We should also remark that to speak of some one being *surfeited*, שׂבע, with tossings to and fro is not a natural use of language. A verbal expression is required as *I toss to and fro throughout the night*.

The associations of the root נדד with sleeplessness in Gen 31:40 and Esther 6:1 seem not to be relevant to the use here. In both of these passages sleep departs from the subject. This is a single event and cannot be related to being sated with נדדים which must imply the repetition of some sort of disturbance. Grammatically, נדוד is the passive participle, so the exact meaning seems to be *those which are chased away* – to wit precisely the חזיונות לילה, the visions of the night described in 20:8. We must therefore discard the idea that this verse relates to any illness of Job, having identified the distortions of Hebrew which have led to it.

3. I am Like a Wineskin?

13:28 deserves short shrift, for the mistranslation in JPS is brash. The Hebrew והוא כרקב יבלה, which means *But it wears away like a rotten thing* (or, more correctly I think, *It wears away as by a termite*), is there translated *Though I am like a wineskin that consumeth*. We need look no further than the personal pronoun to realise that there is no correspondence between the Hebrew text and the idea which the translators (the version is actually from LXX and Vg) have fixed upon, that Job's skin is rotting.

The resemblance between this verse and Hosea 5:12, *Therefore am I unto Ephraim as a moth and to the House of Judah as a termite* is so close, with the reversal of the order of the insects typical of the technique of intra-Biblical quotation[3], that there seems sound reason to look upon it as a momentary lifting of the allegorical veil, and to identify the mysterious "it", הוא, with the Israelite nation and the House of Judah, but this is not our concern in this essay. Wine-skin in Aramaic is רקבה, but in Hebrew (Job 32:19) is אוב.

4. I am Shrivelled up?

16:8 is one of a very obscure pair of verses:

אךְ־עתה הלאני השמות כל־עדתי	16:7
ותקמטני לעד היה ויקם בי כחשי בפני יענה	16:8

and is translated in JPS:

> *And Thou hast shrivelled me up, which is a witness against me*
> *And my leanness riseth up against me, it testifieth to my face*

The two key words which testify to disease are תקמטני, rendered *Thou hast shrivelled me up*, and כחשי, rendered as *my leanness*. The verb קמט is found only once elsewhere in the Bible, in the Pu'al conjugation, also in Job, 22:16. Here in the context there is no possibility of its meaning *shrivelled up*, and it is always translated *snatched away*. It needs no particular principle of consistency to dictate that so rare a word, used twice in the same book, must bear at least approximately the same meaning on both occasions. It is true that rabbinic Hebrew features the root with the meaning *wrinkle*[4], but even this is not nearly the same as *shrivel*, and this is Biblical, not rabbinic Hebrew.

    כחש properly conveys a sense of deceit or falsehood. The only basis for *leanness* is one dubious use of the <u>verb</u> in Ps 109:24, and the use of the corresponding <u>Aramaic</u> word to describe the lean kine of Gen 41:27 in the Targum. In Ps 109 the verse certainly implies the wasting of flesh – בשרי כחש משמן, but כחש does not bear the whole burden of the meaning, which is *fails of fat*. Had it said *fails of redness* the same logic would have כחש meaning *pallor*. In Hab 3:17 the same sense, *fails* is to be found, but again for the verb. The normative sense of deceit or falsehood is to be found in every use of the <u>noun</u> – Hosea 7:3, 12:1 and 10:13, (the latter verse being one quasi-quoted in Job 4:8) and in Nahum 3:1 and Ps 59:13. We have to conclude that the translation of this single word as *leanness* is a serious error.

    Although 16:7-8 is very difficult, it is possible to provide a translation which respects the normal meanings of all the words, without recourse to anachronistic or foreign lexicons.

> *And now I am wearied.*
> *When You ravaged all my congregation*

> *You snatched me away. It has become evidence*
> *And witnesses against me.*
> *My false position testifies to my face.*

Here *snatched away* is as a brand from the burning, so that Job is again complaining of his survival in contrast to the destruction of his people. The possessive suffix of כחשי is an example of the "objective genitive[5]". The first line of v.7 is most simply treated as a passive. Literally *He has wearied me.*

Both LXX and Vg accept the normal Hebrew meanings of the words. Again, all reference to disease, even in the least specific sense of loss of weight, disappears if the Biblical Hebrew sense of the text is respected.

5. My Members are as a Shadow?

17:7, ויצרי כצל כלם   ותכה מכעש עיני, runs in JPS:

> *My eye also is dimmed by reason of vexation*
> *And all my members are as a shadow.*

The first line, if taken literally, would imply that Job was going blind, but everyone is content to accept it as metaphorical. Indeed, they must, for it is virtually a quotation of Psalm 6:8, *Mine eye is dimmed because of vexation (כעס); It waxeth old because of all mine adversaries.* In the second, the English reader sees Job wasting away, because of the rough hyperbole of the English idiom of the shadow. In Biblical use the shadow (where not an image of protection) is always employed to signify ephemerality, not thinness, see Job 8:9, Ps 144:4, Ecc 6:12, etc. Of course *all my members* are not ephemeral, but the mismatch is due to the mistranslation of יצרי as *members*, not to any misinterpretation of the import of the shadow simile. יצר is a form of the imagination or will (Peshitta), and here might be translated *plan* or *purpose*. All Job's plans and hopes have fled like a shadow. The form of the word appears to be the passive participle. (This explanation first proposed by Levi Ben Gershom, *1288 – 1344).*

C after considering the various possibilities opts for *members* essentially on the basis of the need for an anatomical parallel for *eyes*. The dictate of parallel ought, I suggest, to lead to the opposite conclusion. As stated at the head of the section, a literal reading of *eyes* would lead to an unacceptable conclusion about Job's condition, that he was going blind; hence *eyes* must be understood in a non-literal sense and the discomfort described in the first line is clearly to be seen as <u>emotional</u>, not physical. Hence an anatomical parallel creates an almost ludicrous cross-purpose in the verse.

Yet another indication of Job's illness is unable to survive scrutiny in the light of the accurate meaning and use of Biblical Hebrew.

6. I am Loathsome and Abhorrent?

19:17 רוחי זרה לאשתי   וחנותי לבני בטני

emerges as the extraordinary:

> *My breath is abhorred of my wife,*
> *And I am loathsome to the children of my tribe.*

We shall discuss the distortion evident in *children of my tribe* in the second section of this chapter. Here we must concentrate on the indications of putrefaction in *abhorrent breath* and *loathliness*.

None of the significant words here is translated in accordance with Hebrew usage. רוחי is not *my breath* in the sense of the air which I exhale; זרה has no connection with abhorrence; still less does חנן relate to loathing. Indeed, reading translations like this sedulously repeated by generations of scholars inspires a sense of wonder and even distress. There is absolutely no problem about the verse, and the words are all familiar common Biblical Hebrew words. They are correctly translated in many early versions (e.g. T).

The rendition of each of the verbs is usually justified on the basis of a cognate in Arabic. C even has the effrontery to appeal to the parallel between them as confirmation of the meaning of the first! But see comments on vv. 13 & 16 on p.408, showing how the v. combines the two *leitmotifs* of the chapter in these two words. The meaning of this verse is:

> *My spirit seems strange to my wife,*
> *And my favour to the children of my body.*

and the parallel is in the reversal of the normal relationships of intimacy with the wife and respectful gratitude from the children. The context of the verse is one of alienation and distance, in which Job complains of the way in which all his erstwhile intimates avoid him. There is no justification in it for these exaggerated renditions of the key words which, besides falsifying the text and introducing further spurious evidence of Job's disease, go a long way towards destroying the pathos of Job's complaint.

7. My Bone Clings to my Skin and Flesh?

בעורי ובשרי דבקה עצמי   ואתמלטה בעור שני   19:20,

literally, *My bone clings to my skin and my flesh, And I am escaped by the skin of my teeth,* does appear at last to convey physical wasting, although it contains no reference to skin disease. It is appropriate here to quote Psalm 102:4-12 which has much in common with this and several other passages of complaint by Job, but which is correctly interpreted as a lament for Zion as the later vv. 14-23[6] make apparent. Indeed this Psalm throws much light on the Biblical conventions of poetic lamentation. In the following, the comparable passages from the Book of Job are cited on the right.

4.	*For my days are consumed like smoke*	7:6
	And my bones are burned as a hearth.	30:30
5.	*My heart is smitten like grass, and withered;*	
	For I forget to eat my bread.	3:24, 33:20
6.	*By reason of the voice of my sighing*	
	My bone cleaves to my flesh.	19:20
7.	*I am like a pelican of the wilderness*	30:29
	I am become as an owl of the waste places.	30:29
9.	*Mine enemies taunt me all the day;*	
	They that are mad against me do curse me.	16:9,10
10.	*For I have eaten ashes like bread*	
	And mingled my drink with weeping.	3:24
12.	*For my days are like a lengthening shadow*	
	And I am withered like grass.	14:2

If this passage is wholly metaphorical, a lament for the peril and destruction of the nation, as it surely is, then the companion expressions in the Book of Job, including 19:20, *My bone cleaves to my skin and my flesh*, may, if not must, properly be considered so also.

עצמי, literally *my bone*, but at the very least a collective, stands for the whole *persona*, the self (BDB,3, p.782) much as in Modern Hebrew, and it is very likely, therefore, that Job is not complaining of emaciation, but of survival *My ghost clings to my skin and my flesh; and I am escaped by the skin of my teeth* – I continue reluctantly, precariously, to live, because the life-force won't depart. There is little different in this sentiment from the *You snatched me away* of 16:8. It is likely that much the same is to be understood in the Psalm, with דבקה, *clings*, again implying a precarious hold. I.e., my sole sustenance, holding body and soul – flesh and "bone" – together, is the sound of my sighs, not corporeal food, which I forget to eat.

Only in this way can we extirpate the *non sequitur* element from this verse. The use of *flesh* בשרי, in both texts raises doubts whether they really refer, even as a metaphor, to physical wasting. The expected organ is the skin as in <u>he is all skin and bone</u> implying he has no flesh. In the Job verse, if wasting is intended, the combination of *skin* and *flesh* produces self-contradiction.

In 19:20 there is no mistranslation, or illegitimate recourse to cognates, but there is a high probability of a misinterpretation. We might mention also that in the similar passage in Psalm 102, the "wasting" which, if there is any, is in any case metaphorical of the distress of the nation, is attributed not to disease, but to anguish which makes the speaker forget to eat. So on several counts, we should not accept that any reference to Job's emaciation, if we find it, necessarily implies physical disease.

8. The Neck of my Tunic Fits my Waist?

30:16-18 is a most complex and difficult passage, but one which well repays careful examination. JPS gives us:

> And now my soul is poured out within me;
> Days of affliction have taken hold upon me.
> In the night my bones are pierced and fall from me,
> And my sinews take no rest.

> *By the great force (of my disease) is my garment disfigured;*
> *It bindeth me about as the collar of my coat.*

NJPSV pithily renders the last line *The neck of my tunic fits my waist.*
The first two lines present no particular problem, nor do they
refer to anything but spiritual distress. In the next couplet the word
translated *sinews* is עֶרְקִי, another word which appears only twice in the
whole Hebrew Bible with the second example also in the Book of Job,
this time earlier in the same chapter. In 30:3 occurs the expression
הָעֹרְקִים צִיָּה , commonly taken to mean *those that gnaw the desert*. Again
we are obliged by the customary liberty taken by translators to
repudiate the idea that so rare a word could have two entirely different
meanings in two contexts in the same book, and so must render עֶרְקִי
as *my gnawers* = "my teeth" (cf. the *grinders* of Ecc 12:3). H has the
same translation, but sees *gnawers* as *the pangs which gnaw me*. The
second verse seems to be a description of great cold in the night, with
Job saying that his teeth chatter endlessly and the cold pierces him to
the bone. It is apparent from the next verse that this is indeed the
meaning of the second.

30:18 is   בְּרָב־כֹּחַ יִתְחַפֵּשׂ לְבוּשִׁי   כְּפִי כֻתָּנְתִּי יַאַזְרֵנִי

It is the second stich which has given rise to many improbable
versions, of which NJPSV above is perhaps the neatest, with the first
stich usually faring well in translation, although with its unwarranted
of my disease, old JPS is preserving an ancient impertinence. Some
modern authors seek to change יתחפש to תפש or חבש to gain *seize*
instead of *change* or *disguise*, but in so doing they have not really made
the verse easier to decipher. The meaning essentially is *By great force
is my garment changed*, and it is from <u>misinterpretations</u> of this line
that <u>misrenditions</u> of the next derive.
       If we look at 18b only in its immediate context, it is indeed
mysterious. The form כְּפִי is elsewhere usually idiomatic, meaning
either *according to the word of* or *in the same measure as*, but there is
no gainsaying that its literal sense is *as the mouth (or opening) of*, and
as such it is found in Ex 28:32. It is from attempts to mate this literal
sense (perhaps in despair of mating an idiomatic sense) with כֻתָּנְתִּי, *my
tunic*, that strange and awkward phrases emerge, dependent upon the
identification of the "mouth" of the tunic with the collar or neck[7].
יַאַזְרֵנִי means *it girds me*, the word usually used in *gird up your loins* or

gird yourself for battle, and has a more martial sense than merely *clothes me*, to which it is not a synonymous parallel alternative elsewhere in the Bible[8]. There is, as in English, a residual sense to the word which relates to protection from potential attack.

Considering the dominant meanings of these words, it is certainly possible to deduce a translation which makes perfect sense in isolation – *It girds me in just the same measure as my tunic*, meaning either that it provides me with no more protection than my tunic, or with no less. Accepting this as the meaning, we note that it admits of only one possible referent for "it", and that is my changed garment. This surely brings us to the nub of the verse. What is this changed garment? What was it before and what is it now? What protective virtue has it gained? or lost?

Here it becomes necessary to widen perspective and consider the function of Chapter 30 as a whole, and in <u>its</u> context. Job is in the process of winding up his case against God, against his friends, and in his own defence. In doing so he delivers two consecutive speeches, Chapters 29 and 30, which form a contrasting pair. One might almost speak of a secondary degree of parallelism in this before-and-after arrangement. Chap. 29 describes the wealth, the harmony, the intimacy with God, and above all the high repute among men which Job enjoyed before his downfall. Chap. 30 describes the poverty, the anguish, the rejection by God and above all the contempt of men which has become his present lot.

In the nostalgic Chapter 29, Job describes his dress in the following terms:

> *I clothed myself in righteousness and it clothed me;*
> *Like a cloak and a turban was my justice.* (29:14)

This surely is the raiment which has been changed by great force from God. We are dealing here with appearances, not inner reality. Job avers that he presented himself to the world as a righteous and just man – *I clothed myself*, and that his righteousness in turn earned him a recognizable panoply, in effect his prosperity, which gave him a special status and, by implication or extension, immunity – *and it clothed me*.

By *force majeur* this external appearance has been radically changed. Accepting the criteria of his comforters, he implies that while his former prosperity and tranquillity were readily interpreted as the signs of righteousness and justice, his present poverty and distress are consequently accepted as the reverse. With his losses has come the loss of his immunity – from such assaults and insults as the friends have been heaping on him. That prosperity which <u>girded</u> him in the past has been <u>transformed</u> (*transformed itself*, the most accurate rendition of התחפש) into poverty, which now protects him no better than a worthless shift. A magic garment has lost its special virtue by being reversed by God.

Now the chattering teeth in the night is revealed as a brilliant extension of this dress metaphor, by which the inadequacy of the non-magical garment is translated onto a purely physical plane where, as in a new metaphor, cold is revealed as a symbol of rejection and want.

It is apparent that this passage too has nothing at all to do with disease of any kind, and all reference to it or to emaciation is illusory.

9. *Is my Skin Black?*

,עורי שחר מעלי   ועצמי־חרה מני־חרב 30:30,

which JPS translates *My skin is black, and falleth from me, and my bones are burned with the heat*, is part of a companion piece to 30:16-18 just quoted. It too is introduced by the expression ימי־עני, *Days of privation*, which now *confront me* (30:27), and it deals with Job's experience of heat during the daytime in contrast with cold in the night.

It is not possible to be absolutely certain that the JPS translation, with its implication that Job is being seared black by heat (no indication of disease even then) is not correct, but it appears to infringe the Hebrew language.

The verb שחר does not mean *to be black*, but *to seek diligently*, as thrice elsewhere in the Book of Job (7:21, 8:5 and 24:5)[10]. When Hebrew wishes to say *it is black* it simply uses a noun clause and the adjective שחור. So the first stich may mean *He (God) seeks the skin off my back*, and indeed it is difficult to see how the essentially particulate מעלי can mean all of *and falleth from me*. In the second stich עצמי, as in 19:20 is singular and has no anatomical significance – *My soul is scorched in the heat* or something of the kind must be read. The <u>bone</u> stands for the whole essence. A non-literal sense is made compulsory by the impossibility of the literal image. This passage echoes Ps 102, v.s. *My bones are burnt like a hearth*, while the preceding verse:

> *I am a brother to the jackals*
> *And companion to the daughters of the ostrich*

invokes the Psalm's *pelican of the wilderness* and *owl of the waste places.*

Alternately, Job's bones are chilled and afire, but with the ice of loneliness and fear, and the fire of fury and resentment, not with physical agents.

10. Elihu's Testimony

Unless one includes complaints so vague as to be mere expressions of grief, the above nine references constitute the only possible allusions to Job's illness in the Dialogue itself. There remains Elihu's description of what happens to the sinner admonished by God, for which there is a reasonable presumption that it is intended to resemble what has happened to Job. This is 33:19-21, describing not skin disease in any sense, but pain in the bones, loss of appetite, and physical wasting. Elihu is painting a picture of the physical accompaniments of guilt and anxiety common in Biblical writings. The same syndrome of pain in the bones and physical wasting is drawn in Psalms 6, 31, 32 and 38. Here it is particularly relevant to recall that the plural *bones* in the Bible *is considered as a seat of disease or pain especially of personified Israel, for example in* Ps 22:15, 31:11, Lam 1:13 and Hab 3:16 (BDB).

We find Job himself complaining of lack of appetite and, as we have seen in several of the examples above, there are vague complaints in which *bone* or *bones* make their appearance, but we have found no acceptable reference to wasting.

11. Conclusion

One thing is certain. There is no reference in the poem of Job to any disease of the skin. It is almost as certain that there is no reference to physical disease of any kind. It is indeed striking that of the ten passages which are commonly translated in such a way as to support or convey the impression of illness, no fewer than eight have been able to achieve this result only by translating known Hebrew words in ways which do not correspond to any parallels within the corpus of Biblical literature. The statistical probability that this is mere coincidence is effectively zero. It is impossible to escape the conclusion that scholars have, for generations, been deceived by their convictions regarding illness into abandoning the true principles of faithful translation whenever they have scented even the faintest odour of decay or corruption in Job's words.

Job's illness is a metaphor for the ravaging of his country and community, and Job 2:7 is a true quotation of Deuteronomy 28:35.

Job's בנים

The problems of interpretation provoked by Job's children are quite different from those raised by his illness. In the case of references to the latter we were confronted by a statistically impossible frequency of words which have had to be assumed to be of foreign origin in order to sustain the illusion of literal continuity between Prologue and Dialogue. In the case of Job's children there is no such evidence of systematic error. There is a considerable number of references to Job's בנים at intervals throughout the discussion, and a number of inferential references also.

There is, however, a fundamental difficulty with this word בנים, for although this is the word for sons, and often for children in the sense of offspring rather than of young people, it is also used frequently to denote a tribal or even a national or supra-national group, as we have seen with בני־ישראל or בני־קדם, a sort of genus as in בני־האלהים, a subordinate or diminutive class as in the usual understanding of בני־רשף as *sparks*, a filial-like relationship as when Saul called David בני, a God-people relationship as in Deut 32:5, and also to imply a destiny in בן־מות. The only ambiguity we shall be concerned with is whether, when Job's בנים are mentioned, this refers to his biological offspring or to the inhabitants of the district, tribe or nation of which he is leader, or to neither consistently.

We are perhaps entitled to draw some conclusion also from the fact that there is no mention except in Prologue and Epilogue of Job's daughters.

The relevant passages are 5:25, 8:4-7; 8:17, 14:21-22; 17:14; 19:17; 29:5; 31:8 and, in a special sense 15:33; 18:19; 20:11; 21:21; 27:14,15. We must examine them all. There are surprisingly no references whatever to this subject in either the speeches of Elihu or those of the Lord.

B. The Children

1. Eliphaz's Promise

In 5:25 Eliphaz promises Job that, if he turns to God, *You will know that your seed is abundant and your descendants as the grass of the earth.* Apologists for the literal connection with the Prologue are obliged to suggest that Eliphaz is carried away by his own eloquence, and has forgotten that Job has no surviving children![11] Alternatively, it may be seen as a prediction of the reconstitution of Job's family as actually described in the Epilogue. This, however, would be more than a penetration of the Dialogue by the literal details of the Prologue; it would imply the penetration of the down-to-earth verisimilitudes of the Dialogue by the schematic fantasies of the Frame story, and this would be hard to credit. The evidence of 5:25 suggests that the Job of the Dialogue has living children.

2. Punishment of the Children

8:4-7 is difficult, for the verses feature a syntactical conundrum אם בניך חטאו־לו וישלחם ביד פשעם. It has been usual to read this *If your children sinned against Him, He delivered them into the hand of their transgression.* This defies the logic of the situation which surely requires *If He punished your children, they must have sinned against Him.* The syntactical problem arises because there is in the Bible no other example of a conditional sentence with prostasis in the perfect tense and apostasis in the imperfect consecutive. Both problems can be solved by assuming that the second part of the verse is actually a part of a continuing and lengthy prostasis whose resolution is postponed by a further verse and a half to yield the following[12]:

> *If your "children" sinned against Him*
> *And He visited them with the consequences of their transgression;*
> *If you yourself seek earnestly to God*
> *And appeal to the Almighty -*
> *If you are pure and upright -*
> *Then surely He will rouse Himself for you*
> *And restore the habitation of your righteousness;*
> *And be your beginning never so small,*
> *Your end He will greatly enlarge.*

As long as we are able to accept an entirely non-committal meaning for ישלחם ביד פשעם, *cast them into the power of their sin*, with שלח ביד consider-ed as cognate with נתן, נפל and הביא ביד, this passage is compatible with both hypotheses about the children – that they were Job's offspring who were slain for their sins, with Bildad foretelling the slow reconstitution of Job's home and family, or that the children are Job's people sent into exile and subdued in their land, and Bildad is forecasting the ultimate resumption of their sovereignty. The apostasis is a promise of restitution, and the expression *the habitation of your righteousness* is better under-stood as a national homeland than Job's "tent". We must further consider that *restoration* is not possible when the consequence of transgression has been death, the irreparable. Thus this homily perhaps fits better with the hypothesis that Job's "children" means his people, and that the Dialogue Job has not lost biological children by death, but territory and citizens by conquest and exile.

On the other hand, reading ישלחם literally as *He expelled* (Jer 24:5, 29:20), that is, sent them into exile, provides a complete harmony with the allegorical interpretation of the work, and gives to the phrase *restore the habitation of your righteousness* the unmistakable sense of return from exile.

3. Prospering in Exile

We have had occasion to discuss 8:17ff previously (Chap I. p. 104f) and have shown that its probable purpose is to assure Job that, assuming his righteousness, his "children" or his "roots and shoots" will prosper in exile.

4. The Future Fate of the Children

In 14:21-22, Job, speaking from the depths of self-pity, declares that God destroys a man and

> *His children come to honour and he is unaware,*
> *Or they are humbled, but he knows nothing of it.*
> *But his flesh upon him feels his own pain*
> *And his spirit within him mourns.*

These words, I suggest, could not have been spoken by, nor given by
a great writer to be spoken by, a man who had just been bereaved of
all ten of his children. Such detachment would be inhuman. Again
there is a strong likelihood that by *his sons* is meant *his people after
him*. There is in this passage a trace of the same self-centredness
towards the future of the nation after his own death that we find in
Hezekiah's atrocious reaction to Isaiah's prediction of the subjugation
of Judah by Babylon – *Good is the word of the Lord which thou hast
spoken, if but there shall be peace and truth in my days* (Isa 39:8).

5. *Whom Job will meet in the Grave*

17:14 is one of the most haunting verses in the book. Spoken by Job *de
profundis*, it reads: *(If) I had greeted corruption*[13] *"You are my father",
Called the worm "my mother", "my sister"*... There are at least two ways
of reading this. One suggests the scaling of heights of poetic sophistication so lofty as to be beyond belief for the period – that it expresses,
like Blake's *Book of Thel*, a fellowship with all the Universe based on
common origin and destiny which extends even to the earthworm in the
grave. If this is what the poet intended, then it is irrelevant to the issue
of this chapter. The other is that Job is referring to literal parents and
sister who have predeceased him, and whom he will meet, gruesomely,
in the grave. If this is the meaning, then the failure to refer as well, or
by preference instead, to his recently lost children is powerful negative
evidence that the Job of the Dialogue is not a recently bereaved father.

6. *The Sons of my Body*

19:17 unmistakably refers to the children as still living. רוחי זרה לאשתי
וחנותי לבני בטני. We have discussed the verbs above on p.125f. Here our
concern is with the nouns. The complaint, we have noted, is of
alienation. The phrase בני בטני is clearly a deliberate parallel with אשתי,
my wife, so that even were it written in an unknown tongue, we
should be justified in translating it confidently "my (biological)
children". Only here the ambiguity we have been trying to resolve
surrounding the word בנים in other contexts has been deliberately
removed by the addition of the word בטני, which means variously
"belly", "womb" and "body". The phrase פרי בטנך, *the fruit of your body*

occurs repeatedly in Deuteronomy, addressed to the community of
Israel, with the force of the sense of "womb" attenuated as here to
refer simply to the power of generation, without regard to gender. E.g.
Deut 28:11, quoted above.

Many attempts have been made to deflect attention from the
devastating significance of this verse. D provides a lengthy justification
for following several other German commentators in understanding
the phrase as *my (mother's) womb* as בטני is surely to be understood in
3:10, and hence *my brothers* rather than *my sons*. C is the latest to
support this. There are two powerful arguments against it. First
because it creates the asymmetric parallel, *my wife - my brothers*, and
second because Job has already described his deteriorated relationship
with his brothers earlier in the same passage (v.13) in these terms *He
has removed my brothers* (אחי) *far from me*. This is insuperable. We
cannot have it both ways. W. Robertson Smith[14], citing an Arabic
parallel, reads *the children of my clan* but has attracted few supporters
(JPS numbered among them). Dillman[15] essays *my grandchildren*, but
as C remarks, there is no suggestion that any of Job's children was
married. Carey[16], makes the interesting suggestion that Job is referring
to the past when he says *My spirit* (when I worshipped God after
learning of the death of my children) *was strange to my wife, though I
had been gracious to the children of my bowels*, but this defies context.
G[17] comes close to the truth of the matter when he writes "The death
of Job's children in the prologue is no objection to this interpretation
(my own children), since the poet does not trouble to harmonize every
detail of the prose tale with the poetry," but the wideranging implications of this casual observation and the yawning void it opens are
given no attention. The reader is compelled to ask: if Job has not lost
his children; if he is not suffering from a skin disease; of what on earth
is he complaining in these twenty chapters of pain? NJPSV, H and
Hartley all adopt this translation, but none attempts to face its
consequences for the story as a whole.

The truth is that the death of Job's children cannot be fitted under the
rubric "every detail of the prose tale". It is the central tragedy of the
whole book and Gordis's proposition bespeaks a carelessness on the
part of the author of ridiculous proportions. It is one thing to have
mislaid a few thousand camels, or a few hundred she-asses, or the
Satan, between Prologue and Dialogue, but ten children is too much!
One must have sufficient respect for the author of this greatest of all

books to believe that a discrepancy of this magnitude means something.

7. No Consolations After Death

21:21 is the conclusion of the passage already mentioned in relation to the election of Israel, and it is discussed further at some length in Chap. XI. Having said that *God saves His strength for His own children* (i.e. His people, cf. Deut 32:5), Job goes on to describe the feelings of one who receives the mark of Divine recognition – *His own eyes see his ruin as he drinks the wrath of the Almighty* – and then in v.21 *For what will be his pleasure in his House after him When the tale of his time is told?* What this means is that Job rejects the consolation which has been offered to him of a bright future in store for his posterity (v.s. 5:25, 8:17, etc.), not on the grounds that he has no posterity remaining, or in prospect, but simply on the human grounds that death closes all. If Job is speaking personally here at all, he is speaking as a man with surviving children.

8. Servants, Disciples, or Children?

In discussing 19:17, Clines (p.449) asserts that the death of Job's children "is alluded to in the Dialogues", and refers to 8:4 (v.s.) and 29:5. 29:5, part of Job's reminiscence of happier times says בעוד שדי עמדי סביבתי נערי, – *While yet the Almighty was with me, Around me my young men*. Not a few translators and commentators[18] render נערי as *my children*, making of the verse an indication that Job has lost his sons by death, exile, or otherwise. It is true that Job's children are called הנערים by the servant in 1:19, but this translates naturally as *the young people*, and certainly not *the sons and daughters*. The reference usually quoted to support "my children" as an acceptable meaning is II Sam 18:5, where David says *Deal gently for my sake with the young man (לנער), even with Absalom*, but here the absence of the possessive suffix makes the expression quite different, expressive of just the right distance we should expect the worried sovereign-father to maintain from his trusted captains. There is no example where נער could simply be translated *offspring* or *son*. In 29:5, either servants or disciples is indicated particularly as the next verse details the duty of the first or the privilege of the second class – *to wash my feet* (בחמה = *in the heat*, probably, rather than "with butter").

9. Job Pledges his Offspring

31:8 contains one of the curses which Job invokes on his own head in the great clearance oath which concludes his testimony. If any spot has adhered to his hands, he begs, *Let me sow and another eat, and let my descendants be uprooted!* This is clear evidence of a surviving posterity through whom Job may still be harmed. In many modern versions[19] the word *descendants* is replaced with *produce*, giving the line a novel form which might be described as contradictory or incompatible parallel. The word in Hebrew is צאצאי, literally, *that which goes forth from me*. ארץ וצאצאיה (Isa 42:5) means *The earth and its produce*, but this does not confer the meaning *produce* (in the sense of merchandise) on the word in a different combination, for the pronomial suffix to this word is no normal possessive, but a true ablative. While it is possible to imagine a degenerative corruption overtaking such a word in the course of the development of the language, this can hardly have occurred between the writing of Job 5:25 (v.s.) and 27:14, where צאצא unquestionably means descendants, and Job 31:8. The sowing and eating are symbolic, and the first line of the verse means "Let me diligently plan and accumulate for the future, and let strangers rather than my own House profit by it."

10. The Children of the Wicked

The references in the second cycle of speeches and Chapter 27 – 15:33, 18:19, 20:11 and 27:14,15, are all secondary references to the fate of the children of the wicked, predicting their obliteration. 15:33 says it through a poetic mix of metaphor and simile: *He will rob, as a vine, his own grapes; He will shed, as an olive tree, his own blossom.* As in Ps 128:3, vine and olive are respectively wife and children[20].

20:11, employing an unusual gender partitive device speaks of the children of the wicked thus: *His life will end in his youth, and she will lie down with him in the dust.*

18:19 states baldly *No offspring will he have, no posterity among the people, nor any survivor in his home.* There are other more oblique references in these chapters to the blasting of roots and branches which may be intended to have similar significance.

Any or all of these can easily be credited as a *double entendre*, a snide attempt to exploit a resemblance between Job's state and that proverbially due to the wicked. They may therefore be accepted as contributory evidence that Job has indeed been bereft of his children, although in these cases a national interpretation is equally valid. With regard to 15:33, the linking of vine and olive must militate against any literal interpretation, for we know both from Prologue and Epilogue, quite apart from 19:17, that Job's wife did not die during his trial. It would be the height of perversity to accept the children as the olives in 15:33 but reject the wife as the vine.

The alternative interpretation of these passages is that they are straightforwardly what they appear to be, predictions of the downfall of Job's enemies, the wicked, who are discussed fully in Chap. 4 below. Job refers to his friends' dissertations on the fate of the wicked as *vain comfort* (21:34), and this explicitly because the lives of the wicked are, according to him, untroubled, while punishment reserved for their posterity does not touch them. From this it is fair to infer that Job would be comforted by the thought that the wicked reap their due reward if only he could credit it. There is thus sound reason for believing that the bitter dispute between the two sides in the second cycle is a dispute over the facts rather than over the interpretation to be given to these assertions. Again, nothing else is spelled out explicitly, and whatever conclusions the reader reaches are, as it were, on his own responsibility.

27:14, also discussing the fate of the children of the wicked, *If his children be multiplied, it is for the sword, and his offspring shall want for bread* is not spoken by one of the comforters, but by Job himself[21] (see Chap. 9 below). Here he emphatically affirms that the deserts of the wicked are visited not on himself, but on his posterity. Thus the destiny in store for the posterity of the wicked is perhaps the only common ground between the comforters and Job. This makes the interpetation of the comforters' remarks as mocking Job with his own bereavements very difficult to sustain. The logical conclusion is that Job accepts this part of the comforters' case because it does not apply to himself, but rejects all the other descriptions of the lives of the wicked because they do.

11. Conclusion

Unless we accept Gordis's cavalier view, which is in essence that the
author was simply careless of details and allowed all sorts of contradictions to jostle one another in his work, we are faced with a considerable body of evidence, some of it absolutely explicit, that the Job of the
Poem, unlike the Job of the Prologue, had living children at the time
of his conversations with his friends. We have to conclude that 1:18-20,
describing the slaying of his children and Job's reaction to it, is, like
the illness, to be understood allegorically.

Notes Chapter III

1. The family of Goliath is described in two places in the Bible, I Chron 20, and II Sam 21:15-21. The two citations are in sharp conflict, but as II Sam attributes the slaying of Goliath to Elhanan, making nonsense of the famous earlier passages I Sam 17:4ff, 21:10 and 22:10, and removing all reason for his pedigree to appear in the Hebrew Bible, and repeats the word ארגים, once in a completely meaningless way, it is apparent that the authentic version is that of Chronicles, and that the Samuel passage (which incorporates the name Lahmi into the phrase בית־הלחמי, the Bethlehem-ite) is corrupt.

2. pp. 136-7.

3. The reversal of the order of a parallel pair is an example of a common, if not the common device in intraBiblical quotation and allusion. See P.C. Bentjes, *Inverted Quotations in the Bible: A neglected stylistic pattern*, Biblica 63/4, 1982, pp.506-523, and M. Weiss, *The Bible from Within*, Magnes Press, Jerusalem, *1984*, quoting M. Seidel: *When an author uses the expressions of a verse which echoes in his mind, he uses them in reverse order, the later expression appearing earlier and the earlier one later. (Maqbilot Ben Sefer Yeshaya Lesefer Tefillim*, Sinai XXXVIII (*1956*), p.150.

4. B.J. p.176.

5. Gesenius #135m.

6. *Thou wilt arise and have compassion on Zion;*
> *For it is time to be gracious unto her, for her appointed time is come.*
> *For Thy servants take pleasure in her stones,*
> *And love her dust.*
> *So the nations will fear the name of the Lord,*
> *And all the kings of the earth Thy glory;*
> *When the Lord hath built up Zion,*
> *When He hath appeared in His glory;*
> *When He hath regarded the prayer of the destitute,*
> *And hath not despised their prayer.*
> *This shall be written for the generation to come;*
> *And a people that shall be created shall praise the Lord.*
> *For He hath looked down from the height of His sanctuary;*
> *From heaven did the Lord behold the earth;*
> *To hear the groaning of the prisoner;*
> *To loose those that are appointed to death;*
> *That men may tell of the name of the Lord in Zion,*
> *And His praise in Jerusalem;*
> *When the peoples are gathered together,*
> *And the kingdoms, to serve the Lord.* Ps 102, 14-23.

7. This error begins to be seen in the ancient Greek and Latin versions, and has been consistently echoed down to the present. There are very few exceptions. T-S somehow contrives to take פי as "my mouth", meaning "my attorney", he who speaks for me, but this version is absurd. D&G refuse to translate the verse at all, declaring it to be hopelessly obscure or corrupt. R ignores כפי entirely and produces *(Grief) tightens around me as does my coat.* The variety of subjects proffered for יאזרני is

impressive, and includes in addition to the garment itself and God, *despair* (M), *grief* (v.s.), *the multitude of my pangs* (Vg), *phlegm*(NEB) and *my kin* (Moffatt). The closest any translator or commentator has come to a correct understanding is V-S who writes *God is like an armed robber who strips me, lonely traveller, of my clothes* (cf. Mic 2:8) *and only leaves me a piece of shirt to cover my shame. He has deprived me of my dignity.*

8. Except in the expression *Clothed in majesty, clothed in strength, He has girt Himself*, Ps 93:1. The abstract use of "gird", i.e. without specifying girt with what, as in this passage, is epitomised in Isa 45:5: *I engird you though you have not known Me.* The sense of protection becomes dominant.

9. The common use of the Hithpa'el is "to disguise oneself by changing garments." In this case the garment has been changed by external force, but the strictest reading would be *By* force majeur *has my garment disguised itself.*

10. While the examples in Job are all of the Pi'el conjugation, the Qal has this sense in Prov 11:27.

11. V.E. Reichert, *Job*, Soncino Press, London etc. *1946.*

12. B alone seems to have recognized this.

13. See A p.187, n.3, for authority for preferring this to *the pit.*

14. W. Robertson Smith, *Kinship and Marriage in Early Arabia*, new Edn. Ed. S.A. Cook, A & C Black, London, *1903.* 34 (quoted by C).

15. A Dillman, *Hiob*, Leipzig, *1891.*

16. C.P.Carey, *The Book of Job*, Wertheim, Mackintosh & Hunt, London, *1858*, 261.

17. p. 202.

18. E.g. T-S, G.

19. JPS, NJPSV, G, NEB, D&G etc. Earlier versions giving a similar meaning are E.J. Dillon, *The Sceptics of the Old Testament*, Isbister & Co., London, *1895*, p.225 and S. Cox, *A Commentary on the Book of Job*, C.Kegan Paul & Co., London, *1880*, p.371. D resolutely affirms this meaning. Presumably all these translators have been influenced by the parallel line, *Let me sow and another eat*, without considering the probability that this was to be understood metaphorically rather than agriculturally.

20. See Note 3 above.

21. See also D. Wolfers *The Speech-cycles in the Book of Job*, VT, XLIII, 3, *1993*, pp. 385-402.

IV
The Identity of "the Wicked"

In his final speech, the Lord issues a lofty challenge to Job which concludes (40:12-14) with the invitation to *Expose every one that is proud; abase him, and crush the wicked beneath them (or in their place); Bury them in the dust together; Swathe their faces in Perdition - Then shall even I laud you For your right hand will have brought you victory.* This final speech of the Lord is expounded at length in Chap. V, and its hidden meaning explained. But without first understanding who is represented by the word רְשָׁעִים, "the wicked", in this challenge, scant progress towards understanding the speech can be made.

The words רְשָׁעִים, רָשָׁע, occur with great frequency in many Biblical books. It is customary to translate them by the English word "wicked". However, if we examine carefully the many contexts in which the words appear, it is apparent that they have a quite distinct secondary meaning in some of these, notably in some prophetic books, and in Psalms. In Habbakuk 1:4, 1:13 and 3:13, the word is used as a synonym for the Chaldeans, the heathen foreign enemy of Israel bent upon her conquest. In Isaiah 14:5 exactly the same synonymity is clearly stated, and again in Isa 48:22. Jeremiah inveighs against a whole continent of heathen enemies categorized by this term in 25:31 and again in 30:23. Ezekiel 7:21 displays the same convention. Most explicitly in several of the Psalms is this equivalence employed. Thus Psalm 9:6 *Thou hast rebuked the nations; Thou hast destroyed the wicked; Thou hast blotted out their name for ever,* and v.18, *The wicked shall return to the Netherworld - Even all the nations that forget God.*

The singular and plural רָשָׁע are used with quite remarkable frequency in the Book of Job - more than half as many times as in the whole corpus of the prophetic portion of the Bible. Four and a half of the forty-two chapters of the Book of Job are devoted entirely to the consideration of the lives and deaths of the wicked, and several key passages in other chapters. Each of the speakers, Job, the three comforters, Elihu and the Lord, has something important to say about them. I shall be demonstrating in this chapter that although there are occasional references to the wicked in which the word may be understood as it is in English, as those who have deliberately turned their backs on virtue, in the majority the word is employed either exclusively or ambiguously as code-name for the foreign idolatrous foe besetting Israel (Judah), that is specifically for the Assyrians.

1. The Crux in Chapter 15

The fate in store for "the wicked" is introduced as a major theme of the Book of Job in the second half of Chapter 15, and this introduction itself constitutes a major crux in the comprehension of the description which follows it, and of the book as a whole. It will be necessary therefore to delay examination of the passages incorporating the term the wicked until we have explained this introduction.

Chapter 15 comprises Eliphaz's second speech. Unlike any other in the book, it is divided into two equal sections (v. Chap. IX). The first of these represents the conclusion of the first cycle of speeches, the second the opening of the second cycle. In the first cycle the comforters have addressed the question of the significance of suffering, with the assertion that it is invariably an indication of sin. They have coupled this with exhortations to Job to repent and amend his ways, promising him that if he does so, his (unspecified) losses will be recouped. Job's ripostes have taken the form of asserting his innocence, assailing God for indifference or active malice towards him and other inoffensive men, and reproaching his friends for unsympathetic reactions to his unprovoked agony.

In Chapter 15 Eliphaz devotes the first twelve verses to the attempt to change Job's attitude to the "wise" advice which he has been receiving, warning him of the danger which his hostility to God is inviting. Verses 14-16 consist of a perororatorical recapitulation of his opening message - the dream sequence - which expressed the idea that no man is innocent in the eyes of God. These verses form the conclusion of the comforters' first attempt to cope with Job's reversed situation.

Verse 17 introduces the new theme which will dominate the second cycle of speeches - the life-experiences of the wicked. It demands Job's attention with these words: אֲחַוְךָ שְׁמַע־לִי וְזֶה־חָזִיתִי וַאֲסַפֵּרָה - *I shall tell you. Listen to me, and what I have seen let me recount.* The word חָזִיתִי cannot be detached from the idea of seeing although it admits of several modes - with the eye, in a vision, or by experience. It does not, however, include the possibility of learning by instruction. This is of some importance in interpreting what follows.

In Ezekiel 11:15 = 33:24 it is recorded that the remnant of Judah left in the land after the exile to Babylon were claiming לָנוּ נִתְּנָה הָאָרֶץ לְמוֹרָשָׁה - *To us was the Land given as an inheritance!* In Joel 4:17 there is the prophecy: *Then shall Jerusalem be holy, And there shall no foreign foes pass through her any more -* וזרים לא־יעברו־בה עוד. In a letter to Tirhakah, King of Nubia, Pharaoh Necho and other Assyrian appointees in Egypt invited him to come to an agreement with them to exclude the Assyrians[1] - *Let there be peace between us and let us come to a mutual understanding; we will divide the country between us, no foreigner shall be ruler among us!*

Job 15:19, the next-but-one verse after the above introductory exhortation, is: להם לבדם נתנה הארץ ולא־עבר זר בתוכם, which is to say, *To them alone was the Land given, and no foreign foe passes among them!*

The word זר does admit of a less extreme reading than "foreign foe", but this is the usual nuance of the word.

There seems a generic resemblance at work in these passages, expressing defiance of external threats and claims against the integrity and sovereignty of a land. We have to take a look next at the way in which the Job verse is introduced, 15:18 - אשר־חכמים יגידו ולא כחדו מאבותם.

Almost the sole problem with this verse is the determination of all translators with no exception that I have been able to find to reject the natural syntax of the collocation כחד מ־ - hide something from - in favour of contortions such as *Which wise men have told from their fathers and have not hid it[2]*. With this piece of work done, it then becomes easy to apply *To them alone the Land was given* to the "fathers", discarding the ambience of defiance, and achieving a sense of vast antiquity for the alleged traditions about to be recounted - notwithstanding the "seen" of v.17.

There is no such expression in Hebrew, any more than in English, as יגיד מ־, "say from", and if there were, it would still be over-ridden in the sentence above by the force of כיד מ־, "hide from" in direct continuity. A common recourse of those seeking to overcome this is to appeal to the fiction of an "enclitic מ", but in fact there is no such animal in Hebrew. We must conclude that what 15:18 says is something like *What wise men are saying and do not hide from their elders*, and that it is followed immediately by what they are saying.

Therefore, instead of amplifying the authority of the "fathers" (with a spurious tradition v.i.), v.19 is the indirect speech report of what "wise men" are saying, and not concealing (from Eliphaz and his friends, the self-satisfied elders of v.18). *(That) to them alone the Land was given, and no foreign foe passes among them!* which may be read as anything from an expression of intention to resist invasion with guerrilla warfare, to a mere expression of confidence that all will be right in the end. It is however an authentic echo of Joel and Ezekiel, and not comprehensible at all except in the context of an historical allegory.

The claim to seniority by the comforters derives from v. 10 of this chapter, where the lofty exaggeration is made that they are *much older in years than your own father*. Job gets his own back for this at the beginning of Chapter 30, when he characterises his tormentors as *younger in days than I, whose fathers I disdained to set with my sheep-dogs!* If we overlook the element of "contest" in statements such as these, we are not following what is going on at all. So when Eliphaz tells Job what חכמים are saying, he is not referring to any particular group of men, he means in contrast to what you, who are very unwise, say. His לא כחדו is meant to remind Job of his own spineless self-indulgent לא כחדתי of 6:10. Every step in this dialogue is replete with *double entendres*, cruel or witty, or both. As for "the fathers" living before foreigners trod the land, the traditions of the Middle East, including those of Israel, far from recalling periods when land was held in unchallenged possession, are records of ceaseless migrations and conquests, heroic resistances and tragic defeats.

These verses are important in the dynamics of the debate which is the Book of Job. They are not only the introduction to the second cycle of speeches, but also the introduction to that consideration of the wicked which is the second part of Eliphaz's speech. This is a recital, either of the defiant predictions of the resistance, or much more likely Eliphaz's own comments on the fate which will overtake the invaders.

2. *The Wicked – Eliphaz*

In 15:20 we encounter the first use of the word רשעים, in parallel with ערין. *All the days of the wicked he shall writhe, and few shall be the years in store for the tyrant.* עריץ is a political term, tyrant, elsewhere used in Job in parallel with רצ, "foe" (6:23). There follow three verses of wild predictions essentially cataloguing the extreme insecurity of his position, culminating in יבעתהו צר ומצוקה תתקפהו כמלך עתיד לכידור, v.24, which evidently means *The enemy will frighten him, anxiety overwhelm him, like the ruler about to topple*. The word כידור is hapax, but its Arabic cognate relates to swift descent - a hawk, a shooting star, or an attacking army. The shooting star reminds us of Isaiah 14:12, *How art thou fallen from heaven, O daystar, son of morning!* and suggests the

Assyrian monarch as the subject. An alternative is *about to engage in battle*, where the mental state of Saul on the eve of his last battle comes inevitably to mind. What is important about this verse is its concentration on a military image, developed in the ensuing verses.

v.25 *For he stretched out his hand against God, and against the Almighty he played the hero.* If indeed we are dealing with a defiant contemporary statement, there is no doubt from this that the context is the Land of Israel, for it is only by attacking this land that an enemy can be said to be attacking the Almighty.

Vv. 26,27 are very difficult, and have led to many implausible versions. ירוץ עליו בצואר is readily decipherable as *He ran at him full tilt* or similar, but בעבי גבי מגניו is almost impenetrable, the only really recognizable word being "his shields". The usual rendition, *with the thick bosses of his bucklers* has little to recommend it. If עבי derives from עבה to be thick, it is the noun "thickness", not an adjective. A גב, even if it relates to roundness (which is highly doubtful, see Chap. 3.IX) would not be the boss of a shield. A man, no matter how wicked, uses only one shield at a time; and a shield, with no matter how many bosses, is no weapon of attack. I make two suggestions - one being that עבי is a beam and גב a tall object, giving *with the beams of his tall ones of shields* = with the battering rams of his siege engines (cf. the Sennacherib reliefs of the siege of Lachich); the other that גב, as in 13:12 (v. p.198f) is an idol, that on analogy with איש מגן, a גב מגן is a protective idol, and that עבי does mean "thickness", to yield *in the density of his protective idols*.

(v.27) כי־כסה פניו בחלבו   ויעש פימה עלי־כסל

assuredly does not mean *For he covered his face with his fatness and made collops of fat on his loins* (D&G) or anything similar, a picture of obesity and self-indulgence at variance with every other line of the description of this villain. The verse in fact is a further stage in the description of the *preparation for battle* to which this section is devoted, and refers to the practice of smearing armour and body with grease in anticipation of hand-to-hand combat (cf. II Sam 1:21; Isa 21:5). C quotes Terrien as seeing in the verse a reference to painting the face with a warrior-mask, and T-S sees him greasing his body for the swim in order to aid *Leviathan*. There is nothing in the verbs כסה or יעש to encourage the view that the fat in this verse is internally produced adiposity. So we translate *Though he smear his face with his fat and grease his cuisse.*

From here, the chapter having described his mental state and
his preparation for battle, moves to the physical fate of the invader,
the so-called wicked. He will live in abandoned dwellings (v.28),
neither he nor his troops (חילו) will enrich themselves or become
established in the land (v.29). The plural suffix of מנלם attests this
reading. Both these propositions are appropriate when applied to an
invader, but very difficult indeed to relate to the ordinarily wicked
man. *He shall not evade the darkness; His shoot will wither in the searing
flame, And he will depart at a puff from His mouth (v.30).* This last
phrase, ברוח פיו, is a startling contraction of the last two lines of Isaiah
11:4:

והכה־ארץ בשבט פיו   וברוח שפתיו ימית רשע

And he shall smite the Land with the rod of his mouth,
And with the breath of his lips shall he slay the wicked,

where "he" is not God but the promised descendant of Jesse.

At this point we reach the end of the extended description of
what is awaiting the wicked, and it should be clear that this has not
been a recitation of any ancient tradition handed down from remote
forebears, for it has little resemblance to anything else in the Bible. It
is Eliphaz's own homily. From now on this can be in no doubt at all.
We next encounter another verse to which scant justice has been done
in the past, v.31.

אל־יאמן בשו נתעה: כי־שוא תהיה תמורתו

The two (א)שׁs tell us that there is a pun in this sentence. It reads: *Let
him not believe that he is being misled by vanity* (in the sense of bluster),
For vanity (in the sense of frustration) *will be his recompense.* Eliphaz
seeks to confirm all the predictions he has recorded above. *Before his
time it shall be fulfilled, nor shall his high one flourish* (lit. *nor shall his
top branch be leafy*).

Verse 33 ironically introduces the summary conclusion:

He will rob - as a vine his own grapes;
He will shed - as an olive-tree his own blossom.

where, as in Ps 128:3 vine = wife, olive = children.

For the company of the godless is forlorn, And fire will consume the tents of traitors[3]. Then the final message, unmistakably Eliphaz's own (see 4:8 and 5:6), *They conceive trouble and bring forth sorrow, and their womb gestates rebellion.* (Cf. Ps 7:15 & Isa 59:4).

Looking back over this hemi-chapter, to which I have devoted considerable space, it becomes difficult to sustain the illusion that it is truly a discussion of the traditional fate of men who depart from the paths of virtue. For apart from the quite serious difficulties entailed in trying to understand the introduction in this way, there is about the whole description an atmosphere of open conflict, of battle, and a treatment of the problem of the wicked as though on a scale far greater than that appropriate to a discussion of civil evil. The picture of the wicked dwelling in desolate cities and uninhabitable houses (v.28) is surely the picture of a harrassed invading army unable to gain a foothold in the occupied and defended cities, while the reference to "his army" is quite explicit, unless one refuses the commonest meaning of חיל, and is satisfied with something like *his wealth will not endure* (G, JPS, P, D&G, T-S, R, D, H, LXX, Vg, NJPSV, C etc.). The great objection to this reading is that *He will not become rich and his wealth will not endure* is nothing if not absurd, and there is no escape from *He will not become rich* for לא־יעשר. "His substance", used by many as a substitute for wealth, is both unattested and unhelpful, not really changing the contradiction. A real alternative would be *His strength will not endure.*

What is especially interesting in the description of the fate of the wicked as given by Eliphaz is that there is almost nothing in it which resembles Job's own fate either as we know it from the Prologue or from his complaints in the Dialogue. That is, the description seems intended as genuine consolation, promising Job the downfall of those whom he sees as his enemies. The same does not apply so surely to the later descriptions of Bildad and Zophar. However, as H has pointed out in his definitive examination of the strategic use of the verbal echo in the Book of Job, Eliphaz conveys his suggestion of Job's identification with the wicked by mimicking in his description of the plight of the wicked the vocabulary of Job's complaints.

3. *The Wicked: Bildad & Zophar*

The two speeches, Chapters 18 and 20, essentially reinforce Eliphaz's recital of the experiences of the wicked. In Ch.18 Bildad starts with the proposition *The light of the wicked* also *shall be extinguished.* This "also" (גם) surely means *as well as* your *light.* The remainder of the dissertation is merely a recapitulation in rather more flowery language of Eliphaz's predictions of the harrassment the wicked will suffer and the terror which will accompany his every step. Beyond this he pictures the end of the wicked with the blotting out of his posterity and memory from the earth. Both the atmosphere of perpetual fear, to which both Job and his friends testify, and the death of Job's children as described (albeit allegorically) in the Prologue, intensify the suggestion of *double entendre* in the words of so-called comfort being offered. Job is silently invited to compare his own fate with that being described as the fate of the wicked, and draw the obvious conclusion.

In Chapter 20, Zophar has little new to contribute, but there is an interesting description of the activities of the wicked which will lead to his downfall - *Because in dereliction he crushed the poor, He robbed his House[4] and never built it up. Because he knew no quiet in himself, He will not let him escape with his treasures. Nothing could escape his devouring; therefore his happiness is insecure.* Zophar concentrates more on the fortune of "the wicked" than on his physical fate - *He swallowed riches but will vomit them back* but does not neglect to wipe him and his posterity out. The motif of his speech is *That the exultation of the wicked is brief and the joy of the godless momentary.* There are better grounds for suspecting that Zophar is attempting to draw a picture of the wicked in which Job will recognize his own plight than apply to the other two comforters' harangues on the subject.

4. *Job's Answer*

Neither in Chaps. 16-17, nor Chap. 19 does Job pay any real attention to the dissertations on the wicked with which his friends are regaling him. Apart from a cursory protest at the beginning of Chap. 16 that they are "sorry comforters", and a complaint at the general tenor of their words at the beginning of Chap. 19 - *These ten times have you reproached me!* - Job waits until Chap. 21 to respond, and then presents his own version of the life-experiences of the wicked". *Whenever I think about it, I am horrified*, he declares, *And my body is seized with trembling*. Job then paints an idyll of peace, prosperity and prolificacy which, he claims, characterises their lives. *How often*, he asks, *is the light of the wicked extinguished?* and answers his own question *God reserves His strength for His (own) children*. This much misunderstood passage is discussed in detail in Chap 11, p. 275ff. Verses 21:27-30 go a long way towards clarifying what all this discussion of the wicked is really about:

27   If I understand the workings of your minds
       And the secret thoughts with which you wrong me,
28   Then you will say, "Where is the princely house?
       And where the canopy⁵ of the dwelling-place of the wicked?"
29   Have you not asked the travellers?
       And do you not accept their intimations
30   That the evil is deferred to a day of retribution;
       They are escorted to a day of wrath?

The first two verses address the hidden suggestion in the comforters' versions of the life of the wicked that Job is enduring precisely that life. What Job is saying in v.28 is "You will look contemptuously around my ash-heap and ask 'Where is all this idyllic prosperity of the wicked which you are describing?'" This is the only explicit reference to the *double entendres* of the friends' comfort. It is a rare genuine example of what G calls a virtual quotation, and it is not left to the reader to guess this.

The next two verses identify the other sense in which the wicked have been cited, as the foreign pagan foes, living in a distant land, information about whose lives is only to be obtained from travellers (עוברי דרך). It is the evidence which they can bring which Job cites in v.30, that the wicked are being, as it were, fattened for the slaughter of some final day of retribution. This carefully crafted last argument of Job seems to leave no doubt that the word wicked is being used in a semi-punning sense to stand both for what the comforters wish to imply Job to be, and for a distant predatory people, nation and/or ruler.

Note carefully that Job does not claim that their ultimate fate is an enviable one. The clear implication is that they live happy and protected lives until their appalling destiny is ready for them. In the ensuing vv. 31,32, Job registers his deep dissatisfaction with this mechanism for dealing with such people:

But who will confront him with his ways, And now He has acted, who will requite him? When he has been escorted to the cemetry?

A long-delayed vengeance which is visited on the posterity of "the wicked", a post-mortem punishment, is no consolation at all to Job, just as, in v.21 before, he objected that a long-delayed recompense paid to his posterity was no consolation to him for his personal suffering (v. Ch. XI). It is to this insistence by Job on the punishment of the wicked that Elihu refers in the puzzling 36:17, *But you are laden with the cause of the wicked.*

In Chapter 27 Job returns to the question of the wicked, this time giving his views of their ultimate fate - a matter entirely distinct in his mind from their easy life. This portion of Chapter 27 is denied to Job by most commentators, but the reader is confidently referred to Chap. IX below for a discussion of the whole question of the authenticity of the attributions of Chapters 24-27.

Here in vv. 11-13, Job declares his intention to put his friends right on what the lot of the wicked really is, what God has stored up for them:

Let me teach you (pl) what is in God's Hand;
What is with the Almighty I shall not conceal.
Look, you all have witnessed it;
Why then do you vainly mouth vanity?
This is the portion of the wicked man from God,
The heritage of tyrants, which they receive from the Almighty.

Let us re-emphasise that in Chap. 27 Job has nothing to say about the lives of the wicked, nor does he in any way contradict the idyll which he painted in Chapter 21. The destiny of the wicked is that his posterity will be despoiled and wiped out; his plunder will end up in the hands of the just and innocent, and at his death not even his widows will lament him. When he dies, he will do so in panic and terror and to the accompaniment of the contempt of mankind. This description can apply equally to, say, Sennacherib and to a private individual who had devoted his life to the unjust accumulation of wealth.

5. The Wicked: Elihu

There remains one further reference of great significance, this time not
to the fate of the wicked, but to their role in history. This is in Elihu's
Chapter 34.

34:24ff. - תחת רשעים

Of the many key passages in the Book of Job where innocent
mistranslation has conspired to hide the true significance of what is
going on, Elihu's description of God's ways with those who disobey
him is one of the most important.

In 34:23 Elihu declared *For He does not offer to man a second
chance to come before God in judgement*, and then proceeds to describe
what, in his view, is God's practice in such cases. Using the strange
adjective, peculiar to Job and to proto-Isaiah, כבירים, *the mighty*, he says
*He destroys the great without trial (לא־חקר) and sets others in their place
(תחתם)*. It is hard to doubt that the process being described is the
conquest of "the mighty" by "others" as punishment (unless perhaps
something like the passing of the throne of Israel from Saul to David
is intended). The "without trial" comment is certainly directed straight
at Job's repeated call to God for a legal hearing, a trial between them.
Elihu expands on what Job regards as the absence of due process in the
next verse

לכן יכיר מעבדיהם: והפך לילה וידכאו

To this end He familiarizes Himself with their deeds is the sense of the
first stich, explaining why God's omniscience renders the whole legal
process of enquiry, search, trial, redundant. In the second stich *They
were crushed* is וידכאו and the remainder probably spells out *when the
night turned over* i.e. at midnight, see v.20, an indication of great
suddenness.

The next verse is assuredly the most important in the passage,
but it has defied all attempts to coerce it into making real sense, and
this is because the political nature of what is being discussed has evaded
the consciousness of the commentators who have worked on it.

Using the *tempus historicum*, the perfect tense, the verse runs:

תחת־רשעים ספקם: במקום ראים

There is little problem with the verb ספק and its suffix. *He* (God) *chastised them* (the mighty). The trouble starts with תחת. Almost all (I might say all, for I know of no dissenters) commentators have assumed somewhat the same meaning here as in verse 24, "in place of", i.e. "instead of". Accepting this reading opens a gulf of inanity in the verse, and most seek to close it either by assuming a corruption of the text (D&G) or by wheedling some strange variant of meaning from it as *in return for their wickedness* (G, H), *with the wicked* (NJPSV), *as criminals* (P).

תחת, however, has the very simple primary meaning "under", and the phrase תחת־רשעים is in every way cognate with the way the word is used in Psalm 47:4:

ידבר עמים תחתינו: ולאמים תחת רגלינו

He subdues peoples under us, and nations beneath our feet.
The meaning of the first stich of v.26 therefore is *He chastised them under the wicked* - i.e. under the heel of the wicked, and here there is no choice of meanings for the wicked. They have to represent the foreign idolatrous foe of the people of Israel, under whose heel God punished the Israelites from time to time.

In the second stich occurs the familiar word, ראים. This is, of course, the plural participle of the word "to see", but it is used as such almost only where there is an object of vision expressed or implied. Where the word stands absolute, as unquestionably here, it is the noun "seer", the exact archaic synonym of "prophet":

For he that is now called נביא *was beforetime called* ראה.
I Sam 9:9.

The meaning is still current in the time of Isaiah (30:10).
The assumption that ראים means anything other than prophets has led to strange readings of this stich also, for there is no natural sense to the phrase במקום ראים with ראים the participle. So we have *In the sight of all men* (G), *In the place of all beholders* (D&G), *In the public place* (P, H). But these are nothing but embarrassed guesses.

The correct reading is quite simply *instead of the prophets*, with במקום having the same meaning as in Hos 2:1, as also in Modern Hebrew. In an ironic verbal interplay במקום takes on the meaning of תחת abandoned from v.24. Ehrlich adopts this meaning, but ruins it by changing רָאִים to רָעִים to achieve a fatal parallel with תַּחַת רְשָׁעִים!

What we now have is the statement that God punished the mighty, using as His instrument "the wicked", instead of, i.e. taking the place of, the prophets. Why?

אֲשֶׁר עַל־כֵּן סָרוּ מֵאַחֲרָיו: וְכָל־דְּרָכָיו לֹא הִשְׂכִּילוּ

> *Which was because they turned aside from following Him*
> *And did not attend to any of His ways,*
> *Causing the cry of the poor to come to Him,*
> *And He does hear the wail of the afflicted.*

This emphatic assertion that God indeed is sensitive to the cry of the עֲנִיִּים would appear as a rebuttal of Job in 24:12, while the emphasis on the lapse of duty of those being punished restricts their identity to groups which owed fealty to God - the Israelites.

It is impossible to imagine a more orthodox view of matters than this. When the Israelites, despite the continuous admonition and guidance of the prophets, persisted in the practice of injustice towards the poor, God sent a foreign enemy to afflict them. This is the scourge of God, the main theme of Biblical history in a nutshell.

Elihu is not yet satisfied that he has made matters absolutely clear, nor provided adequate justification for God:

וְהוּא יַשְׁקִט וּמִי יַרְשִׁע   וְיַסְתֵּר פָּנִים וּמִי יְשׁוּרֶנּוּ
וְעַל־גּוֹי וְעַל־אָדָם יָחַד   מִמְּלֹךְ אָדָם חָנֵף מִמֹּקְשֵׁי עָם

> *And if He did nothing*, who would condemn?*
> *Or who would notice it if He averted His gaze*
> *- And this applies to nation and man alike -*
> *From# the rule of a godless man,*
> *From# the seduction of the people?*

* Essentially unchanged if we assume "to give silence", to cause quietness", as are often read. The inspiration for this strange but incisive statement is Psalm 50:21 אֵלֶּה עָשִׂיתָ וְהֶחֱרַשְׁתִּי, *These things thou hast done, and should I have kept silence?* A non-causative translation of יַשְׁקִט is therefore surely correct. Cf. also the almost mimetical 21:31b.
# In the above it has been necessary to assume that the מs of v.30 are governed by the aversion of God's gaze in v.29. This expression, הַסְתִּיר

פנים, is normally followed by מין (BDB 711), and here the construction should be understood as similar to that in Ps 51:11, הסתר פניך מחטאי - *Hide Thy face from my sins.*

Elihu has now said all he has to say on the role of the wicked in Job's situation. God is the only One Who can correct the situation (of recidivist sin in Job's land) once the prophets have failed. If He were to ignore the matter, no-one would understand what was going on or take steps to correct it. Elihu has reached his objective - ascribing righteousness to his Maker (36:3). At the same time he has slipped in what seems to be the identification of Job as the "godless ruler" of the (i.e. God's own) people. The end of the chapter sees Elihu asking if there has been the slightest sign of repentance or recognition of wrongdoing by this ruler (confirming his identity as Job), together with an invitation to Job to answer, *For it is up to you to choose, not me!*

6. *The Parallels*

In Biblical poetry, very often the only way of knowing the precise sense in which a word is being used is by examining the term which is used in the other line of the distich as its "parallel". Thus our certainty that "the wicked" in the citations provided at the beginning of this chapter are not domestic criminals but foreign enemies derives as much from such evidence as from context. In Hab 3:13 *the House of the wicked* is placed in opposition to *Thy people.* In Isa 14:5 *the staff of the wicked* is paired with *the sceptre of the rulers.* In Jer 25:31, as in Ps 9, *the wicked* are simply matched with *the nations* while Ezek 7:21 is the most explicit of all with *to strangers (זרים = foreign foes) for a prey* being parallel to *to the wicked of the earth for a spoil.*

It is therefore imperative to inspect the way in which the term (רשע(ים is coupled with other terms in the Book of Job if we are to elucidate with certainty the way in which it is used there. The following Table 1 is the result. In brackets are the initials of the speakers in each case.

First cycle

3:17	(J)	The spent of strength
8:22	(B)	Those who hate you
9:22	(J)	The innocent

9:24	(J)	-
10:3	(J)	The work of Your hands (= Job himself)
11:20	(B)	You (Job)

Second cycle

15:20	(E)	עָרִיץ
16:11	(J)	עֲוִיל
18:5	(B)	-
20:5	(Z)	חָנֵף
20:29	(Z)	-
21:7	(J)	-
21:16	(J)	-
21:17	(J)	-
21:18	(J)	-
21:28	(J)	נָדִיב
22:18	(E)	-

Job's monologue

24:6	(J)	-
27:7	(J)	עֲוִיל
27:13	(J)	עָרִיצִים

Elihu

34:26	(El)	The prophets (רֹאִים)
36:6	(El)	The poor, or the righteous
36:17	(El)	-

The Lord

38:15	(L)	Uncertain, probably the poor (v. p.456)
40:12	(L)	The proud

What is absent from this list is even more striking than what is present. Thus there are no examples of a parallel which indicates sin or crime, and there is only one example of the natural antithetical parallel צדיק. Most striking of all is the very high proportion (40%) of times when the word is used without any sort of parallel expression. This in itself suggests a substantive rather than an adjectival sense for these. We shall look in vain for a similar incidence for any adjective in Biblical poetry. In Psalms and Prophets, the incidence of unmatched uses of the word is only 14% of the total.

There appears a considerable difference in practice between the first and second cycles. In the first, the word seems to be used essentially as an opposite for Job himself. The word *innocent* (תם) in 9:22 is how Job describes himself in the preceding verse (תם אני). In both 8:22 and 11:20 there is an implication of hostility between Job and the wicked, rather than a simple contrast, so that the idea of a foreign foe is already present even at this early stage of the discussions.

In the second cycle, and Job's last answer to it (Chap. 27) fall most of the unpaired uses of the word, together with the three synonymous parallels, חנף, עו(ל)ל, עריץ. These words, taking their definitions from BDB, mean respectively *profane, godless; unjust, unrighteous one, especially of oppressive ruler;* and *awe-inspiring, terror-striking,* with the note that the plural is used as a substantive *in bad sense of formidable adversaries, personal (parallel with רעים and צר)* *and national (parallel with זר).* BDB notes that עריצים is especially frequent as a term for the Chaldeans.

It needs, I suggest, only the assumption that the author knew precisely what he was about in his use of language to deduce both from the presence of the parallels which are there and from the absence of others that are not, that the secondary meaning of רשע - the foreign heathen foe - is dominant in this section of the work.

We have discussed in some detail the passage in which Elihu speaks of the wicked as the alternative to the prophets. In 36:6, the word is almost certainly used in its ordinary sense, but in 36:17, which accuses Job of excessive concern for the due punishment of "the wicked", it is probably better to understand it as referring to his enemies (v.s.). The Lord's first use of the word in 38:15 (discussed on p. 455f below) is neutral, but in His challenge in Chapter 40, it is assuredly the Assyrians who are intended (see Chap. 5).

It might be argued that the associations established by the parallels in the second cycle between the wicked and the exercise of political or military domination merely serve to identify Job as a ruler whose wickedness, if he were wicked, would necessarily consist in being an oppressive and terror striking tyrant. There is even some support to be gained for this from 22:5-9, from Job's own description of his former status in 29:25, and in the passage quoted above from Elihu, 34:30-33. This argument does not however, take into account the unquestionable duplicity of the comforters' three speeches in the second cycle. When Job speaks of *secret thoughts with which you wrong me* (21:27), and refers to the dissertations on the fate of the wicked as *mischievous comfort* (16:2), *mockery,* and *empty consolations* (21:34), he is surely referring to the other dimension of the friends' words whereby they are pretending to comfort Job with the prediction of the discomfiture and destruction of his enemies.

Thus for the majority of its uses, the term (רשע(ים in the Book of Job signifies a dangerous foreign foe. Other clues in the book identify this foe as the Assyrians under Sennacherib.

Notes Chapter IV

1. Pritchard, p.295

2. The literature on this subject is full of complaint. G writes "MT is usually rendered *What wise men declare, without hiding it from their fathers (D&G)*." This is to say precisely, or nearly so, the translation which I would assert *no* commentator employs! D&G does indeed have this version, but with the minute but counteractive addition of a comma between "it" and "from". The translation comes with a note identifying the meaning of *from their fathers* as *having received it from their fathers"*. D also complains that "all the other" (not the Targum of the Antwerp Polyglott) "old translations, including Luther's have missed the right meaning", which he takes with a comma like D&G. However, not even C's compendious and reference-rich commentary records any specific translator or commentator who supports the literal version. Both AV and RV, old enough versions, have *Told from their fathers*, while the oldest of all, LXX and Vg concur that it is the fathers who do not conceal the story to be told.

3. אהלי־שחד. The word שחד properly refers to bribery, but presumably collaborators of some kind are implied here.

4. בית גזל ולא יבנהו cannot possibly refer to a physical home, for to *rob* such a dwelling and to *build* it, are in no sense opposites. On the other hand, where "House" represents nation, clan or even family, the head of such an aggregation has a duty to *build* it, and if instead he robs it (cf. Marcos in the Phillipines) this is indeed a suitable antithesis.

5. אהל משכנות רשעים. Not as habitually translated *the tent where the wicked dwell* or even more simply *the dwelling of the wicked*. As indicated by the singular אהל, משכנות must be the intensive plural, implying a superlatively imposing residence (Ps 132:5 *Until I find a place for the Lord, a dwelling [משכנות] for the Mighty One of Jacob)*. אהל in construct with another word for dwelling is a splendid tented entrance - Dan 11:45 אהלי אפדנו *The canopies of his palace*, and David, again in Ps 132 (3) אהל ביתי *the entrance to my house*.

The phrase is intentionally contrasted with Bildad's משכנות עול, 18:21, where משכנות is a true plural. The only other use of the intensive plural is for the dwelling of God. We are encountering here a sarcastic attribution of sarcasm! But unlike the limp *Where is the dwelling of the wicked?* this question, equivalent to "Where is all this magnificence which you attribute to the wicked?", is absolutely to the point. See LXX *Where is the covering of the tabernacles of the ungodly?*

V
The Identities of Behemoth & Leviathan

The second speech of the Lord, comprising almost the whole of Chapters 40 and 41, is the conclusion of the great debate which is framed between Prologue and Epilogue. In literature, in music, in dance, in every art form which operates in the dimension of time, conclusions serve particular functions, and share common characteristics. They are used to resolve the dissonances that precede them, to solve the mysteries that have been posed, to unite the separate threads of narrative or melody, to put to rest the agitation or passion. Their functions sum to leaving the "audience" with a sense of completion and satisfaction.

As currently understood, this second divine speech does none of those things. Instead, after a promising opening, it tails away into a wordy description of two beasts, *Behemoth* and *Leviathan*, whom the majority of scholars identify as hippopotamus and crocodile[1], celebrating their strength and invulnerability. So read, Bernard Shaw's description of the speech as a "noble irrelevance"[2] is perhaps the best that can be said of it. There are three possible explanations for this disappointment in the conclusion of a great work of art.

1. The author either did not understand, or deliberately chose to disregard, the canons which determine the nature of a conclusion.

2. The speech was not composed by him as the conclusion of the debate - i.e. it has been interpolated by another writer, or additional material which is the true conclusion has been lost.

3. The current understanding of the speech is fundamentally in error.

It is the third of these explanations which is adopted here, with the fault in understanding the speech dependent upon wrong identifications both of *Behemoth* and *Leviathan*, compounded by failure to appreciate the complex allegorical nature of the speech at any level.

1. Behemoth & Leviathan - Mythical or Real?

There has been a long-standing tug-of-war between scholars over the identities of the two "creatures" who dominate these chapters[3]. In effect, two almost equally mistaken theories have been contending. One holds that *Behemoth* and *Leviathan* are mythical monsters of pagan origin, the other that they are real creatures, with the favourites for the past 350 years being hippopotamus and crocodile. As there is without question a mythical monster one of whose names is *Leviathan* (= *Lothan*), and as it appears in the Book of Job both by that name (3:8), and by a number of *aliases* (*Rahab, Yam, Tannin, Tehom, Nahar*)[4], there is certainly a very strong case that can be made out that the mythical monster theory is at least half-right. On the other hand, there is no mythical creature called *Behemoth* nor anything like it in pagan mythology, and despite Pope's and Day's attempts to identify the creature with "the ferocious bullock of El" or "El's calf"[5], no convincing evidence of a terrestrial partner for *Leviathan* by any name. It is true that Talmudic speculation treats the two "beasts" as of the same *genre*, but there is no evidence that such treatment derives from anywhere but Job 40,41 itself.

If however *Leviathan* is a mythical monster, and *Behemoth* is not, does this necessarily mean that *Behemoth* is therefore a natural animal? that the second theory is also half-right? Not only are there other possibilities, but such a resolution would leave nothing in common between the two cyphers, making their juxtaposition in God's speech inexplicable. In all logic there has to be a connection between the two, and it is apparent that neither of the two contending theories has dug deeply enough to uncover it.

The mythological theory rests on the very simple evidence of *Leviathan*'s name and its use elsewhere in Biblical and pagan literature. The "real" theory rests principally upon the actual descriptions of the two "beasts" in Job 40, 41. Additionally, the name *Behemoth*, the plural of ordinary domestic animals, is suggestive of a natural creature. On the other hand its form, the feminine plural parsed as a masculine singular - hence an intensive plural - does not concur. The descriptions of the animals exhibit characteristics of terrestrial and aquatic beasts respectively. But *nihil ex nihilo*; it is scarcely conceivable that no resemblance to any animal would be found in a description of even the most imaginary basilisk. There are anomalies as well[7], and the proponents of hippo and crocodile have had to invoke hyperbole, ignorance, and poetic licence to sustain their identifications.

Before entering into the question of the true identities of the two "animals", and the justification for their partnership, if that is what it is, in these two chapters, I propose to examine the macroscopic structure of God's second speech as a whole, starting, as the speech does, with 40:7. There are five distinct sections. 40:7-14 is a majestic challenge to Job, accusing him of seeking to set aside God's judgement (without specifying what it is) and to condemn God in order to prove himself right. Thus it addresses four-square a central problem of the Book of Job and is a suitable *introduction* to a true *conclusion* to the great debate. But instead of progressing along any of the lines we might naively have anticipated, it shocks us with a challenge which effectively asks Job if he has the *power* to match God. *Have you an arm like God's? and can you thunder with a voice like His?* and then:

> *Deck yourself in majesty and grandeur,*
> *And in splendour and glory be clad!*
> *Scatter abroad the fury of your wrath!*
> *Expose every one that is proud and bring him low;*
> *Expose every one that is proud; abase them!*
> *Crush the wicked beneath them![8]*
> *Bury them in the dust together!*
> *Swathe their faces in Perdition!*

If Job can succeed in this, then God will *laud* Job, for his own right hand has brought him victory.

From this challenge alone, it is apparent that there are meanings - whole subjects of discourse - in the Book of Job which have not been taken into account in forming the conventional understanding of the book, for while we may think the book is about the unjust suffering of a solitary man of unblemished virtue who perhaps stands in some sense for all humanity, the Lord is epitomising it here with talk of abasing the proud and crushing the wicked!

The Lord's rhetorical questions,

> *Have you an arm like God's?*
> *And can you thunder with a voice like His?*

are the counterparts of Job's

> *Do You have eyes of flesh?*
> *Do You see as a man sees?*
> *Are Your days as the days of a man?*
> *Are even Your years as man's days?*

from 10:4,5, and show God entering into the spirit of "contest" by appropriating Job's demonstration of the incommensurability between them.

The next section, 40:15-24, continues without break from *brought you victory* with the introduction of the first of the "beasts", *Behemoth: Behold now:* Behemoth *whom I "made with" you* (v.i.) *eats grass like the cattle,* providing what is on the face of it one of the most extreme and incomprehensible *non sequiturs* in all literature. *Behemoth* is then described in the following nine verses. We shall be placing this description under the microscope later in this chapter, so let us move to the third section (40:25-32), which apparently also arises as an absolute *non sequitur.*

This is a second challenge to Job, this time asking him how he expects to be able to conquer *Leviathan,* who apparently materialises in the text out of thin air. This second challenge is redolent of undisguised, abrasive, but also humorous sarcasm, but it offers no sort of reason for God's apparent conviction of Job's conviction that he will indeed be able to conquer this new member of the *dramatis personae* of the chapter. One can only wonder if Job is intended to be as bewildered as the reader of his book by the interpretation which God appears to be placing on it. The Lord's sarcasm abruptly gives way at the end of the section to what reads like a desperate warning: *Lay but your hand on him! Remember the battle! Do no more!*

The fourth section, a mere four verses, 41:1-4, is in essence a bridging passage, largely occupied by a personal boast by the Lord. It is in fact a very important ingredient in the resolution of the problem of the book, but this is not apparent without a proper understanding of all of Chapter 40.

The final section, 41:5-26, which brings the speech to its strange and opaque conclusion, is the description of *Leviathan,* a fire-breathing monster, invulnerable to attack, who ראה (the same word we have translated *expose* in relation to God's challenge to Job to subdue the proud), he *exposes* or *he surveys all who are lofty,* and *is lord over all the sons of pride.* It is possible dimly to perceive that *Leviathan* is apparently able to do, is constitutionally endowed with the ability to do, what God challenged Job to do in 40:9-14. Dimly indeed, but this arouses the feeling that perhaps *Leviathan* himself is in some way "the mighty arm and the thunderous voice" of God.

Thus there are five apparently disconnected and independent sections to the Lord's second speech. In this chapter, I shall demon-

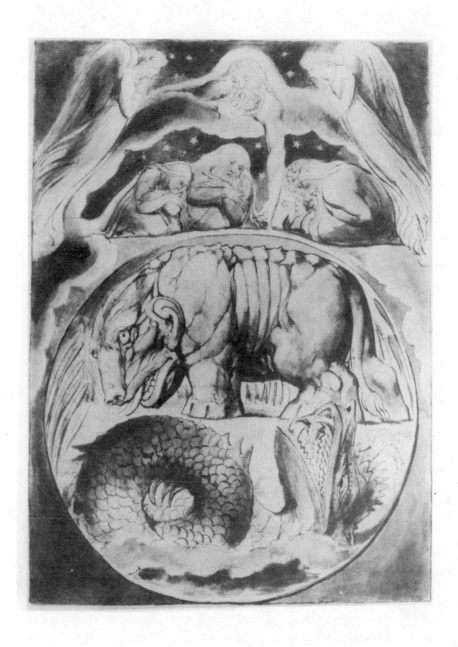

Plate 1: *Behemoth and Leviathan.*

William Blake, 27,5 x 19,7 cm, Fogg Art Museum, Harvard University

strate that in fact the whole speech is a single sequence, each section arising logically from its predecessor and all tending to a final resolution by the Lord of the central problem of the Book.

2. Chapter 40: the Description of Behemoth

The most intriguing question about *Behemoth*, from a literary point of view, is the mystery of the *non sequitur* of his introduction. As we shall see, there is a solution to this mystery, and we shall find that *Behemoth* is the Lord's own reply to the challenge to Job which immediately preceded his abrupt entry into the book.

The name *Behemoth* parsed as a masculine singular occurs twice in the Bible outside the Book of Job, and I suggest that both these citations are helpful in identifying the intention of the word here. The first of these is Psalm 73, v.22, in the phrase *I have been a* Behemoth *with Thee.*

It is well worth pausing a moment to examine this Psalm in some detail, for it is written from the same point of view as Job's speeches. It is the lament of a man who could not abide the injustice of the prosperity of the wicked and the hard lives of the virtuous.

> *I envied the wanton;*
> *I saw the wicked at ease.*
> *Death has no pangs for them;*
> *Their body is healthy.*
> *They have no part in the travail of men;*
> *They are not afflicted like the rest of mankind* etc.
> (NJPSV) [Cf. Job 21],

and then

> *It was for nothing that I kept my heart pure*
> *And washed my hands in innocence,*
> *Seeing that I have been constantly afflicted,*
> *That each morning brings new punishments.*
> [Cf. Job 7:13-19].

Finally, realising the error of his views particularly in the light of the terror-stricken end of the wicked, he makes the confession to God in v.22, *I have been a* Behemoth *with You*. As we shall note again in Chapter IX, Ps 73:17-19 and Job 27: 20-23 are virtually twin texts.

In this Psalm, the word *Behemoth* clearly implies "a beast", with the quintessential qualities of beasthood (as contrasted with human qualities) as is to be expected of an intensive plural. The phrase בהמות אשר־עשיתי עמך (Job 40:15) is so evocative of בהמות הייתי עמך (Ps 73:22) that it is hard to doubt that the evocation is intentional. The parallel in the Psalm is בער ולא אדע - *brutish and ignorant*.

It has been the practice of translators and commentators to understand the introductory phrase in Job 40:15 strictly literally as *Behemoth which I made with you*, and to deduce from this either that the creation of Job and *Behemoth* occurred simultaneously, or that they are alike fashioned of flesh and blood. Even accepting the literality of the phrase, neither of these interpretations is demanded. The real meaning, I suggest is "fashioned as your other half", hence "moulded with your clay". Another way of looking at it is to take לעשות עם as an idiomatic expression. In the same chapter as that in which Job challenged God with his *Do You have eyes of flesh?*, he also tells God חיים וחסד עשית עמדי - *Life and favour You bestowed on me* (10:12). Now God tells Job what else He bestowed on him - *Behemoth* the Beast in the two senses in which this designation is to be understood, that of Psalm 73 and that of Isaiah 30:6 (v.i.).

This reference in Psalm 73 alone sufficiently explains why verse 15 follows verse 14 without pause. It removes the *non sequitur* completely. If *Behemoth* is "the beast in man", and the Lord is telling Job that this beast is in him as in all men - *Behold: the beast which I bestowed on you...* [or *moulded with your clay*], then this in itself is an adequate answer to His own question *Have you an arm like God's? And can you thunder with a voice like His?* The posing of questions followed by the proffering of answers to them is so frequent in the Book of Job as to qualify as a stylistic identifying pattern[10]. The introduction of *Behemoth* as a part of Job's (humanity's) character is sufficient answer to the great challenge at the beginning of the speech. No man has the glory and majesty of God because all are tied to their own bestial natures.

This brings us to the second Biblical use of *Behemoth intensive* in Isaiah 30:6.

Amos referred to the people of the Northern kingdom as פרות בשן, *kine of Bashan* (4:1). In 30:6 Isaiah refers to the people of Judah as בהמות נגב, *the beast of the South*, doubtless intending a deliberate parallel[11]. We must bear in mind therefore, that a second meaning of *Behemoth* (or indeed the true meaning) in this context is the people of Judah, and that בהמות אשר־עשׂיתי עמך really means *This people with which I saddled you*. This equally would provide an adequate explanation for the abrupt entry of *Behemoth*. Job cannot perform a Godlike role because he is weighed down by the defects of his people. In the first case, *Behemoth* is part of Job; in the second, Job emerges as a part of *Behemoth*, but either explanation solves the staggering *non sequitur* posed by both of the conventional readings of the word. I suggest that these two uses define the semantic character of the word, as a symbol of man betraying his highest nature - in the Psalm as an individual, in Isaiah as a nation.

There is, however, an indispensible proviso to be fulfilled before either (or perhaps both) of these meanings for *Behemoth* can be accepted. *Behemoth* cannot be that immensely strong and invulnerable creature which emerges from the usual commentaries and translations. For him so to handicap Job that his own right hand cannot make him victorious, he must be a creature of weakness and vice. The picture of the unconquerable *Behemoth* is not without its dissidents among the scholars[12]. We shall, however, form our own opinions.

The first information given about *Behemoth* is that he eats grass like the cattle. The first level meaning of this statement should be clear. He chews the cud. Incidentally, the hippopotamus does not. In English, the suggestion that a person chews the cud is a derogatory comment, indicating indolence. In the Bible, the phrase is used only once of a human being, and that in very special circumstances. Nebuchadnezzar, when deprived of his senses, went out into the fields and ate grass like the cattle[13]. Assuming, as we are entitled to, that that story is allegorical rather than historical, it leaves the probability that *to eat grass like the cattle* is a metaphor for less than human behaviour.

Next we learn: 40:16. כחו במתניו ואונו בשׁררי בטנו

His strength is in his loins while usually, but illogically taken to mean that he is very strong, actually bears a remarkable resemblance to the colloquial vulgarism *His brains are in his balls*. If it does not mean that he concentrates, wastes, his strength on reproductive exercise, it is tough indeed to find any proper meaning for the expression. If *Behemoth* is about the beast in man nothing could be more appropriate. If about the people of Judah we must expect some metaphorical allusion to *whoring after false gods* or the like.

The second stich of the verse presents the problem that שריר is hapax to this passage. The facts that the root שרר in both Aramaic and NH means "to be firm, hard" (BDB) and that שרר appears in Song 7:3 in anatomical progression between *thighs* and *belly* strongly suggests that the word signifies *genitals*, forming a synonymous parallel with *loins*, and that therefore the second stich merely echoes the first. Most modern versions follow modern Hebrew with *muscles* - giving the again meaningless *his power is in the muscles of his belly*. Judaism and the religions of the surrounding countries were religions of animal sacrifice. The common facts of comparative anatomy were therefore well-known, especially to such highly educated men as the author of the Book of Job. He must therefore have been expected to be well aware - as most modern men are not - that the only animals which have or need muscles in their bellies are bipeds. The usual translation of the phrase is therefore not only meaningless, but also about as inappropriate as speaking of the wings of a worm!

In the light of the incorporation of *Behemoth* with Job or *vice versa*, 40:16 might be seen as God's ironic reply to 6:12 in which Job asks if his strength (כה) is the strength of stones and his flesh (בשרי cf. בשרירי) bronze.

The next verse, 40:17, leads into the terrain of "Humpty Dumpty" linguistics (see p.30), in which words are given meanings according to the whim of the commentator:

יחפץ זנבו כמו ארז: גידי פחדו ישרגו

Literally this seems to mean *He delights in his tail like a cedar-tree; his sinews of fear are intertwined*. Some slight objection may be raised against the first line on the grounds that יחפץ ought to be followed by ב, but there are several precedents[14]. Taking *his tail* as a stock euphemism, the line then becomes a third with the previous verse expressing excessive preoccupation with sex, with the cedar-tree (renowned for its erect stiffness) an appropriate if much exaggerated phallic equivalent. Biblical scholars have never been able to accept this meaning for חפץ, and even those who are prepared to concede the sexual connotations of *tail* accept[15] either Rashi's *hardens*, or *bend* or *depress* from an Arabic root. These latter two do not accord well with the characteristics of the cedar. I am at a loss to know why *delight* has not been universally

accepted, not only as the true meaning of the Hebrew חפץ, but as the
mot juste.

The word פחד in the second line has been subjected to much the
same denaturalisation process, and is usually translated *thighs* from an
Arabic word of some similarity[16], with Vg, T, Rashi, and a few recent
followers reading *testicles* from the Aramaic פחדין. The basic error
which has been made in interpreting this line is the belief that the
intertwining of sinews or tendons signifies great strength (see William
Blake's magnificent *Behemoth* with its decussating fibres[17] Plate 1, page
164a). In fact the intertwining of sinews, like the tangling of guide
ropes, is a metaphor for paralysis! *His sinews of fear are intertwined*
means, as we shall see reinforced later, that he fails to respond
appropriately to situations of danger. The Book of Job is written in
Hebrew.

40:18 states

עצמיו אפיקי נחשה   גרמיו כמטיל ברזל

I believe this verse to be more difficult than at first appears. The word
אפיק poses a real problem of decipherment, for this use does not correspond with anything similar in the Bible (See Chapter 3.IX, Lexicographical Anomalies). Usually taken as a *river-bed*, but perhaps more
properly a *water-hole*, the word is found exclusively in connection with
water except in two further citations in the Book of Job - 12:21 where
the plural perhaps means *the strong* and perhaps *the legions*, and 41:7
where linked in construct with *shields* it seems to refer to a mouthful
of teeth, and so might be translated *phalanxes* to match *legions*.

The least committal translation seems to be *His bones are strong
ones of brass; His skeleton like cast-iron*. This certainly appears to be a
tribute to brute strength, but before accepting this, the Biblical use of
brass and iron as metaphors applied to human beings should be
investigated. The description cannot be intended to be literal - this is
not the bionic animal!

Iron by itself is used as a metaphor for strength on several
occasions, נחוש once only, Job 6:12; נחושה, נחשת, נחושת, never. Whether
these terms, variously understood as *brass, bronze, copper* are freely
interchangeable or not is uncertain. The combination of iron and brass
used figuratively is found in Isa 48:4:

> *Because I know that thou art obstinate,*
> *And thy neck an iron sinew,*
> *And thy brow brass,*

in Jer 6:28,

> *They are all grievous revolters,*
> *Going about with slanders;*
> *They are brass and iron;*
> *They all of them deal corruptly,*

and in Ezek 22:18:

> *Son of man, the House of Israel is become dross*
> *unto Me; all of them are brass and tin and iron*
> *and lead in the midst of the furnace; they are*
> *the dross of silver.*

These passages suggest that these base metals are not intended always as complimentary designations, but it may be cogently argued that what is an insult when applied to a sinew may be a compliment when applied to a bone. Strength and rigidity are proper to the latter. Even so *bones* in Biblical poetry has the additional significance of representing the whole man, the personality, so that if *Behemoth* is indeed a symbolic rather than a real animal, the description is almost certainly unkind.

There is also an uncertainty about the word גרם. In Aramaic this is *bone* but it may not have exactly the same meaning in Hebrew. *Issachar is* חמר גרם (Gen 49:14) more plausibly means *a stubborn ass* than a *bony* or a *large-boned* one, neither of which carries much meaning. There is further the difficulty that, reading גרם as *bone* leaves us with the unacceptable literal reading *His bones are brass; his bones like cast-iron!* Thus a radical translation here could run: *His bones are pools of brazenness, his stubbornness like cast-iron*, with *brazenness* from Ezek 16:36 נחושתך.

The description of *Behemoth*'s bones and sinews is an intentional reference to 10:11b preceding the verse in which Job tells God that He conferred life and favour on him (v.s.) *And guyed me with bones and sinews* making the former allusion to חיים וחסד עשית עמדי unmistakable. The irony in this diatribe, in which God is taking Job to task for having taken for granted His past favour is striking.

Verse 19 brings the reader up with a shock with the wholly unexpected הוא ראשית דרכי־אל - *He is the first/chief/firstfruits of the ways of God*. This portentous identifying-tag has not, I suggest, caused commentators as much reflection as it ought. They have been altogether too ready to accept the hippopotamus as answering to this description[18], whereas in reality he has no qualifications for it whatever. There is good evidence of the meaning of the phrase *the ways of God* in the Book of Job (21:14; 23:11; 34:27), where it is used to refer to the moral and legal demands of God on man. If this meaning applies here also, then it is unquestionable that this descript-ion applies to the people of Israel and Judah and to no other entities.

> *Holy is Israel to the Lord,*
> *His first-fruit (ראשית) of the crop.*
> *All that devour him shall be held guilty.*
> *Evil shall come upon them, saith the Lord* (Jer 2:3).

Moreover, as the first nation to accept the Torah - the ways of God - Israel merits this description in the sense of *first* as well as *first-fruits*. On the other hand to attempt to apply the description to *the beast in man* would be grotesque. The text is moving the reader, therefore in the direction of conceiving of *Behemoth* as an allegorical figure for the people of Judah, embodying their defects, just as the word is employed in Isaiah 30.

The next line (40:19b) is particularly difficult: העשו יגש חרבו. העשו is a defective form of העשהו *He that made him* or of העשוי *he that was made*. The former seems more likely, particularly in view of the form of the following verb, which is jussive. Thus, *Let Him that made him bring His sword*. This is the version of D&G, who add in their note *viz. to assail him*. LXX certainly has the second version, but with *made to be played with by His angels*, no reliance can be placed on this.

There seems in the text so far no justification for any murder-ous enmity between God and His first creation, or the first-fruit of His ways. We shall see that the following verse allows for the possibility that his Maker should bring His sword to *protect* him, which accords well with the relationship implied in the first line of the verse, or to punish him which, in the Jewish understanding of "election" is also compatible with it. G[19] makes the suggestion that עשו does not derive here from the verb "to do or make" but from a putative "to cover", the origin of the name Esau, but the version which emerges *Only the one well-covered (with armour) may bring his sword near to attack him* has nothing to recommend it. Those versions which see *Behemoth* in some way as the sword-bearer of God and at the same time as the hippopotamus have crossed the borders of absurdity. There are many yet more *recherche* and imaginative versions, depending on quite extensive amendments to the Hebrew[20].

Verse 20: כי־בול הרים ישאו־לו: וכל־חית השדה ישחקו־שם

Note that the opening כי carries a promise of an explanation or a justification for the preceding verse - why his Maker should bring his sword. The intention of the verse depends crucially upon the meaning of the word בול. There has been a universal consensus that the word, both here and in Isa 44:19 is a corruption (or contraction) of יבול, "produce", as found for example in Job 20:28, giving *For the mountains yield him produce* (NJPSV) or, by somewhat wild extrapolation of meaning justified by appeal to the Akkadian (Dhorme) *The mountains yield him tribute*, almost but not quite making sense (H). The objections to this assumption of corruption have hardly ever been canvassed. The occurrence of the same corruption twice in two different books is improbable, while the use of the correct form in 20:28 discounts the idea that this is an accepted contraction. יבול as "produce" only once occurs in absolute form. Elsewhere it is always either *the earth and its produce*, or construct, as in Job 20:28 *the produce of his House*. Here it would be no less than a misuse of the word. The riverine habits of *Behemoth* are incompatible with his obtaining his food from the mountains. There is a deadly pointlessness about the information that the mountains supply him produce, and the entire sequence from 19a to 20b is reduced thereby to a string of disconnected statements.

בול is the name of the 8th Canaanite month (I Kings 6:38) and as such by the common pagan convention of naming months, is likely to be the name of a god. In both Phoenician and Palmyrene, בול means "god", and is found in combinations such as עבדבול, ירחבול, זבדבול (BDB). In Isa 44:19, where בול עץ is commonly treated as *the produce of a tree*, what is actually being conveyed in the phrase is "a god made from a tree".

The author was in considerable difficulty in finding a Hebrew word for a pagan god which had not already been appropriated in his text for the God of Israel. As I point out in commenting on 12:6c (p. 292) אלוה (also אל) cannot be God Almighty throughout the book and then mean a pagan god in one position to suit a particular understanding of the context. Here both the need for a hitherto unused name for a deity, and the author's fondness for archaisms, are satisfied together. The most likely explanation of 20a is that it means either *Gods of the hills sustain him* with a collective sense for בּוּל, or yet more simply *The hills supply him a god*. Again we should turn to the second chapter of Jeremiah which introduced the first-fruits image to find *Upon every high hill and under every leafy tree thou didst recline, playing the harlot (2:20)*. *Playing the harlot* of course means worshipping other gods so that here we begin to find the alternative significance of the sexual accusations of vv. 16 & 17. The next verse (21) of Chapter 40 brings us yet closer to the Jeremiah passage.

And all the wild beasts sport there implies that the hills are places of extreme danger. By worshipping false gods, the people of Judah have exposed themselves to attack by their neighbours - wild beasts in this allegorical jungle - perhaps the beasts of Chapter 39. Herein is the most probable reason why their Maker has to intervene with His sword. However the possibility still cannot be discounted that the sword will be used, or has been used, with hostile intent against Judah to punish him for his harlotries. At this point we should recall 5:23 where Eliphaz promised Job that if he turned to God, the *wild beasts* would be at peace with him. By turning to mountain-gods, Job's *Behemoth* has lost him this compact.

תחת־צאלים ישכב   בסתר קנה ובצה is v. 21.

צאלים is believed to be a thorny lotus. The second stich suggests the activity in the first is furtive - *Concealed in reed and fen*. The first is simply another way of saying Jeremiah 2:20 (v.s.). The nettle should be firmly grasped and the translation should be

He prostitutes himself to the trees.

The next two lines have a special significance and a special flavour which is seldom brought out in translation.

יסכהו צאלים צללו: יסבוהו ערבי־נהל

The *significance* is that of protection, or defence. *The lotus-trees screen him as his defence.* D&G[21] point out the syntactical form of the line as

above, but comment "But this is rather pointless". It is frequently to
be observed that scholars of Job, while knowing the exact sense of a
verse or a word, yet reject it in this fashion. צל of course could mean
no more than *shade* from the sun, but even this has the sense of
protection. *The willows of the brook surround him* also seems to convey
a sense of *guarding*. There is certainly no possibility of this being a
hostile encompassment. The inadequate and illusory nature of these
flimsy screens as protection gives the verse its *flavour*, that of irony.

3. *Nahar and Jordan*

Verse 23 introduces a new "character" and fresh controversy.

הן יעשק נהר לא יחפוז: יבטח כי־יגיח ירדן אל־פיהו

If Nahar *oppresses, he does not become alarmed; He is confident that*
Jordan *will gush forth at his command* seems to be the essential
meaning. הן may be read as *Behold*, but this does not materially alter
the sense. אל־פיהו[22] is often read rigidly literally as *to his mouth* but this
leads only to preposterous exaggerations such as Ibn Ezra's suggestion
that the verse refers to *Behemoth* hyperbolically drinking down an
entire river! Surprisingly, G favours this fantastic solution. The clue to
the meaning of the verse is surely the significance of the word *Nahar*.
    Nahar is the Hebrew word for a river, but a river cannot
oppress. One solution might be to change the word *oppress*, but the
only other sense of עשק is *extort* which if anything mates to a river
even more improbably. On the other hand either word fits very well
indeed with *he does not become alarmed*. Various amendments have
been suggested, most commonly to translate עשק *overflow*[23], but עשק is
a regular Biblical Hebrew word, similarly used in an absolute sense in
10:3, and therefore must not be changed.
    Before despairing either of the text or of lexical definitions of
Hebrew words, it is desirable to see what additional senses there are to
the word *Nahar* which may mate better with *oppress/extort*. In fact, as
for *Behemoth*, there are two, and I shall suggest once more that both
are to be understood.

Isaiah 8:6-8:

> *And the Lord spoke unto me yet again, saying:*
> *Forasmuch as this people hath refused*
> *The waters of Shiloah that go softly,*
> *And rejoices with Rezin and Remaliah's son;*
> *Now, therefore, behold, the Lord bringeth upon them*
> *The waters of The Nahar, the mighty and the many,*
> *Even the king of Assyria and all his glory;*
> *And he shall come up over all its channels*
> *And go over all its banks;*
> *And he shall sweep through Judah*
> *Overflowing as he passes through.*
> *He shall reach even to the neck;*
> *And the stretching out of his wings*
> *Shall fill the breadth of thy land, O Immanuel!*

In this passage which, like Job 40:23, is a figure based on a contrast between a Judean and a foreign river, *Nahar* is identified as the king of Assyria and his army in the guise of the River Euphrates (Jos 24:15).

The second identity of *Nahar* is from Ugaritic mythology, in which *Prince Yamm* and *Judge Nahar* are inseparable. *Yamm* of course is the Sea and equivalent mythologically to the sea-monster, that is to *Leviathan*[24]. Thus *Nahar* is one of the many alternative names for *Leviathan*. That this indeed is a major part of the significance of the word in this verse is dramatically confirmed two verses later in the otherwise incomprehensible *non sequitur* of v.25.

We have now become enmeshed in the extraordinary allegorical complexity of this speech, but at the same time light is appearing on the question of how the partnership between *Behemoth* and *Leviathan* can be justified when one is a mythical monster and the other a symbol of certain national vices, little more than a piece of name-calling. Some of the quasi-identities which underly these characters are becoming clear. *Behemoth* is both Job and Judah, while *Leviathan* is apparently to be identified with the Assyrian king, which places him on the same level of reality as *Behemoth* in his character as Judah. *Nahar* is juxtaposed against *Jordan*, the river of Israel, which in this verse must stand for the king of Judah and all his glory! The image of a national river *gushing forth*, implying an aggressive martial spirit reappears in Ezek 32:2 in connection with the Nile, and the same word is used of the Sea in rebellion in Job 38:8.

Verse 23 therefore means that Judah is not worried when Assyria makes demands upon her (*extorts*), for she is confident that she has the military means to defend herself successfully. The confrontation between the two nations is depicted as a confrontation between two rivers, Euphrates and Jordan, and two "beasts", *Nahar (Leviathan)* and *Behemoth*. The verse ties in with and explains v.17b *His sinews of fear are intertwined*. The historically accurate picture of the absurd overconfidence of Judah in the face of the threat from the overwhelmingly more powerful Assyria is thus presented in a novel allegorical form. There is an additional ironic element in the contrast between Jordan in this passage and Shiloah in the Isaiah passage to which it relates (v.s.). Shiloah stood for the *protective* function of the Lord, in which Judah chose not to trust[25]. Jordan alludes to the *aggressive* function which has not been offered.

Because there is considerable embarrassment in the reference to Jordan for all who maintain that the book's characters are all Edomites, that the action takes place well away from *Eretz Israel*, that as wisdom literature the Book of Job is timeless and placeless, and even sometimes that its author was not an Israelite, there has been a concerted attempt to show that *Jordan* in 40:23 does not really mean the Jordan river, but stands for any river at all. G for instance maintains that *Jordan* was used "unconsciously" by the author as a synonym for "river", and compares this demotion from proper to common noun to the very frequent use of *carmel* as a common noun. P supports this view, deriving comfort from the absence of the definite article, but then there are fewer than two dozen definite articles in the whole Book of Job. T-S seems the most emphatic proponent of the idea, referring *Jordan* back to its root - to descend - and deducing from this that it simply means "a river". D before him refers to this derivation, but rightly adds יִרְדֵּן *does not here signify a stream (rising in the mountain) in general; the name is not deprived of its geographical significance*. Robert Alter (pers. comm.) has adopted the view uncritically, writing "Yarden frequently serves as a poetic synonym for river". The Jordan is mentioned over two hundred times in the Bible, and there is not a single example where it is devoid of its geographical locus. This idea is refuted by the evidence and must be rejected.

The description of *Behemoth* is now also moving towards the specification of the "proud" and the "wicked" of the opening challenge of the speech. Clearly *Behemoth* himself as described in allegory, is exhibiting the sin of pride in at least two ways - by choosing his own gods (of the hills) in preference to the Lord, and by being confident in his own unaided capacity to confront *Nahar* (Assyria). This allows us to identify the wicked (who were to be "crushed beneath the proud" by Job) as the Assyrians, a usage of the term which conforms to its use throughout the Book of Job (see Chap. IV).

Corresponding to the identity of Job with *Behemoth*, we should see that the pride of *Behemoth* (= Judah) reflects a similar quality shown by Job which he lacks the capacity to overcome. This pride is manifest in his arraignment of God, and his inability to concede his own share in and responsibility for the sins of his people - seeking to *set aside My judgement* which we are at last able to explain as the chastisement of Israel and Judah under the Assyrians (cf. 34:26).

The final verse in the description of *Behemoth* is obscure.

בעיניו יקחנו: במוקשים ינקב־אף

The commonest view is that it is a rhetorical question, relating to the capture of *Behemoth* by his eyes or nose. It is, however, quite illegitimate to assume without evidence in the text both a change from affirmative to interrogative and the reversal of subject and object in this way. The dissenting view sees it as a statement that one or other party will or can capture another (T-S, *Behemoth* captures the river; H *El* captures *Behemoth*; Vg *Jordan* captures *Behemoth*; LXX, *Behemoth* is captured[26]) by the medium of these organs.

But. The word בעיניו is a self-contained idiom (II Sam 10:3, etc.) meaning, just as in English, "in his opinion", and the first line is an amplification of the confidence expressed in the preceding line. He is confident because, *in his opinion, he can seize him.* That is to say, *Behemoth* can seize *Nahar*, as T-S more or less read. D&G recognized this as the true sense of בעיניו, but, being unable to accomodate this phrase to their interpretation of the passage, in which they saw an overflowing river, converted the word to לעיניו[27]. This is the sort of exegesis we should by now be without.

If בעיניו has nothing to do with corporeal "eyes" then *mutatis mutandis* אף can hardly be a physical "nose". In a way this is fortunate, for מוקשים is plural, and can therefore hardly be a physically actual "trap" for the "piercing" of the nose of *Behemoth* - even were it the function of traps to pierce rather than to capture. Being plural, we must surely translate מוקשים as intellectual rather than physical traps -

"ruses", and אף as "anger". The solution, *By ruses, he will puncture wrath* is not ideal, but it is certainly far more plausible than the alternative image of a beast being caught by the eyes (with the ב inexplicable) and having his nose pierced in multiple traps.

There is another aspect to the habitual reading of this verse as relating to the capture of *Behemoth* by eyes and nose, which is that it steals the thunder and surprise from the ensuing v.26, which asks of the capture of *Leviathan* by nose and jaw, and that it conveys a misleading idea that the description of *Leviathan* is no more than a re-rendition of the *Behemoth* passage with increased force. There is in fact no reference of any kind to the capture of *Behemoth*, the subject is never raised.

4. Leviathan, the Second Challenge

The last two verses of the description of the people of Judah under the insulting title *Behemoth* then testify to their confident belief that they can cope with Assyria, referred to by the name *Nahar*. What follows is a brutally sarcastic demand by the Lord for the specifics of how this coping is to be done, what "ruses" will be employed, but the names of the protagonists mutate, and Judah now quits *Behemoth* to revert to "Job", and Assyria abandons *Nahar* to assume its *alter ego, Leviathan:*

> *Will you land* Leviathan *with a fish-hook*
> *Or lassoo his tongue with a line?*

is more or less the meaning of v. 25 (The apparent indicatives here are interrogatives as v. 26 demonstrates).

In the Lord's "eyes" the idea of a victory of Judah over Assyria is preposterous, not least, we must assume, because Assyria is acting as His own agent in flagellating Judah. He therefore sets out to inflate Assyria in this challenge and to diminish Judah, insinuating the vast incommensurability between them by means of a series of devastating jibes. Assyria is known to be the chaos-monster, *Leviathan*, while Judah is now reduced back to the solitary broken hero of the story, Job, waving a fishing-rod:

> 25   *Will you land* Leviathan *with a fish-hook*
>   *And lassoo his tongue with a line?*

26   *Will you slip a reed through his nose*
        Or pierce his jaws with a bramble?
27   *Will he make endless supplications to you*
        And will he address you tenderly?
28   *Will he enter a pact with you*
        That you take him as a servant for ever?
29   *Will you make sport with him like a bird*
        And will you cage him for your maidens?
30   *Will partnerships buy and sell him?*
        Will they divide him among the merchants?
31   *Can you fill his skin with harpoons*
        Or his head with fishing-spears?
32   *Lay but your hand on him!*
        Remember the battle! Do no more!

This is truly a remarkable passage.

On the face of it is a series of sneers at the long-suffering victim of the Lord's injustice, demanding how on earth, by sea or in heaven he expects to be able to capture, confine, slay, dispose of *Leviathan*. If we have been blind to the allegorical battledoring which has been going on around us, we can only allow this to flow over our heads, either confessing, if we are modest, that we understand nothing of it, or suggesting, if we are not, that the author has strayed from his point. One of the few commentators to grapple with the problems of the passage is H who recognizes the true nature of *Leviathan* as a mythic chaos-monster and sees the deliberately ludicrous in the serial pictures of Job's control of this creature. He does not, however, provide any satisfactory solution to the question of why God should challenge Job here with this impossible task, seeing the conquest of the sea-monster as a form of parallel to the conquest of the land-monster. But the only evidence he is able to find for the latter is the more than questionable 40:24.

It has first to be realised that this challenge to Job in vv.25-32 is the specification of the task referred to in the earlier challenge of vv. 9-14. The conquest of *Leviathan* is the *crushing of the wicked*, for both the wicked and the chaos-monster are code-names for the Assyrians. The multiple mockeries in 25-31 each (except first and last) refers in a distorted way to some feat of the gods in the containment, conquest and destruction of the chaos-monster. The last line of the passage demonstrates that this is no imaginative interpretive extravaganza, but the real intention of the author, for when He says *Remember the battle!* this can only refer to the primal battle of Creation, between Marduk and Tiamat, between God and Yam (38:8-11; 7:12 & Ps 74:13,14).

There is rather more to say about v.26 than each of the others, so I shall postpone discussion of this until the last. V. 27 refers to the submission of the monster and is a reflection of Job 9:13

> *The helpers of* Rahab *grovelled before Him*

and of the claim that when Marduk defeated Tiamat, her "helpers" wailed for mercy[28].

V. 28, the acceptance of the obligation of perpetual service and the signing of a pact to that effect matches the decree of the Lord when

> *He set a bound which they* (the waves) *should not pass over,*
> *That they might not return to cover the earth* (Ps 104:9)
> [See also Job 38:8-11).

V. 29 הֲתְשַׂחֶק־בּוֹ? *Will you make sport with him like a bird?* is a literal allusion to Ps 104:26 לִוְיָתָן זֶה־יָצַרְתָּ לְשַׂחֶק־בּוֹ.

> Leviathan *whom Thou hast made to sport with*[29].

Verse 30 *Will partnerships...divide him among the merchants?* is to be referred to Ps 89:11

> *Thou didst crush (or break in pieces)* Rahab *as one that is slain*

and Isa 51:9, addressed to the arm of the Lord

> *Art thou not it that hewed* Rahab *in pieces,*
> *That pierced the dragon?,*

or to the Creation Epic

> *He split her* (Tiamat) *like a shellfish into two parts:*
> *Half of her he set up and ceiled it as sky*[30].

Thus, except for the framing vv. 25 and 31 which pretend to practicality, but yet mock by suggesting an idiotic failure of appreciation of scale by Job, the Lord is taunting Job with twisted versions of His own accomplishments against *Leviathan/ Rahab/Yam/Nahar*, and asking him if, in his own world, he can match God's achievements in His.

This then is the context in which v. 26 also is spoken, and it seems hard to doubt that in the same way as vv. 27-30 invoke other Biblical references to the ways in which *Leviathan* in one guise or another was humbled, this verse is an invocation of Isaiah 37:29, addressed to the Assyrian king, Sennacherib:

> *Because of thy raging against Me*
> *And for that thine* hubris* *is come to Mine ears,*
> *Therefore will I put My hook in thy nose*
> *And My bridle in thy lips,*
> *And I will turn thee back by the way*
> *By which thou camest.*

* שַׁאֲנַנְךָ, translated *uproar* in JPS. The true meaning is something like self-satisfaction, smug sense of security. It is certainly a reference to the *hubristic* speeches delivered before Jerusalem (Isa 36:14-20, 37:10-13 = II Kings 18:19-25, 29-35, see pp. 206f.)

For more than 2000 years, scholars have been twisting and turning to avoid a literal reading of Job 40:26, finding all sorts of alternatives to the *reed* and *bramble* of the text[31], not recognizing that the absurdity of these implements set against the *hook* and *bridle* of the Isaiah passage matches to perfection the caricature of Job playing with *Leviathan* like a bird compared with the Lord sporting with him in the deep, or of *Leviathan* consenting to serve Job for ever, compared with the Sea obeying the Lord's decree to remain forever behind prescribed boundaries, and so on. The literal meanings of these words fit the context far better than any of the imaginative amendments which have corrupted the literature from *Qumran* to the 1980s. There is, however, another and important significance to the choice of implements in v.26, for they emphasise the identity of *Behemoth* and Job in this chapter.

In the description of *Behemoth*, his defences are said to be the (thorny) locust-trees and the willows of the brook, and his furtive activities take place *concealed in reed and fen*. These are the sources of the *reed* and *bramble* of v.26. Had Job been accused of writing purple-passaged letters to the Assyrians to keep out of trouble, *Will you thrust a pen through his nose and pierce his jaw with a quill?* would have been readily understood as a jibe at this activity. This is the spirit in which v.26 is written, and it reveals its full riches only on condition that we accept both the equivalence of *Behemoth* with Job and Judah and of *Leviathan* with Assyria and Sennacherib.

The significance of *Leviathan* in the Hebrew Bible has never been fully elucidated. The crucial passage is Isaiah 27:1 *In that day the Lord with His sore and great and strong sword will punish leviathan the slant serpent, and leviathan the tortuous serpent; and he will slay the dragon that is in the sea.* Kaiser's commentary on this passage[32] fairly discusses the multiple possibilities which it embodies.

Many commentators have seen in this passage three different monsters, which represent three kingdoms. Thus the dragon in the sea is taken to be Egypt (cf. 30:7; Ezek. 29:3; 32:2), the wriggling snake the Seleucid kingdom, and the fleeing snake the kingdom of the Parthians. Other interpretations sometimes understand the epithets allegorically: the fleeing snake means the rapidly flowing Tigris, the wriggling snake the meandering Euphrates. We cannot exclude the possibility that the apocalyptic writer had to use a secret language in order to refer to the kingdoms which he really meant, because the political situation left him no other choice, but it is by no means certain that his list contains three different references rather than three parallel symbols, and really refers to different beings and not to a single being described in different ways. After dwelling on all these considerations, one may ask whether the passages are concerned only with the monster which lives deep in the sea, or with world empire. Strictly speaking this is not the question that should be asked, because we are dealing with a mythical symbol which can be effective on different levels (simultaneously, DW). But the apocalyptic writer, it should be noted, does not go beyond his prophecy of Yahweh's victory in the final age over the monster in the deep, a victory which he gains in a duel with His powerful sword.

> *Behind 26:20f we saw Yahweh's judgement upon the nations; and it follows from the logic of mythical thinking that after the incarnations of evil, the evil itself must be conquered, and that God has to destroy the last enemy, if "that day" is really to bring the final turning point of history.*

There should, I suggest, be little doubt that in political terms the sea-monster, in various guises and under various names, is a very flexible symbol, to be attached to the enemy of the day. We even find such casual references as that identifying Egypt as *Rahab couchant* in Isa 30.

Reading *Leviathan* in the second speech of the Lord as a symbol for Assyria may appear to be a revolutionary innovation in the interpretation of the Book of Job in the light of the customary understanding of that speech, but it is in fact no more than the acceptance of conventional Biblical usage. The periodic hostility which Israel suffered from the pagan empires which surrounded her was always seen as a manifestation of divine displeasure, and *Leviathan* was employed as a metaphor for the transmission of power from God to them. The way in which the sea-monster relates to the inimical nation becomes yet clearer later in God's speech.

The last verse of Chapter 40, *Remember the battle!* can have one referent only. It refers to the titanic struggles between the Lord and the Sea *(Yam-Rahab-Leviathan-Nahar)*, (= *Marduk v. Tiamat)* in the remote past. Finally abandoning sarcasm, the Lord refers plainly to the scale difference between Job and his adversary, and warns him to abandon all pretence that he can tackle this primal force unaided. The first verse of Chapter 41 follows this without a break, and continues the allusion to this primaeval battle.

5. Chapter 41: the Lord's Affirmation

Ostensibly, the whole of Chapter 41 is devoted to the description of *Leviathan*. But the opening four verses have always created difficulty. They are best read as two tristichoi followed by a distich:

הן־תחלתו נכזב הגם אל־מראיו יטל?   לא־אכזר כי יעורנו?

I have found no reading of these lines which has fully respected either words or syntax of the Hebrew. D e.g. gives *Behold, every hope becometh disappointment; Is one not cast down even at the sight of him?* while 120 years later NJPSV has much the same. G makes the wholesale misconception of the text most explicit with *Indeed, he who attacks him loses all hope, since at the mere sight of him, he is laid low, No-one is foolhardy enough to stir him up.*

It is difficult to locate an authority who has not misread the passage in this way. Tur-Sinai stands out in the recognition that it is *Leviathan*'s hopes in the struggle with the Lord that were dashed, but his insight does not extend to a correct understanding of the remainder of the tristich[33]. The commentators who have followed him have not accepted his example.

The circumlocutory rendering of תחלתו as *the hope of capturing him,* or the transference of the possessive suffix to his "assailant" (when the only assailant in prospect now is Job who has been addressed as "you" throughout the preceding eight verses) are obviously wrong, the one defying the language and the other the logic of the text.

Accepting as the indisputable meaning of the Hebrew Tur-Sinai's version of the first line, *Behold, his hope was in vain* we now require simple and literal versions of the second and third. There is a Hebrew saying: אין גם אלא רבוי - *There is no גם without amplification*[34]. One might add that there is no ? without interrogation. The conventional versions discount the הגם? which conditions the second line. It means "Is it also?" and the remaining two words "at the sight of him" and "he is cast down". These fit together beautifully for the entity whose hopes were dashed in a conflict with God *Must he also be cast down at the sight of him?*

This *him* is a mystery only until we have accepted who he is. It is of course obvious that there are two characters involved, one of whom is *Leviathan*. Once we have determined that the <u>he</u> is *Leviathan*, there are no alternatives for <u>him</u> but *Behemoth*, or Job himself, or the people of Judah, all of whom are the same. The sense is immaculate - just because he was worsted in the encounter with Me (the battle), do not for a moment imagine that he will be too cowed to put up a fight against you, a fight you have no hope of winning:

לא־אכזר כי יעורנו - *Not fierce when he arouses him*

and here, as the logic of language demands, the he and the him are reversed, and we find to our amazement that we are referred all the way back to 3:8, the עתידים ערר לויתן, those (Judeans) who were prepared to *arouse Leviathan* - revealed as a very dangerous game indeed!

> *Behold! His* (Leviathan's) *hopes were dashed.*
> *Must he also be cowed at the sight of him (*Behemoth*),*
> *Not fierce when he arouses him?*

This accurately renders every part of the verse and effectively amplifies the Lord's warning in the preceding verse 40:32. It also overcomes the otherwise insurmountable fact that the third line lacks a verb.

The subtle play by which Job and *Behemoth* are treated by God as both distinct and the same is epitomised by this use of "him". We find the Lord using the same device in reference to Himself when He speaks of the ostrich in 39:17, and in His challenge to Job in 40:9, and the description of *Behemoth* in 40:19. In all these places He speaks of God in the third person, as though repudiating His own Unity.

The three lines above are treated as a tristich verse. Their own internal logic demands this, but the next three lines even more strongly declare that they hold together in a single theme:

ומי הוא לפני יתיצב: מי הקדימני ואשלם   תחת כל־השמים לי־הוא

Here the Lord draws Himself up to His full height as it were to demand:

> *But who is there who can stand up to Me?*
> *Who ever confronted Me and I submitted?*
> *Wheresoever under the heavens, he is Mine!*

Perhaps this last line is intended to be read *Whatsoever is under the heavens is Mine!* In either case, it is a resounding affirmation of the Lord's complete control over *Leviathan* and so also over good and evil. This is, from the point of view of the allegorical reading of the Book of Job, a vitally important statement. It has to be understood as a repudiation of Job's repeated complaints of abandonment by the Lord, of the earth being handed over to the wicked, and an affirmation of the familiar "scourge of God" theory of Jewish history in general and the Assyrian conquest in particular. Whatever *Leviathan* has been able to do has been because the Lord willed it. Job, who is not consistent, has asserted this too, in Chapter 12 in the passage beginning, *With Him are strength and sagacity: His, misleader and misled!* (12:16).

The distich finale of this bridging passage has also proven difficult:

לא־אחריש בדיו   ודבר גבורות וחין ערכו

It is customary to understand לא־אחריש as *I shall not be silent*, but a better sense is achieved by *I am not deaf to*. The line is a quotation of 11:3 בדיך מתים יחרישו - *Men have ignored your ranting*. Men may have ignored Job's ranting, it says, but I, the Lord, am not going to ignore *Leviathan*'s ranting. G sees in this verse a description of the physical qualities of *Leviathan*[35], but with three words for speech, דבר, בד and ערך, and the repeatedly pointed reference to Isaiah 36 and 37, this is flouting the evidence.

The word חין is unknown, but appears to be related to חן, "grace". Thus the sense of the verse seems to be:

> *I am not deaf to his vainglory,*
> *Nor his doughty speech, and the grace of his oratory*

and is to be read as a second direct invocation of the Lord's threat to Sennacherib as recorded in Isa 37 (see comment on 40:26 above).

> *But I know thy sitting down, and thy going out,*
> > *and thy coming in,*
> *And thy raging against Me.*
> *Because of thy raging against Me*
> *And for that thine* hubris *is come into Mine ears ...*

and to be understood as a specific reassurance to Job that the day of the Assyrian is over, and with it, his trials. For His speech to Sennacherib ends with this assurance to Judah:

Thus saith the Lord concerning the king of Assyria:

Plate 2: *Leviathan*

Ovadia Maybar, 1982, Tel Aviv

> He shall not come unto this city, nor shoot an arrow there, neither shall he come before it with a shield, nor cast a mound against it. By the same way that he came, by the same shall he return, and he shall not come against this city, saith the Lord.

6. The Description of Leviathan

Verses 5 and line 6a form another tristich, although not so punctuated in the MT. They are usually taken as forming a minor discontinuity. The three lines are three questions, each containing the interrogative מי? It is important to distinguish this from מי־הוא? which is the appropriate form of a rhetorical question emphasising the difficulty or impossibility of some action as, e.g. 41:2 above. Nonetheless, they are always understood as a trio of bombastic questions - *Who can uncover the face of his garment! Who can breach his double curb! Who can open the doors of his face!*

      This reading seems almost impossible to fit into the context - how suddenly does *Leviathan* come to be garbed? and what is this double curb (*bridle* in some versions)? It is all very well to change רסנו to סרינו, "coat of mail" as LXX, P and G do[36], but this merely compounds the improbability of "garment" transforming this dragon into an overdressed St. George!

      As I think with all surprises in the Book of Job, there is a valid explanation for these unexpected appurtenances of the undoubtedly naked and boistrously unconfined sea-chaos-monster. The garment, the double curb and the doors of his face are previously specified in the boast of the containment of Yam in 38:8-11:

> *Who enclosed* Yam *behind <u>doors</u>*
> *When he burst forth and departed the womb?*
> *When I ordained the vapour as his <u>garment</u>*
> *And the swagging cloud his swaddling-band?*
> *And set my surf to surround him*
> *And put <u>bar and doors</u>?*
> *And said "Hither shall you come and no farther,*
> *And here shall it stay in the pride of your waves!"*

Just as the Lord asks Job in this passage *Who placed these restraints on the Sea?*, with the directed answer *I alone did*, so now he asks who removed them, who set *Yam/Leviathan* free to animate the Assyrian assault on Judah, with the same directed answer, *I, the Lord*. In the catechism of which the above *Yam* passage is a part, the word מִי?, Who? occurs three times, as it does in 41:5,6a. Further the tense of those questions is the perfect, while for such pseudo-questions as *Who can uncover...!* the imperfect is mandatory (*vide* 41:2, etc.[37]). In 41:5,6a the first and third questions employ the perfect tense while the middle one is imperfect. A further technical point of some importance is the use of the Pi'el of פתח implying unfastening rather than forcing open. Only He Who locked can open without force.

Thus the sense of this triplet is as follows:

> *Who unwrapped the face of his garment?*
> *Who penetrated his double curb?*
> *Who unlocked the doors of his face?*

which is to say, "Who liberated this brute?" and the answer to all these questions is again *I, the Lord*.

It should not be overlooked, if we search for elements of contest in the Lord's speeches, that Job before him, in 30:18, spoke of לבוש, *a garment*, in a sense which could only be deciphered by reference to the preceding chapter (see p. 127ff).

From this point onward, the Lord celebrates the vast destructive power and the invincibility of *Leviathan*, and so doing achieves the extraordinary poetic feat of separating *Leviathan* entirely from Assyria, so that he reverts to being that embodied primal force which is the manifestation of the power of God Himself. This is the last ambiguity in the poem. The separation may be taken as symbolising the withdrawal of *mission* from Assyria.

There is little in the remainder of Chapter 41 which has not been soundly translated innumerable times. LXX mistakenly referred v.7 to the creature's scales, and most have followed suit. It is in fact a continuation of the description of the monster's mouthful of teeth, as v.8, which asserts that no air can come between them, makes clear. The idea that no air should be able to penetrate between the scales of his body is literally unthinkable, for it involves the wrong element - it is no water which might penetrate between his scales. The term *shields* for teeth in v.7 derives from the similarity in shape. The description of *Leviathan*'s scales is found in v.15. A reasonable translation of the teeth passage is:

> *His circle of fangs is Terror;*
> *Pride, those phalanxes of shields,*
> *Closed with a tight seal.*
> *One is so close to another*
> *Than no air can come between them.*
> *Each clings fast to its brother;*
> *They are fused together, inseparables.*

The description continues, borrowing from Ps 18 (= II Sam 22) the fire and smoke pouring from the mouth and nostrils of the Lord Himself in the guise of a destructive engine. It was into these incandescent organs that Job was asked if he proposed to insert a reed and bramble!

> *When he rears up, the mightiest are in terror*
> *The wild waves in turmoil!* 41:17

with its vivid picture of the serpent rearing out of the sea in a maelstrom of countercurrent billows (Plate 2, see page 186a), is a reminder of the earlier origins of this myth. With a little imagination it is possible to see in the monster cutting a swathe through the deep, sowing fire and terror, and leaving behind a hoary wake of destruction, the rampaging of a vast invading army.

There is a significant reminder of the confrontation between Assyria and Judah (*Behemoth*) in v.19 which declares

> *He treats iron as straw and brass (נחושה) as rotted wood.*

This is an unmistakable allusion to 40:18, where *Behemoth*'s "bones" are described as composed of these two substances, specified, as demanded by Biblical convention, in the reverse order. The image of Job *filling his skin with harpoons and his head with fishing-spears* now meets the boast that swords, spears, darts and javelins, arrows, slingstones, clubs and lances, are nothing to him (vv. 18,20,21).

At the end comes the expected reference back to the challenge to expose the proud and bury the wicked beneath them in this summary of God's agent of evil, *Leviathan*.

> *None upon earth is his peer,*
> *His, that was made fearless.*
> *All that are lofty he surveys*
> *He is lord over all the sons of Pride.*

But even in this very last word, the ambiguity of allegory is reasserted. The expression is מלך על־כל־בני־שחץ[38]. שחץ is a strange and ambiguous word, unknown in Hebrew outside the Book of Job, and in cognate languages meaning variously *pride* and *lion*.

What is not ambiguous about *Behemoth* and *Leviathan* is the fact that rather than parallel illustrations of any principle or parable, they are depicted in these two chapters as mortal foes, with *Leviathan* the inevitable victor in any contest between them until the Lord enters the lists with His sword (40:19), as champion of *Behemoth*.

The second speech of the Lord emerges from this analysis as a speech couched in allegorical cyphers already well-established principally through the writings of (the first) Isaiah. It provides for Job a reassuring resolution, not of the problems raised by a literal reading of the Prologue loss of possessions, family and health - but of the problems which they concealed behind their own facade of allegory - the Assyrian victories over Israel and Judah in the 8th Century B.C.E. (See Chaps. I & II). The ambiguity with which the author was able to conceal his true subject for the greater part of the book is not sustained in God's speeches, the first of which does indeed address the personal questions of the justice or injustice of the Universe, and man's unjustified expectations of it, to the almost complete exclusion of political material; but the second is devoted wholly to the political scenario.

Its theme is the orthodox prophetic concept of Israel and Judah punished for their faithlessness towards their God, and for their refusal to rely patiently upon Him to extricate them from a threatening political confrontation with Assyria. Assyria is depicted exactly as in the Book of Isaiah as the agent of God's wrath who becomes *hubristic* and will be brought to heel. *Leviathan*, who functions first as the animating spirit of Assyria, and then as the watchman who will bring him under control, is essentially an Angel of the Lord, a detached part of His Unity. *Behemoth* is the errant people of Judah, no match for Assyria, *Leviathan* or God. Job remains enigmatic, the innocent who must suffer for the guilty; valiant spokesman for his people; the remnant that kept faith and was rewarded in the restoration of sovereignty, independence and empire when the dust of the pagan tyrants was finally laid to rest.

Notes Chapter V

1. Samuel Bochart, *Hierozoicon, 1663,* Book 5, Ch. 15.

2. G.B. Shaw, Preface to *Parents and Children (Misalliance), 1910.*

3. P, p.320ff, provides an excellent summary of the case for mythology, while G, p.569ff, and A, p.288ff, present the opposite point of view.

4. 7:12; 9:13; 26:12; 28:14; 38:8-11; 40:23.

5. John Day, *God's conflict with the dragon and the sea,* Cambridge U. Press, Cambridge, *1985,* p.80ff.

6. Louis Ginzberg, *The Legends of the Jews,* JPS, Philadelphia, *1938.* See Index for numerous references.

7. Eating grass like the cattle, having a tail in any way comparable to a cedar, having any contact with the mountains, and relating to the Jordan River, are all incompatibilities between *Behemoth* and the hippopotamus. Underside like sharpest potsherds, swimming in sea rather than river, and breathing fire and smoke, are incompatibilities between *Leviathan* and the crocodile.

8. The more common reading of v.12b (חתם) is *Crush the wicked in their place,* whatever this means.

9. נם־אני אודך The sentence is from Ps 71:22, addressed to God, and significantly following *Who is like unto thee?* in v.19. The ם in Job 40:14 seems to serve little purpose other than to draw attention to this reference.

10. Other examples are: 4:6; 6:5,6; 6:11-13; 7:1; 7:12; 8:3; 8:11; 9:2; 9:14; 9:29; 11:2; 11:10; 13:7-9; 15:2,3; 15:8-13; 18:4; 19:22; 21:17; 21:22; 22:2-4; 22:5; 24:1; 25:4; 26:4,5; 27:8-10; 28:12; 28:20; 31:2; 35:6-7.

11. The identity of *Behemoth of the Negev* with the people of Judah is not accepted by all authorities. G, for instance, asserts that this *Behemoth* is also the hippopotamus (p.476), but this is quite out of the question. The *Burden of the Beast of the Negev,* Isa 30:6-18, is clearly directed against the people of Judah for sending to Egypt for help rather than relying on God - *For it is a rebellious people, Lying children, Children that refuse to hear the teaching of the Lord* (v.9); and *For thus saith the Lord God, the Holy One of Israel: In sitting still and in rest shall ye be saved, In quietness and confidence shall be your strength; But ye would not* (v.15). The surrounding texts also berate the people of Judah for seeking their salvation from Egypt, and it requires considerable ingenuity in contorting the text to avoid the identification of this *Beast of the South* with the *rebellious people* who are berated in the ensuing passage.

12. P (p.323) draws attention to Albertus Magnus's treatment of *Behemoth* as *the natural animal representing sensual impurity* - essentially *the beast in man* as in Ps 73. Other writers (e.g. H) have not been able to overlook the sexual inuendo in the first part of the description of the beast.

13. Dan 4:29.

14. Isa 58:2; Ecc 8:3; Ps 68:31.

15. *Hardens*, from Arabic *hafita; bend or depress*, Arabic *hafasa*.

16. *Thighs* from Qere פחדיו, and thence, Arabic *afhadh*.

17. William Blake *The Book of Job, 1825*, Plate 15.

18. The idea that the hippopotamus merits the description *First of God's ways* is impossibly strained, for there is no other mention of the beast in the Bible. As the largest of the land animals the elephant might qualify, but this identification *pace* Aquinus, will not stand up, for no description which omits trunk and tusks could possibly refer to the elephant.

19. G, p.477

20. *Who made him, that he might fetch His sword*, T-S; *He that made him hath given him a scythe*, Samuel Cox (*A Commentary on the Book of Job*, C.Kegan Paul, London, 1880); *His Creator has given him his own sword*, R; *Made to be tyrant over his peers*, NEB.

21. D&G, phil. notes, p.330.

22. Idiomatically a variant of על־פי found elsewhere exclusively in Joshua. The literal use is more common, usually in the phrase *hand to mouth* also understood literally.

23. *Overflow* is derived from ישפע, according to the suggestion of G. Beer.

24. John Day (*op.cit.*) insists that *Leviathan* and *Yam* are mythologically distinct creatures, of Canaanite origin. While this may have been correct initially, a conflation of them has surely taken place at some time. In the Ugaritic poem about *Baal and Anath* (Pritchard), we find (p.137) *Crushed I not El's beloved* Yamm? *Did I not, pray, muzzle the Dragon? I did crush the crooked serpent*, Shalyat *the seven-headed*, which strongly argues the identity of *Yam* and *Leviathan*. Likewise, the identity of *Yam* and *Nahar* is explicit in the same source, pp.129ff.

25. Otto Kaiser, *Isaiah 1-12, A Commentary*, SCM Press, London, *1972*, p.13.

26. *He took it by the eyes, pierced through its nose with snares*, T-S;
El takes him by the mouth with rings, He pierces his nose with hooks, H;
Yet one shall take him in his sight; One shall catch him with a cord and pierce his nose, LXX;
Like a lure it would charm his eyes, though it should pierce his nostrils with sharp stakes, Mgr. Ronald Knox, (*The Old Testament Newly Translated from the Latin Vulgate*, Burns Oates & Washbourne Ltd. London, *1949*).

27. D&G, phil. notes, p.331.

28. Pritchard, p.67, *The Creation Epic*, Tablet IV, 107-120.

29. Meir Weiss (*The Bible from Within*, Magnes Press, Jerusalem, *1984*, p.78-93) argues that *Leviathan* in Psalm 104 represents those sea-creatures which accompany and disport around ships – tunney fish, dolphin, pilot fish. Thereby he rejects the previous associations of the name *Leviathan*, and any significance for the use of the otherwise unknown expression שחק־בו twice in relation to creatures of the same name.

30. Pritchard, pp. 137-140.

31. See pp. 5,6.

32. Otto Kaiser, *Isaiah 13-39, A Commentary*, SCM Press Ltd. London, *1974*, pp. 221-223.

33. T-S, p.566, relates the second line also to the battle *When he attacked his master, he was thrown down*, but to do this he outrageously reads הגם as Arabic, "to attack" and מראיו as Aramaic, "lord, master"!

34. Reuben Alcalay *The Complete Hebrew-English Dictionary*, Massada Publish. Co. Ramat-Gan/Jerusalem, *1975*, p.361.

35. G, p.483f.

36. LXX: *Who can enter within the fold of his breast-plate?* has been assumed to have been based on this metathesis. P and G have adapted it to "chain-mail".

37. All similar rhetorical questions in the book employ the imperfect (see 11:10, 13:9, 23:13, 26:14, 38:37). See for contrast מִי questions with the perfect, 36:23, 39:5, etc.

38. בְּנֵי־שָׁחַץ is unique to the Book of Job, and appears also in the misplaced verse (see pp. 493f) 28:8, where it is parallel to שַׁחַל, *lion*. There it probably means *proud beasts*, but *mighty conquerors* is a possible alternative, for the accompanying verb הִדְרִיכוּהוּ - *trodden it down* is most appropriate to this.

The Identity of Job's Comforters

We are at the beginning of Chapter 18. Job's three comforters, Eliphaz the Temanite, Bildad the Shuhite and Zophar the Naamathite are growing increasingly frustrated by their inability to dent Job's confidence in his own vaunted integrity, and feeling increasingly battered by the cumulative effect of the brickbats he keeps throwing at them. It is Bildad's turn, and this is what he says:

עד־אנה תשׂימון קנצי למלין: תבינו ואחר נדבר
מדוע נחשבנו כבהמה: נטמינו בעיניכם?

There is no doubt whatever that Bildad is speaking in the plural - on behalf of the three friends one must suppose - to Job also in the plural. There are three natural plurals "we", and three most unnatural plurals "you" (תבינו, תשׂימו, עיניכם). If one accepts the representative role of Job and the allegorical nature of the Book of Job, these plurals can be accomodated relatively easily. But if one is wedded to the literal theory of the book, they are remarkably indigestible.

D, who overlooked almost nothing in his commentary, accepts that Bildad is treating Job here as "a type of a whole class", but considers this to be sarcastic - Job as representing the whole universe of virtuous men. As we shall see when we decipher the verses, this does not fit the situation. Nor does P's conjecture that Bildad is treating Job as a representative of the class of sinners! G mentions that there are "some grounds for assuming that the pl. was used at times in direct address even to one person", but he obviously does not believe his own explanation. The LXX treats these plurals as singular, and D&G think that this must have been the original, but it is impossible to imagine how such pluralisation could have crept into the text by accident. However, C, who lists no fewer than eleven different suggested solutions, comes to the same conclusion, and cites the QT as well as the LXX. The Vg dissents from the LXX. H suggests that Bildad is using "a traditional exordium style", but cites no precedent. Perhaps wisely, many commentators ignore the whole matter, or refer to it without offering an explanation; so R, A, NEB, Hartley.

The text I have quoted contains two unique words, קנצי and נטמינו. The first has caused no end of trouble, but there should be no doubt of the meaning of the second, so let us dispose of that first. The

verse asks *Why are we assessed as beasts,* נטמינו *in your eyes?* There have
been three possibilities considered; one that it is a spelling variant of
נטמאנו - *we are unclean;* the second, that it means *we are considered
stupid* from טמם (G); the third that it is a corrupt form of נדמינו (LXX),
we are compared. It is the following line which decisively demonstrates
that the first of these is correct. It characterises Job scornfully in these
words - *You who tears himself in his anger!* As a beast which is *torn*,
טרף, is itself unclean, it is to be understood that Bildad is throwing
back an accusation of unleanness on Job - `commending the ingre-
dients of his poisoned chalice to his own lips!' The origin of the idea
that Job is "torn" is 16:9, where he complained that God's anger had
torn him. Bildad is also contradicting this in this brilliantly vicious
line.

As long ago as LXX and V, קנצי has been treated as a variant
or corruption of קץ, *end.* But in order to fit the sentence to this, it is
necessary to add the word לא. - *Until when will you not make an end
of words?* Job's riposte in 19:2 should have put an end to this speculation. More recently, *For how long will you lay snares for words,* a most
unappealing and improbable version, has attracted scholars. Already in
1864, D attributed this version to "Castell., Schultens, J.D. Mich.", and
"most modern expositors", but himself preferred to vary it with *hunt
for words.* Castell is 17th Century, and J.D. Michaelis and Schultens,
18th.

The trouble, I suggest, has been an unwavering concentration
on the expression תשימון קנצי, when the phrase is really תשימון למלין -
meaning either *relegate to (mere) words* or *make into bywords,* taking the
pejorative meaning of מלין from Job 30:9, ועתה נגינתם הייתי ואהי להם למלה!
- *And now I am become their burlesque, and I am a byword to them!*

For how long will you turn the קנצי *into bywords?* merely
requires that we find an excuse for letting קנצי represent the comforters, and we shall have at last a solution to the line which meets the
needs of the occasion. The consonantal form of the word קנצי is that
of tribal groups, as the Edomite is אדמי and the Egyptian מצרי. These
words may also convey a collective meaning as do כנעני חתי פרזי יבוסי
עמני מאבי מצרי אמרי in Ezra 9:1, and as does קנזי *et al* in Gen 15:19. This
קנזי drops like a penny into the slot we have been holding open for it.
The interchange of ז and צ is unremarkable in Biblical Hebrew, see for
example such dual forms as עלץ/עלז and צעק/זעק, and also Job 6:17, and
therefore I propose to treat קנצי as a spelling variant of קנזי, the
Kenizzite(s). The vocalization is hopelessly wrong for this, קנזי having

two *dageshim* and two *hireq*s while קנצי is provided with a *seri* and a *hireq* and no *dagesh*.

How does Kenizzite come to represent Temanite, Shuhite and/or Naamathite? The important Kenizzite in the Bible was Jephunneh, the father of the Caleb (Num 32:12, Jos 14:6 & 14, I Chron 4:15). In this last spot is written: *And the sons of Caleb the son of Jephunneh: Iru, Elah, and Naam.* For some reason which has always escaped me, commentators seem to be unanimous in deciding that Zophar the Naamathite did not come from the city of Naamah established in the Judean lowlands in the region of Lachish (Jos 15:41). But this is the only known town which bears the name. Putting two and two together and remembering the decision (See Chap. II) to regard Job as the prototypical Jew, it seems most likely that Naamah was connected with the Kenizzites of Hebron, and that Zophar started his treck to visit Job from the lowland of Judea.

When we examine the pedigree of Kenaz, from whom these Kenizzites sprang, we find to our astonishment that his father was one Eliphaz first born of Esau, and his brother, one Teman, first born to Eliphaz (Gen 36:10,11), which may or may not allow us to consider Eliphaz the Temanite to have been at least well-connected with the Kenizzites. Only one further coincidence is required, and this is to be found in I Chron 4:11, where Chelub, whose name is a variant of Caleb, is described as the brother of Shuhah, from whom perhaps the designation of Bildad as Shuhite derives.

We may now understand what is going on in these two verses. There is a racial conflict coming to the surface. The Kenizzites, better known as the Calebites, remained a recognizable non-Judean minority within the territory of Judah many centuries after the conquest of Canaan (*vide* I Sam 30:14). As we know from the incident involving the Rechabites described in the Book of Jeremiah, the situation of such minority groups was precarious; they had to watch their steps carefully, and undoubtedly they were subject both to discrimination, and contempt, particularly for their failure to observe the ritual of the host tribe, when they would be considered unclean.

This interpretation immediately brings the strange second line, always read as a surly imperative *Consider, and then we shall speak!*, into clear focus. It is the specification of the complaint against Job, based perhaps on his furious insult in 13:5 *If only you would hold your tongues, and that would stand to you for wisdom!* תבינו ואחר נדבר simply states *You make up your minds, and afterwards we speak* which is to say you do not take our opinions into account in forming yours.

Here finally is some explanation for the apparent brutality of the "comfort" offered by the three friends of Job. Secretly, we may surmise, they are delighted at the downfall of a leader, perhaps *the* leader, of the smug and superior majority, and will not forgo one jot of the opportunity offered to quote back at Job the Jew, the texts with which his people have been lecturing the Kenizzites for centuries. *Remember I pray, who, being innocent, perished? And when were the upright cut off?* sounds far more pointed on Eliphaz's lips if we realise that he is quoting back at Job what Job and his people have been dinning into him for ages. This surely is the reason, too, why the Biblical quotations which lard the speeches of the friends are all slightly garbled, why they are forever appealing to the wisdom of preceding generations. Here we see the true point of Eliphaz's first words

> *Behold you have instructed many,*
> *And exhorted the weaklings;*
> *Your words have sustained the fallen*
> *And strengthened the weak-kneed.*
> *But now it is your turn, and you despair;*
> *It touches you, and you take fright.*

Most important of all, here is the explanation of these three singular plurals. Job is being addressed as the representative neither of the class of virtuous men nor of the class of sinners, but as the representative of the Jews. "For how long will you Jews treat us Kenizzites with such contempt?" is the dominant sense of this passage.

There is only one other significant passage in the Book of Job which throws any real light on the identities of the comforters. This is 13:7-12, in which Job advises them to drop their advocacy of God lest He turn on them and terrify them. In this passage Job speaks as an initiate to people outside the circle of mystery - *without doubt His magnificence will terrify you and the awe of Him overcome you.* This warning is followed by a verse with an intriguing twist. It reads:

זכרניכם משלי־אפר   לגבי־חמר גביכם

Both זכרון and גב in this verse have proved enigmatic. The problem may be solved by the application of the process of synthetic parallelism (see p. 175f). There is no other verse in the Bible in which these two words are used in parallel, but by happy "chance" it is possible synthetically to create one.[1] thus:

> *Behind the door and the post hast thou set up thy* זכרון
> *And hast built thyself thy* גב *at the head of every street.*

The first line is Isa 57:8, the second Ezek 16:31. The contexts of the two component lines are identical, with the prophet berating the people for their harlotries with other gods, and it is clear in each context that the word in question represents an object of deviant worship, the זכרון a miniature household image, the גב a publicly erected idol or mound or phallic symbol. The derivation of זכרון is obvious; it is simply a specialised use of the word *reminder*, as the *mezzuzah* of Jewish custom. גב probably derives from גבה, "to be high", see Chap. 3.IX.

An appropriate reading of this strange verse might therefore be:

> *Your household gods are figures of ash;*
> *Like columns of clay your minarets.*

and it again attests to the religious tension between the two communities, casting light on two further matters - the impatient disrespect with which Job listens to his friends' advice on the subject of his relations with God, and the fact that all the quotations from the Bible placed in the mouths of the comforters are slightly inaccurate.

Notes Chapter VI

1. This concept of *synthetic parallel* has not so far as I know been used before, and must stand or fall on its merits. Less obvious examples (see pp. 145 and 166f) are Job 15:19, amalgamating a portion of Ezek 11:15 with Joel 4:17d, and Job 40:15 which reflects a parallel between Amos 4:1 and Isaiah 30:6.

VII
The Identity of the Satan

The non-Jewish reader, confronted with the Satan as a character in a story, is equipped with a store of associations which effectively identify him as "the devil", an independent fallen angel devoted to the promotion of evil in the universe and the corruption of the souls of men with the objective of populating his domain - Hell. To come to grips with the Satan in the Book of Job, he has the difficult task of abandoning all these associations, and understanding the character within the framework of the uncompromising monotheism of prophetic Judaism.

The role of the Satan in the Book of Job is brief but crucial. He appears in two scenes in the supernatural realm in Chapters 1 and 2, and then disappears from the stage as though he had never been. His actions are attributed, both by the several human characters in the book, and by God Himself, not to him, but to God. There is ambiguity about the Satan from the very beginning: *There came the day when the "heavenly host"* (בני האלהים) *came to present themselves before the Lord, and there came also the Satan among them* (Job 1:6). We do not know whether the Satan is one of the "heavenly host" or a different order of being. From the way in which he is immediately singled out by God for interrogation, it seems likely that we are intended to understand the latter.

The expression בני האלהים, which has been at the centre of perpetual theological controversy does not mean *The sons of God*, which might be בני אלהים (38:7), although this distinction may be no more than a function of the difference between prose and poetry. It seems that in the phrase here, אלהים functions as a true plural of אלוה. The word בני in these phrases implies a class of being (cf. בני רשף, Job 5:7) and "the heavenly host" seems the most appropriate way of rendering the expression. This heavenly host is, as it were, a survival, whereby the pantheon of pagan peoples has been absorbed into the character of the Hebrew Deity, and forms a celestial council whose functions seem entirely ceremonial, and where the identities of the most powerful gods of pagan nations are degraded to the equivalents of the shades in Sheol. The Satan in Job 1,2 does not conform at all to this description.

The scene in what we now think of as heaven in Job is a reflection of a similar scene in I Kings 22:19-22 in a story told to King

Ahab by the prophet Micaiah:

> *And he said: Therefore hear the word of the Lord. I saw the Lord sitting on His throne, and all the host of heaven (צבא השמים) standing by Him on His right hand and on His left. And the Lord said: "Who shall entice Ahab, that he may go up and fall at Ramoth-Gilead?" and one said: "On this manner"; and another said: "On that manner", And there came forth the Spirit (הרוח), and stood before the Lord, and said: "I will entice him." And the Lord said: "Wherewith?" And he said: "I will go forth and will be a lying spirit in the mouth of all his prophets" And He said: "Thou shalt entice him, and shalt prevail also; Go forth and do so."*

It is easy to recognize, in their *modus operandi*, the virtual identity of "the Spirit" of this passage and the Satan of the Book of Job. But in Kings, the Spirit is an extension of God's own personality, specifically the Spirit of prophecy, of Divine inspiration, perversely invoked there as a spirit of subtlety, treachery and deceit in His council, qualities which could not with propriety be attributed directly to God.

The Satan's name in Hebrew means "the adversary", and a careful reading of the Prologue to the Book of Job will show that in this book at least he functions as adversary not of man or Job, but of God Himself. It is to Him that he delivers his challenge. It is God, not Job, whom he reproaches, in effect accusing Him of so mishandling the situation on earth that He can never be sure of his position *vis-a-vis* His creatures:

> *Have not You Yourself placed a fence about him*
> *and about his House, and about all that he has...?*

The very form of the question, phrased in the negative, is an accusation. Thus the licence which the Satan enjoys is itself remarkable, making of him the equivalent of the court jester, an institution which, incidentally, antedates the Book of Job by thousands of years[1]. But this cannot be the whole significance of the Satan, for in Chapter 2 it was the Satan himself who *left the precincts of the presence of the Lord and smote Job...*, while in Chapter 1 it is strongly implied that the Satan brought about the destruction of Job's possessions and children, and not that God Himself destroyed them merely at the instigation of the Satan. God's instructions to the Satan were: *Behold all that is his is in your power, only to his person you shall not extend your hand* (1:12). We are back at the same situation as in I Kings where "the Spirit" not only makes the appropriate suggestion, but is also the operative who carries it out.

Yet even as we reach this conclusion, we are obliged to note that in Chapter 1 v.16 the loss of Job's sheep is described in the following terms by the surviving servant:

> *A fire of God fell from the skies and burned*
> *the sheep and the servants and consumed them.*

Are we to imagine that the Satan, as an individual antagonist of God, actually had the power to command *the fire of God*? or was the escaping servant mistaken? Apparently not, for when God meets the Satan for the second time He utters the reproach *although you incited Me to destroy him*, not *although you incited Me to allow you to destroy him*. In the last chapter of the book, the author himself is speaking when he says *They* (Job's friends and relations) *comforted him concerning all the evil that the Lord had brought upon him* (42:11).

All this apparently irreconcilable ambiguity is by no means confined to the nature of the Satan in the Book of Job. We find the same thing on many occasions when an angel of the Lord is mentioned in the Hebrew Bible. Here we should quote somewhat extensively from Meir Weiss[2], who has written with great clarity and conviction on the penetration of the disguise of the Satan in the Book of Job. He considers the nature of the angel of the Lord, the apparent precursor of the Satan, in Numbers 22:

> As we have seen, the name שטן is related to a heavenly being even in its original usage: in the story of Balaam, שטן is used to indicate the angel's attitude of opposition to Balaam. The verse reads, "God's anger was aroused at his going, so the angel of the Lord placed himself in his way as an adversary" (Num 22:22).

While the subject of the first clause is God's anger, the subject of the second is the angel. The juxtaposition of God and His angel is not unusual in biblical narrative, for example "And God heard the voice of the lad, and the angel of God called to Hagar" (Gen 21:17); "God tested Abraham..and an angel of the Lord called to him from heaven" (Gen 22:1,11); "an angel of the Lord appeared to him...and when the Lord saw that he turned aside to look" (Ex 3:2,4); "Then Manoah knew that he was an angel of the Lord. And Manoah said to his wife: `we shall surely die, for we have seen God'" (Jud 13: 21,22). The interchanging of God and His angel reflects the idea that God's emotions, thoughts, will, speech, and action are made known to mankind not by God Himself but through His angel. The angel is nothing more than a manifestation of God Himself. God's objection to Balaam's mission is not expressed by God appearing in person "in his way as an adversary", but through the offices of an angel of God. The consistency of this phenomenon, confirming its significance as a feature of style, is evidenced in I Chron 21, where the incitement of David to take a national census is attributed not to God Himself, as in the parallel account in II Sam 24, but to Satan. It would appear that the account in Chronicles was made to accord with the belief that God does not tempt man to sin in order to punish him. What is done by God Himself in the first account is done by Satan in the alternative version, just as it was God's anger that was aroused against Balaam and yet Balaam's "satan" was not God, but His angel.

Weiss goes on to make a fine distinction between the early identification of God and His angel and the later situation, intermediate between this and full autonomy on the part of the angel, where for example Satan in Chronicles is "not an image of God but the embodiment (hypostasis) of opposition to God's will". While he writes that "in both the prophecy of Zechariah and the story of Job, Satan is an independent personality, an entity in himself, who has a mind of his own", he proceeds from there to the position that in these contexts "Satan is indeed a hypostasis - not of actual opposition to God, however, but of one of the contrary, ambivalent traits of God Himself."

Here, I suggest, he has arrived at the true nature of the Satan in the Prologue to Job. He is the projection of the spirit of doubt and scepticism within the complex mind of the Deity itself. Unable to determine - or, as we shall discuss later in this chapter, perhaps only unable to demonstrate publicly - the quality of Job's devotion to Himself, God uses the device of the Satan to test Job in a way which would have demeaned Him had He been seen to have devised it spontaneously. We are encountering here a defunct convention, one which was perfectly understood between author and his readers at the time of the composition of the book, but which we are now hard put to recover in its full subtlety. This is why it was possible for the author to dispose of the Satan completely once his role as instigator of God's abuse of His servant, Job, had been accomplished.

Weiss raises one further aspect of the Prologue which points to the identity of the Satan as but a facet of God's personality. This is the meticulously crafted symmetry between the scenes on earth and in heaven. Thus while there is a manifest equivalence between God and Job, בני אלהים and Job's children, the days of feasting and the days of God's assemblies, there seems to be no equivalent for the Satan. From the point of view of literary analysis this omission is more important than it appears on the surface. It suggests strongly either that the Satan is the central character mediating between heaven and earth, or that what is manifest in the Satan yet exists concealed in the earthly scene. As Job himself is afflicted by doubt sufficient to arouse him early in the morning of each feast day to make sin-offerings for his children, saying *Perhaps my children have sinned, and cursed God in their hearts,* we find the symmetry fully restored by the interpretation of the Satan as the projection of God's doubt about what is going on in the heart of Job.

This analysis yet has one apparently fatal flaw. It suggests a naivete and ignorance on the part of God which are incompatible with the Jewish concept of an omniscient and omnipotent unique Deity. How can it be that God entertained real doubts as to the quality of Job's devotion to righteousness? This situation, too, has its parallel in an earlier incident of Biblical story. That is the tale in Gen 22, the *akeda,* the *binding* when God "did prove Abraham" by requiring him to sacrifice his son, Isaac. In this story also God appears to doubt the quality of the devotion of His servant, and test him to the limit to establish it. But in the *akeda* we can readily detect a secondary "real" motive behind God's actions - to achieve the disestablishment of the pagan practice of child-sacrifice. This could not effectively have been achieved by interdiction, for the public effect would have been to suggest a less demanding Deity, an easier Master to serve, which cannot have been the intention of God (or of those subtle minds that guided the formation of this religion). It was necessary to demonstrate that a worshipper of the Lord was at least as willing to sacrifice his most precious possession to his God as any idol-worshipper, but that such sacrifices were not acceptable. The story achieves this.

There is similarly a secondary "real" motive behind God's testing of Job. If we consider the relationship between God and the people of Israel on the one hand, and the aspiration of God to universality on the other, it is apparent that there was, before the events discussed in the Book of Job, an incompatibility between them, one which becomes very obvious on reading Sennacherib's messages to Hezekiah and the people of Jerusalem (Isa 36 = II Kings 18).

Hear ye the words of the great king, the king of Assyria. Thus saith the king: Let not Hezekiah beguile you, for he will not be able to deliver you; neither let Hezekiah make you trust in the Lord, saying: The Lord will surely deliver us; this city shall not be given into the hand of the king of Assyria. Hearken not to Hezekiah; for thus saith the king of Assyria: Make your peace with me and come out to me... Beware lest Hezekiah persuade you, saying: The Lord will deliver us. Hath any of the gods of the nations delivered his land out of the hand of the king of Assyria? Where are the gods of Hamath and Arpad? where are the gods of Sepharvaim? and have they delivered Samaria out of my hand? Who are they among all the gods of these countries that have delivered their country out of my hand, that the Lord should deliver Jerusalem out of my hand?

and

Behold thou hast heard what the kings of Assyria have done to all lands, by destroying them utterly; and shalt thou be delivered? Have the gods of the nations delivered them, which my fathers have destroyed, Gozan, and Haran, and Rezeph, and the children of Eden that were in Telassar? Where is the king of Hamath, and the king of Arpad, and the king of the city of Sepharvaim, of Hena and Ivvah?

Sennacherib regards and speaks of the God of Israel as exactly on a par with the gods of other lands. Indeed, up to this point in history, this is precisely what He was. Bound by "treaty" to His people, He ensured their prosperity in peace and their victory in war. If they displeased Him, they might expect to experience calamities, which penitence, sacrifices, and a return to the right path would then reverse. This, of course, is precisely the sort of national order which Job's comforters propound. Inevitably it invites consideration of the relative strengths of different gods, which is what Sennacherib was doing. This aspect is raised by Job in 12:4-6 (see p. 288ff.) and by Elihu in 37:21-24 (see p. 264ff). The best that God might ever hope to achieve in this situation was recognition as the most powerful of the gods, *primum inter pares.*

God's ambition (or should we rather say the ambition of Isaiah and the other prophets of the period, and of the author of the Book of Job?) was that God should receive recognition as the sole, unique and universal God. The thesis of the Book of Job at its deepest level is that the time had arrived historically for the severance of this tribal bond, the rupture unilaterally of the covenant, the treaty, between God and Israel, to free the way for the demonstration of that unrequited love of God, fear of God, worship of God, which Job at the end of his trials personifies. This is the hidden motive behind God's testing of Job. Just as the testing of Abraham appeared to betray God's promise to him that he would raise up nations out of his seed, so the testing of Job seems to betray the comprehensive promises of the Deuteronomic covenant which is explicitly invoked in the first two chapters of the book.

There are thus three levels on which the allegory of God and the Satan may be understood. The simple literal level leaves the Satan as an enigmatic independent spirit who functions simply to start the story moving. The first allegorical level makes of the Satan a projection of a genuine spirit of uncertainty in the mind of a God seeking reassurance that he is loved for Himself alone. The second makes of that uncertainty itself a deception aiming to justify the transformation of the relationship between God and His people from one of physical dependence to one of mature symbiosis. So the Book of Job emerges as the record of the eliciting from the Jewish people of that genuine love of God which could never have been discovered or revealed as long as the covenantal relationship remained intact in unmodified form. It is a vital document in the history of religion, marking the first appearance of devotion as a free-will offering, and of the extension of the concept of the one national god to that of One God for all.

Notes Chapter VII

1. The earliest references to the institution of court fool go back to the 5th. Egyptian Dynasty (c. 2500-2350 B.C.E.). *Encyclopaedia Britannica*, 15th Edn. Micropaedia, IV, p.220.

2. M. Weiss *The Story of Job's Beginning*, Magnes Press, Jerusalem, *1983*, pp.37-42.

VIII
God's First Speech

Chapters 38 and 39 of the Book of Job stand alone and unimitated, perhaps inimitable, in the whole of literature. Although there have been numerous fictional speeches put into the mouth of God, and of the gods, there has never been anything resembling the tumultuous intensity of this strange speech, the poetic climax of this great work.

1. *The Emotional Tenor of the Speech*

The most startling aspect of God's first speech is that, quite apart from its content, it exudes a pungent emotional odour which is wholly at variance with every orthodox conception of the character of the Creator. The speech displays what the modern psychologist terms "inappropriate affect". The Lord, in a welter of sarcasm and abuse, sets out to diminish Job from His first words, *Who is this that is obfuscating wisdom in words without knowledge?* He knows of course exactly whom He is addressing.

In 13:22 Job offered the Lord His choice of weapons in the confrontation he sought with Him - *Then summon, and I shall answer, Or I shall speak and You respond.*

This engaging invitation is accepted in 38:3 in what is perhaps the most extreme example of sarcasm possible:

אשאלך והודיעני

I shall question you, and you reveal to Me!

We shall have occasion to explore the significance of להודיע in connection with 37:19. Literally it is *make known*, but it is an unthinkable word for any communication from man to God, being essentially reserved for messages sent from on high in the opposite direction. Thus already at this early stage in the speech, the Lord is planting the idea that Job is attempting to usurp His own role, first as dispenser of all wisdom, later as we shall see, as conductor of the orchestra of the universe, and finally (see Chap. V *supra*) as dispenser of summary justice to the proud and the wicked. In no time at all Job and his friends are reduced to the status of farm-animals questioning the way the farm is run. Intermixed with this abuse is a strong strain of Self-praise and Self-glorification. God in this speech seems actually to measure Himself against Job and rejoice in the demonstration of His own superiority.

Within the Book of Job, the anaemic fore-runner of this speech is Chapter 26, in which Job attempts to do to Bildad what the Lord succeeds in doing to Job[1]. The great majority of the specifics in Chapter 26 - the attributes or accomplishments of God which Job pretends to apply to Bildad - reappear in Chapter 38. What is missing is the mythological element, *Rahab* and the slant serpent, for everything in the Lord's first speech is natural. It is not *Leviathan* whom the Lord tames there, but *Yam*, the Sea itself. In Chapter 26 vv.5 & 6 are matched by 38:16,17; v.7, by 38:4; vv.8,9, by 38:34; v.10 by 38:19,20. v.12a is answered by 38:8-11, while 12b has to await Chapter 40 for its pair.

On the very well-founded twin assumptions that the author of the Book of Job knew exactly what he was doing, and that he was intuitively familiar with human psychology, the one conclusion which might be drawn from the emotional content of the speech is that the author wished to portray a God afflicted with a sense of guilt towards Job, One Who had determined upon attack as the best form of defence. One may also suspect that he had no patience or sympathy for the sentimental libel that "God is love". A much more extreme view of the affect has been expressed by Jung[2], who accounts for what he calls the "divine darkness unveiled in the Book of Job" by sketching an unquestionably psychotic nature for the Deity.

> *One would have to choose positively grotesque examples to illustrate the disproportion between the two antagonists. Yahweh sees something in Job which we would not ascribe to him but to God, that is, an equal power which causes Him to bring out His whole power machine and parade it before His opponent. Yahweh projects on to Job a sceptic's face which is hateful to Him because it is His own, and which gazes at Him with an uncanny and critical eye. He is afraid of it, for only in face of something frightening does one let off a cannonade of references to one's power, cleverness, courage, invincibility, etc. What has all that to do with Job? Is it worth the lion's while to terrify a mouse?*

To Jung, the Lord's problem is a fear of consciousness, an awareness of a lesser intensity of being than man experiences, and the principal illustration of God's problem is this first speech in the Book of Job. For the lay person, however, even after reading his preface *Lectori Benevolo*, it is extremely difficult to know what Jung is up to when he sets out to psychoanalyse the Deity. If there is a degree of unreality in attempts to psychoanalyse Hamlet and Macbeth, how much more so God! It is all very well to treat God as a real character, but there can be no doubt that a speech such as Chaps. 38, 39 of Job was written by a man, and that the numerous sources from which a picture of God may be built, were in fact different men who in all logic must have had different pictures of God in their minds as they wrote. Therefore, even granting the autonomy of God as an evolving part of the "collective unconscious", we are on safer ground if we treat the speech as a consciously composed fiction, and attempt to discern what manner of God this one author was trying to project, without assuming any sort of reality to it.

The Wizard in *The Wizard of Oz* (= Uz) is modelled on the Lord in the Book of Job (*The Wizard of Oz* is a gentle parody of the Book of Job). The wisest course is to observe them both with the same appreciative eye as literary devices designed to produce a zenith of tension in their respective tales. Avoiding the explosive extremism of Jung, it can be fairly said that the author of Job presents a picture of God which, taken at face value, depicts Him as seriously emotionally immature. The violence of the language used by the Lord in "correcting" Job seems impossible to justify.

Mitchell[3] sees something quite different in the *Voice from the whirlwind*. Dismissing the brutality and sarcasm of the catechism into which the speech is cast, he writes:

> *First we should notice how the answer consists mostly of questions (a good Jewish trait). In their volume and insistence, these questions acquire a peculiar quality. They sound in our ears as a ground bass to the melody of their content, and eventually function as a kind of benign subliminal message, asking a fundamental question that will dissolve everything Job thought he knew. The closest we can get to this question is What do you know?*

It would be fair to comment that the "Jewish trait" of answering a
question with a question operates in a different emotional climate from
this - there is a brutality in the Lord's questions which belongs with
the inquisitor, not his victim.

    Nonetheless, M's image of a ground-bass carrying a message
undermining Job's every certainty is appropriate, even if it is difficult
to perceive it as being benign. The reader who identifies with Job, and
most do, finds the speech painfully hostile and contemptuous. To see
the benign aspect it is, I suspect, necessary to identify with God!

    What however seems to have been overlooked in assessing the
emotional ambience of the Lord's speech is how well it fits into the
emotional tenor of all the exchanges between Job and his friends. The
Lord's speech is composed in the same spirit of "contest literature" as
the major exchanges of the preceding debate. We have seen in Chapter
V how the Lord repeatedly fences in Chapters 40 and 41 with Job's
earlier remarks about his relationship with Him. In the *ad hominem*
sarcasm of 38 and 39, a similar descent to the human level is apparent.
We may properly postulate that in this speech the Lord is acting a role
as a participant in the debate, and that what appeals to us as unwarranted and brutal abuse may in fact be no more than a display of superior
skill in a specialised medium of intercourse. We may speculate on how
this would have seemed to contemporary readers, but we have no way
of knowing.

2. Chapter 38, the Inanimate Universe

We must now turn to the intellectual and imaginative content of this
great speech, obliquely conveyed in harsh catechism. That is we shall
pay attention to the melody and block out the bass. The speech divides
itself into two almost equal halves, the division between them not
corresponding to the present chapter division. The first part, which
discusses the inanimate universe, comprises Chapter 38 from v.4 to 35.
The second, concerned exclusively with the biological world, runs
from 38:39 to 39:30, the end of the speech. 38:36-38, between these
two sections, are generally regarded as referring to inanimate aspects
of the universe, but, see below, I suggest they in fact discuss the
beginnings of life.

    The first four verses celebrate the creation of the earth; vv. 4,
5 and 6 employ architectural imagery, speaking of foundations,

measurements, lines and corner stones, while the final verse of this vignette soars in matchless jubilation:

> *When the stars of the morning rang out in unison*
> *And all the host of Heaven gave voice.*

This is the God characterised for all time by Blake[4] with *Eternity is in love with the products of Time*. The crude, mechanical and inappropriate terminology of the first three verses is a "put-down" of Job who, unlike God, only knows how to build with these instruments and devices.

The next section boasts of the containment of the Sea (*Yam*) in magnificent cadences:

> *And who enclosed* Yam *behind doors*
> *When he burst forth and departed the womb?*
> *When I ordained the vapour as his garment*
> *And the swagging cloud his swaddling-band?*
> *And set my surf to surround him*[5]
> *And put bar and doors*
> *And said: "Hither shall you come and no farther*
> *And here shall it stay in the pride of your waves!"?*[6]

But in this the imagery of the caparisoning of the infant sea, though still tailored to Job's comprehension, is poetic rather than contemptuous.

A third four-verse stanza follows, discussing the place by which seems to be intended the purpose, of the dawn[7]. But this purpose is only an incidental function of the dawn, related to the exposure of the nakedness of the poor and the wicked at his work, and seems to look back in both these particulars to Chapter 24, vv. 7 and 8 and to the discussion of light and dark, and that devastating claim by Job that God imputed nothing amiss to the sufferings of the poor (24:12).

From here on the images flow thick and fast, for the most part in single lines or distichoi. The depths of the Sea, the portals of Death, the whole wide world, follow one another in swift succession. The pace slows with the residences of alternating light and darkness, a punctuating burst of venom: *You know! Because you were born then! and the number of your days is vast!*, and then snow and hail depicted as armories laid up for a future battle, investing the metaphorical representation of inanimate forces with ominous significance. This battle is surely not Napoleon's attack on Moscow as Charlotte Bronte wittily suggested in Shirley, but the anticipated apocalyptic renewal of that with *Leviathan* whose recollection concludes Chapter 40.

The lightning and the East wind merit but one line each, with their interpretation none too sure, but the flash-flood and the thunderbolt are allotted three verses, and also accorded a purpose, and a most telling one in this context.

> *To bring rain to the land without men,*
> *To the desert wherein is no man,*
> *To satisfy desolate wastes*
> *And bring forth shoots of grass.*

This introduces what is perhaps the primary theme of this first speech, which comes to dominate Chapter 39, the concept that man is not the sole, nor even necessarily the central, preoccupation of the Creator. This is no longer the familiar God of Genesis, all of whose labours were concentrated upon fashioning a fitting setting for the crown of creation, Mankind. Here, for the first time in literature, is introduced a clear-sighted view of the true place of man, species and individual, in a necessarily interdependent and interacting matrix of non-empathetic parts.

> *Has the rain a father?*
> *Or who conceived the dew-drops?*
> *From whose womb emerged the ice?*
> *And the hoar-frost of heaven, who begot it?*

re-employs the device from the beginning of the chapter which postulated inappropriate mechanisms for phenomena not understood by humankind, thereby emphasising that not only the Creation but also the daily round of nature are altogether outside human capacity to know or understand. This is החכמה which in Chapter 28 eluded all human search. The speech is no longer addressed to any individual man, but to man as a species. M[8] finds these questions richly and subtly humorous, gently mocking the ideas of God as Father (or Mother) (sic!). But in reality the third line with its feminine image rules out this interpretation. Both Carl Jung and the women's liberation movement lie far in the future, and a feminine element in the Jewish Deity was unthinkable and unthought. These are rhetorical questions of denial emphasising the miraculous, the supernaturality of God's works.

> *Like stone the waters become still,*
> *And the face of the Deep is frozen*

is the extraordinary following couplet, leading us to wonder from what far source this image of a frozen sea reached the author dwelling close to the sub-tropics.

The next two verses ask Job if he can pilot the stars around the heavens, and the following three, the last in the cosmological section, if he can command rain and lightning.

Clearly the main message of this first part of God's speech is the incommensurability between God and Job - God and Man; the vastly superior knowledge, "wisdom" and power of God. In this, the chapter looks forward to 40:9-14, the great challenge to Job in the second speech. It vivifies the "arm" and the "thunderous voice" of God which Job is asked to match. A second aim, as we have said, is to begin the process of removing man from the centre stage of the universe, a process which almost dominates the next chapter. A third aim is surely quite simply to rejoice in the wonder of the universe, to display it in its majesty and complexity. A fourth theme, a reflection of the consensus of the times, is the unknowability of the mechanisms of the cosmos and metereology, a state of scientific ignorance which was accepted as irremediable.

Chapter 38 does therefore provide an answer, albeit a dismal one, to Job's questioning and criticism of God's actions. No man can ever have more than a partial picture of the grand design. Therefore he will inevitably be *obfuscating counsel in words without knowledge* when he presumes to correct his Lord. This is no more nor less than the timeless parental evasion.

3. *The Mysterious Bridging Passage, Verses 36-38*

The essentially indecipherable verses 38:36-38 are:

מי־שׁת בטחות חכמה   או מי־נתן לשׂכוי בינה?
מי־חספר שׁחקים בחכמה   ונבלי שׁמים מי ישׁכיב?
בצקת עפר למוצק   ורגבים ידבקו?

which in the RV (a typical translation) is given as:

> *Who hath put wisdom in the inward parts?*
> *Or who hath given understanding to the mind?*
> *Who can number the clouds by wisdom?*
> *Or who can pour out the bottles of heaven,*
> *When the dust runneth into a mass,*
> *And the clods cleave fast together?*

The three ideas in this version are all almost equally offensive to the dignity of God - that He spends His time counting the clouds and considers this a task worthy of "wisdom", that to make rain He pours out bottles in the sky, and that He enjoys making mud-pies!

The unknowns in these three verses are: נבלי שׁמים; שׂכוי; בטחות; and many different versions of the first verse have been engendered by these uncertainties. The word טחות is not hapax, but occurs in Psalm 51:8, the Psalm in which David voices his repentance for the sin he committed with Bathsheba:

> *Behold thou desireth truth בטחות.*
> *Make me to know wisdom בסתם*

The two Hebrew words are conventionally rendered *in the inward parts* and *in the inmost heart*. סתם refers to things closed, covered, secret, while טוח, which is presumably the root of טחות, means cover in much the same way as טפל which is to plaster or whitewash. Both these words are used for the metaphorical sense in which *whitewash* is used in English. In view of the subject of Psalm 51, there is a possibility that these references to secret or covered places in which the Lord requires the implantation of truth and wisdom in fact are intended to be to the sexual organs.

Rabbi Lakish and Rabbi Judah speaking in the name of R. Joshua b. Levi claimed that טחות are the reins and שׂכוי the cock. "*Who hath put wisdom in the טחות - these are the reins;* "*or who hath given understanding to the שׂכוי*" - *this is the cock.*[9] This reading, produces almost a compulsion to read "cock" not as the bird, but as the symbol of male potency, for its parallel with "reins" which is another word for "kidneys" requires almost mandatorily an anatomical part as its meaning. The "reins" are regarded as the seat of the feelings or affections. It is therefore possible to read the initial couplet of this passage as a novel question about the implantation of reproductive skill to the organs which require it, dealing both with attraction and performance.

I propose to skip to line 37b at this point and to examine the word שכיב which is usually understood as "tilt" or "pour out" and enlisted in a metaphor so primitive that it belongs rather with the Aborigines of Australia than with the sophisticated author of Job - *Who can pour out the bottles of heaven?* as a question about rain. We have to contrast this with 36:27-30, two chapters earlier where Elihu describes the rains of the great flood and how God terminated them:

> *He sucked up the droplets of water;*
> *They distilled into the rain of His "mist"*
> *Which the skies poured down...*
> *Then He displayed His light (*the rainbow*) across it*
> *(*His pavilion, the sky*).*
> *And stopped the sluices of the (upper) sea.*

This brilliant combination of naturalism and myth is in sharpest contrast with the inane image supposedly found in 38:37.

The Hiph`il of שכב has two meanings - to lay, usually the dead, or to make to lie down. The frequent use of שכב in other conjugations as a euphemism for sexual congress certainly allows the interpretation here *make copulate.* To "make to lie down" is a very poor circumlocution for "tilt" while "pour out" is derived from an Arabic cognate and therefore may not be considered. If we accept the meaning

> *Who makes* נבלי שמים *couple?*

we find immediately that it has the sterling virtue that it changes automatically the meaning of verse 38 from the making of mud-pies to the formation of the foetus in the womb or the egg! - *To pour dust into the mould, that the particles cleave together* - yielding a memorable and poetic metaphor far worthier of both the author and the Deity into whose mouth it is placed, than the pointless *when the dust hardens into a mass and the clods cleave fast together?* which is the usual version. The definite article with מוצק favours it.

What are נבלי שמים? It is usual to understand them as "the bottles of heaven" but this is a real absurdity, for no mythology is so crude as to see clouds in this way, least of all that of the Book of Job which deals again and again with the phenomenon of rainfall and its mechanism in far more sophisticated imagery than this. נבל may indeed mean a vessel, and as in English the meaning becomes transferred to human beings (Lam 4:2; Isa 22:24; Jer 48:12), and perhaps even further to any living creatures. But another meaning of נבל, which is to be found elsewhere in the Book of Job (2:10), is *foolish* or *senseless* which is precisely the meaning required to illuminate this image - those without the wit to work things out for themselves. In this version the word מוצק comes into its own. The word is very specific in its meaning, being a shaped mould (I Kings 7:37). This is a beautiful image of the formation of the foetus in a preordained shape as replicas of a sculpture are created by the use of such a מוצק. In accordance with biblical usage, the living being is formed from dust. Nowhere is there a more vivid and poetic portrayal of the process than this.

This leaves unexplained only 37a, about which the first thing to say is that יספר (Pi`el) does not mean "to count" but to recount, and the second that שחקים is used in the Book of Job only as "the heavens", not as "clouds", and that wherever it is "clouds" in the Bible, it is a uniform cloud cover, not a collection of individual "countable" discreet aggregations of vapour. Therefore, not only is the version *Who can count the clouds by wisdom?* silly, but it is also no translation of the Hebrew. The correct translation is to be found in NJPSV:

Who is wise enough to give an account of the heavens?

and the line functions much as the third line in a Khayyam quatrain, as a parenthetical observation. We now have:

Who put wisdom in the covert place?
Or who gave skill to the cock?
Who shall recount the empyrean in wisdom!
And the fools of heaven, who makes them copulate
To pour dust into the mould
That the particles cleave together?

4. Chapter 39, the Animal World

The second section of God's first speech, starting with this description of the processes of conception, deals with the biological world or, more explicitly, the animal world. It consists of carefully graded references to five pairs of animals and birds - the lion and the raven, predators; the wild-goat and the hind, gentle and secretive herbivores; the wild-ass and the wild-ox, varieties of domestic beasts which have themselves defied domestication; the ostrich and the horse, animals aloof and perverse in their habits; and the hawk and the vulture, scavengers.

The pairing of the animals, an advanced form of parallelism, has the special effect of concentrating the reader's attention on the qualities which are peculiar to each pair. He is not being asked to consider the lion or the raven in its totality, but simply the quality which they share.

While almost every section of this second part of the speech is expressed, as in the first section, in questions addressed to Job, somehow all the venom has gone out of them. There is a deflation of emotion; the questions are no longer aggressive, but come over almost as though the Lord were genuinely seeking to probe Job's knowledge rather than to expose his lack of it.

At the same time as these animals are being described, each in a limited fashion, there is being developed the idea of the natural life-cycle. 38:36-38 refers to conception (v.s.); 38:39-41, somewhat out of sequence, to the feeding of the young by their parents; 39:1,2 deals with pregnancy; 39: 2b, and 3 refer to delivery. Verse 4 describes the development of independent and self-reliant life by the young. Verses 5-12 describe adult animals fulfilling their several potentials in accordance with their simple natures, neither serving, nor served by man.

Verses 13-18 describe the perversity of the ostrich, which consists of her vain attempts to protect the eggs which she has laid in the dust. First she wishes she were other than she is and could fly like a stork and so provide a safe nest for her young, and second she makes fearless but futile efforts to protect the young from intruders without realising that they are unnecessary because *(God) has hardened her young to do without her.* As we shall see this description of the ostrich has a special significance above that of the others.

The perversity of the horse (vv.19-25) lies in his love of war. Again it is the adult animal and his mode of fulfilling his nature which is described, but like that of the ostrich, this description stands out vividly from the rest.

Finally the life-cycle arrives at the point of death, with the vulture whose young *lap blood, and wherever the slain are, there is he!*

Two aspects of animal life recur in these descriptions the care of the young, and the non-interaction of these creatures (other than the horse) with men. Will Job hunt the prey for the lion? Who prepares his prey for the raven when his young cry to God (אל) and faint for want of food? The offspring of the mountain-goat and deer *grow up amid the corn; they wander away and do not return to them.* The wild-ass *seeks his pasture in the hills and searches for every verdure.* The ostrich is concerned to protect her young but God has denied her wisdom, so her efforts are futile. Finally that chilling suckling of the vulture's brood.

The theme of independence from man is emphatic and explicit in the case of the third, the central pair of animals. The wild-ass *can scorn the din of the city; he does not hear the shout of the muleteer* and *will the wild-ox consent to serve you? Will he stable in your stall?*etc. Here is the apparent revocation of the first of all the covenants between God and man, Gen 1:28

> Have dominion over the fish of the sea, and over the fowl of the air, and over every living thing that creepeth upon the earth.

The one animal that interacts with man in the chapter is the horse, whose delight in war must be satisfied in association with men. But who is making use of whom in this symbiosis?

Another important thread running through these descriptions is the concept of appropriate times, which rises to the surface in 39:1-4. In each species there is an appropriate time for birth, an appropriate time for the assumption of independence, an appropriate time for death. Everything in the chapter is proceeding in its own preordained tempo and fashion without the interference of man or God. This lesson is to be applied by Job to his own predicament. The umbilical cord between Israel and God also had to be severed at the right time; the parental bond of protection and sustenance had at some time to be ruptured. The implication is that that time has come.

The Book of Job abounds in animal imagery, but in every case the animals are introduced as metaphors or similes of men - from the lions of Chap. 4, the asses of Chaps. 11 and 24, the *proud beasts* of Chap. 28, to the monsters of Chapters 40 and 41. In the animals of Chaps. 38 and 39, we may detect prototypes - miniature allegories of the nations of the Middle East. The idea is suggested by the eccentric vignette of the ostrich, whose resemblance to Job himself is striking.

The ostrich passage is not usually translated faithfully, so I insert the translation here (reading with the consensus כְּנַף־רְנָנִים as that bird).

> *The ostrich-wing would rejoice*
> *If she were stork-wing and feather,*
> *For she leaves her eggs to the earth*
> *And warms them in the dust,*
> *And forgets that the foot might scatter it (the nest)*
> *Or the wild beast trample it.*
>
> *He has toughened her young to do without her;*
> *Her fearless efforts are for nothing,*
> *Because God denied her wisdom*
> *And apportioned her no understanding.*
> *Now she flaps away in safety;*
> *She jeers at horse and rider.*

Job's fearless efforts on behalf of his people are likewise for nothing, for God (the understood masculine subject of הִקְשִׁיחַ) has toughened the people of Judah to survive without his intervention. He too forgot until it was too late that his people had natural enemies within and without (12:4,5; 24:23). He too longs to be what he is not, the effective champion of his people (see 40:8-32 and the comments in Chap. 5 *supra*). Job too lacks wisdom and understanding, certainly in God's eyes - he has *obfuscated counsel in words without knowledge*. The ostrich passage is set apart from the descriptions of all the other animals by the fact that no questions are asked of Job concerning her. God tells about the ostrich, a series of home-truths.

If the ostrich is Job = Judah, the horse is surely Assyria who delights in battle, especially with horse-drawn chariots. The one is animal pressed into the service of man, the other nation pressed into the service of God. Each revels too enthusiastically in his role.

The falcon that spreads her wings to the south can only be Edom, forever hoping for a share in the carcass of Judah, and the vulture that descries death from far away and appears wherever the slain are is the Philistines, real jackals in their role in the time of Hezekiah, eager to feed on the dead and desolate cities laid waste by Sennacherib.

The wild-ass, whose home is the desert, who scorns the din of the city and submits to no muleteer, is that פרא אדם the Ishmaelite (Gen 16:12), the Arabian nomad, and the wild-ox who will never submit to Job perhaps the Aramean whom Israel never successfully mastered for long, perhaps Egypt.

The raven and lion are the nations perpetually at war with Israel, seeking pieces of her, Ammon and Moab perhaps, while the deer and the mountain-goat represent those lands, such as Tyre and Sidon, whose greatest desire seems to have been to have been left in peace to pursue their own unaggressive ends.

The whole family of allegorical nation-animals reappears momentarily in 40:20: כל־חית השדה ישחקו־שם.

Chapter 39 and the last verses of Chapter 38 constitute a simple lesson in ecology. Prey has to be found for predators, grass must be grown for herbivores, wars must be fought for horses, and corpses must lie unburied that vultures may thrive. The universe is fundamentally cruel, and randomly so. It is, I think fair to say that it is this message, commandingly conveyed in the first speech of the Lord, that was responsible for the sequestration of the Book of Job from the mainstream of Jewish religious development. It portrays a God whose involvement with His human dependants is so different from that whose spirit infused all Israelite writings which preceded this book that reconciliation between them was more or less impossible. It was not until the arrival of 19th Century Rationalism that a religious system was evolved which could digest this unpalatable fare.

In summary, the first speech of the Lord conveys a medley of overt and concealed messages to Job.

1. Job's knowledge and comprehension are not adequate to justify his taking the Creator to task. In this, Job is Man.

2. The Divine responsibility for the universe extends far beyond the human sphere, and Divine justice is therefore expressed in terms of economy and ecology rather than in human terms of retribution and restitution.

3. The centrality of Man to the universe is relativistic. While true for Man himself, it is not true either for God or for any of the creatures which share the world with man.

4. Relationships evolve, and as between parents and offspring there arrive times when sucessive loosenings of bonds and severance of dependencies are required, so between God and the people of Israel. There is here a definite implication of attenuation of the covenantal relationship, a distancing of the Deity from *His children*.

5. Just as there is a great variety of animal species, docile, aggressive, predatory, parasitic, so there is a great variety of forms which human societies may take, all equally valid, equally independent. Judah has been behaving like the ostrich in terms of this zoological metaphor, a monument of unwisdom.

6. Over all, there broods the novel, truly anthropomorphic personality of God, irascible, vain, resentful at having been drawn from His proper preoccupations, and yielding not an inch to the sentimental dream of His having created a world in which each receives according to his merit. In allowing His theophany to take place on an equal emotional footing with the human protagonists of his drama, the author came closer to an anthropomorphisation of the Deity than any other Biblical writer.

Notes Chapter *VIII*

1. This interpretation of Chapter 26 is discussed at length in Chapter VIII, and in D. Wolfers *Job: The Third Cycle* in *Dor Ledor* XVI, 4, *1988*, 220-222, and in D. Wolfers, *The Speech Cycles in The Book of Job*, VT, XLIII, 3,*1993* p. 385-402.

2. C.G. Jung, *Answer to Job*, Routledge & Kegan Paul Ltd. *1954* p.4.

3. *The Book of Job* p.xix.

4. William Blake, *The Marriage of Heaven & Hell*, c. 1793 Proverbs of Hell, No. 10.

5. ואשבר עליו חקי. No plausible, still less convincing, explanation for the unexpected verb שבר "to break", with "my decree" or "my boundary" as object, has been advanced. Perhaps the most plausible is that it refers to the appearance of rupture in the line of cliffs which marks the boundary between land and sea. But in the Eastern Mediterranean and the Red Sea, such shore lines are exceptional (v. Jer 5:22 in the next paragraph).

The translation given is experimental. משבר is a breaker, found in 41:17. The suggestion is a nonce-use of the verb to mean *I made breakers* with the breaking being of the sea's waves rather than the land. חק as a bounding limit for the sea, and hence a surrounding circle, occurs both in Job 26:10, where it is the horizon, and in Jer 5:22 where it is the sand.

6. ופא-ישית בגאון גליך. Most authors essay some emendation here because of the grammatical problems. But the phrase most usually attacked, בגאון גליך, *In the pride (or majesty) of your waves* is so typical of the style of the author that it surely must not be sacrificed. P's comment on this line is exceptionally full and fascinating. In the present state of our knowledge, there does not seem to be a single version which commands complete conviction.

7. See p.455f.

8. p.xxv.

9. Talmud: *Rosh Hashannah*, 26a.

The question as to to what person, animal, or organ, God might attribute חכמה and בינה is a very vexed one. Certainly He declares that the ostrich was denied her share of these qualities. The cock (as bird) has no special claim to wisdom as, perhaps the owl does, though some see its ability to distinguish night and day as indicating this quality! Those who regard שכוי as the bird, naturally seek a similar meaning for שחות and claim that the word stands for the ibis, the symbol of the Egyptian moongod who was also the patron of learning, *Thot*, but this derivation is almost unthinkable. The ibis in Biblical Hebrew is ינשוף (Lev 11:17). It is, I think, most unlikely that God would concede wisdom to the human heart or mind in this chapter as many versions suggest, nor does such a concept fit anywhere into its concerns. On the other hand, the raising of the mystery of animal reproduction is exactly appropriate at this point, as the beginning of concern for the animal kingdom.

IX
The Speech-Cycles of Job

The structure of the discussions between Job (J) and his three comforters, Eliphaz (E), Bildad (B), and Zophar (Z) in Chapters 3-31 has generally been regarded as follows:

J: E:J:B:J:Z:J E:J:B:J:Z:J E:J:B:J:?:J

The regularity evident in the first thirteen speeches, and the unfulfilled promise of its persistence contained in the next four, have led most modern scholars to follow Kennicott[1] in postulating errors in the transmission of the text to account for the non-fulfillment of that promise[2]. These suggestions have attracted so much support that the loss by disruption of an original "third cycle" of the form E:J:B:J:Z:J has almost attained the status of a dogma of modern scholarship. Of recent writers, only F.I. Andersen[3], and he somewhat unwillingly, has expressed satisfaction with the traditional transmitted text. Later in this chapter we shall raise the question whether the true form of a cycle of speeches in this book is as assumed above, or whether there are not in fact seven speeches to each cycle, with Chapter 15 compressing two separate addresses by Eliphaz into the one chapter.

The hypothesis of disruption does not depend only on the unexpected introduction of irregularity into a hitherto regularly alternating sequence of conflicting speeches, but is supported by the detection of a number of apparent anomalies, and apparent illogicalities or self-contradictions, in the speeches themselves. These difficulties afflict Chapters 24, 25, 26 and 27; that is the second part of Job's reply to Eliphaz, Bildad's speech, and both the two chapters attributed to Job in the MT which follow it. Chapters 22 and 23, by Eliphaz and Job respectively, have been accepted as the authentic commencement of the hypothetical cycle. The status of Chapter 28, the "independent poem on Wisdom", remains equivocal, but it has rarely been suggested that it forms an integral part of the debate between Job and his friends. That is, by common consensus, it lies outside the boundaries of any "third cycle".

Because there has been no dissension surrounding the first two speeches of this "cycle", I propose briefly to summarise only the four disputed speeches, drawing attention to the difficulties in acceptance of the transmitted text which they have provoked, and to show how each of these difficulties is to be overcome.

1. *Chapter 24*

This is acknowledged to be one of the least well-understood chapters of the Book of Job. In the recent NJPSV translation no fewer that eight of the twenty-five verses are noted as conjectural, and a further one treated as misplaced.

The chapter opens with a very ambiguous verse which is commonly interpreted as a complaint that *God's saints do not see the promised hour of retribution coming upon the sinners* (G). There follow ten verses which in general bewail the oppression of the poor, presumably (but this is never made explicit) by the wicked. Many students claim to have perceived in this passage an alternation of descriptions between the malfeasance of evildoers and the sufferings of the poor and weak[4], but the absence of any specific mention of evildoers makes this position difficult to maintain.

After this comes verse 12, a tristich in which the first two lines refer to the sufferings of those either in, or far from, the populous city (מעיר מתים ינאקו), and the third line records God's callous indifference to their plight - *God sees nothing amiss*. This is followed by the passage familiarly known as "the rebels against the Light", which is usually treated as a fresh start, pointing to the classes of habitual sinners - murderers, thieves, adulterers and perhaps burglars - about to be catalogued in vv. 14-16.

Verses 17-24 are the most disputed part of the chapter and are taken as describing the signal punishment visited by God upon these "rebels against the Light". Under this interpretation there is a clear conflict with Job's fundamental thesis as expounded in Chapter 21 and elsewhere, that there is no mechanism operating for the direct punishment of the wicked. One can only agree with those commentators who insist that Job could not have been made to express these views.

The matter has been dealt with in various ways, some of which are discussed in the Introduction. P bodily transports these verses to form a part of the hypothetical lost speech of Zophar which is required for the integrity of the "third cycle". H goes so far as to treat the whole of the chapter in this way. Hoffman[5] adds them to Bildad's speech in Chapter 25. NJPSV, following LXX and Heath[6] transforms them into the optative mood, while G, seduced by his own theories, treats them as a "virtual quotation" by Job of his opponents. Some have even gone to the extent of denying the authenticity of the entire chapter. I propose to show that these verses do not refer to the fate of the sinners described in the "rebels" passage, but to the fate of their victims, and to God's attitude to it, and to God Himself.

Much of the difficulty with Chapter 24 springs, as with so many other difficulties in the Book of Job, from an initial unwillingness to understand the text literally. When this reluctance is exerted on a word or phrase which is crucial to the sense of a verse, passage, or even a whole chapter (e.g. Chapter 26 below), the most extreme misunderstandings are apt to arise. In this case a crucial error has been made in the translation of the word חמאו (v.19). There are other sources of difficulty in this chapter. One has been failure to perceive its unalloyed unity, that it is concerned from start to finish only with the fate of the poor and oppressed, and with God's tolerance of and responsibility for that fate. The interpretation of the chapter is also prejudiced by what at first sight appears an almost random alternation of singular and plural verbs, often in circumstances which seem to suggest that the subject is unchanged.

The theme of Chapter 24 is the plight of poor vagrants living on the border of the desert, and the injustices which they suffer. I suggest that these vagrants are the remnant of Judah left in the land after the exile of 200,000 intellectuals recorded by Sennacherib[7]. Characteristically, Job attributes their sufferings to the apathy of God, and has no real interest in the human agents He allows play. The chapter as a whole resembles an Israelite version of the Egyptian *Lamentatons of Ipu-wer*[8], although the emphasis is ethical rather than aristocratic. To Job the situation he is describing is

> *The day of the Lord...*
> *Cruel and full of wrath and burning anger;*
> *To make the earth a desolation*
> *And to destroy the sinners out of it.* Isa 13:9

The complaint in the first verse is not the savagely voyeuristic one that God's saints do not witness such days; quite the reverse. It is that, although God has made a practice in the past[9] of sparing *those who know Him* such sights, in the case of Job He has not seen fit *to cut me off before the darkness, Nor did He cover my face from the gloom.* (23:17, the immediately preceding verse). Job's purpose in the chapter is to demonstrate that God has missed His aim, and is visiting the punishment supposedly reserved for "the wicked" on harmless men who have simply not had the opportunities which are required for piety and ritual observance - to *know the ways of the Light.* Let us follow its development.

Verses 2-11:
In none of those verses in the first ten-verse section which have been considered as describing the iniquities of the wicked, or of the evildoers, is either of these parties mentioned. The section is entirely expressed with subjectless third person plural verbs; all such sentences may properly be understood as being in the passive voice, with the victims as the subjects rather than the objects[10]. This way of reading the section is confirmed by line 4b where a passive Pu`al form, חבאו, is used.

> *Boundary stones are moved,*
> *And the flock seized and devoured[11].*
> *The ass of orphans is driven away;*
> *The widow's ox taken in pledge.*
> *The poor are shouldered out of the way;*
> *The destitute of the earth are run to ground together.* 24:2-4.

Interrupting this litany of misery is v.5 which contains the first of the comments on God's attitude.

> *See! Wild asses in the wilderness,*
> *They set off on their business, scrounging for prey.*
> *To Him the desert is food for young men!*   (ערבה לו לחם לנערים)

This begins to set the tone of the chapter. The first two lines are sarcastic; they mean "See how wicked they are, searching, of all things, for food to keep themselves alive!" The comment that in God's eyes the desert is adequate sustenance for young men is Job's opening broadside against Him for His misjudgement of the unfortunate as deserving punishment. By ignoring the word לו, the majority of commentators have allowed themselves to miss the point of this verse.

The next six verses pursue the recital of the deprivation, starvation, exposure, and exploitation to which the poor are subjected. Then comes v.12, the second of the tristichs, which contains the next comment on God's attitude, and serves also as the introduction to the so-called "rebels against the Light" passage.

Verses 12-16

---

12   *Far from the crowded city they groan,*
        And the soul of the victims cries aloud,
        But God imputes nothing amiss! (וֵאלוֹהַ לֹא־יָשִׂים תִּפְלָה)
13   *(He says) "They were among the rebels against the Light."*
        They knew nothing of its ways
        Nor did they dwell in its paths.   [24:12,13.]

The evidence that 13a must be regarded as what G would call a "virtual quotation" of God's thoughts on the subject of all this misery, apart from the fact that the device imparts coherence and continuity to the chapter, lies in the tense *They were*. In the Hebrew, this is הֵמָּה הָיוּ, which is unmistakable, and the many deviations to be found in translations *They are; Those are; Some there are; These are*[12] - simply do not correspond with the Hebrew text. All of these variants are designed to throw the referent of הֵמָּה forward to the categories to be enumerated in the ensuing verses, and away from the souls in torment of v.12 and its predecessors. But, although G claims otherwise[13], there is only one genuine example in the Bible of the pronoun הם anticipating its referent (Prov 30:24 & 29), and there it is, as must be mandatory for such a construction, a part of a timeless noun clause. As we know that it is not Job's opinion that these unfortunates are wicked, and as we have just read God's opinion being introduced, albeit with a negative in line 12c, it seems that l.13a likewise is, as it were, reading God's mind.

אלוה לא־ישים תפלה is recognizable as one of the rare crossrefer-ences between Prologue and Dialogue. In 1:22, after all his disasters, the narrator comments that *For all this, Job did not ascribe (נתן) תפלה to אלוהים*. There is a marked contrast apparent. Job's tolerance of injustice applies to injustice done to himself; God's tolerance is of injustice done to others. Job's tolerance of injustice does not however extend to that done to others. Thus concealed in the irony of v. 12 is that Job now does ascribe תפלה to אלוהים. Balancing v.5 chiastically in form, lines 13 b,c are no amplifications of 13a, but Job's refutation of God's assumed opinion - they note the ignorance and lack of opportunity of the victims - They knew nothing of the ways of Light nor did they dwell in its paths. This is no rebellion.

The next three verses are remarkable, for they show Job instructing God who are the true rebels against the Light. Not, says Job, the poor and needy, but those who kill the poor and needy, and those who break the fundamental commandments:

---

14   *It is the murderer who revolts against the Light.*
        He kills the poor and needy,
        *Or at night it might be, say, a thief**

15   *And the eye of the adulterer awaits the dusk,*
        Saying, "No eye shall see me,
        *And He puts a veil over His face."***

16   *He breaks in the dark into houses.*
        *The daytime is sealed against them.****

        They know not the Light.

---

* The Hebrew is ובלילה יהי כגנב

** This phrase is commonly translated to convey that the adulterer puts a veil over his own face. It has not, apparently, been recognized that the whole passage is related to Ps 10 in which the context is similar. So, Ps 10:11:

> *He hath said in his heart "God hath forgotten;*
> *He hideth His face (הָסְתֵּר פָּנָיו); He will never see."*

The variation here, סְתֵר פָּנִים יָשִׂים is a pregnant recollection of 12c אֱלוֹהַּ
לֹא־יָשִׂים תִּפְלָה, telling us again what God does יָשִׂים.

    *** This is admittedly a most unusual version of line 16b,
יוֹמָם חִתְּמוּ־לָמוֹ, which is almost always understood as *By day they seal
themselves up*. But, despite 3:14, לָמוֹ is not a reflexive pronoun, nor does
the Pi`el of חתם admit a reflexive sense, nor does it seem right under
these circumstances to precede the accusative with ל. Again the
subjectless 3rd person plural imports a passive voice, in this case with
יוֹמָם (which is noun as well as adverb) as subject. לָמוֹ may be singular
or plural, referring only to the last mentioned villain, or to all who
rebel against Light. The daytime is sealed to them because they dare
not go abroad in it, but they do not seal themselves up. Either way,
this resolves the first of the puzzling alternations of number. The
plural חִתְּמוּ is not in conflict with the preceding singular חתר. The form
of the sentences is not "He does this, They do that", but "He does this,
that is done to him/them."

    There is a certain amount of punning on Light as the path of
righteousness and as the simple opposite of darkness in the above,
which sets the stage for the mysterious verses which follow.

Verses 17-20
It is vv. 17-20 which pose the most severe problems in Chapter 24.
The Hebrew is:

17	כי יתדו בקר למו צלמות
	כי יכיר בלהות צלמות
18	קל־הוא על־פני־מים
	תקלל חלקתם בארץ
	לא־יפנה דרך כרמים
19	ציה גם־חם יגזלו מימי־שלג
	שאול חטאו
20	עוד לא־יזכר

Very little of these verses has ever been correctly deciphered. Coming as they do immediately following the passage describing murderers and adulterers, they have always been assumed to record the summary justice meted out to them, and therefore to stand in direct contradiction of those passages in Chapter 21 in which Job laments the absence of any mechanism for the punishment of the wicked in their own persons and lives. It is for this reason that so many suggestions have been made for the reattribution or amendment of this passage.

It will also be noticed that it is in this passage that the most extreme and vertiginous alternations of number occur, 17a, 18b and 19b apparently having plural referents, and 17b, 18a and c and v. 20, singular. While the usual practice has been to shrug the shoulders at this and regard it as no more than an extreme example of the inconsistent way in which collectives are treated in the Book of Job, if this were the explanation, it would represent a mischievous piece of mystification by the author which would be hard to forgive. In fact, as will be demonstrated, with the exception of v. 20, all the singular lines refer to a singular, and all the plurals to a collective subject.

The probable reasons why so little effort has been expended on confirming the identities of the wayward referents of these lines have been first, the wrongful assumption that vv. 2-12 have referred to oppressors as well as their victims – the reluctance to translate 3rd. person plurals as passives, and second, the failure to appreciate that vv. 14-16 are no more than an "aside" intended to demonstrate the relative innocence of the victims in v.12, rather than an integral part of the central theme of the chapter. Accepting that the chapter is about victims, about God's reaction to their sufferings, but not about their oppressors, it becomes much more questionable that these verses might elaborate the fate of the latter.

The first thing to note about line 17a is the strange order of the words. יחדו, an expression of commonality, is separated from the word למו by בקר, and bears a disjunctive accent. The usual assumption that יחדו...למו implies *to all of them* is therefore very suspect. Indeed it looks very much as though this word order was chosen deliberately to prevent precisely this reading. Nor is *all of them* properly the sense of יחדו which, at its weakest, implies a sort of togetherness, an association based on some sort of identity. I therefore conclude that יחדו must be read as modifying the whole phrase בקר למו צלמות, as indeed the accentuation suggests. Its meaning is therefore *alike, as one* (Cf. I Sam 30:24), and implies that to them morning (light) and deep darkness (the Shadow of Death) are indistinguishable. To the criminals who do their work in the dark, the arrival of dawn is what צלמות is to ordinary men, the time of terror. *To them the morning is as deep darkness..*

The second point to be pondered in this line is the introductory כי which is the first of a pair in this verse. כי in this book is usually "for", but כי...כי is hardly probable as "for...for". After a negative, כי is characteristically "but", and the preceding line לא־ידעו אור is negative.

The best solution here, dictated by the sense of the lines, is to take the first כי as "for", because it explains "their" lack of knowledge of Light, and the second as "but", for it introduces an incompatible proposition:

כי יכיר בלהות צלמות

which means *But he is acquainted with the terrors of deep darkness.* For three excellent reasons, the subject of this line cannot be the same as the preceding referent of למו.

1. It is singular and that was almost certainly plural.

2. The כי heralds a contrast.

3. The sense of this line flatly contradicts the sense of the preceding line unless their subjects are different entities.

Thus we have in effect:

> *They* confuse morning and the Shadow of Death,
> But *he* is well acquainted with the Shadow of Death

Who then is the "he" of this line? The sense precludes the possibility of its being any of the criminals listed in the preceding verses, therefore it must be either one of their victims or the God Who keeps popping up in this chapter and Who was last referred to in v.15.

There are two further lines with singular subjects in this short section, 18a and 18c, and there should be, I suggest, little doubt that their subjects are God. But 24:18 has sound title to being one of the most difficult verses to decipher in the whole Book of Job.

קל־הוא על־פני־מים

He is swift[14] on the face of the waters

has all the appearance of a totally irrelevant observation, floating into the text from outer space, until we realise that its very irrelevance is its purpose, for it is followed by the statement

Their portion is accursed in the earth

If we place the emphasis on the triple contrast between these lines, we see what they are saying.

> *He* was *swift* on the *waters*,
> (But) *Their* portion is *cursed* in the *land*.

This, like 7:12 (*Am I Yam? Or Tannin? That You set a watch over me?!*) is a reference to God's accomplishments in the containment of the Sea and the Sea-Chaos monster who appears at intervals throughout the Book of Job under various names. We are encountering a reference which would have been instantly comprehended by contemporaries, but which is puzzling in the light of the culling of mythological elements from the Bible and their excision from mainstream religious thought. But there seems no doubt that the conflict with the Sea was a far more significant ingredient of God's reputation in the time and place of the writing of the Book of Job than can be deduced from other surviving Biblical literature. T-S considered this verse to be related to certain "titans" who were assistants to *Leviathan*, but made no attempt to integrate this strange idea into the flow of the chapter. The line may additionally be read as a recollection of Gen 1:2. What Job is saying, with bitterness, is that God was very successful in combatting evil in the sea-monster, but that is not much help in rectifying the injustice of those whose suffering takes place on the dry land - the victims who are the central concern of Chapter 24. That is, he is crying out against a God whose concerns are irrelevant to suffering mankind. Those whose *portion is accursed in the land* are assuredly the victims, and not their persecutors as is so often assumed. Those versions (based on LXX) which proceed in the optative *May they be flotsam on the face of the water; May their portion in the land be cursed; May none turn aside by way of their vineyards* (NJPSV) cannot be countenanced at all, for whatever may be said in favour of converting the imperfects in 18b and 18c into jussives, nothing can justify so treating the noun-clause in 18a. (LXX excludes 18a from the cascade of jussives, but leaves it meaningless).

The use of the verb קלל in 18b is not so much word-play with קל in 18a, as an indication of parallel intent. It directs us towards the realisation that water and land are intended antitheses. It is fascinating to observe how, in the next chapter, Bildad will refer back to this contrast with the immortal עשה שלום במרומיו - *He Who made peace in His high places* [*Leviathan* operates in both sea and sky], and use it to justify God's apportioning of power on earth.

Line 18c also has God as the subject:

לא־יפנה דרך כרמים

and is merely another way of saying that He neglects His duties towards His people: *He does not visit vineyards*, with *vineyards* a reference within the chapter to v.6, where the poor are condemned to glean the after-growth of the vineyard of "the wicked" when God, according to Job, expects them to be satisfied with the food resources of the desert. Job in his reproach against God, not satisfied with accusing Him of indifference, now adds the accusation of wilful ignorance. He cannot bother to inspect the evidence. This reference should be seen as confirmatory that line 18b refers to the poor, not the criminals.

But we should see here also a reference outside the chapter to, e.g. Isa 5:1-7, the Song of the Vineyard, culminating in *For the vineyard of the Lord of hosts is the House of Israel, and the men of Judah the plant of his delight*, and Jer 12:7-10, which shows the image persisting through the years as a recurrent symbol of Israel and metaphor for its people as seen through the eyes of the Lord.

The complete sense is that the Lord does not turn aside from His cosmic concerns to pay due attention to the plight of His people. The intransigent phrase יפנה דרך emerges as entirely appropriate.

If this is correct, then there should be little doubt that the subject of יכיר is also God, whose acquaintance with the terrors of the Shadow of Death derives from His battle with the Sea and the Sea-monster, to which reference is made again in 38:8-11 (*Yam*) and in 40:32 (*Leviathan*). The "sandwich" form of the tristich, v.18, with the central line as it were suspended as an anacoluthon between two related verses, is common in the Book of Job, see especially 26:14 below.

In the next verse, 19, there seems to be the most direct reason to suppose that the whole section does relate to sinners, if not to criminals. This, incidentally, is an important distinction, for the word חטא, when it means "to sin", is never used of such serious crimes against man as are listed in vv.14-16. It usually refers to transgressions against God, but where human offences are involved, they seem to amount to little more than being at fault to a fellow man, to having done something requiring confession and perhaps restitution.

ציה גם־חם יגזלו מימי־שלג שאול חטאו

The laconic שאול חטאו has invariably (with one brave exception[15]) been regarded as a verbless sentence, borrowing גזל, "snatch away" from the previous line, with the Underworld as the subject and with חטאו performing the role of noun-object, "the sinners" or "those who sin". There are two compelling reasons why this version cannot be.

חטאו is 3rd person plural perfect indicative of the verb חטא, occurring in just this form in Job 1:5 and 8:4. It is neither a noun nor a participle, and cannot suitably be construed as such[15]. Also the verb יגזלו is masculine plural in form, and cannot rightfully be "borrowed" to service a sentence with a feminine singular subject (שאול).

In the Book of Job the passage to שאול is invariably expressed without a preposition between the verb of motion and the destination

(שאול יורד: 7:9; שאול תרדנה: 17:16; and most specifically שאול יחתו 21:13). שאול חטאו is cognate with each of these, but is an intended contrast or antithetical parallel to the last, with which it displays conspicuous assonance. Many commentators from D on have noted the contrast between this passage and parts of Chapter 21 describing the fate of "the wicked", but none has referred to this specific antithesis.

The sense "to sin" is neither the only, nor the primary meaning of the word חטא. The fundamental meaning is "to miss the way," "to go astray," from which the concept of sinning is derived. This sense is unquestionable in Job 5:24. *He who hastens with his feet goes astray* (Prov 9:12) well illustrates this use. Very simply we may translate שאול חטאו *They stray into Sheol* - they wander there in an aimless fashion, an accidental fate in sharp contrast with the directional שאול יחתו, *They descend to Sheol* in 21:13, implying in due process and due time. They here is the same entity whose portion in the land is accursed, the only other genuine plural in the passage, the same souls in torment as those of v.12.

The first line of this verse has its own fascination *Drought and also heat consume the snow-waters* is first of all an image drawn from the desert, and so relates specifically to those driven into the desert, of whom Job has already said that God considers this an adequate environment for them. The desert is their bread (ערבה לו לחם לנערים, v.5c); now comes the consideration of their water. Other aspects of the line are of interest - the word גזל, by no means the expected word in such an image, is used here for the third time in the chapter. Their flocks are seized; their fatherless children snatched from the breast; and now their water is stolen by the inanimate agents of God, drought and heat. Are we to ignore the fact that Job's flocks and children were seized and slain before he personally was placed in peril? Not only are Job's sympathies evident in this, but his very identity is inextricably interwoven with that of the unfortunates of Chapter 24.

Line 19a is not, as often assumed, a simile; nor is it a parallel. It is a condition. When the climatic stringency becomes extreme, with the coincidence of drought and heat, these people, depending on unreliable sources both of food (bread) and water (snow-water, not river or cistern), simply perish. The whole is designed to reflect the insignificance, both in reality and in God's eyes, of these victims of an injustice which He Himself sanctions. God alone is responsible for drought and heat.

We are not entitled to overlook either, even if we cannot account for it satisfactorily, the similarity between this description and the vignette of Job's "brothers" in 6:15-20, with its discussion of streams and snow and ice and those who were "snuffed out" in the (his, ?His) heat.

Verse 20 is the first in which the collective is treated as singular, and for this too there is a reason. The first two lines, coming immediately after the record of the trivial death of the victims read:

The "womb" forgets him; the worm מתקו him;
He is no longer remembered.

While difficult to decipher in detail, there is no doubt as to their drift - he disappears totally from the earth and all remembrance of him vanishes. Perhaps we should revocalize רחם to give a proper parallel: *When the vulture is done with one, the worm enjoys him*, or perhaps רחם here is an allusion all the way back to 1:21 where the earth itself is figured as the womb (but there it was בטן). There is surely an intended contrast between מתקו רמה and מתקו־לו רגבי־נחל of 21:33; perhaps the victim is sweet to the worm, while the earth itself is sweet to the wicked coming to it when a long and prosperous life has made it a welcome resting place, but our understanding of the verb is too deficient for certainty. The connection between the two uses of this rare word is pointed by the use of the masculine form with the feminine subject, רמה.

The reason for the use of the singular in the couplet is that, of the singular worm and vulture, each is responsible for the forgetting or consuming of only one of the victims. To say the worm feeds sweetly on <u>them</u> is making altogether too much of a feast!

Injustice is broken like a tree, the third line of v.20, a somewhat clumsy image, has a dual message. The injustice of the death of the victims is obliterated with the rapid disappearance of all trace of them, but it is obliterated like a broken tree - in reality eternally resurgent,

> *Though there is hope for the tree,*
> *If it be cut down, that it will again renew*
> *And its shoots not cease.*
> *If its root grow old in the earth*
> *And in the dust its trunk die,*
> *At the scent of water it will bud*
> *And put forth boughs like a sapling* (14:7-9).

The water, whose lack finished off the victims, revives injustice (the tree) by its very scent. We are doubtless also expected to remember in this connection that *men lie down to rise no more* (14:12).

We now have for these verses:

> 17   *For as one to them are the morning and the shadow of Death*
>   *But well He knows the terrors of the shadow of Death.*
> 18   *Swift was He on the face of water*
>   *Their portion is accursed in the land -*
>   *He does not turn aside to visit vineyards!*

> 19   *When both drought and heat consume the snow-waters*
>   *They stray into Sheol.*
> 20   *Mother-earth forgets each one, the worm edulcorates him;*
>   *He is no more remembered,*
>   *And injustice is smashed like a tree.*

Verses 21-24

The next section begins with the Janus-like word רעה. This has the primary, and by far the more common meaning, *to care for, to feed tenderly*, and secondarily the opposite sense, *to devour* (v.2). If we accept that the discussion of the *rebels against the Light* ended in v.17, there is no justification for ascribing the secondary meaning here, and we should read *He tended...* or, perhaps better, following the form in Gen 49:24, *He Who tended...*

Part 2

There is little doubt that the principal subject of vv. 21-24 is God, Whose behaviour is more and more being revealed as the passionate preoccupation of the chapter. It is surely He Who *is aroused and trusts not the living*, Whose *eyes are upon their ways*, and Who ‫אישׁ‬ - *is gone* (not *They are gone* which is ‫אינם‬, and in any case absurd when followed by their being *brought low*). With this understanding the passage runs quite easily and logically, with the final figure of a brief flowering and a speedy culling following desertion by God being a restatement of 12:23 *He increased the nations and destroyed them; Spread the nations abroad and then abandoned them.*

The passage proceeds:

---

21   *He Who tended the barren who bore not*
      And the widow whom none rejoiced,
22   *And dragged down the mighty in his prime,*
      Is aroused, and He trusts not the living.
23   *One may give Him His due for security, and rest easy,*
      But His eyes are upon their ways.
24   *When they rise up a little, He is gone;*
      And they are brought low, like all men. They retract
      And are lopped off, like a head of corn.

Again the alternation of singular and plural is deliberate and purposeful. It is one man, Job (whoever he stands for), who has paid His due to God, and thought he might rest securely (cf. 12:4-6), but it is the nation upon whose ways the eyes of God are fixed.

The idea of the *arousal* of God was implicit in the reference to His days at the beginning of the chapter. In this sad and beautiful conclusion to Chapter 24, Job recalls the compassionate God he once thought he knew, and shows his bewilderment at the turn of events which cut off the Jewish state in full stride (and cut him down in the allegorical parallel). Of especial interest is the juxtaposition of the two apparently contradictory statements - *He is aroused* and *He is gone*. The contradiction is only apparent, for *He is gone* means that He has severed the intimate relationship between Him and His people (Deut 31:18), a complaint made earlier in this speech (23:8,9), while *He is aroused* shows Him in His daemonic aspect, judging the whole earth.

The chapter ends with these final words of defiance, which

reveal unquestionably that what Job has been saying has been in contradiction, not of what he himself has said previously, but of the theses of the comforters:

> 25   *And if it is not so, then who will give me the lie*
>   *And reduce my words to nought?*

With this reinterpretation of the entire second half of the chapter, from v.13 to v. 24, we observe that all reason for disqualifying it from Job's mouth, or for tampering with it in any way, has disappeared. It is not the exemplary fate of the wicked, but the melancholy fate of the poor that the speaker is describing, and this is a topic appropriate only to Job, who is now in a mood to arraign divine injustice wherever he thinks he perceives it.

2. Chapter 25

Bildad's speech is so short that we may quote it in full:

> *It is His to decide who should rule and who tremble[16],*
> *His, Who made peace in His high places.*
> *Is there any limit to His armies?*
> *And upon whom does His light not shine?*
> *How then can man be justified with God?*
> *And how shall he be acquitted that is born of woman?*
> *If He drapes the moon that it shine not*
> *And the stars are not bright in His eyes,*
> *How much less man, the worm!*
> *And mankind, a maggot!*

The assault on this speech has been based entirely on its brevity[17], and emendations suggested have consisted of the addition to it of large portions either of Chapter 24[18], or of the following Chapter 26[19]. It is appropriate to quote D&G's assessment[20] for it underlines that there is no ground in the speech itself for suspecting its completeness, but that suspicions depend only on the characters of the adjacent speeches.

> *In the brevity of Bildad's speech and the absence of the attribution of any third speech to Sophar, it has frequently been held that the poet provided a formal indication that the friends had exhausted their arguments and thrown up the case. This explanation might be more favourably entertained if everything else in 22-27 containing the third cycle of speeches were in order; but this is not so.*

Bildad's speech has two components. The first two verses take up Job's challenge to prove him a liar. The first line asserts that it is God's prerogative to decide who shall be "on top" and who underneath - Job's protests against the current ordering of society are illegitimate. The second line refers to the subjugation of God's celestial rivals recorded mainly in Akkadian mythology, but also fully integrated into the Book of Job[21]. The implication is that God has proved His statecraft in a harder school than earth, justifying His assumption of the power specified in the first line.

The second verse is intended as a refutation of the plea, implicit throughout Chap. 24, explicit in 24:13b,c, that if the poor have neglected to "follow the Light", it is because they have had no opportunity. The opportunity is universal, declares Bildad. God's Light (=Sun) rises on all, and His troops (? = stars or angels) are numberless. No-one has the excuse of ignorance. The addition to this section of the bulk of Chap. 26, as for instance G proposes, would merely dilute this argument with a large number of "facts" about God which are irrelevant to the point Bildad seeks to make.

The last three verses are, as innumerable commentators have remarked, a paraphrastic amalgamation of Eliphaz's statements in 4:17-19 and 15:14-16[22]. That is first, they are quite unoriginal, and second, they recapitulate the opening argument of the comforters' case. These two considerations add considerable weight to the contention, referred to by D&G, that the brevity of this speech and the absence of Zophar's are indications of the exhaustion of the friends' case. The fact that Bildad's speech ends with a quotation, indeed a quotation of a quotation, is, as we shall see, of great importance to the understanding of Job's response to it, while the fact that Chapter 26 does open with a riposte to each of the two sections of Bildad's speech as it now stands in the MT makes it scarcely feasible to do as P recommends, and attach the bulk of Chapter 26 after these verses. However, as the attack on the integrity of Chap. 25 has always been predicated on errors of attribution in Chaps. 24 and/or 26, its defence must in the end rest on the establishment of their authenticity.

3. Chapter 26

Chapter 26 has always puzzled readers because, rather like Chapter 28, no matter where positioned or to whom attributed, the bulk of it (vv. 5-14), apparently a hymn of praise to God, has no realistic connection or relevance to the book. Attribution to Job seems at first sight the least likely of all possibilities.

The opening two verses clearly do belong to Job, for they consist of generalised abuse of Bildad as one whose friendship, help and counsel are worthless. This seems a reaction to Bildad's dismissal of Job's excuses for the ignorance of the poor - an angry accusation of lack of charity. Likewise there is no reason to doubt that v.4 *With whose help did you utter your words? And whose spirit (נשמת־מי) issued from you?* is spoken by Job, as a contemptuous charge of unoriginality, apparently of plagiarism of the words of Eliphaz.

Many commentators simply pass this verse by, but D remarked more that 100 years ago that Bildad is using the words of Eliphaz here, and therefore read the second stich as a sneer at this plagiarism. D&G contradict this and claim that Job is telling Bildad he had God's help in speaking, but this seems pietistic, pointless, and out of place. The true point of the verse lies one step beyond D's insight. When Eliphaz delivered this message for the first time in 4:17-19, he claimed that it was told to him by a spirit (רוח) which visited him in the middle of the night (4:12-16). Now, when Bildad delivers the same message, Job is asking him, in the nastiest way, which spirit dictated the message to him! Job did not appreciate this message - that all men are sinners in God's eyes - the first time he heard it. Now he is truly enraged at having it forced upon him for the third time.

With this understanding we are able to approach the intriguing v.5 from a novel angle of vision. It reads:

הרפאים יחללו   מתחת מים ושכניהם

This is always read: *The shades writhe under the waters and their inhabitants*, which contradicts everything that is recorded about the state of the shades of the dead in Sheol in Middle Eastern literature, and seems supremely disconnected from anything within a hundred miles of the Book of Job. It is somehow usually interpreted as honouring God!

Whether the initial ה is correctly the definite article (avoided where possible in Hebrew verse, especially in Job, and even in prose not used with רפאים), or properly a mark of interrogation, it is impossible to be certain. The question form found in LXX makes the intention even clearer, but there is little to choose between sarcastic question and sarcastic assertion. In this verse again a crucial word has been consistently mistranslated. יחוללו is the always passive Po'lal form of the verb חול, and means on this and every occasion where it is employed in the Bible (including Job 15:7) *They were brought forth*. It would be hard to find a clearer example of translators giving precedence to interpretation over accuracy than this, as attested by D&G when they declare that *to be brought forth* is *not a suitable sense*, a rare example of scholars rejecting the concordant evidence of MT and LXX. The meanings *writhe, tremble* are legitimate for the Qal and the active Po'lel, but neither Po'lal nor Hophal means anything other than essentially "to be born". Thus the meaning of the verse, if affirmative, is:

> *The shades have been brought forth*
> *From under the waters and their denizens*

Alternatively, it asks if this is so. There is no difficulty in interpretation. Job is answering (or extending) his own question as to the identity of Bildad's spirit-prompter. He must have been (or was he?) one of the shades of the dead, released from the Underworld to "help" this hapless victim of Job's irony. But "released" is not quite what this diabolical author has in mind! Nor is it the true meaning of יחוללו which, in connection with the dead, is a first-class paradox.

The next verse seems to follow innocently and logically:

> *Sheol is naked before him*
> *And Abaddon uncovered!*

Before Bildad, not God, for so far it is apparent that the speech is all about Bildad and not at all about God, and that, by corollary, it is most certainly spoken by Job himself. The verse is based on Prov 15:11.

This is: שאול ואבדון נגד יהוה - *Sheol and Abaddon are before the Lord - How much more then the hearts of mankind?* Job 26:6 is ערום שאול נגדו ואין כסות לאבדון. As always, it is upon the difference that we must concentrate if we are to find out the last nuance of meaning. The Underworld is *before the Lord*, but it is *naked before* Bildad. Abaddon is *before the Lord*, but it is *uncovered* to Bildad. These are very strange metaphors for the accessibility of places, or of knowledge about them. They are in fact sexual images, and joined to יחוללו of the preceding verse they suggest that Bildad has actually engendered the spirits who have been born of the Underworld and Abaddon, and delivered from under (מתחת) the waters. This veiled accusation of mental necrophilia must be designed to make Bildad regret his *lese majeste* in accepting Job's rash invitation to anyone to prove him a liar.

From v.7 to v.13, the speaker seems to be recording the principal accomplishments of the Deity, each verse emphasising that "he" did this, or "his" rebuke, power, understanding, spirit, hand, as the active agent. Most significantly, God is mentioned nowhere in this section. It is of course possible to argue stubbornly that nevertheless these verses are about God, even though we cannot know why or by whom they are spoken, and this stand will perhaps lead to the retention of the conviction of disorder in the text, even though vv. 5 & 6 have now been accounted for satisfactorily. It is equally possible to argue that Job's sarcasm continues to soar to ever greater heights, and that he is lampooning Bildad's pretensions as he himself was lampooned when asked if he was *born before the hills* (15:7), and as he is yet to be lampooned by God Himself with *You know, because you were born then, and the number of your days is vast!* (38:21), and a dozen brutal and unanswerable questions. Such certainly seems to be one of the techniques of this debate, so that it is probable that Job is jeering that if the man is like God in that the secrets of the Underworld are open to him, then he must be like God in his powers and accomplishments! Job's venom at his friends' falsity is finally gushing forth in this chapter like pus from a lanced carbuncle. At last Job loses his temper.

The author has provided us with an adjudicator for this dispute, the final verse 14:

> *If these be but the fringes of his ways*
> *And what a whisper of a word was heard of him!*
> *Who, then, will understand the thunder of his might?*

The middle line betrays the secret, for in describing his night-message, Eliphaz used these words:

> *Now a word was secretly brought to me*
> *And my ear received a whisper thereof.*

With Eliphaz's message re-presented to the reader's attention, there should be no doubt that the *whisper of a word*, שמץ דבר, is an intentional reference to the דבר...שמץ מנהו of 4:12. By this time Bildad and his spirit counsellor have become hopelessly intertwined in Job's diatribe. The Book of Job is woven together by gossamer threads linking the chapters, and this is one of them. The word שמץ occurs nowhere else in the Bible.

There is thus every probability that the whole of Chapter 26 has been correctly ascribed to Job in MT, QT and LXX.

4. Chapter 27

Contrary to the practice found elsewhere in the Dialogue, this chapter, although following without interruption another speech attributed to Job, has a fresh formal introduction, *And Job resumed (יסף) his parable, and said:* The form of this introduction differs from all preceding chapter introductions which are in the uniform style, *And Job answered and said:*. This feature has frequently been taken as indicating that there is indeed a missing speech between Job's undoubted 26:4 and this chapter. But far from accounting for it, that hypothesis leaves the departure from uniform style unexplained. It would indeed be fair to state dogmatically that, were we confronting the disordered fragments of what was once a regular third cycle of speeches, and if the beginning of Chap. 27 were the beginning of Job's final speech in reply to Zophar in that cycle, then the introduction to Chap. 27 has to be in the uniform style of all "cycle speech" introductions, and the existing form of the introduction is incompatible with the third cycle hypothesis. That is, unless one chooses to make the assumption that the introduction has been altered by a redactor so incompetent that he has made confusion worse confounded.

It is possible to account for the present form of the introduction as follows: Instead of thinking in terms of a "third cycle" it seems proper to consider the entire section from Chap. 23 on as an interrupted monologue. The variation in style of the introduction to Chap. 27 should be taken as an intended clue to the monologuic nature of the post-second cycle speeches. In this analysis, Job and the author consider the friends' case to be concluded at the end of Chap. 22, which is Eliphaz's final summing up. Chaps. 23 to 31 are one long monologue by Job, his "parable" (מֹשֵׁל), interrupted by Bildad's brief and unoriginal speech of Chap. 25, and the furious response (Chap. 26) which this elicited from Job. Looked at in this way, the variant form of the introduction does not at all suggest that a speech has dropped out.

The first five verses (2-6) of Chap. 27, a magnificent oath of moral independence, are incontestably Job's. They assert righteousness, no longer out of fear of God, but despite Him. These verses may well be considered a landmark in the history of ideas, the development of moral philosophy.

> *Until I die, I shall not doff my integrity from me.*
> *To my righteousness I cling, and never let it go.*
> *My heart shall not reproach me all the days of my life.*

The remainder of the chapter has been treated in various ways by modern scholars, but almost all have agreed in assigning a large part of it to the "lost speech of Zophar." The problem which has worried all commentators is the close resemblance between the later part of the speech and the propositions advanced by the comforters about the fate of the wicked throughout the second cycle. They have taken the view that these sentiments are quite inappropriate for Job.

In what follows I shall seek to demonstrate that only Job could have spoken these words. There are two sections. The first, vv. 7-10, opens with the sentence: *Let my enemy be as the wicked and him who rises me up against me as the unjust.* This is a firm denial of the accusation (22:15-20) that Job is in sympathy with the wicked. Job may believe that the wicked control their own earthly destinies (21:16), but it was an unjust and untrue deduction from this that he envied or sympathised with them. A is probably also correct in seeing it as a reference to the custom whereby a false accuser was made to suffer the penalty for the offence with which he had charged the accused.

The remainder of the section is devoted to the explanation of why Job has no wish to associate himself with the fate of the wicked, but wishes it on his enemies instead. This is essentially because the wicked man lives in a state of alienation from God and cannot call upon Him and expect an answer when in trouble, as Job always has done and still does (12:4b).

> *Will God hear his cry*
> *When trouble comes to him?*
> *Will he have pleasure in the Almighty?*
> *And call upon God for all seasons?*

So 27:9,10.

Therefore, and only for this reason, the profit of wickedness is not worth the loss. This is nothing like what the friends have been saying. Job puts forward a spiritual reason for virtue while they advance practical ones. Job's reason follows logically and directly from the opening fanfare of the chapter. He will maintain his integrity, he will not commit sin, for thereby he would forfeit the right to accuse God, to appeal to God, even at this late stage to expect recognition from God. *The ungodly cannot come before Him* (13:16). In the certitude of his rectitude Job can and does call upon God *for all seasons* (בכל־עת), even from the pit of despair into which that same God has cast him. There is no real difficulty in accepting Job as the speaker of this section. Indeed far greater problems are caused by the assumption that it is spoken by any of the friends.

It is the second section, commencing at v.11 and dealing with the fate of the wicked at the hand of God, which has caused the greatest trouble. The first impression it gives is that Job is merely repeating what the comforters themselves have been saying *ad nauseam* on this subject, even to the extent of an almost *verbatim* quotation of Zophar's last words (20:29) near the start of the section (27:13). If we are to be made to accept that what follows is authentically Job's, it is necessary that two propositions be demonstrated - that the description does not materially contradict anything else that Job has said, and that it does materially conflict with the descriptions of the same phenomenon by Eliphaz, Bildad, and Zophar. Certainly the introduction to the section, if read straightforwardly, threatens an all-out contradiction of the comforters' thesis, and the repetition of Zophar's last words, with the emphasis shifted, reinforces this promise:

> *Let me teach you (pl.) what is in God's hand.*
> *What is with the Almighty I shall not conceal.*
> *Behold you all have witnessed it*
> *Why then do you vainly mouth vanity?*
> *This is the portion of the wicked man with God,*
> *The heritage of tyrants, which they receive from the Almighty.*
>
> 27:11-13

Plainly "this" in v.13 means "this (penalty) and not what you have said", and by extension, "this and only this". The singular "me" and the plural "you" show beyond doubt that this is Job speaking to his friends, so that if we cannot accept the remainder of the chapter as Job's rival version of the fate of the wicked, we must postulate (as G actually does) yet another lost section of this insupportable "Third Cycle" which does contain that version.

The subsequent verses make only two points:

(a) vv. 14-18: that the posterity of the wicked will not profit from his depredations, but rather will suffer to the point of ultimate extinction.

(b) vv. 19-23: that ultimately the wicked man will die suddenly and in terror.

The first of these points Job has never contested; his concern has always been for the punishment of the wicked to be meted out in their own lifetimes, and this, he has claimed, does not happen (21:13, 17-18, 30-31). A justice postponed is no justice in his eyes.

The second point is new, and at first sight seems to conflict with 21:13, 22-26 and 32 in all of which Job seems to be describing the easy and honoured death of the wicked. Let us examine these more closely.

21:13 reads: יבלו בטוב ימיהם וברגע שאול יחתו. *They spend their days in prosperity, and on a sudden go down to Sheol.* Many translators, from LXX to H contrive to read ברגע as *in tranquillity* or similar, and indeed this adds to the suggestion of formal parallel in the verse, but the meaning of the word is not to be found elsewhere. The words for "tranquillity" deriving from the root גרע are מלגוע and בלגע, like כלגע, is most simply read as "in a moment", its literal translation, so that it is most likely that it was the suddenness of his death that Job was admiring, not its ease. If his death is accompanied by terror, it is only momentary, and it did not serve Job's purpose to mention it before. לילה (27:20, cf. 34:25) expresses this same suddenness, but now fully accompanied by terror. The ideal Biblical death is not sudden, but indeed tranquil (e.g. Gen. 48,49).

21:22-26 is a description of the fate of the רמים, the eminent men of their generation, not of the wicked (see p. 283ff below). The two men described, one who lives well and dies easily, the other who dies *in bitterness of soul* after a life of hardship, are to be understood as equals in vice and virtue, subject to random destiny, and thus useless as didactic examples.

21:32 gives only an external picture of the funeral of the wicked, conducted with pomp and respect, in accordance with the principle well marked by all men, that the sins of the wicked are blotted out by death. There is nothing here to deny the agony and terror of his last moments, of his abandonment *in extremis* by God.

Job thus merely seems to be setting the record straight by asserting that the death of the wicked is not to be envied.

In what way does this version differ from that of the friends? Why does he describe their dissertations on the subject of the wicked as הבל - *vanity* (21:34 as well as 27:12)? The descriptions of the wicked are contained mainly in the three speeches of the second cycle.

In Chap 15, Eliphaz paints the direst picture of misery and fear in which the wicked are destined to wallow, as the people they have plundered hound them into poverty, isolation and despair.

In Chapter 18, Bildad describes how horror and terror dog the brute's footsteps, with the earth conspiring against him.

In Chapter 20, Zophar depicts the vengeance of man and God pursuing him to a violent end in battle.

Add to these 4:8, 5:2-7, 8:11-15, and 11:20, lines from earlier speeches of the friends, and we find that they seek to overwhelm Job with the impression that the wicked suffer for their crimes during their own lifetimes. This is the הבל which Job so despises and resents, a sentimental view of life at odds with all experience, especially his own.

There is nothing to envy in the life, or the death, of the wicked, but reality must not be denied, the true penalty must be understood, and Job's own case must be sharply distinguished from that of the wicked. The penalty for a life of evil is the loss of something infinitely more precious than any that has yet been taken from Job - the right, reserved for upright men (13:16, 23:7, 27:9) to approach God, the certainty of continuity through the ages for his posterity, and the embrace of death as a friend.

The speech, I believe, can only be Job's, and while the method of argumentation is not as clear and explicit as a modern writer would have made it (he would have said "This and only this..."), it follows a clear logic and makes the same sharp point - this and this alone is how

God punishes evil men, and the rest of what you have said on the subject is eyewash!

Another reason may be adduced to show that the MT is correct in attributing Chapter 27 in its entirety to Job. Despite its limitless originality, the Book of Job is not by any means composed in a void. It is tied to the rest of the Hebrew Bible by innumerable quotations, allusions and references. This is very much the case with Chapter 27, which is intimately related to the so-called Job-Psalm, No.73[23]. This Psalm is a beautiful and epoch-making meditation by one who, like Job, had endured great suffering and who, like Job, came close to the conclusion that wickedness was better rewarded than virtue.

> *Surely in vain have I cleansed my heart*
> *And washed my hands in innocence;*
> *For all the day I have plagued,*
> *And my chastisement came every morning.*
>
>   Ps 73:13,14

Unlike Job, this sufferer kept silent about his feelings, saying that if he spoke out he would have been *faithless to the generation of Thy children* (v.15). He finally came to exactly the same conclusion as that given in these last verses of Chap. 27 of Job:

> *Panic makes him ebb, like the flood.*
> *One night a tempest will steal him away.*
> *A wind from the east will carry him off and he depart,*
> *And it will whirl him away from his home.*
> *He will hurl it at him without stint.*
> *He will fly, fleeing from its power.*
> *He will clap His hands at him*
> *And hiss him off the stage.*

Psalm 73:17-19 is:

> *Until I entered the sanctuary of God*
> *And considered their end.*
> *Surely Thou settest them in slippery places;*
> *Thou hurlest them down in utter ruin.*
> *How are they become a desolation in a moment!*
> *They are wholly consumed by terrors.*

In the Psalm the avoidance of the agnoy of death in a state of alienation from God more than compensates for all the material advantages of an evil life. This is exactly the same statement that is to be found more vividly in Chap. 27 of the Book of Job. This coincidence of views between the speaker of Chap. 27 and one whose situation was similar to Job's and whose earlier train of thought had run parallel to his, lends the strongest support to the contention that Job is the speaker of the entire chapter.

5. *The Architecture of the Dialogue*

The final aspect of this "Third-Cycle" problem which must be addressed is that of the actual composition of the two cycles which have, presumably, been properly preserved. If we judge entirely by the chapter divisions of the modern Hebrew Bible, there seems every reason to accept the conventional view of the structure, that the Job speech-cycle contains six speeches. Chapter divisions are, however, a late imposition on the original text. In QT, except for blank lines between Chaps. 26 and 27 and Chaps. 31 and 32, and blank spaces between Chaps. 19 and 20 and lines 40:5 and 6, there is no sign of such divisions. Unfortunately all of QT earlier than Chap. 17 has been lost. It is a simple deduction that where a change of speakers occurs there is intended something like a chapter division, but under all other circumstances it seem likely that the judgement of one "editor" is responsible for the existing state of the text in this regard.

If we examine the first two cycles from a thematic point of view, we find that, while Job veers from theme to theme within each cycle, the two companions of Eliphaz merely repeat the respective themes of Eliphaz's speeches in each of the two cycles. Thus in Chaps.

4 & 5 Eliphaz discusses the inevitable association between suffering and
sin, the universal tendency of all mankind to sin, the reciprocity
between the mercy and the justice functions of God, and the efficacy
of repentance if only Job would undertake it. In Chap. 8, Bildad
appeals to Job to make repentance in confidence that he will be
restored if he does so, points out the inevitable association between sin
and suffering, and renews the appeal to repent. Zophar tells Job that
he must be guilty, that man cannot penetrate the secrets of God but
that God knows when men have sinned, and then adds his appeal to
Job to repent and turn to God for forgiveness, promising in his turn
Job's restoration.

In the second cycle Eliphaz from 15:17 onwards describes the
terrible state in which the wicked is condemned to live (see Chap. 4
above), while in Chaps. 18 and 20 Bildad and Zophar do no more than
repeat this description in their own words. Thematically, each of the
two cycles is hermetically distinct, but the first half of Chapter 15
disturbs this neat arrangement, being wholly related to the themes of
the first cycle, reproaching Job for his reactions to the comfort which
has been offered to him, and winding up by repeating in fresh words
the "dream message" of Chapter 4.

From this, it seems that the best way of regarding Chap. 15 is
that it comprises two distinct speeches, vv. 2-16 and vv. 17-35. In this
regard v.17 has all the hallmarks of an opening salvo rather than a part
of any continuity: *I shall declare to you! Hear me! And let me relate
what I have seen:*

If then we take Chapter 15 as a dual speech, half related to the
first cycle and half to the second, we discover a speech cycle of the
form E:J:B:J:Z:J:E, which must then assign to Chapter 22 the role of
Eliphaz's final address in the second cycle, and not that of the opening
of the third. What Eliphaz actually does in Chapter 22 is first to bring
out into the open the hidden elements of the second cycle; that is he
boldly accuses Job of the sins of the wicked - tyranny over a nation,
and then, returning to the dominant feature of the first cycle, he again
appeals to him to repent and promises him God's mercy if he does so.
Thus Chap. 22 serves not only as a conclusion for the second cycle,
but a conclusion to the entire case of the three comforters.

There is nothing in Chapter 22 which resembles either Bildad's
Chapter 25 or any of those parts of Job's speeches in Chaps. 24, 26 and
27 which have at various times been suspected of belonging to the
comforters' speeches in a Third Cycle. That is to say, it is impossible

to construct from any extant material a Third Cycle which is thematically consistent in the way that the first and second cycles are. This being the case, it appears that each cycle consists of seven speeches, beginning and ending with Eliphaz, and that there is nothing left of Chapters 22-27 to justify the long- and widely-held theory of a third cycle of speeches.

Each separate item of the case for a mangled "Third Cycle" of the Book of Job can be countered, and the transmitted text and its attributions justified. There is no disorder in the last exchange between Job and his friends, no missing speech, and no "Third Cycle". The probable plan of the debate is an introduction by Job, two cycles of speeches each opened and closed by Eliphaz, in which each of the other friends speaks once and Job replies to each of the three separately. Thereafter Job begins a monologue which is interrupted briefly by Bildad, and then by Job himself angrily retorting to the interruption. The monologue then resumes, modulating in Chap. 29 into a soliloquy which continues until we read in 31:40:

The words of Job are ended.

Notes Chapter IX

1. B. Kennicott *Remarks on Select Passages of the Old Testament, 1787,* pp.169-70.
2. See D&G pp.xxxviii - xl.
3. p. 208
4. For example, G, T-S, H, Hartley, etc.
5. J.G.E. Hoffman, *Hiob, 1891.*
6. T. Heath, *An Essay Towards a New English Version of the Book of Job, 1756*
7. *Annals of Sennacherib* Pritchard, p.288.
8. Pritchard, pp.441-444.
9. There are two Biblical references to God's protecting His favourites from the sight of His vengeance: II Kings 22:20, Hulda the prophetess to Josiah, and Isaiah 57:1. See pp.99.
24:1 is מדוע משדי לא־נצפנו עתימם דיעיו לא־חזו ימיו, but there is the disjunctive accent Dehi on משדי, suggesting a pause after "Why?" *The times are not hidden from the Almighty* is an incontestable proposition. *Why are the times not hidden from the Almighty?* is indefensible. *Why are the times not laid up* or *reserved by the Almighty?* is difficult to understand, and leads to uncharacteristic calls for Job to have the pleasure of witnessing His judgement executed. Such an introduction to the chapter is in complete contradiction of its contents.
10. Gesenius #144 f,g. Translating these as passive obviates any necessity for supplying imaginary subjects for them. The common resource of providing an impersonal subject is not satisfactory as the "they" who are doing these things cannot be characterless, and are therefore not truly impersonal.
11. The Hebrew is וירעו which is usually taken to mean *and they pasture them.* Some commentators maintain that this makes sense in the context (e.g. H) but I am unable to accept it. This is a recital of the injuries done to the subjects of the chapter, and the feeding of their stolen flocks is out of these bounds. This secondary meaning of ורעיו is usually wrongly assumed for 24:21.
12. *They are*: AV, P, NJPSV; *Those are*: D&G; *Some there are* : NEB; *These are*: JPS; *The evildoers rebel*: G.
13. BJ p.265, etc.
14. The verb קלל is to be *light* in any of several ways, but the adjective קל, found twelve times apart from this passage, never means anything but *swift*. In Jer 3:9 where the meaning seems to be lightness of moral character, the word functions not as an adjective but a noun. The reading *He is flotsam (*or perhaps better, *foam) on the face of the waters* is very attractive, particularly if the subject is taken to be the poor who *stray* aimlessly into Sheol in the next verse. But such a solution infringes the consistency of number most grievously, as well as invoking a wholly novel sense for קל.
15. Bernard, p.218 is the exception. He translates *They glide down to the grave*, but no explanation is given for the exotic *glide*. The interpretation which he gives is that this is a figure for the ease of the death of the sinner.
J. Emerton (pers. comm.) draws my attention to Gesenius #155n as a possible authority for taking the verb as functioning nominally, but none of the examples there is so stark as this.

16. ‫המשל ופחד עמו‬. Usually rendered *Dominion and fear are with Him*, but ‫ המשל‬is properly the conferring of dominion as in Ps 8:7, so that this seems to be the meaning. The non-causative reading leaves the statement purposeless in the context. Also it surely cannot be right to accept a causative sense for "fear" and reject the same for the Hiph`il-derived "dominion". Although the intensive sense is supported by the Lexicons, there is no good reason for making this exception. Indeed all that is achieved is to sever Chap. 25 from the theme of the preceding chapter which deals, *inter alia*, with social hierarchy. T-S "corrects" the word to the Hiph`il participle to yield much the same sense as this version.

17. G, BGM, p.96; P, p.xx; D&G, quoted in text below, etc.

18. Hoffman *op. cit.*

19. Credit for this suggestion seems to belong to A. Elzas *The Book of Job, 1872* p.83. An unusual proposal of Stuhlman (*1804*) is the addition of Chapter 28 to Bildad's speech.

20. P, xxxviii.

21. Cf. the various references to *Leviathan, Rahab, Yam*, etc. A.S.Peake, *The Century Bible: Job, 1904*, may have been the first to connect this line with the mythical battle between Marduk and Tiamat. See especially, however, 24:18.

22. *Shall man be more just than God?*
   The creature more pure than its Maker? etc. 4:17-19
and
   What is man that he should be clean?
   And he that is born of woman that he should be right? 15:14-16.

23. The expression is Gunkel's (quoted in O.S. Rankin, *Israel's Wisdom Literature*, Schoken Books, NY, *1969*, p.148).

X
Elihu's Last Words

Biblical poets are not always meticulous in observing the jingle-warning of the Victorian moralist:

> If you your lips would keep from slips
> These things observe with care:
> Of whom you speak; to whom you speak;
> And how, and when, and where.

That is to say that they do not always make clear who are the referents of pronouns used as subjects, objects or owners, datives or ablatives, or of those Hebrew verbs which incorporate their own subjects within their forms. What is more, many of them have a habit of changing these referents in the midst of a sentence or a passage, sometimes leaving the reader to follow a path rather like a ski slalom. The alternation of singulars and plurals in Job 24:15-20 (v.s. Chap. IX) has exactly this effect, and has led many scholars to conclude that the author simply disregarded number altogether! The most attentive student of a text may become lost as the poet modulates from one subject to another without notice.

Such problems are particularly numerous in the Book of Job in which there are many sections in which the subject of discussion is unspecified, and where the context allows of more than one solution, and some of these are crucial to the understanding of the work as a whole.

There is an ever-present danger that an unidentified referent, one which is not spelled out beyond ambiguity by text or context, will become a misidentified referent, to the almost irreparable confusion and distortion of the text. The following chapter is an analysis of one such accident.

הודיענו מה־נאמר לו!
לא נערך מפני־חשך

This *cri de coeur* must be one of the outstanding examples of a misidentified referent in the Hebrew Bible. I know of no speculation by any commentator as to to whom this call is addressed nor who might be the "him" of לו other than the assertion by T-S that the verse refers to "it" - the darkness - against which Job's friends are incapable of composing spells! All others have automatically assumed that Elihu in this verse 37:19 is demanding from Job instruction in how to address God, although many, seeing the extraordinary incongruity of this idea, have assumed the question to be deeply sarcastic. H and G embrace this resource with enthusiasm.

It is not difficult to see that the verse:

Reveal to us what we should say to him!
We cannot order our speech because of (or compete with) the
                                                                      darkness

can hardly be a straight request by Elihu to Job for advice on how to address God. There is no occasion for him or any of the three comforters to address Him, and still less for Job to wish them to do so, or to seek their help in his suit with God as is sometimes assumed. Job has in 13:7-12 warned them of what will happen to them if they attempt to draw His attention to themselves. Not only for this reason is Job the last person on earth to whom they would turn for advice in such an enterprise - Job whose *own mouth condemns him*, (15:6) who *reels off words without thinking* (35:16), who *talks without sense and whose words are without discernment* (34:35), and who *follows the way of the wicked* (22:15; 34:36). Every word which Job has addressed to God has sent shivers down the spines of all four of them.

Were the verse "ironic" (G) or "deeply sarcastic" (H) it would constitute a betrayal of Elihu's promises in 32:14 and 33:7 that he would not address Job in the way that the friends have done and that his "pressure" would not be heavy on him. But more important than this is the fact that the idea of a sarcastic appeal at this point does not dovetail with any other aspect either of Elihu's strategy towards Job, or that of the friends, nor is it a comprehensible riposte to any pronouncement by Job.

If we look at the ways in which the Hiph'il of the verb ידע is employed elsewhere in the Book of Job, and elsewhere in the Bible as a whole, we shall also find no support for this interpetation. להודיע is literally to "make known" which is very much the same as to "reveal". There are two classic examples of this use, in Job 10:2 and 13:23, where Job asks God to reveal to him *wherefore You contend with me* and *my transgression and my sin*. The expression אשאלך והודיעני is used twice by the Lord, in 38:3 and 40:7, and quoted by Job in 42:4. *I will ask you and you reveal to Me* is indeed brutally sarcastic, but as such it fits perfectly into the strategy of the Lord's speech to Job which repeatedly seeks to suggest that Job aspires to usurp God's roles. Revelation is supremely one of God's prerogatives. The inaccurate translations "you <u>answer</u> Me", "<u>tell</u> Me", "<u>declare to</u> Me" for הוֹדִיעֵנִי[1] blunt the point of this barb. When God asks a man for revelation, sarcasm has reached its uttermost.

The word is also used in 26:3 by Job sarcastically when he tells Bildad how well he has *revealed sound wisdom* to the masses, and by Elihu in a neutral way when he refers to his lost belief that the task of revealing wisdom was appropriate only to the aged. In this context it is often translated "teach" (cf. its use in Proverbs, v.i.).

The incongruity between the Biblical use of this word and the assumptions made about its use in 37:19 is most acutely exposed when we look at the sixty-two other examples of the Hiph`il throughout the Bible where the word is used in a very restricted way. Forty-two of the sixty-two uses refer to <u>revelations</u> by God[2], by one of His prophets, or by priests (in one case revelations by priests and diviners of the Philistines to those seeking their advice). Five relate to the <u>instruction</u> of children by parents (of the deeds and demands of God) and three to the <u>revelation</u> of God's doings by Israel to the other nations. Two have essentially *no-one* as the subject, being used in rhetorical questions asking who revealed anything to God. In one there is revelation of the Law through the Torah, and in one <u>disclosure</u> by the Psalmist of his sin to God (Ps 33:5) [this is unique in that it does involve providing information from man to God but it is information privately held by the man]. Four are in the Book of Proverbs of which three are <u>teachings</u> by the Proverbialist or by Wisdom and one <u>teaching</u> the righteous. In one, King David fails to <u>disclose</u> to the Prophet Nathan who is to succeed him. Two of the three remaining uses are somewhat eccentric or doubtful. Gideon <u>teaches</u> the elders of Succoth with switches cut from the forest, a humorous use of the word, and in II Chron 23:13 the musicians perhaps <u>display</u> - make heard rather than make known - the praises of God. Only once is the word used in a wholly secular way, in I Sam 14:12, where men of the garrison offer to <u>show</u> Jonathan something.

In no case at all is there the suggestion of making known something as yet speculative. All sixty-two uses relate to the transmission of an established truth or principle or historical fact or body of knowledge. Even in the case of Gideon, the Judge was <u>revealing</u> to the men of Succoth the truth - who was boss! *Make known to us what we should say to Him* would therefore be an unprecedented way of using the word, for in reality it asks for an opinion.

If we are to bring this sentence into harmony with the established meaning of the word, and with the general context of the Book of Job, and, as we shall see, the local context of its own chapter, we must re-orient it so that it reads as a request to <u>God</u> for information about what should be said to <u>Job</u> rather than *vice versa - Reveal to us the truth of the matter so that we can pass it on to Job!*

This is of course the burning question which troubles Elihu - how to get through to Job, how to persuade him to save himself from the inevitable consequences of his obduracy. But, so great is Job's loss, suffering and grief that all their arguments have failed to penetrate. They cannot find an approach which is commensurate with Job's <u>darkness</u> (15:23; 17:12; 19:8; 20:26; 22:11; 23:17; 30:26). לא נערך is a strange expression, but in the light of the use of the verb elsewhere in Job, it is probable that its sense is *We cannot compose our speech* as is generally understood. *We cannot equal - we cannot match the darkness* are also possibilities.

An address to God at this point in Elihu's speech is plausible and does not materialise out of thin air. Chapter 37 is largely devoted to a description of a thunder-storm which is actually taking place at the time the speech is delivered, and which will be the whirlwind from which the Lord will speak in Chapter 38. Here is the thunder:

שמעו שמוע ברגז קלו   והגה מפיו יצא

Hearken well to the turmoil of His voice
and the roar that issues from His mouth! 37:2

Elihu uses the gathering storm as subject of a series of homilies to Job on the power and care of the Lord. He hears God in the storm, and a few verses later the Lord speaks out of the storm (38:1). It is natural therefore that Elihu should seek to address the apparition of which he has become aware, and appeal to Him for help in what has come to be understood by all four of Job's interlocutors as an impossible task.

There is another good reason why we should be prepared to consider that this part of the speech is addressed not to Job but to the Deity. Try as one may, it is impossible to extract a reasonably coherent sense from the remainder of Chapter 37 on the assumption that it is addressed to Job. It can readily be appreciated that the two following versions, both very recent, have achieved only the most partial and dim sense, the most fragmented continuity, and have achieved even these at the cost of numerous sacrifices of the accuracy of translation of Hebrew words and phrases.

19 *Educate us in what we should say to Him*
    We cannot prepare a case in the dark.

20 *Can He be informed when I would press charges?*
    Does a mortal testify when confused?

21 *Now, one cannot look at the sun,*
    Brilliant in the clouds,
    When the wind rises and clears them away.

22 *From the North the gold appears*;*
    Around Eloah the splendor is awesome.

23 *Shaddai - we cannot reach Him!*
    Great in His might and justice
    Mighty in His righteousness -
    He does not answer!

24 *Therefore mortals fear Him;*
    But even the wise of heart cannot see Him. H.

* Note: in the N. hemisphere the sun is never in the North.

19 *Inform us, then, what we may say to Him;*
    We cannot argue because [we are in] darkness.

20 *Is anything conveyed to Him when I speak?*
    Can a man say anything when he is confused?

21 *Now, then, one cannot see the sun,*
    Though it be bright in the heavens,
    Until the wind comes and clears them [of clouds].

22 *By the north wind the golden rays emerge;*
    The splendor about God is awesome.

23 *Shaddai - we cannot attain to Him;*
    He is great in power and justice
    And abundant in righteousness; He does not torment.

24 *Therefore, men are in awe of Him*
    Whom none of the wise can perceive. NJPSV

Let us, however, examine these verses on the assumption that they are addressed to God.

היספר־לו כי אדבר   אם־אמר איש כי יבלע?

The Pu'al of ספר means to be related or recounted, not told, so that all those versions which depend on the verb to imply the simple communication of a single fact to God are not faithful to the real meaning of the word. G has pointed out that there seems to be a parallel in the verse between כי אדבר and אם אמר, and that כי...אם form a pair of particles. This is indeed true, but the function of this pair is to introduce conditions of which that or those with אם is/are more specific than that with כי[3]. Read in this way, the verse comes to mean:

> *Will it be explained to him if I speak out?*
> *If a man says that he is nonplussed?*[4]

There are in fact three possible ways of reading the line, each assuming a different referent for the nondescript word איש, and there are good logical reasons to support each one of them. The logic of the verse itself supports the idea that איש refers to Elihu himself and the meaning is as given above. The logic of the associations of the word לבע in the Book of Job favours Job as the referent of איש, and the meaning *If man* (or *a man) says he has been destroyed*, while the logic of the following couple of verses suggests that perhaps איש here means simply "men" in general - *If people are saying that he has been destroyed*.

In this verse Elihu is asking God if, provided he, Elihu, joins his pleas to Job's, God will appear to give Job his answer. It is here that we find the essential function of Elihu in the Book of Job, as the second witness to summon God to trial:

One witness shall not rise up against a man for any iniquity, or for any sin, in any sin that he sinneth; at the mouth of two witnesses, or at the mouth of three witnesses, shall a matter be established. Deut 19:15.

The progressive dynamic of Elihu's address to God cannot be understood beyond this point without a correct understanding of the

force of the first word of the next verse, 21, וְעַתָּה. This innocent-look-
ing word is simply translated throughout the Bible as "And now; but
now; so now; now therefore," and presents no problems of comprehension at all. These meanings do not seem to apply so simply either
here or in Job 35:15, for in both cases the word occurs in the course
of indirect speech. There are therefore the two possibilities - that עַתָּה
belongs to the quoted speech, or that it is being used as an introduction to a later section of the quoted speech - *He said this, and now (he
says) this* or *and then (he said) that* (See p.33f).

There is some similarity to the use of the word in Isa 43:1 and
49:5. In Job 35:15, although this line is not generally followed, by far
the most probable solution is achieved by taking *And now* as the
introduction to a fresh quotation, viz.

13. *Surely God does not listen to vanity*
    Nor does the Almighty regard it.
14. *How much less when you say you cannot perceive Him,*
    The case is before Him and you will summon Him forth!
15. *And now that His anger punishes no-one*
    And that He takes no note of great iniquity.

followed by the comment on the quoted words - *But Job opens his
mouth in vain, and reels off words without thinking.* In the above, the
presence of כִּי, *that,* after עַתָּה really leaves little choice, as also the fact
that 35:15 is an obvious reference to Job's thesis in Chapter 21, with
15a referring directly to 21:17. Likewise, 14a refers to Chapter 23 and
14b to 16:19ff. Nonetheless this reading is often vigorously opposed
(e.g. by G). Dhorme translates more or less in this way. P copies.

In 37:21 there is no כִּי, but otherwise the situations seem very
similar. However 20b is to be read, it is apparent that יְבֻלָּע is what אִישׁ
said and that it is therefore open to us to proceed with "and then
(that)" and expect what follows to be a further statement which may
have been made in the past or might be made in the future, and could
influence whether God would relate matters to Job. 21a is לֹא־רָאוּ אוֹר
- literally *They do not see (the) light* but also quite possibly *The light is
not seen,* which may be taken both as an explanation of why "we
cannot order our speech because of the darkness", and also why Elihu
or another אִישׁ is confused.

This word light is more than ambiguous. It may be the simple
opposite of literal or figurative darkness - that is it may mean

straightforward *illumination*, or *understanding*, or, in one way that darkness was used in v.19, *salvation*, as we might speak of *light at the end of the tunnel*. In Chapter 24, in what is generally referred to as the "rebels against the light" passage, light stands both for the light of day and for *law* and *right behaviour*, for *God's will* and almost for *God Himself*. In 25:2 these meanings are punned with the *sun*. Although אור is several times used for "lightning" in the Book of Job, this sense is not applicable here.

It is more likely than not that here a double meaning is intended for the word, one sense being the sun, as the immediately following reference to skies implies. I suggest that the second meaning is very closely associated with God - His values, His ways, all that those who followed Him stood for.

The plural ראו, unless איש is taken as plural in sense[5], is quite without a trace of plural subject, and therefore must be regarded as passive[6]. If we are to follow the assumptions above, the figurative meaning of this line must be that, because of the *darkness* which has been inflicted upon Job, men in general have lost sight of the advantages of virtue - that is of God's way, the light. This same sentiment has been expressed by Job twice, but in each case has been generally misunderstood. This is in 17:8,9 in the passage commencing *Upright men are astonished at this*[7], and in 12:4-6 where Job demonstrates that following the path of virtue and trusting God has made him a laughing-stock to God's adherents (friends)[8].

If we follow the consensus and regard בהיר in the next line בהיר הוא בשחקים as meaning, as in modern Hebrew, *bright*, we encounter a prodigious contradiction if we also take the tense of this noun clause to be the present, and הוא to be an anomalously masculine pronoun for אור. The view, advanced vigorously by G that men cannot see the sun after a wind has cleared away the storm-clouds (line c) because it is too bright in the skies is very ingenious, but totally unconvincing. On the other hand, NJPSV makes excellent sense with *One cannot see the sun, though it be bright in the heavens, Until the wind comes and clears them (of clouds)*, but is untrue to the Hebrew text. *Waw* never means "until", and "though" and a subjunctive cannot be supplied *ad libitum*.

Considering the structure of this sentence, the tense of the noun clause is the past. The following line commences with a waw so we should accept that whatever is described in the first line is antecedent to it. The noun clause implies a state of affairs, and the active verb in the perfect tense in the following line represents an event. The invisibility of the "light" in 21a has to be explained in lines b and c, and the statement that a wind cleared the sky [שְׁחָקִים] (of clouds), apart from posing an etymological absurdity (שְׁחָקִים, always in the Book of Job *skies*, originated as an undifferentiated cloud-cover) is the exact opposite of what is required to explain it.

Let us look at where this leads us: the light was bright in the skies *But a wind passed by and purified them*; purified them, that is, of the light which is now not to be seen. If we take the light as representing God, then we have indeed here a vigorous statement designed to bring Him to his own defence, particularly if we interpret this *wind* as the same as that wind which blew down the house of Job's children at their feasting - the Assyrian invader[9]. As a quotation of what people are saying as a result of God's destruction of His own people, this makes excellent sense. Nonetheless, there are several things wrong with it.

One is the masculine pronoun. אוֹר is a feminine noun, and the masculine word with this spelling means <u>fire</u> (and, if QT is to be trusted, occurs at least twice in the Book of Job[10]). The second is the word וַתְּטַהֲרֵם. This verb occurs no fewer than 88 times in the Bible, most frequently in Leviticus where it relates to *ritual* purity and purification, diet, and rules relating to infections. It may also refer (as classified in BDB) to *ceremonial*, or *moral* purity. The Pi`el, which is the form here includes *ceremonial* and *moral* purification, but also according to BDB *physical* cleansing, of which the examples found in the Bible are the purification of metals from dross; of the land from corpses; the Temple from unclean things; the land and city from Asherim and images; the Temple from household stuff, and of the priesthood by the exclusion of alien blood.

With the exception of the single late example (Mal 3:3) where the purification of the sons of Levi is likened to the extraction of gold and silver from dross, all examples of what BDB terms *physical* cleansing or purification are in fact related to ritual purity or uncleanness in some way. There is no single example in the Bible of this word being used for the sort of secular cleaning which is implicit in the blowing away of clouds from the skies, or even in the expulsion of a bright vision. The word is exclusively concerned with purity, and not at all with cleanliness.

Taking these two anomalies together, and furthermore examining the form of the word בָּהִיר, which is that of a *qatil* noun, I conclude that בָּהִיר is no adjective, but a masculine noun. The word

בהיר is unique to this passage, but there is the feminine form בארת
which, in Lev 13 and 14, is a skin lesion which may be either טהר or
טמא, *pure* or *impure*. While the custom has developed of understanding
this to mean a "bright spot" in the skin, the fact that it is sometimes
כהה, "dull" (Lev 13:6, 21, 26, 28, 39) is hardly compatible. Likewise, the
variety of colours which such a spot may have indicates that its
meaning is probably simply a discoloration, or more likely just a
blotch. G, in describing the word, wrote of its being "an instance of
addad, 'a word of like and opposite meaning.' The root means 'shine,
be bright' in Arabic and Ethiopic (with metathesis) and 'be obscure,
dark' in Syriac." This is perhaps the only example of a figure of speech
which requires two languages at once to illustrate it!

הוא in this sentence is *God*, not the feminine אור, so that "light"
comes to mean God as well as His ways. Elihu is thus suggesting that
what is being said is that God Himself is no longer detectable; He was
once a בהיר in the heavens, and we cannot be sure whether this was a
luminary or a *blemish*, but the Assyrian assault swept by and purified
them (of Him). In examining the next verse, 37:22, we are obliged to
keep in mind certain norms and rules of word-order in Hebrew, for
the usual understanding of this verse accepts a serious double violation
of those rules. The verse is:

מצפון זהב יאתה   אל־אלוה נורא הוד

and a typical translation will run, incomprehensibly oriented: *Out of
the north comes gold(en splendour); About God is terrible majesty.*

The Hebrew expression נורא הוד is grammatically shocking, for
Hebrew, like French, places the adjective (and the participle used
adjectivally) *after* the noun, with only rare and special exceptions[11].
Here נורא is Niphal participle and הוד noun, and the only legitimate
way of combining them is in the expression הוד נורא. Almost equally
ungraceful, if not downright prohibited, is זהב יאתה, where the placing
of the subject before the verb sounds wrong even in English, a
language where this is the normal sequence. It is, however, to be
conceded that the extant accentuation favours these readings.

There is an entirely different way of reading this verse which
avoids both of these improbable infringements of Biblical practice and
at the same time reinforces Elihu's argument to God that His
destruction of Job coupled with His failure to explain it is leading to
the defection of His followers.

There is an expression associated with the use of the word arwn in connection with God which is to be found in both Psalm 96:4 and Psalm 89:8. At the beginning of an exultant song of praise in Ps 96 is נורא הוא על־כל־אלהים *He is more terrible than any of the gods*, and Ps 89 על־כל־סביביו *More dread than all about Him*[12]. Taking the hint of these expressions, we may read על־אלוה נורא as *More terrible than God,* and conjecture that the reason for the inversion was that נולא על־אלוה is almost unpronouncable because of the succession of glottal stops.

In the first stich we may well read bhz צפון, as a construct phrase, *Zaphon of gold*, the site of the *gold* and C dwelling place of Baal[13]. Note that the North (צפון) is the direction from which the Assyrian invasion, as indeed almost all invasions, of Israel came. The verse emerges as:

> *From Zaphon of gold there comes*
> *A majesty more awesome than God!*

and is a statement, like those of Isa 37:8ff, well-calculated to arouse the jealousy of the God of Israel. The well-judged addition of "of gold" to צפון invokes the pagan god under whose banner the invading army marches. A valid alternative for stich a is "From the north there comes gold" - i.e. the product of the process of purification, but again the Assyrian monarch, *A majesty more awesome than God!*

Then the final scornful verses, still what Elihu attributes to those who are gossiping about Job:

23 שדי לא־מצאנהו שגיא־כח   ומשפט ורב־צדקה לא יענה

24 לכן יראוהו אנשים   לא יראה כל־חכמי־לב

Verse 23 is syntactically convoluted. Usually the phrase לא־מצאנהו is regarded as an *anacoluthon*, but it is hard to imagine Elihu, or any of the three comforters whom he associates with himself in the "we", who have been expressing their certainty about God and His ways throughout the debate, suddenly saying that they cannot find, or reach, or understand Him. This is particularly so if v.22 has already been translated, as it usually has, to describe the splendid appearance of God in the skies. It is therefore far more likely that *Shaddai* in this sentence is *pendens*, and the sense is something like this:

> *The Almighty, we have not found Him great in strength*
> *And justice and great righteousness, nor that He does not oppress.*

It is to be noted that the Pi`el יענה cannot accept *Justice and great righteousness* as its objects. Throughout the Bible this verb, meaning "oppress", is used only with human victims, as in every other language. The traditional readings of this line *Right and Justice He perverteth not* (D) or *to judgement and plenteous righteousness He doeth no violence* (JPS) are either untrue to the meaning of the verb, or nonsense.

In fact, of all the verses in the Book of Job, none seems a better candidate for correction than this which, if read without vowels emerges very simply with no complex figures of speech thus:

> *The Almighty is no more powerful than His flock,*
> *And does not respond to justice and great righteousness.*

which is precisely, in both dimensions of the book, what Elihu is required to say at this point - politically, that the failure of God to defend Israel and Judah against the Assyrians shows Him incapable in terms of power, and morally, that His abandonment of Job the man shows Him indifferent to right and wrong.

The following verse casts a very clear light on this one, for it reads:

> *That is why men have feared Him;*
> *He paid no attention to any of the wise at heart*

The "that is why" carries the intention that what follows (if anything) will be a recapitulation of what came before, while *He pays no attention to any that are wise at heart* is much the same as *He does not respond to justice and righteousness*. This means that He does not distinguish between Job and the wicked. This concluding statement seems a reinforcement of the proposition that God makes no distinction between right and wrong (24:17 [see Chap. IX]; 9:22). There is a play on the word "fear" which has the special sense when applied to God in addition to its common sense of terror. To be God-fearing is essentially the same as to be *wise of heart* (cf. 28:28; & Pr 9:10 *The fear of the Lord is the beginning of wisdom*.). This final verse should be accepted as confirming that the whole passage from v. 20b to 24 is indeed an attempt to convince God of the urgency of His explaining His actions to Job, the Jewish people, and the world at large.

Notes Chapter X

1. *Answer* Me: LXX, Vg, AV, NEB, etc.
Tell/inform Me: D, P, G, H, etc.
Declare to Me: RV, D&G, T-S, etc.
2. In one of these, Dan 8:19, the speech is attributed to the Angel Gabriel.
3. Gesenius, #159bb.
4. That is to say, *confused*, the common sense of the Pi`el of בלע, especially as employed by Isaiah. For this use of the Pu`al, see Isa 9:15. In Job the Pi`el is twice employed to describe what God has done to Job, once in 2:3 by the Lord, and once in 10:8 by Job. In these the meaning is surely *destroy*.
5. As in Deut 27:14, etc.
6. Gesenius #144f,g.
7. See Chapter XI, Misidentified Referents.
8. See Chapter XI, Misidentified Referents.
9. See Introduction, p.72.
10. 24:13 and 37:11.
11. Gesenius #132a.
12. It is likely that the author of Job had Ps 89 particularly in mind, for 37:23, the next verse, seems designed as a refutation of Ps 89:14,15:

Thine is an arm with might;
Strong is Thy hand and exalted is Thy right hand.
Righteousness and justice are the foundations of Thy throne;
Mercy and truth go before Thee.

---

13. The building of Baal's house, in Pritchard 131-135.

XI
Misidentified Referents

In Chapters 15, 24, 26 and 37, and elsewhere in the Book of Job, we have already encountered a number of passages where the failure correctly to identify the referents of pronouns has led to vast confusion in interpreting the text. In this chapter I propose to deal with a number of additional examples of the same flaw, in most of which the consequences for the understanding of the book have again been far-reaching.

1. The Views of the Righteous

17:8,9 is one of a number of short passages in the Book of Job where, as traditionally understood, the second part seems to contradict the first. In the preceding three verses Job has been describing what God has been doing to him (see below, p. 278ff), and he now states:

יִשֹׁמּוּ יְשָׁרִים עַל־זֹאת   וְנָקִי עַל־חָנֵף יִתְעֹרָר
וְיֹאחֵז צַדִּיק דַּרְכּוֹ   וּטֳהָר־יָדַיִם יֹסִיף אֹמֶץ

The first of these four stichoi is straightforward and asserts that *Upright men are astonished at this*. That is to say, they are taken aback at the sight of a righteous man (and/or God's own people) suffering so dreadfully. The זֹאת is the same as in 12:9 and 19:26 - Job's trials. This line, like 12:4ff (v. p. 288ff) plays the theme that God is destroying His reputation with His own party by what He is doing to Job. We should expect it to be followed by a report of the defection of God's friends, of righteous men, from their adherence to Him.

The second stich, however, has always been understood as follows: *And the guiltless is aroused against the godless*, which is not so much a *non sequitur* as a rebuttal[1]. If we have understood the first stich as recording an undesirable effect of Job's discomfiture, how can we accept that the second reverses this and shows a highly desirable, if unaccountable, effect? Unaccountable, for how should Job's downfall arouse the guiltless against the godless rather than against either God or Job? Taking any other passage in the book in which Job describes the reactions of his erstwhile friends (19:14-19 for example), we shall encounter a report opposite to this one. A closer look must remind us that התערר elsewhere never means "to be aroused", at least not in this sense. While it may mean to "awaken" (reflexly) [Isa 51:17], in its only other use in the Book of Job (31:29) it means "to *exult*" or "*triumph*".

There is therefore a different meaning altogether possible for this line. If we take the verb of the first stich to be governing the second also, and the על in the second stich to be performing the same function as in the first[2], the line means:

> *And the guiltless, that the heathen triumphs*

and all contradiction of sense has disappeared.

The next verse is usually taken as maintaining the contradiction introduced by the above line, on Job's lips self-defeating, for he surely cannot wish to show what stirling effects his own downfall has had on other righteous men. So we find usually *The righteous holds to his way, and the clean of hands gains strength.*[3] Apart from its perverse sense, there is one important anomaly in this version of this verse also. אחז does not mean to hold tightly to something already grasped, but to take tight hold of something. The word for maintaining a tenacious grip is לחזיק (2:3,9; 8:15,20; 27:6). אחז is frequent in Job with its standard meaning (see 16:12; 18:9; 18:20; 21:6; 26:9; 30:16; 38:13). 23:11 alone is equivocal. See esp. n. to 18:20, p.407. The righteous therefore is not clinging to his own ways, he is seizing upon a new way - that of the heathen in the preceding line. Likewise the טהר־ידים of the next stich is not gaining in strength but, by becoming a recruit to his party, increasing the strength of the heathen; the pronominal suffix of דרכו serves also for אמץ.

Now all four sentences join in harmony to demonstrate how God is alienating His own followers by His public disgrace of Job. In v.10 Job exempts his friends as too stupid to comprehend who has wronged whom in the affair. Verses 11 and 12 confirm Job's intention, for they declare that when he is dead, all this will come to an end. For this reason *My conclusions*[4] *Turn night into day. The light is near by very reason of the darkness!*

> *Upright men are appalled at this*
> *And the guiltless, that the heathen triumphs,*
> *So that the righteous embraces his ways*
> *And the pure of hands reinforces his strength*
>
> 17:8,9

is answered by Eliphaz in 22:19,20 where, in flat contradiction of exactly these sentiments in relation to the prosperity of the wicked, he declares:

> *Righteous men look on and jeer,*
> *And an innocent man would deride them*:*
> *`Surely our enemy is gone to Perdition,*
> *And the fire will consume their remnant!'*

* Cf Ps. 2:4

In 18:20 Bildad also refers to this passage with *Those in the West will be appalled at his fate (עֲל־יוֹמוֹ), and in the East they will be seized with horror* (אָחֲזוּ שָֽׂעַר). יֹמוֹ stands in for זֹאת and שָׂעַר for the way which the righteous seizes. This has to be the way of the heathen, not of the righteous.

2. Whose Children? (1)

Principal part of that loveliest of Hebrew names, Hepzibah, the root חפץ has not fared well in the Book of Job. In Chapter 40 (v.s. Chap. V) it is constrained to adopt alien meanings "bend" or "stiffen", while in Chapter 21 there has been a perennial tendency to strip it of its intrinsic sense of "delight", and substitute a neutral or anxious "care" or "interest". The reason for this is that its context has suffered distortion, again through the misidentification of a crucial referent, so that the true meaning of מַה־חֶפְצוֹ בְּבֵיתוֹ אַחֲרָיו? no longer seems appropriate. But the attractive sense of חפץ is so undeniable that it is imperative that we seek and find that context which justifies the only possible translation of the line,

> *What is his pleasure in his House after him?*

The trouble starts in earnest only with 21:19:

אלוה יצפון לבניו אונו   ישלם עליו וידע

Job has been complaining that God does not punish the wicked (רשעים), or at any rate not with any consistency -

> *How often is the lamp of the wicked put out*
> *That their deserts come upon them?*

a rhetorical question demanding the answer *Not often!*, and then this v.19. The great majority of scholars has understood this as a statement, attributed by Job to his friends, that God visits the sins of the <u>wicked</u> upon *their* sons, and this despite a serious disagreement of number, for the *wicked* have been treated as plural in the preceding two verses, and this verse unquestionably speaks of *his* sons. We have encountered such a severe clash of number before in Chap. 24 and found that the best solution by far was achieved by accepting the integrity of the text. The interpretation which is obligatory if we do this here is that בניו means *God's own children* - His people. (See also 17:5, immediately below).

The word אונו, with its underlying implication of reproductive vigour, hints at this. It does not mean exactly "punishment", but "iniquity", "sorrow" or "strength". In this case, linked to the word יצפן, it is surely His strength (though certainly His punishing strength) which God <u>reserves</u> for His own, rather than the wicked man's sins which God stores up for his children. The image is the obverse of that in Ps 31:20 טובך אשר־צפנת ליראיך - *Thy goodness which Thou hast laid up for them that fear Thee.* With this grammatically consistent reading, the remainder of the passage proceeds with no problem, and it is easy to recognize that Job is describing himself when he refers to one of God's בנים.

Taking 19a as referring to the children of the wicked puts an unbearable constraint on line 19b, which then must be treated as desiderative, as also verse 20; so we find such versions as:

> *You say,*
> *"God saves His punishment for his children"*
> *Let Him recompense <u>him</u>, that <u>he</u> may know it!*
> *Let his own eyes see his downfall,*
> *And he himself drink of the Almighty's wrath.*

In this accepted version, which treats 19a as a quotation of the friends' alleged statements (although there have been no such statements) the last verse 21 has to serve as a refutation of the idea that the *wicked* will be distressed by the dire fate in store for his posterity after his death. So the word חפץ cannot be allowed its true meaning. The sense demanded by this context is *distress*, or even *grief*, more or less the opposites of the true meaning, although most translators make do with the less extreme *what does he care about the fate of his house after him?*

It is important also to correct a wrong impression which the proponents of the traditional version repeatedly canvass. The idea that God reserves (i.e. postpones) the punishment due to the wicked for their children is in fact to be *Job's* statement of God's custom, and never the comforters' (27:14 which [v.s. Chapter IX] is spoken by Job). The burden of the comforters' thesis regarding the wicked, and hence of the quarrel between them and Job, is that, regardless of what will happen to their posterity, they themselves, in their lifetimes, will suffer to the full the devastating wrath of God (Chaps 15, 18, 20, etc.).

A faithful translation of this passage therefore will be:

> *God reserves His strength for His own children,*
> *When He gives one his quietus, he knows!*
> *His own eyes see his ruin*
> *As he drinks the wrath of the Almighty.*
> *For what pleasure does he have in his House after him*
> *When the tale of his time is told?*

In this version we note that חפצו in v.21 is restored to its correct meaning of "pleasure" or "delight", and that there is no longer the least temptation to regard v.19a as a hypothetical quotation of words which in fact none of Job's friends has uttered, nor to contort 19b and v.20

into jussives which the consonantal form of יִשְׁתֶּה (the jussive is יֵשְׁתְּ) decisively refutes. This verse has been the subject of some caustic comments in the Introduction.

The version above, which sees God's punishment (although this is not the word used) as reserved for His own (people) is an iteration of the authentic principle of the election of Israel:

> *You only have I known of all the families of the earth.*
> *Therefore will I visit upon you all your iniquities.*
>
>   (Amos 3:2)

Now the last verse becomes a refutation of the comfort which <u>has</u> been offered to Job in the promise of the restoration of his posterity (5:25, 8:19), that comfort being signified by the word חפץ. But what comfort is there, what delight, Job asks, in a posthumous reward?

3. Whose Children? (2)

In this next example, we again encounter the word בניו in a context which gives several good reasons for suspecting that God is the true referent of the possessive pronoun.

At the beginning of this chapter we dealt with verses 8 and 9 of Chapter 17, and noted that they referred to grievances of Job described earlier in the chapter. We shall now turn to verses 3-7 of that chapter, where, in miniature, we encounter as profound a misunderstanding of the text as anywhere in the Book of Job. Verse 3 is:

שׂימה נא ערבני עמך   מי־הוא לידי יתקע?

The verse is addressed to God and the first stich contains two pleas, using the imperative mood. שׂימה נא takes its object from the "pledge" which is an intrinsic part of the verb ערב. לשׂים אות is to display a sign. God's "pledge", like the rainbow, or the pledge given to Hezekiah is an אות, a sign. It would of course be very convenient to misread ערבני, the verbal imperative with suffix, for the noun ערבון with possessive, to achieve *Establish, I pray, my pledge with You!*, and many do just this. But not only is this contrary to the principles of translation upon which this book is built, but, as we have remarked in the Introduction (p.57), ערבני is a direct quotation from the words attributed to Hezeki-ah. "Give a pledge for me" he asked, and the shadow on the sundial retreated ten degrees. ערבני עמך means "Give (them) a pledge (for me) with You!" and as a request, receives its justification in the second line of the verse.

3b means essentially *No-one (else) will shake my hand*. To "strike hands" with someone is to conclude an agreement with him. Job asserts that no-one on earth will trust him (i.e. believe him), and therefore he asks God as it were to restore his credibility by some visible sign of confidence. Cf. Ps 86: 17 עשה עמי את לטובה! *Show me a sign for good, that those who hate me may see it and be confounded!*

From here ideas move at breakneck speed. 4a seems to explain why no-one will believe Job - *Because You hid their hearts from Understanding*. While this may seem an adequate explanation, it is not the one that Job really has in mind. Rather it is the consequences which God visited upon those whose hearts He hid from understan-ding which explain why none will believe Job - and it is here that the mischief of mistranslation and misinterpretation begins its work in earnest. 4b reads: על־כן לא תרומם

Therefore You did no exalting

The present tense *You do not exalt*, is equally effective.

This line has hitherto always been translated into the future tense - "You will not, cannot, dare not exalt (them)." (Sometimes varied unjustifiably by "they will not exalt You"). What is being said here is much the same as the burden of Chapter 24; that because the bulk of the population is ignorant (in Chap. 24 they knew nothing of the Light), God abandons them to their oppressors. Here He does not fulfil His promise to lift them above the nations around (in praise, renown and honour). The relevant reference is Deut 26:19 = 28:1. In the apparent injustice of God's punishing the people because He Himself hid their hearts from understanding, there is the same doctrinal paradox as when He hardened the heart of Pharaoh to refuse to allow the departure of the Children of Israel from Egypt, and then savagely oppressed the Egyptians for their intransigence. In the admission by Job that the people have lacked Understanding there is an important concession to the idea that God's oppression of the Jewish people may not have been חנם after all. These uncomprehending people are the *Behemoth* of Chapter 40.

There is a temptation to add a stage direction to vv. 5,6, 7 - "ASIDE", for it is exactly in the spirit of a stage "aside" that the specification of how God did not exalt is conceived. This is why there is no necessity for the mention of God, who is the subject of the verb in v.5. What follows is all Deuteronomic:

לחלק יגיד רעים

To a portion He said "(You are My) friends!"

חלק יהוה עמו *The portion of the Lord is His people* is Deut 32:9, and should be considered wherever חלק occurs in association with God. The usual ways of reading the word - "for a spoil" "a share (of reward, of a feast, etc)" or "to flattery" are all eccentric. Under normal circumstances the verb הגיד takes the preposition -ל for the party addressed, and so, if at all possible, we should accept here. What the sentence means in plain language is that He proclaimed friendship to His portion (the people of Israel). The suffix is to be borrowed from בניו in the second stich. The "saying" or "proclamation" contains within it <u>the intention to exalt.</u>

This reading of the line is quite impossible to accept without also accepting the national allegory of the Book of Job. Thus the universal view of v.5 is that it is a proverb with any one of half a dozen possible contingencies spelled out in the first stich whose result is the "failing" of the eyes of someone's children.[5] All of these, however, depend upon the word יגיד playing a part of speech to which it is not adapted. Thus the common form of this first line is:

<u>He who</u> *informs on/gives/invites/denounces (his) friends...*

assigning the role of a participle to the indicative verb. The paradigm of the proverb as a Hebrew literary form is to be found in the book of that name. In all, there are some 165 examples of the phrase "He who..." amongst these proverbs – that is to say occurring in proverbs of much the same form as is deduced for Job 17:5. With the exception of four, all of these employ the participle in preference to the active verb. Three of these exceptions have the same verb יפח (14:25, 19:5 =9) and feature the active verb in the second half of the proverb where no ambiguity is possible, while the fourth, מצא אשה מצא טוב (18:22), is made clear by its repetition. There is no proverb at all whose form parallels exactly that of Job 17:5. This should cast great doubt on that interpretation. Now after the promise of friendship comes the reality:

> But the eyes of His children fail

His children, בניו, as the people of Israel is Deut 32:5, while the whole is Deut 28:32, addressed to the Children of Israel: *Thy sons and thy daughters shall be given unto another people, and thine eyes shall look, and fail with longing for them all the day.*

Verse 6 opens with a waw. On the whole, however, it seems that almost all translators and commentators have elected not to notice it. Indeed, several have gone so far as to place a break in the text between verses 5 and 6 (NJPSV; C), while G even goes to the extent of placing verse 5 in quotation marks and verse 6 outside them. Amongst those versions which I have seen, only two, D and Kissane[5], acknowledge the existence of this conjunction, D by adding "And" in a quite meaningless fashion, and Kissane by recognizing that the subjects of verses 5 and 6 *must be the same.* Indeed there is but one possible explanation for this waw, other than the assumption that it has appeared out of nowhere with no meaning at all, and that is that it is *waw copulativum* and links v. 6 to v. 5 in this way.

Verse 6 exactly parallels the report of promise and betrayal of verse 5:

והציגני למשל עמים

is *not And He exhibited me as a byword to the peoples*, a contraction of Deut 28:37. The vocalization of משל, appropriately that of the noun in Deuteronomy, is here that of the infinitive construct of the Qal verb. The משל from which "proverb" derives, meaning "to resemble", is not found in the Qal, but in the Niphal, Hiph'il and Hitpa'el.

Few commentators bother to refer to this discrepancy, and in this they are abetted by the great Lexicon of BDB which allows the word so vocalized to mean "a by-word" in the construct case. But this does not conform with Hebrew language and usage. Most simply assume a corruption. This assumption, however, defies the principles enunciated in the introduction to this book, for there *is* an authentic

Qal verb למשל - *to rule* in which (as often the participle) the infinitive construct takes the genitive, here (cf. Ps 105:20), עמים[6].

The Qal verb משל has nothing to do with proverbs or bywords, and the only possible <u>literal</u> meaning is

---

And He set me to be a ruler of peoples

---

and the reference is now Deut 15:6 ומשלת בגוים רבים *And thou shalt rule over many nations (but they shall not rule over thee)*. This interpretation is only to be found in the mediaeval commentary attributed to Berechiah[7], who understood it only in a moral sense and did not allude to Deuteronomy. Again, as in 5a, we find a promise by God of the exaltation of the people of Israel. When Job says He designated <u>me</u> a ruler of nations, this <u>me</u> is not personal but collective, and he speaks as the Israelite nation.

With this line, as with so many in the Book of Job, the true solution remains unthinkable - is automatically rejected - until the idea is admitted that Job is not merely an individual man, but a symbol and surrogate of the nation.

Again in the second stich, the speaker reports on the reality, ותפת לפנים אהיה. This either means (NJPSV)

But I have become like Tophet[8] of old

---

or,

But I have become one in whose face they spit.

This latter is the version adopted by most, but there is no verb "to spit" from which תפת might be derived. Ibn Ezra suggested a <u>tabret</u> in the sense of a musical instrument used to drum up laughter or scorn for תפת but this, although accepted by AV, is far-fetched.

It is not far-fetched to see in this final stich 6b of the quatrain the reference to Deut 28:37 which we have denied to v.6a - *Thou shalt become an astonishment, a proverb, and a byword, among all the peoples whither the Lord shall lead thee away,* but if the reference is not to be detected here, it certainly is in 17:8 which picks up the word *astonishment,* שמה, from the Deuteronomy verse to give us ישמו ישרים על־זאת (see section 1 of this chapter above).

It is fascinating that the flavour of this passage resembles that in the Book of Jonah when the prophet found that his predictions, delivered to the inhabitants of Nineveh at God's behest, were not to be fulfilled. Here the speaker, whoever he is intended to represent, is complaining that his own credibility has been destroyed because God's promises have not been fulfilled. Obviously he is one who has backed these promises to the hilt and broadcast them to the nation and perhaps to the world. Nor is it difficult to imagine, looking in 700 B.C.E. through the eyes of a contemporary Jew at the wreckage of his nation for which so much was promised in Torah and by the prophets, that all this must have rung true in its pathos and pain.

4. God's Responsibilities

The next passage we shall consider is intimately linked to 21:17-21 (v.s.). It is the immediately following v.22:

הלאל ילמד־דעת   והוא רמים ישפוט?

What is the subject of ילמד in this verse? Indeed what is its grammatical structure?

Perhaps 22:2 will help: הלאל יסכן־גבר כי־יסכן עלימו משכיל?
But this too is full of ambiguous possibilities.

Then does 34:9 provide any assistance?:

.כי־אמר לא יסכן־גבר   ברצתו עם־אלהים

Here at last is a verse with an undoubted meaning - *For he said: "It does not profit a man to be in the good graces of God".* This may also be read *Man does not profit when...,* but the essence of the sentence is that it is man whose profit is being discussed here, not God.

If יסכן־גבר unquestionably has this meaning in 34:9, it is not at all legitimate to translate the same phrase in 22:2 in an opposite way. גבר, therefore is in logic if not in syntax the <u>object</u> of יסכן with the causative meaning *to benefit*. Therefore 22:2 cannot be read "Does a man profit God?" or similar, as most versions desire. Not, however, LXX which reads *Is it not the Lord who teaches understanding and knowledge?*, but this is certainly no correct translation of the verse. Very strangely, however, it is the identical translation which LXX gives to line a of 21:22, the sentence at the head of this section, although there can be no valid explanation for the introduction of the negative there. What LXX has done, however, is to assert boldly that יסכן־גבר and ילמד־דעת are more or less identical in meaning. This in fact is true in so far as "the teaching of wisdom" belongs in the category "the benefitting of man". Furthermore, we must read the LXX version as drawing our attention to the nature of 22:2 as a riposte to 21:22. However, by treating הלאל as though it were הלא לאל, LXX has fatally compromised its ability to make real sense of the interchange.

I propose to deduce backwards from 34:9 to 22:2, and thence to the key verse 21:22. Assuming that the recipient of benefit, notionally the predicate, in the phrase יסכן־גבר is גבר, (a) man, then הלאל in 22:2 cannot by any means embody any part of the predicate of the sentence, and must indeed be somehow related to the subject. The preposition ל, expressing the dative and movement towards, is also used ascriptively and possessively in Hebrew, as in שיר לדוד, "A song of (? by) David".

In 22:2 and 21:22, the introductory הלאל is compounded of the interrogative particle, the ל, and the name of God. The same word order is found in 13:7 *Is it for God that you speak unjustly*, but the full significance of this ל must be speculative. I suggest that the correct sense to be attributed to this compound word in Chaps. 21 and 22 is *Does it pertain to God?*, as one could well ask הלדוד השיר זה?, where the interrogative is correctly placed before the word about which the doubt exists. This gives us for 22:2:

Does it pertain to God that He be of benefit to man? or, more succinctly: *Is it God's obligation to profit man?*, followed by *On the grounds that a wise man profits Him?*

and for 21:22:

Does it pertain to God that He teach wisdom through His judgement of the eminent?, or, again more succinctly, *Is it God's aim (or duty) to teach...?* We are, I think, justified in translating this very non-specific preposition of appertainment by different words when it used by Eliphaz and by Job, for certainly their intentions are dia-metrically opposed. Eliphaz is excusing, where Job is accusing.

If now we follow what Job is saying in Chapter 21, we find that this interpretation makes a perfect fit, and illuminates a whole section of the chapter. In vv. 17-21 Job asserted that God does not punish the wicked, but exposes them to a random fate - He reserves all His punitive attention for His own people (v.s.). In vv. 23-26 he illustrates the fates of two different members of the class רמים, which we may interpret either as <u>eminent</u>, with neutral implications of vice and virtue, but implying those in the public eye - from whose fate conclusions are likely to be drawn - or as <u>proud</u> being some sort of equivalent for "sinful" or "wicked". One of these men lives and dies well, the other *dies with a bitter soul and has never tasted good. Alike they lie down in the dust and the worm covers them up* (a reference to Isa 14:11, the celebration of the death probably of Sennacherib).

I suggest then that the purpose of these two vignettes is the demonstration of the proposition that *in judging the eminent*, God teaches no lessons to mankind about the sort of behaviour He will reward or punish. One seems rewarded and one punished, but Job has nothing to say of any distinction between them. Job is refuting the thesis, as he does throughout this chapter, that a sticky end is a sign of wickedness, and a happy life and an easy death a sure indication of virtue. In 22:2, however, Eliphaz is sliding out of his untenable stance in the dispute by asserting that, because God has nothing to gain from a man's virtue, He therefore has no occasion to reward it, making a debating point while failing to defend his original thesis.

The general way of reading 21:22 is quite different, seeing both דעת and אל as objects of ילמד, the first direct and the second indirect. D relates the line to Isa 40:14 (מי למדהו דעת?) and so has some precedent for *Shall one teach God knowledge?* but his justification for the translation in the context of the chapter is unconvincing. All modern scholars seem to have followed him, but very unhappily. D&G comment that "in its present context the verse seems to defy explana-tion". It is of considerable interest that QT appears to support LXX (though without the negative). What has survived of 21:22a is *Is it for God...?*, and again we find that Berechiah follows this route, with *Is it for God to teach knowledge?*

The only satisfactory way out of the dilemma caused by the irrelevance of the question *Can any teach God knowledge?* is to accept, stripped of its negative, essentially the sense of LXX and to treat אל as the subject of ילמד.

In accordance with the principle of consistency, we should have expected the verbal relationship between 21:22 and 22:2 to reflect an organic or thematic relationship, and indeed this does exist. חלאל does have the characteristic of a reference used by one party to a debate against the other. For Eliphaz is contesting Job's implicit complaint in Chapter 21 that God does not use the opportunity provided by the existence of prominent men to teach moral lessons to mankind in general - by asserting that God has no obligation to confer benefits on mankind. This example of "quotation" of one speaker by another ramifies afar from here, for these two passages are both linked thematically to Elihu's use of the phrase יסכן־גבר in 34:9, and with the parallel expression יסכן־לך in 35:3. The former deals explicitly with the fate of man as did 21:22f, firmly contradicting Job with *For the works of man He requites to him, and He causes each to receive according to his way*, while the latter leads into an amplification of Eliphaz's contention in 22:2ff with *If you sin, what do you do to Him? And if your iniquities multiply, what have you wrought against Him? If you are righteous, what do you give Him? And what does He gain at your hand?*

Here the sequence of mini-quotations comes full circle back to Job who, in 7:20, asked plaintively of God, *Suppose I have sinned, What have I done to You? (חטאתי מה אפעל לך?)*. Elihu's words, אם־חטאת, מה תפעל־בו?, correspond precisely, and his continuation is the perfect logical "put-down" to Job's complaint - if your sin is of no concern to God, why should you expect your righteousness to be of such interest to Him? But it was Eliphaz, not Job who spoke 4:6b: *your hope, surely it is the integrity of your ways*.

5. *The Transfixed Gallbladder*

In their descriptions of the fate of "the wicked", there is no doubt that Job's friends engage in a certain amount of exaggeration, with literal fire and brimstone in Chapter 18, and the poison of asps and the viper's tongue and such-like delicacies being prepared for him in Chapter 20, but somehow the description of his mortal wounding in battle as generally understood for 20:25 does not ring true even as hyperbole. Perhaps this is because in for example the NJPSV translation, no fewer than twelve of the fourteen elements of the verse have been misrendered, leaving only two pronominal suffixes correct! Zophar is cursing the wicked man, and threatens him with God's vengeance in battle:

> Let him flee the iron shaft,
> The bow of brass will impale him! 20:24

and then: שלף ויצא מגוה וברק ממררתו *יהלך עליו אמים

* Aleppo Codex joins this word to the preceding line.

This is the NJPSV translation:

> Brandished and run through his body,
> The blade, through his gall,
> Strikes terror into him!

If, however, we translate the verse simply and literally, exactly as the Hebrew runs, we should obtain the following:

He draws (a sword)	שׁלף
and he departs	ויצא
from pride	מגוה
And a flash of lightning	וברק
from his bitterness	ממררתו
He goes forth.	יהלך
Upon him	עליו
Terrors!	אמים

There is little justification required for these renditions. These are all the accepted and normative meanings of the words. גוה as *pride* is in Job 22:29 and 33:17, and in Jer 13:17, whereas it is nowhere to be found as either "back" or "body". Nonetheless, LXX has *somatos* (body), while Vg ignores the word. Vg does, on the other hand translate מררה *amaritudo* which means "bitterness". The Hebrew word מררה, vocalized with *Sere* and *Qames* under the two רs (Job 16:13) does mean <u>bile</u> (not <u>gall</u> which is either figurative, or the secretion of the <u>animal</u> liver), but there is no reference in the Bible to the organ, the gall-bladder. In this passage the word is vocalized in the same way as in 13:26 where Job accuses God of *writing against me <u>bitter things</u>*. We might translate here *bitter deeds*.

The word ברק is pre-eminently related to lightning, which indeed, is its meaning. In Deut 32:41 occurs the phrase ברק חרבי, literally *the lightning of My sword*, but usually weakly translated *My flashing sword*, and similarly for *spear* in Habbakuk and Nahum. In the latter *the lightning of the spear* is parallel to *the flame of the sword*. In Ezekiel its ברק becomes a feature of the sword, especially nurtured by polishing. None of this provides licence for translating the word as though it were itself the weapon or its blade.

The word אמים, the regular plural, appears to be *terrors*, while the intensive plural *terror* is אימות.

Looking at the literal translation, it is not difficult first to deduce that there are two different referents for the two "he"s of the first line - God and the wicked man, and second, that two different weapons are referred to, each obliquely. What is <u>drawn</u> is the <u>iron shaft</u> of v. 24 and what shoots the flash of <u>lightning</u> is the <u>bow of brass</u> from the same source. There is not of course, nor ever has been, a bow made of brass, copper or bronze, save for decorative purposes (Ps 18:35 notwithstanding)⁹.

The double image of departure from pride and bitterness is a correct and natural one in the context, and the "body" and "gallbladder" of most versions illustrate a straining after parallel which, when one word of a pair has been misconceived, brings about inevitably the ruin of the other. Our final version will be:

> *When He draws, he will depart his pride;*
> *And at a flash of lightning, he will quit his bitterness;*
> *Terrors assail him!*

6. Job the Laughing-stock

If we have not been able to accept Job as complaining that he has been exhibited as a by-word to the peoples in Chap. 17, there can be no doubt that he asserts he has become a laughing-stock in Chapter 12. There is no more fascinating nor significant confusion of referents than follows this statement in vv. 4-6, and again it is the inability of scholars to consider any political or military background which forces them into disagreeable confusion.

שחק לרעהו אהיה   קרא לאלוה ויענהו   שחוק צדיק תמים
לפיד בוז לעשתות שאנן   נכון למועדי רגל
ישליאהלים לשדדים   ובטחות למרגיזי אל   לאשר הביא אלוה בידו

The first line states

> *I have become a laughing-stock to his friends*

There should be no problem with this, but there is. The great majority (Gordis is a welcome exception) seek to read it either as

> *I am as one who is a laughing-stock to his friends* or
> *I am become a laughing-stock to my friends.*

We find <u>His friends</u> as God's people in 17:5 above, and one who adheres to Him is <u>His friend</u> in 36:33. The appearance of God in the second stich should make it clear that this is the referent of the suffix of רעהו. This is the first of several passages in which Job endeavours to persuade God that what He is doing to him is alienating His own constituency - (v.s. 17:8,9). We therefore accept Gordis's insight that Job is, as it were, a scandal to <u>God's</u> friends.

There should be no difficulty in perceiving that the second and third stichoi of v.4 constitute together a noun clause with subject in line b and predicate in line c.

> *He who calls upon God and He answers him*
> *(Is) a just and innocent jest*

and this is precisely the joke being made at Job's expense.

This same form is apparent in verse 5, which also lacks an active verb and where stich b means *(Is) ripe for stumbling.* I draw attention here to the *oxymoron* achieved by the use of the word נכון - "fixed, firmly established", before "slippings of the foot". This figure of speech is a harbinger of the paradoxes in the expressions to come in v.6.

It remains to decipher the first stich which ought, if this deduction is correct, to specify forms of virtuous attitudes or behaviour which (in Job's cynical frame of mind) predispose those who harbour them to disaster.

There are two phrases in 5a, לפיד בוז and לעשתות שאנן. שאנן is "at ease" and בוז is "contempt". Plainly the ל of לפיד specifies at what the scorn is directed, and therefore we must assume the ל of לעשתות serves a similar function indicating in respect to what someone is at ease.

> Scorn of disaster; carelessness of favours
> (Is) ripe for stumbling

is the most likely reading, though certainly we might be more comfortable with participles in the first stich. As it is, the text seems to assert that it is the (normally) praiseworthy attitudes of mind which predispose towards a fall, rather than that the person who harbours them is destined for it. Alternatively we might regard the two phrases as intended to function as nick-names much in the spirit of Isaiah 7:14 or 8:3. שאנן may, like בוז serve as a noun (Isa 37:29). It is important to recognize the distinction between scorning disaster, meaning rising above it, and scorning the person to whom disaster occurs, which is how this phrase is usually understood. פיד cannot stand for a person overwhelmed by disaster.

The word עשתות as vocalized here is the plural of עשת, a word of uncertain meaning, found only in Song of Songs 5:14 in the sentence מעיו עשת שן. This is a very difficult image of erotic poetry, usually understood as *his belly is a plate of ivory*. It is suggested that the root means either "smooth" or "fat", based on Jer 5:28 where it is parallel to "fat"[10]. But the adjective עשות in Ezek 27:19, cannot mean anything like this, although "polished" (NJPSV) is possible. The alternative suggestion is that the word derives from an Aramaism, "to think", found in Jonah 1:6[11]. But in that context *favour* seems much more likely than the traditional "think of", as also the word עשתון in Ps 146:4, where the immortal *Put not your trust in princes* is followed by the statement that in the day they die, their עשתנות perish. Here favours is surely the *mot juste*. Favour in its old-fashioned sense as "something given as a mark of *favour*" would satisfy the sense both in the Song of Songs and in Ezekiel, while "fat and *favoured*" is an acceptable alternative to "fat and sleek" in the Jeremiah verse.

Secure in thought is what we might call a fall-back position here.

At this point it should be apparent that what is being said here is <u>the specification of the taunts</u> which are being directed against Job (or God) by God's erstwhile friends. Exactly the same format is to be found in 22:19,20 where Eliphaz says of the prosperity of the wicked that *righteous men look on and jeer, and an innocent man would deride them: "Surely our enemy is gone to Perdition, and the fire will consume their remnant"*. There also the specification of the taunt follows the record of it with no interpolated "they say".

Verse 6 continues this record of the mocking of Job, and as we shall see, its content <u>is</u> mockery.

ישליו אהלים ׀ לשדדים. I am constrained to print the vital disjunctive accent, *'azlah legarmeh* in this line, for it absolutely prohibits the reading, which we find in all modern versions of Job *The tents of robbers*. Nor is this accent the only factor which ought to cause us to reject this possibility. "The tents of robbers" is אהלי שדדים and, despite Gesenius's contrary assertion (# 129b)[12], there is no Biblical example of the substitution of a genitive ל in circumstances where no ambiguity would be caused by the use of the construct, as is certainly the case here. Of those who have written on this verse, only Berechiah has respected this accent. It has, however, been quite impossible for anyone to arrive at a correct understanding without first realising that he is facing a passage redolent of contemptuous sarcasm. Berechiah did not understand this, and consequently accepted that (his) tents are secure <u>against</u> robbers. The true sense is that his tents are secure <u>for</u> robbers! This is שׁחק. "His", which is understood, refers to him who calls upon God and is answered.

The next line may be understood in either of two ways, although again the ל, the second of a set of three which matches those of verse 5, is the key to the general understanding of the verse. The ambiguity depends on the word בטחות, which is hapax to this verse, and may be read as a noun parallel to אהלים (with the verb ישליו penetrating to this b stich) or as suggested by D as the intensive "perfectly secure", making a parallel for ישליו. Our alternatives are:

And his fortresses - for those who provoke God
And perfectly secure - for those who provoke God

I suggest that, because of the <u>waw</u> which seems to foretell an addition rather than an intensification, we should accept the first, regarding בטחות as meaning "secure places". Note that again there is a disjunctive accent, Dehi, on this word.

The last line of v.6 is one of the most important in the book, being one of a few select references to the historical crisis the analysis of which is its main purpose.

לאשר הביא אלוה בידו

has caused untold havoc. D&G follow a popular fashion in translating "Who brings his god in his hand".

We have to remember two things *ab initio* with this line. First that throughout the Book of Job אלוה represents the One God of Israel, and it cannot be downgraded to any old god just for the sake of this one verse, particularly when it is patently the parallel equivalent of אל. Second that the line is introduced by that same ל which we have encountered in each other of the stichoi of the verse. The conclusion which we derive from this is that מרגיזי אל, שדדים, and the whole of this line as one unit, are three parallel expressions describing those to whom the possessions of the man who trusted God are in pawn.

The ways this one line has been treated present a millenial history of outstanding examples of culpable error. They are summarised in these terms by G:

(a) the idolator "who makes his God with his hand" (Ra.); (b) the idolator "who brings his God in his hand"; (c) "who holds God in his power" (D-G)*; (d) "who sees his God in his strength"; (e) "who makes might his God" (Buttenweiser, Moffat**); (f) "God's terror-spreaders, whom God brings up for him" (T-S). G then lists four suggested amendments, and comments "The totally unconvincing character of these interpretations and emendations has, predictably enough, served to suggest deleting the clause, or the verse, or the entire section, as a gloss, leaving unexplained how or why these inexplicable words were interpolated into the text. G then adds to the list of improbable resolutions one rather more unlikely than any other, that the line means "all those who have deceived Him".

*   This is not the version of D&G, nor do I know whose it is.
**   Nor is this the version of Moffat.

Since G wrote this, NJPSV has essayed "Those whom God's hands have produced," H, "Those who try to control Elohah," Hartley, "Those who bring God in their hands" and C "Those whom God has in His own power."

All these mistranslations are culpable because all translators have either shied away from, or have dismissed in incredulity, the blasphemy of the true translation.

That there is a connection between the expression נתן ביד (9:24), שלח ביד (8:4), נפל ביד (I Chr 21:13), and הביא ביד is more than probable; it is virtually certain. As the first three mean "Give into the power of", "deliver into the power of", and "fall into the power of", there must be a very strong presumption that the fourth means "bring into the power of", that is, "subdue to the power of".

How are we to accommodate the concept of some man subduing God to his own power to Job's uncompromising faith in the One God, and He omnipotent, as 12:9 (*Who knows not of all these that the hand of the Lord wrought this?*) asserts? That passage in which Job declares his faith in the omnipotence of the Lord is in fact the whole of 12:7-9, the passage immediately following that which we are now examining. This suggests the presence of an internal debate in the speech, with vv. 7-9 designed to refute v.6, and perhaps what precedes it. The introductory word of v.7, ואולם, a strong adversative, "however", while an embarrassment to every other version, confirms this. The internal debate of the speech is between Job speaking for himself in vv. 7-9 and Job reporting what is being said about him, the שׂחק, those jests, in vv. 4-6.

6c can only be translated:

> *For whomever subdues God to his power!*

None of this makes any sense at all unless we accept that these tents and fortresses belong to a people whom God is pledged to protect - the people of Israel. It is worth noting the cumulative rhetorical and musical vigour of this triplet in which three parallel lines are displayed, the first with subject, verb and predicate, the second with only two of these, and the last shorn of all but this astounding predicate (cf. "Because I do not hope to turn again; Because I do not hope to turn; Because I do not hope" T.S. Elliot).

As we have had occasion to note elsewhere, in 701 (or 700) B.C.E., Sennacherib sent *via* his lieutenant, Rabshakeh, the following message to the defenders of Jerusalem:

> *Do not let Hezekiah delude you by saying: The Lord will save you. Has any god of any nation saved his country from the power (יד) of the king of Assyria? Where are the gods of Hamath and Arpad? Where are the gods of Samaria?...Tell me which of all 'the gods of the countries have saved their countries from my power, for the Lord to be able to save Jerusalem?*

Among those faithful friends of God who heard these words ringing out across the valley to the walls, there must have been many who believed that here indeed was the one who could subdue God to his power, and that to this robber, who had already devastated and seized forty-six cities and countless villages throughout Judah, who (a veritable provoker of God) was now laying siege to the city and the very house of God, the tents and fortresses of Judah were indeed secure trophies.

How orthodox now becomes the next passage, the retort in which the "scourge of God" theory is upheld, that all this, the זאת which returns in 17:8 and 19:26, is the work of the hand (יד) of God. This becomes the preoccupation of the entire remainder of this chapter, which concludes in vv. 17-25 with the logical demonstration that the mighty catalogue of reverses of the people of Judah which underlie the allegorical reverses of Job, is also God-given.

> *I have become a laughing-stock to His friends.*
> *(They are saying) "He who calls upon God and He answers him*
> *"Is a just and innocent jest.*
>
> *"Scorn-of-disaster, disdain-of-favours*
> *"Is ripe for stumbling.*

> *"His tents are secure - for robbers;*
> *"And his fortresses - for those who provoke God,*
> *"For whomsoever subdues God to his power."*

7. The Prophet Elihu

The expression להגיד לאדם ישרו in Elihu's speech, 33:23, has been the occasion for considerable controversy. The full verse in the context of a man chastised and wounded by God as warning that he is standing into danger because of his prideful ways, runs:

אם־יש עליו מלאך   מליץ אחד מני־אלף   להגיד לאדם ישרו

and is followed by

> *Then He will be gracious unto him and say*
> *"Save him from going down to the pit;*
> *I have found a ransom".*

The difficulties of the verse centre first on what is the מלאך מליץ, human or angelic? Then is "one in a thousand" an expression of rarity or abundance? Then to whom does the "interpreter" make his declaration - man, God, or the heavenly host? and finally what is the referent of the possessive pronoun of ישרו? Does it refer to man's righteousness, God's righteousness, or the right path to follow?

The favoured version of the present day identifies the interpreter as angelic; there is no sort of consensus for the meaning of the one in a thousand; the declaration is regarded as made in heaven to testify to a man's righteousness; a common variant of this is that it is made to the man to show him the right way (D, D&G).

The implications of this dominant version need to be considered carefully. We are discussing the case of a man whose behaviour has led God to administer a severe admonition; so severe that he is declining into death. The suggestion is that at a heavenly court, attended by one or more thousands of angels, if one of those attending vouches for the innocence (or righteousness) of the accused, God will reverse His decree and allow his restoration to health and prosperity. There is no precedent whatever in Biblical tradition for such a procedure. Although H refers to Zech 3:1-5, there is nothing in that scene which resembles this situation. He refers also to Enoch 9:3ff and 15:2, but this is no authority for Biblical tradition.

The function of intercessor, or defending counsel (paraclete [T]) is nowhere else assigned to an angel. Indeed it is indisputable that Hebrew tradition assigns the role of spokesman <u>for</u> God to the angelic beings, and that the only member of the heavenly host who ever adopts an adversary relationship to Him is the Satan. Obviously the מלאך מליץ here is not the Satan. In the Bible, the only beings ever recorded as intervening with God on behalf of the condemned are human prophets, notably Abraham in the case of Sodom and Gomorrah. It is true that in the degenerated and superstitious Judaism of the post-Biblical era, as to folk-Christianity, such fancies were acceptable, but they are absolutely heterodox to Biblical Judaism. Duhm, making the assumption that the mediator is angelic, concludes from it that Elihu must be a very late interpolation: *The idea of spirits hostile to or protective of the soul can hardly have originated without foreign influence, though we can hardly determine whether we have before us Persian, or Egyptian or other ideas.* Indeed they must be seen as detracting from the wisdom and omniscience of the Deity, implying that He could wrongfully initiate the process of warning and punishment against a man who was in fact righteous, later accepting correction from one of His minions. For these reasons, the alternative that this functionary is human is preferable to the assumption that he is semi-divine.

Interestingly Vg regards the functionary as an angel who delivers his message to the man in question, showing him where "man's good lies", and this is essentially the version accepted by D and D&G (v.s.). While this version retains a correct role for the angel, and avoids ascribing error to God, it puts a severe strain both on "one in a thousand" and on ישרו. There is actually little room for doubt that the expression אחד מני אלף implies rarity. It certainly does in Ecc 7:28 (*One man in a thousand have I found, but a woman never!*), and in Job 9:3, whether the referent be taken as men or questions. But if this is so, the expression has no proper application to an angel, for it implies that the role of spokesman for God can only be carried out by the exceptional angel, whereas the very word for angel, מלאך, *messenger*, testifies to this as the normative role of all angels.

ישר with the possessive suffix is hardly the word of choice to express the idea of a man's duty, or the right path for him to follow. We should expect דרכו or something similar. The expression *the paths of uprightness* does indeed occur in Proverbs twice (2:13; 4:11), but in each case ישר is preceded by a word for "paths". It is very doubtful if the noun alone can support this sense. Prov 14:2, הולך בישרו *Who walks in his uprightness* is not comparable. The image is of a garment (Cf. Job 29:14). The normal meaning of ישרו is simply "his uprightness" and so the majority of commentators render it, and if it is taken as Job's, this more or less rules out an angel as the testifier.

The word מלאך is equally at home with an angelic messenger and a human one, with a messenger between men, and one conveying the word of God, a prophet (e.g. II Chr 36:15,16.). מליץ, a word strangely derived from the verb "to scorn", is an interpreter of languages in Gen 42:23, and a foreign emissary in II Chr 32:31. In Isa 43:27 it refers, perhaps more likely to priests than to prophets, to intercessors from man to God, while Job in 16:20 speaks of his tears (understood) as his intercessors with God[13]. There is no precedent in the Bible for this word to represent a supernatural voice.

If Elihu, in speaking of a messenger-interpreter, an intercessor of some kind, does have a human in mind, who or what can this be? The expression *one in a thousand* fits very well with this assumption, suggesting that only the exceptional human being can perform such an office, and this raises the possibility that he intends a prophet. Now it is clear that the unspecified "man", who is languishing on the point of death because of visions conveyed to him *in a dream, in a night-vision* (33:15, cf. 7:3-5; 13-15) is intended to be Job, which leaves the role of prophet who is to save him from *going down to the pit* as Elihu himself. This then is the other side of Elihu's modesty, an overweening vanity in which he sees himself, not only as vastly the intellectual superior of the three comforters, but as an elect prophet of God who has been sent to accomplish Job's salvation. According to D, this is the view put forward by an array of earlier commentators, none of whose works is available to me - Schultens (1737), Schnurrer (1781-2), Bullier, Eichhorn (1816-19), Rosenmuller (1806), Welte. D&G refer to Schultens, and consider that Dillmann (1891) has provided a sufficient refutation of this line of reasoning.

Despite this confidence, the theory seems to fit the text better than any of the alternatives. But what is the message that the "intercessor" delivers, and to whom? Here the text is powerfully supportive of the view, attributed to Hitzig (1874), that we should read *declare unto (the) man His* (i.e. *God's*) *uprightness,* for ל- הגיד in Biblical as in modern Hebrew mean to tell to someone, not to tell about someone, or on behalf of someone. G mentions Gen 20:13 as a precedent: אמר-לי אחי הוא *Say of me, 'He is my brother',* and this has some merit, but the usage of אמר is not the same as of הגיד and the example is unique. However, the crucial test of the sense of the passage lies in the general purpose and drift of Elihu's intervention, which is to demonstrate the righteousness of God.

> *Far be God from evil or the Almighty from iniquity* 34:10
> *For the works of man He requites to him*
> *And causes each to receive according to his way* 34:11
> *Truly, God would not act wickedly,*
> *Nor the Almighty pervert justice* 34:12
> *Attend to me a little longer, and I shall declare to you*
> *That there are still things to be said for God.*
> *I will bring my evidence from times of old*
> *As I ascribe righteousness to Him who framed me.* 36:2,3
> *Behold, God is pre-eminent in power,*
> *Who is a teacher like Him?* 36:22

Indeed, if we examine the whole of Elihu's speeches from this point of view, it is apparent that they are dominated by the intention of demonstrating to Job the justice and righteousness of God. There is, however, nowhere in the Book of Job the slightest sign of anyone but Job, God Himself, and the narrator seeking to testify to Job's righteousness.

How can instruction in the righteousness of God save a man from going down into the pit? That is, how can the fact of the instruction induce God to say *Save him from going down into the pit; I have found a ransom [כפר]* (33:24)? The first thing to remember is that Elihu has charged neither Job nor his hypothetical "man" with active evil. The charge against Job is his disdain for God and the denial of His justice; the charge against the man is "pride" (33:17), which is much the same thing. Further very specifically, Elihu has described the purpose of God's nocturnal visitations of the man as to *restrain his soul from the pit and his life from perishing by the sword* (33:18). But man is prone to failing to receive the message - *God speaks once, yea twice, if he (man) has not perceived it* (33:14), which is why specifically an interpreter is required. His task must be to secure the effect which God sought to achieve by sending His ambiguous dreams and night visions - i.e. to induce "the man" to abandon his prideful views, which is to say, to accept the righteousness of God. In the Bible, dreams characteristically need interpretation. The specific task of the מלאך מליץ is to persuade the man of God's ישר, which is precisely what Elihu is trying to do throughout his intervention.

The only remaining obscurity lies in the word כפר, usually taken as "a ransom". This concept recurs in 36:18 *Do not let the magnitude of the כפר deflect you*. The word denotes the price paid for a threatened life (Ex 21:30), and most often implies a monetary exaction. This is certainly not the case here or in Chap. 36. As it seems that what is required is that the man abandon his previous views, and accept what he previously denied, it seems that the "ransom", the price of salvation, is penance. Indeed, this penance is described exactly later in Chap. 33 - he is to make a public recantation of his views *He will say, "I have sinned and perverted the Right, and He has not requited me"* [QT][14] (33:27). *He redeemed my soul from going down to the pit, and my spirit sees in the Light* (33:28).

I conclude therefore that the מלאך מליץ is Elihu himself in the role of the interpreter of God's dream-messages to Job; that *one in a thousand* emphasises the rare qualities required for this role; that the message is delivered to Job, and that it consists of the evidence of God's righteousness.

8. *The Treachery of Job's Brothers*

There are no Homeric similes either in the Book of Job or in the Bible as a whole. Typically a simile in Job is a single word or a single line of verse. The way in which the passage Job 6:15-21 has commonly been treated therefore sets it apart as a figure of speech unique in the Bible.

The passage starts with a simple simile - indeed with two:

אחי בגדו כמו־נחל   כאפיק נחלים יעברו

My brothers have defaulted like a wadi

---

is the first stich. *Defaulted* for בגדו conveys the required sense here of
the sort of treachery provided by an intermittent stream which
disappears just when it is most needed. This simile is much the same
as is found in Jer 15:18. We do not know with certainty who is
intended by Job's "brothers". The assumption that this is the comforters is difficult to credit. Job's three friends have just come to comfort
him, and only one has so far spoken. Could he be so ungracious as to
accuse them all of having deserted him in these circumstances?
Nowhere else in the whole Dialogue does Job refer to them as
"brothers"; and the other reference to brothers, in Chap. 19 - הרחיק *He
(God) has removed my brothers far from me* is certainly not applicable
to them. "Brothers" in Biblical Hebrew has a very wide applicability
beyond sons of the same parent - friends, allies, relatives, descendants
of related tribes may all be referred to with this word.

Strange things start to happen in this passage from this point
on. The second stich, instead of being accepted as approximately
parallel with the first, with יעברו echoing בגדו, and further illustrating
the treachery of the brothers, seems always to be taken as continuing
the illustration of the treachery of the stream! Thus we have:

As the channel of brooks that overflow JPS
Like a bed on which streams once ran NJPSV
As the bed of torrents which vanish away D
Like freshets that pass away G
Like the channel of wadis that pass away D&G
Like wadi channels they overflow P

etc. But LXX has no difficulty in recognizing the true subject of יעברו
They have passed me by like a failing brook. However the singular אפיק
followed by the plural נחלים does pose a problem. The word אפיק is
discussed at some length in Chapter 3.IX, Lexicographical Anomalies.
There the conclusion is reached that it means not "channel", but a
standing body of water, from water-hole to lake. These are bodies of
which one can be fed by several wadis, justifying the phrase אפיק נחלים,
which certainly is not true of stream-beds and channels. Thus, we
should read for 6:15b:

Like a water-hole of the wadis, they passed away

which starts to do what the reader has every expectation of reading next, to explain in what way Job's "brothers" have betrayed or deceived him or let him down.

Now comes the devastatingly difficult: הקדרים מני־קרח

Which are black by reason of the ice JPS
They are dark with ice NJPSV
They were blackish from ice D
They grow dark with ice G
Which are turbid by reason of the ice D&G
They run turbid with ice P

One does not require to be a great observer of nature to know that all these versions are wrong. First of all, frost apart, there is no such thing as ice on a wadi, a נחל. Second, ice is dazzling white, and while it may be possible to point to some obscure reference testifying to ice turning water dark, no poet would ever use such an image. The favoured reference here is a description of streams of Lebanon by A. Geikie[15]. But even if this is read as describing the blackening of water with ice (actually all it does is speak of the turbulence caused by the melting of snows) these mountain streams have nothing in common with the desert wadis being discussed.

Then there is the problem that קדר does not mean "black", or "turbid", nor "dark" in anything like the same sense as would be applicable to rivers. The word represents a combination of grief, darkness, and a lowered posture which has no one-word equivalent in modern western languages[16]. Its darkness is the absence of lustre, not a dark colour. The word here is the plural participle, which is found only in Job 6:16 and, by what may be an amazing coincidence, but is far more likely to be by design, in Job 5:11. If, however, we consider the possibility that these two uses of this otherwise unique word ought to have the same meaning, we have to regard 6:16 in an entirely new light. For whatever the specific meaning of קדרים in 5:11, and this is by no means sure, it is sure that it refers to a group of people, either so identified, or so characterised.

If this is so also in 6:16, then the apposition of הקדרים is not with rivers or channels, but with brothers. Indeed given the choice of apposition with a singular אפיק or a genitive נחלים, it is difficult to say which is syntactically less acceptable! We may play with this word in many ways (see note 16), but the striking thing about it as the designation of people is that there is a tribe, the *Bene Kedar*, בני קדר, in whose territory are situate Tema and Sheba[17], both of which cities are mentioned in Job 6:19, a part of this same passage. The arm of coincidence is becoming excessively elongated! The *Bene Kedar* are Arabs; they live in Bedouin tents - black and low, crouching into the landscape. קדרים, if we respect its participial form, may be read as "the kedar-tented ones".

Verse 16 declares (perhaps once it asked?):

> *The Kedarites are made of ice*
> *There is snow concealed upon them*

a contention to be explained immediately:

בעת יזרבו נצמתו   בחמו נדעכו ממקומם

> *As soon as they were singed, they vanished,*
> *In his heat they were snuffed out of their place.*

יזרבו, Pu`al, has to be taken as a variant of צרב, "to scorch". Of course ice and snow are pre-eminently what disappears in heat. *In his heat they were snuffed out of their place* reads as an accusation of cowardice, of desertion in the first heat of battle. By no means may the pronominal suffix of חמו be disregarded. We continue to unfold a version in which the referent of the subjects of all these verbs is the same brothers who are the proper subject of the discussion, rather than the intrusive rivers. The usual translations of this last v. 17 hardly differ from the above except in ignoring the his (or His or its) of חמו, but it is always assumed that the treacherous streams are the subjects.

Verse 18: ילפתו ארחות דרכם   יעלו בתהו ויאבדו

This easily carries the sense:

> *The paths of their roads turned back[18],*
> *They went up into the wilderness and were lost.*

Again it takes a great deal of imagination to believe that this figure is intended to describe rivers, especially when we consider the word יעלו, which is the one thing that rivers can never do! Likewise דרך is not elsewhere associated with rivers. It is necessary also to keep in mind the nature of the image with which the proponents of the Homeric simile started-intermittent streams whose flow is absent when needed. Now we seem to be talking about rivers whose beds twist and turn and peter out in the desert sands, an entirely different form of waterway (if such exists) and of betrayal. As a description of the brothers, the picture is one of headlong desertion and retreat back through the desert to their own homeland in the hilly country of northern Arabia which is Kedar.

הביטו ארחות תמא   הליכת שבא קו־למו

In order to adapt this verse to the prevailing theory of the Homeric simile, it has been necessary to understand ארחות and הליכת as "caravans" or "processions", but in neither case is this a correct translation. Both words mean *paths*, either literal or figurative. ארחות in this verse is the same word as in the preceding one. Differently vocalized it means <u>caravans</u>, but from the root הלך, only תהלכת (Neh 12:31) has the requisite meaning. With these two false exchanges the common way of reading the verse is *The caravans of Tema looked; the companies of Sheba waited for them*, suggesting nomads searching in vain for the driedup wadis. Even then to achieve this it has been necessary to understand הביטו, which means *They beheld*, unfaithfully and uniquely as *looked in vain*, which is the reverse of its true sense, i.e. *they did not behold!*

It is also to be considered that the trading tribes of the Arabian desert knew the ways of desert wadis with an intimacy which matches the Cockney's knowledge of his London streets. Far from being a familiar illustration of trusting people betrayed by fickle friends, the "wadi" image as usually understood defies the known habits of the area. It is the unwary stranger who is likely to be let down by "treacherous streams", not caravans from Tema and Sheba.

Verse 19, still with the brothers, the Kedarites, reads:

> *They beheld the paths of Tema;*
> *The ways of Sheba awaited them.*

which conveys exactly the sense of the Hebrew and confirms the destination of their retreat - homewards to Kedar.

Verse 20: בשו כי־בטה   באו עדיה ויחפרו

with its mixture of plural and singular verbs is usually, if not always, treated as though בטח were plural[19] - *They were put out because they had hoped* is the sort of meaning we read for the first line, but its true translation is

> *They were ashamed because he trusted,*

or perhaps *was confident*, or even *was steadfast*. This <u>he</u> must be the same as formed the suffix of חמו, the person in whose "heat" they were snuffed out of their place, and the meaning is surely that the deserting brothers were shamed because their ally remained confident and held his ground while they deserted the field. *They came thither (*home to Kedar - Tema and Sheba*) and were confounded.* The same emotion is exactly described in Macauley's jingle:

Back darted Spurius Lartius; Herminius darted back:
And, as they passed, beneath their feet they felt the timbers crack.
But when they turned their faces, and on the farther shore
Saw brave Horatius stand alone, they would have crossed once more.

Now Job turns to his comforters and says:

6:21כי־עתה הייתם לו   תראו חתת ותיראו

The expression כי־עתה with <u>maqqeph</u> means "for then," "in that case" or, alternatively "otherwise". Here it seems to mean "in that case" in the unusual sense "if you were in that case", hence

> *In such a case you would have been for him,*

and here is the third appearance of this unspecified "him", and it should not be doubted that this is the same person who experienced heat and remained steadfast. The explanation of this apparently benign judgement of the friends is given in the second stich, and proves to be appropriately barbed:

> *(After all) when you see someone in terror, you take fright!*

I.e., As you are so prone to be infected by the spirit of whomever you are exposed to at the time, being scared at the sight of my fear, you would presumably have been moved to constancy by the sight of "his" resolution or trust. We are, however, on weaker grounds in trying to understand this verse than any other part of the passage. Equally valid is "otherwise", i.e., if they had not fled.

The verse appears to be a riposte of some kind to 4:5:

כי עתא תבוא אליך ותלא   חגע עדיך ותבהל

But now it comes to you and you despair;
It touches you and you take fright.

and carries the implication that while Job at least had to be afflicted before he caught fright, the friends take fright at the mere sight of someone else in distress. Whether the absence of the *maqqeph* in 4:5 is significant is hard to tell.

It is, I think evident, that if this interpretation of the passage is correct, then it refers to a real historical incident in which Arab troops deserted an ally who "trusted" or remained steadfast. Exactly such an incident is recorded in the history of Judah and at the right time. Hezekiah, shut up in Jerusalem awaiting the seige of Sennacherib, was deserted by his *amelurbu* (translated in Cambridge Ancient History[20] as "Arab") troops (Annals of Sennacherib)[21], but with the help of Isaiah, remained resolute and defiant. Hence, when Sennacherib's envoys reached Jerusalem, they prompted his stewards to demand of Hezekiah:

> *What is this confidence in which you trust?* - (Isa 36:4)

מה הבטחון הזה אשר בטחת?

It is the existence of this well-known quotation which enables the author to employ the laconic כי־בטח in the apparently not-too-well-founded belief that he would be understood.

In weighing the version of these verses given here against that to be found in all other studies of Job, not only must the unique eccentricity of a Homeric image in the Bible be taken into account, and the uncharacteristic abandonment of the complaint which Job begins to a natural history lesson, but also the multiple mistranslations of Hebrew words which are involved in the simile version. These include הליכת, ארחות, הביט, לפת and are compounded by the rejection of the number of one word and the pronominal suffix of another.

Let us retain the assumption that the above version and its interpretation[22] are more or less correct. In that case what is the meaning of 5:11, and how does 6:16 reply to it?

If 6:15-21 is somehow a debating reply to 5:11, we must assume that 5:11[23] refers to the same event but gives it an entirely different significance. We have there the Kedarites (or the kedar-tented ones) being lifted to a place of safety by the miraculous hand of God. What is this but a celebration of the safe extrication of the Kedarites from the peril to which the Sennacherib invasion exposed them? The Land of Kedar is an elevated plateau in Saudi Arabia, and whether we consider the divine act to have been the elevation of this plateau in the remote past to serve as a safe retreat, inaccessible to a pursuing enemy (treating שפרים as *lowlands* and קדרים as the whole tribe together with its abode), or simply the ensuring of the safe return of the deserting troops to their mountainous funk-hole, makes no difference to the dynamics of such a debate. The comforters are themselves taking comfort from the safety of Job's allies, as it were identifying with them, while Job perforce dwells on the treachery which left his champion and his people to face the music alone.

The passage in Chapter 5 continues for several verses describing the failure of Sennacherib and his men successfully to pursue and punish the Kedarites. 5:12-16:

> *Frustrating the plans of the crafty*
> *That their hands achieved nothing lasting;*
> *Trapping the smart ones in their own guile*
> *That the schemes of the crooked were swept away;*
> *In the daytime they encountered darkness*
> *And they groped in the noontide as in the night;*
> *And he saved from the sword, from their own mouth,*
> *And from the hand of the mighty, the poor,*
> *That the helpless had hope*
> *And injustice held her tongue.*

Notes Chapter XI

1. G argues fiercely for the contradiction as "one of its (the book's) most fundamental contributions to the problem of evil". "The truly good man will be aghast at Job's misery, but he will not on that account be deflected from the path of righteousness. The good life is its own reward and justification - it does not require the prop of a false theodicy with the cruel distortion of reality" (BofJ, Special Note 14, p. 524f).

2. על in this second stich governs a complete clause, as in 16:17 and Isa 53:9. BDB considers it to be functioning as a conjunction in such cases.

3. This use of יוסף, particularly in the phrase יוסף לקח - *increases learning*, to refer to the acquisition of more of a particular quality, is found several times in Proverbs, and once in Ecclesiastes.

4. מורשי לבבי is literally *What I inherit from my heart*. As the heart is the seat of understanding in Biblical Hebrew, *My conclusions* is the probable meaning.

5. *He that denounces his friends for the sake of flattering*
He invites his friends to share his bounty
Who denounces his friends for a reward
He who gives his friends for a spoil
A man bidding his friends to a feast
He that speaketh flattery to his friends

are the versions of JPS; G; P, H and NJPSV; D, D&G and RV; C; and AV respectively. Others are similar.

6. The use of the infinitive construct to serve as a *nomen regens* in this way is irregular, and the verbal forms of משל take only indirect objects. Revocalization as the participle would satisfy the grammatical purist (v. Bib. Heb. Stutt.).

7. Berechiah reads "And He placed me to rule peoples", but comments:

> *has not God caused me to stand in the past, when I was in my glory, to rule and correct peoples with the rod of reproof. And a Topheth, and a blaze of fire, burning like the Topheth, which blazes for ever, I was to them formerly; so much were they afraid to approach me, for I used to remove the wicked from the earth.*

The greatest problem with this interpretation is the plural עמים which, as <u>peoples</u> means <u>nations</u>, a term quite inapplicable to any sheikh-Job.

8. *Topheth* is the high place in the Valley of Gehinnom (outside my window as I write) where children were sacrificed to Moloch both before and after the time of Hezekiah, but not during his reign. Hezekiah *removed the high places, and broke the pillars, and cut down the Asherah, and he broke in pieces the brazen serpent that Moses had made; for unto those days the children of Israel did offer to it* (II Kings 18:4). Half a century later, Josiah did the same, and in his case the record specifically mentions *Topheth - And he defiled* Topheth, *which is in the valley of Hinnom that no man might make his son or his daughter to pass through the fire to Moloch.* (II Kings 23:10).

9. An excellent summary of the techniques of bow-manufacture in the ancient Middle East is in Yigal Yadin, *The Art of Warfare in Biblical Lands*, McGraw Hill, NY, *1963*, Vol.I, 6-8. The essence of the bow is, of course, its tensile strength, of which brass, bronze and copper have effectively none.

10. BDB, p.799.

11. Ibid.

12. Gesenius provides three supposed examples, I Sam 14:16, Ps 37:16, and II Chron 28:18, but concedes that in the third the circumlocution clarifies the text. But in I Sam 14:16 the circumlocution is necessary to clarify whether it is Saul or the watchmen who are in Gibeath-benjamin, while in Ps 37, the expression is not even a true genitive -

טוב מעט לצדיק מהמון רשעים רבים

is best read *To the righteous a little is better than the abundance of many wicked men.*

13. A sensitive and beautifully poetic image, which has not been understood correctly.

מליצי רעי   אל־אלוה דלפה עיני
ויוכח לגבר עם־אלוה   ובן־אדם לרעהו

The first line, consisting simply of two nouns - *My intercessors; my friends*, is to be understood grammatically as the direct object of דלפה, *weeps*. While others weep tears, what Job weeps is friendly intercessors with God. That is, quite simply, Job hopes that his tears will suffice to plead with God, *as a man might with his neighbour.*

14. The more regular understanding of לא־שוה לי is *But it has not profited me*, but this has little or no justification.

15. A. Geikie, *Holy Land and the Bible, 1887*, i, 124, simply wrote:

> *The streams of Lebanon send down great floods of dark and troubled waters in spring, when the ice and snow of their summits are melting; but they dry up under the heat of summer, and the track of the torrent, with its chaos of boulders, stones and gravel, seems as though it has not known a stream for ages.*

Desert wadis are not snow-fed, but run intermittently in the wake of cloudbursts.

16. Other than proper names, there are fifteen examples of derivatives of the root קדר in the Bible. In every case they are associated with one or more of the three concepts "to be bowed down", "to be dark (of lights, extinguished)," and "to mourn". In Jer 14:2 קדרו לארץ has the gates of Judah <u>bowing down</u> to the ground in antithesis to the cry of Jerusalem which has ascended. In Ezek 32:8 *All the bright lights of heaven* אקדירם עליך, *And set darkness upon thy Land*, exhibits the sense of darkening by extinguishing light. There are four examples of the phrase קדר ללכת (including Job 30:28), all of which are traditionally understood as "go mourning", but nothing in any of their contexts suggests mourning as distinct from grief and a sense of persecution.

"Walk bowed" or "Walk in darkness" are both possibilities therefore.

The sense of mourning is explicit in the noun קדרות, which is a mourning garment or material - *I clothe the heavens with קדרות, and I make sackcloth their covering.* (Isa 50:3).

17. Isa 21:14-16 firmly establishes Tema as Kedarite. This passage, the conclusion of the brief *Burden upon Arabia* properly runs:

> To greet a thristy man, bring water!
> The inhabitants of the Land of Tema met the fugitives with its* bread (= war**),
> Though they fled from the swords, from the drawn sword,
> And from the bent bow and from the grievousness of war.
> So thus saith the Lord to me: Within a year, according to
> the years of a hireling, and all the glory of Kedar shall fail...

* Arabia's
** A pun, war being the staple diet, or bread, of the Arabs, and the root לחם doing double duty for <u>war</u> and <u>bread</u>. As with חמו in Job 6:17, it has been customary to ignore the suffix of לחמו here.

There is of course no sense in cursing Kedar for the inhospitality of Tema unless the former included the latter.

The close geographical (and presumably also tribal) relationship between Sheba and Tema, and hence also Kedar, is attested not only in v.19 of the passage under consideration, but also in the Annals of Tiglath-Pileser III who, in listing the distant nations which paid him tribute, twice recorded in the one phrase *The inhabitants of Tema and the inhabitants of Saba* (Pritch. pp. 283f). This Sheba is distinct from the southern Arabian Kingdom of the Queen of Sheba. Presumably it is the same that is mentioned as the raiders of Job 1:15.

18. The verb לפת occurs only thrice in the Bible, once as the Qal in Judges 16:29 where Samson <u>grasped</u> the two pillars before demolishing the temple. No-one really has any idea of the significance of the choice of this word for Samson's action. The other two examples, Job 6:18 and Ruth 3:8 are in the Niph'al conjugation. In Ruth the meaning appears to be "turned round", with a reflexive sense which is proper to the Niph'al. NJPSV has *pulled back*, but both LXX with *etarachte*, and Vg with *conturbatus*, regard the word as indicating internal turmoil rather than any change of posture. But neither of these ancient versions has anything for Job 6:18 resembling its translation of the same word in Ruth.

The clues to meaning here are therefore confusing. What Samson undoubtedly did was to grasp the pillars with his hands <u>turned outwards</u> to give himself the purchase needed to force them apart. He did not encircle them as one would if grasping for support. In the case of Ruth, Boaz was startled, then וילפת, and only then *Behold, a woman lay at his feet.* The versions of LXX and Vg seem only to be compatible with a record of his reactions <u>after</u> seeing Ruth. What a person startled in his sleep does is either turn over, if he is on his face or side, or sit up, if he is on his back. Boaz, having eaten and drunken and having a merry heart (v.7), was probably asleep like one somewhat inebriated, on his face. But this is straining the sort of detective work which is possible with Biblical texts too far. However a change of posture seems virtually certain in that *Behold* follows rather than precedes the verb.

Most interpreters understand "turn" in the sense of twisting and turning, but the image does not appear to add anything to their picture of truant rivers. For a version to which it could be appropriate, see note 22 below.

19. Without comment, Berechiah quotes the Hebrew here as the deviant plural, בטחון, which is apparently what was present in the manuscript he employed.

20. *Cambridge Ancient History*, Ed. Bury, Cook, Adcock, Cambridge U. Press, *1976*, Vol III, p.390:

> *Though the events that followed are not quite clear, and different views can be maintained, it would seem that the foreign Urbi troops (Arabs) introduced...to defend the city were thoroughly untrustworthy. Hezekiah was shut up "like a bird in a cage", and forty-three of his western cities were cut off and allotted to the pro-Assyrian kings of Ekron, Ashdod and Gaza. 200,150 men are stated to have been taken captive and a heavy tribute was imposed.*

21. Annals of Sennacherib, Pritch. p.288:

> *Hezekiah himself, whom the terror-inspiring splendour of my lordship had overwhelmed, and whose 'amelurbu' (translated as "irregular") troops which he had brought into Jerusalem, his royal residence, in order to strengthen it, had deserted him...*

While I am surely no expert on the Assyrian language, I am constrained to comment that "Amal" as a god, is apparently related to the corvee, or system of conscripted labour (Pritch. p.268) and if this syllable is removed, <u>urbu</u> has the right consonants to represent the Arabs. "Impressed Arab" troops is therefore a likely meaning.

22. There is a second possible explanation for the passage which in some ways is more satisfactory. This is that the incident referred to in the two passages 5:11-16 and 6:15-20 is the same as that alluded to in Isaiah's *Burden upon Arabia*, see note 17 above. In that case, it is not desertion of which Job's "brothers", the people of Kedar, are guilty, but falling upon a fleeing and defeated army which made its way to them expecting succour. In this case there must be two different plural subjects in the passage in Chapter 6. Verses 15-17 refer to the behaviour of Kedar, and vv.18-20 refer to the fugitives who are "confounded" (בשו ויחפרו) by their hostile reception, and the singular בטח and חמו are references to the leader of the band of fugitives, even perhaps Job himself.

The people of Kedar, descendants of Ishmael, are naturally accorded the title "brothers" by the Israelites (cf. Deut 23: 8). It is on this basis also that their succour might have been expected.

23. 5:10 and 11 may well be intended as descriptions of God's actions at the time of the Creation:

הנתן מטר על־־פני ארץ   ושלח מים על־־פני חוצות
לשום שפלים למרום   וקדרים שׂגבו ישע

There are several ambiguities. The word חוצות may have a simple domestic sense such as fields or even (T-S) streets, or an almost cosmic as open spaces (G), the earth (LXX), or less specifically than any - surrounds. With ארץ as its mate in parallel, streets and fields seem very inadequate. To understand what is intended by חוצות one must first accept the sense of שלח. The rain in the first stich falls vertically from heaven onto the face of the land. The water (no synonym for rain) in the second stich is sent forth horizontally onto the face of what? Surely the answer must be the area surrounding the dry land. Bearing in mind that a succession of verbal participles most frequently describes single events in the past rather than repeated and habitual practices (see Chap. I, n.22, p.108), the entire passage from v.9 to v.16 may properly be read in the past tense as a celebration of specific actions of God on specific occasions in the past, rather than, as is usually taken, in the present as a celebration of what He does constantly. If this is right, v.10 may well be a description of the primaeval watering of the land with the *flight* of the waters (Gen 2:6 and Ps 104:7). In Ps 104 the flight of the waters is accompanied by and presumably causally related to the rising of the mountains and the sinking of the valleys. It is this which may give relevance to the otherwise puzzling lamed of לשום (most ignore it; G inventively calls it an <u>infinitive consecutive</u>).

In the Psalm (v.10) occurs המשלח מעינים בנחלים בין הרים יהלכון - *That sends forth springs into the wadis that run between mountains* (NB, not into the <u>valleys</u>; these do not *run*). This is another possible source for שלח in Job 5.

There are good grounds for insisting that 5:10 does refer to the primaeval watering of the earth, for the verse is mentioned by Job in 12:15. The dynamics of Job 12 are explained in Chapter I above, where it is shown that the posing of two contrasting proverbs is followed by four "quotations" from the words of the comforters, which are then used as the evidence on which a choice between the proverbs is made. One of these "quotations" is וישלחם ויהפכו־ארץ - *If He send them (the waters) forth, they overturn the earth.* The overturning of the earth surely means the raising of mountains and the sinking of valleys.

On analogy with the Psalm, we might now read 5:11a: *To set the lowlands on high*, with full purposive significance attached to the lamed. This would force upon us a very eccentric meaning for קדרים. Although שפל is most frequently used as an adjective or noun, *lowly, humble,* applicable to living beings, the feminine form is used as a proper name for a particular area of Lowland, so the sense is certainly not foreign to the root. The alternative *setting the lowly on high* allows no significance to the lamed and provides no continuity of thought to the passage.

The second stich contains the expression שׂגבו ישע. ישע, like ישועה, is primarily *salvation* and secondarily *safety*. *Victory* (BDB) is unsubstantiated, while *prosperity* (D) is quite without foundation. The word שׂגבו reinforces the impression of safety, for it implies being set on high out of reach of danger (מרום in 11a is capable of a similar connotation, see Isa 26:5, Job 39:18). It seems certain then that we are not dealing with an accidental secondary meaning in reading the expression as implying the elevation of some people to a place of security or safety. There are implications attached to the raising of the people in the second stich which are not explicit in the first.

Were we dealing with an entirely unknown word in קדרים, there would be little hesitation in translating *Setting the lowly on high and raising those in peril to safety*, and discarding all the above speculation about the connection between the preceding verse and Ps 104 or Job 12:15. קדרים is not, however, a hapax legomenon, and there is nothing in common between the root קדר and peril, and neither mourners, nor those bowed down, nor the dejected (NJPSV) nor the forlorn (P, H) nor the crushed (T-S), the afflicted (G) nor the lost (LXX) gives any real relevance to the theme of safety. Perhaps crushed makes some sort of fit, but T-S has reached this by assuming that not only here, but in a variety of Biblical passages, קדר is an error for קדד, and we cannot accept this assumption of wholesale corruption.

PART 3

TRANSLATION

I
Translation

THE BOOK OF JOB

Chapter 1

1. A man there was in the Land of Council. Job was his name, and it was so that this man was innocent and upright, and one who feared God and shunned evil.

2. There were born to him seven sons and three daughters.

3. His possessions were seven thousand sheep, and three thousand camels, and five hundred yoke of oxen, and five hundred she-asses, and a very large number of servants. This man was greater than any of the Children of the East.

4. And his sons went and held feasts, each in his house on his (birth)day, and they sent and invited their three sisters to eat and to drink with them.

5. It transpired that as the days of feasting came around, Job sent and purified them, and rose early in the morning, and sacrificed burnt-offerings according to the number of them all, for Job said, "Perhaps my children have sinned, and cursed God in their hearts". In this way did Job act on each of the days.

6. There came the day when the heavenly host came to present themselves before the Lord, and there came also the Satan among them.

7. The Lord said to the Satan, "From where have you come?", and the Satan answered the Lord and said, "From roaming on the earth and from tramping around upon it".

8. The Lord said to the Satan, "Have you given your attention to My servant, Job, for there is none like him on the earth, a man innocent and upright, who fears God and shuns evil?"

9. And the Satan answered the Lord and said, "Is it for nothing Job fears God?

10. "Have not You* Yourself placed a fence about him, and about his House, and about all that is his, all-encompassing? The work of his hands You have blessed, and his possessions burst bounds in the Land.

11. "However, just extend Your hand and touch all that is his, I declare he will curse You to Your face!"

12. Then said the Lord to the Satan, "Behold, all that is his is in your power. Only to his person do not extend your hand". Then the Satan left the precincts of the presence of the Lord.

13. There came the day when his sons and his daughters were eating and drinking wine in the house of their oldest brother;

14. When a messenger came to Job and said, "The oxen they were ploughing, and the asses they were grazing at their side,

15. "When Sheba fell and seized them, and the servants they put to the sword, and I am escaped, only I alone, to tell you".

16. While this one was still speaking, another came and said, "A fire of God fell from the skies, and burned the sheep and the servants, and consumed them, and I am escaped, only I alone, to tell you".

17. While this one was still speaking, another came and said, "Chaldeans formed three columns and plundered the camels and seized them, and the servants they put to the sword, and I am escaped, only I alone, to tell you".

18. Before he had finished speaking, another came and said, "Your sons and your daughters were eating and drinking wine in the house of their first-born brother,

19. "When behold, there came a great gale from beyond the desert and struck the four corners of the house, and it fell upon the young people, and they died, and I am escaped, only I alone, to tell you."

20. Then Job arose and ripped his gown, and shaved his head, and fell to the ground and prostrated himself,

21. And he said:
"Naked came I from my mother's womb,
And naked shall I return thither.
The Lord gave, and the Lord has taken away.
Blessed be the name of the Lord."

22. In all this Job neither sinned, nor ascribed anything amiss to God.

Chapter 2

1. (Again) it was the day when the heavenly host came to present themselves before the Lord, and there came also amongst them the Satan to present himself before the Lord.

2. The Lord said to the Satan "Where is it you come from?" and the Satan answered the Lord and said, "From roaming on the earth and from tramping about upon it".

3. The Lord said to the Satan "Have you given your attention to My servant, Job, for there is none like him on the earth, a man innocent and upright, who fears God and shuns evil, and who still holds fast to his innocence when you incited Me against him to destroy him for nothing?"

4. And the Satan answered the Lord and said, "One pelt for another! Surely all that a man has he will give in exchange for his life.

5. "However, just extend Your hand and touch his bone and his flesh, I declare he will curse You to Your face!"

6. And the Lord said to the Satan, "Behold him in your power. But guard his life!"

7. Then the Satan left the precincts of the presence of the Lord, and smote Job with a sore boil from the sole of his foot to the crown of his head,

8. And he took for himself a shard with which to scratch himself, and he sat among the ashes.

9. Then his wife said to him, "Are you still clinging to your simplicity? Curse God and die!"

10. He said to her, "You speak with the speech of one of the doltish women! Shall we accept the good from associating with the God, and the evil not accept?" In all this Job did not sin with his lips.

11. When three friends of Job heard of all this evil which had come to him, they came each from his place, Eliphaz the Temanite, and Bildad the Shuhite, and Zophar the Naamathite, and they came together by appointment to share his grief, and to comfort him.

12. When they lifted their eyes from the distance and did not recognize him, they lifted up their voices and wept, and each ripped his gown, and they flung dust upon their heads skywards.

13. And they sat with him upon the ground seven days and seven nights, and none uttered a word to him, for they saw that the pain was very great.

Chapter 3

1.   After this, Job opened his mouth and cursed his day,

2.   And Job spoke and said,

3.   Perish the day in which I was born
And the night that declared "A boy is conceived"!

4.   That day, let it be darkness.
Let not God seek it out from above;
Let no radiance brighten it!

5.   Let darkness and the shadow of Death reclaim it;
Let a cloud abide upon it;
Let those who make Cimmerian# the day overwhelm it!

6.   That night, let palpable dark seize it!
Let it not rejoice among the days of the year;
Let it not enter the calendar!

7.   Behold! Let that night be barren,
No celebratory sound come to it!

8.   Let those who curse daylight cast a spell against it
Those ever-ready to arouse Leviathan!

9.   Let the stars of its dawn be darkened;
    Let it await light, but there be none,
    Nor let it glory in the sight of the eyelids of sunrise!

10.   For it did not shut fast the gates of my womb
    Nor hide sorrow from my eyes.

11.   Why could I not have died from the womb!
    Emerged from the belly, and perished?

12.   Why did knees receive me?
    And why breasts, that I should suck?

13.   Else should I have rested and been still;
    I should have slept then, there had been repose for me

14.   With the kings and councillors of the earth
    Who built up the wastes to themselves,

15.   Or with princes, who once had gold,
    Who filled their houses with riches,

16.   Or as a concealed abortion I might never have existed,
    As the infants that never see the light.

17.   There the wicked cease from raging
    And there rest the spent of strength.

18.   Prisoners take their ease together
    Not hearing the shout of the overseer.

19.   The small, he is there with the great,
    And the slave, free of his master.

20.   Why is light given to one in travail,
    And life, to the bitter of soul?

21.   To those who await death when it is not there,
    Though they dig for it more than for hidden treasure?

22.   Who would rejoice, unto exultation,
    They would jubilate, to have found the grave?

23.   To the man whose way is hidden
    And whom God has hedged about?

24.   For I confront my bread with sighing
    And outpoured like waters are my groans.

25.   For I feared a horror and it came to me,
    And that which I dreaded is upon me.

26.   I did not rest, nor was I quiet,
    Nor did I relax, but tumult came.

Chapter 4

1.   Then spoke Eliphaz the Temanite, and said:

2.   Will the attempt to speak to you try your patience?
    But who could refrain from words?

3.   Look, you have instructed many
And lent strength to weaklings.

4.   Your words have sustained the stumbler
And you have invigorated the weak-kneed.

5.   But now, when it comes to you, you rebel.
It reaches you, and you are afraid.

6.   Is not your fear your folly?
But your hope, surely it is the integrity of your ways?

7.   Remember, I pray, "Whoever perished, being innocent?
And where were the righteous cut off?"

8.   Going by what I have seen, it is they who plough sorrow
And sow trouble, who reap the same.

9.   By the breath of God they perish
And by the gust of his anger they are consumed.

10.   The roar of the lion! The growl of the king of beasts!
And the teeth of the cubs erupt#.

11.   When the old lion perishes for lack of prey
The whelps of the lioness disperse.

12.   Now a word was brought to me by stealth
And my ear caught a whisper of it

13.   In agitations from those visions of night
When deep sleep falls upon men.

14.   Fear came upon me, and trembling,
Filling my whole frame with terror.

15.   Then a spirit passed in front of my face.
The hairs of my flesh stood on end.

16.   It stopped, but I could not discern its shape.
A form was before my eyes.
Silence! Then I heard a voice:

17.   "Is mere man more just than God?
The mortal more pure than his Maker?

18.   "If He is uncertain of His servants,
And to His messengers imputes misdeed

19.   "How much more those that dwell in clay,
Whose foundation is in dust!
They are crushed more readily than a moth;

20.   "Between morning and eve they are swatted.
Without warning, they perish for all time.
"Surely their life-line is uprooted in them.
They die - and not in wisdom!"

Chapter 5

1.   Call by all means! Is there any to respond to you?
      And to whom among the holy ones will you turn?
2.   For it is anger that slays the foolish man
      And zeal that kills the simpleton.
3.   When I see a fool settling in
      I curse his habitation abruptly.
4.   His tribe are far from safety
      And crushed in the Gate with none to help them.
5.   What was their harvest, the hungry eat
      Or carry it to the common store#,
      While their troops long for capture#.
6.   For sorrow does not sprout from the dust,
      Nor trouble spring from the ground,
7.   But when a man is born to Trouble
      The brood of Pestilence ride high.
8.   However, for my part I would apply to the Deity;
      Yes, to God would I commit my cause,
9.   Who did great works past discovery,
      Miracles numberless.
10.   Who gave rain over the surface of the earth
      And sent forth water over its surrounds
11.   To set the lowlands on high
      That the Kedarites# were raised out of reach to safety,
12.   Frustrating the plans of the crafty
      That their hands achieved nothing lasting;
13.   Trapping the smart ones in their guile
      That the schemes of the crooked were swept away.
14.   In the daytime they encountered darkness
      And they groped in the noontide as the night.
15.   But He saved from the sword, from their own mouths,
      And from the power of the mighty, the poor,
16.   That the helpless might have hope
      And injustice hold her tongue.
17.   Look, "Happy is the man whom God correcteth;"
      And "Despise not the chastisement of the Almighty."
18.   For He causes pain, but He binds it up.
      He wounds, but His hands heal.
19.   In six troubles He will deliver you;
      Even in seven no evil will befall you.
20.   In famine He ransomed you from death,
      And in war from the power of the sword.

21. You will be protected from the lash of slander,
     Nor need you fear devastation, that it is on the way.
22. Laugh at ruin and dearth,
     And fear not the beasts of the earth,
23. For you will have a covenant with the stones of the field
     And the beasts of the wild will be at peace with you;
24. And you will know your dwelling to be inviolate,
     And administer your habitation and not be remiss,
25. And you will know your seed abundant
     And your posterity as the grass of the earth.
26. You will go in strength to the grave
     Like the ascent of a hay-stack in its season.
27. Attend to this! We have studied it. It is so.
     Hearken to it and you bind it to your heart!

Chapter 6

1.   Then Job spoke and said:
2.   Oh that my provocation were truly weighed
     Together with my disaster in a balance!
3.   For then it would outweigh the sea-sand.
     This is why my words are wild:
4.   That the arrows of the Almighty are with me
     Whose poison my spirit drinks.
     The terrors of God are arrayed against me!
5.   Does the wild-ass bray when he has grass?
     Does the ox low over his fodder?
6.   Can anyone stomach the unseemly unseasoned?
     What taste is there in the rheum of one desperate for death?
7.   My gorge refuses to touch!
     They are like the deformities of Lahmi!
8.   Would that my request were allowed
     And that God would grant my hope
9.   And that it would please God to crush me,
     To loose His hand and cut me off,
10. And that I might still have my comfort
     While I recoiled in the anguish He does not stint,
     That I never disowned the words of the Holy One.
11. What is my strength, that I should linger?
     And what will be my end, that I prolong my life?
12. Is the strength of the stones my strength?
     Is my flesh brass?

13.   Can I not even help myself?
     And is sagacity so far driven out of me

14.   That I become one to despair of mercy from his Friend,
     Or abandon the fear of God?

15.   My brothers were treacherous like a wadi;
     Like a waterhole of the wadis, they fled away.

16.   Are* the Kedarites# made of ice?
     Is snow hidden on them?

17.   Once they were singed#, they vanished,
     In his heat, they were snuffed out of their place.

18.   The paths of their roads turned back;
     They went up into the wilderness and were lost.

19.   They beheld the paths of Tema;
     The ways of Sheba awaited them.

20.   They were disconcerted because he was steadfast;
     There they came and were confounded.

21.   Otherwise# you would have been for him.
     When you see terror, you take fright.

22.   Is it that I said, "Give to me!"?
     Or, "Offer a bribe on my behalf from your wealth!"?

23.   Or, "Rescue me from the hands of the foe!"?
     Or, "Ransom me from the tyrant's grip!"?

24.   Instruct me, and I shall be silent,
     And where I have erred, make me understand.

25.   How is straight speech grievous?
     And what does reproof from you prove?

26.   Do you think your words are convincing,
     And the cries of a desperado mere wind?

27.   Would you even cast lots over an orphan
     As you haggle over your friend?

28.   Now be so kind as to look at me -
     Would I lie to your faces?

29.   Come again, let there be no injustice!
     And again! My righteousness is at stake!

30.   Is there anything unjust in my speech?
     Have I not the wit to recognize disaster?

Chapter 7

1.   Is there not service assigned to Man upon the earth
    With his days as the days of a hired man?

2.   As a servant, he longs for the shade,
    And as a hired man he hopefully expects his wage.

3. But me! My portion is months of vacuity,
   And nights of trouble are allotted me.

4. If I lie down, then I say "When shall I arise?" But the night is endless
   And I am surfeited with nightmares until dawn,

5. My flesh clad in worm and dust-clod;
   My body inert and discarded.

6. My days are swifter than a weaver's shuttle,
   And draw to an end without hope.

7. Oh remember! For my life is but a breath,
   My sight will not return to seeing good.

8. The eye that now sees me will behold me no more.
   While Your eyes are (yet) upon me, I am not.

9. As a cloud is consumed or flees away,
   So he who descends to Sheol will not arise.

10. He will return no more to his shell,
    Nor shall his abode know him again.

11. So shall I not spare my voice.
    I will speak in the anguish of my spirit;
    I will complain in the bitterness of my soul:

12. Am I Yam? Or Tannin?
    That You post a guard over me!

13. For when I say, "My couch will console me,
    My bed will alleviate my plaint",

14. Then You terrify me with dreams
    And affright me with visions,

15. So that I prefer suffocation,
    Death to my bodily form#.

16. I reject that I should live for ever!
    Lay off me! For my days are vain.

17. "What is man that You magnify him?"
    And that You set Your mind on him?

18. And examine him every morning
    And try him every moment?

19. For how long will You not turn from me
    And let up on me long enough for me to swallow?

20. Suppose I have sinned. What have I done, to You,
    O gaol-warden of Man?
    Why have You made me Your target
    That I have become a burden to myself?

21. And why do You not lift my transgression
    And pardon my sin?
    For then could I lie down in the dust
    Where You could enquire for me, but I should not be.

Chapter 8

1.　　Then Bildad the Shuhite spoke and said:
2.　　How long will you go on bellowing these things?
　　　Such a tempest are the words of your mouth!
3.　　Does God pervert judgement?
　　　Or the Almighty pervert the right?
4.　　If your children sinned against Him
　　　And He consigned them to the consequences of their transgression,
5.　　If you yourself seek earnestly to God
　　　And appeal to the Almighty -
6.　　If you are pure and upright -
　　　Then will He rouse Himself for you
　　　And restore the habitation of your righteousness,
7.　　And be your beginning never so small,
　　　Your end He will greatly enlarge.
8.　　For ask, I suggest, the generations past,
　　　And ascertain what their fathers discovered
9.　　For creatures of yesterday are we, and know nothing,
　　　For our days upon earth are but a shadow
10.　 Surely they can teach you, and speak to you,
　　　And utter these words from their hearts:
11.　 "Can the papyrus grow without the marsh?
　　　Can the reed shoot up without water?
12.　 "While yet in its prime and not plucked,
　　　It will wither ahead of all other grasses.
13.　 "Such are the ways of all who forget God.
　　　Thus the hope of the godless will perish.
14.　 "He who despises# his Troth,
　　　And whose trust is in a spider's house,
15.　 "When he relies on his House, it will not stand,
　　　When he holds fast to it, it will not endure.
16.　 "(The righteous) is full of sap as long as the sun endures.
　　　And about His garden, his shoots spread forth.
17.　 "Around His spring his roots weave.
　　　He beholds a House of rock.
18.　 "If one destroy him from his place
　　　And repudiate him: - *I know you not!*
19.　 Behold, this is the joy of his way -
　　　That from alien soil they will sprout anew".
20.　 See! God will not reject the innocent,
　　　Nor will He strengthen the power of evildoers.

21. So much so that He will fill your mouth with laughter
    And your lips with triumph.
22. Those that hate you will be clothed in shame,
    And the dwellings of the wicked will be no more.

Chapter 9

1. Then Job spoke and said:
2. Truly I know that it is so -
   "How can a mere man be justified with God?"
3. If one desired to dispute with Him
   He could not answer Him, not one in a thousand.
4. However wise at heart and mighty in strength,
   Who has stood up to Him and come out whole?
5. Him, Who removes mountains and they know it not
   When He overturns them in His rage?
6. Him, Who rattles the earth from its place
   That its pillars stagger?
7. Him, Who commands the sun that he not rise
   And seals the isolation of the stars?
8. He stretched out the heavens, He alone,
   And trod down the pretensions of the Sea.
9. He ordained the Hyades, Orion,
   And the Pleiades, as well as the Chambers of the South.
10. "He did great works till past discovery,
    And miracles numberless" -
11. See! He trampled me down, and I did not see!
    And He violated, while I did not perceive Him.
12. See! He has robbed; who will restore it?
    Who will say to Him, "What have You done?"?
13. God will not recall His anger;
    The confederates of Rahab grovelled beneath Him.
14. How much the less shall I prevail
    And set out my case against Him?
15. When, though I am in the right, I cannot answer.
    I shall throw myself upon the mercy of the court!
16. If I were to summon, and He acknowledge me,
    I should not credit that He would listen to my voice
17. Not that One Who bruises me with the whirlwind
    And multiplies my wounds for nothing;
18. Who will not leave me to draw my breath,
    But sates me with bitterness.

19.   If it be a matter of force, well, there is the power!
    But of justice, who will receive my testimony?

20.   Am I righteous? My mouth condemns me;
    Am I innocent? It shows me perverse!

21.   Am I innocent? I know not myself.
    I despise my life.

22.   It is all one. Therefore do I declare:
    He makes an end of innocent and guilty both.

23.   If disaster slay suddenly,
    He derides the ordeal of the guiltless.

24.   The land is given into the power of the wicked.
    He has covered the faces of its judges.
    If not, then who did?

25.   Yet my days hasten swifter than any runner.
    They flee without glimpse of good,

26.   Speed by with the swift skiffs,
    Like the eagle that stoops on its prey.

27.   If I say, "I will forget my complaint,
    I will discard my frown and be of good cheer,"

28.   I dread all my tribulations.
    I know You will not acquit me.

29.   I shall be condemned.
    Why then do I waste my efforts?

30.   Though I wash myself with snow
    And cleanse my hands with lye,

31.   Still You will tumble me into a ditch
    That my very garments* will abhor me!

32.   For This is no man like myself, that I should rebut him,
    And we come together in judgement.

33.   There is no mediator between us
    Who might deal evenhandedly for us two.

34.   Let Him remove His whip from me,
    And let not His terror un-man me -

35.   I long to speak, and not be in fear of Him,
    But that is not how I am with myself.

Chapter 10

1.   I loathe my life!
    I will unleash my complaint.
    I will speak in the bitterness of my soul,

2.   Saying to God, "Do not condemn me!
    Reveal to me why You prosecute me.

3.   "Does it do You some good to persecute,
That You reject the work of Your hands
But shed radiance on the counsel of the wicked?

4.   "Do You have eyes of flesh?
Do You see as a man sees?

5.   "Are Your days as the days of a man?
Are even Your years as man's days

6.   "That You grub for my guilt
And search for my sin?

7.   "It is within Your knowledge that I am not wicked,
And none can rescue from Your power.

8.   "Your hands shaped me and fashioned me;
At the same time You turn and engulf me.

9.   "Reflect that like clay You have moulded me,
And that to the dust You will return me;

10.   "Surely like milk You did pour me
And like cheese curdled me;

11.   "In skin and flesh You arrayed me;
With bones and sinews guyed me;

12.   "Life and favour You bestowed on me
And Your providence watched over the spirit within me.

13.   "But these things You hid in the heart of You;
I know that all this was from You!

14.   "If I erred, then You would mark me,
And of my sin would never acquit me;

15.   "If I were wicked, woe unto me!
And even if righteous, my head should not lifted be.
Oh! Have enough of my shame and consider my agony!

16.   "As it mounts, like a lion You hunt me
And renew Your marvels upon me;

17.   "You refresh Your accusations against me
And whip up Your anger towards me -
Both service and wages laid on me!

18.   "Why then from the womb did You extrude me?
I had died and no eye seen me!"

19.   I should have been as if I had not been;
I should have been born from womb to grave.

20.   Will not my brief day cease?
Or He desist from me, that I may take a little comfort

21.   E'er I go whence I shall not return,
To the land of darkness and the shadow of Death?

22.   The land of Stygian gloom, as of palpable dark,
          The shadow of Death, and chaos,
          Where the shade is as palpable dark.

Chapter 11

1.   Then Zophar the Naamathite spoke and said:
2.   Shall a spate of words go unanswered?
          And must a voluble man be accounted right?
3.   Your ranting has silenced the people;
          You have blasphemed, with none to shame you;
4.   You said, "My doctrine is pure,
          And I have been spotless in Your eyes".
5.   But if only God would speak
          And converse directly with you,
6.   Then He would tell you the secrets of wisdom,
          For manifold is sagacity.
          Know then that God has remitted to you some of your sin!
7.   Can you encompass the range of God?
          Can you explore to the furthest bound of the Almighty?
8.   High as the heavens - what can you do?
          Deeper than hell - what can you know?
9.   Longer than the earth is its measure
          And broader than the sea.
10.   If He violate, or deliver (one) up,
          Or summon (another), who shall reverse Him?
11.   For He knows worthless men,
          And shall He see iniquity and pay it no heed?
12.   But every empty man thinks himself wise,
          And a wild ass's colt a man is born!
13.   If only you would set your heart to rights,
          And stretch out your hands to Him,
14.   If, iniquity being on your hand, you thrust it from you,
          And let not injustice dwell in your tents,
15.   Then you will lift up your countenance free from blemish,
          And you will be steadfast, and need no longer fear.
16.   Therefore forget your trouble;
          Remember it as water under the bridge.
17.   Then the future will dawn brighter than noon;
          The shade will be as the morning,
18.   And you will trust that there is hope
          And search for security no more;

19.   And you will couch with none to make you afraid
       And many will entreat your favour.
20.   But the eyes of the wicked will long in vain
       And there will be no escape for them,
       And their hope will be the breathing out of life.

Chapter 12

1.   Then Job spoke and said:
2.   Truly, but you are the people,
       And with you, wisdom will die out!
3.   I also have understanding, like you;
       In no wise do I fall short of you;
       And who does not know things like these?
4.   I have become a laughing-stock to His friends
       (They say) "He who calls upon God and He answers him
       Is a just and innocent jest!
5.   "Scorn of Disaster, Disdain of Favours,
       Is ripe for stumbling!
6.   "His tents are secure - for robbers!
       And his fortresses - for those who provoke God!
       For whoever subdues God to his power!"
7.   However, ask the beasts, and they will teach thee,
       And the fowl of the air, and they will tell thee,
8.   Or speak to the earth, and it will teach thee,
       And the fish of the sea, they will recount to thee:
9.   Which does not know of all these
       That the hand of the Lord wrought this,
10.   In Whose power is the spirit of all that lives
       And the breath of all mankind?
11.   Does not the ear test words
       As the palate tastes its food?
12.   "Wisdom is with the aged
       And length of days has understanding"?
13.   "With Him is wisdom and might;
       He has counsel and understanding"?
14.   "If He throw down, it shall not be rebuilt".
       "If He confine a man, he shall not be released".
15.   "If He restrain the waters, they dry up".
       "If He send them forth, they overturn the earth".
16.   (So) with Him are strength and sagacity;
       His, misleader and misled!

17.   He it was Who led councillors away barefoot
     And made fools of judges.

18.   Who slackened the bond of kings
     And bound their loins with a slave-band.

19.   Who led priests away barefoot
     And subverted those established of old;

20.   Who robbed the faithful of speech
     And diverted the judgement of elders,

21.   Pouring contempt upon princes
     And undermining the morale of the legions#.

22.   It was He uncovered deep things out of darkness
     And brought out into light the shadow of Death!

23.   He increased the nations, and destroyed them,
     Spread the nations abroad, and abandoned them*,

24.   Disheartening the chiefs of the People of the Land
     When He left them to wander a trackless waste.

25.   They groped in the dark, for there was no light,
     And He made them to stagger, like drunkards.

Chapter 13

1.   Look, my eyes have seen it all,
     My ears have heard and understood it.

2.   What you know, I know, I also;
     In no wise do I fall short of you.

3.   Nonetheless, myself, I would speak to the Almighty,
     Indeed, it pleases me to dispute with God.

4.   And nonetheless, you lot are whitewashers with lies,
     Fine physicians, all of you!

5.   If only you would hold your tongues,
     And that would stand to you for wisdom!

6.   Be so good as to listen to my accusation
     And attend to the pleadings of my lips!

7.   Is it for God that you speak unjustly
     And on His behalf that you voice deceit?

8.   Would you curry favour with Him?
     On God's behalf would you enter the lists?

9.   Would it be good if He searched you people's souls?
     Or, as one deceives a man, would you deceive Him?

10.   Oh, but you people will receive His censure
     If you hypocritically curry favour!

11.   Without doubt His magnificence will terrify you people
     And the awe of Him overcome you -

12. Your household gods are figures of ash,
    Like columns of clay your minarets#!

13. Keep silent with me! For it is I, I that must speak,
    And let come on me what may.

14. Why do I put my heart in my mouth
    And take my life in my hands?

15. If He intends to slay me, I cannot wait,
    But I will defend my ways to His face.

16. Even this would be as good as deliverance to me,
    For the ungodly cannot come before Him.

17. Hear ye! Hear ye! My speech!
    Be attentive to my declaration!

18. Let it be known that I have prepared my case.
    I know that I shall be vindicated.

19. Is there anyOne to contend with me?
    If not, I shall hold my peace and perish.

20. Only two things do not do with me -
    Then shall I not hide from Your presence:

21. Withdraw Your hand far from me,
    And do not intimidate me with Your terror.

22. Then summon, and I shall answer,
    Or I shall speak, and You respond.

23. With what sins and transgressions am I charged?
    Reveal to me my iniquities and my sins!

24. Why have You averted Your face
    And reckoned me as an enemy to You?

25. Would You strike terror from a driven leaf
    And pursue dry chaff

26. That You indite against me bitter charges
    And make me inherit the guilt of my youth?

27. You put my feet in a hobble
    And then scrutinize my ways!
    On the soles of my feet You engrave Yourself,

28. While it is wearing away as by a canker,
    Like a garment consumed by a moth!

Chapter 14

1. Man that is born of woman,
   Short are his days and full of turmoil.

2. Like a flower, he comes forth and withers;
   He fleets like a shadow and does not abide.

3.   And to this You devote Your vigil!
       And me You would bring into judgement with You?

4.   Would that the pure were distinguished from the defiled!
       Not blent!

5.   If his time is decided,
       The number of his months is at Your discretion,
       You have ordained his limit which he shall not pass,

6.   (Then) look away from him - and he will cease
       While he fulfils, like a hired man, his contract.

7.   Though there is hope for a tree,
       If it be cut down, that it will again renew,
       And its shoots not cease;

8.   If its root grow old in the earth
       And in the dust its trunk die,

9.   At the scent of water it will bud
       And put forth boughs like a sapling;

10.   But a man dies and lies flat.
       Yes; man perishes; and where is he?

11.   Let the waters depart the sea!
       Let the river be wasted and dry!

12.   But man lies down to rise no more.
       Till the heavens pass away they will not waken
       Nor be roused from their sleep.

13.   Oh, that You would preserve me in Sheol!
       That You would conceal me until You repent of Your wrath,
       Set me a limit, and then remember me!

14.   If a man dies, will he ever revive?
       All the days of my bondage I would wait
       Until my reward came.

15.   You would call, and I would answer You;
       You would yearn for the work of Your hands.

16.   For then You would take note of my ways;
       Not watch for my every flaw.

17.   My transgression would be sealed in a bag
       And You would whitewash over my iniquity.

18.   But in truth the fallen mountain wears away,
       And the cliff moves from its place.

19.   The water erodes the stones,
       And its own springs wash away the dust of the earth;
       And You destroy the hope of man.

20.   You subdue him, and he departs into eternity;
       Changing his state, You dismiss him.

21. His children come to honour, and he is unaware;
    Or they are humbled, but he knows nothing of it,
22. But his flesh upon him feels his pain,
    And his spirit within him mourns.

Chapter 15

1. Then spoke Eliphaz the Temanite and said:
2. Shall a wise man answer the ravings of the wind
   And encumber his belly with the sirocco,
3. Argue with pointless chatter
   Or words that can lead nowhere?
4. Indeed, you must discount fear
   And moderate your complaint in the presence of God;
5. For your chastisement must teach your lips
   And you must select the language of the prudent.
6. Your own mouth condemns you, and not I,
   And your lips testify against you.
7. Were you the first man born?
   And brought forth before the hills?
8. Did you eavesdrop at the council of God
   And reserve wisdom for yourself?
9. What do you know that we know not?
   You understand, and it escapes us?
10. Among us are both old and grey-haired men,
    Weighted with more years than your own father.
11. Is the consolation of God too little for you
    That you find my speech too gentle?
12. Why are you so beside yourself?
    And why do your eyes flash fire
13. That you would forfeit your spirit to God,
    And spit such speeches from your mouth?
14. What is mere man that he should be clean,
    And that he should be right, that is born of woman?
15. If He is uncertain of His holy ones,
    And the heavens are not pure in His sight,
16. How much less the abominable and obscene -
    Man that swills iniquity like water!
17. I shall declare to you. Hear me;
    And let me relate what I have seen:
18. That which those in the know are saying,
    And do not hide from their elders:

19.   "To them alone the land was given
        And no foreign foe trespasses among them!"
20.   All the days of the wicked, he shall writhe,
        And few shall be the years in store for the tyrant.
21.   The cry of alarms is in his ears;
        In peacetime the destroyer will come for him!
22.   Never certain of returning from darkness,
        He will be sought by the sword.
23.   A vagrant in search of bread, lost,#
        He senses that the day of dark is near at hand.
24.   The enemy will frighten him; and anxiety
        Overwhelm him, like a ruler about to topple
25.   For he stretched forth his hand against God,
        And against the Almighty he played the hero.
26.   He runs at Him in stiff-necked pride
        In the density of his protective idols#.
27.   Though he smear his face with his fat
        And grease his cuisse,
28.   Yet will he live in ghost-cities,
        In uninhabitable houses
        That are ripe for ruin.
29.   He shall not become rich, nor shall his army prosper,
        Nor shall any of theirs# become established in the Land.
30.   He shall not evade the darkness.
        His shoot the searing flame will wither,
        And he will depart at a puff of His mouth!
31.   Let him not imagine he is being misled by vanity,
        For vanity will be his recompense!
32.   Before his time it will be fulfilled,
        Nor shall his high one flourish.
33.   He will rob - as a vine - his own grapes.
        He will shed - as an olive-tree - his own blossom.
34.   For the company of the godless is forlorn
        And fire will consume the tents of traitors#.
35.   They conceive trouble and bring forth sorrow,
        And their womb gestates rebellion!

Chapter 16

1.   Then Job spoke and said:
2.   I have heard much of the same sort,
        Mischievous comforters, the lot of you!

3.   Have we come to an end of windy words?
        Or does something ail you that you keep on answering?

4.   Much as I too might have liked to have spoken as you do
        If only your lives were where mine is,
        I might have conspired against you with words
        And wagged my head at you,

5.   I would (in fact) have strengthened you with my mouth,
        And compassion would have restrained my lips.

6.   Had I spoken, my pain would not have been eased,
        And had I forborne, what relief should I have had?

7.   Howbeit, now it has tried my patience.
        When You ravaged all my congregation

8.   You snatched me away. It has become evidence
        And witnesses against me.
        My false position testifies to my face!

9.   His anger tore me; and so He resents me.
        He gnashes his teeth at me.
        My enemy sharpens his eyes on me.

10.   They gape at me with their mouths.
        They strike my cheek in contempt.
        Everyone, they surfeit themselves on me!

11.   God delivered me to the ungodly
        And abandoned me into the hands of the wicked.

12.   I was at ease, and He battered me;
        And He took me by the nape and He shattered me;
        And He set me up as a target for Himself.

13.   His archers surround me;
        He cleaves my reins unsparingly;
        He spills my bile upon the ground.

14.   He breaks me with breach upon breach,
        Runs at me like a hero.

15.   Sackcloth I have sewn to my skin
        And thrust my horn in the dust.

16.   My face boils over with weeping,
        And on my eyelids sits the shadow of Death

17.   Although there is no wrongdoing on my hands
        And my prayer has been pure.

18.   O earth! Cover not my blood!
        And let there be no home for my cry!

19.   Already, behold, my brief is in heaven,
        And my record on high.

20.   My interpreters, my friends,
        My eye lets fall to God,

21.   Pleading for a man with God
        As a man might for his friend.
22.   For the lean years have come,
        And I set out on that path from which I shall not return.

Chapter 17

1.   My spirit is destroyed; my days extinguished;
        I am ready for the grave -
2.   Unless I am harbouring delusions
        And my eye assents to their deceptions#.
3.   Display (some sign)! Give a pledge (for) me with You
        No-one will trust me!
4.   For, having hidden their hearts from understanding,
        You therefore will not exalt them.
5.   To His portion He said "Friends!"
        But the eyes of His children fail,
6.   And He set me to be a ruler of nations,
        But as Tophet of yore I have become,
7.   And my sight is dimmed with frustration
        And all my purposes are as a shadow.
8.   The upright are appalled at this,
        And the innocent, that the heathen triumphs,
9.   So that the righteous embraces his ways
        And the pure of hands reinforces his strength.
10.   But as for you lot, turn back and come again
        For I cannot find one with gumption among you!
11.   When my days are past, the conspiracy parts.
        My conclusions
12.   Turn night into day.
        The light is near by very reason of the darkness!
13.   If I am awaiting Sheol as my home;
        If I have spread my couch in the darkness;
14.   Have greeted corruption, "You are my father!"
        Called the worm, "My mother!" and "My sister!",
15.   Where then should be this my "hope"?
        And that my "hope" who then should see it?
16.   Will they descend to the babble of Sheol?
        Shall we be at rest together in the dust?

Chapter 18

1.   Then spoke Bildad the Shuhite and said:

2.   How long will you (Judeans) treat the Kenizzites* as bywords?
   You make up your minds, and afterwards we may speak!

3.   Why are we accounted as beasts,
   Unclean in your sights?

4.   You who tears himself in his anger!
   Shall the earth be depopulated for your sake
   And the cliff moved from its place?

5.   The flame* of the wicked also shall be put out
   And the blaze of his fire not shine.

6.   Light shall be darkness in his tent
   And his lamp shall be put out above him.

7.   The strides of his strength will be shortened
   And his own cleverness cast him down,

8.   For he is consigned to a net by his feet
   And he trudges in its toils.

9.   A trap grabs him by the heel
   And a web holds him fast.

10.   His destruction is concealed in the earth
    And his undoing by the way.

11.   Terrors affright him on all sides
    And harry him at the heels.

12.   Let his strength grow faint
    And retribution will be ready for his stumbling.

13.   Piecemeal it will consume his body;
    Piecemeal shall the Firstborn of Death consume him!

14.   His surety will be torn from his tent,
    And panic impel his steps to Moloch.

15.   It will dwell in his tent when he is no more.
    Brimstone will be strewn on his habitation!

16.   From beneath will his roots dry up,
    And from above his branches wither.

17.   The memory of him will perish from the earth,
    And there shall be no name for him on the face of the disc.

18.   They will thrust him out from light into darkness
    And send him fleeing from the world.

19.   No offspring will he have; no posterity among the people,
    Nor any survivor in his home.

20.   Those in the west will be appalled at his fate,
    And in the east they will be seized with horror.

21.   Such, be assured, are the dwellings of the unjust,
          And this the destiny of him who acknowledges not God!

Chapter 19

1.   Then Job spoke and said:
2.   How long will you grieve my soul
          And pulverize me with words?
3.   These ten times you have insulted me.
          Are you not ashamed that you misrepresent# me?
4.   And all the more truly if I have erred -
          I have to live with my error!
5.   If you must glorify yourselves at my expense,
          And advance my disgrace as evidence against me,
6.   Know, then, that God has cheated me,
          And that His siegework surrounds me.
7.   Behold, I cry "Violence!", but I am not answered;
          I cry for help, but there is no law.
8.   He has blocked my road that I cannot pass,
          And over my paths He has imposed darkness.
9.   He has stripped me of my honour
          And lifted the crown from my head.
10.   He has demolished me from all sides, and I depart,
          And He has rooted out my hope like a tree.
11.   And His anger is kindled against me
          And He reckons me as His foe.
12.   En masse His raiders come
          And throw up their ramp against me
          And encamp about my keep.
13.   He has removed my brothers far from me
          And my acquaintances are quite estranged from me.
14.   My neighbours have failed
          And my familiars have forgotten me.
15.   My household and my maidens treat me as a stranger.
          I am as an alien in their eyes.
16.   I summon my servant, but he does not respond.
          I entreat him with my mouth!
17.   My spirit seems strange to my wife,
          And my favour to the children of my body!
18.   Even criminals despise me.
          Let me arise, and they speak against me.
19.   All my old cronies abominate me,
          And those whom I love turn their backs on me.

20. My ghost clings to my skin and my flesh,
    But I escaped by the skin of my teeth
21. Pity me! Pity me! O you my friends!
    For the hand of God has touched me!
22. Why do you pursue me, the same as God
    And do not weary of my life?
23. Would then that my words were written;
    Would that they were inscribed in an archive,
24. With iron pen and lead,
    Carved in the rock for ever!
25. And me, that I might know my Redeemer alive,
    And that in the end He will arise upon the dust,
26. And that after my body, this might be restored,
    And in my flesh I should see God,
27. Whom I myself should see for myself
    And my eyes behold, and no stranger.
    (For this) do my reins perish in my bosom.
28. Because you say, "How are we persecuting him?"
    And that the root of the matter is in me,
29. Be in fear yourselves of the sword,
    For spite is (made) a sword-worthy sin,
    That you may acknowledge His might#.

Chapter 20

1. Then spoke Zophar the Naamathite and said:
2. It is my agitation which makes me reply,
   And because of the urgency within me.
3. I have heard my insulting rebuke,
   But an inspiration from my understanding answers me
4. Do you know this from olden time,
   Since man was set upon the earth?
5. That the exultation of the wicked is brief,
   And the joy of the godless momentary?
6. Though his pride mount up to the heavens
   And his head vaunt itself to the clouds,
7. Like his dung, he shall perish for ever.
   Those who once saw him will ask, "Where is he?".
8. Like a dream, he will fly away and none find him,
   And he will be put to flight like a vision of night.
9. The eye that descried him will do so no longer,
   Nor shall his home behold him more.

10.   His children will curry favour with the poor
              Whose hands will repay his affliction.

11.   His life will end in his youth,
              And she will lie down with him in the dust.

12.   Though evil exude sweetness in his mouth,
              And he secrete it under his tongue,

13.   Though he cherish and will not relinquish it
              And hoard it within his palate,

14.   His food will be changed in his bowels -
              The bitterness of vipers is within him!

15.   He swallowed riches, but will vomit them back;
              God will expel them from his belly.

16.   He sucks the poison of vipers;
              The adder's tongue will slay him!

17.   Let him not gloat over his rivers -
              The overflowing streams of honey and butter!

18.   Not him who will disgorge the fruit of his labour and not digest it;
              As his wealth, so his restitution, and he shall not profit.

19.   Because in dereliction he crushed the poor,
              He robbed his House and never built it up.

20.   Because he knew no quiet in himself,
              He will not let him escape with his treasures.

21.   Nothing could escape his devouring,
              Therefore his prosperity is insecure.

22.   In the abundance of his sufficiency he will be in straits;
              The hand of every downtrodden man will come at him.

23.   Let this be for the filling of his belly!
              He will visit him with the ferocity of His anger.
              It will rain down on him when he is embattled#!

24.   Let him flee the iron shaft,
              The bow of brass will impale him!

25.   When He draws, he will depart his pride;
              And at a flash of lightning, he will quit his bitterness.
              Terrors assail him!

26.   All-dark is kept hidden for his treasure.
              The unfanned fire will consume him!
              The survivor of his tent will fare ill.

27.   The heavens will disclose his iniquity
              While the earth rises up against him.

28.   Let the wealth of his House be carried away,
              Flotsam in the season of His wrath!

29.   This is the portion of the wicked man from God
              Yes, the heritage of his verdict from the Supreme.

Chapter 21

1. Then Job spoke and said:
2. Listen carefully to my words
    And let that be your condolences -
3. Indulge me while I speak,
    And after my speech, mock on!
4. Have I a quarrel with men?
    So why shouldn't I be short-tempered with you?
5. Attend to me, and be appalled
    And clap hand to mouth.
6. Whenever I think about it I am horrified
    And my body is seized with trembling.
7. Why do the wicked live?
    Make their way and gain great wealth?
8. Their seed is established with them in their sight
    And their descendants before their eyes;
9. Their houses are safe from fear
    Nor is the rod of God laid on them.
10. Their bull impregnates and does not balk;
    Their cow calves and does not miscarry;
11. They spawn their babes like the herd
    And their children go a-dancing;
12. They raise the clamour of timbrel and harp
    And rejoice to the tune of the pipe;
13. They pass their days in prosperity,
    And on a sudden go down to Sheol.
14. But they said to God, "Leave us alone!"
    And "We desire no knowledge of Your ways!
15. "What is the Almighty that we should serve Him?"
    And "What will it profit us if we entreat Him?"
16. If their prosperity is not in their own hands
    Then I am far from understanding the wisdom of the wicked.
17. How often is the lamp of the wicked put out
    That their deserts come upon them?
    Lots He apportions in His (blind) rage.
18. They are as straw in wind
    And as chaff whipped away by storm.
19. God saves His strength for His (own) children;
    When He gives one his quietus, he knows!
20. His own eyes see his ruin*
    As he drinks the wrath of the Almighty.

21.   For what will be his pleasure in his House after him
        When the tale of his time is told?
22.   Is it God's aim to teach wisdom
        Through His judgement of the eminent?
23.   This one dies in full strength;
        His end in ease and peace,
24.   His organs# full of fat
        And his limbs well-padded;
25.   And this one dies with a bitter soul
        And has never tasted good.
26.   Alike they lie down in the dust
        And worms cover them over.
27.   If I understand the workings of your minds
        And the secret thoughts with which you wrong me,
28.   Then you will say "Where is the princely house?
        And where the canopy of the dwelling-place of the wicked?"
29.   Have you not asked the travellers?
        And do you not accept their intimations
30.   That the evil is deferred to a day of retribution;
        They are escorted (unharmed) to a day of wrath?
31.   Who will confront him with his way?
        And when He has acted, who will requite him
32.   When he has been escorted to the tombs
        While He kept watch over his harvest-heap?
33.   The nuggets of the stream edulcorate him,
        And all mankind may loot his leavings,
        But to his face was never an account.
34.   How then do you offer me empty consolations?
        For of your answers all that remains is falsity!

Chapter 22

1.   Then spoke Eliphaz the Temanite and said:
2.   Is it God's duty to benefit man
        On the grounds that a wise man benefits Him?
3.   Is it a joy to God if you are righteous?
        Or a windfall to Him if you make blameless your ways?
4.   Is it because of your fear that He rebukes you,
        Enters into judgement with you?
5.   Is it not that your evildoing is great
        And without end your iniquity?
6.   That you have indentured your brother for nothing
        And stripped the naked of clothing?

7.   Given no water to the weary
     And withheld bread from the hungry?

8.   Yes, the strong-armed man owns the land
     And whom he favours dwells therein!

9.   Widows you have dispatched empty
     That the support of orphans was crushed.

10. That is why there are snares around you
     And sudden terror affrights you,

11. Or impenetrable darkness,
     Or copious waters cover you.

12. Is not God high as heaven?
     And behold, the topmost stars, how high they are!

13. But you said "What does God know?
     Can He judge through the cloud-cover?

14. "The cloud veils Him and He sees nothing
     While He parades the vault of heaven!"

15. Will you keep to the perpetual pathway
     Which the companions of evil keep?

16. Who are gathered in before their time -
     Whose footing was spilled as a river?

17. Those who said to God, "Begone from us!"
     And (you ask) "What does the Almighty do to them?"

18. And (you answer) "He fills their houses with prosperity,"
     Yet (you say) "The wisdom of the wicked, far be it from me!"

19. Righteous men look on and jeer,
     And an innocent man would deride them,

20. (Saying) "Surely our enemy# is gone to perdition,
     And the fire will consume their remnant!"

21. Submit yourself to Him and sue for peace;
     What you earn thereby will be good.

22. Accept the Law from His lips
     And lay up His words to your heart.

23. If you return to the Almighty, you will be restored.
     Dispel unrighteousness from your tents,

24. And leave treasure to the dust
     And gold to the stones of the stream;

25. Then shall the Almighty be your treasure,
     And riches *in excelcis* to you;

26. For surely you will find delight in the Almighty
     And lift up your countenance to God.

27. When you supplicate Him, He will hear you
     While you honour your vows;

28.   And when you make a decree, He will uphold it for you,
        And light will shine on your paths,
29.   For humbled, and you will concede it#, is pride,
        And He saves the meek in spirit.
30.   He will deliver (even) him who is not innocent,
        And he will be delivered through the purity of your hands.

Chapter 23

1.   Then Job spoke and said:
2.   So this time too my complaint is rebellion!
        The heavy hand upon me is because of my groaning!
3.   Would I might know where I might find Him!
        I would come to His establishment;
4.   I would set out my case before Him
        And be fluent in my pleading.
5.   I would understand the words with which He answered me
        And comprehend what He said to me.
6.   Would He use force majeur to refute me?
        No, on the contrary, He would respect me.
7.   Then the upright may reason with Him;
        So should I be discharged* for ever by my Judge.
8.   Behold, I go east, and He is not there;
        West, and I do not discern Him;
9.   North, where He labours#, and I cannot behold Him;
        He is concealed from the South, that I cannot see.
10.   But He knows the nature of my way;
        If He tried me, I should emerge like gold
11.   My foot has clung to His path;
        I followed His way unerringly;
12.   Nor have I departed from the commandment of His lips;
        I treasured the words of His mouth above my own decree.
13.   But He is One, and who can annul Him?
        And His spirit wills, and He does it.
14.   Thus will He execute my decree,
        And He has myriads of the like to deal with.
15.   Therefore am I nervous in His presence;
        When I think it over, I am terrified of Him.
16.   Yes, God dissolves my courage
        And the Almighty intimidates me
17.   Because I was not cut off before the darkness,
        Nor did He cover my face from the gloom.

Chapter 24

1.   Why were the times not held back by the Almighty
    That those who know Him did not see His days?

2.   Boundary stones are moved
    And the flock seized and devoured.

3.   The ass of orphans is driven away;
    The widow's ox taken in pledge.

4.   The poor are shouldered out of the way;
    The destitute of the earth are run to ground together.

5.   See! Wild asses in the wilderness
    They set off on their business, scrounging for prey!
    To Him, the desert is food for young men!

6.   They forage for his fodder in the open field,
    And glean in the vineyard of the wicked.

7.   They lodge naked, for lack of clothing,
    Without cover in the cold.

8.   They are drenched with the downpours of the mountains
    And resort to rock for want of refuge.

9.   The fatherless is snatched from the breast
    And pledges taken from the poor -

10.   Naked, they tramp unclad,
    And hungry, they hump the grain.

11.   Between the bullocks# they trundle the olive-press;
    They tread wine-presses, and thirst.

12.   Far from the crowded city they groan,
    And the soul of the victims cries aloud,
    But God imputes nothing amiss:

13.   (He claims) "They were among the rebels against the Light"
    They knew nothing of its ways
    Nor did they dwell in its paths!

14.   It is the murderer who revolts against the Light
    He kills the poor and needy,
    Or at night it might be, say, a thief.

15.   And the eye of the adulterer awaits the dusk,
    Saying, "No eye shall see me,
    And He puts a veil over His face."

16.   He breaks in the dark into houses.
    The daytime is sealed against them.
    They know not the Light

17.   For as one to them are the morning and the shadow of Death
    But well He knows the terrors of the shadow of Death!

18.   Swift was He on the face of water!
        Their portion is accursed in the land!
        He does not turn aside to visit vineyards!
19.   When both drought and heat consume the snow-waters
        They stray into Sheol.
20.   Mother-earth# forgets each one; the worm edulcorates him;
        He is no longer remembered,
        And injustice is smashed like the tree!
21.   He who tended the barren who bore not,
        And the widow whom none rejoiced,
22.   And dragged down the mighty in his prime,
        Is aroused, and He trusts not the living.
23.   One may give Him His due for security, and rest easy,
        But His eyes are upon their ways.
24.   When they rise up a little, He is gone;
        And they are brought low, like all men. They retract
        And are lopped off, like a head of corn.
25.   And if it is not so, who then will give me the lie
        And reduce my words to nought?

Chapter 25

1.   Then spoke Bildad the Shuhite and said:
2.   It is His to decide who should rule and who tremble,
        His, Who made peace in His high places.
3.   Is there any limit to His armies?
        And upon whom does His light not shine?
4.   How then can man be justified with God?
        And how shall he be acquitted that is born of woman?
5.   If He drapes*# the moon that it shine not
        And the stars are not bright in His eyes,
6.   How much less man, a worm!
        And Mankind, a maggot!

Chapter 26

1.   Then Job spoke and said:
2.   How helpful you are to the powerless!
        How you deliver the helpless!
3.   What a counsellor you are to the unskilled!
        How you reveal sagacity to the multitude!
4.   With whose help did you utter your words?
        And whose spirit issued from you?

5.   Have* the shades been brought forth
         From under the waters and their denizens?

6.   Sheol is naked before him
         And Abaddon uncovered!

7.   It was he who stretched out Zaphon over chaos
         And suspended the land over the void!

8.   He who constricts waters in his nimbi,
         The cloud never splitting under its load!

9.   He who shrouds the face of heaven*,
         O'erspreading it with his cloud!

10.   He traced the line on the face of the waters
         To be the frontier between light and dark!

11.   The pillars of heaven tremble
         And are astonished at his rebuke!

12.   By his power, the sea is quiet,
         And by his mastery he shattered Rahab!

13.   By his breath, the heavens are clarity;
         His hand pinioned the serpent as it fled!

14.   If these be but the fringes of his ways
         And what a whisper of a word was heard of him!
         Who then shall comprehend the thunder of his might?

Chapter 27

1.   Then Job resumed the thread of his parable and said:

2.   By the living God, Who has denied me justice,
         And by the Almighty, Who has embittered my soul,

3.   I declare that for all the time my spirit remains within me,
         And the breath of God in my nostrils,

4.   My lips shall not utter falsehood,
         Nor my tongue voice deceit.

5.   Far be it from me to put you in the right! Until I die,
         I shall not doff my integrity from me.

6.   To my righteousness I cling, and never let it go;
         My heart shall not reproach me all the days of my life.

7.   Let my enemy be as the wicked!
         And him who rises up against me as the unjust!

8.   For what is the hope of the godless, though he pillage,
         When God requires his life?

9.   Will God hear his cry
         When trouble comes to him?

10.   Will he have pleasure in the Almighty
         And call upon God for all seasons?

11.   Let me teach you what is in God's hand!
        What is with the Almighty I shall not conceal.
12.   Look, you all have witnessed it;
        Why then do you vainly mouth vanity?
13.   This is the portion of the wicked man with God,
        The heritage of tyrants, which they receive from the Almighty:
14.   If his children are multiplied, it is for the sword,
        And his offspring will want for bread;
15.   Those who survive him will be buried in death,
        And his widows will not weep.
16.   Though he heap up money like the dust
        And store raiment like the dirt,
17.   He may lay it up, but the just will wear it,
        And the innocent share out his wealth.
18.   He built his House like the moth,
        And like the shelter the watchman frames.
19.   He will die rich, but will not be gathered (to his people)#.
        When he opens his eyes, he is no more.
20.   Panic makes him ebb, like the flood.
        One night a tempest will steal him away.
21.   A wind from the east will carry him off and he depart,
        And it will whirl him away from his home.
22.   He will hurl it at him without stint.
        He will fly, fleeing from its power.
23.   He will clap His hands at him
        And hiss him off the stage!

Chapter 28

1.   Though there is a source for silver
        And a place for the gold that they refine,
2.   Iron is extracted from dust,
        And from molten rock, copper.
3.   An end (man) puts to darkness
        As he explores to every frontier;
        The very stone of the Underworld
4.   Erupts a stream from near some vagrant exile.
        These forgotten ones, off the beaten track
        They languish; they wander away from humankind.
5.   The earth - from her comes bread,
        But her subterrain is raked over like a fire;
6.   Her stones are sources of sapphire
        And she yields him dust of gold.

9.   Man sets his hand to the granite,
         Turns the hills upside down;

10.   He hews out conduits in the rocks
         And all that is precious his eye sees.

11.   He dams the rivers from weeping,
         And what was concealed, he brings to light.

12.   But Wisdom, where shall she be found?
         And where is the place of Understanding?

7.   That pathway the hawk knows not,
         Nor has the falcon's eye beheld it;

8.   The sons of pride have not trodden it down
         Nor the lion attained to it.

13.   Man does not know her value
         Nor is she to be found in the land of the living.

14.   Tehom says, "She is not in me!",
         And Yam says, "Nor with me!"

15.   She cannot be bartered for darics
         Nor shall silver be weighed as her price

16.   Not to be equated with gold of Ophir,
         With precious onyx or sapphire.

17.   Bullion and glass are not her peer,
         Nor gilden vessels equal exchange for her.

18.   Coral and crystal need not be mentioned,
         For the price of Wisdom is beyond rubies.

19.   The topaz of Ethiopia is not her peer;
         She is not to be equated with pure gold.

20.   Then whence comes Wisdom?
         And where is the place of Understanding?

21.   That she is hidden from the sight of all the living
         And concealed from the fowl of the air?

22.   Abaddon and Death declare:
         "With our ears we have heard her fame".

23.   God understands her way,
         And He knows her place,

24.   For He gazed to the ends of the earth,
         And surveyed every place 'neath the skies

25.   When He assigned its weight to the wind
         And confirmed the waters' measure;

26.   When He set for the rain its limit
         And its path for the bolt of thunder.

27.   Then did He see her and announce her;
         He established her and explored her also,

28.   And He said to man:
        "Behold, the fear of the Lord, that is wisdom,
        And to shun evil, understanding".

Chapter 29

1.   Then Job resumed the thread of his parable and said:
2.   Would that I were as in the times of old,
        As in the days when God watched over me,
3.   When His lamp shone over my head
        I walked through the darkness to His light;
4.   As I was in the days of my prime#,
        When familiarity with God was with my dwelling;
5.   While yet the Almighty was with me,
        Around me my young men,
6.   When my steps were washed in fever,
        And the Rock gave me forth rivers of oil#.
7.   When I set forth to the Gate in the city,
        When I laid out my seat in the square,
8.   Youngsters saw me and withdrew,
        And the aged rose and remained standing.
9.   Nobles refrained from speaking
        And put their hands over their mouths;
10.   The voice of the governors was hushed
        And their tongues clave to the roof of their mouths,
11.   For when the ear heard me, it accounted me blessed,
        And when the eye saw me, it testified to me,
12.   For I delivered the poor when he cried for help,
        And the fatherless, that had no helper.
13.   The blessing of the dying came upon me
        And I made the heart of the widow jubilant.
14.   I clothed myself in righteousness and it clothed me;
        Like a cloak and a turban was my justice.
15.   Eyes was I to the blind
        And I was feet to the lame.
16.   A father I was to the needy,
        And the case that I did not understand I explored;
17.   And I broke the teeth of the unjust
        And tore the prey from between his jaws.
18.   And I said, "I shall die with my nest,
        And like the phoenix I shall multiply my days;
19.   "My roots will be open to the water
        And the dew will lodge on my boughs.

20. "My honour will renew itself in me
     And my bow in my hand be refreshed".
21. They heard me, and waited for me,
     And kept silent for my counsel.
22. After my speech, they would not resume,
     And my discourse dropped upon them.
23. Yes, they waited for me as for the rain
     And opened wide their mouths as for the spring rain.
24. When I scorned them, they could not stand firm
     Nor give me cause to frown.
25. I made their decisions and sat as chief,
     And I dwelt as the king in the host,
     As he that comforts the mourners.

Chapter 30

1. But now I am an object of scorn
    To those younger in years than I,
    Whose fathers I disdained
    To class with my sheepdogs.
2. Why is even their energy directed against me
    When they are at their last gasp?
3. Wasted with want and famine,
    These gnawers# of the desert -
    A twilight# of ruin and desolation!
4. They garner salt-wort from the scrub
    And the root of the broom is their bread.
5. They are driven beyond habitation,
    Bayed at like thieves,
6. To dwell in the gutters of wadis,
    In holes in the earth and in caves.
7. Between the bushes they bray;
    They meet among the nettles -
8. Fools! And also scoundrels,
    They were scourged out of the land.
9. And now I am their burlesque,
    I have become a byword to them.
10. They abominate me. They shun me,
    Not omitting their spittle in my face!
11. For He has unleashed His dregs# to afflict me,
    And they have thrown off all restraint before me.

12.   Against the Right these captive bulls# arise;
        They disdain my course
        And cast up against me their own paths to perdition.

13.   They have dismantled my way of life;
        They contribute to my ruination though it does them no good.

14.   As a vast eruption they come;
        Like a tornado, they circumvolve.

15.   Terror is dumped on me!
        It whirls away my renown like the wind
        And my credit culminates like a cloud.

16.   And now my soul is spilt within me;
        Times of privation possess me.

17.   The night wrenches my bones out of me
        While my teeth# know no rest.

18.   By force majeur is my raiment transfigured.
        It armours me no more than my gown.

19.   He has thrust me into the mud
        And I have become as dust and ash.

20.   I cried out to You, but You did not answer me;
        When I persisted, You noticed me#.

21.   You have changed Yourself into a Being cruel to me;
        With all Your strength, You detest me.

22.   You mount me on the wind and make me ride it
        And dissolve me back into chaos!

23.   For I know that You will consign me back to Death,
        And to that home appointed to all the living.

24.   On the other hand, He would not set His hand to a ruin,
        Nor in its extremity ignore# its cry.

25.   Did I not weep for him whose days were hard?
        My heart grieved for the poor,

26.   Yet when I looked for good, there came evil,
        When I expected light, there came a palpable dark.

27.   I am in turmoil without surcease;
        Times of privation confront me.

28.   Darkling I wander, lacking the day-star;
        I rise in the assembly - to cry for help!

29.   I am a brother to the jackals
        And companion to the daughters of the ostrich.

30.   He seeks the skin off my back
        And burns my soul more than the searing heat.

31.   So let my harp be tuned to the mode of mourning
        And my flute to the tone of tears.

Chapter 31

1. I made a contract with my eyes;
    How then could I dance attendance on the Virgin?
2. For what is the portion of God above
    And the inheritance of the Almighty on high?
3. Is there not retribution for the wrongdoer
    And rejection for him who performs idolatry?
4. Does not He Himself see all my ways
    And count all my steps?
5. I vow I have not walked with vanity,
    Nor has my foot sped to treachery.
6. When I am weighed in a just balance
    God will realise my innocence.
7. If my step has strayed from the Way,
    Or my heart has followed my eyes,
    Or if any stain has adhered to my palms,
8. Let me sow and another eat,
    And may my descendants be uprooted!
9. If my heart has been seduced to a woman
    So that I lay in wait at my neighbour's door,
10. Let my wife grind to another,
    And let others go down on her!
11. For he (who so acts has done) vileness,
    And she a capital offence.
12. Sure it is a fire that burns to Abaddon,
    And would consume all my gain.
13. If I dismissed the cause of my manservant or my maidservant
    When they disputed with me,
14. What then should I do when God appears?
    And when He calls for an account, how should I reply?
15. Did not He Who made me in the womb make them?
    And did not the One fashion us in the belly?
16. I have withheld nothing from the desire of the poor,
    Nor left the widow's eyes full of longing,
17. Nor eaten my rations in solitude
    And the fatherless not shared in the eating;
18. He would vow "From my youth he brought me up as a father",
    And she "From my mother's womb" that I cared for her.
19. If I have seen one perishing for lack of clothing,
    Or the poor without covering,
20. If his loins did not bless me
    And he was not warmed with the fleece of my sheep,

21.   If I have condemned the fatherless
        Because I saw myself supported in the Gate,

22.   Let my shoulder part from my shoulder,
        And my arm be broken from my trunk!

23.   For terrible to me was the vengeance of God,
        And I could do nothing out of line with His magnificence.

24.   I have not placed in gold my trust,
        Nor said to the yellow metal, "My security!"

25.   I did not rejoice that my wealth was great
        And my hand had attained riches.

26.   Had I beheld the sun when it shone
        Or the moon in splendour pacing,

27.   And my heart were secretly enticed
        And I had kissed my hand to my mouth,

28.   This too would have been a capital offence,
        For I should have been false to God above.

29.   If I rejoiced in the downfall of one that hated me
        Or exulted when evil befell him,

(29a.   Then may my curse fall on my own ears
        And let my affliction be a byword for my people,

29b.   I did not revile him in my anger
        And I held my peace before his peers,)ª

30.   Nor did I allow my mouth to sin
        To call for his life with a curse!

31.   Surely the men of my household would say,
        "May it be that he has not wearied of his life!"

32.   No stranger slept abroad;
        I kept my doors wide to the wayside.

33.   Never did I hide my sin like Adam,
        Concealing, by my evasion#, my iniquity,

34.   That I should tremble before the gossip of the rabble,
        Or be in terror of the contempt of the gentry,
        And keep silent, and not creep out of doors!

35.   Oh grant me that someOne is listening to me!
        This is my talisman! Let the Almighty respond to me
        And the indictment of my accuser!

36.   Shall I not raise it aloft on my shoulder!
        I shall twine it about me like a garland!

---

a.   Bracketed verses are reconstructed additional verses as found in the Qumram
        Targum.

37.   I shall give Him account of all my steps.
          Like a prince I shall approach Him!
38.   If my land has cried out against me
          And the furrows thereof wept together,
39.   If I have consumed its product without payment
          And caused the spirit of its tenants to expire,
40.   Let thistles grow instead of wheat,
          Garlic instead of barley!

Ended are the words of Job.

Chapter 32

1. So these three men ceased to answer Job, because he was righteous in his own eyes.
2. Then was kindled the wrath of Elihu, the son of Barachel the Buzite, of the family of Ram. Against Job was his wrath kindled because he esteemed his own righteousness greater than God's;
3. And against his three friends was his wrath kindled, because although they had found no answer, they had condemned Job.
4. And Elihu had held back from Job with words, for they were older in days than he,
5. But when Elihu saw that there was no answer on the lips of the three men, his wrath was kindled,
6. And Elihu, the son of Barachel the Buzite, spoke and said:
          I am young in days, and you are aged,
          Therefore was I reticent, and in trepidation
          At declaring my opinion to you,
7.   I said: let age speak
          And profusion of years teach wisdom.
8.   But in truth it is His spirit in man
          And the breath of the Almighty that informs them.
9.   It is not the great who are wise
          Nor the old who exercise judgement.
10.   Therefore I say: listen to me;
          I will declare my opinion, even I.
11.   See, I waited for your speeches;
          I gave ear to your dissertations
          While you fumbled for words,
12.   And I followed your testimony closely,
          But note, there was no refuter of Job,
          None who answered his words, among you.

13.   And don't you say, "We have found wisdom,
        Let God fix him, not man!"
14.   But he has not composed words against me,
        Nor would I reply to him with your kind of speech.
15.   They are dismayed! They answer no more!
        Speech is removed from them!
16.   And I waited till they did not speak,
        Until they ceased, and answered no more.
17.   I too will put in my oar,
        I shall declare my opinion, even I,
18.   For I am full of words;
        The wind in my belly inflates me.
19.   Look, my belly is like wine that has no vent;
        It will spout forth like new wine-skins.
20.   Let me speak, and I shall have relief,
        I shall open my lips and reply.
21.   Forgive me if I do not ingratiate myself to any,
        Or give titles to a man,
22.   For I do not know how to betitle,
        For if I did, my Maker would soon whisk me away.

Chapter 33

1.   Nonetheless, hear my speech, O Job,
        And attend to all my words.
2.   Observe, I have begun to speak,
        My tongue has uttered in my mouth.
3.   The uprightness of my heart, the words I choose,
        And the knowledge of my lips, will speak what is pure.
4.   The spirit of God made me
        And the breath of the Almighty quickened me.
5.   If you can, answer me;
        Pit yourself against me; take your stand.
6.   Behold, I am as you in God's eyes;
        I too am a snippet of clay.
7.   See, my terror will not frighten you,
        Nor will my pressure be heavy upon you.
8.   Now surely you have said in my hearing,
        And I have heard the sound of your words:
9.   "I am pure, without sin;
        Clean am I, and there is no iniquity in me!
10.   "Lo! He finds pretexts against me
        And reckons me as an enemy to Himself.

11. "He puts my feet in a hobble.
     He watches all my paths."

12. Behold, this does not make you right! I answer,
     For God is greater than man.

13. Why have you quarrelled with Him,
     Saying that He will not answer for any of His deeds?

14. For God speaks once,
     Yes, twice, if one has failed to perceive it,

15. In a dream, a vision of the night,
     When deep sleep falls on men,
     In slumbers in bed.

16. It is then that He opens the ears of men
     And terrifies them* for their correction,

17. To turn man aside from his works,
     And suppress the pride in the strong,

18. That He may restrain his soul from the pit,
     And his life from perishing by the sword,

19. And he is chastened with anguish on his bed
     And the turmoil in his bones is endless,

20. And his life makes bread repugnant to him
     And good food to his appetite.

21. His flesh wastes from sight
     And his unseen bones are laid bare.

22. But though his spirit draw near to the pit
     And his life to extinction,

23. If there be one to speak for him,
     An intercessor, the one in a thousand
     To declare His uprightness to man,

24. Then He will be gracious to him, saying,
     "Save him from going down to the pit;
     I have found a ransom!"

(24a [And if the terrors have prepared] the fire,
     He will snuff it out,
     And they will be filled [with confusion])ᵃ

25. His body is made fresher than a youth's;
     He returns to the days of his vigour;

26. And he will appeal to God and He will accept him,
     And He will see his face with joy,
     And restore to man his righteousness,

---

a.   Bracketed verse reconstructed from Qumram Targum

27.   Being more righteous than men.
    While he will say,
    "I have sinned and perverted the right,
    And He has not requited me.
28.   "He redeemed my soul from going to the pit,
    And my life sees in His Light."
29.   Behold, all this will God do
    Twice, three times, with a man,
30.   To bring back his soul from the pit,
    That he be enlightened with the light of life.
31.   Mark well, Job, hear me;
    Be silent, and I will speak.
32.   If you have words, answer me;
    Speak, for I desire your justification.
33.   If not, you listen to me.
    Hold your peace, and I shall teach you wisdom!

Chapter 34

1.   And Elihu spoke and said:
2.   Hear my words, geniuses!
    And knowing ones, give ear to me!
3.   For the ear tries words
    As the palate tastes its food.
4.   Let us exercise our judgement;
    Let us decide for ourselves what is good.
5.   For Job has said, "I am righteous,
    And God has turned aside my judgement."
6.   According to my judgement, I lie (if I say)
    `The arrow within me is deadly, though without sin!'
7.   What man is like Job?
    He drinks derision like water!
8.   And he keeps company with evildoers
    And associates with wicked men.
9.   For he said, "It is no benefit to a man
    To be in the good graces of God!"
10.   Therefore, you men of understanding, hear me!
    Far be God from evil,
    Or the Almighty from iniquity!
11.   For the works of man He requites to him
    And causes each to receive according to his way.
12.   For goodness sake! God would not act wickedly
    Nor the Almighty pervert justice.

13. Who burdened Him with the governance of the earth?
    And who entrusted Him with the care# of the whole of it?
14. If He were to set His heart against him,
    Gathering to Himself His spirit and breath,
15. All flesh would perish together
    And Mankind would return to the dust.
16. So if (you have) understanding, hear this!
    Give ear to the sound of my words!
17. Could it be that One Who hates justice is in control?
    And would you condemn the Great and Righteous?
18. Him Who says* to the king, "Scum!"
    And calls princes wicked?
19. Who does not respect the mien of nobles
    Nor consider the burgher before the poor,
    For all of them are the work of His hands?
20. In a moment they die, and at midnight
    The people are convulsed, and pass away,
    And the mighty are carried off powerless.
21. For His eyes are on the ways of men
    And He sees all their movements.
22. There is no darkness, nor no shadow of death
    Wherein the workers of iniquity may hide.
23. For He does not offer to man a second chance
    To come before God in judgement.
24. He destroys the great without trial,
    And places their successors in their stead.
25. To this end He familiarizes Himself with their deeds,
    So when the night turned over, they were crushed.
26. He chastised them beneath the wicked,
    Instead of the prophets.
27. Which was because they turned aside from following Him
    And did not attend to any of His ways,
28. Causing the cry of the poor to come to Him,
    And He does hear the wail of the afflicted.
29. And if He did nothing, who would condemn?
    Or who would notice it if He averted His gaze?
    - And this applies to nation and man alike -
30. From the rule of a godless man,
    From the seduction of the people?
31. For has he said to God, "I have been arrogant.
    I do not wish to act badly.
32. "What I do not perceive, You teach me.
    If I have done wrong, I shall do it no more"?

33. Are you sure that He will restore it because you reject Him?
    Well, it is for you to choose, not I,
    So say what you know!
34. Any reasonable person will say to me -
    Yes, any sensible person who hears me -
35. "Job is talking without sense,
    And his words are without discernment."
36. Sire, Job is being tried to the limit
    Because of his responding like a man of sin.
37. For he has added rebellion to his iniquity,
    He goes mocking among us,
    And multiplies his words against God.

Chapter 35

1. And Elihu spoke on, and said:
2. Do you consider this to be (good) judgement,
   That you say "I am more righteous than God!"?
3. That you ask what use is it to you
   "What profit is there in my avoiding sin?"?
4. I shall return you the answer,
   And your friends with you:
5. Regard the heavens and see,
   And behold the vault, it is higher than you!
6. (You asked) if you sin what do you do to Him?
   And if your iniquities multiply what have you wrought against Him?
7. If you are righteous, what do you give Him?
   And what does He gain at your hand?
8. Your wickedness relates to men like yourself,
   And your righteousness to human beings.
9. Men called out under the weight of oppression;
   They cried for rescue from the arm of the mighty.
10. But he never said "Where is God, my Maker,
    (Who apportioned His spirit among us)[a]
    Who gave songs in the night?
11. "Who taught us beyond the beasts of the earth
    And enlightened us more than the fowl of the air?"
12. There they cried out, but He did not answer
    Because of the pride of evil men.

---

a. Bracketed line reconstructed from Qumram Targum

13.   Surely God does not listen to vanity,
         Nor does the Almighty regard it.
14.   How much less when you say you cannot perceive Him,
         The case is before Him and you will summon Him forth,
15.   And now that His anger punishes no-one,
         And that He takes no note of great iniquity*!
16.   But Job opens his mouth in vain,
         And reels off words without thinking!

Chapter 36

1.   And Elihu continued, saying:
2.   Attend to me a little longer and I shall declare to you
         There are still things to be said for God.
3.   I shall bring my evidence from times of old
         While I ascribe righteousness to Him Who framed me.
4.   For truly my words are not false.
         A man of rectitude is with you.
5.   Look, God is mighty, but He does not reject out of hand,
         Mighty in the power of His understanding.
6.   He will not preserve the wicked,
         But He gives justice to the weak.
7.   He does not waver in His vigilance for the righteous,
         But with kings upon a throne
         He seats them, and they are exalted to eminence[a],
8.   And if they are restrained in fetters
         And confined with cords of affliction,
9.   Then He recounts to them their deeds
         And their transgressions, how they have vaunted themselves,
10.   And He opens their ears to correction
         And directs them to return from wrongdoing.
11.   If they listen to Him and obey Him,
         They round off their days in prosperity
         And their years in pleasantness[b],
12.   And if they do not listen, they perish by the sword[c],
         So they die, unenlightened.

---

a.   ' Joseph

b.   Joseph and the butler

c.   The baker

13. But the godless of heart harbour anger^c.
    They will not cry for help though He confine them.
14. Their life is extinguished in their youth,
    And their existence ends among the gigolos#!
15. He delivers the afflicted by His affliction
    And opens their ears by tribulation.
16. But anger tempts you from the voice of distress
    To the broad place whose depths are without form,
    And you with your table laden with rich fare!
17. But you are laden with the cause of the wicked.
    Justice and judgement will lay hold of them!
18. "For spite..." (you said and now I say)#, lest it tempt
    you against chastisement,
    Nor must you let the magnitude of the penance deflect you.
19. Would you have Him adjudge your cry to be not from distress
    And all the resources of your strength?
20. Do not long for the night,
    To follow the nations into oblivion^d.
21. Take heed! Do not dwell upon iniquity,
    For that is why you have rejected affliction.
22. Look, God is pre-eminent in power;
    Who is a teacher like Him?
23. Who supervises His way?
    And who can say, "You are doing wrong?"
24. Remember that you (too) have glorified His work
    Of which men sing.
25. All mankind observed it;
    Mortal man descried it long ago.
26. See, God is great and unknowable,
    And the tale of His years defies search.
27. For He sucked up the droplets of water;
    They distilled into the rain of His `mist'^e
28. Which the skies poured down;
    They flooded over the multitudes of men^f.
29. Yes, beyond understanding were the outspreadings of cloud,
    The crashings of His pavilion!

---

d. Literally "To go up to the nations in their place"

e. The Creation, Genesis 2:6

f. The Great Flood, Genesis 7:11

30.   Then He displayed His light^g across it
       And stopped the sluices of the sea^h.
31.   For by these means He executes judgement on peoples,
       And provides food for the masses.
32.   He swathed His hands in lightning
       And commanded it to be His agent^i.
33.   His friend would testify to Him
       As do even cattle when offered on the altar!

Chapter 37

1.   How much more at this my heart trembles
       And is moved from its seat.
2.   Listen! Hear well the turmoil of His voice
       And the roar that issues from His throat!
3.   He unleashes it under the whole of the heavens,
       And His lightning to the corners of the earth.
4.   After it rumbles the voice.
       It thunders with the voice of His majesty,
       And none can outpace them, for His voice shall be heard!
5.   God thunders with His voice; Marvels
       He accomplishes - great things and unknowable.
6.   For to the snow He says, "Seek the earth!",
       And to the torrent, "Rain!", the torrent which is
       His guard of strength#.
7.   He sealed a compact with all mankind
       That all men should know His work.
8.   Then the beast slinks to his covert,
       And huddles in his den.
9.   Outside that chamber comes the whirlwind,
       And away from the predators#, the cold.
10.   By the breath of God He creates ice,
       And the expanse of water is forged hard.
11.   Likewise He loads the cloud with moisture,
       And projects abroad His thundercloud,

---

g.   The rainbow, Genesis 9:13

h.   The upper sea, Genesis 1:7; 8:2

i.   Igniting the altar at Mt. Carmel, I Kings 18:38

12.   And it whirls about, gyrating at His control,
        To do those things, whatever He commands,
        On the face of the wide world.
13.   Whether for chastisement, or for His earth,
        Or for mercy, He makes it come to pass.
14.   Give ear to this, O Job!
        Pause, and consider the wonders of God!
15.   Do you know how God instructs them,
        And causes the lightning of His clouds to burst forth?
16.   Do you know anything of the manoevrings of the clouds
        The wonders of Him Who is perfect in skill?
17.   You who, warm clad
        In the still silence of the South Land,
18.   Used to hammer things out with Him under skies
        Adamant as a mirror of bronze?
19.   Reveal to us what we should say to him!
        We cannot compete with the darkness.
20.   Shall it be explained to him if I speak out?
        If a man says he has been destroyed[a]?
21.   And now that men cannot see the Light.
        It was once bright in the skies,
        But a wind swept by and purified them?
22.   - "From Zaphon the gold there approaches
        A majesty more awe-ful than God's!
23.   "The Almighty, we have not found Him mighty in power
        Or justice or great righteousness, nor that He does not oppress.
24.   "That is why men have feared Him.
        He paid no attention to any of the wise at heart"?

Chapter 38

1.   Then the Lord spoke to Job out of the whirlwind, saying:
2.   Who is this that is obfuscating counsel
        In words without knowledge?
3.   Gird up your loins like a man,
        And I shall question you and you reveal to Me.
4.   Where were you when I founded the earth?
        Say whether you know Understanding!
5.   Who determined its measurements - if you know?
        And who stretched out a yardstick on it?

---

a.   Or: "that he is nonplussed?"

6.   Into what are its pedestals sunk?
       And Who laid its corner-stone

7.   When the stars of the morning rang out in unison
       And all the host of heaven gave voice?

8.   And Who enclosed Yam behind doors
       When he burst forth and departed the womb?

9.   When I ordained the vapour as his garment
       And the swagging cloud his swaddling-band?

10.   And set My surf# to surround him,
       And put bar and doors,

11.   And said, "Hither shall you come and no farther,
       And here shall it stay in the pride of your waves!"?

12.   In your time did you ordain the morning?
       Instruct the dawn* in its place?

13.   To gather up the coverlets of the earth
       That the poor* are exposed upon it?

14.   The woman revolves like a seal on clay,
       And the men brazen it out like one who is clothed*.

15.   But their ‘light' is witheld from the wicked,
       And the haughty shoulder is broken.

16.   Have you been down to the whirlpools of the Sea?
       And have you paraded in the recesses of the Deep?

17.   Have the portals of Death been rolled back for you?
       Have you seen the portals of the shadow of Death?

18.   Have you surveyed the whole wide world?
       Say whether you know it all!

19.   Where is the path to where light lodges?
       And darkness, where is its home?

20.   That you can conduct it to its perimeter,
       And know the direction of its den?

21.   You know! Because you were born then,
       And the number of your days is vast!?

22.   Have you visited the treasuries of the snow?
       Or seen the armories of hail

23.   Which I have stored against the time of trouble,
       Against the day of battle and war?

24.   In what ways is the lightning forked?
       The East wind broadcast over the earth?

25.   Who cleaved the fosse for the flash-flood?
       And the pathway for the bolt of thunder?

26.   To bring rain to the land without men,
       The desert wherein is no man.

27.   To satisfy desolate wastes
        And bring forth shoots of grass.
28.   Has the rain a father?
        Or who conceived the dew-drops?
29.   From whose womb emerged the ice?
        And the hoar-frost of heaven, who begot it?
30.   Like stone the waters become still,
        And the face of the Deep is frozen.
31.   Can you fasten the links of the Pleiades,
        Or loosen the belt of Orion?
32.   Can you lead forth Venus in due time,
        And can you guide the Bear with her litter?
33.   Do you know the decrees of heaven?
        Do you apply its authority to the earth?
34.   Can you lift up your voice to the clouds
        That copious waters cover you?
35.   Can you dispatch the lightnings and they go forth
        And say to you, "Here we are!"?
36.   Who put wisdom in the covert place#?
        Or Who gave skill to the cock?
37.   Who shall recount the empyrean in wisdom!
        And the fools of heaven, Who makes them couple#
38.   To pour dust into the mould
        That the particles cleave together?
39.   Will you hunt the prey for the lion?
        Or satisfy the appetite of the cubs
40.   When they crouch in their dens?
        When they remain in the thicket to lie in wait?
41.   Who prepares his prey for the raven
        When his young cry out to God
        And faint for want of food?

Chapter 39

1.   Do you know the season of birth of the mountain-goats?
        Have you marked the calving of the deer?
2.   Have you counted the months that they fulfil?
        And do you know the season when they bring forth?
3.   They crouch down and split forth their young
        And dispose of their navel-strings.
4.   Their offspring dream away, and grow up amid the corn;
        They wander away and do not return to them.

5.   Who drove the wild-ass free?
        And who unbridled the onager

6.   To whom I assigned the desert as his home
        And the salt-flats for his dwelling?

7.   He can scorn the din of the city;
        He does not hear the shout of the muleteer.

8.   He seeks his pasture in the hills
        And searches for every verdure.

9.   Will the wild-ox consent to serve you?
        Will he stable in your stall?

10.   Can you yoke the wild-ox in a furrow with a thong?
        Will he harrow the valleys at your behest?

11.   Can you trust him, though his strength is great?
        And can you leave your labour to him?

12.   Will you rely on him to cart home your seed
        And plenish your threshing-floor?

13.   The ostrich-wing would rejoice
        Were she stork-wing and feather,

14.   For she leaves her (clutch of) eggs to the earth
        And warms them in the dust,

15.   And forgets that the foot may scatter it
        Or the wild beast trample it.

16.   He has toughened her young to do without her;
        Her fearless efforts are for nothing

17.   Because God denied her wisdom
        And apportioned her no understanding.

18.   Now she flaps away in safety;
        She jeers at horse and rider.

19.   Did you give the horse his strength?
        Did you clothe his neck with thunder?

20.   Did you make him burr like a locust?
        The majesty of his neigh is terror!

21.   He paws in the valley and exults in strength;
        He goes forth to greet the battle.

22.   He laughs at fear and is never dismayed,
        Nor turns back from the sight of the sword.

23.   The quiver resounds upon him,
        The glittering spear and javelin.

24.   In storm and fury he laps up the ground;
        He cannot hold still when the trumpet sounds.

25.   At the sound of the horn he cries "Aha!"
        And he snuffs the battle from afar -
        The thunder of chieftains, the clarion.

26.   Does the falcon wing by your wisdom?
        He spreads his pinion to the south.
27.   Is it at your command that the vulture soars
        And makes his nest in the heights?
28.   In the cliff he dwells, and lodges there,
        In the cliff-crag and rampart.
29.   From there he scans for food.
        His eyes descry it far away,
30.   And his fledgelings lap blood;
        And wherever the slain are, there is he.

Chapter 40

1.   And the Lord spoke to Job, and said:
2.   Shall strife with the Almighty be set aside#?
        Let him who argues with God answer for it!
3.   Then Job spoke to the Lord and said:
4.   Behold, I am contemptible.
        How can I reply to you? I lay my hand on my mouth.
5.   Once I have spoken, but I cannot answer;
        Even twice, but I can no more.
6.   Then the Lord spoke to Job
        Out of the whirlwind, and said:
7.   Gird up your loins like a man.
        I shall ask, and you will reveal to Me!
8.   Shall you indeed annul My judgement?
        Shall you condemn Me, that you be found right?
9.   Yes, but have you an arm like God's?
        And can you thunder with a voice like His?
10.   Deck yourself in majesty and grandeur
        And in splendour and glory be clad,
11.   Scatter abroad the fury of your wrath
        And expose every one that is proud and bring him low,
12.   Expose every one that is proud; abase him,
        And crush the wicked beneath them!
13.   Bury them in the dust together!
        Swathe their faces in Perdition -
14.   Then should even I laud you
        For your right hand will have brought you victory!
15.   Just look:
        The beast whom I mixed with your clay
        Chews the cud like the cattle.

16.   Just look, his strength is in his loins
        And his vigour in the private parts of his body.
17.   He delights in his 'tail', like a cedar-tree.
        His sinews of fear are intertangled!
18.   His bones are ingots of brass.
        His skeleton cast-iron.
19.   He was the first-fruit of the ways of God
        Needs must his Maker bring His sword,
20.   For the hills provide him his god,
        And the whole menagerie of wild beasts preys there.
21.   Under the thorny lotus he prostitutes himself,
        Concealed in reed and fen.
22.   The lotus-trees screen him as his defence.
        The willows of the brook guard him round about.
23.   Behold, if Nahar oppresses he does not become alarmed;
        He is confident that Jordan will gush forth at his command!
24.   In his opinion he can seize him;
        By ruses, he will puncture wrath#.
25.   Will you land Leviathan with a fish-hook
        And lassoo his tongue with a line?
26.   Will you slip a reed through his nose
        Or pierce his jaw with a bramble?
27.   Will he make endless supplications to you
        And will he address you tenderly?
28.   Will he enter a pact with you
        That you take him as your servant for ever?
29.   Will you make sport with him like a bird?
        And will you cage him for your maidens?
30.   Will partnerships buy and sell him?
        Will they share him out among the merchants?
31.   Can you fill his skin with harpoons
        Or his head with fishing-spears?
32.   Lay but your hand on him!
        Remember the battle! Do no more!

Chapter 41

1.   Behold, his[a] ambition was thwarted:

---

a.   Leviathan

          Must he[a] also be daunted at the sight of him[b],

2.   Not fierce when he[b] arouses him[a]?
          But who is there can stand up to Me?

3.   Who ever confronted Me and I submitted?
          Wheresoever under the heavens, he is Mine!

4.   I am not deaf to his[a] vainglory,
          Nor his doughty speech, and the grace of his orato

5.   Who[c] unwrapped the face of his[a] garment?
          Who breached his double curb?

6.   Who unfastened the doors of his face?
          His circle of fangs is Terror,

7.   Pride, those phalanxes# of shields,
          Closed with a tight seal.

8.   One is so close to another
          That no air can come between them.

9.   Each clings fast to its brother;
          They are fused together, inseparables.

10.   His sneezes flash flame
          And his eyes are as the eyelids of dawn.

11.   From his mouth issue blazing torches
          And sparks of fire escape.

12.   Out of his nostrils pours smoke
          As from a fanned brazier with reeds.

13.   His breath will ignite coals
          And a tongue of flame darts from his mouth.

14.   In his neck dwells strength,
          And before him capers despair.

15.   The scales of his flesh adhere;
          They are cast upon him, unshakeable.

16.   His heart is cast like a stone;
          Yes, hard-cast like the nether millstone.

17.   When he rears up, the mightiest are in terror,
          The wild waves in turmoil!

18.   Approach him with the sword, you will not prevail,
          Nor spear, dart, nor javelin.

19.   He treats iron as straw
          And brass as rotten wood!

---

b.   Behemoth

c.   The Lord

20.   The brood of the bow cannot make him flee;
        To stubble he converts the balls of the sling.
21.   As though straw were esteemed a club,
        So he scorns the rattling of the lance.
22.   His underside is the blades of a plough;
        He dredges a swathe through the mud.
23.   He makes the ocean boil like a kettle;
        He sets the sea a-seething.
24.   Behind him, he lights up his wake;
        One would think the Deep become hoary!
25.   None upon earth is his peer,
        His, that was made fearless.
26.   All that are lofty he surveys.
        He is lord over all the sons of pride.

Chapter 42

1.   Then Job answered the Lord, and said:
2.   I knew that You were capable of anything,
        And that no plot could be concealed from You.
3.   "Who" (You asked) "obscures counsel without knowledge?"
        That is why I propounded what I did not understand,
        Things too wonderful for me, which I knew not.
4.   (You said) "Hear Me and I will speak.
        I shall question you and you reveal to Me!"
5.   With the hearing of the ear I hear You,
        And now my eye sees You,
6.   Therefore do I despise, and am comforted
        For, all that are dust and ash.

7. And it was after the Lord had spoken these words to Job that the Lord said to Eliphaz the Temanite "My wrath is kindled against you and against your two friends, for you have not spoken rightly of Me, as has My servant, Job. 8. "Now therefore take for yourselves seven bullocks and seven rams, and go to My servant Job, and offer up for yourselves a burnt-offering, and Job My servant will pray for you. For to him will I be gracious that I do not do to you anything unrighteous, for you did not speak rightly of Me, as did My servant, Job." 9. And then went Eliphaz the Temanite and Bildad the Shuhite, Zophar the Naamathite, and did that which the Lord had told them, and the Lord was gracious to Job. 10. And the Lord turned the captivity of Job when he prayed for his friends, and the Lord gave Job twice as much as was previously his.

11. Then came all his brothers and all his sisters, and all those who had been his acquaintance before, and they ate bread with him in his house; and they consoled him and comforted him for all the evil that the Lord had brought upon him; and each one gave him a *kesitah*, and each one a golden ring.

12. So the Lord blessed the latter end of Job more than the beginning, and he had fourteen thousand sheep and six thousand camels and a thousand yoke of oxen and a thousand she-asses.

13. And he had seven sons and three daughters.

14. And he called the name of the first Jemimah, and the name of the second Keziah, and the name of the third Keren-Happuch;

15. And there were not found women so fair as the daughters of Job in all the land, and their father gave them inheritance with their brothers.

16. And after this Job lived a hundred and forty years, and saw his sons and his sons' sons to four generations.

17. So Job died, being old and full of years.

II
Footnotes to Introduction, Chapters 1-3

Chapter 1

3. ויהי האיש ההוא גדול מכל־בני--קדם

BDB does not equivocate in asserting that in comparative sentences such as this כל is not "all" but "any". See p. 88f.

5. ...ויהי כי הקיפו ימי המשתה וישלח איוב ויקדשם והשכים בבקר

ככה יעשה איוב כל־הימים

The conventional translations of this verse do not result in a coherent and comprehensible, let alone believable, story. הקיפו, which is related to surrounding and encompassing and rounding (the corners of the head), is always understood here as implying the completion of a round of seven feasts rather than the advent of a single one. This makes of Job's ritual an annual event* rather than a frequent one. This in turn renders כל־הימים inappropriate.

כל־הימים (see p. 498) is an idiom meaning "continually", but this is not suitable here however we read the passage. It must, therefore be taken literally as <u>all the days</u> - i.e. all the days of feasting - each one of them. The only way that consistency and sense can be imparted to the verse is by assigning to הקיפו the meaning "<u>came</u> around" instead of "<u>went</u> around". We then have a clear picture of Job's actions either on the morning of the day of each feast, or on the morning after.

* T and Berechiah and others consider the feasts to have been daily events, each son having one day of the week as "his day". All that supports this is the fact that Job had as many sons as the days of the week. When Job curses "his day" [3:1] (surely intended to be a similar expression), it is his birthday against which he inveighs.

12. ויצא השטן מעם פני יהוה

The expression, מעם פני, literally <u>from with the face of,</u> is a little more elaborate than מלפני.

16. אש אלהים

The destruction of Sodom and Gomorrah is attributed to fire from the Lord (Gen 19:24), although modern scientific opinion favours an earthquake. Numbers 26:10 may be helpful:

> *Whereupon the earth opened its mouth and swallowed them up with Korah - when that band died, when the fire consumed the two hundred and fifty men - and they became an example.* (NJPSV translation)

It is possible that *fire from God* stood for any violent natural cataclysm.

עד זה מדבר וזה בא ויאמר .18

Berechiah explains the variant עד (in vv. 16 and 17 the formula has עוד) in this way.

בכל־זאת לא־חטא איוב ולא־נתן תפלה לאלהים .22

For comment on תפלה and its cognates in Job, see p. 470ff.

Chapter 2

8. A <u>shard</u>, symbol of a broken home, and <u>ashes</u>, of a burnt city. The latter is foreign to the patriarchal scene (p.74).

עדך מחזיק בתמתך? ברך אלהים ומת .9

תמה is certainly *integrity* in 2:3, 27:5 and 31:6. In Prov 11:3 *simplicity* reads better, and here, one must suspect that Job's wife had something less flattering than *integrity* in mind.

10. אחת הנבלות. Implies moral folly here and in 30:8. If this is the word also in 38:37 (see pp. 217ff.), it signals merely want of sense or knowledge. מאת האלהים is essentially a more modern way of saying מעם, *from with*. I have read here *From (being) with*. The definite article is unusual but cannot justify such versions as *from the hand of God* (AV *et al*). The expression *The God* is surely expressive of the sort of extreme respectful distance that Blake sought to portray in the <u>before</u> engravings in his series *The Book of Job*.

Chapter 3

יגאלהו חשך וצלמות תשכן־עליו עננה יבעתהו כמרירי יום .5

In the first stich (and wherever the word צלמות occurs in the Bible) there is a fashion at present to read some form of darkness in preference to the older *shadow of Death*. But the vocalization of this word in the MT demands *The shadow of Death*. If we abandon this vocalization here, we lose the anchor of the MT entirely, and cannot contest any emendation of vowels anywhere. The traditional meaning is therefore employed throughout this translation.

There are no good reasons for preferring any of the meanings suggested in the literature for כמרירי. The three favoured suggestions embrace derivations from *kamar*, a Syriac word, to be black; from מרר, Hebrew to be bitter, and *mara*, Arabic to be hostile. In the circumstances, this seems to leave the field open for even more *recherche* speculation.

The Cimmerians (Cimmerii) were

> *a nation on the western coast of Italy, generally imagined to have lived in caves near the sea-shore of Campania, and there, in concealing themselves from the light of the sun, to have made their retreat the receptacle of their plunder. In consequence of this manner of living, the country which they inhabited was supposed to be so gloomy, that, to mention a great obscurity, the expression* Cimmerian darkness *has proverbially been used. Homer, according to Plutarch, drew his images of hell and Pluto from this gloomy and dismal country, where also Virgil and Ovid have placed the Styx, the Phlegethon, and all the dreadful abodes of the infernal regions.*

F.A. Wright: Lempriere's Classical Dictionary, Routledge & Kegan Paul Ltd. London (*1949*) 149.

6c. במספר ירחים אל־יבא

The literal "Let it not appear in the number of the months" cannot be applied to a "day". C understands it as "in the reckoning of the months", and NJPSV "in any of the months". But the expression מספר ירחים probably had the simple and direct meaning given in the text. The verse is important in demonstrating that Job's curse is forward-looking. He is cursing the day every time it reappears annually, not retrospectively. Hence *his day* is the birthday in the same sense as it is now understood.

8b. העתידים ערר לויתן

Leviathan appears here in his capacity of the slant serpent, the probable cause of eclipses.

> *If thou smite Lotan, the serpent slant,*
> *Destroy the serpent tortuous,*
> *Shalyat of the seven heads...*

Poems about Baal & Anath, Pritch. p.138.

21. In Proverbs 2:4, this expression was used for the seeking of Wisdom.

23. The use of this expression by Job as an illustration of his distress is made ironic by its use in 1:10 by the Satan to signify God's protective net cast about him.

24. כי־לפני לחמי אנחתי תבא

The phrase, split but undeniable in this line, בוא לפני, while literally *come before*, may also have the idiomatic sense of *confront.* That is to say it may as well mean to *come before* in the spatial sense of *into the presence of*, as in the temporal sense of earlier in time.

III
Footnotes to First Cycle,
Chapters 4 - 15:16

Chapter 4

5. כי עתה תבוא אליך ותלא   תגע עדיך ותבהל

Note that כי עתה without <u>maqqeph</u> has no idiomatic force. The verb לאה is to be *weary* only in the sense of being impatient of something, hence rebellious... In v.2 above the word is used with apparent solicitude. This verse reveals the falsity of that. נגע עד, see Isa 16:8, is "reach as far as".

6. ‏הלא יראתך כסלתך?

In denying to this expression the meaning: *Is not your fear (of God) your (source of) confidence?*, I am well aware that I am defying virtually all commentators of Job (but not Rashi nor LXX). Nonetheless, the fact that there is no precedent for יראה unmodified to stand for יראת אלהים (we shall reject Job 15:4 likewise, v.i.); the fact that the only other example of the feminine form כסלה (Ps 85:9) bears indisputably (despite BDB's unaccountable <u>confidence</u>) the meaning *folly*; the fact that the last thing that Job mentioned before Eliphaz began to speak was his <u>fear</u> in the normal sense of the word, and the fact that to make sense of the "Godfearing" solution it is necessary to supply not one, but two phrases as understood, all conspire to convince me forcefully that the meaning of the line is *Is not your fear your folly?* - more or less exactly what LXX has.

It is true that this inflexible reading of the line produces an antithesis rather than a synthesis with the second line of the couplet - תקותך ותם דרכיך *And your hope the integrity of your ways?* But why not? Having pointed out that Job's fear is foolish, it is natural that Eliphaz should then show him his way out - the source of his hope. Note that the word תקוה <u>can</u> stand for "source of hope" as well as hope (Ps 71:5). "Fear" as "piety", or "religion" is to be found nowhere in any language, culture, or system of belief. An Israelite might indeed derive confidence from his "ways", but, unlike a Christian, not from his faith or his fear (even of God).

7. It is difficult to find the source of this apparent quotation. Perhaps Eliphaz is thinking of Psalm 37.

8. The first of a series of references, see 5:6 (p. 367), and 15:35.

10. שאגת אריה וקול שחל   ושני כפירים נתעו

11. ליש אבד מבלי־טרף   ובני לביא יתפרדו

Two translational problems are raised by these two couplets. What is the significance of the strange grammatical form of the figure? And what does נתעו mean?

The first line consists of two pairs of construct phrases - i.e. four consecutive nouns without a verb. *The roar of the lion; the voice of the king of beasts;* this is surely the poetic invocation of a scene by which the absence of all verbal components serves to increase the immediacy and terror of the audible proximity of a lion or pride of lions. It is in a way a device to heighten the present tense - the scene an inescapable presence.

In the second line a verb appears and opens the path to the development of the situation. It is usual to understand נתעו as *are broken*, on the suggestion of an unattested Aramaic form of the Hebrew נתץ. This translation hurtles the image on to its end before it is properly established. The "breaking of the teeth" of כפירים is borrowed from Psalm 58:7 which prays for this. There is another, and I think better alternative. The distinction between כפיר and גור, a lion's whelp, is the eruption of the teeth - a כפיר being old enough to hunt its prey. I suggest therefore that נתעו is a spelling variant of נטעו *are planted*, implying <u>are established</u> - erupt. With this meaning the two lines reinforce each other in emphasising the power and terror of the pride of lions in their prime.

The verses now bear a remarkable resemblance to Isa 40:24, the only other Biblical source for the Niphal of נטע.

That bringeth princes to nothing
He maketh the judges of the earth as a thing of nought.
Scarce are they planted (נטעו),
Scarce are they sown,
Scarce hath their stock taken root in the earth;
When He bloweth upon them, they wither,
And the whirlwind taketh them away like stubble.

The animal image of Job 4 is essentially the same as the agricultural image of Isaiah. The lions, who are of course men or nations (who *plough trouble and sow mischief*, v.8) do very nicely for a short while (v.10 = the lines beginning "Scarce"), but then they wither (11a) and are blown away like stubble (11b). The image records the collapse of the state and the exile of its population. The same history is told in Job 12:23 and 24:24. The <u>lion</u> is the symbol of <u>Judah</u> (Gen 49:9, Num 23:24, 24:9) or of her foes (Jer 2:15).

12-16. The vignette of Eliphaz's spooky dream has imposed upon innumerable scholars and readers, but not on Job! (see Chapter 9, p. 243). The "dream" is a fraudulent device with the double purpose of granting supernatural authority to Eliphaz's rebuke to Job, and of deflecting Job's anticipated resentment onto an absent third party. There is evidently a convention associated with this, as Jeremiah's attack on false prophets attests:

> *I have heard what the prophets say, who prophesy falsely in My name: "I had a dream, I had a dream." How long will there be in the minds of the prophets who prophesy falsehood - the prophets of their own deceitful minds - the plan to make My people forget My name by means of the dreams which they tell each other...?*

Jer 24:25-27.

17. האנוש מאלוה יצדק? אם־מעשׂהו יטהר גבר?

There is some pietistic objection to the idea that man might be purer than God, even when phrased as a rhetorical question clamouring for a negative reply (JPS, NJPSV, H, G, etc.). Num 32:22 is cited in support. But when Elihu asks (35:2) הזאת חשבת למשפט אמרת צדקי מאל?, it is hardly possible to avoid *Do you think this is judgement - that you say "I am more righteous than God!"?*; and once we accept this there, it is as well to admit it elsewhere also.

20. מבלי משׂים

is obscure, and usually considered to stand for משׂים לב, paying attention - either they themselves or any potential observer. I suggest that the figure here is closer to that of 34:23f

> *For He does not offer man a second chance (ישׂים עוד)*
> *To come before God in judgement.*
> *He destroys the great without trial (לא־־חקר)...*

Chapter 5

The passage, 5:1-8 is discussed at greater length in Chapter 3.IX.1, pp. 465-470.

1b. ואל־מי מקדשׁים תפנה?

Conceivably *To whom, rather than the Holy One, will you turn?* The verse is, in the first place, a reproof to Job for appealing to the powers of darkness in Chapter 3. The argument from v.1 to v.8 needs to be followed very closely. v.8 is in fact the rebuttal of the suggestion in this verse.

2. כי לאויל יהרג־כעשׂ ופתה תמית קנאה

This is usually, and understandably, taken as a warning to Job that his intemperate (angry) language is likely to lead him to destruction, but it is much too early for Eliphaz even to hint that Job is אויל and פתה. The convention being established between them is that Job is being victimised by God because of the errant behaviour of his children or his nation. This we find explicit in Bildad's forthcoming speech (8:4).

The purpose of this verse therefore is to instruct Job, as from one ruler to another, in what is required to put down folly in his realm whenever it shows its head. The two emotions, כעש and קנאה, are what are necessary to do this. כעש, we should note, is <u>anger</u> when it is God's, but not when it is man's, where something like <u>irritation</u> fits the contexts better. קנאה (zeal) is a supremely divine quality, and is never found in a pejorative sense. The Biblical usage of these words is illustrated by Deut 32:21:

הם קנאוני בלא־אל   כעסוני בהבליהם

They roused Me to jealousy with a no-god;
Angered Me with their vanities.

which essentially says what Job 5:2 does - these are the qualities needed to deal with these follies.

<u>Zeal</u> and <u>anger</u> being essentially divine qualities, Job's appeal to lesser creatures for help (קדשים) is doomed.

3. אני ראיתי אויל משריש   ואקוב נוהו פתאם

This verse is never translated accurately. We have to note first the reduplicated pronoun אני ראיתי which indicates a contrast between the speaker and someone else - here the person addressed, Job; second the <u>waw</u> introducing the second stich, which in this case gives the v. the form "when stich a, stich b." In the conventional reading of this passage, for Eliphaz to admit to cursing the home of the foolish is equivalent to his admitting to cursing Job. This is not possible.

Eliphaz is continuing his instruction of Job by telling him his own practice in such cases as have befallen him - in contrast to Job's spineless moaning! The assumption we must make is that it is by now too late for Job to copy Eliphaz in coping, and so (v.8), his only remaining hope is to rely on God.

4,5. These are the specifics of Eliphaz's curse, which reveals itself as a true חרם, as described in Ezra 10:8 -

יחרם כל־רכושו והוא יבדל מ(ה) קהל

all his substance should be forfeited, and himself
separated from the congregation.

This fate is not dissimilar from Job's. See espec. 19:13-19.

5c. is quite obscure; ושעף צמים חילם. The number demands that חילם, and not צמים be the subject of שעף. The verb requires a sentient subject, so (unless we accept a metaphorical longing by <u>their wealth</u>) חילם must be their <u>army</u> (cf. 15:29). This now relieves us of the necessity for emending צמים to צמאים, "the thirsty".

The suggestion here is that the impressed or mercenary forces of the dissident group - no individuals but a sizeable rebellion - welcome the end of their isolation by becoming prisoners of war. The verse remains problematic.

6. Eliphaz is providing the justification for his practice of <u>cursing</u> the habitations of such people as are responsible for trouble immediately. But we must bear in mind that the sort of curse of which he speaks is no ineffective outburst of blasphemy, but a social sanction of ferocious efficacy, as well as being the closest approximation that human agents can make to the application of כעש and קנאה.

7. For a full discussion, see pp. 465-470.

8. Again a reduplication of the 1st person pronoun, revealing Eliphaz recommending to Job a different course from that upon which he seems to have embarked. <u>Were I in your place</u> is the implication.

10,11. See pp. 306f.

15. וישע מחרב מפיהם   ומיד חזק אביון

The first of several examples in the book of a trio of items punctuated as in English, a, b and c (see, e.g. 8:10). While AV respects this literal reading, few later writers do so. D speaks for them all in being convinced that the first מ of מפיהם is as he calls it "local". He cites Ps 64:4 and Ps 57:5 where the tongue is parodied as a sword. But these swords are directed against their enemies, not themselves. God is saving the poor from the hand of the mighty in the second stich; he must be saving them from a real, hostile sword in the first. Saving "from their own mouth" must be seen as an early dig at Job for the intemperance of his speech.

21. בשוט לשון תחבא   ולא־תירא משד כי יבוא

שוט לשון, literally *the scourge of the tongue.* שד כי יבוא is a reference to Isa 13:6, the day of the Lord. Eliphaz knows precisely the nature of the fear (p 97ff.) that haunts Job.

23a. Poetically a perfectly acceptable image. P finds the idea strange and seeks to substitute "field-sprites" - an unwarranted pagan intrusion. A quotes Blommerde as suggesting אבני as בני with prosthetic א, and proposes a number of new examples of this bi-form.

26b. כעלות גדיש בעתו

A very strangely-worded simile, as though the גדיש rose of its own accord. Perhaps a recognition that the harvesting of human lives is also managed by a husbanding Power.

Chapter 6

6. See pp.470ff.

7. See p.120

10. Cf. Ps 119:50-52

> *This is my comfort in my affliction,*
> *That Thy word has quickened me.*
> *The proud have had me greatly in derision;*
> *Yet have I not turned aside from Thy Law.*
> *I have remembered Thine ordinances of old, O Lord,*
> *And have comforted myself.*

The sandwich form of the verse, with parenthetic middle line, is not unique, see 15:30, 24:18.

11. מה כחי כי איחל   ומה־קצי כי־־אאריך נפשי

The two stichoi say the same thing. This is the first of several references to Job not waiting. Here it clearly means waiting to die - delaying death. אאריך נפשי is surely not *I should be patient* (JPS etc.).

13. האם אין עזרתי בי   ותושיה נדחה ממני

14. למס מרעהו חסד   ויראת שדי יעזוב?

These two verses have proved perennially difficult. If however we take 6:14 in isolation, depriving it also of its connecting preposition, it gives us the reasonably straightforward:

> *One who despairs of mercy from his friend*
> *And abandons the fear of the Almighty?*

In this formulation it is also probable that "his friend" is also the Almighty. If we now restore the preposition ל, it appears that its significance may be to indicate the transition <u>into</u> one who despairs, giving for תושיה נדח ממני ל- the grammatically daring *Is wisdom so far driven out of me that I am become,* or *that I am changed into, one who despairs...* Note that the sequence of participle and finite verb is found "almost as a rule" (Ges. #116x).

15-21. See pp. 299-307.

22,23. הכי־אמרתי הבו לי   ומכחכם שחדו בעדי

ומלטוני מיד־צר   ומיד עריצים תפדוני

The third and fourth of these four questions are inconsistent with the literal Job, being appropriate only to a captive, an exile or a hostage. The only way this can be circumvented is by treating them as deliberately fantastic and therefore having no relevance to Job's actual situation. Such a solution would be far more appealing were it not that the first two questions are entirely appropriate. Job has been reduced to destitution and might well have asked his friends to help him in a material way.

27. ‏אף על־יתום תפילו   ותכרו על־ריעכם?‏

The ‏אף‏ (represented by *even* in the translation) is a conjunction which joins this verse to the preceding. Hence it, too, must be treated as a question.

29. ‏שבו נא אל־תהי עולה   ושבי* עוד צדקי־בה‏

The *Qere** calls for ‏ושבו‏. It is worth considering the meaning of the unamended text. ‏שבי‏ is <u>captivity</u>, and the line might mean *As for captivity, my righteousness will still be preserved in it*. However, the accent links ‏עוד‏ to ‏ושבי‏. But what other referent than <u>captivity</u> is there for ‏בה‏? This version of ‏צדקי־בה‏ is RSV.

30b. ‏אם־חכי לא־יבין הוות‏

Somehow this has been misunderstood. ‏הוה‏ is <u>disaster</u>, or <u>destruction</u>; there is little to choose between them. It is the same word as in Ezek 7:26 ‏הוה על הוה‏ ‏תבוא‏, and is also in 6:2, to which this is a reference. Job has asserted that he is facing total ruin (6:2-11), while Eliphaz has presented the situation as remediable by a little repentance, and has told him that his fear is folly (4:6). In this verse Job is maintaining that his view of the situation is correct - he knows the taste of disaster, and the friends are being unjust in claiming that he is overdoing his distress and protest (4:5). The metaphor of taste has already appeared in 6:6,7.

Chapter 7

4,5. See pp. 121f, and for 4a, p.114.

9. ‏כלה ענן וילך   כן יורד שאול לא יעלה‏

Repeatedly in this book, as in sundry poetic passages, the passage to the Underworld is expressed without a preposition between verb and noun. This is important for 24:19.

12. ‏הים־אני אם־תנין?!‏

By no means to be translated *Am I the sea? or the dragon?* <u>Yam</u> and <u>Tannin</u> here are proper names. Reading the line aloud in Hebrew reveals its indignation and fury.

15. ‏ותבחר מחנק נפשי   מות מעצמותי‏

A difficult construction. Evidently ‏נפשי‏ is the subject of *chooses*, and *death* is effectively in apposition with *strangling*.

16a. ‏מאסתי לא־לעלם אחיה‏

‏מאסתי‏ is usually read as an absolute *I reject it!* and taken as supporting an absolute reading of ‏אמאס‏ in 42:6. The suggestion here is that the sentence contains a supportive double negative and what the speaker rejects is ‏לעלם‏ ‏אחיה‏, that he should live for ever.

20. See p. 286.

Chapter 8

(v.4) אם־בניך חטאו־לו   וישלחם ביד פשעם .4-6
For the possible alternative significance of <u>children</u> in this v. see p. 134. The
translation treats 4b, v.5, and 6a, as a part of the extended prostasis, both on
logical grounds (p.133), and because of the imperfect consecutive tense of
וישלחם. Berechiah alone of those I have read does the same.

6b. ושלם נות צדקך
It is possible that when Jeremiah wrote (31:23)

> *Thus saith the Lord of Hosts, the God of Israel:*
> *Yet again shall they use this speech*
> *In the Land of Judah and in the cities thereof*
> *When I shall turn their captivity:*
> *The Lord bless thee, O <u>habitation of righteousness,</u>*
> *O mountain of holiness.*

he had Job 8:6 in mind. The use of the expression *habitation of righteousness*
for Judah, and that in association with return from captivity (as in Job 42:10),
is not to be dismissed out of hand as of no significance. It is also important
to register that Jeremiah is using it as a well-known designation of Judah.
Whether this derives from Job or not, it makes the use of the expression to
mean the dwelling of a single sheikh improbable. The only other use of the
phrase is also by Jeremiah (50:7), where the Lord Himself is referred to as the
<u>Habitation of righteousness</u> (נוה־צדק).

14. אשר־יקוט כסלו   ובית עכביש מבטחו
The verse also presents two problems - the meaning of יקוט, and why the
general term בית עכביש is used in preference to the specific קורי עכביש, a spider's
web (Isa 59:5).
The second of these questions can be answered confidently, but not the first.
The appearance of the verse is that of true *parallelismus membrorum*, with כסלו
and מבטחו making one pair of equivalents, and יקוט and בית עכביש another. This
requires that יקוט function as a noun, but there is no nominal form in Biblical
vocabulary which is close enough to the word to justify even an assumption
of corruption. The best which has been suggested is that it is a derivative of
the Aramaic קיט, equivalent to Hebrew קיץ, *summer*, from which the more
daring derive *gossamer*. This is not convincing.
Vocalised with *sureq* instead of *holem* the word is the 3rd person singular
imperfect Qal of the verb קוט which, however, is nowhere (else) found
without a following preposition (e.g. Job 10:1, Niph'al). The verb means,

apparently the same in Qal and Niph'al, "to loathe", and it is this that I have adapted to yield *He who despises his Troth* - translating כסלו to mean that to which his allegiance and trust are owed. This is perhaps the closest it is possible to get to the text, but the probability that there is a word יקום of which we have no knowledge, of which no trace but this has survived, is great. The fact that the following images refer only to בית עכביש from this verse, and not to anything for which the יקום might stand as a noun, militates somewhat against the idea of a strict parallelism.

The second problem is more easily resolved. In v.15 the evil-doer *leans upon his בית, but it does not stand; he holds fast to it, but it will not endure.* In this image the בית is both the spider's web of the preceding verse and the House the family, tribe or nation of the man. Later still in the passage the virtuous man *beholds a house (made) of stones*, an enduring posterity (this may also be read, with a prosthetic א, as *the House of his children*). The whole edifice of word-play is impossible without the word בית in v.14.

With the whole picture before us, the verbal solution for יקום is less unattractive. A man who trusts in his own House, but despises the help from God which he should seek is the paradigm of Isaiah 22:8-11:

> *...you did look in that day to the armour in the house of the forest. And you saw the breaches of the city of David, that they were many; and you gathered together the waters of the lower pool. And you numbered the houses of Jerusalem, and you broke down the houses to fortify the wall, and you made also a basin between the two walls for the water of the old pool.*
>
> *But you looked not to Him that had done this Neither had you respect to Him that fashioned it long ago.*

or more simply Kipling's *valiant dust that builds on dust, and guarding, calls not Thee to guard.*

16. Both Saadiah and Berechiah recognized that two different plants (as in Ps 1 and Jeremiah's copy of it in Jer 17:5-8), and two different types of man, are the subjects of Bildad's homily. G devotes Special Note 10 (BJ p.521) to a judicious demonstration that this is correct. Although H and M accept this, C, NJPSV, and V-S, amongst the most recent translators still maintain either that only one plant is described, or that both plants described are symbols of the wicked. So little faith does any scholar have in the author's accuracy in the use of number, that none mentions the decisive fact that (v. 19) משוש דרכו, *the joy of the way* (of the second plant), is that מעפר אחר יצמחו, *from other soil they will spring forth*, with the only possible referents for they

being its roots and shoots (or בנים). This therefore is true joy, not sarcasm, and so the way which is symbolised by this plant is the way of the righteous.

אם־יבלענו ממקמו   וכחש בו לא ראיתיך .18

This is a picture of conquest and exile. Note the use of the verb בלע, as in 37:20.

ומעפר אחר יצמחו .19b

Perhaps in deference to the disjunctive accent on ומעפר, the only two solutions that seem to have been considered for this line are to treat אחר as plural (after Vg) or יצמחו as singular (after LXX). The accent, however, seems mischievous. There is an accepted phrase עפר אחר (Lev 14:42) which means "fresh soil" - here more appropriate is *alien soil*.

The subject of the agricultural יצמחו is those items in the preceding verses which can indeed "spring forth" from the soil - יונקתו and שרשיו, his roots and shoots of vv.16,17. They go forth over His garden and wrap around the spring, and if the plant is destroyed in its place, they will shoot forth again in foreign soil.

The purpose of the whole picture is to console Job that, if his protestations of virtue are really true, then his "children" who have been exiled, will prosper in their new environment. This a familiar use of Biblical imagery. A similar picture of the original transplantation of the Israelite nation is painted in Ps 80, vv.9-12.

Thou didst pluck up a vine out of Egypt;
Thou didst drive out the nations and did plant it.
Thou didst clear a place before it,
And it took deep root, and filled the land.
The mountains were covered with the shadow of it,
And the mighty cedars with the boughs thereof.
She sent out her branches unto the sea
And her shoots unto the River.

חן־אל לא ימאס־תם   ולא יחזיק ביד־מרעים .20

In itself, this verse, which is surely the summary of the tree simile which precedes, is compatible only with the idea that two different plants, one corresponding to evil and one to good, are described in it. חן־אל ... ימאס is quoted by Elihu in 36:5.

Chapter 9

אמנם ידעתי כי־כן   ומה יצדק אנוש עם־אל .2

The spirit of contest requires deliberate misunderstandings of words with several alternative meanings. Here Job takes up the צדק of 4:17 and affects to understand it as to be *justified*, instead of to be *just*.

 3. It is obscure whether this means that a mere man could not answer one in a thousand of the accusations of God, or that not one man in a thousand could answer God. One in a thousand is, however, an expression of rarity (see 33:23 and discussion of it on p. 295ff.).

 4. חכם לבב ואמיץ כח   מי־הקשה עליו וישלם

This v., like 4:10, features an opening line devoid of a verb, but here there is no vivid picture to be brought dramatically to our eyes or ears (see comment on 4:10, p. 380). The only question the verse raises is to which of the two parties in line b is line a intended to apply? The second stich is something like *Who has stood up to Him that He submitted?* JPS, for example reads *Wise in heart and mighty in strength* as characteristic of Him, but better justification for the existence of the line is provided by attaching the description to Who? - *Who is so wise and mighty that...?* This probably reinforces the phrase *one in a thousand*, and shows it to mean (not) one man in a thousand.

 7. האמר לחרס ולא יזרח   ובעד כוכבים יחתם

Probably the only genuine example of חרס for sun in Hebrew (Jud 14:18 is suspect). Perhaps from the Egyptian sun-god *Horus*. בעד in stich b is frequently ignored in translations and commentaries. One way of looking at it would allow בעד exactly its theoretical meaning, *in separation from*. The sun is sealed by God in separation from the stars. While they are shining He bids the sun not rise. Alternatively we could understand, with the usual weak sense of בעד, *(First) He bids the Sun not rise, And (next) He seals up the stars*. The line celebrates the inviolable distinction or alternation between night and day. Cf. 24:16b, q.v.

The usual idea, that God at one time capriciously holds back the dawn, and at another obscures the night sky, defies the known facts of nature. The reading "shine", as an alternative for יזרח, relegates the first stich of the verse to a consideration of eclipses, for which there is no equivalent in relation to the stars.

A similar image is to be found in Le Gallienne's translation of the first of the Rubaiyat of Omar Khayyam:

> *Wake! for the sun, the shepherd of the sky*
> *Has penned the stars within their fold on high.*

 8. נטה שמים לבדו   ודרך על־במתי־ים

This verse is helpful in dating the Book of Job. There are passages in

Deutero-Isaiah and Jeremiah which resemble it, but each with a crucial difference. Isa 42:5 is

> *He that created the heavens and stretched them forth*
> *He that spread forth the earth and that which comes out of it,*
> *He that gives breath unto the people upon it,*
> *And spirit to them that walk therein.*

and Isa 44:24:

> *I am the Lord, that maketh all things;*
> *That stretched forth the heavens alone;*
> *That spread abroad the earth by Myself.*

while Jer 10:12 is:

> *He that hath made the earth by His power,*
> *That hath established the world by His wisdom,*
> *And hath stretched out the heavens by His understanding.*

The coupling of the creation of the heavens with the containment of the Sea in the Job passage, reveals an earlier mythology, which in post-exilic writings was excluded from most texts (but see Jer 31:35, p.327). Insofar as there is any dependency in these passages, the prophetic writings appear to depend on Job as a source, not vice versa.

8b. is literally *Trod down the high places of the Sea.*

10. Quoting Eliphaz, 5:9, with deep irony to follow.

11,12. הן יעבר עלי ולא אראה   ויחלף ולא־אבין לו

הן יחתף מי ישיבנו?   מי־יאמר אליו מה־תעשה??

Not the relatively bland *He passes by me...He moves on* (AV, NJPSV, G, etc.) The first verse is dependent on Isa 24:5: עברו תורה חלפו חק - *They have transgressed the Law, violated the statute.* This is bitter complaint of wrongs done to Job. Each verb, especially יחתף, "robbed" has an understood object. The people's sins in Isaiah become God's in Job.

13. A reference to the Akkadian Creation Epic, which details the titanic battle between Marduk, the volunteer champion of the "good" gods against Tiamat, her helpers ("bad" gods), and the monsters which she created especially for the fight. *Rahab* is the Israelite equivalent of Tiamat.

After he had slain Tiamat, the leader,
Her band was shattered, her troupe broken up;
And the gods, her helpers who marched at her side,
Trembling with terror, turned their backs about,
In order to save and preserve their lives.
Tightly encircled, they could not escape.
                 Tablet IV lines 105-110   Pritchard, p. 67

The one Biblical reference is Ps 89:11.
         15b. למשפטי אתחנן
The translation is loose, but reflects the intention.

17. *For nothing* - חנם. The word is like a refrain in the earlier part of the book: 1:9, 2:3, here, and 22:6.

19. A second glance at Psalm 89, this time well askance:

Thine is an arm with might;
Strong is Thy hand and exalted Thy right hand.
Righteousness and justice are the foundations of Thy throne;
Mercy and truth go before Thee. (vv.14,15)

The associative technique whereby one reference to the Psalm conjours up a second, makes of the Bible a dimension of added depth to the Book of Job.
         21. תם אנ. לא־אדע נפשי אמאס חיי
The dynamics of 9:20,21 favour reading תם אני as an interrogative, but it may be an emphatic assertion. Stich b is a subtle *double entendre*. Prov 15:32: פורע מוסר מואס נפשו - *He who refuses correction despises his own life*.

23. פתאם as *suddenly* seems to miss the point both here and in 5:3. T-S suggested *carelessly*, with a possible derivation from פתה, essentially "silly". *Faut de mieux*, I have accepted this.
         27,28. יגרתי כל־עצבתי
Although 28a uses the word עצב rather than עצם, there is a remarkable resemblance between these verses and Isa 38:13, in Hezekiah's prayer (see p.

37):

> *The more I make myself like a lion till morn,*
> *The more it breaks all my bones.*
> *From day to night You will make an end of me!*

     30. The *Qere* gives *snow-water*. Some scholars object to both versions and seek to read שלג as nitre, on the grounds that neither snow nor snow-water cleans any better than other kinds of water (e.g. G). This contention must be seen as a manifestation of the 20th Century passion for expunging the poetry of the Bible. Snow-water is poetically cleaner than water from other sources. Cf. *Gilgamesh*, Tab XI, 240: *Let him wash off his grime in water clean as snow.* (Pritch. p.96).

     34. The same stipulations that Job will make directly to God in the second person in 13:21.

Chapter 10

     1. נקטה נפשי בחיי   אעזבה עלי שיחי   אדברה במר נפשי

In stich a, as in 7:15, נפשי is simply "I", but in stich c it is the exact counterpart of Isa 38:15 (see p.57) where Hebrew comes as close to the concept of the soul as can be. In stich b, עלי gives the interesting idea of Job unleashing his complaint upon himself.

     4,5. Perhaps the most daring words of the poem. This statement of the incommensurability of man and God is, in the spirit of contest, matched by the Lord Himself in 40:9 when He demands: *Have you an arm like God's? And can you thunder with a voice like His?*

     7b. ואין מידך מציל

אין מציל is a frequently encountered collocation. This particular phrase recurs in Isa 43.13.

     8-18. Of the 24 stichoi in this passage, all except two (13a and 13b) conclude with the same syllable י - *me* or *my*. The two lines of the centre verse of the eleven each ends with ך, *Your* and *You* respectively. I have attempted to preserve this assonance as well as possible.

     8b. יחד סביב ותבלעני!

8a is *Your hands shaped me and fashioned me.* 8b is difficult, but יחד סביב must, I suggest, be treated as modifying תבלעני - *You destroy me*, not as the limp *altogether round about* embellishing *fashioned*, which is favoured by most scholars. I suggest the thrust of the phrase is to imply a Janus-like duplicity on God's part, that the intention to destroy Job existed יחד, simultaneously and co-extensively, with the intention of creating him. סביב then applies to God, all of Whose facets (His roundaboutedness, as it were) are יחד. The essence of the phrase is to show the unity of God's contradictions, and might be translated *in the Unity of Your multiplicity*.

12a. חיים וחסד עשית עמדי

Little more than 1 1/2% of some 2500 uses of the verb עשה in the Bible are coupled with the preposition עם. Of these about half relate, as here, to the bestowing of חסד (kindness) upon someone. Rarely this is joined to truth. In Psalm 86:17 we find *Bestow on me a sign of good*, and there is one example where God works marvels for, with or upon the people. There are several examples where there is no object for עשה, but merely an adverbial phrase attached *Deal with Thy servant according to Thy mercy* (Ps 119:124).

Although חסד is a noun, it is usual to translate it adverbially in the phrase עשה עם חסד to yield *Deal kindly with*, sacrificing the grammatical purity of the noun to preserve the literal sense of the preposition. This is impossible where the object of עשה ס חיים or, אות לטובה (v.s. Ps 86:17). Then, an idiomatic sense for עשה עם is unavoidable. With regard to the crucial 40:15 (See Chap. 5), note that there is no phrase in the Bible, עשה עם, where the probable sense of עשה is *make*. There are two other examples of עשה עם in Job, 13:20 and 42:8. Neither of these is unproblematic.

16a. ויגאה כשחל תצודני

Many scholars struggle to interpret this line as though the subject of יגאה were the relatively remote "my head". It makes better sense if "my agony" is taken in that role. The verb most commonly refers to involuntary raising, and the sense in Ezek 47:5, of rising waters, is similar to that of mounting affliction here.

17c. חליפות וצבא עמי

This line is evidently a complaint against God, and almost certainly for something which He Himself has done to Job, rather than for someting which He has allowed to happen to him. This distinction is prompted by the two preceding lines: *You refresh Your accusations against me And whip up Your anger towards me*.

Most read the line in terms of warfare (צבא), but none provides a convincing role for חליפות in that connection. However in Job 7:1 and 14:14 (the only other times the word is used in the book) Job uses the word צבא for the bondage of service which is life itself (*All the days of my* צבא *I would wait Until my relief [?reward, ?wages, ?translation] came*). It must not be overlooked that the word usually translated *relief* in this verse 14:14, is the same חליפה as in 10:17. Therefore the relationship of the two words in 10:17 should exactly mirror that in 14:14. This leaves only one possible way of understanding this verse - essentially (with the literal words underlined):

Responsibility both for providing the <u>service</u> (of virtue) <u>and</u> paying the <u>wages</u> (of sin) are laid <u>upon me</u> (by You).

The sense of חליפה in both passages is the same as that of the masculine חלף (Num 18:21,31) - the reward of service.

19b. מבטן לקבר אובל.

Epitomises the true quality of יבל, which is to transport, with no overtones of splendour (cf. 21:32).

20a. הלא־מעט ימי יחדל.

This daring construction has caused endless trouble. The subject of יחדל, *cease*, is מעט, literally "fewness", but let us say "brevity". So *Will not my brief day cease!* would be a fair English rendition. We must remember that the context is one in which Job complains that he was not allowed to die at birth. The next line (Qere) ושית ממני ואבליגה מעט is probably also governed by הלא which in both lines exerts a desiderative force.

22. This verse is a demythologised version of the ritual description of the Underworld found both in *Gilgamesh* (VII, iv, 34-39, Pritch. p.87) and in *The Descent of Ishtar* (I, 4-11, Pritch. p.107).

Chapter 11

10. אם־־יחלף ויסגיר   ויקהיל ומי ישיבנו.

An interesting trio of verbs, seemingly a comment on 9: 11,12. We must understand a much blander intention, however, for this is a part of the technique of interpersonal attribution which courses through the book. The two Hiph'il verbs, יסגיר and יקהיל, are transitive, so, as with 9:11,12, we must supply, if only mentally, objects for them. They are probably antithetical, so we should prefer the meaning *deliver up* to *imprison* for יסגיר. Nowhere in this book has anyone been imprisoned, but Job or the people of Judah, has (have) been delivered up to the wicked.

12. ואיש נבוב ילבב   ועיר פרא אדם יולד.

This strange verse has come to receive a conventional translation as a proverb: *A foolish man will gain understanding when a wild ass's colt is born a man.* C recently substitutes *tame* for *a man* in stich b, but the amendment does not help. The rendition of the second stich depends heavily on the disjunctive accents in the MT separating the words פרא and אדם, for פרא אדם, *a wild ass of a man* is a collocation familiar from the description of Ishmael (Gen 16:12). Without the accents, we should perforce read פרא אדם as the subject and עיר as the object of יולד. This, however, is not one of the crucial questions to be asked about the verse.

The first is, what is the true sense of the Niph`al of the verb לבב? The only other form known is the Pi`el where the meaning is essentially *enhearten* = *encourage*. Correctly, the essence of the Niph`al is to impart a reflexive sense to a verb (Gesenius #51), and according to the same source *Equally characteris-*

tic of the Niph`al is its frequent use to express emotions which react upon the mind. With these hints, it seems more likely that what is meant here is *attributes wisdom to himself - thinks himself wise*, rather than *receives wisdom*, which is a purely passive sense.

A second vital question is the real form of the verse, particularly the force of the <u>waw</u> with which the second stich begins. The proverb into which the verse is conventionally turned places the second stich earlier in time than the first - when b then a. I doubt if this sequence is permissible. See e.g. comments on 5:3 and 5:7 (pp. 382 & 468). If there is a temporal sequence here it is surely: when a, then b.

There is however, no need to assume any temporal sequence. In the translation given, stich a states what man attributes to himself, and stich b contradicts it with the speaker's generalisation about man. איש is better regarded as distributive than translated *a man*; נבוב incorporates the idea of "man".

13,14. אם־אתה הכינות לבך   ופרשת אליו כפיך

אם־און בידך הרחיקהו   ואל־תשכן באהליך עולה

The reduplication of the second person singular pronoun, here and elsewhere - notably 15:4,5 - seems to impart a quasi-imperative sense to the verb, reinforced here by the two following imperatives in v.14. See next note.

16. כי־אתה עמל תשכח   כמים עברו תזכר

It is scarcely avoidable here to translate as a pair of imperative verbs. Again the reduplicated pronoun indicates this. The imperfect, however, is capable of this mood even without its assistance (Ges #107 m,n [1]).

19a. ורבצת ואין מחריד This, linked to 18b, וחפרת לבטח תשכב is a quotation from the Covenant of Leviticus 26:6: If you follow my laws and faithfully observe My commandments, ... I will grant peace in the land, and you shall lie down untroubled by anyone (NJPSV).

Chapter 12

The dynamics of Chapter 12 are discussed on pp. 101ff.

4-6. Any translation of these ambiguous verses must provide justification for the strongly adversative ועולם which introduces verse 7. That is it must in some way propound the proposition, refuted there, that man, not God, was responsible for Job's calamities. See Chapter XI, pp. 293ff. for a full consideration.

9. Identical with Isa 41:20c, and closely resembling Deut 32:27d. Many assume that the name יהוה used here uniquely in the Dialogue testifies to its being a quotation of Isaiah. But we still have not dated either passage with certainty, and see discussion of the names of God, pp. 75ff., for another explanation.

11. For the function of this verse, see p. 101.

14b. יסגר על־איש ולא יפתח

A reference to 11:10 - ‏?אם...יסגיר...ומי ישיבנו, but with a deliberate change in the conjugation of סגר.

15b. (referring to <u>waters</u>) וישלחם ויהפכו־ארץ

A reference to 5:10,11a וְשֹׁלֵחַ מַיִם עַל־פְּנֵי חוּצוֹת לְשֹׁם. See pp. 311-313, Note 23, for a discussion of this specific passage.

17-25. A crucial passage which is invariably understood as the recital of the habitual actions of God. Most of the verbs are in the form of participles, of which only one, מגלה, can be certainly identified, and it is verbal (see p.108, n.22). In v.18 פתח is perfect tense and, being followed by imperfect consecutive, can hardly escape rendition as <u>tempus historicum</u>. In a way, in 13:1 *Look, my eyes have seen it all, My ears have heard and understood it*, there is confirmation that the whole passage is to be read as what God has just done.

17a. מוליך יועצים שולל

Cf. Isa 20:1,2:

> *In the year that Tartan came unto Ashdod...the Lord spake by Isaiah the son of Amoz, saying: "Go, and loose the sackcloth from off thy loins, and put thy shoe off thy foot." And he did so, walking naked and barefoot.*

21. מזיח אפיקים רפה

אפיק is in a wholly unfamiliar context here (see p.508). It is usually read as <u>the strong</u>, but the word has a sense of things held or bound together, as מזיח would seem to be the cord that binds. The interpretation can only be a guess.

23b. שטח לגוים וינחם

וינח is the **B** Hiph'il of נוח (BDB p.628), and means "to leave alone", "abandon". In Num 32:15 it has exactly the sense required here, when Moses threatens the people of Israel that God will leave them in the desert as He did their fathers for forty years. The MT Job vocalizes the word as the **A** Hiph'il, which appears to have a more benign meaning, "to set at rest". Most read "leads them away", presumably to destruction, from the root נחה.

24. מסיר לב ראשי עם־הארץ

עם־הארץ, the "People of the Land" formed a sort of fourth estate after the nobility, the military and the prophets. During the exile to Babylon they asserted themselves as the true inheritors of the land. Note here it is the <u>chiefs</u> of the people of the land who are condemned to exile. The casual mention of this class is powerful evidence of a Judean setting for the story.

Chapter 13

4. For טפל see p.470ff.

5. The use of the impersonal מִי־יִתֵּן for something asked of the friends is, I suspect, exceptionally discourteous. It is perhaps to this that 20:3 is addressed.

7. הלאל תדברו עולה ולו תדברו רמיה?

Preserving the word-order of the Hebrew which undoubtedly has its significance. See also pp. 283ff.

9-12. It is vital to the comprehension of the Book of Job to understand that in these verses Job is speaking from within the circle of God's intimates to a group outside. His friends are acquainted with the worship of the One God only by hearsay.

In these four verses, Job uses the word אתכם three times (cf. *If thou thouest him thrice...* Shakespeare) and follows this barrage with זכרניכם, עליכם and גביכם. It may well be that a conventional form of insult is involved.

10b. אם־בסתר פנים תשאון

In secret for rtsb has no relevance, and H's *If you reveal a hidden bias* is unsupported. We must understand פנים as two-faced like the subject of the sentence. !ynp rts carries the sense of hypocrisy, while פנים נשא is to demonstrate partiality (in this case still to God as in v.8).

12. This verse is considered several times elsewhere, notably p.198. Both זכרון and גב are objects of worship. <u>Minaret</u> is to be understood in a transferred sense here.

13. Essentially the same as 5. v.s.

14a. Not a literal rendition.

15. There is no reason not to be absolutely literal in translating this famous crux. Job is explaining the urgency of his drive to defend himself to God. הן, either *behold!* or *if,* cannot introduce the subjunctive as in AV and RV.

19. מִי־הוּא יָרִיב עִמָּדִי כִּי־עַתָּה אַחֲרִישׁ וְאֶגְוָע!

There is a perfect ambiguity in this verse, for כִּי־עַתָּה may as well mean *otherwise* (3:13) as *in that case* (6:3), and מִי־הוּא, while it could call for the negative reply "no-one", could also be a genuine question. In neither case does it provide a proposition to which כִּי־עַתָּה in either sense provides a logical continuation! We are thus left in doubt as to whether Job is stating that he will give up if anyone disputes with him, or that he will give up if he is left thrashing the air without an opponent in court. From what follows, it seems that the second is intended, but there is no certainty. 31:35a apparently supports.

20a. אַךְ־שְׁתַּיִם אַל־תַּעַשׂ עִמָּדִי

Another example of the rare conjunction of עשׂה with עם. In this case it seems unequivocally to mean "do <u>to</u> me" as in Gen 20:9 and II Sam 13:16. Vv. 20-22 are the proposition rehearsed in 9:34.

23. The proposition rehearsed in 10:2.

27. ותשם בסד רגלי   ושמור כל־ארחתי   על־שרשי רגלי תתחקה

By far the best explanation of the third line is provided by T-S who sees in it an analogy with the branding of the owner's name on the body of a slave. T-S quotes Isa 49:16 in support, but there it is the slave owner (God) who claims to have engraved the name of the slave (Zion) on the palms of His hands. The practice (if it ever existed) of branding the sole of the foot would have made tracing a runaway easier. T-S's explanation brilliantly justifies the otherwise inexplicable use of the hithpa'el form of the verb. This is the only instance of the uncertain term שרש רגל.

Many commentators have noted the contradiction between 27a and 27b, but there is no reason to doubt that it is an intentional intensification of protest. Even after immobilising me, you still scrutinize my every movement!

28. והוא כרקב יבלה   כבגד אכלו עש

The idea that רקב here is an Aramaic <u>wineskin</u> is unconscionable (see p. 122). The image of rottenness, which is so similarly expressed in Hosea 5:12 is not to be evaded. In the prophet the רקב is parallel to the moth, and as a simile for God is almost indisputably an active and animate agent of rot rather than the rot itself. Hence I suggest termite, or some other agent of decay, as the true sense of רקב. No other citation impedes this interpretation. Indeed, Prov 12:4. *A virtuous woman is a crown to her husband; but she that does shamefully is as a* רקב *in his bones*, also cries out for a living agent.

Chapter 14

4. See pp.477ff.

6. שעה מעליו ויחדל   עד־ירצה כשכיר יומו

This verse is an oddity in that it contains an interpolated conclusion. The natural order of thought is *Look away from him while he fulfils his contract, and then he will cease to be.* Strangely, the whole of the rest of the chapter depends and enlarges upon this conclusion *he will cease* which is, as it were, carelessly thrown into the sentence any old where! *He will cease* is foretold in the preceding verse. A less likely meaning is *he will cease to exist for you.*

7a. כי יש לעץ תקוה

This is <u>the</u> tree, not <u>a</u> tree. The tree is that of 8:16-19 whose roots and shoots will spring forth from "alien soil". Job is drawing attention to the limitations of analogy! He does not challenge the truth of what Bildad has claimed, but he will not accept what is effectively a posthumous consolation, cf. 21:21 (see p. 276f).

11. It is uncertain exactly what image the author is seeking here. Surely not, as almost every authority concludes, *As the waters fail from the sea and the river is drained dry*. These are two contingencies as unthinkable as

עד-בלתי-שמים, *Till the heavens pass away* in the next verse. Thus the <u>waw</u> opening v.12 must be taken as <u>But</u>.

14. אם-ימות גבר היחיה? כל-ימי צבאי איחל עד-בוא חליפתי

A verse important mainly because of its testimony to other passages. For צבא and חליפה in tandem see 10:17. The two verses reciprocally support. איחל is an intentional reference to 13:15 - "As I am to die, I cannot wait; on the other hand, were there to be a resurrection, I would wait indefinitely for it." Finally the tentative wish for the impossible here and in v.13 lurks behind the famous 19:25ff, traditionally *I know that my Redeemer liveth*, but see p.485ff.

16,17. The verses are replete with ambiguities. The text gives what seems the most likely solution.

18. ואולם הר-נופל יבול

The image is difficult enough to visualize without speaking of the "falling mountain". The geological portrait in this and the following verse is stunning in its appreciation of slow erosion. In this respect it is in advance of Greek science at its best. The first "scientific" presentation of the concept of slow geological change was in the unfinished masterpiece, *The Theory of the Earth* by James Hutton in 1785.

19b. תשטף-ספיחיה עפר-ארץ

ספיחיה, literally "those that come forth spontaneously from her", exactly as in Lev 25:11. Linked to the verb שטף which is to overflow, to rinse, or wash away, these must be *springs* of water rather than seedlings. Much the same problem is raised by the similar word צאצאיה, which is *descendants* when the suffix is a woman, but agricultural *produce* when it is the earth.

21b. ויצערו ולא-יבין למו

למו here is surely singular. Most modern scholars agree.

Chapter 15 (1-16)

2. Continuing the distinctly unedifying pit-humour exchange about wind. This comes to a deplorable climax in 32:19,20.

4. אף-אתה תפר יראה ותגרע שיחה לפני-אל

This is the second example of the word "fear" accepted by almost the whole assemblage of scholars as standing for "fear of God". This, and the following verse 5, are considered in detail on pp. 479ff.

7. הראשון אדם תולד? ולפני גבעות חוללת?

Another example of conventional contest wit. These exchanges about age and experience continue until the Lord's heavy-handed 38:21 *You know! Because you were born then And the number of your days is vast!*

The word חוללת, the po'lal form of חול is a crucial clue to the correct understanding of Chapter 26, see pp. 243f.

8b. ותגרה עליך חכמה

A rare example of the same word, תגרה (4b supra), used consecutively with entirely different meanings. See pp. 44 and 479ff.

    10. See Note to 15:7.

    11. ‏המעט ממך תנחומות אל   ודבר לאט עמך?‏

The syntax of stich a demands a resolution in stich b, as in Jos 22:17,18: ‏המעט‏ ‏...לנו‏? - *Is the iniquity of Peor too little for us...that...?* There is a possibility of error in the text, for ‏לא טעמך‏ (*that my speech is not to your taste?*), referring back to 6:6, fits in all ways better than ‏לאט עמך‏.

    13a. ‏כי־תשיב אל־אל רחוך‏

‏רוח‏ is never "anger" and the Hiph`il ‏השיב‏ never means "to direct" which are the implications of the conventional reading <u>That you turn your spirit against God</u>. Job has been asking repeatedly for death - to *return his breath (of life) to God*. These are the natural meanings of the words of the text, and they make impeccable sense. There can be no justification for any other reading, despite its antiquity (LXX).

Ehrlich has this version, and H concludes his comment with

> *a play on the formula of Eccl 12:7 seems to be intended. For by "turning" (‏שוב‏) his "angry spirit" (‏רוח‏) on El, Job is inevitably returning (‏שוב‏) his spirit (‏רוח‏) to God in self-destruction.*

But Job does not need to be told he is seeking self-destruction; his seeking is active and intentional, and it is this which most merits Eliphaz's rebuke. If any word-play is intended, it is in the reverse direction to H's suggestion.

Chapter 15, 17-35

Chapter 15, 17-35 is considered extensively on pp. 144ff.

24. יבעתהו צר ומצוקה   תתקפהו כמלך עתיד לכידור

In Zeph 1:15b the phrase צרה ומצוקה, and in Ps 119:143a, צר־ומצוק occur, in each case meaning *Trouble and anguish*. The mixed masculine and feminine forms in the Job passage may be devised intentionally to distinguish from these probably familiar phrases. Certainly the two verbs, one masculine and one feminine in form, demand that we do not combine the two subjects into one. צר, as a collective can be the sole subject of the plural יבעתהו, but צר ומצוקה cannot be joint subjects of the singular תתקפהו. The military images which follow also seem to support *foe* for צר. On the other hand the word order, placing תתקפהו after מצוקה is discouraging. Other aspects of this verse are discussed on pp 146f.

25ff. The image of a warrior attacking God Himself strongly suggests that the wicked is the enemy <u>pro tem</u> of Israel.

27. כי־כסה פניו בחלבו   ויעש פימה עלי־כסל

Eliphaz describes the assault made by the "wicked" man against God - *He runs at Him in stiff-necked pride in the density of his protective idols* is the version we have hammered out for the preceding line (see p.147f). The common understanding of v. 27 leads to such versions as:

> *Because he hath covered his face with his fatness*
> *And made collops of fat on his loins.*

The picture is one of gluttonous fatness, the mark of spiritual insensibility (cf. Deut 32:15, Jer 5:28), or the way the evil-doer battened on his victims. (V.E. Reichert, *Job*, Soncino Press, London, *1946*, p.77.)

This version is suspect <u>first</u> because properly understood the references to fatness in Deuteronomy and Jeremiah are actually references to the condition of prosperity which preceded the fall from grace, while in the verse as translated here the fatness is itself a part of the offence; <u>second</u> because חלבו is not *his fatness*, but *his fat*, the literal substance of grease; <u>third</u> because כסה ב- implies the external application of a substance, not distortion by internal excess of it; <u>fourth</u> because if one wishes to describe a badly overweight man, one does not speak of fat on his face and thighs, but mainly on his belly; <u>fifth</u> because of the incompatibility of his *running* at God and the state of extreme adiposity postulated; <u>sixth</u> because of the incompatibility between the picture of gross prosperity conveyed by the fatness, and that of deprivation, if not starvation, conveyed by the remainder of the descriptions of the condition of the wicked in Chapter 15; and <u>last</u> because as understood in this way the verse is atrocious poetry!

What then is the meaning of the verse? I suggest (v. p. 147) it literally refers to the preparations made by a warrior for battle. Battle in Biblical times was man-to-man physical enounter, not greatly different from wrestling except for the addition of weapons. As the modern wrestler greases his body to prevent his adversary from gaining a grip on him, so did the ancient warrior grease both his body and his armour. There are traces of this practice to be found in the Bible. It is noted in II Sam 1:22 that the shield of Saul was vilely cast away *not anointed with oil*. This might be read as a reference to a way of preserving the shield when not in use, but in Isa 21:5 *Rise up, ye princes, anoint the shield!* is a battle cry beyond doubt.

There is another possibility for this verse, which depends on there having been a metaplasm in the word חלבו, but which brings the quality of the verse up to that of the remainder of the book, and takes into account the sense of the phrase כסה פניו ב- as in 9:4 or Isa 29:10 - <u>to blindfold</u>. It is not likely, for it also requires an adjustment for what becomes the suffix of פימה (Note, however, that פימה as a word in its own right is very dubious). We must consider the version therefore:

> *For he has blindfolded himself to his destruction*
> *And set his mouth to folly.*

29. לא־יעשר ולא־יקום חילו   ולא־יטה לארץ מנלם

The usual version of this - *He shall not become rich nor shall his wealth endure* does not make sense. The plural suffix of the unique word מנלם (Berechiah declares that it means *of that which is theirs*) requires a plural referent, while all the way from v.20 to v.33 the wicked man is singular. Only חילו as *his army* can supply this. See also 5:5.

32b. וכפתו לא רעננה

כפה, literally a branch or palm-frond, is only found elsewhere in contrast with עגמן in such phrases as *high and low, root and branch*. It is doubtful if it admits a non-figurative meaning.

35. הרה עמל וילד און   ובטנם תכין מרמה

Eliphaz's last statement on the subject of the origin of עמל and און, see 5:6,7 and 4:8. See also Ps 7:15 where the similar הרה עמל וילד שקר leads to ישוב עמלו בראשו - *His mischief will rebound to his own head*. Also Isa 59:4.

Chapter 16

3. A sarcastic shot aimed at 8:2 in which Bildad characterised Job's words as "a tempest". See note to 15:2.

5. אאמצכם במו־פי   וניד שפתי יחשך

ניד evokes 2:11 where the three friends came לנוד ולנחמו. שפתי יחשך derives from

Prov 10:19, חושך שפתיו משכיל *He who curbs his tongue shows sense* (NJPSV trans.).

The poverty of Biblical Hebrew in respect of tenses cannot be better illustrated than in these verses 4-6. The translation must depend entirely on context in this respect.

7,8. See pp. 123f.

9. אפו טרף וישטמני   חרק עלי בשניו   צדי ילטוש עיניו לי

The first stich does not say *He tore me in His anger*. The distinction is important. This is much the same as 9:23 with its suggestion that Job regards his misfortunes as an incidental effect of God's activities against a third party. Certainly he does not maintain this position consistently, but it emerges from time to time (e.g. 23:17).

There is considerable doubt about who is the gnasher of teeth and sharpener of eyes in the second and third stichoi. In stich c it is specified to be Job's foe (צרי), but is this God or his earthly foes? Verse 10 surely refers to the same foe, but here they are plural, while v. 11 makes a clear distinction between them and God Who delivered Job into their power. Stich b appears to apply to God, but the grossness of the anthropomorphic description casts great doubt. Psalm 37 reports that:

> *The wicked plotteth against the righteous,*
> *And gnasheth at him with his teeth.*

On balance it seems best to treat the whole passage from 9b to 10c as referring to human enemies - perhaps the "friends".

13c. ישפך לארץ מררתי

Humans do not excrete a liquid called "gall". This has only a figurative sense for them. The human excretion is <u>bile</u>. The attempt to subvert מררה into meaning <u>gall-bladder</u> in 20: 25 is unjustifiable. See p. 287.

16a. פני חמרמרה מני־בכי

It is a general rule that nonce-words such as חמרמר (Lam 1:20, 2:11), formed by rare poetic conjugations for special occasions, cannot possibly bear more than one meaning. This is the Pe`al`al of חמר *to boil over*, which makes perfectly acceptable sense in the context. On the other hand there is no known Hebrew root חמר - to be red - from which the universally accepted *red with weeping* might be derived.

17b. ותפלתי זכה

This is the correct word for *prayer*. Cf. 15:4.

18. The intention here is the same as in 19:23,24, where Job expresses the craving for immortality for his protest, if not for his person. The verse owes a debt to the first recorded murder - *The voice of thy brother's blood cries unto Me from the ground* (Gen 4:10). The full significance of leaving blood uncovered is to be found in Ezek 24:7,8:

> ...*that it might cause fury to come up, that vengeance might be taken, I have set her blood on bare rock, that it should not be covered.*

Job's passion in summoning the earth as witness against the injustice of God is quintessentially Hebraic.

20f. See p. 309, n.13.

22. כי־שְׁנוֹת מִסְפָּר יֶאֱתָיוּ   וְאֹרַח לֹא־אָשׁוּב אֶהֱלֹךְ

It is doubtful if the second stich is to be regarded as something to be fulfilled after the first stich. NJPSV *A few more years will pass and I shall go the way of no return* summarises the usual understanding, but יאתיו is come, not go, and the idea that Job expects to die only in a few years seems immediately contradicted by 17:1. Therefore I suggest the phrase שְׁנוֹת מִסְפָּר means "years of counting", i.e. of dearth.

Chapter 17

2. אִם־לֹא הֲתֻלִים עִמָּדִי   וּבְהַמְּרוֹתָם תָּלַן עֵינִי

A very difficult and uncertain verse. הֲתֻלִים is almost always taken as the personified "mockers" (cf. 13:9), referring to the comforters, or if accepted as "mockery", allowed much the same sense; אִם־לֹא is then taken as an affirmation. But this concept has little or nothing to do with what is said in vv. 1 and 3. The translation given, while radical, yet respects the meaning of the Hebrew and attributes continuity to the passage.

NJPSV *I close my eyes* for חֹלֵן עֵינִי is surely wrong, while P's *The Mounds loom before me, On the Slime-Pits my eye dwells* shows a truer appreciation of the demands of the context than of the text. Moffatt gives *illusions* for הֲתֻלִים, but does not thereby produce a more relevant verse.

3-6. See pp. 278ff.

7. וַתֵּכַהּ מִכַּעַשׂ עֵינִי   וִיצֻרַי כַּצֵּל כֻּלָּם

יצֻרַי is commonly understood here as "my limbs" (even by such authorities on Hebrew as Rashi and Ibn Ezra), but this is a far cry from the range of meanings associated with the root, which relates to creative and imaginative forms. Scholars have been misled by the modern hyperbolic simile utilizing the thin-ness of a shadow. In biblical use the metaphor, where not of protection, relates only to ephemerality (e.g. 14:2), and so can scarcely refer to "limbs". Job means that all his dreams have passed away (cf. Terrien). Being too anatomical in the second stich should by rights reflect back on the first, and lead interpreters to see Job as going blind! Strangely, NJPSV seems to accept this even without assuming an anatomical second stich. Their 7b is *All shapes seem to me like shadows*, ignoring the suffixed yod.

In truth, "limbs" and "eye" form a false parallel in these translations, for "eye" must be metaphorical. כעש - vexation or frustration - does not cause physical deterioration of the eyesight.

8,9. See pp. 274ff.

10. Not accepting Job as a victim of injustice, the friends are in Job's eyes too stupid to react as men of virtue do.

11a. ימי עברו זמתי נתקו

זמה is always an evil purpose, so that זמתי surely means the evil purposes devised **against** me - the objective genitive (Ges. # 135m). A sarcastic implication (what you think of as my זמות) is just possible in the light of v.15, which is surely sarcastic, and v.14, an ironic parody of Prov 7:4. *Say to Wisdom, Thou art my sister, and call Understanding thy kinswoman."*

11b,12. מורשי לבבי   לילה ליום ישימו   אור קרוב מפני-חשך

11b is certainly part of a sentence and forms the perfect subject for 12a, while 12b is a comment on the proposition. The heart is the seat of understanding and ירש has a dominant sense of inheritance - *What I inherit from my understanding* is thus the meaning of 11b, hence *my conclusions*. The figure taken as a whole expresses Job's satisfaction in the thought that when he dies the whole scandal described in 17:8,9 will fizzle out. The idea of this turns gloom into rejoicing – night into day. It is because of his imminent death (the darkness), that relief of the situation (light) is near.

13-16. These verses are designed to refute the often expressed assurance of the friends that, if Job will only put his own house in order, all will be well again. If (as he has assumed in this chapter) he is in articulo mortis, what sense is there in talking about this hope or that hope (15a and 15b)?

15. At first sight there appears to be a contradiction between the satisfaction expressed in vv.11,12 at Job's imminent decease, and the evident dissatisfaction in the rejection of all hope in the concluding verses. The resolution of this lies in the neglected waw of verse 15 - ואיה אפו תקותי?. This murt be read as But, with the implication "This is all very well for the rest of mankind, but what about me personally?" It throws the emphasis onto the word "my".

16a. בדי שאול תרדנה

Awarding בדי the same meaning as in 11:3 and 41:4. There seems no better solution.

Chapter 18

2-4. See Chapter 6, pp. 195-199.

5. גם אור רשעים ידעך   ולא־יגה שביב אשׁו

Twice in QT אור is translated "fire" rather than "light", as though written with *sureq* rather than *holem*. Both because of context, and the masculine verb, this variation fits particularly well here.

9. יאחז בעקב פח   יחזק עליו צמים

The verse could have been designed to illustrate the difference between אחז to seize, and חזק to retain. See ad 17:9, p. 274. צמים is related to צמה a veil; hence *net*.

10. טמון בארץ חבלו   ומלכדתו עלי נתיב

The author is not ringing the changes of synonyms tediously, as most versions suggest. Neither חבל nor מלכדת has a proper claim to be a form of trap. Strictly, the first is destruction, and the second capture. A similar passage is Ps 140:6, where "cords" is correct, but the cords are to bind him when captured, not to ensnare him. A noose or cord buried in the ground is in itself harmless.

The Hebrew has his חבל and his מלכדת, which also weighs heavily against their being mechanical devices to trap him. The distinctions are not of vital importance but they reflect the high quality of detail in the book. The deeper implications are that he is an offence to the earth which will avenge itself on him, and that his way of life contains the seeds of its own ruin.

13. יאכל בדי עורו   יאכל בדיו בכור מות

The verse poses two problems - what is בכור מות, *the firstborn of death*? and what is the meaning of בד? Fortunately we are not obliged in translation to identify the firstborn of death. The idea that it is some specific skin disease such as elephantiasis is untenable on numerous grounds. I suggest that rather than disease, or still less any specific disease, the term means *fire*, hence its coupling with the word אכל, commonly used of fire, but only once (Ezek 7:15) of pestilence (and famine). See note to v.14 below.

The usual translation of בדים as *members* is too concrete and too specific. The sense is *bit by bit - piecemeal*.

14. ינתק מאהלו מבטחו   ותצעדהו למלך בלהות

A subject must be found for the feminine verb תצעדהו, and תשכון, the first word of 15a (T-S writes *There is no instance of a subjectless verb in the feminine*). The only candidate, but that an appropriate one, is בלהות which appears plural. See, however, Ges. #145k, under whose umbrella this case seems to fall. It is construed as singular in 27:20, 30:15 and three times in Ezekiel. Only in Job 18:11 is the noun plural, and there it is the subject of two masculine verbs! This obliges us to sacrifice the attractive, but incomprehensible phrase, "The king of terrors", and return to the known reality of Middle Eastern horrors, with "the king" being Moloch. NJPSV has much the same solution. Encyclopaedia Judaica (Vol. 12, pp.230f) cogently argues that Melech was probably the original vocalization for Moloch, with this "tendentious misvocalization" introduced long after the writing of Job. See also Isa 57:9, immediately after a description of the sacrifice of children (57:5).

> *And thou wentest to the king with ointment, and didst increase thy perfumes, And didst send thine ambassadors far off, Even down to the Netherworld.*

Assuming that these "ambassadors" are the sacrificed children, as they surely are, then in this passage Melech is assuredly Moloch, who or whose furnace becomes identifiable as בכור מות, "The Firstborn of Death" in the previous verse. This, then, is a second Jobian reference to Tophet.

15. תשכון באהלו מבלי־לו   יזרה על־נוהו גפרית

Again with panic as the subject. מבלי־לו - The ל here is probably to introduce what passes for the object, so simply *without him*. The phrase surely cannot function as a noun and so be the subject of תשכון (RV etc). The purpose of strewing brimstone (or salt) on land is to make it forever uninhabitable. Panic dwelling in his tent after his death - a most uncompanionable ghost, is a compatible concept.

20. על־יומו נשמו אחרנים   וקדמנים אחזו שער

It is difficult to accept קדמנים as those before him, for what could they have known of him? We should be haoppier with "horror" as the subject and קדמנים the object of אחז, but the sense is undoubted, and there is good reason, as follows.

נשמו is the same word Job used in 17:8 for the reaction of the upright to his own fate, while in 17:9 he has the righteous taking hold of (אחז) his (the heathen's) ways (most have him holding to his own way, but they have overlooked this reference). Horror is Bildad's equivalent for his ways. There can be no doubt here that Bildad is sneering cruelly.

Chapter 19

2. עד־אנה תוגיון נפשי   ותדכונני במלים

A riposte to 18:2, עד־אנה תשימון קנצי למלין (see Chap.VI). Effectively this refutes the negative version of LXX.

3b. לא־תבשו תהכרו ־לי

There is no known root הכר. The choice seems to be between תכרו (as in 6:17) or תנכרו (as in 21:29). The latter has been assumed. T. has the witty *that you are acquainted with me* as though תהכירו. C reports that three Mss have תַחכרו,

and postulates a Hebrew root חכר, "illtreat", on the basis of an Arabic cognate. *This*, he says, *is a satisfactory sense, and emendations are gratuitous*!

7. הן אצעק חמס! ולא אענה   אשוע ואין משפט

It is not just the absence of justice that Job decries here, but the absence of every feature of law - no police, no courts, no judge, no-one to appeal to, no sign of an organised state in the moral world.

9b. ויסר עטרת ראשי

As in Lam 5:16 the "from" is understood. Note that the whole passage 19:6 to 19:20 is a lamentation in much the same conventional form as the book of that name; see espec. Lam 3.

13. אחי מעלי הרחיק   וידעי אך־־זרו ממני

As with 6:15, who Job means by his "brothers" is not specified, but it cannot be the comforters. It is the statement in this verse which rules out the possibility of בני במני in v.17 being a reference to the children of Job's mother's womb (see p. 135). This is the first of three uses of the root זור *to be a stranger* in this short passage - זרו here, לזר in v.15 and זרה in v.17. There is to be a fourth, ולא־זר, in v.27. The existence of this unmistakable leitmotif is another reason for rejecting the usual mistranslations of זרה in v.17 as from a cognate Arabic root.

16. לעבדי קראתי ולא יענה   במו־־פי אתחנן־לו!

The servant does not come when Job claps his hands to summon him. This is the first of three uses of the root חנן, *to be gracious* in this short passage - אתחנן here, חנותי in v.17, and חנני in v.21. The existence of this second unmistakable leitmotif is yet another reason for rejecting the usual mistranslations of חנותי in v.17 as from a cognate Arabic root.

17. See pp.125f. and 135f., and notes to vv. 15 and 16 supra.

18. גם־עוילים מאסו בי   אקומה וידברו־בי

עוילים is either wrong-doers, or sucklings, the latter being impossible here. The idea that it might mean boys, youngsters, urchins, which seems to have been adopted almost unanimously, may have arisen in the search for needless parallels with the preceding verse. The word is the same as in 16:11 - God has delivered me to the עויל, where (despite D), boys is absurd. QT has *evil people*. ידברו־בי is an unusual form. *Interrupt* is a valid alternative, see 29:7-25, detailing the respect Job was wont to receive when he rose to speak in the Gate.

20. See pp. 126f.

21. The climax of pathos in the work.

22b. ומבשרי לא תשבעו

An unexpected expression, whose meaning appears to be no more than *Are you never going to tire of using me as your butt?* In 31:33 the same expression is found, but it is the man himself who might "weary of his flesh" - grow tired of life. The subtlety of this "Why are you not tired of my life?" is exemplary.

23-27. See pp. 485 - 491.

למען תדעון שדין .29

Clearly the three <u>nuns</u> are there for the sake of assonance of which the author is fond (see 10:8-18), but what is שדין. I suggest it is the intensive plural of שדי, and that the assumption that this word means *The Almighty* is correct, שדין signifying His might.

The suggestion that it means *that there is a judgement* (D et al) is very improbable both because -ש does not occur in the Book of Job elsewhere, and also because the idea contradicts 19:7 flatly. Indeed it is the friends' thesis, not Job's.

Chapter 20

מוסר כלמתי אשמע   ורוח מבינתי יענני .3

Again the objective genitive - it was Job's rebuke, probably in Chap 13 (q.v.). It is interesting that the answer is given to <u>Zophar</u> by his understanding. No biblical verse better illustrates the way in which the faculties were regarded as independent of the person.

עין שזפתו ולא תוסף   ולא־עון תשורנו מקומו .9

An invocation of 7:8: לא־תשורני עין ראי. שזף is a very rare word - Job 28:7 and Song 1:6 being the only other examples.

בניו ירצו דלים   וידיו תשבנה אונו .10

The first stich of this verse, *His children will curry favour with the poor*, is <u>post mortem</u> as far as he (the wicked) is concerned (vide vv.7-9). The second stich *And his hands will restore his wealth* seems to resurrect him. This does not quite make sense. A man (even if alive) cannot restore or return his own wealth. There are two alternatives. <u>His hands</u> may be those not of the wicked man, but his son, who is destined to restore his father's ill-gotten wealth to the poor. Note that in v.11 "his life" refers to the life of the son, followed by the note of the early death of the daughter also (v.i.). The second alternative is that "his hands" are those of the poor, who will *repay his affliction* rather than *restore his wealth*. In each case the singular "his" refers to an individual of the collective noun in the preceding stich.

11. PARTITIVE GENDER

There are four apparent examples of a novel figure of speech in the Book of Job, each of which, unrecognized, has contributed to the confusion which the book has consistently evoked in serious readers. They are 20:11, 31:11. 31:18 and 38:14. All these verses have in common (a) that they contain a feminine form for which there is apparently no trace of a referent in the context, and (b) that they are preceded by a verse which refers collectively to a group of people necessarily embracing both sexes.

In 20:11 the <u>children of the wicked</u> are under discussion, and Zophar states:

עצמותיו מלאו עלומיו   ועמו על־עפר תשכב

This evidently means *His life will end in his youth, and she will lie down in the dust with him.*

All sorts of devices have been employed to extract sense from the sentence, but in fact it creates no difficulty at all if we assume that the common noun בניו, his children, in the preceding verse is being partitioned by gender in this one, so that the true sense of the verse is *His son will die in youth and his daughter will lie down in the dust with him.* In 27:14,15 the same sentiment is expressed by Job himself.

14b. מרורת פתנים בקרבו

It is a small matter that snakes do not have gall-bladders or gall, but the translation of מרורה here as <u>gall</u> is quite without foundation. In 16:13 the vocalization of מררה, which there can be nothing but <u>bile</u>, is entirely different. This is the word found in 13:26 - God writes מררת against Job. It is whatever is bitter in the viper. There is a deliberate contrast with the sweetness in his mouth of v.12 - it turns bitter in his intestines. No translation but *bitterness* is acceptable.

16. This is not a surprising physiological error. It was well-known that the poison of a serpent was transmitted by its bite (Prov 23:32, Ecc 10:11) and that it was innocuous when swallowed. To suck the poison of serpents is to follow their deceptive advice. The serpent's tongue is the symbol of temptation (Gen 3). This passage may be compared to Ps 140:3: *They have sharpened their tongues like a serpent: adder's poison is under their lips.*

17. אל־ירא בפלגות נהרי נחלי דבש וחמאה

Of the twenty-odd translations in my library, only four – NJPSV, LXX, D&G and Budde, respect the sense of אל as a prohibition rather than a negation in this verse. G states baldly *אל is emphatic, "surely not, never"* but the Bible lends scant support to such a view.

The significance of ירא ב- depends very much on context, which in this case is the statements in vv. 15 and 18 that all his gains will be reversed in short order. This enables us to find a clear and very relevant meaning for the verse in:

> Let him not <u>gloat over</u> his rivers etc. of honey and butter!

This is not quite the same as NJPSV *Let him not enjoy...* which seems to be a plea to outside powers to prevent his profiting from his wealth. *Let him not gloat...* is best understood as a piece of unfriendly advice. See BDB p.908, ראה, 8a (6). <u>Enjoy</u> is very far from the usual meaning of ראה.

19. כי־רצץ עזב דלים בית גזל ולא יבנהו

As very often in the Book of Job, בית is not the physical structure of a house, but stands for the commonweal of a family, tribe or nation. See, e.g. 3:14. 8:15, 20:28, 21:9, 21:21, 22:18, 27:18. Once the word in this verse is understood in this way, all its difficulties melt away.

Because in dereliction he crushed the poor, or some similar expression, now becomes a genuine explanation or illustration of the second stich: *He robbed his House and did not build it up.* One who does not care for the welfare of his own poor is robbing his own House, unwittingly preparing its downfall. This is an impeccable proposition of social theory, and of Hebrew prophetic doctrine, and again identifies Job as the responsible leader of a group, probably national.

20b. בחמודו לא ימלט

The verb is Pi`el and an extraneous subject is needed.

23b,c. ישלח־בו חרון אפו   וימטר עלימו בלחומו

בלחומו corresponds to no known form. The suggestion is a derivative (infinitive construct) of לחם, to <u>war</u>. Zeph 1:17, which is quoted as the justification for the impossible <u>bowels</u> for this word, really speaks of <u>flesh</u> - *Their blood is poured out like dust and their bowels like dung* is a genuinely impossible figure. עלימו is singular.

24,25. Fully discussed on pp. 286ff.

Chapter 21

4b. ואם־מדוע לא־תקצר רוחי?

A puzzling construction. G offers some similar expressions from other sources. Job is apparently defending the rudeness which nettled Zophar.

5,6. Job speaks here as a man who has just woken up to the facts of existence as the nursery tales fade into unreality.

11. ישלחו כצאן עויליהם   וילדיהם ירקדון

עויל derives from עול to <u>suckle,</u> and therefore cannot represent the half-grown children of almost very version. שלח here is an irreverent word for delivering the young - they cast their young in an animal fashion. The image is one of prolific, easy and successful reproduction, and only the second line refers to children sporting on the green. See also note to 19:18. The inspiration is Ps 17:14.

13. יבלו בטוב ימיהם   וברגע שאול יחתו

ברגע is often taken as "in tranquillity", but the words derived from the root רגע which might mean this are מרגוע and מרגעה (Isa 28:12 and Jer 6:16 respectively). The contexts of these single citations are equivalent, and Vg translates them identically <u>refrigerium</u>, more or less *lassitude*. LXX has *calamity* for the first and *purification* for the second.

רגע vocalized as in 21:13, is always "a moment", and so it should be translated here. The matter is of some importance, see p. 250. The apparent parallel of sense between בטוב and ברגע is deceptive.

16. הן לא בידם טובם   עצת רשעים רחקה מני

What this probably means is "If they are not the masters of their own destinies, I certainly have thoroughly misunderstood the principles by which they operate!" הן, whether Hebrew or Aramaic, leans towards the meaning "If", and certainly appears frequently in Job as such. Ges. considers that this sense requires that the apodosis be introduced with <u>waw</u>. A possible alternative sense is something like *Behold, their good fortune does not derive from anything they have done*, and then *Their modus vivendi is the opposite of mine*.

Insistence on reading הן as *Behold!* has led others either to propose considerable emendation, or deleting the verse altogether. 22:18 depends entirely on this verse.

17. ‏כמה נר־רשעים ידעך   ויבא עלימו אידם   חבלים יחלק באפו?‏

Stich a is a direct rebuttal of 18:5.

חבל is usually taken as pangs, but the word is tied to the pangs of birth. Coupled with the word חלק which is used for the careful apportioning of plots of land, portions of spoil, fortune in general, this seems the best interpretation - that destiny is determined by a God in a wild fury rather than with calm discretion. Cf. 18:21 & 20:29. Also perhaps 7:3. For איד here and in v. 30, see Chap. 3.IX. עלימו is plural in this context.

18. The referent of יהיו is ambiguous - the wicked, or whatever God distributes in His rage. This image is often used of the wicked.

19-21. See pp. 275ff.

22-26. See pp. 283ff.

24a. ‏עטיניו מלאו חלב‏

Probably עטינים will remain forever an object of doubt. The rare agreement of LXX and Vg and the need for an anatomical parallel leads me to favour "organs". G's speculation that the word is an euphemism (olives) for testicles, with milk equivalent to semen is certainly plausible.

26. ‏יחד על־עפר ישכבו   ורמה תכסה עליהם‏

Cf. Isa 14:11, of the king of Babylon:

> Thy pomp is brought down to Sheol,
> And the noise of thy psalteries;
> The maggot is spread under thee,
> And the worms cover thee.

27,28. ‏הן ידעתי מחשבותיכם   ומזמות עלי תחמסו‏
‏כי תאמרו איה בית נדיב?   ואיה אהל משכנות רשעים?‏

Again the הן is best understood as "If". Job is telling the friends that he has penetrated the hypocritical veneer of their consolations to the brutal equation of himself with the wicked which lies behind them. "What you are going to do now, after what I have said, is to look around my ash-heap and sarcastically ask *Where is all this splendour you say the wicked enjoy?*" For the phrase ‏אהל משכנות‏ see p.160, n.5.

30. כי ליום איד יחשך רע   ליום עברות יובלו

The first stich contains the phrase, יחשך רע. I suppose, taken in isolation, everyone would agree to its meaning *The evil is held back*. Surprisingly, however, in the context of the full line רע has always been regarded as an adjective, to stand for "the evil man", forcing the translators to struggle with the inappropriate verb, giving *The evil man is reserved for the day of calamity* (but for איד v.s. ad v.17). This is entirely unnecessary; the wicked, but in the plural, are already in this discussion and there is no call to refresh the subject. The meaning of the verse is that *the evil* which is due to the wicked *is deferred to a day of retribution: they* (the wicked) *are escorted* (unharmed) *to a day of wrath!* In this version, the preposition ל is correct, and does not require excusing (see e.g. H p.323, n. 30b).

31-33. Little thought is devoted to these verses nowadays, but looking back over the literature, it is apparent that a good deal of effort has been spent in arriving at the present comfortable consensus as to their meaning. D employed more than three pages to discuss the phrase ועל גדיש ישקוד (32b) alone. Unfortunately, the consensus does not correspond at all closely with the text. There are in all seven lines to this passage, and of these only two are unproblematic.

31. מי־יגיד על־פניו דרכו   והוא־עשה מי ישלם־לו?

31a is clear as *Who will confront him with his way?* though even here there is an ambiguous possibility in that it may be God's way of virtue rather than his own of sin that no-one has shown to him. By contrast, 31b is weird, with הוא־עשה wellnigh indecipherable. The usual way of looking at it is as *What he has done*, followed by *who will pay back to him?* but this is surely illiterate. הוא־עשה can never be a substantive form. On the other hand עשה does exist quite often as an intransitive absolute; indeed it seems possible that the הוא־עשה of this verse is a contra-quotation of Ps 37:5 which reads:

גול על־יהוה דרכך ובטח עליו והוא יעשה-

> *Commit thy way to the Lord;*
> *Trust also in Him and He will bring it to pass.*

This is JPS, and *Trust in Him and He will act* seems more accurate. Psalm 37 is that Psalm par excellence which upholds the principle of God's dispensation of justice on earth to the righteous and the wicked, and contains those supreme expressions of wilful human blindness *I have been young and now am old, but I have not seen the righteous forsaken, nor his seed begging for bread,* and *The meek shall inherit the earth.* It is therefore a natural target for Job! In Job 21:31b there should be an immediate question. Who is הוא? I believe it to be God for several reasons. First, the use of the pronoun itself suggests a change of subject; second הוא in the Book of Job is very often God; third, the attractive idea that this is a contra-quotation of Ps 37 requires this reading, making of הוא־עשה a mirror image of הוא יעשה where God is the subject. Finally by far the best sense is achieved by accepting God as subject rather than the wicked with

> *Who will confront him with his way?*
> *And now He has acted, who will requite him?*

God's action being specified both before and after as escorting the wicked unharmed to the day of wrath (30b), and to the place of tombs (32a), and deferring his deserts (30a) and guarding his possessions (32b).

There seems a very close resemblance between the awkward והוא־עשה followed by מי ישלם־לו? and והוא ישקט followed by ומי ירשע in 34:29. In the latter God's action-inaction (silence) is hypothetical, but leads to the rhetorical question who? (i.e., if not He?). In 21:31 God's action-inaction is accomplished, but also leads to the rhetorical who? with the implied answer *not He, therefore no-one.*

32. והוא לקברות יובל   ועל־גדיש ישקוד

32a has also given rise to little discussion or reflection in recent years: *When he is born (in pomp) to the sepulchre,* with קברות as an impressive tomb, has been generally accepted. There is, however, no precedent for קברות as intensive plural, and no fewer than twenty examples from Numbers to Chronicles where it is a simple plural. Both LXX and Vg treat it as a true plural [but NB, both Herodotus and Sophocles use the (Greek) plural for a single grave. Liddel & Hart Lexicon].

Another objection is that יובלו in v.30 immediately preceding has been understood as escorted (unharmed), and the principle of consistency requires us to understand יובל in this verse in much the same way. There should therefore be no suggestion of an elaborate funeral procession read into the verb, merely a passage to the grave which has been unaccompanied by hardship or the רע (evil) so well-earned. When Job despairingly cried מבטן לקבר אובל! *I would (or should) have been borne from the womb to the grave!* there was certainly no suggestion of any elaborate transfer. Evidently this is a routine word for the removal of a corpse to the cemetery with no implication as to the form of ceremony.

For ועל־גדיש ישקוד scholars have settled on *And a watch is kept over his tomb,* but there are no fewer than three textual objections to this version, as well as one of sense. Most difficult, of course, is that גדיש does not mean a tomb at all, but something of the kind of a haystack or cornsheaf. The fact that the rising of a גדיש is used as a simile for a man coming to his tomb in due season in 5:26 rules out of court for ever the idea that גדיש can mean a tomb. A word cannot be used as a simile for itself.

The second objection is the mild one of the absence of the possessive suffix. The third is the singular form of ישקוד, which rightly rules out the passive and leaves either him who was borne to the grave or God Himself as the subject. To have him watching over his own tomb is of course farcical.

LXX provides a more or less literal translation of the verse, which at first sight seems to make no sort of sense - *He has been led away to the tombs and he has watched over the heaps*, but ultimately it is the literal translation which must prevail. P suggests that the tomb keeps watch over him.

The meaning of the common version - a watch kept over his tomb - elevates the sinner to very high rank indeed. As D remarked *the placing of guards of honour by graves is an assumed, but not proved, custom of antiquity*. One can certainly imagine that the graves in the Valley of the Kings, or the pyramids, with their fabulous riches, were guarded night and day, but before accepting that the wicked in Chapter 21 is of this class, it is as well to think out the implications for the whole debate, the whole Book of Job, of such an assumption.

Out of all this speculation, the solution of treating God as the subject of ישקוד, and seeing in this stich as it were a summary of vv. 1-13 describing the security and prosperity of the wicked, seems by far the best. So we should understand *And He keeps (or kept) a watch over his accumulations*.

33. מתקו־לו רגבי־נחל   ואחריו כל־אדם ימשוך   ולפניו אין מספר.

33a is perhaps yet more difficult. Here we are not sure of the meaning of the verb מתק, and the usual rendering of נחל as the valley is not sound, either philologically or from the point of view of public health! It cannot too strongly be emphasised that no-one would bury a body in a wadi-bed, which is what a נחל is when it is not the stream itself. (Commentators are keen on referring to the burial of Moses in a valley {גי} [Deut 34:6] as evidence that burials often took place in valleys. This may or may not be true, for no more than one swallow makes a summer does one body, no matter how distinguished, make a cemetry, but burials certainly did not take place in נחלים).

For that matter, our knowledge of the word רגב is remarkably sketchy, depending entirely on this verse and Job 38:38 where the best guess we can make is particles, perhaps of dust, but a possessive suffix is lacking. Thus *The clods of the valley are sweet to him* (AV, RV, JPS, P, G, D&G, D, H, Rowley, NJPSV & Hartley [wadi for valley], LXX [stones for clods], etc.), besides being maudlin, and although very well attested, rests on none too secure a foundation. How troubled one at least of the ancients was by the verse is demonstrated by the Vulgate translation: *Sweet (to him) was the gravel of Cocytus.* Cocytus, according to Lempriere's Classical Dictionary was a river of Epirus.

> *The word is derived from kokuein, to weep and to lament. Its etymology,*
> *the unwholesomeness of its water, and above all its vicinity to the Acheron,*
> *have made the poets call it one of the rivers of hell.*

Altogether a strange choice for Vg to have made.

In 24:20, מתקו is generally accepted as *feeds sweetly on him*, with the worm as the subject, despite the disagreement of gender. The sense of sweetness is surely the essence of the verb, but the transitive use is puzzling. Feeds sweetly borrows half its sense (to suck) from the Aramaic, and somehow one doesn't imagine worms sucking. The simplest explanation of 24:20 is surely that the worm sweetens him in the sense opposite to that of Anthony's *The evil that men do lives after them, the good is oft interred with their bones*. There the word would be "edulcorates" which means to make sweet, but with the added sense of removing what is harsh and acrid (Shorter OED). Is there any reason why the same sense should not apply in 21:33? We have noted in Chap. IX above considerable interaction between Chaps. 21 and 24 of Job. It is possible that a decisive contrast is intended between רמה, the worm of Chap. 24, and in Chap. 21 as agents achieving the same result for the inadvertent sinner of Chap. 24 and רגבי־נחל the truly wicked man of Chap. 21. For this to be so, we must accept מתקו־לו as the equivalent of מתקוהו (Ges #117n). The problem now is to locate the meaning of רגבי־נחל which fits this hypothesis.

22:24 reads: ושית־על־עפר בצר ובצור נחלים אופיר - *So leave treasure in the dust, and gold to the stones of the stream*. Could רגבי־נחל be nothing but alluvial gold?

> *Alluvial deposits of native gold found in or along streams were the*
> *principal sources of the metal for the ancient civilizations of the Middle*
> *East.*

(Encyclopaedia Brittanica,*1979*, Macropaedia, Vol 8, p. 237.)

If we simply translate רגב as nugget, this sense will emerge in English. With this interpretation the line becomes a suitably cynical observation of the way in which wealth washes out most stains from the reputation.

The next line, ואחריו כל־אדם ימשוך, is likewise not quite so simple as the consensus suggests. The verb משך seems sadly out of place if the sense is to be that all mankind follows either in his wake - to the grave, or in his footsteps - by taking his unpunished way of life. The suggestion (BDB) that משך in Jud

4:6 is the intransitive *proceed* is probably incorrect for, as in Ex 12:21 the verb is coupled with the verb לקח, and means *draw out of the herd and take;* i.e. משׁך there conveys select from a larger number. It seems that משׁך should be considered as always transitive. Jud 20:37, where the intention of the verb is obscure, may be an exception.

It is therefore very likely that an object for משׁך lurks somewhere in the text. As for the meaning of the verb, the probability is that it is the same as that in Chap. 24 - yet another link between these two chapters - *to drag down (to ruin)* (24:22, where the object is אבירים). There are two possible objects - כל־אדם *He drags down all mankind to ruin after him* or, with the plausible but unprecedented meaning for אחריו (as though אחריתו) "what comes after him", *All mankind may loot his leavings or drag down his survivors to ruin.* אחריו here might then be treated as a direct quotation of the same word in 21:21, and as an abbreviation of the whole phrase ביתו אחריו *his House after him.* The sentiment in this formulation is identical with that which Job later expresses in 27:13ff when he lectures his friends on the true fate of the wicked.

33c. does not seem to have given rise to any speculation, the inconsequent *As there were innumerable before him* or something like *Before him marches an innumerable host* (G) being more or less universally accepted. Gordis's version (H also) is absurd; for we cannot have all mankind behind him and innumerable hosts in front! If we accept (with D) that all that this means is that all men in the past have met death, and all in the future will, it seems both banal and out of place in a discussion of the fate of the wicked. Versions which see the line beginning with "As" do not account for the use of <u>waw</u> rather than the comparative particle.

לפניו is only rarely *before him* in time, almost exclusively in Kings and Chronicles referring to the conduct of kings in comparison with those earlier and later in time than they. In these expressions, it is usually coupled with אחריו as here. Much more often it means *in his presence.* A secondary sense here may therefore be *But to his face was never an account,* cf. 21:31 above, על־פניו, and 31:37, where מספר has precisely this sense.

Taking all these considerations together, the safest solution seems to be to accept כל־אדם as the object of משׁך, but to take as its subject God, as in Chapter 24, and to regard the couplet as a reflection on the universality of death with its squaring of accounts. However...

Chapter 22

2. The whole complex which revolves around הלאל? is discussed on pp. 283-286, q.v.

4a. המיראתך יכחך?

There is a perfect and unresolvable ambiguity in the word יראתך - *your fear* or *the fear of you.* The question is certainly sarcastic, but the question is, how sarcastic? Again there should be no question of "Your fear (of God)".

6. Again חנם

16. אשר־קמטו ולא־עת   נהר יוצק יסודם.
See 16:8. This is the only other use of the verb קמט.

18. The attributions here seem unavoidable. This last recognizable quotation (of 21:16b) is another deliberate misunderstanding, with Eliphaz pretending to believe that Job there was claiming not to subscribe to the philosophy of the wicked.

19. יראו צדיקים וישמחו   ונקי ילעג־למו
20. אם־לא נכחד קימנו ויתרם אכלה איש.
As a natural progression from the statement that one party jeers at another, or otherwise comments on or addresses him, this verse quotes the derision as direct speech, cf. 12:4, 15:19, 24:13, none of which has been generally recognized. There has, however, been no difficulty about recognizing the intention of this passage. Thus if קים means, as has been proposed by D and numerous others, "adversary", it is our adversary, not theirs. This view of the reaction of the צדיק and the נקי to the revelling of the wicked is a reply to 17:8,9, which records the נקי and צניק reacting to the same events by throwing in their lot with the wicked. Cf. ישמחו with ישמו (17:8). Cf. also 18:20.

22. קה־נא מפיו תורה   ושים אמריו בלבבך.
Torah is not necessarily the Law of the Pentateuch, but see the Midrash Teruma, Exodus 25, where God's לכח is the Torah.

24. ושית־על־עפר בצר   ובצור נחלים אופיר.
Lay your treasure in the dust and gold among the stones of the stream makes no sort of sense, particularly as Job is now destitute, but we do know that the stones of the stream is the source of gold. Hence "leave" rather than "lay".

25b. וכסף תועפות לך.
Not silver, which is anticlimactic after gold.

29. כי־השפילו ותאמר גוה   ושח עינים יושע
The first stich is essentially indecipherable. Note the word גוה as pride, as in 20:25, see. p. 287.

30. It is this verse which appears to have prompted Ezekiel (14:14,20) [see pp.52f].

V
Footnotes to Chapters 23 - 31
Job's Monologue

Chapter 23

2. גם־היום מרי שחי   ידי כבדה על־אנחתי
At first sight this opening verse of Chapter 23 appears to forewarn us of the change of mood in the ensuing long speech. Time has passed and circumstances, perhaps, have changed. Job's indignation has become self-conscious. *Yet today my mood is mutinous.* The catharsis has advanced to the point of exhaustion. This is one way of interpreting the first stich. The verse is especially interesting from two points of view.

a. The use of the expression גם היום, literally *also,* or *yet today,* suggesting perhaps that the work was designed for public performance over a number of days and that Chapter 23 opened a new session, the third (P, D&G).

b. The phrase על־אנחתי which is most ambiguous, and might mean *despite* (P) or *because of* (JPS) my groans, or *upon* (D) or *more than* (G) my groaning.

If we are to accept מרי as *rebellion* rather than as an unknown form of "bitter" (D points out the combination of שיח with מר in both 7:11 and 10:1) then we must either avoid "complaint" for שיח (Job would not voluntarily characterise his complaint as rebellion) or accept R's excellent suggestion that Job is alluding to the accusations of Eliphaz in Chapter 22 stet.

Even now my complaint is (treated as) rebellion.

This version fully accomodates the גם with which the verse starts (cf. similar problems afflicting 24:19, 30:2 and 41:1 which have led to some devaluation of the word in this book).

The real meaning of ידי כבדה, *my hand is heavy* or *my heavy hand,* is a teasing problem. Following LXX many commentators amend the phrase to *His (God's) hand is heavy.* Among them is P who notes the close resemblance to the opening of the 3rd tablet of *Ludlul Bel Nemeqi, His hand was heavy (upon me). I was not able to bear it.* The closest Hebrew expression is Ezek 3:14 where describing what seems to be a classical migraine aura culminating in a severe headache, he declares ואלך מר בחמת רוחי ויד־יהוה עלי חזקה - *And I went bitter, in the heat of my spirit, and the hand of the Lord was strong upon me.* The only example of the actual phrase יד כבדה in the Bible is Ex 17:12, where Moses' hands grow heavy with fatigue. The general but not invariable sense of כבד in the Bible is passively "wearisome" rather than actively oppressive. The word is also used to describe what is overnumerous or too prolonged. יד

420   *Part 3*

itself is a very imprecise word in such contexts as this, being a metaphor for all sorts of things of which hands are capable. But without doubt someone else's hand being heavy upon one is a description of affliction, oppression, or punishment.

The idea that the suffix of *my hand* is an error for *His hand* (or, less justifiably, with Blommerde, that ׳ is an alternative way of writing the 3rd person possessive suffix) is hardly tenable despite its antiquity. Both the sense required (however vaguely) by the requirements of parallel, and the music of the verse require ידי. The verse is all about Job's subjective state. Besides, the expression *His hand is heavy* על can hardly escape being cognate with the Ezekiel passage above and *my groaning* as the target of God's heavy hand (D&G) is the <u>reductio ad absurdum</u> of this theory. Only if "his" were to mean Eliphaz's could the phrase be acceptable, and then only in the context of Renan's insight. What is possible is that ידי is the objective genitive. D in 1864 says *all modern expositors explain the suffix as objective*. This is as כלמתי in 20:3, and כשחי in 16:8. In this view "My heavy hand" = the hand which is heavy on me, a circumlocution for my oppression, with no personal owner of the hand at all.

If these speculations are accurate, then the purpose of the verse is to caricature the comforters' thesis with the proposition that Job's complaining is itself the cause of his suffering.

3. מי־יתן ידעתי ואמצאהו   אבוא עד־תכונתו

The phrase מי־יתן ידעתי authenticates the continuity between 19:23,24 and 19:25.

תכונה is not a normal word for a dwelling. In Ezek 43:12 it is an attribute of the Temple, and in Nahum 2:10 it seems to refer to the rich contents of palace or city. *Establishment* fits all these contexts.

4-7. A pleasant and meandering dream.

7. שם ישר נוכח עמו   ואפלטה לנצח משפטי

D raises the question as to whether שם is local or temporal in this sentence, but I suggest it is, as it were, neither and both - "in those circumstances", i.e. *in that time and place*. We translate "then", because it can carry this more comprehensive meaning. *Reason* (JPS) for נוכח seems to convey exactly what Job is after.

אפלטה is Pi`el, and in all other uses causative. There is a great temptation to revocalize משפטי to be *my judgement* (LXX, Vg) rather than *from my Judge*, which is the MT. We are in very deep water here. The only way Job can escape his Judge is by dying. לנצח is a refrain in Job which up till now always refers to death (4:20, 14:20, 20:7; but see also 34:36). Job does not want to get away from God, but close to Him, and this fantasy in fact depends on a restored intimacy. What absolutely rules out the change to "judgement" is the following two verses which employ "my Judge" as referent.

We must, therefore, assume that Job expects to escape God the Judge, but not God the friend. I have attempted to resolve these difficulties in the translation.

8,9. The terms קדם, אחור, שמאול, ימין offer the choice of compass points (see, e.g., Isa 9:11) or self-oriented directions. While no-one knows exactly what the phrase שמאול בעשתו means, it evidently describes some activity of God's which is confined to שמאל. This must be North rather than left. (G's assertion that it means *where he is covered* seems farfetched.)

10b. בחנני כזהב אצא
Literally *In His trying of me*. The sentence is surely conditional. It might also be regarded as governed by *He knows*.

11. באשרו אחזה רגלי   דרכו שמרתי ולא־אט
This verse is a paraphrase of Ps 17:5:

תמך אשור במעגלותיך   בל־נמוטו פעמי

translated: *My steps have held fast to Thy paths, My feet have not slipped.* The Psalm and the Job verse exhibit the same apparent anomaly, the use of a word which means to grasp (אחזה; תמך) in a sense which seems like "to hold fast to". In the Psalm it is God's מעגל that the poet's אשור has followed. In Job it is the Lord's אשור that the poet's רגל has followed. We find it easier to visualise these in terms of adherence than grasping, largely, I suspect, because the Biblical convention of the independence of the faculties from the total personality is foreign to our way of thinking. In modern jargon, we might translate both these words with the expression *locked on* to. The issue is important because of 17:8,9, where the meaning of אחז should condition our understanding of whose way the righteous follows.

12. מצות שפתיו ולא אמיש   מחקי צפנתי אמרי־פיו
The whole verse is Job's answer to 22:22, *Accept the Law from His lips and lay up His words to your heart*, but stich b incorporates a reply to 22:28 as well. *When you make a decree He will uphold it for you.*
The word חקי in this stich has caused much difficulty and led to many proposals for amendment. We should translate the disputed word in exactly the same way as we shall when it is repeated in v. 14. There it is *my decree* in the sense of what is decreed <u>for</u> me rather than <u>by</u> me. The verse means that Job was always ready to retract his own decisions if he found they conflicted with God's word.

15,16. Job's fear, which has been repeatedly referred to by him and as often decried as unjustified by the comforters, is now to be defined and specified.

17. This important verse is discussed on pp.99f and 227.

Chapter 24

Chapters 24-27 are extensively discussed in Chapter IX.

1. מדוע משדי לא־נצפנו עתים   וידעיו לא־חזו ימיו

This strange verse has consistently been understood in the reverse sense to that intended. The disjunctive accent which isolates מדוע from the rest of the sentence has not been accorded sufficient importance, while the tautologous and obvious nature of the proposition that "the times" are not hidden from the Almighty has also received too little recognition. Why? is a comment on the previous verse. *Why has He exposed me to such sights?* is Job's question, and then, *it is not as though he didn't know what was coming,* and it is His usual practice that *His friends do not have to see such sights.* (The explanation of this is on pp.98,99). The verse has none of the unpleasant voyeuristic elements which are usually seen in it.

An alternative way of reading it to the same effect, but disregarding the accent, and with the alternative meaning of the word נצפנו, is:

> *Why were the times not held back by the Almighty*
> *That those who know Him did not see His days?*

גבולות ישיגו · עדר גזלו וירעו 2.

The idea here seems simple - they move landmarks. Obviously in order to enclose within their own lands what belongs to others - see Deut 19:14 and 27:17. *They steal the flock and pasture it* is quite pointless, though H maintains it makes sense, claiming *The act of "carrying off" flocks and pasturing them as one's own is a prime example of exploiting the weak as Nathan's parable illustrates.* But in Nathan's parable the one ewe lamb was roasted and served to the rich man's guests, not pastured.

The sort of sequels to stealing a flock which would make sense are selling or eating or branding or concealing, or merely retaining, but not pasturing. It is strange that the majority of commentators accept רעה in verse 21, where it means "to shepherd, to tend", as meaning "to devour", but do not employ this appropriate translation here. LXX *With the shepherd* is neither accurate nor pertinent. See Note 11 to Chapter 9.

הן פראים במדבר יצאו בפעלם משחרי לטרף ערבה לו לחם לנערים. 5.

The overtones and subtleties of this pivotal verse must not be disregarded. *Wild-asses* are twice used as symbols of Israel and Judah (Hos 8:8,9 and Jer 2:24) lusting after false gods, and already Job has likened himself to a wild-ass deprived of its grass and braying (6:5).

The association of the herbivorous wild-ass with the word טרף, which is properly prey (although in Ps 111 and Prov 31 it is simply food) is a deliberate impossibility, emphasising the unreasonableness of the whole thesis of the verse. (See 40:26-31 for an extended example of this technique). The subject is the poor, who are driven out into the wilderness, where they are obliged to "search diligently" for the wherewithal to survive. By calling this "prey", the author is demonstrating how God blames his people for what they cannot help - essentially for their misfortunes. The third stich is a direct reproof to God for His apparent expectation that they can survive in the desert on its resources alone. Cf. Jer 31:2, מצא חן במדבר עם שְׂרִידי חרב *They have found grace in the desert who survived the sword.*

How completely inattention to natural history can lead to misunderstanding is epitomised by Gersonides who writes

---

these wicked are like wild animals in the desert which are evil beasts, and are ready to devour weaker animals, and likewise are the wicked constantly seeking to prey upon men.

---

6. בשדה בלילו יקצירו   וכרם רשע ילקשו

Portrays them as outcast and outlaw. A specification of the second stich of v.5. The apparently unnecessary suffix of בלילו may be a second reference to 6:5. Its referent is either <u>the field</u> itself - *They harvest its fodder in the field* - or <u>the wicked</u> of the next line. I have assumed the latter.

The opposition here between the wicked, whom we have identified as the conquerors of the land, and the poor, who have been dispossessed, identifies the latter as the people of the land. Their vineyards have passed into the hands of the wicked, who, we may assume, do not carefully leave gleanings for their former foes. The pickings are lean.

10. ערום הלכו בלי לבוש   ורעבים נשאו עמר

11. בין שורתם יצהירו   יקבים דרכו ויצמאו

30:12. על־ימין פרחח יקומו   רגלי שלחו   ויסלו עלי ארחות אידם

Of these two citations each contains a quadriliteral hapax legomenon, and there is a remarkable resemblance between them. Neither has yet been confidently identified. This leaves the way open for a somewhat <u>recherche</u> speculation. For שורתם in 24:11, the common guesses are <u>rows</u> (of trees), or <u>walls</u>, with a suggestion by Dhorme of <u>millstones</u>. Vg somehow introduces <u>the midday sun.</u>

24:10-11 is pervaded with irony. This is explicit in *Hungry they hump the sheaves* (10b) and *They tread the winepress and thirst* (11b). The first line, *Naked they tramp about unclad* seems devoid of this character. We are concerned now with the third stich, *Between the שורתם they press the oil.* Apparently שורתם is either plural or collective and, as thirst and wine, also hunger and wheat, are in a sense opposites, or at least antidotes, so should be שורתם and olive oil. The sense of the verse is surely reflective of Micah 6:15 *Thou shalt tread the olives, but shall not anoint thee with oil,* and Deut 28:40 *Thou shalt have olive-trees throughout all thy borders, but thou shalt not anoint thyself with oil.*

The process of olive-pressing in ancient Israel involved pressing the olives with enormous stone wheels, pierced in the centre with a square hole through which passed a beam. (The process is still [1992] to be observed at Kibbutz Ein-Dor at the foot of Mount Carmel, where a functioning olive-press has been re-assembled, and teams of school-children visit the museum and work it.) The rotation of these wheels was heavy labour, to which it is reasonable to assume that animals were impressed. If we imagine the poor of Chap. 24 being employed to turn the presses alternating with these animals, or in tandem with them, we should then have an image in which the contrast between the sweet-smelling, cleansing and refreshing properties of the oil would fitly be contrasted with the stench and squalor of labouring as lower animals and with them. The word שורתם then emerges as a portmanteau word שור תם, a tame or gelded bull, an ox. In later Hebrew, שור תם is a bull not known to gore.

Another Hebrew word for bull is פר, the first syllable of פרחח, the hapax legomenon in 30:12. חח, the second syllable means a hook, ring or fetter (see the discussion of 40:26 on p. 26ff)). Speculation about this word has been fascinating. G, plagiarising D&G, who in turn accepted a version without acknowledgement from D, takes it as a variant of פרח, a bud or bloom, relates it plausibly to אפרח, a young bird, asserts it to be semantically interesting that the Arabic *farhun* means both a young bird and a base man, and arrives from this circuitous path at *young rabble* for פרחח. Much the same interpretations are to be found in Berechiah, and who knows how far back their origins lie? If we examine the preceding verse, we can reasonably identify who it is that "arise" in this one, *For He has unleashed His dregs to afflict me, and they have thrown off all restraint before me.* Job claims that he is being persecuted by the lowest among human creatures, in thrall themselves to starvation and every kind of human want. To him they behave bellicosely like bulls, but in every other sense they are fettered and restrained (see 11b, literally *They have cast off the bridle in my presence*). Cf. v.2.

12a. מעיר מתים ינאקו

The context dictates that this be *Far from the city*, not *from within the city*.

12c. ואלוה לא־ישים תפלה

It would not be unreasonable to conclude on the basis of the irony of this line alone, that Prologue and Dialogue were composed by the same author. See 1:22. For a discussion of תפלה and its family, see p.470ff.

13. As pointed out on p. 229f, the first stich of this verse must be understood as what God does impute. The past tense of המה חיו and the fact that it refers to those already spoken of, are not to be gainsaid.

אור is used with multiple sense. As the ensuing descriptions show, it is intended to include in its meanings the simple sense of daylight, while in Bildad's reaction to it in 25:3 it is apparent that the sun is also implied.

However the main intention is, as T. actually translates the word, Law, or enlightenment, or, see 37:19, even God Himself.

The second and third stichoi are Job's attempted refutation of God's (assumed) unreasonable condemnation of the victims. This view is confirmed by the tenor of Bildad's 25:3 which in its turn attempts to refute this defence.

14. לאור יקום רוצח   יקטל־עני ואביון   ובלילה יהי כגנב

An excruciatingly difficult verse. The first problem it poses is the meaning of יקום לאור in stich a. Most regard it purely as an indication of the time of day when the murderer performs his foul deeds, with scholars about evenly divided as to whether it is dawn or sunset! In this respect, both the intrinsic meaning of the word, אור, and the apparent antithesis with <u>night</u> in stich c should settle that dispute in favour of the dawn. But this leaves the sense of the passage in tatters.

"לקום אל someone" is to rise up against him, as is "לקום על". But "לקום ל-" seems only to be used in the sense of being guaranteed to someone, and one of the three such uses is in Chapter 22, v.28.

Both senses *The murderer rises against the Light* and *The murderer is pledged to the Light*, although almost exact opposites, fit this context. The first would be Job's reply to God's imputation that the poor are rebels against the Light. Not so - it is those who kill the poor who are such. The second would be a sarcastic corollary of God's imputation - If the poor are rebels against the Light, then their killers are champions of the Light. But the first sense is much more likely, as the remainder of this passage up to the revealing line לא ידעו אור proceeds to detail other criminals.

Stich c is also problematic. Almost all commentators solve their problems by ignoring the jussive form of the verb and the comparative כ which introduces the thief, producing *And at night he is a thief*. This is really very unlikely, for even forgetting the two unaccountable anomalies, the speaker is surely not so short of villains that he has to double up the occupations and make one both a thief and a murderer! I suggest that what we have here is a subtle use of grammatical devices to accomodate a modulation from the figurative to the literal meaning of light and dark. Taking the literal sense of לאור, the poet provides the alternative condition - לילה and proposes another rebel against the light who will operate under that condition - so he might say "Or, at night, let it be, say, a thief".

15-19. Fully discussed on pp. 230ff.

20. ישכחהו רחם מתקו רמה   עוד לא־זכר

The first clause seems to evoke 1:21a - ערם יצתי מבטן אמי וערם אשוב שמה *Naked came I from my mothers womb and naked shall I return thither*. The alternative is to treat רחם as the carrion vulture (Lev 11:18), providing a good parallel. The literal *The womb forgets him* seems meaningless.

21-24. Discussed on pp. 239f.

21. רעה עקרה לא תלד   ואלמנה לא ייטיב

רעה is the participle in the verbal form, perhaps because, as Gesenius puts it (# 128a): *The language prefers to avoid a series of several co-ordinate genitives depending upon one and the same* nomen regens. Nonetheless, רעה is the first subject of יקום in v. 22. The outstanding skewed parallelism between עקרה לא תלד and אלמנה לא ייטיב is a faithful guide to sense.

22b. יקום ולא־יאמין בחיין

יקום, in a similar context is Ps 110 vv. 12 & 14

Arise, O Lord; O God, lift up Thy hand
Forget not the humble...
Unto Thee the helpless committeth himself;
Thou hast been the helper of the fatherless.

The form חיין is unique, and more likely the plural of חי, *the living*, than the fixed word חיים, *life* (Cf. Isa 8:19).

24a. רמו מעט ועיננו

The last of the apparent discrepancies of number. Again to be solved by faith in the text.

Chapter 25

Chapter 25 is discussed in full on pp. 241f.

5. הן עד־ירח ולא יאהיל   וכוכבים לא־זכו בעיניו

There is a resemblance to 9:7 in the first stich, which perhaps refers to the waning of the moon. עד as a verb is possibly related to עדה, *to ornament*, usually reflexive, but see Ezek 16:11. In the Hiph'il it means *to doff* in Prov 25:20, perhaps a paradoxical use like ברך in Chaps. 1 & 2.

Chapter 26

Chapter 26 is discussed on pp. 243-246. Of all chapters in the Book of Job, this is that which has been most consistently and most completely misunderstood. There is a Middle Eastern (now Arabic) form of 'folk-art' which consists of a verbal duel between two parties in which not so much arguments as insults are exchanged. The parties vie with each other in inventing the most scurrilous, wounding, and yet poetically imaginative fantasies about their opponent. The debate is rigorously *ad hominem*, and an audience, as excited as at a cock-fight, awards the palm.

Many of the speeches in the Job Dialogue have partaken in small measure of this *genre*, usually in a few verses at the opening or closing of a speech.

Chapter 26 is wholly of this class. Job is determined to put an end to this nonsense once and for all. He will not consider starting again at the beginning, as Bildad's vv. 4-6 appear to portend.

7. נטה צפון על־תהו   תלה ארץ על־בלימה

Again a description of nature which seems to shame Greek science!

12. בכחו רגע הים

What is the meaning of the verb רגע? BDB gives here and in Jer 31:35 = Isa 51:15 *disturb*, but in this v. the parallel states that *by his understanding he shattered Rahab*, and *Rahab* is another name for the Sea-monster. Thus shattering *Rahab* and stirring up the Sea are explicit contradictions. It should therefore be seen that he calmed the Sea rather than disturbed it. In the Jeremiah passage just three characteristics of God are given - He gave the sun for a light by day; He gave the rules of the moon and the stars for a light by night, and He רגע the Sea ויהמו his waves. This is a description of the most fundamental of Divine gifts; Jeremiah is talking of the Creation in this passage. In Middle Eastern mythology, the Creation was achieved by the victory of the Creator God over the chaotic Sea (monster). Thus the proper reading of this verse would be *Who stilled the Sea when his waves roared*, not *Who stirs up the Sea that his waves roar*, which is both irrelevant and inadequate in company of the setting of sun, moon and stars in the heavens. It is an interesting commentary on the practice of translation by committee that NJPSV has in Job 26:12 *By His power He stilled the sea* but in Jer 31:35, *Who stirs up the sea into roaring waves*. G supports this dual attitude to the verb. Most modern commentators choose *calmed* in the Job passage, as did LXX.

Note that in v. 12 the chaos-monster is a denizen of the sea, while in v.13, as נחש ברח (Isa 27:1), it is to be found in the sky.

Chapter 27

Chapter 27 is discussed on pp. 246-253.

1. See p. 246 for the significance of this variant form of introduction.

2. Job's oath has no parallel in previous literature. It asserts a stubborn reconciliation between faith in God and a reality which is incompatible with all He is supposed to stand for. In psychoanalytic terms it might be described as a resolution of the collective human Oedipal conflict.

7. A (p. 221) points out that the penalty in Israelite law for malicious prosecution was "the punishment attached to the crime wrongly chrged", and suggests this as an invocation of it.

15. שרידיו במות יקברו

What does it mean, to be *buried in death*? Simply, I suggest, to be obliterated from human memory, to have what you built broken down, and what you accumulated dispersed. See also 27:18. The *moth's house* is the coccoon, a temporary dwelling destined to be abandoned. Likewise the *watchman's shelter* - the harvest <u>succah</u> - is pulled down, dismantled after the briefest of occupations. Cf. 20:7, יאבד לנצח. The translations of מות as "pestilence" or the god *Mot* are wild.

16,17. Cf. 20:10,11. Job has no quarrel with any of the comments on the ultimate fate of the wicked and his "House", only with statements declaring that he receives his deserts personally in his lifetime. This quatrain is a poetic *tour de force*, with parallelism simultaneously abab and abba.

18. The pun on "House" which first appeared in Chapter 8 is made explicit here with the wicked man "building" his House (which is his name, his family, his nation) with similes drawn from the construction of physical "dwellings" (v.s.). This is in the spirit of the modern rule against the mixing of metaphors.

19. עשיר ישכב ולא יאסף   עיניו פקח ואיננו

The verse seems almost incomprehensible. *His wealth*, as the putative subject of איננו (T), is not present in the verse, nor does G's speculation that איננו means *he is not (so) any more* commend itself. As vv. 14-18 describe what is essentially the fate of his heirs and assigns, we should accept the old version which sees ישכב as an indication of his dying, and the Niph'al יאסף as having its most usual sense of being gathered to one's ancestors, etc. The popular idea that the verse depicts the end of the man's fortune overnight, leaving him alive but poor, is incompatible with Job as speaker of these lines.

20a. תשיגהו כמים בלהות

תשיגהו is almost always rendered "overwhelm him", or similar, but the verb שׂוג = סוג, of which this is the Hiph'il, has as its simplest sense, *to retreat*. Thus the natural sense of the Hiph'il is *make to retreat* (cf. 24:2 *supra*). Where the simile is with waters, *make ebb* is the most appropriate translation.

20b. לילה גנבתו סופה

The same phrase as in 21:18 when Job spoke of *chaff whipped away by the storm*.

22,23. God is the subject of these verses.

23. An unusual example of assonance by the selection of suffixes. Note also use of עלימו for the singular.

Chapter 28

Chapter 28 is discussed on pp. 491ff.
    3-4. Discussed at length, pp. 494ff.
    5. Unlike the remainder of this poem, this verse does not exhibit a real parallel between the lines. The meaning of the verse is that while it is the function of the earth to provide food, man (in his greed?) turns it upside down as one rakes a fire to bring the live embers to the surface, to quarry the riches beneath. The image with its subtle invocation of the glow of precious

stones, is poetry of a high order.

10-11. The verse form of this quatrain is abab.

11a. מבכי נהרות חבש

It is not clear to what procedure this refers. The term בכי does not correspond to anything familiar when applied to rivers. Many now follow P in reading as Ugaritic, "sources".

12,20,28. Wisdom with capital W translates החכמה and with a small w, חכמה. William Blake's answer to v.12 (in *The four Zoas*) is not to be missed:

> What is the price of experience? Do men buy it for a song? Or Wisdom for a dance in the street? No, it is bought with the price Of all that a man hath, his house, his wife, his children. Wisdom is sold in the desolate market where none comes to buy, And in the wither'd field where the farmer ploughs for bread in vain.

7,8. The reasons for considering these verses displaced are presented on p.493ff.

8. לא־הדריכוהו בני־שחץ   לא־עדה עליו שחל

שחל is certainly a lion, though more often figurative than literal. בני־שחץ is known only through its two parallels, here and in 41:26 (גבה). *Lordly animals* is a possible interpretation, but, with הריכוהו as its verb, *conquerors* cannot be ruled out. For a path to be "trodden down" by animals it must be their habitual resort, whereas a conquering army does it in one visit. In 41:26 no form of animal fits the context. I have left the translation non-committal. עדה seems to be the only Biblical example of this meaning for the verb.

13. "She" is used here for Wisdom, while "it" is the pathway or route to her.

14. With the personification of תהום, The Deep, and ים, The Sea, it seems best, as in 7:12 (*Yam* and *Tannin*) and 38:8, *Yam*, to preserve their names. *Tehom* also is *Leviathan*.

15. Four different words for gold are used in the Hebrew. The *daric* is a Persian gold coin mentioned in Ezra (8:27). The translation is inexact, but appropriate to time and place.

17,19. Awkwardly, the Hebrew uses the phrase לא־יערכנה in both these verses. This sense of the verb ערך - *match* or *equal* - may also be present in 37:19, q.v.

24b. תחת כל־השמים יראה

It is important, more for the sake of 41:3 than of this verse, to note that this phrase is different in meaning from כל־תחת־השמים. The first means everywhere, while the second is everything. See 37:3, where the meaning is beyond doubt.

28. Cf. 1.1.

Chapter 29

כאשר הייתי בימי חרפי   בסוד אלוה עלי אהלי .4

In modern Hebrew חרף is bleak winter but in Biblical Hebrew it is autumn, harvest-time. How such a change could occur is a linguistic mystery! Here Job almost seems to be using the word as though it meant springtime! Another sense entirely may be intended, "my prosperity" from BDB חרף IV.

5b. סביבתי נערי

There is no excuse for being more specific than the text allows. נערי means *my young men*. It is the task of interpretation, not translation, to identify them. Many appeal to 1:19, where Job's children are spoken of by the servant as הנערים, *the young people*. 1:15, 16 & 17, where the servants are referred to by the same term, are evidence against this view. See also p. 137f.

ברחץ הליכי בחמה   וצור יצוק עמדי פלני־שמן .6

No-one's feet were ever washed in butter. This is no misspelling of חמאה. The word רחץ refers to washing with water (once with milk [Song 5:12]). Job's נערים used to wash his feet in the heat, cf. Gen 18:4, 19:2, 24:32, 43:24, Jud 19:21. See especially Abigail who, upon receiving a proposal of marriage from David, said *Behold, thy handmaid is a servant to wash the feet of the servants of my lord* (I Sam 25:41). Nor is the exaggeration of the rock pouring forth rivers of oil in stich b in the style of this chapter. Most probably the misspelling lies with צור which, as a parallel to feet, is a contraction of צואר, *neck* (cf. Neh where the א, which unlike that of חמאה is not of the root, is missing). This gives Job's neck being anointed for him with oil. If we are to insist on the rock, we should spell it with a capital R, and make of the line a pious acknowledgement of God's part in his prosperity. In this reading vv. 5 and 6 form a chiastic quatrain abba.

For חמה, see Note to 30:28.

ואמר עם־קני אגוע   וכחול ארבה ימים .18

With my nest has a maudlin sound to our ears, but it is possible that it was a manly expression in ancient times. Jewish tradition persistently translates stich b as referring to the *phoenix*, rather than to *sand* which is the normal translation of חול (e.g. Rashi).

21-25. After what appeared to be the conclusion of the chapter, vv. 18-20, Job resumes the description which preceded it. That this is not a misplacement of verses is attested by 31:38-40 which do exactly the same thing to the conclusion of that chapter. The two passages authenticate each other.

Chapter 30

גם־כח ידיהם למה לי?   עלימו אבד כלה .2

In the preceding verse, Job complained that his juniors "whose fathers he disdained to class with his sheepdogs" hold him in derision. The only appropriate way of understanding v.2 is as a development of this.

We have first to decide whether this verse 2 continues the description of the fathers or resumes that of their sons. This depends crucially on the reading of stich b. כלח (only here and Job 5:26) cannot be "old age" as many suggest, for it must be something which can אבד, perish. Strength or health are the best candidates. Preferably strength, for 5:26, as *You will go the grave in good health* is not quite the blessing called for by the context. Taking the word as strength, then v.3 and those that follow all constitute the exposition of this proposition. Thus we have to regard v.2 as being about the characters who are the main subjects of the chapter, viz. the sons.

This being so למה לי כח ידיהם, if read as *of what use to me is the strength of their hands?*, would become another of those deplorable *non sequiturs* which have given Job the bad aspects of its reputation, and driven G as he does again here, to see "virtual quotations" as the solution to numerous obscurities, and have driven others to find more corruption in the Book of Job than in a cemetery. In this chapter, G in fact treats five problematic passages as "virtual quotations".

"Of what use to me ..." is the meaning of למה לי in Gen 27:46, Isa 1:11, Jer 6:20 and (simil.) Amos 5:18. Here it would seem that a different meaning must be understood.

In this verse למה has its regular meaning Why?, and לי means concerned with me rather than of concern to me. The concern is of course hostile, as v. 1 indicates. A similar use of the preposition is in Ps 137:7. This interpretation brings the word גם , otherwise obtrusively redundant, to life. In addition to all his other legitimate and gratuitous enemies, why these, of all people, also? (cf. 19:22). In the second line of the verse the על of עלימו probably implies *although*.

There is a secondary puzzle posed by these lines, and indeed by the bulk of Chapter 30. Who are the degenerates whom Job attacks so comprehensively in the chapter? It is true that their description bears a distinct resemblance to that of the unfortunate poor driven into the wilderness in Chap. 24, but it would be unthinkably inconsistent should Job show such compassion and understanding in one chapter, and then heap abuse on the same people in another.

The בני בלי־שם of 30:8 are, in fact, the three comforters, and the clue to this is strangely conveyed in what seems from v.2 to be the total impossibility of their being so - the phrase *those younger in years than I, whose fathers I disdained to class with my sheepdogs*. Correctly read, this brutal slap is a direct riposte to 15:10 *Among us are both old and grey-haired men, weighted with more years than your own father*, involving a struggle for seniority which we would consider infantile!

These two expressions, juxtaposed, reveal themselves as ritual forms of insult, with no true implications regarding the ages of either speaker or addressee. There is really every reason to believe that Job and his three friends were of approximately the same ages; very rarely are friends made cross-generationally. It is apparent that the claims to seniority are a form of "one-upmanship" in which, in 30:2, Job more than successfully competes with his persecutors. In 38: 21 the Lord takes advantage of this exchange to join in the fun with the sarcastic *You know...because the number of your days is vast!*

3. בחסר ובכפן גלמוד   הערקים ציה   אמש שואה ומשאה

Setting the stage for the richly poetic hyperbole of the whole chapter. ערק occurs only here and in v.17 of this same chapter (where it is often given an entirely different meaning). The meaning *gnaw* is deduced from cognates. אמש elsewhere (Gen 19:34, 31:29,42 & II Kings 9:26) is *yesterday*, or *last night*. Neither is applicable to this context, and we have to confess complete ignorance as to what the word is doing here. The translation is designed to maintain the mood.

4b. ושרש רתמים לחמם

Some (e.g. G, Hartley, RSV) render לחמם as "their fuel". This is quite certainly wrong, for it defies the spirit of the passage.

6. בערוץ נחלים לשכן   הרי עפר וכפים

ערוץ seems to be the passive participle of the verb ערץ, *tremble* or *cause to tremble*, usually with awe. It is unknown except for this verse. Wadis are the beds of intermittent streams, and are characteristically strewn with boulders and frequently show overhanging sides where the violence of sudden torrents has carved away the soft soil. The only reasonably comfortable lodging place for the night such a locale offers is beneath these overhangs. I suggest this is what is intended here. They are unsafe, because the "roof" is unsupported.

9. ועתה נגינתם הייתי   ואהי להם למלה

מלה in parallel with נגינה clearly has this pejorative meaning. See also 18:2, p. 196. Cf. Ps 69:12,13.

11a. כי יתרו פתח ויענני

What is יתרו? The *Qere* is יתרי, while the vocalization of the *ketib* applied to the *Qere* yields *the Ithrite* (II Sam 23:38 [bis] = I Chron 11:40). Nothing is known of the *Ithrite* except for the names Ira and Gareb in David's band of thirty-seven. יתרו is either a name, first attributed to Moses' father-in-law, or simply *his* יתר, with יתר being a cord, a remnant, excess, or pre-eminence. It seems highly probable that the singular subject of the two verbs is God, especially as all other referents in the context are plural. We may essay then *He has loosened my (or His) cord* or *He has unleashed His remnant* or *He has undone my pre-eminence, to afflict me* or *and afflicts me*.

As the second stich is literally *And the bridle before me they have cast off*, there is a great temptation to see the subject of this first stich in the word יתרו interpreted as *His dregs* (remnant) an appropriate term for those described so bitterly in the first seven verses of this chapter. Before settling on this, however, we must recognize that no matter how metaphorical the bridle of stich b may be, it is a fine parallel for יתר as a cord, not a remnant. D argues strongly that it is never the sort of cord which could parallel bridle. Some read it as a bowstring - essentially therefore *He has unstrung my bow* - the bow of 29:20. In the light of the contrast between Chapters 29 and 30 (see particularly pp. 129ff.), this is an attractive supposition. But so is *undone my pre-eminence*, for Job's pre-eminence is what Chapter 29 is all about.

All of the above seem plausible, and one may well claim for the verse a multiple meaning. In this translation, however, preference is given to possible *ketivs* even over probable *qeres*, so *His dregs* has been selected.

על־ימין פרחח יקומו .12a

For פרחח see note to 24:11. The only meaning which fits ימין in the context is *the Right* as a moral concept. This sense is not found elsewhere before the Book of Ecclesiastes, but this does not mean it was not known to Hebrew speakers long before that time.

להיתי יעילו לא עזר למו .13b

היתי here is the same as in 6:2, and probably identical with the הוות of 6:30. It means *my destruction* or similar. The construction of the sentence is almost unique, featuring a negative participle. H, who translates the last part of the line *There is no-one to deliver me from them!* succinctly sums up recent comment on it as follows:

> This line literally seems to mean *there is no helper for them* which makes little sense. Fohrer, Driver & Gray, and others emend 'ozer, helper, to 'oser, "one who hinders". Pope now rejects this emendation, arguing that the root 'zr, like its Arabic cognate, can mean both "help" and "hinder". The best suggestion however, is that of B. Baisas that the preposition le here means "from" and that 'ozer, as elsewhere (29:12) means "liberator, deliverer". (Ugarit-Forschungen 5 1973, 43).

It is certainly difficult to agree with this final sentence, or any of the suggestions for upending the meaning of עזר. There is also a prevalent opinion that the verse should be rearranged into three lines, with להיתי יעילו as a separate sentence. Thus H has as a separate line *and work towards my downfall*. There is, however, a good reason why MT places all five words in one line. The clause להיתי יעילו means essentially what H has deduced - *They contribute to my ruination*, but היתי (or even the whole clause) then becomes the referent for עזר, a participle in apposition, and we must read the rest of the line first literally as *not a helper to them*, and then literately as *though it does them no good.* There is no reason that "a helper" must be a person rather than a thing, or as in this case an action. As in v.2 of this same chapter (see p. 430f), it is the gratuitous - almost disinterested - nature of the assault (by the comforters) to which Job is drawing attention, and which particularly offends him.

15. ההפך עלי בלהות   תרדף כרוח נדבתי   וכעב עברה ישעתי

Again the apparently feminine plural בלהות is construed as feminine singular (v. note to 18:14, p. 406.).

16-18. See pp. 127ff.

20. אשוע אליך ולא תענני   עמדתי ותתבנן בי

The second stich is very problematic. Vg inserts a negative before תתבנן, and G postulates that the לא of stich a penetrates to b. LXX testifies against this, but many authors take this route.

We cannot translate עמדתי as *I ceased*, for Job has not stopped bemoaning his fate since Chapter 3. The sense *persist* for עמד is in Deut 25:8, Ruth 2:7, and Ecc 8:3. It seems best to treat the verse as an example of antithetical parallel, for תתבנן בי seems very much the opposite of תענני.

24.

I did not strike the poor	
When they cried out to me in their disaster	H
O then that I might lay hands on myself	
Or at least ask another, and he should do this for me!	LXX
Surely none shall put forth his hand to a ruinous heap	
Neither because of these things shall help come in one's calamity.	JPS
Doth one not, however, stretch out the hand in falling?	
Doth he not raise a cry for help on that account in his ruin?	D
But surely Thou dost not exert Thy power only to destroy	
Surely Thou hast mercy on the fallen.	Vg
Yet I always believed	
"Surely if a man pleads, one must extend one's hand	
When he cries out under the affliction of God."	G
One does not turn his hand against the needy	
When in his distress he cries for help	P
Vain prayers! He stretcheth forth his hand.	
What good is it to protest against his blows?	R
But not with destruction does he stretch forth His hand;	
If with His misfortune, He would dandle them. RASHI	
"Only let him not stretch out his hand against the ruin!"	
When he (thus) cried out over them in his calamity.	T-S
Yet God does not stretch out His hand in destruction	
If one cries to Him for help in his disaster.	Hartley
Howbeit, will not (one sinking) stretch out a hand?	
Or in his calamity (will not one) cry for help?	Budde & D&G

Surely against a ruinous heap He will not put forth His hand
Though it be in his destruction, one may utter a cry because
of these things.   RV

Howbeit He will not stretch out His hand to the grave
Though they cry in His destruction   AV

And yet a sinking man will stretch his hand
Crying for help in his calamity.   Moffat

Yet no beggar held out his hand
But was relieved by me in his distress   NEB

Did I ever strike down a beggar
When he called to me in distress?   M

Prayer is vain when He stretcheth forth His hand
When men cry out at His calamity.   Cox

Yet have I ever laid a hand on the poor
When they cried out for justice in calamity?   JB

Surely there is no begging off His putting forth (His) hand;
Though they cry out when He destroyeth.   Carey

The polyphiloprogenitive Hebrew verse which has begotten the above twenty different translations on twenty-one translators is the following:

אַךְ לֹא־בְעִי יִשְׁלַח־יָד   אִם־בְּפִידוֹ לָהֶן שׁוּעַ

Apart from the question of whether one has faith enough to accept the authenticity of this text, the verse really only raises three problems - the significance of ב־ יד שלח the meaning of the unknown word להן, and שוע (see p. 449). As can be seen there is a wide divergence of opinion about the first: it seems it might mean to stretch out the hand for help, to stretch out the hand in falling, to stretch out the hand to help, to stretch out the hand to strike someone, to stretch out the hand in charity or for charity. By far the largest consensus is that the hand is stretched forth to strike a blow, and this interpretation has the merit of according with its use in other Biblical contexts (Gen 37:22, I Sam 24:11, Est 2:21). The Pi`el of שלח in the same idiomatic form has the sense of making use of something (Prov 31:19). No other use of ב־ יד שלח is non-hostile.

We are justified on these grounds in disregarding the versions of Budde and D&G, of Delitzsch, of Gordis, Moffatt and NEB. We may also dismiss LXX which translates אשלה, and Habel, and Mitchell, and Jerusalem Bible, which follow LXX.

Then there are those versions which treat בעי as though a part of a verb בבעה, which is non-Hebraic. These too, Renan and Cox, may be disposed of.

עי is a ruin, usually rendered a heap or a ruinous heap. Because Carey ignores this word, we must reject his version. There is no precedent for the word being applied to a man, the two places referred to by the word being Jerusalem (Micah 3:12, Jer 26:18 [quoting Micah], and Ps 79:1) and Samaria

(Micah 1:6). Given the historical background argued in this work for the Book of Job, there is every reason to believe that the conventional use of the word is being observed here and that what Job is saying is "surely He (God) will not put forth His hand (i.e. deliver a *coup de grace*) against an already ruined city (Jerusalem) or nation (Judah)".

That the subject of יִשְׁלח is God seems almost unavoidable. V.19 treats of God in the third person; vv. 20-23 address Him in the second person with bitter complaint against His treatment; v.24 apparently brings the discussion of God's conduct to an end, and v.25 opens a new phase of Job's argument with a description of his own compassion. The only possible alternative is an impersonal "one" as the subject of יִשְׁלח, but, unless pointing a contrast between the behaviour of "one" - a decent human being - and God - a fiend, this version does not fit the context at all. So we may rule out Vg, which has "you" as the subject, and JPS and P which have the impersonal "none" and "one".

What remains at this point of the examination is, for stich a

Surely He would not strike a ruin	NJPSV
"Only let him not stretch out his hand against the ruin"	T-S
But not with destruction does He stretch forth His hand.	Rashi
Yet God would not stretch out His hand in destruction.	Hartley
Surely against a ruinous heap He will not put forth His hand	RV
Howbeit He will not stretch out His hand to the grave	AV

As is so often the case when examined, T-S version is both wildly eccentric and almost impossible to understand, while Rashi, Hartley and AV have invented new meanings for עִי.

But when we examine the context, we find a calamitous contradiction between *Surely He would not strike at a ruin* and the preceding verse which says that Job knows that God will bring him to death. For this reason the *surely* of both NJPSV and RV cannot be admitted when the rest of the line asserts that God will not strike a ruin (i.e. Job or the political entity for which he stands). This *surely* translates אַךְ, which allows also an adversarial sense to what precedes it. This is expressed in the oldfashioned *Howbeit* of AV. What is required is the good argumentative *On the other hand*, which exactly expresses one of the senses of אַךְ.

I know You are going to kill me...On the other hand (musing) He would hardly waste His strength on a heap of ruins seems to be the sense and drift of the passage, and properly accomodates the change from You to He. So with the small change from *Surely* to *On the other hand* we may accept RV and NJPSV as the proper meaning of stich a.

What is לְהֵן? I do not propose to enter into the speculations by the above authors; their thinking can be deduced from the versions. Stich b, introduced by אִם (perhaps אַךְ..אִם is similar in significance to אִם..הֵ, אִם..כִּי, אִם..אִם) has to be a sentence with a verb, as indeed each of the above versions concedes, but there is no apparent verb in the line. שׁוֹע is a noun. Where there is a sentence without a known verb, and an indecipherable word in it, it is most likely that that word is the missing verb. What verb, and in what form, could לֹהֵן be? There is really only one candidate, for if a verb, it is certainly a contracted form. Such contractions appear particularly in the Hiph'il conjunction, as for example, לְלַבֵּן for לְהַלְבִּין (Ges. #153q). This seems then to be a contraction of the modern לְהָהֵן, which surely cries out for such contraction. The root is הוֹן; the verb only occurs in the Hiph'il, and its meaning is *to treat lightly* - i.e. to disregard. The syntactical form, לֹא followed by the infinitive construct with prepositioned לְ has the special meaning, peculiarly apposite here, *it is not possible to* (Ges. #114[1]).

Note that whether עִיר is regarded as symbolising a city or state, or simply a man, it is correct to write "its" rather than "his".

27a. מֵעַי רֻתְּחוּ וְלֹא־דָמּוּ

Literally *My bowels boil etc.* This is not idiomatic English.

28. קֹדֵר הִלַּכְתִּי בְּלֹא חַמָּה   קַמְתִּי בַקָּהָל אֲשַׁוֵּעַ

For the multiple significance of קֹדֵר see pp. 301f and 309f. n.16. חַמָּה is a very rare poetic word for the sun or the heat of it (Isa 24:23, 30:26,26, Song 6:10, Ps 19:7). It is probable that the same word, mispointed, is in the preceding chapter, 29:6 (v.s.). Stich b seems to be a re-play of parts of verse 20.

29. Cf. Ps 102:7. See also note to 19:20.

30. See p. 130f.

Chapter 31

1b. וּמָה אֶתְבּוֹנֵן עַל־בְּתוּלָה

The translation follows a small minority in accepting the suggestion of G. Jeshurun (JSOR 12, 1928, 153f) that *The Virgin* is *Anath = Ishtar*. The next two verses provide reason for this. Against this view is the fact that Ben Sira (c. 170 B.C.E.) effectively quoted this line as בִּבְתוּלָה אַל־תִּתְבּוֹנֵן (9:5) [G]. But this was sage advice, not a commandment whose transgression would be a serious sin. Jeremiah inveighed against the worship of Ishtar (7:18, 44:17, etc.).

2. וּמֶה חֵלֶק אֱלוֹהַּ מִמָּעַל   וְנַחֲלַת שַׁדַּי מִמְּרוֹמִים?

The first observation of this verse must be that the introductory <u>waw</u> rules out the possibility (see NEB, etc.) that v.1 is out of place. This cannot be the opening verse of the chapter.

The answer to the question asked in the verse would have been as obvious to its contemporary readers as "Who rules the waves and who never shall be slaves?" would have been to a 1920 English readership, or "whose flag was still flying?" to an American. כִּי חֵלֶק יְהוָה עַמּוֹ יַעֲקֹב חֶבֶל נַחֲלָתוֹ Deut 32:9. See also 17:5 and note thereto, p. 280f.

This sentiment is, of course, irrelevant to the observation of virgins, but very much pertinent to the question of whom the people of Judah worshipped. God is entitled to the undivided worship of His people; this is, as it were, the interest on His inheritance.

The common understanding of the verse regards it as what a man will receive from God if he transgresses the commandments - the trouble specified in the next verse, but this would be an unprecedentedly cynical use of the word נחלה, *inheritance*. Besides this, the use of these terms to mean *inheritance from* rather than *of* has only Ps 127:3, הנה נחלת יהוה בנים, to support it.

3. הלא־איד לעול   ונכר לפעלי און.

איד and נכר are non-specific disasters. נכר occurs only once elsewhere in the Bible, in Obadiah 12 where it summarises the fall of Judah; איד is discussed under Lexicographical Anomalies in Chap. 3.IX. Its essential sense is retribution.

עול is unspecified injustice or unrighteousness, while און is wickedness, very often consisting of idolatry. It seems that all four of these terms are too strong for the peccadillo of looking intently at a virgin.

4. The word for "count" in this v. is the Qal יספר. Compare with 38:37, where the verb is Pi'el and has a different meaning.

8. אזרעה ואחר יאכל   וצאצאי ישרשו.

צאצאי - that which goes forth from me. The suffix is no possessive, but a true ablative. This word referred to descendants in 5:25, 21:8 and 27:14, and has the same meaning here. "Produce" is chosen by some because of the reference to sowing in the first stich, but this sowing is metaphorical.

11. Job's repudiation of adultery contains the almost humorous grammatical conundrum כי הוא זמה   והיא עון פלילים.

The Masoretes have found no recourse but to exchange the two pronouns to achieve agreement of gender. G ingeniously suggests the הוא refers to <u>this act</u> understood, and היא to זמה. But in Hebrew the feminine form is more often used than the masculine for the unexpressed subject (cf. זאת in 12:9), and to make זמה, a non-specific word for sin, the subject of עון פלילים is to discard the anchor of the Deuteronomic laws which specify both adultery and the worship of the heavenly bodies, the two sins described here as עון פלילי(ם), as deserving of the death penalty. I suggest therefore that what is to be understood by היא and הוא is the male and female partners in the adulterous act - *For he (who so acts has done) vileness, and she a capital offence*. This is another example of the figure of speech which I have called partitive gender.

12. כי אש היא עד־אבדון תאכל   ובכל תבואתי תשרש.

Most seek to amend תשרש to תשרף, *burns*, although this requires not only the change of שׁ to פ, but also from <u>shin</u> to <u>sin</u>. The image may be slightly more complicated. Abaddon is underground, and a fire which burns all the way to it will certainly affect roots. <u>Destroy the roots of all my increase</u> as a complex quasi-agricultural image should be entertained.

18. Boasts of Job's care of the fatherless, the יתום.

כי מנעורי גדלני כאב   ומבטן אמי אנחנה

The transitive גדלני can mean only <u>He brought me up</u>, and the full expression in stich a is *From my youth he brought me up like a father*. It being beyond contest that the orphan did not rear Job, it seems equally obvious that not Job, but the orphan, the יתום of the preceding line, is speaking here. Thus the introductory כי must be allowed to bear the whole burden of *He would avow:* (cf. 27:3, and 33:13). Revocalization to the Pi`el conjugation seems justified. The second line of the verse, which is broadly parallel to the first, has contributed a great deal to the habit of choosing an illiterate translation for the first line, and the assumption of a preposterous <u>he grew up to me</u> for גדלני. What this second line says is: *And from my mother's womb I cared for her.* Now whatever allowance we make for hyperbole in the expression <u>from my mother's womb,</u> we shall not be able to accept that anyone should boast of looking after orphans from his first day on earth. The logic of the relationship being declared here - that between the rich and powerful landowner and the destitute orphan - requires that the former care for the latter from the day of the latter's birth, as in the first stich there was care from my youth. For this to be so, there have to be two speakers in this line, the orphan saying *From my mother's womb*, and Job, *I cared for her*. This is not impossible to accommodate. It is necessary to read the verse as a mix of direct and indirect speech, as in the translation.

The very good reason why this is not all placed in direct speech is that <u>he cared for me</u> does not reveal the sex of the orphan as does <u>I cared for her,</u> a peculiarity of language shared by Hebrew and English.

An interesting alternative is provided by Berechiah who sees the He, which is the subject of גדלני, as God, Who saw to Job's upbringing "like a father". He has no such helpful suggestion for the second stich. A further example of "partitive gender".

23.   כי פחד אלי איד אל   ומשאתו לא אוכל

For איד see Chap. 3.IX. The מ of משאתו is sometimes rendered *by reason of.*

28a.   גם־הוא עון פלילי   כי־כחשתי לאל ממעל

גם links the verse to v.9 which in v.11 is described as עון פלילים. These are the two crimes considered in Deuteronomy as worthy of the death penalty - worship of heavenly bodies (17:3-5) and adultery (22:22). This seems to justify the translation. In this verse the genders agree.

29a & 29b. Verses reconstructed from fragments discovered in QT.

31. Surely the men of my tent said: מי־יתן מבשרו לא נשבע

This verse has been dealt with in quite extraordinary ways. G has taken the *surely* (אם־לא) and turned it upside down to give a question expecting the answer "Never!" - *Did they ever say `If only we had our foe's flesh, we could never gorge ourselves enough!'* This is quite beyond the pale.

JPS has *Who can find one that hath not been satisfied with his meat?*; NJPSV puts the whole verse in brackets and has Job's men saying *We would consume his flesh insatiably!* H follows G in misreading אם-לא to achieve *Did..ever say "May we never be sated with his flesh"?* The ever-sober D has *If the people of my tent were not obliged to say: "Where would there be one who has not been satisfied with his flesh?"!* -, and emphasises that this is the flesh of the cattle of the host, not his flesh. D&G, Moffatt and Hartley have much the same as D but more compactly. NEB, characteristically disdaining the Hebrew altogether, produces *Have the men of my household never said, "Let none of us speak ill of him!".* T-S, for once unoriginal, has almost the same as AV - *Oh that we had of his flesh! We cannot be satisfied.* Astoundingly LXX, rejecting all this cannabalistic nonsense, turns the whole thing into a nymphomaniac orgy: *And if too my handmaids have often said: Oh that we might be satisfied with his flesh:*

The first principle which must be observed in translating this verse is that מי-יתן is <u>always</u> an idiom expressing a wish. Any version which does not have the men of my tent expressing such a wish is wrong. Similarly אם-לא, where it does not mean *if not* or <u>unless</u>, is also an idiom and strongly assertive. What the men of Job's tent say, therefore must be something good, for there is no doubt that Job is defending his character and conduct throughout this chapter. With these constraints, how is the verse to be understood?

The word שבע, while it may simply mean <u>satisfied</u>, can also mean <u>over-satisfied</u> - fed up with, weary of something, as in the immortal verse of Isaiah 1:11, *I am fed up with burnt-offerings of rams* etc., but also in Job 7:4, several of Hezekiah's proverbs, and in Lamentations, some later Psalms, and Habbakuk; also probably Job 19:22, q.v.

The expression שבע מבשרו - apparently *surfeited with his flesh* can very properly mean *weary of his life* - i.e. as is said in English of the burden of the flesh. Now instead of all the gluttonous, cannabalistic, sexual and homosexual images which have been tried out on this poor verse, we can find in it the very simple and pious wish:

May it be that he has not wearied of his life!

The rationale is that anyone who set himself up in enmity to Job at the time when he was God's favourite, under His protection, was risking the divine wrath, effectively committing suicide. Hence the wish is benign, forgiving and appropriate. The "he" of this verse is the משנאי of v.29, *he that hated me.* The verbal form נשבע is ambiguous, either 3rd. masc. sing. perf. Niph`al, or 1st masc. pl. imperf. Qal, and as can be seen above, different authorities take different views.

33. אם-כסיתי כאדם פשעי   לטמון בחבי עוני

As this is exactly what Adam did (Gen 3:8 - *and the man and his wife hid themselves from the presence of the Lord God amongst the trees of the garden*), there is no reason to have truck with such awkward expressions as *after the manner of men* to explain כאדם. They originate with Vg, but T has *Adam*. LXX omits the word כאדם.

בחבי is usually considered to be in my bosom, but its hypothetical derivation from חבב, an almost unknown word for 'to love' (only Deut 33.3), is more than speculative. The context is better served by regarding the word as the infinitive construct חוב = חב, of חבה, another word for hiding, used in Jer 49:10 for exactly this situation - Edom hiding from the wrath of God.

35. הן תוי

There is merit in mistranslation when it gives rise to felicities like *Man is born to trouble as the sparks fly upwards, I know that my Redeemer liveth,* or *Would that mine adversary had written a book!* This last is the AV of Job 31: 35c, and strangely has been achieved by the opposite error to that which gave rise to *I know that my Redeemer liveth* treating a sentence as though it were governed by פן־יתן when it manifestly is not. Verse 35 is part of the three-verse conclusion to Job's oath of clearance (which is over-run by three more verses of avowal of innocence). The Hebrew is:

מי יתן־לי שמע לי! הן תוי שדי יענני וספר כתב איש ריבי

אם־לא על־שכמי אשאנו אענדנו עטרות לי

מספר צעדי אגידנו כמו נגיד אקרבנו

Modern scholars are all but unanimous in their understanding of these verses. Job wishes that his Accuser (איש ריבי) would put his accusations in writing. He would then display them to the world with pride. תוי in these versions is rendered either as *my signature*, or *my writ* - Job's testimony to which he seeks a reply. This all seems over-subtle. Who would display his indictment with pride to the world? - like a garland around his shoulder and a crown on his head?

איש ריבי is indeed surely *my accuser* - a counsel for the prosecution or an informer. As G states the phrase means an opponent in a law suit. But the word תו means a mark of innocence, of exemption from punishment - see Ezek 9, the only other authentic source for the word, where in a vision the prophet is told התוית תו - mark a mark - on the foreheads of all who have deplored the abominations of Jerusalem. Only these were then spared. Such a mark must be displayed, so that the Angel of Death as he flies through the land, may recognize those to be spared and passover them.

When Job cries הן תוי! *Behold my sign!*, he is referring to the foregoing oaths of innocence which he believes, or wishes to believe, will serve as a protective *talisman* against divine wrath. He is asserting his faith in the efficacy of the oaths he has just delivered.

Let the Almighty answer me! This יענני is to be understood in much the same sense as the אענגו in 9:14,15 - respond to a legal charge. As Job's oath is to be regarded as <u>proof</u> of his innocence, so it becomes an accusation against God and requires His response. Now, as the <u>waw</u> implies, the next phrase, איש ריבי וספר כתב, is also governed, not by *Grant me...*, but by *Let the Almighty answer...* I.e., Let Him answer both me and the writings of my accuser, my indictment. Up to this point there is only scant evidence that Job has imagined any accuser other than God Himself, but he can hardly be asking God to respond to His own accusations. Also the phrase איש ריבי sits very oddly as a reference to God *Who is not a man, as I am* (9:32).

There is, however, in 27:7, one prior suggestion of a third-party accuser, *Let my enemy be as the wicked, and he who rises against me as the unjust.* There Job wished the fate of the wicked on this third party, who may be Eliphaz (and his friends), but may also be an unknown informant who, Job suspects, has poisoned his reputation in God's eyes - that is, Job may have penetrated something of the Satanic plot of the Prologue.

However this may be, having delivered his oath of innocence, Job expresses the desperate wish that it shall have reached the <u>ears</u> of God, and that God will now feel obliged to respond to it by accepting his innocence, and then to respond to the list of charges against him - the ספר כתב of line c - as his defender. Again we refer to 17:3, שימה נא ערבני עמך where Job sought to make an ally of God in his struggle to vindicate himself.

What Job will twine around his shoulder and set as a crown on his head is thus not the indictment of his foe but his own testimony, the תו upon which he is relying to win God to his side, Chap. 31 in its entirety. With this talisman on display, before the <u>eyes</u> of God all the time, he will approach God like a prince and give Him account (מספר) of all his deeds.

VI
Footnotes to Chapters 32-37, Elihu

Chapter 32

2. Elihu's name translates "He is my God, the son of God Bless the Scornful, of the family of Haughty".

3. צדקו נפשו מאלהים, literally *his justifying himself more than God.* Cf. 4:17.

8. אכן רוח־היא באנוש   ונשמת שדי תבינם

The רוח in man is the breath of life granted by God, which He may withdraw as He wills. See 33:4, רוח־אל and נשמת שדי, and 34:14, רוחו ונשמתו. אנוש is singular, for the breath is individual to each man, but where it is God's in stich b man becomes a plural suffix, for God's spirit informs them all.

14. This v. is relevant to the interpretation of 34:36 and 37:19.

18,19. Further pit-wit. Note (ad 13:28) the correct Hebrew word for wine-skin, אוב. New wine-skins are elastic, and when opened, spout forth vigorously. From old wine-skins there is only the flow occasioned by the force of gravity.

Chapter 33

3. Again an example of the form a, b and c. See 5:15.

6. הן־אני כפיך לאל   מחמר קרצתי גם־אני

For כפיך, cf. 30:18. For clay, see 10:9 זכר־נא כי־כחמר עשיתני and 4:19 שכני בתי־חמר.

7. Inspired by 9:34 and 13:21.

11. Authenticates the sometimes contested סד of 13:27.

13. מדוע אליו ריבות   כי כל־דבריו לא יענה

The construction here, with the word כי bearing the whole burden of introducing a direct speech quotation (no-one but Job could say this), is important mainly in helping to authenticate the version of 31:18 given. See also 27:3.

15. בחלום חזיון לילה   בנפל תרדמה על־אנשים   בתנומות עלי משכב

Stich b is the same as 4:13b, and the whole verse is a reference to 7:14. Elihu is explaining to Job his experiences and symptoms. See next note.

16. אז יגלה אזן אנשים ובמסרם יחתם

יחתם, seals, does not make sense here, though many valiant attempts have been made. It is, however, probable, from the resemblance between v.15 and 7:14, that the word is misvocalized and is to be read as the Pi'el of חתת as in that verse. So LXX.

17. Pride = גוה; see 20:25, and p. 287.

20. The same idea is in Ps. 107:18.

22. ‏ותקרב לשחת נפשו   וחיתו לממתים‏

There is no reason to read more into ‏שחת‏ than "the grave" or "the Underworld". ‏ממתים‏ as executioners, or Angels of Death, is doctrinally too innovati-
ve. Hence I treat it as singular in sense.

23,24. See pp. 295-299.

26,27. ‏יעתר אל־־אלוה וירצהה   וירא פניו בתרועה וישב לאנוש צדקתו‏
‏ישר על־אנשים ויאמר   חטאתי וישר העויתי   ולא שוה לי‏

The main problem with these verses is that of sorting out the referents. The
first stich certainly has the man as the subject of *appeal*, and almost certainly
God as the subject of *accept*, for these are characteristic actions. Who sees
whose face with joy is more questionable, and most consider that the man
sees God's. However this verse is about penitence which is alleged to cause
God to rejoice, while the penitent may be expected to be more sober in his
reactions. Nor does any man (other than Moses) see God's face. Also, as the
subject of stich c is undoubtedly God, the continuity is better maintained by
making the assumption that God sees man's face with joy.

‏ישר על־אנשים‏ has the natural meaning *More upright than men*, (the strangely
vocalized ‏ישר‏ is probably a defective spelling of the infinitive absolute) which
again is applicable to God only, while it must be the man who declares that
he has sinned, and equally surely it is God who did not requite him. A
deviant version of the last sentence is *it did not profit me*.

The suggestion that ‏ישר‏ somehow = *he will sing* (attributed by H to Michel)
is unsound both lexically and as to sense; he cannot both sing and say the
same words (unless we allow the importation of prohibition-style gangster
slang). Nonetheless, it is impossible not to be uneasy about the translation.

Chapter 34

2. There is surely this element of sarcasm in the use of the word ‏חכמים‏
as a form of address. The word is echoed in verse 34 to follow.

3. As in 12:11 (see p.101) this challenge is followed by the presentation
of a quotation, and then by comment on the quotation - the testing of the
words.

4. ‏משפט נבחרה־לנו   נדעה בינינו מה־טוב‏

This is very much verse 3 in other words. The word ‏משפט‏ as *judgement* in the
sense of discernment recurs in v.6, but in the different sense of the outcome
of a trial in v.5. This is a rare example of translatable word-play.

6. ‏על־משפטי אכזב   אנוש חצי בלי פשע‏

A very difficult verse. As Elihu has stated he is going to exercise his judgement,
‏על־משפטי‏ is surely his own statement which is to introduce that judgement. ‏אכזב‏,
I lie, must somehow be made to apply to Job. *This "I" lies* (i.e. the "I" of v.5) is
a possibility, but the version given reads more naturally. The second stich also
is obscure and seems to employ the words in unfamiliar ways.

9. Refers to 21:22-26.

12a. אף־אמנם אל לא־ירשיע

Some special form of emphasis is required to do justice to אף־אמנם.

18. האמר למלך בליעל   רשע אל־נדיבים

The vocalization of האמר with the interrogative and infinitive construct is quite irregular and invites the assumption of corruption. While many read this as a question *Can one say to a King (i.e. God) `Scum!'?* etc., the alternative in the text (LXX, Vg, P, etc.) is more plausible. In the light of the whole of Elihu's speech, and especially the examples in Chap. 36, we may tentatively identify the king here as Ahab (Naboth's vineyard), and the prince as David (Bathsheba).

20. גרע ימותו וחצות לילה   יגעשו עם ויעברו   ויסירו אביר לא ביד

The first stich is apparently based on 21:13 (ברגע שאול יחתו) and 27:20 (לילה גנבתו סופה). עם in stich b is unexpected and cannot be translated as one would אנשים. This is very much a collective word rather than a plural. For a similar expression, see 36:20.

אביר which emerges as the subject of this prediction, is also in 24:22 where Job places the destruction of אבירים to the past credit of God. Elsewhere אביר ranges in meaning from the mighty men of Judah (Lam 1:15) through various enemies, to the king of Assyria (Isa 10:13). As here אבירים seem a natural target for God, and to embrace strength and arrogance. לא ביד is not, I think *not by hand*. Cf. Isa 10:13, עשיתי בכח ידי *By the strength of my hand I did it* as the specification of the arrogance of one particular אביר. The expression is closely similar to 4:21b - ימותו ולא בחכמה - *They die - and not in wisdom*. The similarity is evidence of common authorship.

23. Here משפט again as in v.5. עוד is a noun meaning a recurrence. There is no need to amend to מעוה (Reiske).

24. Responding to Job's insistence on a trial.

25b. והפך לילה וידכאו

Cf. חצות לילה of v.20.

26-30. These important verses are discussed at length on pp. 153-156.

28b. Refuting Job in 24:12c.

29. Cf. 21:31b (q.v.). Further evidence of common authorship.

36. אבי יבחן איוב עד־נצח   על־תשבת באנשי־און

I do not think there is a more stark example of the propensity for the professional Biblical scholar from generation to generation to commit mayhem on the Hebrew text than this one. I find no scholar in four centuries who does not reject the absolutely unquestionable translation of the first word of this verse - *My father = Sire!* in favour of a piece of spurious scholarship which would put a schoolboy to shame in any other field. אבי as much means "my father" in English as "my father" means אבי in Hebrew. There is no latitude at all, not a second of a degree, for any other reading. The rewriting of this word to mean *would that!* is equivalent to a claim to the rights of co-authorship of the book! Astoundingly, Rashi looks both ways, accepting *My Father!* and *Would that*, with the latter based on אביונה (Ecc 12:5).

In every translation into English, Elihu is credited with the savage sentence *Would that Job were tried to the end, for answers which befit sinful men* or its equivalent. The sentiment should strike the reader with a profound shock, and not only because it is incompatible with Elihu's avowed intention to seek Job's salvation rather than his destruction. The downfall of Job has been taken, almost since it was written, as the archetype of the human trial by God. The sufferings and sorrows of Job are treated in literature and speech as the ultimate that men can be called upon to endure at the hands of fate or God. And now here comes young Elihu praying that Job be tried to the limit! Not only is the malice of such a prayer almost beyond belief, but there is no possible content for it. *Only his life you shall spare* was God's instruction to the Satan, which is surely to confess that the author, the Satan, and God, could devise no greater trial than that which had already been visited upon Job when Elihu was supposed to make this awful petition. Rowley refers to "the hardness of Elihu's vain spirit", but most authors accept it without comment.

In this "translation", it is noteworthy that *would that!*, which is commonly expressed in Job (11 times) by מי־יתן, and which in Biblical Hebrew may also be לו(א), is the rendition of the single very common word אבי. Nowhere else in the Bible, nor for that matter in any written Hebrew, or in any written cognate language, do we encounter this word as a part of a verb. As Berechiah, with less sense of outrage than I, wrote *Some say that אבי is from the root אבה, but this is as impossible as to form בני from the root בנה*, etc. Nowadays we see the suggestion made that אבי is 1st person imperfect of the (imaginary Hebrew) verb ביי *to entreat*.

See also pp. 43f.

Chapter 35

2. Elihu resumes addressing Job, but continues to employ the *leitmotif* משפט.

6. אם־חטאת מה־תפעל־בו?

An unquestionable example of the unintroduced quotation. 7:20a: המאתי מה אפעל לך נצר האדם?

7. The perfect reply.

8. This statement is a landmark in the development of thought. It is fascinating to observe how this understanding of the valid foundation of ethics arises logically from Job's earlier and to some extent self-serving question to God. Students who are convinced that there is nothing new in the speeches of Elihu would do well to consider this verse.

ולא־אמר איה אלוה עשׁי　נתן זמרות בלילה? .10

The singular here, while it might be taken as revealing a more logical attitude to number than English, which would normally have written "But they never said" (G), in fact denotes Job, as the implications of verse 11 below reveal. The expression נתן זמרות בלילה is of uncanny beauty, and perhaps relates (as G suggests) to the incomparable 38:7. I suggest it firstly refers to poetic inspiration and secondly is an antidote to 7:13,14, referring to terrifying dreams.

מלפנו מבהמות ארץ　ומעוף השׁמים יחכמנו .11

A reference to 12:7

שׁאל־נא בהמתה ותרך　ועוף השׁמים ויגד־לך

Job has appealed to the beasts and the fowl to teach the comforters the truth about the events. Elihu tells him that God is a better teacher, and his failure to appeal to Him is why he has received no relief.

14. Referring to 23:8,9 and 16:19.

תחולל לו as *You are waiting for Him* would be the only example of the Pol`el verb with this meaning (cf. Qal in Mic 1:12). The translation reflects a belief that some variant of the usual "bring forth" is more satisfactory (also in Micah).

ועתה כי־אין פקד אפו　ולא ידע בפשׁ מאד .15

For the significance of ועתה here, see pp. 33 & 265. פשׁ is presumably פשׁע. Elihu has become somewhat incoherent, and it is difficult to be sure of what he is saying. The first stich depends upon 21:17, and the second upon the correct interpretation of 24:13ff.

Chapter 36

כתר־־לי זעיר ואחוך כי־עוד לאלוה מלים .2

Stich a. is a paraphrase of 15:17a, and provides evidence both of the common authorship of the Elihu portion of the book and the Dialogue, but also, as it is the opening of a new chapter, of the division of Chapter 15 into two distinct sections, belonging to the two cycles of speeches (see p. 253).

אשׂא דעי למרחוק　ולפעלי אתן־צדק .3

למרחוק may be temporal or geographical, but there is little geographical in what follows. The examples which Elihu presents in this chapter are Biblical, and all from Genesis and Exodus, the earliest periods known at the time of writing.

Ascribing righteousness to God is the theme of Elihu's entire contribution.

הן־אל כביר ולא־ימאס .5a

The understood object of ימאס is in 8:20, הן־אל לא ימאס־תם, "the innocent". This is the version of LXX. See also 42:6 for the absolute use of this verb.

7-12. The story of Joseph and the butler and the baker is recognizable in this example. Again Elihu is seeking to refute the imputation of indifference in God's treatment of the רמים in 21:22-26. Note in v.22 below that the conclusion drawn is that there is no teacher like Him - a direct reply to Job's assertion that God does not teach lessons in this regard.

9b. ופשעיהם כי יתגברו

The hithpa'el of גבר found elsewhere only in 15:25 and (of God) Isaiah 42:13.

9 & 10. By means of dreams, as the baker and butler.

11. The butler and Joseph.

12. The baker.

13. ויחנפי־־לב ישימו אף   לא ישועו כי אסרם

אף here is the same as in v. 16 below. In stich b ישועו means they cry to God for help, see 35:9,10.

14b. וחיתם בקדשים

ב in the same sense as in 24:13, במרדי־אור, *among the rebels*. Any translation of קדשים here will be a guess.

15. יחלץ עני בעניו   ויגל בלחץ אזנם

A figure similar to Isaiah 63:9, *In all their affliction (צרתם) He was afflicted*. In the variations on the words צר, לחץ and עני, the parallel in Isaiah 30:20, לחם צר ומים לחץ is also important.

16. ואף הסיתך מפי־צר   רחב לא־מוצק תחתיה   ונחת שלחנך מלא דשן

Most (not B) do not consider anger for אף. Presumably it is the word-order which leads to this avoidance of the most relevant reading, but there are ambiguities in אף מיפי־צר, and in the light of v.18a it is important to present the preposition immediately after the verb. It is difficult to make appropriate sense of the verse with God as the subject of הסיתך.

The place to which Job has been tempted throughout the Book of Job is Sheol, appropriately described as רחב *the broad place*, תחתיה *whose depths* (fem. as a *constructio ad sensum*), are לא־מוצק *without form*.

Stich c is strange, but no other interpretation seems better.

17. ודין־רשע מלאת   דין ומשפט יתמכו

Altogether a strange verse, but apparently an accusation that Job is too preoccupied with the desire to see the wicked get their deserts, perhaps a reaction to 21:17,18. There is an ambiguity in the verse, however, for the true reading of stich b is surely *They grasp at law and judgement*, as though a comment on Job's insistence on a trial. But the two stichoi only fit to each other if we read *Judgement and law* as the joint subjects יתמכו of rather than its objects.

18. כי־חמה פן־יסיתך בשפק   ורב כפר אל־יתך

Another worthy candidate for the choice of the most difficult verse in the book. כי־חמה is the phrase which introduced Job's warning to the comforters that *anger*, or *spite* was a crime punishable by the sword (19:29). It may be here that Elihu is invoking this warning with a truncated quotation. Otherwise it is impossible to decipher the phrase, and the assumption must be made that the phrase "Beware of" is to be supplied.

חמה is feminine, and technically disqualified as the subject of יסיתך. However the verb is the same as that in 16a so that the same subject (אף), which is masculine and also more or less identical in meaning with חמה, may be assumed and the word "it" employed ambiguously to signify it. יסית ב- (instigate against) has a quite different meaning from יסית מ- (seduce from), so that the ambiguity of subject is lost in translation.

Stich a warns Job not to allow his resentment of the immunity from punishment of the wicked to cause him to resent his own admonitory chastisement, while stich b adjures him to accept even the enormity of his losses without revolt.

19. היערך שועך לא בצר   וכל מאמצי־כח

The interrogative here requires us to understand *shall?* rather than *will?*, with no little residue of sense from פן in the preceding verse. The subject of יערך is God; its direct object is שועך which, see 30:24, and perhaps also Isa 22:5, means a cry (for help), and never wealth*. This should not be in doubt in view of verse 13 above - לא ישועו כי אסרם - *They will not cry for help though He confine them.* The indirect object is לא בצר. Stich b means nothing more than *and wholehearted.* It is vital that God should accept the repentance that Job is being asked to offer Him. If Job is still full of anger or distracted by secondary considerations, this will not happen. The verse has not been correctly understood.

* The word שוע here and in 30:24 presents unpalatable alternatives. In the verb שוע, to cry for help, the *waw* is consonantal, not vocalic as in the putative noun. און/אונך and עול/עולה are precedents for such a transformation. For wealth as the meaning, we must assume the elision of the initial י of the root, which I believe is impossible (cf. בול in 40:20).

20. אל־תשאף הלילה   לעלות עמים תחתם

The first stich is a reaction to 17:11,12, where Job's reflection on his impending death changed night into day. שאף with an apparently very undesirable object is in 5:5 also (q.v.). This use of לעלות *to go up* in the sense of *to perish* is implicit in the simile of 5:26, and also in the gloriously obscure final verse of this chapter. Cf. Isa 5:24 and esp. Ps 102:25.

In stich b we again see the journey to the world of the dead with no preposition. The use of the word עמים, nations, or peoples would be very puzzling were we not convinced that Job represents another such nation or people. The nations referred to are presumably the Jebusites, Canaanites, Hittites, Amorites etc., and Job is being enjoined not to allow his people to follow them into the no-place to which history has consigned them.

21. A summary of vv. 15-20.

22. Riposte to 21:22ff.

27. כי יגרע נטפי־מים   יזקו מטר לאדו

This is introduced as an illustration of the vast age of God. The word אדו is unique to this verse and Gen 2:6, where it refers to the very first rain after the Creation of the Earth.

אשר--יזלו שחקים   ירעפו עלי אדם רב. 28.

רעף is usually understood as to trickle, but when Isaiah (45:8) calls on the heavens to rain down righteousness, using the two verbs of this verse, he certainly does not mean any niggardly shower. Together with v.29, this refers to the Great Flood. The אדם רב are the multitude which perished.

הן-פרש עליו אורו   ושרשי הים כסה. 30.

The Light, which puts an end to the storm, is surely the rainbow of Gen 9:13 (LXX), while the puzzling expression שרשי הים is not the sea-bed which is worse than meaningless in partnership with *He covers*. It is the source of the sea - the holes in the sky through which the upper sea pours down in rain upon the earth. Cf. Gen 8:2, *The fountains also of the deep, and the windows of heaven were stopped, and the rain from heaven was restrained.* (See also Gen 1:7).

31. The first stich decisively identifies the previous section as a description of the Flood.

על--כפים כסה-אור   ויצו עליה במפגיע. 32.

מפגיע as in Isa 59:16, one who acts as agent for the Lord.

יגיד עליו רעו   מקנה אף על-עולה. 33.

A conundrum with almost as many solutions as aspirants. Taken here as referring to the lowing of cattle (מקנה) on being led to the altar for sacrifice (עולה). Meant as a reproach to Job for showing less fortitude and respect for God than even dumb animals. The sense crucially depends upon the meaning assigned to רעו. The alternative to *His friend* is *His thunder*.
It is because of the following verses 37:1,2 which use the word לזאת - *at this* - in reference to thunder, that the possibility that this verse refers to the thunder which follows lightning cannot be dismissed despite the unmistakable meaning, *cattle*, of the following word in the MT. So a real alternative must be:

> *His thunder tells of it,*
> *Acquiring fury as it dies away.*

Chapter 37

ירעם בקול גאונו   ולא יעקבם כי-ישמע קולו. 4.

ולא יעקבם is more or less impenetrable. The verb in MT is Pi'el, but Vg translates it as passive - *non investigabitur*. With the suffixed מ this does not seem a possible solution, but the device of an impersonal subject seems to be the closest we can come to the intention of the text.

6a. כִּי לִשְׁלָג יֹאמַר הֱוֵא־אָרֶץ

The only authority for fall (to earth) for הוא is the equally hapax Arabian word whose meaning may be either set or rise (of a star or constellation [Koran 53:1]). This is very unconvincing. With ארץ as a direct object, it seems preferable to assume a meaning which accords with both context and Hebrew grammatical usage.

6b. וְגֶשֶׁם מָטָר וְגֶשֶׁם מִטְרוֹת עֻזּוֹ

With apparently four consecutive words for rain, this sentence resembles nothing so much as Shakespeare's rather silly "When first your eye I eyed"! The apparent dynamic of the verse yields *And shower of rain and shower of rains of His strength*. Adding the word "to" to this just allows it to make some sort of sense, but there are several considerations which induce me to believe, much against my will, that the line should be repointed altogether.

One is that, except for here, there is no sign of a plural for מטר, while גשם, the alternative word for rain comes in the plural seven times in the Bible. Each word in all its forms is found 36 times. This discrepancy provides a probability more than 100 to one that מטר, a true collective, cannot be made plural. If it could, the plural is more likely to be מטרי than מטרות. Another, that the phrase גשם מטר - "shower of rain" does not occur elsewhere in the Bible, but מטר־גשם does (Zach 10:1). Also that מטרות עזו as His showers of strength is most unconvincing. Then that the sentence unless supplied with a verb lacks sense and coherence. H e.g. solves this problem by making this entire line the subject of יחתום in v.7.

The assumptions made are that מטר is the Qal imperative of the verb, and that מטרות is the plural of מטרה, "guard", as frequently in Jeremiah. See the word in its alternative sense in Job 16:12.

7. בְּיַד־כָּל־אָדָם יַחְתּוֹם לָדַעַת כָּל־אַנְשֵׁי מַעֲשֵׂהוּ

חתם does not mean to seal up in the sense of imprisoning or confining. With ביד it has every appearance of referring to a compact. The term כל־אדם must be read as what it says - all mankind. The reference then is again to the aftermath of the Flood, *As for Me, behold, I establish My covenant with you, and with your seed after you* (Gen 9:9).

9. מִן־הַחֶדֶר תָּבוֹא סוּפָה וּמִמְּזָרִים קָרָה

There have been innumerable speculations as to what might be החדר from which the whirlwind comes. More likely is that it refers to the dens in which the wild animals are cowering. Similarly with מזרים, literally *the scatterers*. The idea that this means *the winds* again depends on a hapax Arabic word from the Koran (51:1) [D]. The attempts to translate these two words to indicate the sources of storm and cold have not been profitable, despite the convincing association of "comes" and "from". There is no constellation known as The Chamber, nor any m. pl. מזרים (cf. מזרות, 38:32). This and the conventional reading of 37:6a (v.s.) are of the type of target at which Pusey was aiming (v. p.29f).

10. An image derived from far away from the Middle East. Here we may understand the second sense of למרחוק (36:3).

11. QT translates אורו here as *His fire*.

17. אשר־בגדיך חמים   בהשקט ארץ מדרום

השקט as vocalized is the construct form of the infinitive construct of the Hiph'il verb. Strictly ארץ, the genitive, is the subject, yielding, *In the South land's showing quietness* (causative) or as given in the translation (intensive). ארץ מדרום (cf. אלוה ממעל and שדי ממרומים [31:2] and more certainly אל ממעל [31:28]) does not necessarily mean the Land from the South. דרום as South wind is a large, unsupported and misdirected assumption. The hot wind in the Middle East is the East wind, not the South. This is not a conceivable error for an inhabitant to make! The South Land is the Negev of Judah.

18. תרקיע עמו לשחקים   חזקים כראי מוצק

Although vv. 15 and 16 have been interrogative, there is no sound reason to assume that this verse is also a question in its own right. It is essential to find for the verse, in the context which surrounds it, a plausible and logical reason. That Elihu should follow his question whether Job knows anything about the mechanism of storms with a strange remark about his clothing and the sirocco, as is usually understood, and then ask him if he shared in the hammering out of the heavens, is not plausible or logical.

Do you who, warm clad in the calm of the South Land, hammer things out with Him under brazen skies, know anything about clouds and thunderstorms? This seems the thrust of the passage, relying on the heat, and cloudlessness of the sky of the South Land to justify a serious doubt as to whether Job knows anything at all about the vagaries of weather as they affect other climes. It reveals the full significance of ידע־על in v.16. The Negev of Judah, referred to picturesquely by the Beduin as *the anvil of the sun* often sees no cloud from one year to the next. (Cf. the Egyptian conceit of rain in foreign lands as a "Nile in the sky").

The known meaning of רקע, actually to hammer out as a metal, is inapplicable, but what Job used to do עמו - with God - was to call upon Him and He answered him (12:4). A plausible extension of the meaning of the word is to discuss - to hammer out an argument, to debate (this is one of OED's definitions of *hammer*). What Job has been doing in the book is to go at it hammer and tongs with God, and this may be the intention of this unique verb.

לשחקים is usually taken as the object of the verb, though the ל as introducing the object after the verb is otherwise unknown in Job except with the pronoun "him" (9:11, 19:28), and perhaps "me" (19:3). These examples, necessitated by the absence of the *nota accusativa* את, cannot be used as precedents to justify this Aramaism. The absence of the vowel denoting the definite article beneath the ל also weighs against the usual reading *Did you with Him spread out the skies.*

Gordis defies the common view with the claim that the verb is a denomina-
tive formation from רקיע, firmament, and so translates - though it is a long
leap - *Can you fly with Him to the heavens?*. He claims this as the meaning of
the verb in modern Hebrew, but in fact it is used in this way mainly
figuratively, in the sense of fantasizing. But this latter is ruled out by the
descriptive specification of the heavens to which he "soars". NJPSV copies G's
interpretation of the verb, but unaccountably changes "with Him" to "like
Him", as though God were winged.

The gravest objection against these, as against the traditional understanding,
is one of sense. It is not until God Himself speaks that Job has to face
sarcastic hyperbole of this kind. On Elihu's lips, these impertinent questions
are simply out of character and out of place. All his questions to Job have
been reasonable and factual up to now. The question read into this verse by
all scholars is equivalent to asking Job if he participated as an equal with God
in the Creation of the heavens. The Companion Bible, which always shows
good sense, offers the variant reading: *Wast thou with Him when He spread out
the sky?*, a slightly less absurd piece of wit, and Knox's rendition of Vg is *Was
it with help of thine God fashioned the heavens?"*.

The fragment in QT, apparently its version of תרקיע לשחקים, is intriguing -
inflate the fog. This is a little like T, stretch out the hazy clouds. (In Celine
Mangen's translation of the Targum this is followed by the astonishing
apparent anachronism "so that their appearance will be like a clear wind-
ow-pane").

לשחקים as *under skies* is also debatable, but somewhat reminiscent of God
walking in the garden לרוח היום (Gen 3:8).

19-24 These crucial verses are the subject of Chapter X.

VII
Footnotes to Conclusion,
Chapters 38 - 42

Chapter 38

Chapter 38 in its entirety is discussed in Chapter VIII above.

1. ‏מי זה מחשיך עצה במלין בלי־דעת?‏
If we accept Elihu as an integral part of the Book of Job, we have to consider the possibility that this rebuke is directed, not at Job but at him. On the other hand, when Job repeats more or less the same words in 42:3, he certainly appears to be accepting the rebuke for himself. That verse, however, does not appear in the oldest surviving manuscript of Job, QT, while in LXX it is endowed with a wholly different significance.

3b. ‏ואשאלך והודיעני‏
In 13:22, Job offered God the choice of weapons - *Summon and I shall answer, Or I shall speak, and You respond*. In this verse God makes His choice, and twists the knife of sarcasm in Job with the use of the word ‏הודיעני‏ - as though Job could make anything known, reveal anything, to God.

4. The questions which now pour forth from the Lord are not at all what Job had in mind when he issued his challenge. Job was concerned to establish his innocence and righteousness by replying to questions about his conduct - his "steps" and his "way". The Lord affects to consider that virtue lies in knowledge and power!

7. This verse shows how "Eternity is in love with the productions of time" (W. Blake, *Proverbs of Hell*, in *The Marriage of Heaven and Hell* (1793). We are to assume that ‏בני אלהים‏ are both stars and angels. See 25:3 for confirmation.

8. The persistent legends of the Middle East regarding a rebellious Sea and/or sea-monster, whose containment was necessary before Creation could be successfully accomplished, are possibly the result of orally transmitted memories of the time when the Mediterranean was being filled by a vast waterfall through the present straits of Gibraltar, and was seen inexorably to rise higher every day, forcing the inhabitants, human and animal, to retreat, apparently for ever.

10a. ‏ואשבר עליו חקי‏ See p. 224, n.5.

11b. ‏ופא ישית בנאון גליך‏ See p. 224, n.6.

13-15. ‏לאחז בכנפות ארץ   וינערו רש״ים ממנה‏
‏תתהפך כחמר חותם   ויתיצבו כמו לבוש‏
‏וימנע מרש״ים אורם   וזרוע רמה תשבר‏
This is the last, and by far the most complicated of the examples of the device of so-called partitive gender in the book. Note that the two elevated ‏ע‏s are

believed to indicate a conviction on the part of the Masoretes that one of these was present in error (pers. comm., the late Rabbi Louis Rabinovitz). In the translation, the first has been dropped, and the word read, as in Pr 22:7, as "the poor".

The verses discuss the "place", that is the purpose of the dawn (השחר). כנף is taken here as in Ruth 3:9 to be a nightcovering, for what the dawn assuredly does is to take away the cover of darkness from the earth. The accepted *(Four) corners of the earth* is a difficult and improbable image.

The verb נער is enigmatic. While generally understood in the Bible as "shake out", this sense is not, in any of the passages where it occurs, really appropriate, and in some of them it is impossible. The accepted version which sees the dawn "shaking the wicked" out of the earth is almost ridiculous - an absurdly mixed metaphor. The word in all its aspects is discussed in Chap. 3.IX, Lexicographical Anomalies. The sense which fits all the contexts is to "strip, bare, expose", and this last sense is surely most appropriate here. Reference to the exposure of the poor upon the earth would be a direct allusion to Chapter 24, vv. 7,8 describing the way the poor are condemned to lie all night naked to the cold and rain.

It is verse 14 which exhibits the partition by gender of the poor in the preceding verse, with a feminine singular verb in the first stich and a masculine plural in the second. The picture in the first of a woman, discovered naked by the arrival of dawn, and rolling over and over like a cylinder seal to cover her shame, and seeking, as it were, to imprint herself into the earth, is exceptionally lively. Again the accepted version, which sees the earth "changed like clay under a seal" and its colours "standing out like a garment" strains the credulity with its, albeit brilliant, artificiality at every point.

Only in v.15 do the wicked appear, with another reference to Chapter 24, where the wicked are referred to as *rebels against the Light*. Their "light" is darkness (18:6).

21. The Lord joins in the inelegant free-for-all about age.

23. We touch a very primitive level of pagan mythology in this verse. The suggestion must be that the battle between the Lord and the forces of chaos (*Leviathan*) is to be renewed at some time; that they are indestructable, and eternally resurgent.

30. Cf. 37:10 and note to it on p. 452.

36-38. Discussed at length in pp. 215-218.

39-41. There is every reason to believe that these verses, relating to the biological world, belong in the next chapter.

Chapter 39

Chapter 39 in its entirety is discussed in Chapter VIII above.

3. תכרענה ילדיהן תפלחנה   חבליהם תשלחנה

פלח has the sense of splitting or cleavage. *Bring forth* is inadequately vivid. There is no good reason to treat חבל as metonomy for offspring. There is nothing indelicate about the latter! The natural association of birth and the umbilical cord is sufficient to justify the word.

5,6. Cf. 24:5.

13. כנף־רננים נעלסה   אם־אברה חסידה ונצה

The translation, which is as close as possible to a word-for-word rendition conveys what seems to be the intention here. כנף־רננים, *wing of ringing cries* is everywhere agreed to be the ostrich, principally because the habits described in the following verses fit that bird. Note that no questions are asked of Job about this bird, whose ardour to defend its young and inadequacy to do so, match Job's attitude to his people.

15. ותשכח כי־רגל תזורה   וחית השדה תדושה

The objects in both stichoi are singular number. This is a form of *constructio ad sensum*, with *the nest* understood.

16. הקשיח בניה ללא־לה   לריק יגיעה בלי־פחד

The masculine subject of the transitive Hiph'il verb הקשיח is the same אלוה as is the subject of השה in the next verse. This is not the grammatically indefensible *She is hardened against her young* (AV, etc.) which also contradicts the sense of the immediately following stich, as well as of v.13.

Neither NJPSV *Her young are cruelly abandoned* nor H *She treats her young harshly* can be in any way be justified by the text. P (*Her young she harshly rejects*) has an interesting note on the habits, real and reported of ostrichs.

The point of this verse is that her heroic defence of her young (see next verse) is rendered unnecessary by the fact that God has endowed them, as He has all creatures, with the capacity to survive in the conditions to which they are born. The stupid ostrich does not realise this and so makes efforts which, heroic though they are, are in vain. Exactly the same applies to Job, whose fierce defence of his people in the preceding chapters is quite unnecessary because God has hardened the Jewish people also to do without him.

Neither in its only other use (Isa 63:17) nor in the natural sense of the Hebrew, does להקשיח mean to treat harshly.

17. כי השה אלוה חכמה   לא־חלק לה בבינה

There is surely some relationship between this verse and 38:36,37. Is the ostrich one of the נבלי שמים?

18. כעת במרום תמריא   תשחק לסוס ולרכבו

מרום, *height* has the naturally associated meaning of *in safety* (Cf. 5:11, where it is parallel to ישע).

The associative character of Hebrew verse - somewhat like the cinematographic device in which a feature at the end of one scene is used to merge into the next - is well-illustrated by the way the description of the horse follows this casual reference to that animal.

התרעישנו כארבה? הוד נחרו אימה 20.

The strict meaning of the Hiph'il of רעש seems to be to cause to quake (Isa. 14:16, Ps 60:4, etc.). It is hard to see how this might apply here. It seems necessary to find some activity of the horse which resembles that of a locust. רעש in modern Hebrew is all noise and no quake. It is likely that the use of the word to signify the sort of noise which accompanies a quivering action was an early variant of sense. The shivering noise which a horse frequently makes is probably what is intended. The parallel of נחרו in stich b is decisive. For אימה where an adjective is expected, see also 41:6.

וכי ירים קנו סלע ישכן ויתלנן על־שן־סלע ומצודה 27b, 28.
Cf. Obadiah 3,

שכני בחגוי־סלע מרום שבתו ... אם־הגביה כנשר ואם בין כוכבים שים קנך
You who dwell in clefts of the rock, in your lofty abode... Should you nest as high as the vulture*, should your nest be lodged among the stars... and Jer 49:16,

שכני בחגוי הסלע תפשי מרום גבעה כי־תגביה כנשר קנך
You who dwell in clefts of the rock. Who occupy the height of the hill; should you nest as high as the vulture*...
Both these prophetic citations, certainly either dependent upon Job or influencing it, refer to Edom (see p. 222).

* נשר as in the Job passage, usually translated in this context *eagle*. The bird in Job is certainly a carrion eater.

Chapter 40

הרב אם־שדי יסור? מוכח אלוה יעננה 2.

From its punctuation, חסור is the only extant example of the Niph`al of סור, while רב is the infinitive absolute of ריב. Many read it as the participle - *He who argues with the Almighty*, and this is also possible. In either case the sense of the verse is that Job must not evade giving God a reply. The sentiment is a sequel to 38:3 and a demand for the fulfillment of the promise in 13:22a *I shall answer*, אענה.

אזר־נא כגבר חלציך אשאלך והודיעני 7.

Remorseless, the Lord repeats the cruelly sarcastic 38:3.

8ff. The entire passage from 40:8 to the end of Chapter 41 is analysed in detail in Chapter V.

עצמיו אפיקי נחשה 18a.

For אפיק here, in 41:7, and also in 12:21, see Chap 3.IX, Lexicographical Anomalies.

בעיניו יקחנו במקשים ינקב־אף 24.

As the idiom *In his opinion*, בעיניו is common. As usually understood here "by his eyes", it would not only be unique as a meaning of בעיניו but also as a use of the preposition ב with any substantive.

The subject of יקחנו is the same "he" who has been the subject of all the preceding verses from v.15, i.e., *Behemoth*, and the object is the last named third party, that *Nahar*, whose "oppression" does not disturb his confidence. In the second stich במוקשים might be considered as the two words במו קשים - *by stubbornness*. מוקשים otherwise is the plural of snare or trap. These do not operate by piercing (נקב), and certainly not noses. I have assumed metaphorical traps. What is impossible is for the ב of בעיניו to introduce the anatomical feature by which the animal is to be caught in stich a, and the ב of במוקשים to introduce the instrument which will catch it in stich b.

There is no reason and no right to treat the verse as interrogative, but the stich is puzzling.

25b. ובחבל תשקיע לשונו

The literal meaning, "And with a cord will you cause to sink down his tongue?", does not conjour any sort of reasonable picture. It surely refers to some contemporary mode of fishing, but fish, of course, do not have tongues! Nonetheless, it is striking that in this verse we can find all three of hook, line and sinker! On the other hand, neither *Leviathan* nor the popular but erroneous crocodile is a fish.

T has *tear (?out) his tongue with a rope* which makes some sense. Another possibility is *silence his voice*.

Chapter 41

7. For אפיק again, see Chap. 3.IX, Lexicographical Anomalies.

10ff. The image of Leviathan now shows its resemblance to the portrait of the Lord in Ps 18:9-16 = II Sam 22:8-16.

17. משחתו יגורו אלים   משברים יתחטאו

The same expression "reared up" is used of Tiamat's monsters several times in the Creation Epic.

משברים are normally sea-breakers, and in this context particularly should be so translated. However the alternative in the Vulgate *When he rears, angels themselves are afraid, and purify themselves in their dread* is also difficult to dispute. The hithpa'el of חטא has only this meaning elsewhere, and may be taken here as whatever (if any) might be the Israelite equivalent of crossing oneself.

NJPSV renders stich b "as he crashes down, they cringe".

22. תחתיו חדורי חרש   ירפד חרוץ עלי־טיט

A much simpler understanding is achieved by taking חרוץ as in Dan 9:25 (BDB III), than with the commonly agreed "threshing sledge".

Chapter 42

1. ידעתי כי־כל תוכל   ולא־יבצר ממך מזמה

We might read the first stich as a protest of some impatience that God has rattled off His own accomplishments and not directly discussed Job's conduct. In the second stich, the word מזמה is not ethically neutral; it means evil purposes, and refers to the character and conduct of *Leviathan* which the Lord has explicitly acknowledged in 41:4.

מי־זה מעלים עצה בלי־דעת?   לכן הגדתי ולא אבין   נפלאות ממני ולא אדע 2.

Certainly this reads like a confession in reply to the Lord's introductory words in 38:2; but the Lord used the word מחשיך - "obscures" rather than מעלים "conceals", and spoke of "words without knowledge" rather than the yet more brutal "without knowledge". LXX ingeniously relates the first stich to the impossibility of concealing anything from God (v.1), but is obliged to distort the second and third to achieve a consistent version. As noted in the note to 38:2, this verse is omitted from QT, but 40:5 is in its place (40:5 is also present in Chapter 40 of QT). The mechanism by which this particular variation of versions occurred seems unfathomable.

שמע־נא ואנכי אדבר   אשאלך והודיעני 4.

Again quoting the Lord in 38:3 and 40:7, but also his own 13:22.

לשמע אזן שמעתיך   ועתה עיני ראתך 5.

What is going on in this final declaration by Job has puzzled readers and scholars ever since it was written. There is probably little more than associative technique dictating the first stich, but the second clearly heralds some revelation. But first we must recall that this was Job's devoutest wish, expressed in the parallel verses 19:25a and 19:26b. For this Job's *reins perish within his bosom* (19:27c).

That Job has now heard God with his ear and seen God with his eye is probably to be understood in the same way as Ps 73:17 עד־אבוא אל־מקדשי־אל, *Until I entered the sanctuary of God*, where the Psalmist records the change in his outlook which took place when he achieved this intimacy with God. There is, however, no good reason to make a contrast between hearing and seeing with the use of "but". "You ordered me to hear You, and I have both heard and seen You" is what we should understand.

על־כן אמאס ונחמתי   על־עפר ואפר 6.

Job's last words have almost always been translated to convey abject surrender. Curtis (J.B. Curtis, *On Job's Response to Jahweh*, JBL, 98/4 [1979] 497-511) is an important exception.

The phrasing appears to suggest that both verbs are intransitive descriptions of Job's state of mind, and that the second stich is an adverbial modifier. Hence e.g. *Therefore I abase myself and repent in dust and ashes* (G). The verb מאס is found without an object only in Job, 7:16, 34:33 and 36:5. Of these 34:33 is properly a quotation of 7:16, while 36:5 is a quotation of 8:20 so that we should read חם as an understood object (LXX). In 7:16, if truly intransitive, the cry is something like *I am disgusted!*, but with Hebrew's tolerance of the double negative, מאסתי לא־לעלם אחיה gives no good reason to object to *I reject the idea of living for ever*. However we look at 42:6, it is impossible to find a precedent for a reflexive sense to this verse - *I abase/ abhor myself* - while the usual alternatives, *retract/recant* are either not intransitive, or very far from all other uses of the verb.

On the other hand the Niph'al נחמתי, when followed by על can mean *repent*, but in one of the senses, *relent, retract*, not in the modern sense of feeling remorse for a wrong action. Another common use of the phrase is *to be comforted for*; the best known example of this meaning is in Jer 31:15 רחל ... מאנה להנחם על-בניה כי איננו - Rachel ... refuses to be comforted for her children, for they are not. The verse, had it been spoken by God, would be easy to understand - *I reject and repent me of flesh and blood*, but there is no way in which Job can have said נחמתי על-עפר ואפר with this sense to it. As an absolute, נחם is not *repent*, which is שוב. עפר ואפר as a deprecating term for flesh and blood is Gen 18:27.

Respect for the symmetry and integrity of the architecture of the Book of Job leaves no choice but to understand נחמתי explicitly as *I am comforted*. On the threshold of the Dialogue, in 2:11, the friends came to Job לנוד-לו ולנחמו - *to console him and to comfort him*. On the threshold of the Epilogue, in this very last verse of the Dialogue, we must translate Job as saying *I am comforted* - surely not by the comforters, nor in the way they intended, but nonetheless comforted. This is a perfect example of the irony which pervades this work from start to finish.

In Job's mouth therefore, the sentence which is capable of meaning *I reject and repent me of flesh and blood* comes to mean *I despise, and am comforted concerning, flesh and blood*. After God's aweful revelations, in Chapters 38 and 39, of the insignificance of all individual life, and in Chapters 40 and 41 of His intentions regarding the Assyrians and the Judeans, Job perforce accepts the devaluation of the individual and is consoled by the promise of the survival and destiny of the collective. While to a modern mind there may seem a contradiction between contempt and consolation, this is illusion. It was an Oriental poet who, nine hundred years ago with an irony which was the match for Job, wrote

> *To me there is much comfort in the thought*
> *That all our agonies can alter nought,*
> > *Our lives are written to their latest word,*
> *We but repeat a lesson He hath taught.*
> *Our wildest wrong is part of His great Right,*
> *Our weakness is the shadow of His might,*
> > *Our sins are His, forgiven long ago,*
> *To make His mercy more exceeding bright.*

(Omar Khayyam. The translation-paraphrase is by Richard Le Gallienne, *The Rubaiyat of Omar Khayyam* [John Lane the Bodley Head, London, 1914] 33).

לא דברתם אלי נכונה כעבדי איוב 7,8.

This unexpected endorsement of Job's words about God will draw debate as long as memory of the book remains with mankind. It is open to every interpreter to state his own opinion as to what it was that Job said which drew this remark from the Lord, and what the friends.

To me it is their remarks about distributive justice which have been so rightly judged by the Lord. Job has penetrated to the truth about the moral conduct of the world, that the quality of an individual's life is unrelated to his moral deserts; that disaster is a random occurrence as likely to befall the righteous as the wicked; that God does reject the innocent and reward the wicked as individuals as often as He does the reverse. What Eliphaz and his friends have maintained, from 4:7

> Remember, I pray, "Whoever perished, being innocent?
> And where were the righteous cut off?"

to 20:29 *This is the portion of the wicked man from God* is sentimental rubbish, at odds with all experience of life, precisely that speaking unjustly and deceitfully for God against which Job warned them in 13:7ff.

ויהוה שב את־שבית איוב בהתפללו בעד רעהו 10.

ויסף יהוה את־כל־אשר לאיוב למשנה

See pp. 103ff. for the first line and 7 for the second. In the strange conditionality of the Lord's restitution of Job's captivity resides a but-slightly-disguised hint of the purpose of the whole work, of Job, the Jews, of God Himself in His designing of history. To pray for others is the function of priests. The constitution of the Israelite nation is given by God to Moses, before the Ten Commandments, in these words:

> *Thus shalt thou say to the house of Jacob, and tell the children of Israel: Ye have seen what I did unto the Egyptians, and how I bore you on eagle's wings and brought you unto Myself. Now, therefore, if you will hearken unto My voice indeed, and keep My covenant, then ye shall be Mine own treasure from among all the peoples; for all the earth is Mine: and ye shall be unto Me a kingdom of priests and a holy nation.*

The condition of the return of the people of Israel to their land and the restoration of their sovereignty is that they shall perform their role under this Covenant, yet older than the Deuteronomic Covenant which dominates the first two chapters of the book. This is to be the function of the Jewish people in their restored state - to spread the knowledge and doctrines of God to the gentiles, to pray for them. This interpretation is to be found in L. Corey "The Paradigm of Job", Dor LeDor, XVII, 2, 1988/89, p.125

11. For the significance of this as relating to the funding of the return from exile, see p.74f.

12-17. These over-explicit verses are absent, both from QT and from the Commentary of Berechiah. This seems a valid reason for considering them a later addition.

16. See p. 74.

VIII
Special Remarks

1. 5:2-7

The passage 5:2-7 is a self-contained homily, framed almost as a parenthesis between two verses which might well have been juxtaposed consecutively -

Call if you will - who will answer you?
And to which of the qodashim will you turn? (5:1)
However for my part I would seek to God,
And to God I would submit my cause. (5:8)

Verse 1 is a jibe or a reproach to Job for his appeals in Chapter 3 to the powers of darkness, while v.8 is its justification, the principal theme of the first cycle of comfort, that submission to God is the only path to salvation.

Verse 2, which begins the parenthetic homily, opens with the word כי, "for", promising an explanation for the negative judgement on the appeal to the powers of darkness which is implicit in the scornful questions of v.1. It declares, employing (for the Book of Job) an uniquely convoluted grammatical construction, that כעש (anger) and קנאה (zeal or jealousy) slay the אויל (foolish) and the פתה (simple).
The usual way of understanding this is as a warning to Job that by the intemperance of his language he is exposing himself to deadly danger[1]. Implied is that אויל and פתה are descriptions applied at least tentatively by Eliphaz to Job himself. To this point in the passage this is acceptable, but in the next verse a great difficulty is raised when Eliphaz states that he curses the habitation of the אויל. Eliphaz could not admit to cursing anything to do with Job at this stage of the Dialogue. Both words אויל and פתה in Biblical Hebrew convey, besides folly, a distinct sense of sin against God, of deviations from proper respect and exclusivity of worship.
There are in the Bible two references which must be taken into account in attempting to interpret the full implications of this verse 5:2. Prov 1:32:

The tranquillity of the simple (פתים) will kill them
And the complacency of dullards will destroy them (NJPSV)

Certainly at first sight Job 5:2 seems defiantly to contradict this, for the antitheses between tranquillity and complacency and anger and zeal are too marked to be coincidental. But while the Proverbs verse specifically identifies the tranquillity and complacency (משובה and שלוה) as qualities of the fools, the Job verse does not identify the anger and zeal as their own. The source of the anger and zeal which will slay them is at this point left open.
The second reference is Deut 32:16, 21 and 22. In each of these three verses

the verbs קִנְיָא and כעיס are used, twice describing how God has been provoked to anger and jealousy by the backsliding of the people, and once promising to engender those same feelings among the people in retaliation. Other than Job 5:2, these are the only places where these two words are found in combination. As we shall see when we consider 5:7, there is an additional cogent reason for considering an important connection between the two passages. In Deut 32, it is God's anger and jealousy which brings about the undoing of deviants. However, no more does 5:2 refer to God's כעש and קנאה than it does to the emotions of the foolish themselves. An unbiassed reader sees that it is these qualities in the abstract to which reference is made.

Leaving in suspense the question of whose anger and zeal are to kill what fool(s), let us advance to v.3.

אני ראיתי אויל משריש   ואקוב נוהו פתאם

There has been some reluctance to translate what is written here, for it fits ill with the idea of the spontaneous destruction of the fool as a consequence of his own excesses which is the common understanding of v.2. So LXX provides "I have seen foolish ones taking root: but suddenly their habitation was devoured", and many translators seek and find ways to distort Eliphaz's assertion that he, personally, curses the habitation of the foolish as soon as he sees him becoming established.

Indeed this statement is apparently incompatible with, or at least irrelevant to, the idea of the self-destruction of the fool in his own anger and (?) envy. It begins to look perilously as though the anger and zeal either are Eliphaz's, or are mobilized by Eliphaz's curse.

The verse commences with a reduplicated first person pronoun, אני ראיתי. Almost every translation and commentary (but Vg) disregards the redundancy. But the reduplication of the first person pronoun in the Book of Job is used on more than twenty occasions with the express purpose of pointing a contrast between the speaker and another party, as in such simple phrases as "You speak and I shall answer" etc. Here, then, we have to understand "(Unlike you [who go calling on the powers of darkness]) when I see a fool settling in, I curse his habitation forthwith!"

Verse 3 becomes a self-satisfied lesson in statecraft by one ruler (or family head) to another, and the assumption underlying it is that, in Eliphaz's perception, Job's misfortunes have arisen not because of his own sins, but because of his feeble failure to control the sins of those for whom he was responsible - his children (see 8:4) or members of his tribe or nation (see Chap. III, above).

Vv.4 and 5, which contain considerable obscurities, are devoted to describing the effects upon the fool of Eliphaz's curse. It is here that anger and zeal make their reappearance for the verses describe the anger and zeal of the populace inflamed by Eliphaz's exhortations. It is evident that the curse is not an invocation of Divine action, but of a class with the *herem* (Ezra 10:8) *all his substance should be forfeited, and himself separated from the congregation (of the captivity).* The "children" of the foolish (an expression which much diminishes the probability that Eliphaz means Job's own children when he speaks of the foolish) are crushed "in the gate", which is to say by human agency, and their harvest is eaten by the hungry, not, as would be the case were the source of destruction God, blasted by blight.

What we have learnt so far, then, is that anger and zeal are agents which destroy fools, and that Eliphaz claims that he arranges for the destruction of fools in his environment by whipping up the population against them by means of a curse. The proper way of understanding this is surely that Eliphaz succeeds in mobilizing the anger and zeal of the non-foolish part of the people against the fools.

When, then, in v.6, Eliphaz explains *For sorrow does not sprout from the dust, nor does trouble spring from the ground,* there is at the very least an ambiguity about the statement. Sorrow and trouble are what must be inflicted upon fools, if not by man then by God. If we relate this verse to its companion, 4:8:

> *Going by what I have seen, it is they who plough sorrow*
> *And sow trouble, who reap the same.*

there is a strong inclination to assume that it is the secondary reaped trouble and sorrow which Eliphaz is now saying do not spring from the ground - the ploughing and sowing are done among men, not in the soil, and the reprisals come from men also.

This leads to the crucial verse 7, universally familiar as "Man is born to Trouble as the sparks fly upwards", but, as pointed out on p.39f, recently subject to unacceptable amendment to read "Man gives birth to trouble..." The proverb is one of the treasures of the Bible, and of the Book of Job, and it is painful to have to declare that it is no more than a felicitous mistranslation of the Hebrew, but this is so. The Hebrew is:

כי אדם לעמל יולד   ובני רשף יגביהו עוף

The expression בני רשף (rendered "sparks") is unique to this verse, but רשף itself is a familiar name, both from the Bible and elsewhere in the Middle Eastern panthea. The כי at the beginning of the verse, following as it does the negatives of verse 6, means "but", not "for" (BDB p. 474). The expression of the MT אדם לעמל יולד is purposefully ambiguous, for man may be born to Trouble (incidentally also a pagan god) either to receive it or to dispense it. This ambiguity is removed by those who amend יולד to the Hiph'il, but they then lose both the connection with 4:8 and the neat antithetical parallel with the later 15:35 which completes the cycle by claiming that those who are born to Trouble, (defined as the wicked) ultimately give birth to it again.

The second stich is introduced with a <u>waw</u> which is usually taken to mean "as" and, heralding the universal truth that sparks fly upwards, gives to the verse its proverbial form. It is more likely that this <u>waw</u> functions in the same

way as that of v.3, to create the form "when stich a, then stich b". What all
this is about depends entirely on the meaning of the expression בני רשף. *Reshef*
is originally the god of pestilence in several Middle Eastern panthea, including
the Canaanite. That he may also be considered one of the Qadoshim referred
to in 5:1 (v.s.) is suggested by two Egyptian stelae depicting *Reshef* in company
with the goddess *Qedesh*. The word reshef occurs five times in the Bible apart
from here.

In Ps 78:48 the poet recapitulates the plagues of Egypt and says: *He gave their
beasts to the hail and their cattle to the* רשפים. From Ex 9:3, 10, 23-25, we know
that the agents which destroyed the Egyptian cattle were hail, boils and
pestilence (דבר). Some form of disease is therefore the meaning in this citation.
In Hab 3:5 רשף appears in parallel with דבר, pestilence, as one of the attendant
demons going before God.

A vital allusion to רשף, which connects intimately with verse 5:2, which
invoked anger and jealousy as the agents to slay the foolish, is Deut 32:23-25
where the consequences of God's fury are spelled out:

> I will heap evils upon them
> Expend my arrows on them -
> The wasting of hunger,
> The bowels of רשף,
> And bitter destruction;
> And the teeth of beasts will I send them
> With the venom of crawling things of the dust.
> Without shall the sword bereave,
> And in the chambers, terror;
> Slaying both the youth and the maiden,
> The suckling with the man of grey hairs.

The old rendition of רשף as "fiery bolts" is quite out of place in this catalogue
of natural collective disasters and human ferocity, nor can that expression be
mated satisfactorily to לחמי "bowels of". Plague or pestilence (see e.g. NEB)
fits the context far better. It should be recalled too that *the sword, famine, and
pestilence* are a common triad in both Jeremiah and Ezekiel.

But the true significance of the Deuteronomy threat, linked as it is like Job
5:7 with the application of כעש and קנאה, is that Deut 32:23-25 is the very
specification of what בני רשף means - all those diseases and torments which are
associated with the release of the normal restraints which are kept on the
biological foes of mankind - pestilence and vermin and blind disorder.

In Ps 76:4 רשפי-קשת can be nothing but arrows - the *shafts* of the bow. *Fiery shafts*, as in some versions is gratuitous, based on assumptions as to the meaning of רֶשֶׁף derived from elsewhere.

A similar sense is embodied in Song 8:6:

> *Love is strong as death;*
> *Jealousy is cruel as the grave.*
> *The* רְשָׁפִים *thereof are* רִשְׁפֵי אֵשׁ,
> *A conflagration of the Lord!*

In this verse the specification of the רְשָׁפִים as being of fire logically precludes a tautologous fiery meaning for רֶשֶׁף. The verse virtually states "These are special רְשָׁפִים, unlike all others, being of fire". Darts, shafts, pangs, all fit the context.

It is a little difficult to pin down precisely where the illusion began that רֶשֶׁף was/were associated in any way with fire. The only citation which couples them is the Song of Songs passage quoted above, whose true force is to forbid any intrinsic sense of fire to רֶשֶׁף. Berechiah writing around 1300 accepts "sparks", but gives no origin for the idea. T also associates the word with fire. Ibn Ezra, as both LXX and Vg, consider בְּנֵי רֶשֶׁף to be birds. References to רֶשֶׁף are found spanning the whole period from 1850 BCE to 350 BCE[2].

Confusion as to the function of the god *Reshef* has arisen on the assumption that some Egyptian references indicate him (also) to have been a god of war (v.i.). The notion that he is a ruling demon of birds is the basis for LXX and Vg, as also T-S and NEB. It is likely that these are errors which have arisen because of the secondary characteristics of pestilence - the poetic metaphor of arrows and darts which strike the body when it is invaded by disease accounting for the first, and the speed with which illness strikes seemingly from another dimension for the second. The one quotation linking *Reshef* with war *The chariot-warriors are mighty as Rashaps*[3] (speaking of Rameses III's army) in no way rules out pestilence as the image intended.

In a Talmudic discussion[4], there is no dissension on the fundamental meaning of the word as relating to disease, one Rabbi speaking of demons, and the other of painful suffering.

It appears that the only valid senses for רֶשֶׁף are those directly derived from the original identity of the god as presiding demon of pestilence, and in the case of Job 5:7 there are good reasons for identifying בְּנֵי רֶשֶׁף with the collection of dire afflictions spelled out in Deut. 32:23-25.

What of the expression יַגְבִּיהוּ עוּף? The Hiph'il יַגְבִּיהוּ from the verb גבה is to "make high", and the infinitive עוּף is the infinitive construct "flying". The phrase therefore has the literal meaning *make high their flying*. My daughter has drawn my attention to a parallel expression in modern Hebrew הרחיקו לכת, literally *make far their going*, but with the meaning *draw far-reaching conclusions*. On analogy with this, יַגְבִּיהוּ עוּף will probably mean "fly high" in a colloquial sense, enjoy exceptional success.

There is no well-accepted generalisation like "sparks fly upwards" which can
be fitted to pestilence, so we must perforce abandon the proverbial form, and
with it "as" as the meaning of <u>waw</u>. The success, or high-flying, of pestilence
is a conditional occurrence, dependent upon the right circumstances. We are
therefore obliged to accept the <u>waw</u> as partaking of a construction in every
way similar to that of v.3. The two stichoi as understood in the above
discussion join together to produce

> But when a man is born to Trouble
> Pestilences have a field day!

while together the two verses 6 and 7 declare that trouble does not generate
spontaneously but occurs as the result of the catalytic presence of a particular
type of person. The pestilence becomes inevitable if someone like Eliphaz
does not intervene swiftly and decisively to destroy the man born to Trouble;
for otherwise God Himself will inflict it.

2. 6:6 and the תפל־טפל complex.

I have never for one moment been able to believe that the expression, ריר
חלמות, in Job 6:6, means any one of "white of egg", "juice of mallows" or
"slime of purslane", or, still less, "slimy cream cheese" as A.Yahuda[5] relying
on the Arabic *halum* or *hallum*, quoted by P, would have it!
"White of egg" from חלמון is the Targum version, and has the support of the
Rabbis, but both the old JPSV and the new have deserted them in favour of
"juice of mallows", and G, writing of a "riot of gastronomic failures" follows
their example. "Slime of purslane" receives a mention as an alternative in R,
and has the support of BDB and D&G. Hartley cleverly straddles several
horses with "the milk of a weed". Clines quotes Millard[6] as asserting that the
word is cognate with "the unidentifiable *hilimitu* of the Alalakh texts", and
Hartley gives more details of this, but it is difficult to see how this advances
matters. Tur-Sinai alone follows Rashi's grandson and tosses out the *dagesh* in
the *lamed* and boldly translates to "the saliva of dreams". The oldest
translations of all, strangely enough, do not mention any article of food the
LXX has "vain words", and the Vg, "the taste that brings death" *gustatum
adfert mortem*. In that version the word ריר has been rendered as "taste". We
shall advert to this later. None of the translators and commentators exhibits
any enthusiasm for the version which he employs. Many of them mention the
LXX version; T-S even claims that it supports his bold stroke, but the Vg
version is seldom if ever mentioned.
Here is the context. Job woke from his trance and protested to high heaven
at his fate. Eliphaz started with his unctuous reproach, telling him that a man
of his reputation for virtue shouldn't be scared; reminding him that when
others were in trouble he always had the right words for them; then retailing
a dream he claimed to have had in which a spirit told him that all men are

sinners in the eyes of God, and finally informing him that if he would but commit his cause to God, everything would come right in the end. This, he assures Job, the ultimate God-fearing man, he knows because he has researched it!

Job reacts to this by claiming the extremity of his injuries as the cause of the wildness of his complaint. He then asks v.5, *Does the wild-ass bray when he has grass? Does the ox low over his fodder?* The answer to these rhetorical questions is, of course, "No". This brings us to verse 6:

היאכל תפל מבלי-מלח?   אם-יש-טעם בריר חלמות?

which asks *Can one eat* תפל *without salt? Is there taste in* ריר חלמות?

Everything from now on hinges on the decision whether we are to take this as an extension of the discussion of what God has done to Job, or whether it is a reaction to the unacceptable "comfort" which Eliphaz has offered. Commentators seem to be divided fairly evenly on this, but it is hard to contest that v.5 does relate to God's actions which have deprived Job of everything he needs to sustain his life which he there symbolised as the necessary food of animals. Likewise the bellowing of the animals can only be the analogy to Job's own intemperate language. Unquestionably when Job defends the wildness of his words, he is referring to his own speech which antedated Eliphaz's and this cannot have been his reaction to the cruelty of Eliphaz's words; it must have been to the cruelty of God's actions. Does this necessarily mean that vv.6 and 7 also relate exclusively to God's devastations? There seems to be an irresistible logical flow from v.2 to v.7 as follows:

1. My calamity is immeasurable. (v.2,3a)
2. Therefore are my words wild. (v.3b)
3. (Additional reason) Because the terrors of God are arrayed against me etc. (v.4)
4. An animal does not bellow when it is fed. (v.5)
5. Can anyone eat x without salt? Is there any taste at all in y? (v.6)
6. I refuse to touch them. (v.7)
7. (The unexpressed QED) Therefore I bellow instead.

On this logic, there is no alternative but to consider the unknowns, x and y to be surrogates for what God has forced on Job, and it is on this assumption that I proceed.

Crucial to our understanding of ריר חלמות in 6:6b is the meaning to be attached to 6:6a, and in particular to the word תפל.

There are four paths by which we may approach this puzzle which has perhaps been too readily ignored in the past. These are (a) by appeal to authority; (b) by appeal to Biblical Hebrew language; (c) by appeal to the logical requirements of the passage; (d) by appeal to its poetic requirements.

(a) Almost every translator and commentator who has essayed this verse has followed Vg in rendering תפל as insipid food, and the remainder of the phrase as *without* salt or *unseasoned*. But there must surely be a suspicion that this version comes simply as an attempt to find for חפל a fit with *without salt*, not as a known and accepted meaning. The Seventy did not know it. LXX is alone in reading the question *Shall bread be eaten without salt?*. D varies the usual can insipid food be eaten unsalted? with the somewhat better *is that which is tasteless eaten unsalted?* and is emphatic that חפל refers to Job's trials, not to Eliphaz's words, but he leaves the impression that the lack of salt does refer to Eliphaz. Most commentators do not remark on the word חפל at all, but for those who do P's prejudicial assertion that the word is found only in this passage and Lam 2:14 is typical, but see (b) below. H has the most extensive and pertinent comment that I have been able to find. He refers to Ps 69:21,22:

> *I looked for sympathy (נוד) but there was none,*
> *For comforters (מנחמים), but I found none.*
> *They gave me poison for food,*
> *And vinegar to drink for my thirst.*

as a precedent for the symbolisation of comfort as food, and the parallel with Job in this passage is startling. H, therefore, is convinced that חפל itself is to be understood as alluding to Eliphaz's words, not to God's cruelty. He apparently does not consider that Job has already pre-empted the symbolic significance of food in v 5.

> *Job is not describing what is simply insipid or unappetizing, but what is inedible. It is unnecessary therefore to refer this remark to Eliphaz's argument, even though the figure of taste is a natural one for reason and sense (Pope).*

The comment of C is that חפל represents "the pill that God has prescribed". The first part of this last sentence is not compatible with the acquiescent translation which Clines provides "Can one eat tasteless foods without salt?", for even tasteless foods are edible.

The traditional view, the view of the authorities, is clear. They all but unanimously consider the meaning of חפל to be "insipid fare".

(b) Looking at חפל from a literary point of view, it is necessary to take into account the complex תפל־טפל־תפלה and the relationships, if any, between these three words. The majority of authorities evade these relationships by

recognizing two distinct words, תפל, one used exclusively by Ezekiel, representing the concrete substance plaster, or whitewash, and so connected to טפל;
the other meaning, as we see accepted above, tasteless or insipid (food), and
found exclusively here and in Lam 2:14., where it is in parallel with שוא,
"vanity".

It is worth spending a moment on this citation. *Your prophets have seen for
you שוא and תפל* is the first sentence of the verse, and then *They have not
disclosed your iniquity so that your captivity may be returned*, and finally *They
have prophesied for you שוא and מדוחים.* This last hapax word may also have
something to say about the meaning of תפל. The intention here is hardly
disputable, the poet is accusing the prophets of glossing over the sins of the
people and prophesying sweet nothings. The usual assumption is that מדוחים
derives from נדח and means something like enticements. But the meaning of
נדח is banishment, which is exactly what they have not prophesied. I suggest
that the true derivation is from דוח and the sense is cleansing, i.e. of guilt as
in Isa 4:4. As a parallel to this whitewash for תפל is almost perfect. On the
other hand, insipidities, while adequate for the context in Lamentations, lacks
all the specificity of this accusation. Besides, this is some distance from the
insipid food required in Job 6:6.

Vg. does not translate תפל as insipid food in Lam 2:14, but adjectivally as
"foolish" - *stultus*, with שוא as "false". Vg does, however give מדוחים as the
self-defeating "banishments". LXX gives the substantive "folly" for תפל.

We may deduce from the above that the necessity for a second word תפל in
addition to Ezekiel's *whitewash* is not apparent from the usage in Lamentations. If we examine the use of the word by Ezekiel - five times but always in
the same figure - it is immediately apparent that it is the same word as that
in Lamentations, for while Ezekiel speaks of daubing literal plaster on a wall,
he is in reality speaking as plainly of false and lulling prophecies as is the poet
of Lamentations. Readers of the NT are familiar with the concept of covering
corruption with this substance from the *whited sepulchres* of Matt 23:27. If we
refuse to accept this sense for Job 6:6 also, we are undertaking the perilous
game of asserting that a known Hebrew word does not mean in this book
what it means elsewhere in the Bible, and that unnecessarily.

The implication of this is that in its literal sense, תפל is indeed, as Clines
asserted, not an article of food. It is whitewash or plaster, something that can
perhaps be forced down the gullet, but which no-one would ingest voluntarily, and which has no food-value. So asking if one could eat it without salt is
the equivalent of asking if a man can eat his hat without an ample coat of
jam.

The verb טפל is apparently to plaster over, but the word occurs only in Job
(twice) and in Ps 119:69. In Job 13:4 it is a figure for smearing facts with lies,
and in 14:17 a plea that Job's sins be hidden from view - not taken into
consideration - by God. In the Psalm also it is the truth which has been

plastered over with lies. The correspondence between the noun and the verb, in both the concrete and abstract senses, is complete.

תפלה also occurs twice in Job and but once elsewhere (Jer 23:13). Its use in Jeremiah is very similar to the use of lpt in Lamentations.

> *In the prophets of Samaria I have seen* תפלה.
> *They prophesied by Baal and caused my people, Israel, to err.*

The two citations in Job display an unique, almost surreal, interaction between character and author. In 1:22 the author as narrator reports that *for all this, Job did not sin, nor ascribe* תפלה *to God*. In 24:12 Job reports with chilling wit that *God does not impute* תפלה to the pain and suffering of the innocent described in that chapter.

BDB gives the derivation of תפלה as from תפל (given as tasteless), but many seek to derive it from Arabic *tafala*, "to spit" (P). This unsupported speculation is improbable, for the relationship between תפל and תפלה is almost certain in the light of Job 1:22, 6:6 and 24:12, all of which seem to tend together. Where possible Hebrew roots should be sought for Hebrew words.

Pope also declares rightly that in use the word is very nearly the antonym of glory, כבוד. In each of its three uses it represents something shameful, something morally unsightly (rather than unseemly, see Jeremiah *I have seen* תפלה).

I conclude from this evidence that the verb טפל means to hide by plastering over; that the noun תפל is the plaster; and that the noun תפלה is a defect requiring to be plastered over, and that this complex of words is primarily employed poetically and figuratively, in relation to sin and its nondenunciation.

(c) We have reached the conclusion that the whole of vv. 5-7 refer to the treatment meted out to Job by God, and not the cold comfort offered by Eliphaz. Having initially decided to use as an analogy for this treatment the denial of its natural food to an animal, Job proceeds to the logical development of characterising what has been meted out to him also in gustatory terms.

Contradicting, boldly but again surrealistically, the narrator of 1:22, Job asserts he has been fed תפל. This is the same as ascribing תפלה to God. While it is not difficult to see how Job can ascribe unsightly things to God, how is it possible for him to use the specific word תפל which we have just finished demonstrating means the cover-up, not the thing covered? This distinction is quite probably not intended to be made here, but תפל exactly describes the accusation which Job has to make against God in 10:8-13, that all the while He was nurturing Job, *granting me life and favour, these things You did hide in Your heart!*. The logic of the passage then gives to תפל a double meaning, primarily figurative as God's hypocrisy towards him, and secondarily literal as an inedible substitute for the grass and fodder which have been denied him.

It is when we face the addition, *without salt* that we perhaps encounter the contribution of Eliphaz in the suggestion that conceivably one could eat תפל if only it came with appropriate seasoning of good words from a friend. On the other hand such a figurative use of salt is not found elsewhere until NT (Matt 5:13, etc. Mark 9:49, Col 4:6) where it is frequent. Particularly apposite is the last of the above:

"Let your speech be alway with grace, seasoned with salt, that ye may know how ye ought to answer every man".

If this is not the intention of the addition, then it can only be read as an intensification as *unmitigated whitewash, unadulterated whitewash, whitewash without salt to boot!* There is certainly nothing in the logic of the passage which requires that תפל stand for any ordinarily edible, even though unappealing, substance.

(d) It is perhaps from the poetic point of view that the common readings, tasteless food, insipid food, grate most strongly. The essence of poetry is specificity and its associative power. Note how "Can one eat whitewash?" immediately conjours a picture to the mind, while "can one eat insipid food?" fails. The latter is about as far away from the soul of good poetry as it is possible to wander. "Can one eat whitewash (of hypocrisy) without salt (of kindness)?" is good poetry, while the alternative is bad prose.

There is a traditional metaphor connected with taste. We read of the "taste of defeat" as we do of the "scent of victory"; of "tasting death" (this is found in the NT several times); of actions that leave a "bitter taste in the mouth". At the end of this Chap. 6, Job asks if his palate (חך) cannot discern perversity. The most general metaphorical use is that of Ps 34:9 "Taste and see that the Lord is good". In view of the metaphorical ambience of both words, טעם and תפל, it seems unavoidable that some more vivid image than insipid food must be understood.

Indeed, there are not words to describe the weakness of "insipid food", and the subsequent specified slops as symbols of the destruction which has come upon Job. "You have taken all my possessions, killed all my children and left me a physical wreck; it is as though you had fed me with white of egg!" The only possible reaction to this is "Come off it!" This is the master poet of the ages writing? It is no doubt from an appreciation of this awful incompatibility in dramatic force that many commentators elected to read vv. 6,7 as referring to Eliphaz's speech despite the logical problems this raised.

The conclusion of this analysis is that תפל is indeed plaster (or whitewash) in its literal sense. In this it is intended to represent not-food, and thus is an inappropriate partner in parallel for white of egg, slime of purslane, juice of mallow, or any sort of cream-cheese, all of which are food. It also conveys an inseparable metaphorical sense of the concealment of true intentions or actions which are themselves disgraceful.

There are then many good reasons for not choosing from the unappetising menu which has been accumulated in the search for the meaning of חלמות. Perhaps not the least should be that every one of the putative seventy translators of the LXX undoubtedly went to his wife and asked her what sort of food this was, and what seventy housewifes don't know about food, one aristocratic author certainly doesn't!

It is only if we can accept, in defiance of the logic of the passage, that Job is talking about Eliphaz's unseemly "comfort" in Chaps. 4 and 5, that we could entertain the insipids and slops of the usual versions. The same applies to the version of Tur-Sinai which allows us to take ריר חלמות as *drooling of dreams* or *dreamland droolings*, regarding it not as the poisoning by phantoms which T-S has concocted, but perhaps a well-deserved assault on the "dream-sequence" which was the centrepiece of Eliphaz's speech. If, however, we conider that Job has not yet started taking his friends to task but is still explaining why he is "braying" and "lowing" like an animal deprived of his proper diet, this also does not fit into the context.

Let us then consider what is called for in the context. Surely it is either a direct and precise parallel to תפל - a substance at once inedible but ingestible and with a well recognized secondary moral overtone - something of the order of "soft-soap", or it is a specification, something which relates either to the crushing of Job by God, or to the inappositeness of Eliphaz's words. This is why, of all the versions before us, that of LXX, "vain words" even though it grasps what we have deduced to be the wrong horn of this dilemma, is the one that gives the most satisfaction. With it, we know where we are. The assorted foodstuffs of the moderns add only to our confusion. But the best that can be said of the LXX version is that it is an interpretation of what is required by the context, but in no sense is it a translation of the text.

I wish to re-examine the version of the Vg, for in this there is a hint of an entirely novel approach to the analysis of this word חלמות. Vg treats the syllable מות independently, as the word death. The vocalization is all wrong for this, and the verb which Vg supplies - "to bring" does not seem to have any warrant in the verse. But there is that unaccounted *dagesh* in the *lamed*. Let us stretch out the word by supplying the missing letter which the *dagesh* perhaps indicates: חללמות. The MT vocalization of מות gives us the infinitive construct, and adding to it one of the lameds gives us impeccably "to die". This leaves over, as the first part of a portmanteau-word, חל. What would be the meaning of חל־למות?

There is, I suggest, one possibility only which respects the grammar strictly, i.e. which does not require the assumption that a second letter (ה) has dropped out. This is that חל is the poetic form of the Qal active participle of חול, and that it is used here in exactly the same sense as the feminine Qal indicative is used in חלה לטוב in Mic 1:12, "to await anxiously". How appropriate this is to the context may be seen from vv 8 & 9 following, where Job begs:

> *Would that my request were allowed*
> *And that God would grant my hope,*
> *And that it would please God to crush me,*
> *That He would loose His hand and cut me off!*

and from 11a which asks *What is my strength that I should wait* (כי איחל)?
I conclude, therefore, that the second question in v. 6 is "What taste is there
in the saliva of one desperate to die?" a question made even more poignant by
7:19, later in this same speech, when Job complains that God will not leave
him alone long enough to swallow his own spittle (רק). The one word חלמות
is now revealed as the full symbol of all that God has done to Job, the
quintessence of the demands of the context. As for ריר, its only other use in
the Bible is in I Sam 21:14 where King David feigns madness and dribbles on
his beard. The verb also occurs but once (Lev 15:3), and refers to a bodily
discharge. There being no precedent for such fantasies as "slime" or "juice" for
the word, it is as well that we should dispense with them.
In connection with any interpretation or translation of this verse, it should
be remembered that the Hebrew טעם means discernment in the "taster" as well
as taste in what is put in the mouth (see, e.g. Job 12:20), and that while the
palate is usually taken as the site of the sense of taste, it is quite possible that
the saliva was also considered a participant. Hence the strange identification
of ריר with taste found in the Vg (v.s.).
We have then two valid ways of interpreting this last line
- Is there any flavour at all in the saliva of a man desperate to die? or
- Is there any discrimination in the saliva of a man desperate to die?
It is not possible to dismiss altogether two alternative portmanteaux - (a) חלה
למות, conceivably even a direct quotation from Isa 38:1 -
        Then was Hezekiah sick to the point of death
(see p.55), or (b), in the light of 6:4,
        The arrows of the Almighty are with me,
חלל למות, meaning "mortally wounded" (justifying Elihu's חצי אנוש in 34:6).

3. Not one, 14:4

מי־יתן טהור מטמא   לא אחד!
This verse, which follows the serene mourning of vv. 1 and 2 and the
explosive rebellion of v.3 has been translated with little confidence in
innumerable ways.
NJPSV: *Who can produce a clean thing out of an unclean one? No-one!*

LXX: *For who shall be pure from uncleanness? No-one!* G: *Men say 'Who can distinguish the pure from the impure? No-one!'*

There are three considerations which must be taken into account in the translation of this verse, and most versions so far achieved infringe all three. They are:

1. The expression מי־יתן, while grammatically a question, in fact lacks all interrogative force and is a purely desiderative idiom meaning "would that...", or "let it be granted that ..." It expresses what the speaker desires, most frequently, but not invariably (see Job 31:31) an impossibility (e.g. Num 11:29).

2. The word טמא is masculine in form, and therefore cannot be interpreted as the "unclean" woman from whom man is born (relating v.4 to v.1). Nor, I believe, is there any precedent, Biblical or Talmudic, for treating woman *per se* as unclean.

3. The phrase לא אחד is not the Hebrew for *no one*, but means *not one*[7].

The first version given above treats the preposition מן as *from* in the sense of out of, but taking into account the second consideration above, this is improbable, for if woman is ruled out as the unclean source of man, the context provides no plausible alternative. There are, however, other possibilities for מן, one of which is that it has the same force here as in the phrase אחד מני אלף - *one in a thousand* (9:3; 33:23). This gives the phrase טהור מטמא the sense the *pure among the defiled*, according a collective force to טמא while preserving an ambiguous one for טהור - Job alone, or all who are like him? With this conception the verse comes to mean *Let there be of pure among the defiled not one!* i.e. *Let there be not even a single pure man amongst the defiled majority of the human race!* In such a version the sentiment would be Job's interpretation of God's purpose in *bringing me to judgement with Him*. This version, like those which treat the phrase לא אחד as *no one*, does not take into account the true significance of the word אחד. While this is the numeral one, it has an additional significance, or restriction of meaning, based on its own derivation from the verb יחד, *to be united*. Thus not one but two or more things can be אחד when they are in some sense united - treated as alike, or behaving as alike. The split phrase in this verse מי־יתן...לא אחד is therefore a perfectly acceptable way of saying *Oh that a and b not be confounded, not be united in their fates,* or *in the judgements passed on them, not be treated as one!* In such a version, a and b have to be the pure and the impure, leaving open the question why they are joined (or separated) by the preposition מי. The Hebrew language, unlike modern European languages, is fully tolerant of double negatives and double possessives; thus by analogy the use of מי, which implies separation, may tend to reinforce לא אחד which negates identity. The preposition may therefore still be treated partitively to yield *Oh that the pure among the impure not be treated as one (with them)!* Job's meaning then is essentially that he wishes God would not *bring him into judgement with him*, a course of action which he interprets as equivalent to treating him as though he were one with the impure. Because propositions governed by מִי־יִתֵּן are most commonly impossibilities (v.s.), the tense of this verse is best regarded as the past, the irremediable. So our next version will be:

>Oh that the pure among the defiled were not lumped together (with them)!

Some further refinement of this seems still possible. G's version (leaving aside his characteristic and unnecessary reading of the verse as a "virtual quotation"), *Who can distinguish the pure from the impure?* accords another perfectly acceptable sense to מִן, dependent on the grammatical force of יִתֵּן. He has, however, violated the sense of the idiom, מִי־יִתֵּן. By correcting this we would arrive at:

>Would that the pure were distinguished from the defiled!

as the meaning of the first stich, and

>Not amalgamated

for the second. In this version the use of the phrase לֹא אֶחָד is exactly analogous to the use of the phrase לֹא אָכְזָר in 41:2 (see p. 184f), i.e. a phrase apparently in apposition with a verb (there יִטֹּל, here יִתֵּן), that is, in amplification of it. The sense remains that Job wishes that God would show some discrimination between good and bad men.

4. 15:4,5

>*You subvert piety*
>*And restrain prayer to God.*
>*Your sinfulness dictates your speech,*
>*So you choose crafty language.*

This 1980 version of Job 15:4,5[8] differs little from the countless versions which have preceded it and the few which have followed. The first one which is demonstrably much the same as this was the Vg, while LXX gives evidence of having faced a somewhat different Hebrew text. It is therefore a good question why a version which has apparently given satisfaction for nearly 2000 years should be brought up for interrogation and examination now. The Hebrew of these verses is:

אַף־אַתָּה תָּפֵר יִרְאָה וְתִגְרַע שִׂיחָה לִפְנֵי־אֵל

כִּי־יְאַלֵּף עֲוֹנְךָ פִיךָ וְתִבְחַר לְשׁוֹן עֲרוּמִים

It is striking that, in making the version which has held the stage for so long, the following compromises have of necessity been incorporated:

1. תָּפֵר has been afforded a deviant and over-literate translation in *subvert*, and one which cannot apply to fear or to fear of God. G reads *undermine*. C chooses *abandon*, while NEB has *banish*, D&G accept RV's *do away with*, or *frustrate, annul, destroy*. AV has *cast off*, while D, keeping closest to the Hebrew, has *make void*. Both *abandon* and *banish* make good sense of the

line, but they are not known meanings of פרר[9]. These include *break* (an agreement or vow), or *annul, frustrate* or *make ineffectual.* The variety of solutions listed above shows the difficulty writers have experienced in adapting this word to what they believe to be the context.

2. יראה, which everywhere else (except Job 4:6, to which we shall address ourselves later) means *fear* and nothing more, is here required to stand for the phrase יראת אלהים, *fear of God.* This is not so much a kind of fear, as respect and obedience, a mode of conduct. The legitimacy of this ellipsis is doubtful. So is the fitness of the abstraction "you subvert piety" to the spirit of this book. Other translations, while having much the same meaning, are less stark in this respect.

3. גרע, which normally means to reduce or diminish, and somewhat obscurely seems to mean monopolise in Job 15:8, where it is often rendered restrain in the sense of hold back for oneself alone (obj. wisdom), is here required to mean restrain in quite a different sense - holding back altogether, as one might a dog. There is no comparable use. C has *you slight*, suggesting it is another way of saying diminish, but this is farfetched.

4. שׁיחה's claim to mean *prayer* cannot be sustained. The masculine form is *complaint* usually, and the only other use of the feminine is twice in the late Psalm 119 where it seems to mean study in the sense "object of study". No amount of ingenuity will fit this sense to the context. The verb too is dominated by the idea of complaint, with musing or meditating a secondary sense. Both of these, and also devotion, are to be found in translations of this verse.

5. לפני-אל is not how one says *to God.* One prays לאל or אל-אל, but in this context to God seems a tautology. לפני is *before in time or place*, hence here *in the presence of.*

6. אלף is *to teach*, but does not quite fit into the concept of a man's iniquity influencing his speech, hence such words as *dictates* (v.s), *inspires* (C), *exposes* (with reversal of subject-object, D), *reveals*, (similarly, R), *prompts* (Jerusalem Bible.), *declares* (T-S). Nonetheless many, including Vg and T, do use the word *teaches*, but the metaphor is flawed. One does not learn from his iniquity, but perhaps from its consequences.

7. ערום is far more often a complimentary than a derogatory term - prudent, sensible, rather than crafty.

The existence of these multiple discords between Hebrew and English admits of three possible (not mutually exclusive) explanations. 1. The author of Job had a poor acquaintance with the Hebrew language. 2. Our own appreciation of the semantic range of numerous Hebrew words is seriously deficient. 3. There is something fundamentally at error in the translation. Of these possibilities the first is unthinkable. With regard to the second, while it might well apply to a small number of Biblical Hebrew words, the probability that it could apply to so many gathered into so short a passage is too low to be worth considering. In respect of the third, if it is possible to identify a single mechanism which can account for most or all seven of these discrepancies - and the eighth to be described in the next paragraph - this' would be tantamount to proof of the proposition.

These seven discrepancies are not all that is discordant about the verse. Immediately after accusing Job of using crafty language, which means language calculated to conceal the real intentions behind it (cf. the notorious serpent of Gen 3:1 whose speech really was crafty), Eliphaz tells him *Your own mouth condemns you and not I; And your lips testify against you.* This is incompatible. Crafty or subtle language conceals guilt; it does not reveal it.

Job's language in the four preceding speeches has indeed been such that no-one could call it crafty, or subtle, or anything but reckless, and this is surely a meaning which ערום cannot abide. Further, while Eliphaz might well tell Job that his iniquity (עונך) infects his speech, and even that he has abandoned piety (if piety were a recognizable concept at the time), it is very difficult to discern anything in what Job has said which might warrant the accusation that he is interfering in some way with prayer. Thus not only is every line of the quatrain flawed by inaccurate translations of key words, but the sense of every line is in some way woolly and hard to grasp, like an image in a distorting mirror.

All in all, there seems to be more than sufficient reason to justify a fresh look at these two verses. While there are a number of different angles from which an approach might be made, I propose to begin with the apparently unmistakable contradiction of *sense* between the last line and the total content of the Dialogue.

Inasmuch as there is no justice in the use of the word *crafty*, neither as a description of what Job has said, nor as a recommendation as to what he should say, let us start by amending this word back to its commonest sense - *prudent*. Eliphaz could never have said that Job had chosen prudent language, any more than he could have accused him of using crafty speech, but he very well might have recommended to Job that he choose such language in future.

> *And you must choose the language of the prudent.*

while it fits well into what we know of the situation and the relationship between the two men, requires an unusual, but not unknown, grammatical interpretation, for תבחר is the plain imperfect tense, not the imperative[10]. One writer only, so far as I have been able to discern, decided that this line must be read in this way. This was Berechiah, whose comment yields *Thou shouldst have chosen the tongue of the thoughtful.*

It is worth while at this point to see how the whole quatrain would look were it in fact imperative rather than indicative:

> *What is more you must subvert piety*
> *And restrain prayer to God.*
> *Your iniquity should dictate your speech*
> *And you must choose the language of the prudent.*

quite absurd! but let us make a few adjustments, correcting the anomalies we have found in the translations of key words. That is, let us read fear as fear, diminish as diminish, complaint as complaint, לפני as in the presence of and teach as teach. Also we must choose a word for תפר which reflects one of its known meanings. At the same time let us recall the versatility of the word עון. at last here is a plausible speech for Eliphaz to have made, which respects the correct value of all words in the Hebrew text.

> *Furthermore you must discount fear*
> *And moderate your complaint in the presence of God.*
> *For your chastisement must teach your lips,*
> *And you must select the language of the prudent.*

In translating תפר with discount, we are taking the meaning "make ineffectual". Banish (v.s.) would be even sharper. It is Job's own expressed fear (3:25, 7:14, 9:28, 34, 13:21) which he is being admonished to surmount. A better word than diminish for גרע is *moderate*, but there is no real difference in meaning. That Job has been complaining is incontestable, and that Eliphaz and his friends have been criticizing him for this is equally clear. Job's fear and his complaints are organically linked.

The word עון has the triple senses, iniquity, guilt, and punishment. In this case with the verb *teach* as its predicate, punishment is overwhelmingly more likely than iniquity or guilt. Was it not Eliphaz who quoted *Happy is the man whom God correcteth, Therefore despise not the chastisement of the Almighty* (5:17)? and has not the whole thrust of the first cycle of speeches by the comforters been to persuade Job to accept the lesson of his downfall and make his confession and peace with God - that is to let his chastisement teach his lips?

This version is therefore fully in harmony both with the spirit and the letter of text and context.

Also let us lay to rest the reference in 4:6 which is used to support the proposition that יראה may anomalously mean piety - fear of God. See also p. 379.

Job 4:6 is: הלא יראתך כסלתך תקותך ותם דרכיך? and is almost universally given as *is not your fear (of God) your (source of) confidence? And your hope, is it not the integrity of your ways?*

This reads very well, and fits perfectly into the scheme of the speech, and the following propositions, if not into what precedes it. However the word כסלה as a source of confidence is very dubious indeed[11]. There is only one other use of this feminine form in the Bible, in Ps 85:9 where, *pace* BDB, it undoubtedly means *folly*. The context is God speaking peace to His people and His saints, ואל־ישובו לכסלה - *But let them not return to folly!*

Why then should we not read this verse something like

> *Is not your fear your folly?*
> *But your hope, surely it is the integrity of your ways??*

and here at last we can find some learned support, for this is how LXX rendered the first stich of 4:6. There is support also in the precedent context, for not only was Job's last complaint that his worst fear was being realised (3:25), but the very last word which Eliphaz speaks before 4:6 is תבהל, *You are afraid*. After this *Is not your fear...?* is completely consequent and appropriate. Therefore, as there is an eminently satisfactory way of reading the verse without the unsupported assumption that יראתך can mean *your fear of God*, Job 4:6 is very much a broken reed of a precedent to justify treating יראה in 15:4 as any form of piety. In fact neither reference can support the other, and there is no other.

The reduplicated 2nd person pronoun

The Romans and Greeks regarded Biblical Hebrew as a thoroughly barbaric language for one reason, its lack of elegant adornment - its Spartan economy. Their contempt was surely unjustified, but their recognition of a cardinal feature of Biblical language - accentuated yet further in verse - was accurate. What then is the apparently quite unnecessary word אתה doing at the beginning of verse 4 above? The use of the personal pronoun in conjunction with the imperfect, the perfect, or the imperative form of a verb in Hebrew is redundant. Nonetheless, there is a considerable number of these pronouns in the Book of Job, and while the Is and wes, the hes and the theys are of no concern to us in this section, the yous are.

This pronoun is used very sparingly. The first time is in the prose Prologue where it seems simply and appropriately emphatic *Have not You Yourself built a fence about him...?*, emphasising that God Himself is responsible for any doubts he might have about Job. The question form of the sentence sets it apart from the other cases.

With more than 350 examples of 2nd person verbs, there are nine further examples of a redundant 2nd person pronoun in the poem of Job. Of these, most significantly, four support plain imperatives:

5:27 שמענה ואתה דע־לך - *You hearken to it and bind it to your heart!*

19:21 חנני חנני אתם רעי - *Pity me! Pity me! O you my friends!*

33:33 אם־אין אתה שמע־לי החרש ואאלפך חכמה - *If not, you listen to me; Hold your peace and I shall teach you wisdom!*

34:32 בלעדי אחזה אתה הרני - *What I do not perceive, You teach me!* the others are related to indicative forms:

8:5: אם־אתה תשחר אל־־אל - *If you would seek earnestly to God* Strictly speaking this is a conditional sentence, but the אתה apparently imparts a pleading note to it which makes it desiderative if not imperative. *Would that you would seek...* or *If only you would seek...* is implicit. The impression Bildad seeks to convey, and indeed does convey, is not only that he predicts a good outcome for Job if he repents, but that he also wishes Job' repentance.

11:13ı is virtually identical: אם־אתה הכינות לבך - *If only you would set your heart to rights...!*

11:16 כי־אתה עמל תשכח כמים עברו תזכר. At first glance, this seems to offer no justification for the redundant "you". If, however, we take a hint from the preceding examples that it implies a weak form of the imperative, a kind of urging rather than the simple affirmative normal to declarative forms of the verb, we obtain the natural and appropriate *Therefore forget your trouble; remember it as water under the bridge, Then the future will dawn brighter than noon etc.*

27:12 אתם כלכם חזיתם falls into quite a different category, where אתם is required as an anchor for כלכם, giving the emphatic *all of you.*

34:33 כי־אתה תבחר ולא־אני ומה ידעת דבר. This last example clarifies the problem for although the reduplicated pronoun is linked to an imperfect tense indicative verb, that verb itself is in tandem with an imperative. The sense here is clearly *You choose, not I, so say what you think!* It is interesting that the verb תבחר is also in the passage 15:4,5 which we are examining. In 34:33 the pronoun serves the additional function of providing a concrete contrast for אני.

In all, therefore, there are eleven reduplicated pronouns out of a possible 350-odd. One of these in a question may be discounted, leaving ten, of which four are with imperatives and a further five are as well or better read as imperative, or at least cajoling. The conclusion that the reduplicated 2nd person pronoun is capable of acting as an imperative or desiderative vocative seems strongly justified.

Even discounting this possibility, the fact that assuming imperative senses for 15:4,5 repairs eight anomalies in our current understanding makes it almost mandatory to read them in this way. This revision of the meaning of two verses is an application of the principle of "Ockham's razor" - <u>Non sunt multiplicanda entia praeter necessitatem</u> - *Entities are not to be multiplied beyond necessity.*

5. Job's Redeemer, 19:23-27

Waw in Hebrew means a hook. The letter à is accordingly shaped like a hook, and functions in the language as a hook, to join together (or paradoxically to join apart) words, phrases, sentences. It is a versatile letter-word which most often means *and* and sometimes *but*, but also on occasions *that* and *while* and *although* and *seeing that, as*, not to mention *yea!*, and many delicate refinements of these words. When attached to a verb and appropriately vocalized, waw has the strange power of influencing its tense, and in some types of inverted sentences, waw serves a purely formal purpose of introducing the predicate. In both these last two cases, modern western languages can leave the word out in translation, although recognizing and adjusting to its influence. Grammarians have had a fine time with waw, and recognize *waw apodosis, waw copulativum, waw concomitantiae, waw explicativum, waw consecutive*, and others.

The committee which translated the Bible for the JPS in the 1970s and 1980s decided to take a stand on this word, and pointed out: "Always to render it as "and" is to misrepresent the Hebrew rather than be faithful to it. Consequently the committee translated the particle as the sense required, or left it untranslated.[12]" But see in the Introduction (p. 40) the section (9), Massacre of the Particles for a comment on how this wise intention has been translated into practice.

A long time ago, a Jewish teacher said

> *Till heaven and earth pass, one jot or one tittle shall in no wise pass from the Law, till all be fulfilled* (Matt 5:18).

Without doubt this proscription included waws. It is still orthodox Jewish doctrine.

When, therefore, we encounter a waw, we are under an obligation to account for it. The waw which is a central character in this section has, on the whole, been rudely thrust aside by all commentators and translators, and those who have attempted to accomodate it to their understanding of the passage in which it occurs, have still not taken it seriously. It might be said that this is the waw which everyone wishes away[13], waw anathema.

I know that my Redeemer liveth

is one of the best known lines in the Bible. Surprisingly, the Hebrew is not ידעתי כי חי גאלי, but ואני ידעתי גאלי חי. There are no fewer than three important differences, and one minor one. There is the <u>waw</u>; there is the prefixed אני, an apparently pointless duplication of the pronoun, there is the absence of the more or less essential כי, and the less than optimal word order of the final clause. Let us examine these four anomalies gathered into a single stich.

1. In the Bible there are innumerable examples of the verb "to know" followed by a sentence stating what is known. In every instance but two[14], the verb is followed by כי, ש, or an equivalent. Its absence here is therefore a suspicious circumstance which should spur us to seek an alternative reading.

2. The reduplication of the personal pronoun "I" is a fairly common device in Hebrew, and is found some twenty odd times in the Book of Job. It is used, particularly in Job, for the specific purpose of pointing a contrast between the speaker and another subject, usually the person addressed. In v.27 of the present passage there is an unmistakable example of this convention. The אני in this verse should therefore induce us to search the context for a source of contrast to the speaker. I, recognizing this, claims justification for *but* as the translation of <u>waw</u>, writing, "Better, (than for I know...) 'But as for me, I know', since the pronoun is emphatically used and the conjunctive letter <u>waw</u> does not imply a link of logical sequence with the preceding verses, but on the contrary suggests an adversative sense. Earthly wishes are brought to vanity, *but* there is a knowledge to which Job now clings, My Redeemer liveth."

3. The unpopular ו with which the sentence begins and which therefore cannot introduce the predicate, and which is not attached to the verb and therefore cannot influence its tense, demands recognition as a hook, joining the sentence to, or repelling it from, what preceded it.

4. Graceful Hebrew places the subject after the verb (Ges. #142a). Indeed, when this phrase was incorporated by the poet Ibn Gvirol into the hymn אדון אולם (Lord of the Universe), the order was reversed to give חי גואלי. In Job 19:25, the gracelessness of the word order is intensified by the preceding אני ידעתי which also, though in this case quite naturally, gives precedence to the subject over the verb. Frequently in relation to this verse, mention is made of the Ugaritic formula expressing confidence in the fact that Baal lives, but even here both the normal Semitic word order and the missing כי are found:

> wid` khy aliyn b`l kit zbl b`l ars
>
> *And I know that there lives powerful Baal,*
> *Exists the prince, Lord of the Earth!*

In addition to these four textual irregularities, there is a problem with the sense of the passage which is not evident until we reach v.27c, an expression of utter and hopeless longing *My reins perish in my bosom*, which is entirely at odds with the sublime confidence supposedly expressed in vv.25-27b. Only T-S has attempted to reconcile this.

Clearly our next task is to examine the preceding verses, particularly in the light of I.'s rare defence of *but* for <u>waw</u>.

Would then that my words were written;
Would that they were inscribed in an archive
With an iron pen and lead,
Carved in the rock for ever!

The idea that *But as for me I know that my Redeemer lives* is a proper adversative continuation of this is difficult to accept. This prologue does not state or imply *You think my only hope of salvation lies in the perpetuation of my words...* allowing v.25 to contrast you and me ("as for me") and two differing opinions. Nor is there a trace of justification for I's mention of the vanity of earthly wishes; this is the reader's reflection, not the text. Both the desire for the preservation of Job's words and whatever v. 25 has to say are equally Job's appeals, and the adversative sense which I. seeks is not to be found in this way. Rashi proposes that it is adversative to "you persecute me", implicit in 19:22, but this is far-fetched.

Let us therefore look into the possibility that <u>waw</u> here actually does mean *and*, and that there is a logical sequence between the ideas of vv. 23,24, and what succeeds them. This requires that v.25 shall be governed by the same desiderative expressions מי־יתן (Would that!) which govern these preceding verses, and that the contrast which is implied by אני is not with another person (for there is no other person here) but with the subject of vv.23 and 24, Job's words.

This gives us for ואני ידעתי *And as for me, that...* Having, as it were, disposed of his words, Job now declares what he wishes for himself. The first possibility then is that Job wishes he knew that his Redeemer lived - an expression of deep doubt of the very existence of God which is at variance with all else Job has to say in the poem. It, like the accepted *I know that my Redeemer lives*, requires the missing כי, and offends by its word order. Let us break the continuity for a moment and consider the meaning of the Biblical word גואל.

Despite recent variations employing the translation "Vindicator"[15], the word admits of only two correct translations - *redeemer* and *kinsman*; but a redeemer may be such by virtue of any one of several quite distinct legal functions which he performs, as follows:

1. Avenger; the close kinsman who has the duty of avenging a murder.
2. Levirate husband; the brother or close relative of a man who died married but without issue, upon whom devolves the duty to wed his widow and raise up in the deceased's name (יקום על שם) an heir to his property rights.
3. Redeemer of property; again a close relative who has the right of first refusal (? also the duty) to repurchase real estate sold through poverty.
4. Redeemer from slavery; again a kinsman who may repurchase a man who has sold himself as an indentured servant.

There is also the concept of God as Redeemer, first encountered in Ex 6:6, then in Hosea, Deutero-Isaiah and in several Psalms. Here the function of

Redeemer is less restricted, and includes redemption from exile and captivity, from conquest (e.g. the redemption of Jerusalem), from death itself, or simply from nameless misfortune or error. While usually applied to the nation as a whole, there are in Psalms several allusions to God as a personal Redeemer. In the Bible, God is in fact the only entity to be referred to as a Redeemer (the participle), and in Deutero-Isaiah, this word degenerates into an alternative name for Him. While we consider only the literal interpretation of the Job story, there does not seem to be great scope for the operation of a redeemer except in the very last of the senses mentioned. If, however, we consider the allegorical interpretation of Job as representing the nation Judah in the time of Hezekiah, then all the functions of God as Redeemer become relevant, for Judah has been brought to comprehensive ruin.

If we rule out the the inauthentic vindicator ("champion" C) there does not seem a feasible alternative to God as the Redeemer of this verse, not least because Job has disposed of all his relatives and friends as having deserted him in vv. 13-19 of this chapter. In these circumstances *I know that my Redeemer lives* reduces itself to *I know that God lives*. El had good reason to tell Anath that he knew that Baal lived, in that Mot had claimed to have killed him. For anyone to claim that he knew that God lives was impossible in the culture of ancient Israel. The very designation of Him as "the living God" and the invocation "As God lives!" point to the absurdity of such an assurance. The concept that God might be dead, which is implicit in the assertion "I know that He lives" was literally unthinkable. *(Would that) I knew that my Redeemer lived* is, in the light of all the rest of the Book of Job, an even more impossible reading. LXX *I know that He is Eternal who will deliver me* is an attempt to solve both the problem of sense and that of word-order, but חי cannot be "Eternal".

What other meaning can there be for (מי־יתן) ידעתי גאלי חי? The author of the Book of Job had remarkable consideration for those scholars who would spend their lives trying to decipher his work over the millenia, and very frequently used his abstruse words and constructions twice in the course of the book, enabling one citation to throw light on another. The expression מי־יתן ידעתי, unique to the Book of Job, reappears in 23:3 as *Would I might know where I might find Him!*. We are on good grounds then in reading the expression as *Would that I might know!* Let us move now to v.26b, for this line tells us explicitly what (or whom) Job is so desperate to know

ומבשרי אחזה אלוה!

Again the introductory <u>waw</u> indicates that the sentence is governed by the desideratives מי־יתן, so that the verse reads:

And in my flesh I should see God

There is a full and exact *parallelismus membrorum* between this line and line 25a. אלוה, God, means the same as גאלי, my Redeemer; מבשרי, in my flesh, means exactly what חי, *alive*, implies; אחזה, *I might see* is equivalent to ידעתי אני,

I might know. In both lines Job is pleading that he be granted the sight of God while he is alive. The חי of v.25 is thus adjectival, and relates to the subject, I, Job, and not to the object, my Redeemer, in this sentence. There is therefore no call for a כי in the sentence, Job does not wish to know that anything. He wishes to know his Redeemer. Likewise there is no infringment of rules regarding the order of subject and verb, for there is no second verb in the sentence.

There is an interesting complication to this interpretation in relation to contrasting forms of immortality sought by Job for his words and for himself, as indicated by the reduplicated personal pronoun. Verses 23 and 24 ask that Job's words shall be preserved for all time. In 14:13 Job expressed, also with the phrase מי־יתן, a longing that God "hide" him in the Underworld until His wrath was past (עד־שוב אפך), and then resurrect him. This same desire seems to be concealed behind the חי and the מבשרי of this passage. Assuming that a restoration of his situation in his natural lifetime is out of the question (indeed expecting death any moment), Job is asking to be resurrected in the flesh to meet God on a future occasion which will be specified in the two lines enclosed between the chiastic 25a and 26b. This occasion is essentially the same as the contingency expressed in 14:13. It is because of the daring and (at the time) unfamiliar concept of resurrection, that it is necessary, in 27a and 27b, for Job to repeat with exceptional insistence, that it is his own personal body which is to experience this encounter with his Redeemer, with God.

The interior pair of lines 25b and 26a have posed a perennial puzzle, and there is an almost universal assumption that they have suffered some form of damage.

ואחרון על־עפר יקום   ואחר עורי נקפו־זאת

As we see, both of these also are introduced by waw and, in the absence of any better explanation, must be read as wishes rather than statements. Despite the presence of the form יקום על (v.s.), there seems no way in which all this can be related to the levirate function of the redeemer. יקום על, however, has a wide spread of meanings, and is usually taken here as to arise upon or to stand upon, or even (NJPSV) to testify upon. אחרון also is hard to pin down, but surely has an apocalyptic significance in relation to the last day[16]. עפר, dust, is a metaphor, either for mankind, or for the earth, with the former more likely. I suggest that either the wish being expressed in this passage is much the same as that in 14:13, so that its meaning approximates *that His wrath may be past - And that the last thing (or His last) may be fulfilled upon the dust!* - or, more simply and conventionally, it pleads for His appearance *that in the end He will arise upon the dust*

The next line has frequently been abandoned as insoluble "Vs 26a is in a state of textual corruption which defies the resources of exegesis". (I) is a challenge few could resist. The great problem is the verbal form נקפו. This is the only example of the Pi'el of either of the supposedly distinct two verbs נקף[17]. As a third person plural, it lacks any plausible referent in the context, and must therefore be treated as a passive (see e.g. RV which exactly copies Berechiah with *After my skin has been thus destroyed* as though כזאת).

There is also difficulty in determining the subject of the verb in the sentence. This can only be solved if we maintain faith that the text is intact and incorrupt, for then we find the sentence has exactly the same form as e.g. "That after the main course, there will be served dessert." In this, the verb *served* services both nouns, but with implied difference in tense, and with the desiderative applicable only to the second subject. In full the sentence is "(would that) after the main course (has been served), there will be served dessert". Transferring this to Job, we read:

> (Would that) after my body [or skin] (has been נקף),
>
> there will be נפף this.

There must be a strong presumption that the verb implies some form of restoration or reconstitution after God's hostile activities have ceased or the last trump has sounded. זאת, *this*, which Job is so keen to see נקף, is the code-name which he gave to his disasters in 12:9 and 17:8.

Although נקף with the sense of going around occurs twice elsewhere in the Book of Job (1:5 and 19:6), and in the alternative sense of striking off, or harvesting, only in the first Isaiah (10:34 [and the noun in 17:6 & 24:13]), almost all commentators see the latter as the meaning here, and relate it to the stripping of Job's skin or body, thereby driving themselves into a wall of contradiction with מבשרי in the next line. If anything it is the repair of Job's skin (making it the sole authentic reference to skin disease in the Dialogue in contradiction of what I wrote on pp. 119 and 131) to which the phrase refers. Let us examine the alternatives.

In the Qal conjugation נקף means go around in preordained order (Isa. 29:1 - *Let the feasts go around*). In the Hiph`il it commonly means to surround, or to make rounded, but in Job 1:5 it means either complete a circuit or, more likely, come around in due order[18]. There is therefore in both conjugations a sense of returning or recycling which has something in common both with redemption and resurrection. The unique Pi`el form in this verse ought to be related to the Qal sense of the verb, either intensified or made causative. It is perfectly consistent with Hebrew usage for the verb to have the sense *bring back, bring round again*. As this is the sense which best fits the context, this speculation will be accepted here to yield:

> *And that after my body, this might be restored*

The remainder of the passage provides little difficulty, but emphatic confirmation of the correctness of this reading. V.27 amplifies Job's desire to see God *in my flesh* by asserting that he seeks this vision with his own physical organs of sight and, with the second reduplicated "I" of the passage, himself and no other. On the assumption that the occupation of the Land of Judah by Sennacherib is the background of the Book of Job, I take this emphasis on Job himself rather than a זר - a stranger or foreign foe (see 15:19 and comment on it on pp. 145f) as stipulating the restoration of sovereignty as part of Job's plea.

It is the final line of the triplet verse which provides decisive confirmation of the penetration of the מי־יתן of v.23 through the whole of vv. 25, 26 and 27. *(For this) do my reins perish in my bosom* completes a frame within which all the rest is comprehended.

6. The Stone of Darkness, 28:3,4

a) Chapter 28 in general

The reader comes upon Chapter 28 of the Book of Job as upon an enchanted grove in the heart of a wild and hostile jungle. Magically, the passions and problems of Job, the abrasive personalities of the comforters, vanish. All the fret and tumult ceases and an uncanny detachment supervenes. Here in this one chapter is a true example of the mood and form of Wisdom Literature, the *genre* to which the whole book has frequently and unwisely been assigned. It is ironic that the same authors who place Job most firmly in the Wisdom tradition often deny the authenticity of this chapter. Even more ironic is the manifest message of the chapter, that man's search for Wisdom is foredoomed to failure.

Chapter 28 is a formal and regular poem in three stanzas on the theme:
> *Wisdom, where shall she be found?*
> *And where is the place of Understanding?*

The poem poses a real problem in deciding its proper place in the book. Is it, as its position indicates, a part of Job's monologue? Is it an intermezzo, the author's commentary? Is it an interpolation, a wonderful comment by someone else on what has transpired? Or an independent poem by the same author which has somehow been bound with this? Is it perhaps an imitation of a Greek dramatic chorus, evidence of dependence of this work on Greek tragedy?

I believe it is possible to rule out the idea that the chapter is by another hand than that of the author of the Book of Job. The fact that there is one phrase בני־שחץ, which occurs only in this chapter and in Job 41:26, but nowhere else in the Bible, and another תחת־כל־השמים which is found only elsewhere in Job, and in Deuteronomy and Daniel, are powerful witness against the suggestion of a pastiche. The link between 28:28 and Job 1:1 also cannot be accidental. Indeed, perhaps in some early proof version of the drama, the author intended to conclude the whole book with that symmetrical balancing of the opening announcement.

It should pass without question that only if there is incontrovertible evidence to be adduced that the speech is not an utterance by Job in its correct sequence, should any of the alternatives be given serious consideration. Neither the formality, nor the tranquillity of the chapter, nor the fact that אדני, The Lord, is found nowhere else in Job, neither alone nor together, constitute such evidence. This must be looked for in the sense of the chapter, and whether Job could or could not reasonably have spoken it. The position in which the chapter has been placed suggests it is to be considered the continuation and conclusion of Chapter 27. Each of Chaps. 27 and 29 is introduced with a phrase indicating Job as the speaker. We have, I trust, disposed of the idea that Chapter 27 is not authentically Job's in Chapter IX above. It is a part of Job's final monologue. Chapter 28 follows from 27 with only the conjunction כי. If there is a continuity here, it is apparent that the monologue has modulated into soliloquy.

How does the chapter fit into the system of thought and action which underlies Job's character as we know it? It is apparent from the various exchanges which have taken place between Job and the comforters that they all, including Job, set great store by Wisdom. Job resents the pretensions to wisdom of his erstwhile friends, their smug delivery of advice on the nature of man's relations with God and the conduct needed to survive within this framework. His resentment reaches a climax in Chapter 26. But so far Job's own position has appeared to lack logic. The wicked prosper and only their descendants suffer for it; they themselves feel their position only at the last moment. Those who adhere to God - His children - are singled out for ceaseless scrutiny and punishment, and even perfect or near-perfect innocence does not serve as a shield. God is capricious and even actively malign towards those who obey Him. Yet Job maintains both his integrity and his loyalty to his Persecutor. How can he defend, even to himself, this course as being the path of wisdom?

Chapters 27 and 28 together answer this question in perhaps the only way possible, by expressing *a priori* certainty that transcends, and boldly proposes always to transcend, every item of contrary evidence. They insist, in fact, on the superiority of intuitive knowledge (27:2-6) and revealed knowledge (28:28) to Wisdom and Understanding. The process which begins with the stubborn certitude of the first verse of Chap. 27 leads inexorably to the assertion of undiluted faith in the last verse of Chap. 28. The application of observation, analysis, debate, mental or physical energy in whatever form to the central problem of existence is futile. Wisdom cannot be found or even located; only received. Something is going on beyond our powers of comprehension, in a dimension we cannot negotiate. Therefore we must accept the guidance of the One Being Who can comprehend. Cf. Koheleth:

> *Fear God and keep His commandments,*
> *For that is the whole of man* Ecc 12:14.

This is the philosophy by which Job lived before his trial - Godfearing and shunning evil. He may no longer be תם וישר, *simple and straight*, for now he is experienced and broken, but as he emerges from despair, anger and grief, he reasserts that part of his character over which he has retained control. He will continue to fear God and avoid evil: *To my righteousness I cling and will not let it go. My heart shall not reproach me all the days of my life* (27:6). Though all has changed around him, nothing essential has changed within. Job was not righteous from fear, greed for reward, or hunger for human approbation, but out of an indelible passion for righteousness. This chapter, together with 27:2-6 of which it is an exposition, was necessary to establish this, to show us his soul, to demonstrate that God really had won His "wager" with Himself, and to explain to future generations the true meaning of love of God.

b) Verses 7 and 8

Chapter 28 differs from the rest of the Book of Job in that it conveys the strongest impression that it is constructed not as an evolved discourse in a relatively amorphous poetic form, but as a strictly regular and formal poem. The plan of the poem is of three stanzas or cantos, punctuated by a refrain. However, in its present form the poem's divisions are of unequal length, the first containing twenty-four lines in eleven verses; the second sixteen lines in eight verses, and the third nineteen lines in nine verses.

The three stanzas deal with three different aspects of the one theme, expressed in the refrain *Where shall Wisdom be found? And what is the place of Understanding?* With the exception of vv. 7 and 8, the first stanza shows how human exploration of the earth, its surface and its depths, has been comprehensive and exhaustive. It describes the ceaseless activities of human beings in exploring the recesses of the earth in quest of treasure, safety or knowledge, and how this has given every opportunity for locating the "place" of all the various components of the earth. It is a remarkable summary of the technological achievements of the Iron Age. Stanza II asserts that Wisdom is not to be found by or during these activities, nor seen by the animal kingdom, nor is there anything of equivalent value with which it may be bought or for which it may be bartered. Stanza III answers the thematic question by asserting that God alone knows the location and nature of Wisdom and that He gave of it but one guiding principle to Man:

> *The fear of the Lord, that is wisdom[19],*
> *And the avoidance of evil is understanding.*

Vv. 7 & 8, located in the heart of the first stanza, read:

> *That pathway the hawk knows not,*
> *Nor has the falcon's eye beheld it;*
> *Conquerors (or sons of pride) have not trodden it down.*
> *Nor the mighty (or the lion) attained to[20] it.*

It seems almost certain that the pathway to which this verse refers is the way to Wisdom. Indeed, v.21, *Seeing it (Understanding) is hid from the eyes of all the living and concealed from the birds of the air*, has only this verse to justify it. But if this is so, and the pathway is that to Wisdom and Understanding, the verses are unquestionably misplaced thematically in the first stanza and belong in the second. There has been no mention of the pathway to Wisdom before v.7, and therefore this rational solution can hardly be applied if the verses are allowed to remain in their present place. If the pathway is not that to Wisdom, only the most far-fetched alternatives remain - that it is the path of the shaft of the mine supposedly described in v.4 is the favoured, but miserably inappropriate solution (JPS). Others (e.g. H) suggest the way to subterranean mines of gems.

In the first stanza the verses are doubly out of place, for they contradict the whole theme, which is the comprehensiveness of human exploration and the demonstration that there is no (physical) hiding place on earth with which man is unacquainted. We have to conclude (see translation of entire chapter) that vv. 7 and 8 actually belong after the present verse 12. This will be the only assumption of displacement of verses made in the whole translation of the book. It reduces the first stanza by two verses and four lines, and correspondingly increases the second.

c) Verses 3 and 4

The poetic structure of this chapter is uniformly of couplets, almost all of the type termed by Lowth[21] synonymous parallel. That is, the second line of the couplet repeats, in variant, the idea expressed in the first. There is a little, but only a little latitude taken with this form. vv. 10 & 11, *He hews out conduits in the rocks, And all that is precious his eye sees. He dams the rivers from weeping*[23], *And what was concealed, he brings to light*, form a combination of which the parallel form is not aabb but abab, with the a lines in antithetical parallel. Verse 22, *Abaddon and Death declare "With our ears we have heard its fame"*, has no element of parallel, while v.5, *The earth, from her comes bread: but her subterrain is raked over like a fire*, defies simple classification. Otherwise all the verses, apart from those about to be discussed, are examples of the purest and simplest - the most naif - form of Biblical verse. Only vv. 3 and 4 (and the concluding v.28) contain more than two lines.

The evidence of the nature of the poem itself tends to support the conclusion that the major anomalies of arrangement - the existence of the two tristichoi, vv. 3 and 4, and the discrepancies in the lengths of the stanzas - are flaws which have developed during the transmission of the work, and not irregularities in the original composition. The poem bears every hallmark of a work composed within the straight-jacket of a rigid form, like the acrostics of Lamentations and some Psalms, but fails to fulfill our expectations of it because of these anomalies. Additionally, the anomalies introduce definable deformities into the poem apart from those of structure.

We have discussed the incongruity of sense between vv. 7 & 8 and the first stanza. The two tristichoi, 3 and 4, read as such, not only disappoint our expectations of parallelism, the essence of Hebrew poetry, but as tristichoi, they are incomprehensible. The absence of proper parallel in certain verses of Hebrew poetry is, of course, no anomaly in itself; there are scores of verses in the Book of Job which have no trace of parallel. But when we have a poem of twenty-nine verses of which every other is a couplet and almost every other exhibits the simplest form of parallel, the anomaly becomes a real one, as if we were reading a rhymed poem and encountered a verse without rhyme. We should suspect a printing error, as we are entitled to do here. The "restoration" of vv. 3 and 4 into three couplets was first suggested by D. Yellin[24], but he failed to decipher the verses successfully.

A has justly remarked that "everyone is reduced to despair by verse 4, and, comparing several versions, such as AV, RSV, NEB, it is hard to believe that they all had the same Hebrew text in front of them." In fact the same or deeper obscurity applies to the third line of verse 3, which is placed at the head of this section. The much-battered Hebrew text of the two verses is:

3. קץ שׂם לחשׁך   ולכל־תכלית הוא חוקר   אבן אפל וצלמות

4. פרץ נחל מעם־גר   הנשׁכחים מני־רגל   דלו מאנושׁ נעו

The first two stichoi make a perfectly satisfactory and self-contained parallel pair, testifying to the unremitting exploration of the earth by man:

> An end He (man) *puts to darkness*
> And he explores to every frontier.

The third line is a great mystery - *The stone of thick darkness and the shadow of death*[25]. There is just no way in which this can be made to connect, as an integral part of the same verse - its conclusion, with lines a and b. G is, I think, the only translator who has come near to understanding the stich itself, but even he missed the significance of the image, representing it as a situation to which men never come, rather than one to which, despite its remoteness and danger, men nevertheless are witness. Thus he translated it in such a way as to allow the two verses to testify against the theme of the first stanza rather than for it[26].

The expression אפל וצלמות is foreshadowed in the Book of Job twice in Chapter 10, vv. 21 and 22 (q.v.). These verses assert that the Underworld is אפל וצלמות. Mutatis mutandis, אפל וצלמות is the Underworld. The line therefore says *The stone of the Underworld*, and means the one word *Lava*.

If we join this line to 4a, constructing the second of the three distichoi, we find that the first two words of that line (a verb apparently without hope of a subject and an evidently inappropriate object) describe precisely and accurately what lava does, פרץ נחל - it *erupts a stream*, and it is now apparent that the third line of v.3 belongs with the first of v.4, for each is required to make sense of the other. Now we are able to discard all the dubious secondary meanings of נחל which have been invoked to decipher the expression. There is just one form of stone which does what a נחל does - flows in an intermittent torrent אבן אפל וצלמות - lava.

מעם־גר, the remainder of the stich, is not an easy phrase, but it is of help in translating it to keep in mind what the author is trying to establish in this stanza - the ubiquity of man, the inquisitive witness. The word מעם, a combination of "from" and "with", means *from with* or *beside*. The lava, the text claims, bursts in a stream beside a גר. גר spelt with a qames is the participle of גור, to sojourn, and refers, in the place where he is staying at the time, to one who wanders from place to place, or who is a stranger. It is most often used in a verbal sense, often in combination with the noun גר with Sere, but can also be employed, as here, as a substantive. Vg catches the sense of גר here with *wandering people - populo peregrinante*. So restless a creature is he, even a volcanic eruption is likely to be witnessed by some displaced man.

The last two lines of v.4 must now be assumed to form a verse of their own. The first line is deficient of a verb, and the second contains two, דלל, *to be brought low, to languish*, and נעו (see the pathetic Lam 4:14,15) *to wander, to totter*, etc. If not physically, but functionally, we attach the first verb to line a, we obtain a simple, relevant, and satisfactorily parallel reading with:

> The (or these) forgotten ones, off the beaten track
> They languish. They wander away from humankind.

This again attests to the ubiquity of human beings. Who the fogotten ones are intended to be is uncertain. Most likely it refers back to the גר, taken in a collective sense.

The restoration of vv.3 and 4 into three couplets and the displacement of vv.7 and 8 to a probably original position in the second stanza now leaves us with twenty lines in ten vv. in each of the first two stanzas, and nineteen lines in nine vv. in the third. This is the maximum regularity which can be imposed upon fifty nine lines. The last triplet, like the rhymed couplets which end scenes in Shakespeare's early plays, or the "needless Alexandrine" which "ends the song"[27], is an authentic conventional method of conclusion.

Notes Chapter 8

1. T. is a determined exception to this general rule, stating than the anger "of the master" kills the fool and the jealousy "of creatures" slays the simpleton. This over-specification has no good foundation.

2. Encyclopaedia Judaica, XIV, 81f & V, 1524.

3. Pritch. p. 250, n. 27 (Quoting Edgerton & Wilson).

4. *Berakoth* 5a.

5. A.S. Yahuda, JQR 15 (1902-3), 702, 703.

6. A.R. Millard, "What has no Taste?" (Job 6:6). UF 1 1969, 210.

7. G., p. 147, quotes Ps. 139:16 and Mal. 2:15 as evidence that the phrase does have this meaning in late Biblical Hebrew. In Ps. 139 the phrase occurs ולא אחד בהם, meaning *While (yet) there was none of them (my days)*. There is no conceivable analogy with "no one". In Malachi, the phrase לא אחד is followed immediately by עשה giving *Not one who does*. Thus in neither case does the negated word אחד functions as a true indefinite pronoun, giving warrant for treating the phrase as the absolute *no one*. Even modern Hebrew cannot tolerate such a crudity, and *no one* is אף אחד.

8. NJPSV.

9. C. (p. 342, n.4b) quotes G.R. Driver (VT Supp 3 [1955] 77) as finding "a different root פרר with cognates in Arab. and Syr.; hence NEB You banish the fear of God from your mind".

10. See Ges. #107 (a) (1). Job 6:23 is an example.

11. Even the masculine form כסל nowhere certainly has this meaning. Job 8:14 will remain obscure until the word יקוש is successfully deciphered, and in Job 31:24 אם־שמתי זהב כסלי neither "If I have made gold my (source of) confidence..." nor "If I have placed my confidence in gold..." exactly translates the Hebrew, but the latter seems closer.

12. Tanakh, JPS (Cited on Page 79, n. 12).

13. The waw of 19:25a has been variously treated. With sure artistic instinct, Handel simply omitted it from his *aria*. P. and H. follow suit. The AV translated it *for*, as does R., although this is not an accepted meaning for the particle. The alternative favoured by both JPS translations, by NEB and by D&G is *but* which is a normal meaning of waw, while T-S has chosen *yet*. I have found only two versions which translate the word at its most common value *and*, and these are Eduard Konig's *Das Buch Hiob*, 1929, p. 192, and D. Samuel Cox, (*A Commentary on the Book of Job*, Kegan Paul & Co., London, 1880). This latter is a curiosity in that Cox treats vv. 25-27 as the text which Job wishes engraved in stone. Were it not for the intrusive ואני, which Cox perforce disregards. this would be a perfectly proper speculation.

14. The exceptions are Isa. 48:8 and Job 30:23.

15. D&G, NEB, NJPSV all translate the term Vindicator, though equating the term with God. P., who also supplies this word, understands the term as applying to a human third party – an idea which dates from Ibn Ezra. M. has *witness*. There is however nothing in common between the function of a go'el is never in any sense an intermediary; he acts himself, but in the interests of another.

16. There seems a close relationship between this passage of Job and Isa. 30:8 in which the expression יום אחרון appears:

Now come, write it upon a tablet;
Inscribe it for them in a book,
And let it be until the last day
As a witness for ever.

Isa 30. is also related to the description of *Behemoth* in Chap. 40 of Job (see Chap. 5 *supra*).

17. The secondary נקף (I in BDB occurs as a verb only once, in relation to the thickets of the forest (Isa. 10:34), and its meaning there is fairly surely *prune*. The derived noun certainly refers to the <u>harvesting</u> of olives, and as this is done by striking the tree, the idea has been accepted that it means to <u>strike (off)</u>. As both the thinning of vegetation, and the harvesting of fruit are seasonal activities, which return in regular succession, it is not possible to be sure that there are actually two quite different roots here and not two distinct applications of the one.

18. Job 1:5 describes Job's actions כי הקיפו ימי המשתה. It then states *thus did Job on each of the days*. The two expressions fit together only on the assumption that the first means *when (or as) the days of feasting came around*. There is on the other hand a clear contradiction between them if הקיפו is understood as signifying the end of a complete round of feasting. This incompatibility is obscured in most versions because of an insistence upon translating כל־הימים *regularly, always*, or in other ways which divorce the <u>days</u> of that phrase from the <u>days</u> of feasting. Of the translators who employ this idiomatic rendering of the phrase, G. seems to be the only one who feels it needs defending. But this examples, Gen. 43:9, 44:32; Deut. 4:40; II Chron 7:16, 10:7, 12:15, 21:7, all but one (v.i.) illustrate the use of the term to mean *for all of the time*, i.e. as a phrase of <u>duration</u>, not of repetition.

The idiom כל־הימים occurs thirty-seven times in the Bible apart from Job 1:5, and is <u>without doubt</u> a measure of duration on all of these occasions with the possible exceptions of II Kings 13:3 and II Chron 12:15. The latter, however, is a variant of I Kings 14:30 where the phrase <u>is</u> a measure of duration (*There was war... continuously*). The II Chron passage pluralises the war, leaving open a possibility that the meaning is <u>repeatedly</u> rather than <u>continuously</u>. In II Kings 13:3, employing the imperfect consecutive, God delivered them into the hand of Hazael כל־הימים, which certainly could be understood grammatically as <u>repeatedly</u>, but the immediate and subsequent context strongly suggests <u>permanently</u>, a continuing and unremitting subjugation, as the true intent of the phrase. Hazael was not of a character to let his victims loose to fight another day.

There is no way in which כל־הימים in Job 1:5 can be interpreted as an adverbial phrase of duration. Job's actions form a ritual sequence strictly limited in time. He sent and sanctified his children, rose early and offered burnt-offerings, one for each of them. The phrase <u>must</u> therefore imply repetition. Thus it is non-idiomatic, and should be translated literally as *all the days*. As the surrounding verses repeatedly refer to and emphasise the words <u>day</u> and <u>days</u>, and the verse itself speaks of ימי המשתה <u>the days of feasting</u>, there should be no question but that these are those same days (Duhm, D&G).

19. The question asked is *Where shall החכמה be found?* The Lord's message refers to חכמה without the article. G. (Special Note 24) has an excellent discussion of the significance of this distinction. החכמה perhaps is the sum total of natural philosophy,

while חכמה is the practical wisdom appropriate for mankind. The distinction has been preserved in comment and translation by writing wisdom with upper or lower case <u>Ws.</u>

20. The Hebrew says that the שחל has not עדה עליו. עדה is traditionally assumed to mean <u>advanced</u>, but this does not fit very well, neither with the context nor the preposition על. It is possible that the verb is related to the noun עד, <u>booty</u>, and means "plundered".

21. Bishop R. Lowth, <u>Praelectionis de sacra poesi Hebraeorum,</u> Oxford, <u>1753</u>, Lecture 19.

22. יארים, originally streams of the Nile. Thence canals and watercourses. In view of the context here, most probably something like the Shiloam tunnel which carried water from outside Jerusalem to within its walls is to be visualised. A <u>tunnel</u>, which allows visualisation of the interior of the earth, is more appropriate than a <u>channel</u> which does no more than graze its surface.

23. מבכי נהרות חבש. The words here are strangely chosen. Literally it is *He binds the rivers from weeping*, and so perforce, I have translated. The only other example of the Pi'el חבש (Ps. 147:3) means to <u>Bind up</u> (a wound), as does the Qal in Job 5:18. In Job 34:17 the Qal seems to have a much stronger meaning. <u>Weeping</u> does not seem an appropriate word for rivers. LXX speaks of *interrupting the whirlpools of the rivers,* while Vg. skirts the subject skilfully. The intention nevertheless seems clear. Blocking the flow of rivers, man is able to inspect their previously concealed beds.

24. David Yellin, <u>Higre Miqra</u> – Iyyob, 1927.

25. The modern fashion for translating צלמות as <u>darkness</u>, or in some way other than <u>The Shadow of Death</u> is hard to defend. The MT vocalization of every example of the word supports the traditional poetic rendering and refutes the modern variant. Those who reject tradition here are also rejecting the MT.

26. Gordis (BJ) p. 300ff translates אבן אפל וצלמות as *The lava, dark and pitch-black*, not apparently appreciating (a) that the whole phrase is required to identify the stone as lava; (b) that אפל and צלמות retain their substantive grammatical forms and functions in the line; (c) that black is not the colour of lava, neither while flowing nor when solidified; (d) that neither word אפל nor צלמות can function as a colour, not even black. G. follows Yellin in rejecting the Hebrew גר in favour of the Arabic jawra[tun], a deep hole, to produce *cleaves a channel from the crater*, and then translates the remainder in order to achieve the <u>non</u>-observability of this phenomenon *never trodden by human foot, bereft even of wandering men*. In addition to the reversal of sense which this produces, this version is ruled out by the plural forms דלו and נעו, which demand הנשכחים for their subject, not גר.

27.   Alexander Pope *An Essay on Criticism, 1711.*

IX
Lexicographical Anomalies

In the course of these essays, I have had occasion to attack as illegitimate the practice of assigning anomalous meanings to well-known Biblical Hebrew words where the normal and established meanings do not lead to senses for the text which correspond to the translator's view of what is proper. In this chapter I shall be doing what is almost, but not quite, the same thing - deducing from incompatibilities of sense anomalous meanings for well-known Hebrew words. However, in the examples which follow, the variations in meaning which I shall suggest will apply not just to the word in the special context of a passage in the Book of Job, but to it in all its contexts throughout the Bible. That is to say that I shall postulate that the accepted meaning as found in lexicons, translations and commentaries of the Bible as a whole is wrong.

גב

In the Bible, wherever we encounter the word "back" in an unmistakable context, it is גו, vocalized either with *patah* or *seri*. In Modern Hebrew this word has all but disappeared, and the principal word for "back" is גב with *patah*. We shall here examine the Biblical usage of the latter word, and show how its meaning has become distorted until it has usurped the sense of its weaker brother, גו.

According to BDB, and all concordances and dictionaries of the Bible, the root of גב is גבב, meaning "to be curved, convex, or hollowed out". This is conceived as being related to the Aramaic גבבא, "a hill", and to Arabic, Aramaic, Ethiopic and Assyrian words, all meaning "cistern". However the root remains conjectural, for there is no other trace of a Hebrew verb גבב with that or any meaning, and hills are more often high than curved, and only in the artificial Abu Simbel mound, hollowed out. However, in appropriate combinations, גב is always spelled with a *dagesh* in the ב, apparently confirming the hypothetical root.

Possibly the only example of the word גב in the Bible where its meaning is unambiguous is in Lev 14:9, where the phrase גבת עיניו assuredly means "his eyebrows". But whether this phrase derived from the fact that the eyebrows curve or arch, or from the fact that they are set above the eyes, might be debated for ever.

In all, the word גב occurs thirteen times in the Bible, but in only five of its books. Of these no fewer than seven are in Ezekiel and three in Job, leaving one each for Leviticus, I Kings and Psalm 129.

In I Kings 7:33, in the description of the molten sea of the Temple of Solomon, גבs are mentioned as parts of the brass wheels supporting the "bases". These are described as like chariot wheels. The usual well-justified assumption is that the גב is the rim or the felloe of the wheel. The other parts named and described are the axle-trees, the hubs and the spokes.

In Psalm 129:3 the dramatic complaint is voiced:

The ploughmen ploughed upon my גב. They made long their furrows.

It is largely from this verse that the idea derives that גב means back.

The Ezekiel passages belong in three groups - 16:24, 31 and 39; 1:18, 18 and 10:12; and 43:13.

The last of these relates to the vision of a new temple, and specifically to the dimensions of the altar. It comes in the phrase *the גב of the altar*, and the most probable interpretation, as well as I can deduce, is the height. JPS translates "The base of the altar". NJPSV gives "height", but claims a contradictory literal meaning, "bulge". LXX has "height", while Vg inexplicably has *fossa* - "a trench".

In NEB the translation is so dissimilar from the Hebrew that it is not possible to deduce which word corresponds to גב. RV sees the phrase as meaning "the higher place of the altar". None of these versions seems to relate the word to its alleged root, and most seem to suggest an origin in גבה, "to be high, exalted", which is a proper Biblical Hebrew verb. If this is correct then the *dagesh* in the ב is suspect. The references to גב in Ezekiel Chapter 16 are in the context of the prophet's favourite assault on his countrymen the accusation that they go a-whoring after false gods.

You have built yourself your גב at the head of every street,

And made your רמה in every road

is v.31, while v.24 is a slight contraction of this sentence, and v.39 declares:

I shall throw down your גב and break your רמה.

The word used here for *throw down* is הרס, a very strong word, used for altars, cities, and even countries.

In Ezekiel Chapter 16 it is quite certain that the גב is some form of ceremonial object for the worship of deviant deities, and its consistent parallel with רמה (high place) strongly suggests that it is some form of lofty construction, a phallic pillar or similar. BDB essays "mound". Clearly, the גב is something which must be built, and having been built, may be overthrown. A mound does not quite meet this specification. Again it seems that the appropriate root for the word in these passages is גבה rather than גבב.

As a bridge to the next passage, we require to examine Isaiah 57:7,8. Here also a prophet is inveighing against the metaphorical whoredom of the people.

Upon a high and lofty mountain hast thou set thy bed; Thither also wentest thou up to offer sacrifice. And behind the doors and the posts hast thou set up thy זכרון.

The resemblance between this last line and Ezekiel's complaints in Chapter 16 is obvious.

Job 13:12, in an attack by Job on the qualifications of his friends to speak on God's behalf, runs:

Your זכרון *are figures of ash; Like* אב *of clay are your* גב.

This strange insult, and insult it surely is, cannot possibly be comprehended without reference to both Ezek 16 and Isa 57, in which גב and זכרון are used in identical contexts, in verses exhibiting a close parallel between them, and serving the same function in both verses. That is the real parallelism in Job reflects what we shall call a *synthetic parallelism* between the lines of the two prophets, who were contemporaries. Both words, גב and זכרון, unmistakably signify objects of deviant worship, the first as we have noted, a lofty symbol erected in the open air, the second apparently a household image - some pagan equivalent of the Jewish *mezzuzah*, a sinister reminder or remembrance. The Job verse draws attention to the artefactual nature of the objects of worship of his pagan friends, which leaves them wholly unprepared for any confrontation with the living Lord of the Universe (see the preceding v. 13:11). These גבs, therefore, are identical with those of Ezekiel 16.

These are the first two uses of the word in Job. The third is very conjectural. The wicked man *runs at Him (God) full tilt* בעבי גבי מגניו. The accepted translation of this opaque phrase has been *with the thick bosses of his bucklers*, giving to גב the meaning "boss" - the rounded protruberance sometimes to be found in the centre of a shield. There is in the ancient world one illustration of a "thickly-bossed" shield - a relief from the palace of Ashurnasirpal II (883-859 B.C.E.) showing such a shield affixed to the *rear* of war-chariots[1]. All other illustrations show only singly-bossed shields.

The translation is very improbable. עבי, if related to density, is a noun "thickness", not an adjective. One man, wicked or otherwise, carried only one shield, and a shield, bossed or otherwise, is a defensive, not an offensive weapon. It is difficult indeed to imagine any writer selecting thickly-bossed shields as the only weapons to be assigned to an assailant in the description of such an attack. The poet would surely either have illustrated his metaphor with genuine weapons of assault, or with some imaginative figure.

We might essay (treating עבי as "beams" [cf. I Kings 7:6 and Ezek 41:25]) *with the battering-rams of his siege-engines*, i.e. "his tall ones of shields", but this seems very farfetched. Alternatively, we might understand a גב מגן to be a form cognate with איש מגן which simply means a warrior, giving *in the density of his guardian idols*, again according גב the meaning of some object of deviant worship.

This leaves only the repeated use of the word in the description by Ezekiel of the extraordinary vision of the fourfaced creatures with which his prophetic career commenced, and which repeated itself more or less exactly at a later time as described in Chapter 102.

The relevant portion of the JPS reading of Ezek 1:15-20 is the following:

> *Now as I beheld the living creatures, behold one wheel at the bottom hard by the living creatures at the four faces thereof. The appearance of the wheels and their work was like unto the colour of beryl and the four had one likeness; and their appearance and their work were as it were a wheel within a wheel...As for* גביהן, *they were high and they were dreadful; and they four had* גבתם *full of eyes round about. And when the living creatures went, the wheels went hard by them; and when the living creatures were lifted up from the bottom, the wheels were lifted up.*

At the second appearance there is some variation in the description. 10:12 reads:

> *and their whole body* and* גבהם, *and their hands and their wings, and the wheels were full of eyes round about, even the wheels that they four had.*

*בשרם, correctly *their flesh.*

In this vision, Ezekiel twice confirms that this is the same conglomerate creature which he described earlier in Chap. 1.

In the first of these recitals, JPS translates the word גב as "rings", and in the second as "backs", but there can be no real doubt that the same translation must be applied to both citations. LXX treats all גבs in both passages as "backs", but Vg, like JPS, distinguishes the two passages, and indeed what appear to be the masculine and feminine forms of גב in 1:18, one from the other. Vg reads for this verse:

Statura quoque erat rotis et altitudo et horribilis aspectus Et totum corpus plenum oculis in cicuiti ipsarum quattuor.

In this version it is clear that גבהם is being read as their body, but as there is no plural noun in the first Latin stich we cannot tell if the translator considered *statura* (height) or *rotis* (wheel) to be the equivalent of גב. In 10:12 there is no ambiguity, and גבהם is translated *colla*, their *necks*. NJPSV and the Jerusalem Bible treats the first set of גבs as "rims", and the second as "backs". The prophet participated in this apparent confusion. There are three different forms for the three uses of what seem to be the same word. גביהן and גבהם give different genders to the owners of the גבs, while גבתם assigns to the word itself a feminine plural form. To complete the picture, I Kings employs the plene spelling גביהם.

Clearly Vg would have no truck with "back" as a translattion of a word which meant a part of the anatomical equipment of a creature with four faces pointing either in the four directions of the compass, or to the right and the left (1:10). Such creatures can have no backs! We may, I think, also rule out JPS's "rings", for their introduction as fresh features is inadequate, and יראה להם "they were fearsome" is impossible as a description of rings. Much the same objection applies to *rims*. The word appears in the middle of a description of wheels, so that גב appears here, as in I Kings, to signify some part of a wheel, but *Their rims were tall and frightening, for the rims of all four were covered with eyes* is not true to the Hebrew in that "for" is no translation of <u>waw</u>, nor can one speak of rims as "high"; the appropriate word is "thick". The גבs of 10:12, like those of 1:18, are "covered with eyes". I find it inconceivable that the words mean different things in the two contexts - parts of wheels in one and parts of bodies in the second, and the phrasing *their flesh and their* גבs *and their hands and their wings and the wheels* cries out that the גב is part of the creature and the wheel is not.

The possibilities are, I suggest, the *torso* - the *totum corpus* of Vg's rendition of 1:18b - the *head* or *face*, and Vg's *neck*. Of these, only the torso - the height and stretch of the body, can be related to any other use of the word, or to either of the possible roots. The same applies to the description *They were high (or tall) and they were fearsome*. The torso is as appropriate as the back for Ps 129, and possibly also for the pillars or statues of Ezek 16 and Job 13:12.

There are, I suggest, good reasons also for suspecting that there are two distinct words, גב and גבה. Although there seems little consistency in the use of gender in Ezekiel's description of his vision, the fact that the description of גביהן is succeeded in the same sentence by the description of גבתם suggests that the latter are the גבות of the גבים of the חיות.

From this examination, it appears that every example of the use of the word גב may be related to the root גבה with one exception, the description of the sea of brass in I Kings 7:33. Here there is no doubt that the word signifies some part of a wheel, and almost certainly the rim or a part of it - an arc. It is probable that the phrase גבת עינים in Leviticus is of the same derivation as this - the arch of the eye. It is certain that in Ezekiel, Chapter 16 the word implies some tall structure used for pagan worship, and so is derived from גבה, and I believe it is certain that Job 13:12 has the same meaning and derivation. Job 15:26 cannot be deciphered with any confidence. In Ps 129 a derivation from גבה is more probable than from גבב, while in Ezek 43:13 there is no certainty of meaning, but again the balance of probabilities favours something to do with height - גבה. In Ezek 1:18,18 and 10:12, derivation from גבה seems most plausible.

The fact that there are two examples of the construct feminine form and three of the masculine suggests that there may be two distinct words involved - גב and גבה.

אפיק

The root of this word אפק is a verb found only in the Hithpa'el, meaning to compel or restrain oneself, to refrain. It is conjectured that the root meaning is "to be strong" or "to hold". The noun אפיק occurs nineteen times in the Hebrew Bible, of which four are in the Book of Job, seven in Ezekiel, two in Joel, three in three different Psalms, and one each in II Samuel and the Song of Songs.

BDB defines it as a "channel (as holding, confining waters; poetic)". In Job 12:21, where this meaning is patently inapplicable, it is suggested that the meaning is "the strong".

It is striking that in the majority of uses of the word outside the Books of Job and Ezekiel it is coupled with the word מים, *water*, or its equivalent, while in all usages but three of the four in Job, some connection with water is plausible or certain.

The seven exmples of the word in Ezekiel all bear a generic resemblance to one another, and in most cases occur in quadriliteral parallel with mountains, hills and valleys. Of especial interest are 31:12, 32:6, 34:13 and 35:8:

Upon the mountains and in all the valleys his branches are fallen, and his boughs lie broken in all אפיק הארץ. 31:12

I will lay thy flesh upon the mountains And fill the valleys with thy foulness. I will also water with thy blood the land wherein thou swimmest, even to the mountains; And the אפיקם shall be full of thee. 32:6

And I will fill his mountains with his slain; in thy hills and in thy valleys and in all thy אפיקם shall they fall that are slain with the sword. 35:8

In each of these quotations, in its own way, there is a suggestion, almost fully explicit in 34:13-18, that אפיקים do not represent running waters or their river-beds, but standing accumulations of water. Indeed, if we accept that settled waters in 34:18 does refer to the אפיקים of 34:13, as most assuredly the

> *I will bring them out from the peoples, and gather them from the countries, and will bring them to their own land; and I will feed them upon the mountains of Israel, by the* אפיקים *and in all the habitable places of the country. I will feed them in a good pasture, and upon the high mountains of Israel shall their fold be; there shall they lie down in a good fold, and in a fat pasture shall they feed upon the mountains of Israel.....Seemeth it a small thing unto you to have fed upon the good pasture, but ye must tread down with your feet the residue of your pasture? and to have drunk of the settled waters, but ye must foul the residue with your feet?* 34:13-18

good pasture of 34:18 refers to the good pasture of 34:14, then there is no alternative but to understand these אפיקים as lakes, water-holes, pools, etc. There is strong confirmation of this meaning in Joel 1:20, P. 42:2, and Song of Songs 5:12. The first two of these are almost identical - *As the hart panteth after* אפיקי מים (Ps 42:2) and *The beasts of the field pant unto Thee, for all the* אפיקי מים *are dried up.* Deer and "beasts of the field" - i.e. wild beasts - drink by choice at waterholes, not running streams, and it is they, not streams, which dry up in drought times. To the poetically sensitive, the verse in the Song of Songs is conclusive: *His eyes are like doves beside* אפיקי מים, *washed with milk and fitly set..* The picture is quiescent, and it would be a poetic solecism of the first order to describe eyes as like *doves beside the brooks,* as though they exhibited nystagmus!

In II Sam 22:16 = Ps 18:16, אפיקי מים evidently means the "bed of the sea": *And* אפיקי ם *appeared, and the foundations of the world were laid bare.* There is an apparent inconsistency between this use, which carries implications of an empty watercourse or container, and the uses of the similar expression in the passages referred to above, where the water itself is the important element in the phrase.

Psalm 126:4 *Turn our captivity like* אפיקים בנגב, could equally mean streams or pools, but properly understood, Isaiah 8:7 is decisive. Isaiah says (see also p. 176)

> *Forasmuch as this people has refused The waters of Shiloah that go softly...*
> *The Lord bringeth up upon them The waters of the River, mighty and*
> *many, Even the King of Assyria and all his glory; And he shall come up*
> *over all its* אפיקם, *And go over all its banks.*

Not only is the "river" Shiloah famous largely for its principal pool - *The Pool of Shiloah* (Neh 3:15) = The Pool of Solomon, (which is why the prophet refers to its slow movement), but the image virtually precludes any other meaning than pools. Certainly streams is impossible, and beds (NJPSV) even more unlikely.

Joel 4:18 in an "end of days" prophecy uses the word in a way better adapted to moving than to still water - *All the* אפיק *of Judah will flow with (ילכו) water.* The only use of אפיק in Job which corresponds in any way with the fifteen other examples in the Bible is the first, 6:15, where אפיק נחלים is a parallel for נחל, used in the sense of a stream which runs intermittently and may be dried up when needed. The singular אפיק in construct with the plural נחלים by rights rules out the bed or channel of a river, and suggests a pool or waterhole which derives its water from several intermittent streams - *a wadi-fed water-hole.*

In 12:21 some class of men is comprehended in the term אפיקים - *Pouring contempt upon princes and undermining the morale of* אפיקם. Guessing at the meaning from context and the supposed root and the uses of the verb which are known, I prefer to essay *legions* rather than *the strong*, particularly as there are many Hebrew words available for the latter. In one sense, if a lake is an אפיק מים, then a legion or a regiment is an אפיק אנשי-מגן.

In 40:18 the mystery only deepens as Behemoth's bones are described as אפיקי נחשה (and his גרמים as like cast-iron). Some versions attempt pipes or tubes of brass, as derivatives of channel, but I feel that a solid and compact sense must be intended. The word I have used in the translation, *ingots*, suggests, as both lake and legion, something which while capable of being dispersed, is held together by internal or external means.

Job 41:7 has suffered from the fact that it has not been generally recognized that the verse still refers to Leviathan's teeth, introduced in v.6, and is not the beginning of a description of his scales. These are described in v.15, later in the chapter. Thus אפיקי מגנים is a metaphor for the whole mouthful of teeth, described in the next verse as so close together that no wind can come between them. (It is this reference to air which rules out the idea of scales which have to be impenetrable to water, but to which air is irrelevant). מגן, a shield, is an excellent metaphor for a tooth, as the shapes of the two objects are similar. As a metaphor for scales, it is equally valid, but in a functional rather than morphological sense. The chosen translation, using the term phalanx in the Greek military sense, is an admitted anachronism.

איד

The noun איד is a derivative of the root אוד, "to be curved, bent, also trans. burden, oppress" (BDB). It is defined in BDB as "distress, calamity (under which one bends)". The parenthesised explanation is unconvincing. the word is found twenty-two times in the Bible, six in the Book of Job, five each in Jeremiah and Proverbs, three in the one verse of Obadiah, and one each in II Samuel, Psalms and Ezekiel.

The dictionary definition does not fit well with the occurrence in seventeen of the twenty-two citations of the forms אודם, אידו, אידכם, אידך, אידם and אידי. These forms where the word is linked with a possessive pronoun suggest as it were a custom-made disaster for each individual, a concept which does not correspond to the use of the words "distress" and "calamity" in European languages. While "their calamity" as the subject of a sentence (the most common syntactical form) is not impossible, we should expect to find it followed not by a verb indicating the descent of the calamity, but rather by a definition of what their particular calamity was. When we speak of the arrival of some disaster with a pronominal possessive appendage, we think usually of something proper to the person concerned - merited, or in some other way inevitable, and appropriate in nature to the victim.

So in a typical sentence such as Job 21:17:

> How often is the light of the wicked put out
> That their איד comes upon them?

the most natural translation is surely "their deserts".

In 31:3: *Is there not איד for the wrongdoer?*, even with no possessive pronoun, the expectation is the more specific "retribution", and in 31:23 *For terrible to me was the איד of God"*, the even stronger "vengeance" fits well.

All three of these translations carry the sense of a boomerang, something which curves back upon itself - a far more plausible adaptation of the root sense than the idea of one "bent" under oppression.

Similar senses fit well with the three other examples in the Book of Job, although in these "calamity" is less jarring. So in 18:12, either retribution or calamity may well be described as "ready for his stumbling". In 21:30 the evil (not the evil man) may as well be reserved for the day of calamity as the day of retribution, but the latter is undoubtedly the sharper expression. In 30:12 *They cast up against me אידם ארחות* there is no way to be sure exactly what is intended.

Jer 18:17 and 46:21 again feature the expression "their day of איד", with retribution making the most suitable sense. In the second of these there is a distinct flavour of punishment in the use of the word which is made parallel with עַת פְּקֻדָּם, which seems best rendered "their time of reckoning". A sense of punishment or retribution is also applicable to Jer 48:16, while in 49:8 it is made absolutely explicit - *I bring the אֵיד of Esau upon him, the time when I shall punish him."* In Jer 49:32 again either calamity or retribution is possible, but the possessive suffix favours the latter.

In several of the uses in Proverbs it is true that calamity seems a more appropriate sense than deserts, retribution, vengeance or punishment, but in 17:5 *He that is glad at אֵיד shall not go unpunished* there is again the sense of punishment, while in 24:22 *My son, fear thou the Lord and the king, And meddle not with them that are given to change; For their אֵיד shall arise suddenly, and ruin from them both, who knows it?* the use of the genitive to yield אֵיד from rather than of strongly supports vengeance or retribution, not calamity. Indeed, this last is virtually impossible.

Ezek 35:5 and the three iterations in Obadiah 13 all refer to the behaviour of Edom towards Judah at the time of Nebuchadnezzar's destruction of the nation, and speak of this event as יוֹם אֵידָם. This could, of course, be "the day of their calamity", or "their day of calamity", but it is more in keeping with the prophetic interpretation of events, and indeed of the Israelite theory of history as a whole, to read "their day of reckoning", with the sense of when they received their due deserts from God.

The last use is II Sam 22:19 = Ps 18:19 where again "calamity" is an acceptable reading, but "my day of reckoning" is equally plausible.

נער

The verb נער is found only eleven times in the Bible, while nouns apparently derived from it occur three times, twice the feminine and once the masculine. The verb is common in NH where it means to "shake" or "stir up", and in Biblical Hebrew it has long been assumed that its meaning is to "shake out" or "shake off". The occurrences of the verb are three in Isaiah, three in Nehemiah, two in Psalms, and one each in Job, Judges and Exodus.

It is my contention that the word has nothing whatever to do with "shaking", but means "to strip, bare, expose".

Let us consider first the verse in Nehemiah (5:13) which employs the verb in three different forms:

גַּם־חָצְנִי נָעַרְתִּי וָאֹמְרָה כָּכָה יְנַעֵר אֱלֹהִים אֶת־כָּל־הָאִישׁ אֲשֶׁר לֹא־יָקִים
אֶת־הַדָּבָר הַזֶּה מִבֵּיתוֹ וּמִיגִיעוֹ וְכָכָה יִהְיֶה נָעוּר וָרֵק

A standard rendering of this (JPS) is:

> *Also I shook out my lap, and said: "So God shake out every man from his house, and from his labour, that performeth not this promise; even thus be he shaken out and emptied!"*

Taking into account that חצן is actually "bosom" and not "lap", it is fair to say that "shake out" jars on the reader on each of the three occasions that the word is used in this sentence. In far better conformity to sense and usage would be:

> Also I bared my bosom and said, "So God strip every man of his house and of his labour, that performeth not this promise; even thus be he made naked and empty!"

Describing the devastation of the land, Isaiah in Chap. 33 first declares
>   *Your spoil is gathered as the caterpillar gathereth;*
>   *As locusts leap do they leap upon it* (v.4),
and then

> *The land mourneth and languisheth;*
> *Lebanon is ashamed, it withereth;*
> *Sharon is like a wilderness;*
> *And Bashan and Carmel* נֹעֵר. (v.9)

JPS cannot accept the grotesque "shaken out" for this and translates "clean bare". NJPSV follows with "stripped bare", as NEB and the Jerusalem Bible. LXX has "manifest" - i.e. stripped of all covering, but Vg stands by "shaken" with *concussa*. AV and RV treat the active participle נֹעֵר as a transitive indicative with "shake off their leaves (fruits)".
The sense apparently required is simply to be bare. Even "stripped bare" infringes the grammatical form.
Later in the same chapter, 33:15 there is a description of the man of virtue which includes the phrase נֹעֵר (again the active participle) *his hands from holding bribes*. Again "shakes off" is not an appropriate expression. The two following parallel lines make it clear that what is being described is not a man

who, having sinned, shakes himself free of his sins, but one who is immune to sin altogether - *That stoppeth his ears from hearing of blood and shutteth his eyes from looking upon evil.* The real sense then is to keep uncontaminated, thus naked of taint. The man keeps his hands bare of bribes.

In the third use in Isaiah, 52:2, התנערי of *the dust; Arise and sit down, O Jerusalem!* the verb is parallel with התפתחי, with the sure meaning "divest thyself of". Certainly "shake yourself free of the dust" is a possible reading, but "denude yourself" is at least equally acceptable.

In Psalm 109:23, the image of the locust which we met in Isa 33:4 is again invoked, but the translators seem to credit that it is the shaking of a locust out of the clothing, rather than the stripping of vegetation by the insect which is intended by the poet. This is perilously close to a literary impossibility.

> *For I am poor and needy,*
> *And my heart is wounded within me.*
> *I am gone like the shadow when it lengthens;*
> נערתי *like the locust.*
> *My knees totter through fasting;*
> *And my flesh is lean, and hath no fatness.*

In the Hebrew the comparative כ may as well mean "as by" as "as", so "stripped bare as by the locust" is a valid reading, and in every way more in accordance with literary convention than "shaken off as the locust" (JPS, NEB) or "like locusts" (Vg, NJPSV); "tossed up and down like locusts" (AV,RV,LXX); "whirled off like a locust" (Moffatt). The idea of the locust being shaken out of the clothing is especially inappropriate because such an act frees the locust, who welcomes it, while the alternative image of the wind which sweeps the locusts out to sea (Ex 10:19) makes of the complaining poet a proverbial predator, which is absurd.

Ps 136:15 and Ex 14:27 both feature the verb in the context of the drowning of the Egyptian army in the sea which returned to its bed after the Israelites had safely crossed it during their escape from Egypt. In both, God is the subject, and it is stated that He נער the Egyptians in, or in the midst of, the sea. "Shook out" has no applicability. Most versions (from LXX on) read "overthrew", but this is arbitrary, bearing no relationship to any other use of the word. The sense "exposed" is, however, perfectly acceptable.

In Judges 16:20 the use of נער is quite obscure. Woken by Delilah with the information that the Philistines have arrived, Samson says "I will go out as at the other times and אנער". Presumably he intended to say that he would rid himself of them, but no specific meaning of נער can be deduced from this passage.

The noun נערת which is found in Judges 16:9 and Isa 1:31 means "tow" - the fibre of flax. BDB derives this on the assumption that the flax is shaken to produce the tow, but in fact it is beaten. The process may aptly be described as one of *stripping* the fibres of flax from the surrounding woodpulp.

The corresponding masculine noun נער is to be found only in Zech 11:16 in the sentence:

> *For lo, I shall raise up a shepherd in the land, who will not think of the נער, neither will he seek the young, nor heal the broken, nor feed that which stands still, but he will eat the flesh of the fat and will break their hoofs in pieces.*

Valid possibilities for נער here are "exposed" and "naked". "Shaken off" or "out" seem out of the question.

This brings us to the one exquisitely difficult example of the verb in the Book of Job, 38:13. Here the Lord is describing the dawn, which takes hold of the coverlet of the earth and "the wicked" (or more probably "the poor", v. p.413) "ינערו" upon it". The usual reading of this is that the dawn grasps the (four) corners of the earth (כנפות הארץ) and shakes the wicked out of it as one might shake crumbs from a sheet. This strange personification of a four-handed dawn corresponds to no other mythological treatment in any culture.

What the dawn naturally does is to lift the coverlet of darkness from the earth, and expose those who have been hiding on its surface under its protection.

It seems possible that the word נער derives originally from the root עור "to be exposed, bare", and is related to the complex of words ערם, עירם, ערום, and ultimately עור, "skin".

Index of Biblical References

1. The Book of Job

Chapter 7

1.	191, 393.
3.	297 (3-5), 412.
4.	98, 113, 120f, 440.
5.	98, 120f.
6.	56, 126.
7.	56.
8.	56, 409.
9.	237, 385.
11.	419.
12.	100 (12-21), 162, 180, 191, 234, 385, 429.
13.	165 (13-19), 297 (13-15), 447.
14.	98, 443, 447, 482.
15.	100, 298, 385, 392.
16.	385, 460.
17.	32, 50.
19.	477.
20.	286, 446.
21.	130.

Chapter 8

2.	402.
3.	191.
4.	133f (4-7), 137, 236, 293, 382, 386, 466.
5.	130, 386, 484.
6.	386.
8.	101 (8-10).
9.	124.
10.	383.
11.	191, 251 (11-15).
14.	105 (14-17), 386f, 428, 496.
15.	274, 387, 410.
16.	387f, 398 (16-19).
17.	134, 137, 387f, 428.
18.	104f, 388.
19.	104f, 278, 388.
20.	274, 388, 447, 460.
22.	156f.

Chapter 9

Chapter 10

20.   394.
21.   495.
22.   394, 495.

Chapter 11

2.   191.
3.   32, 186, 405.
10.   191, 193, 394, 396.
12.   32, 221, 394f.
13.   395, 484.
14.   395.
16.   395, 484.
18.   395.
19.   98.
20.   157f, 251.

Chapter 12

4.   33, 50, 100, 221, 207 & 240 & 273 (4-6), 248, 266, 288ff, 395, 418,
        452.
5.   221, 266, 289ff, 395.
6.   266, 289ff, 395.
7.   293, 395, 447.
8.   293.
9.   76, 89, 101, 273, 293, 395, 438, 490.
11.   101, 444.
12.   101.
13.   101.
14.   396.
15.   312, 396.
16.   101, 186.
17.   100 (17-25), 294 (17-25), 396 (17-25).
18.   396.
19.   74, 91.
20.   477.
21.   169, 396, 458, 506, 508.
22.   110.
23.   70, 240, 380, 396.
24.   102, 396.
25.   112.

22.   134f.

Chapter 15

2.   191, 254 (2-16), 399, 402.
3.   191.
4.   44f, 97, 379, 395, 399, 403, 479ff, 496.
5.   44f, 395, 399, 479ff.
6.   260, 481.
7.   42, 244f, 399.
8.   191 (8-13), 399f, 480.
10.   146, 400, 431.
11.   400.
13.   400.
14.   144 & 241 (14-16).
17.   144f, 254 (17-35), 447.
18.   145f, 160.
19.   145f, 199, 418, 490.
20.   146, 157.
21.   147 (21-23).
23.   262.
24.   146, 401.
25.   147, 401 (25-27), 448.
26.   147f, 503, 505.
27.   147f, 401f.
28.   36, 148ff.
29.   148, 382, 402.
30.   148, 384.
31.   148.
32.   148, 402.
33.   113, 138, 148.
34.   160.
35.   38, 379, 402, 467.

Chapter 16

2.   150, 159.
3.   402.
4.   403 (4-6).
5.   402.
7.   123f.
8.   123f, 127, 418, 420.
9.   92, 126, 196, 403.

13.   406.
14.   406f, 434.
15.   407.
19.   138.
20.   274f, 407, 418.
21.   160, 412.

Chapter 19

2.   196, 407.
3.   150, 407f, 452.
6.   408 (6-20), 490.
7.   408, 409.
8.   262.
9.   96, 408.
12.   100.
13.   125, 136, 300, 382 & 488 (13-19), 408.
14.   273 (14-19).
15.   32 (15-19), 408.
16.   125, 408.
17.   125f, 135f, 139, 408.
18.   408, 411.
20.   73, 126f, 130, 437.
21.   408, 484.
22.   191, 408, 431, 440, 487.
23.   404 & 485ff & 487 (23-24), 420 (23-25).
25.   74, 93, 398, 460, 486ff, 488ff, 492 (25-27).
26.   56, 101, 273, 294, 460, 486ff, 488ff.
27.   408, 460, 486ff.
28.   56, 452.
29.   42, 409, 448.

Chapter 20

3.   396, 409, 420.
5.   150, 157.
7.   409, 420, 428.
8.   122, 409.
9.   409.
10.   409, 428.
11.   138, 409, 428.
12.   410.
14.   410.

34.   139, 159, 251.

Chapter 22

2.   191 (2-5), 283ff, 287 (2-4), 417.
4.   98, 417f.
5.   158 (5-9).
6.   107, 391, 418.
11.   262.
15.   248 (15-20), 260.
16.   123, 418.
18.   32, 158, 410, 412, 418.
19.   33, 275, 291, 418.
20.   275, 291, 418.
22.   418, 421.
24.   94, 416, 418.
25.   418.
27.   107.
28.   421, 425.
29.   287, 418.
30.   52, 80, 418.

Chapter 23

2.   419f.
3.   100 (3-9), 420, 488.
4.   420 (4-7).
7.   76, 251, 420.
8.   240 & 265 (8-9), 421, 447.
9.   421, 447.
10.   421.
11.   170, 274, 421.
12.   421.
13.   57, 98 (13-17), 193.
14.   421.
15.   421.
16.   421.
17.   99, 228, 262, 403.

Chapter 24

1.   93, 99, 191, 226, 229, 256, 421f.
2.   107, 228 (2-4), 237, 257, 422, 428.

Chapter 25

Chapter 26

Chapter 27

1.	246, 427, 491.
2.	247 & 492f (2-6), 427.
3.	33, 439, 443.
5.	376.
6.	274, 493.
7.	157, 248 (7-10), 427, 442.
8.	191 (8-10).
9.	248, 251.
10.	248f.
11.	152f (11-13), 249ff (11-23).
12.	251, 484.
13.	157, 249, 417 (13-15).
14.	138f, 250 (14-18), 277, 410, 428 (14-18), 438.
15.	140, 410, 427f.
16.	428.
17.	428.
18.	410, 427, 428.
19.	428, 250 (19-23).
20.	169 (20-23), 250, 252 (20-23), 406, 428, 445.
22.	428.
23.	428.

Chapter 28

Chapter.	491ff.
3.	494ff, 494f.
4.	494, 494ff, 494f.
5.	428f, 494.
7.	409, 429, 493ff.
8.	65, 193, 429, 493ff, 493.
10.	429, 494, 494.
11.	429, 494, 494.
12.	191, 429, 494, 495.
13.	429.
14.	162, 429.
15.	429.
16.	93.
17.	429.
19.	429.
20.	191, 429, 494.
21.	494.

22.   494.
24.   429.
28.   65, 76, 89, 270, 429, 491, 493, 494, [2].

Chapter 29

1.   491.
2.   89, 100 (2-5).
4.   430.
5.   137, 430.
6.   137, 430, 437.
7.   74 (7-17), 408 (7-25).
12.   433.
14.   96, 129, 297.
18.   430.
20.   433.
21.   74 (21-25), 430 (21-25).
25.   96, 158.

Chapter 30

Chapter. 110.
1.   146, 430.
2.   419, 424, 430ff, 433.
3.   128, 432.
4.   432.
6.   432.
8.   376, 431.
9.   108, 196, 432.
10.   108.
11.   423, 432f.
12.   96, 423, 433, 509.
13.   433.
15.   96, 406, 434.
16.   127ff (16-18), 274.
17.   396, 432.
18.   36, 96, 141, 187, 443.
19.   436.
20.   434, 436 (20-23), 437.
21.   97.
23.   497.
24.   434ff, 449.
25.   436.

26.   262.
27.   130, 437.
28.   309, 430, 437.
29.   126, 437.
30.   126, 130f.

Chapter 31

1.   437f.
2.   93, 191, 437f, 452.
3.   438, 509.
4.   438.
6.   376.
8.   138, 142, 438.
9.   91 (9-11), 107 (9-11), 439.
11.   74, 409, 438, 439.
12.   438.
18.   33, 409, 438f, 443.
23.   439, 509.
24.   496.
26.   91, 107.
27.   91, 107.
28.   74, 91, 107, 439, 452.
29.   42, 274, 440.
[29a.   439.
29b.   439.]
31.   439, 478.
33.   408, 440f.
35.   397, 441f.
36.   441.
37.   417, 441.
38.   430 (38-40).
39.   74.
40.   25, 255.

Chapter 32

2.   443.
3.   443.
8.   443.
14.   260, 443.
18.   443.
19.   122, 399 (19-20), 443.

Chapter 35

Chapter 36

8.	161, 176, 180 & 187 & 210 & 213 & 236 (8-11), 429, 455.
10.	224, 455.
11.	224, 455.
12.	213 (12-15).
13.	274, 455f, 513.
14.	409, 455f.
15.	157f, 455f.
16.	210, 213.
17.	210, 213.
18.	213.
19.	210, 213.
20.	210, 213.
21.	213, 245, 399, 432, 456.
22.	214 (22-29).
23.	456.
30.	215, 456.
31.	215.
32.	215, 451.
33.	215.
34.	210, 215.
35.	215.
36.	212 (36-38), 215ff (36-38), 219 (36-38), 224, 457.
37.	42, 193, 220, 224, 376, 438, 457.
38.	415.
39.	219f & 222 & 456 (39-41).
41.	76.

Chapter 39

1.	219 (1-2), 220 (1-4), 223.
2.	219 (2-3).
3.	456f.
4.	219.
5.	193, 219 (5-12), 223 (5-12), 457.
6.	457.
7.	220.
8.	220.
9.	220.
13.	219 (13-18), 221 (13-18), 457.
15.	457.
16.	220 (16-18), 457f.
17.	77, 185, 224, 457.
18.	312, 457.

2. Genesis - Deuteronomy

Genesis

Exodus

Leviticus

3. Joshua - II Kings

I Kings

5.	3.	258; 5. 71; 10. 71, 88.
6.	38.	172.
7.	6.	503; 33. 501, 505f; 37. 218.
12.	32f.	117.
14.	30.	498.
22.	19-22.	201f; Chapter. 59.

II Kings

5.	13.	41.
9.	26.	432.
13.	3.	498.
17.	27f.	92.
18.	3.	69, 72; 4. 52, 308; 5. 69;
	19-25.	181; 29-35. 181, 206.
19.	11.	207; 35. 73.
20.	1-11.	55.
22.	18-20.	99, 256.
23.	10.	52, 308.

4. Isaiah - Malachi

Isaiah

1.	5f.	53, 56; 5-8. 115; 6. 22;
	11.	431, 440; 31. 512.
2.	12ff.	99.
4.	4.	473.
5.	1-7.	236; 24. 449.
7.	14.	26, 290.
8.	3.	290; 6-8. 175; 7. 507; 19. 426; 23. 117.
9.	11.	421; 13. 79; 15. 271.
10.	13.	445; 34. 490, 498.
11.	4.	149.
13.	6.	93, 383; 6-22. 99; 9. 227.
14.	5.	143, 156; 11. 285, 412; 12. 146;
	16.	458.
16.	8.	379.
17.	6.	490.

Ezekiel

5. Psalms & Proverbes

126.   4.   307.
127.   3.   438.
128.   3.   138, 148.
129.   3.   502, 504f.
132.   3.   160; 5.   160.
136.   15.   512.
137.   7.   431.
139.   16.   497.
140.   3.   410; 6.   406.
144.   4.   124.
146.   4.   290.
147.   3.   499.

Proverbs

1.   32.   465.
2.   4.   377; 13. 297.
4.   11.   297.
7.   4.   405.
8.   14.   101.
9.   10.   270; 12. 237.
10.   19.   403.
11.   3.   376; 27. 142.
12.   4.   398.
14.   2.   297; 25. 280.
15.   11.   245; 32. 391.
17.   5.   510.
18.   22.   280.
19.   5&9.   280; 12. 237.
22.   7.   456.
23.   32.   410.
24.   22.   510.
25.   20.   426.
30.   24&29.   229.
31.   15.   422; 19. 435.

6. Song of Songs - II Chronicles

Song of songs

1.   6.   409.

8.   27.   429.
9.   1.   196.
10.   8.   382, 466f.

Nehemiah

3.   15.   508.
5.   13.   510.
12.   31.   303.

I Chronicles

4.   11.   197; 15. 197.
11.   40.   432.
20.   4-8.   121, 141.
21.   1.   204. 13. 293.

II Chronicles

7.   16.   498.
10.   7.   498.
12.   15.   498.
21.   7.   498.
23.   13.   261.
28.   18.   309.
29.   2.   69, 72; 20-24. 117.
30.   1-20.   117; Chapter. 92.
31.   21.   69.
32.   31.   297.
36.   15f.   297.

7. The Christian Bible

References to the Apocrypha

Enoch

9 3ff.   296
15.   2.   296

References to the Christian Bible:

Matthew

| 5. | 13. | 475; 18. 485. |
| 23. | 27. | 473. |

Mark

| 9. | 49. | 475. |

Colossians

| 4. | 6. | 475. |

Entries in square brackets [] refer to the Preface.

Abbreviations of Frequent References

A   Francis L. Anderson, *Job,*, Tyndale Old Testament Commentaries, Inter-Varsity Press, England, *1976.*

AV   Authorized Version of the Bible, *1611.*

⋋ B   Berechiah Ben Natronai Ha-Nakdan, *A Commentary on the Book of Job from a Hebrew Manuscript in the University Library, Cambridge*, Ed. W.A. Wright, London, 1905

BDB   F. Brown, S.R. Driver, C. A. Briggs, *Hebrew and English Lexicon of the Old Testament,* Clarendon Press, Oxford, *1977.*

C   D.J.A. Clines *Word Biblical Commentary Job 1-20,* Word Books, Dallas, *1989*

D&G   S.R. Driver, G.B. Gray, *A Critical and Exegitical Commentary on The Book of Job,* T&T Clark, Edinburgh, *1921.*

Del   F. Delitzsch, *Biblical Commentary on the Book of Job,* Translated from the German by Rev. F. Bolton, Wm.B. Eerdmans, Michigan, *1949.* (Original German *1864.*)

G   R. Gordis, *The Book of Job,* Jewish Theological Seminary of America, NY *1978.*

G   (BGM) R. Gordis, *The Book of God and Man,* University of Chicago Press, *1965.*

Ges   *Gesenius' Hebrew Grammar,* (Ed. E. Kautzsch, Revised A.E. Cowley), Oxford U. Press, *1910.*

H   N.C. Habel, *The Book of Job,* SCM Press, London, *1985.*

I   *The Interpreter's Bible,* Abingdon Press, Nashville, *1954.*

JPS   Jewish Publication Society, *Job,* with Introduction and Commentary by Rabbi Dr. V.E. Reichert, Soncino Press, London, Jerusalem, New York, *1946.*

LXX   *Septuagint version of the Old Testament and Apocrypha,* English trans. by Sir L.L. Brenton, S. Bagster & Sons, London, *1976.*

M   S. Mitchell, *The Book of Job,* North Point Press, San Francisco, *1987.*

NEB   *New English Bible,* Penguin Books *1974.*

NJPSV Jewish Publication Society of America, *The Book of Job,* Philadelphia, *1980.*

P   M.H. Pope, *The Anchor Bible, Job,*, Doubleday & Co., New York, *1965.*

Pritch   J.B. Pritchard (Ed) *Ancient Near Eastern Texts,* Princeton University Press, Princeton, *1969.*

QT   M. Sokoloff, *The Targum to Job from Qumran Cave XI,* Bar-Ilan University, Ramat-Gan, *1974.*

R   E. Renan, *The Book of Job,* W.M. Thomson, London, (original publication *1859*).

RV   Revised Version of the Bible *1885*.

T   C. Mangan, *The Targum of Job*, in *The Aramaic Bible, Vol. 15*, T&T Clark Ltd., Edinburgh, *1991*.

T-S   N.H. Tur-Sinai (H. Torczyner) *The Book of Job*, Kiryath Sepher Ltd., Jerusalem, *1967*.

Vg   *Biblia Sacra Iuxta Vulgatum Versionem*, Deutsche Bibelgesellschaft, Stuttgart, *1983*.

V-S   A. van Selms, *Job*, W.B. Eerdmans, Michigan, *1985*.